226 Dwinelle

643-1045
Bonnie F.

TRADITIO

TRADITIO

An Introduction to the Latin Language and Its Influence

PATRICIA A. JOHNSTON
BRANDEIS UNIVERSITY

MACMILLAN PUBLISHING COMPANY
NEW YORK

Macmillan Publishing Company
866 Third Avenue, New York, New York 10022

Collier Macmillan Canada, Inc.

Library of Congress Cataloging-in-Publication Data

Johnston, Patricia A.
Traditio : an introduction to the Latin language and its influence.

English and Latin.
Includes index.
1. Latin language—Grammar—1976– . 2. Latin language—Influence on foreign languages. 3. Language and languages—Foreign elements. 4. Languages in contact. 5. Civilization, Modern—Roman influence. I. Title.
PA2080.J64 1988 478.2′421 87-14107

ISBN 0-02-360560-X

Printing: 2 3 4 5 6 7 Year: 8 9 0 1 2 3 4

ISBN 0-02-360560-X

For Jan Waszink,
magistro optimo.

Preface

Traditio: An Introduction to the Latin Language and Its Influence is designed to give students at the college level a thorough introduction to Latin grammar and some experience translating Latin authors. It includes sufficient materials for courses lasting one school year, but it can also serve as the text for a one-semester review or intensive introductory course. Its exercises and reading passages are based on the themes and—to the extent possible—actual works of the great Latin authors, from as early as Plautus and as late as Copernicus, modified as necessary to conform with the grammar of the Classical period. The forms and constructions covered will be familiar to most instructors. Commonly used forms and constructions that seem to cause some difficulty, such as the subjunctive mood, are introduced in the early chapters and reinforced by frequent recurrence throughout the text.

In each chapter, new grammatical material is followed by exercises (*Scrībenda*). Vocabulary to be memorized by the student (*Verba* [*memoriā*] *tenenda*), with accompanying vocabulary notes (*Notanda*), is listed. Then, beginning with the second chapter, a set of prereading exercises (*Ante legenda*) based on the new vocabulary and grammatical structures in the chapter prepare the student for the connected reading passage(s) (*Legenda*) at the end of the chapter. These passages, in turn, provide a thematic context for future grammatical explanations and exercises.

A *Probanda* follows every third chapter. In this section, students are expected to test themselves on the contents of the three preceding chapters. The correct answers are given at the end of each *Probanda*.

The *Legenda* have been arranged according to loosely interwoven themes. Roman Comedy provides the first major theme, and Education at Rome the second. Ovid's account of the myth of Hercules is then followed by Latin passages containing philosophical, religious, and scientific interpretations and extrapolations of this and other myths. Under the heading, "The Roman Experience," passages concerning literary patronage, social status, and history are gathered.

In addition, a tutorial program keyed to each chapter of this text has been developed for the IBM PC and compatibles. This software provides drills and tests of all conjugations and declensions as well as vocabulary tests. Instructors may obtain copies of this software as well as an answer key to the exercises from the publisher.

Many students have a limited opportunity to study Roman civilization formally after completing their introductory Latin courses. I have therefore attempted to provide some background information for the reading passages and, in the Appendices, a Chronological Table, and a list of Proper Names. Additional sources are included in the footnotes.

Teachers may choose to assign only selections from the *Legenda*. A considerable portion of the *Legenda* should be read regularly, however, as these reading passages provide a context for examples and exercises of future chapters. Another reason for reading the *Legenda* is the invaluable experience they give students in translating connected Latin passages. The student who has mastered all the *Legenda* should be able, with the aid of a good dictionary and commentaries, to translate most of the Latin authors.

I am indebted to a great many people for their assistance at various stages in the development of this book. In particular I wish to thank Professors Sheila K. Dickison of the University of Florida, W. R. Johnson of the University of Chicago, Christine M. Kalke (now at the National Endowment for the Humanities), Anne Leen of Furman University, T. James Luce, Jr. of Princeton University, Richard W. Minadeo of Wayne State University, and Carroll Moulton (formerly of Princeton University), for their criticisms and suggestions in reviewing this text. Professor Wendell Clausen of Harvard University and my colleague Ann Koloski-Ostrow generously made their expertise available to me. Throughout the development of this book, Mrs. Anastasia Sutermeister, also of Brandeis University, and my husband, George Johnston, consistently provided encouragement and assistance. The initial planning and writing of *Traditio* came about through the foresight of Helen McInnis, formerly of Scribner's, now of Macmillan. Dr. Carol Lanham of the University of California at Los Angeles worked closely with me in planning, organizing, and initiating the text. The editorial staffs at Macmillan and at Michael Bass & Associates have shown extraordinary care, creativity, and devotion in producing this text. My students at Brandeis, finally, who cheerfully struggled through the early versions and went on to prove the efficacy of the text, had a major role in determining its final shape. In many ways this is their book.

I have dedicated *Traditio* to a great scholar and teacher of the classics, Professor Emeritus Jan H. Waszink of the University of Leiden. My hope is that *Traditio* will enable others to read and enjoy Latin literature, much as Professor Waszink made this pleasure available to Latin students of my generation.

PATRICIA A. JOHNSTON

Contents

TRADITIO

Introduction: The Latin Language

A Brief History

Latin was originally the language spoken in Latium, a district of central Italy that included Rome. Rome was founded, according to tradition, about 753 B.C. Starting in the fifth century B.C., the Romans gradually consolidated and extended their territory. Latin spread as Roman power grew, displacing various other native languages, first in Italy and later in countries conquered by Rome.

The oldest surviving Latin occurs in inscriptions. Examples of Latin inscriptions before the third century are rare, although some have been found from as early as the sixth, and possibly the seventh, century. Latin became the dominant language of culture in western Europe, and held that position for well over a thousand years. The first known literary work in Latin is a translation from Greek, of the *Odyssey*, about 240 B.C. Around 200 B.C. Latin literature began to blossom with the comedies of Plautus and Terence, which were based on Greek originals. Many of the most famous names of Latin literature—Cicero, Caesar, Vergil, Horace, Ovid—come from the last years of the Roman Republic (which lasted from 509 to 31 B.C.) and the early part of the Roman Empire (which lasted from 31 B.C. to the fourth century A.D. in the West, and until the fifteenth century A.D. in the East). The fame of these authors is due in part to the fact that they were the main authors read by school children.

By A.D. 200 Christianity was creating a whole new vocabulary and style with which to address the masses. A succession of compelling preachers and thinkers gradually constructed a vast body of exegetical and doctrinal works in Latin to stand beside St. Jerome's great achievement, his translation of the Bible into Latin, known as the Vulgate Bible. Meanwhile, children continued to learn their Latin from pagan grammars, and to read pagan literature and pagan mythology.

As the universal language of education, Latin had truly remarkable staying power. Secular literature began to bloom again in the eleventh

The Ancient World.

century, and the twelfth century experienced such a renewal of learning and creativity that it has been called the Latin Renaissance. Grammars and commentaries written in the third and fourth centuries A.D. remained in use throughout the Middle Ages, and as late as the seventeenth century scholars all over Europe could correspond and converse in Latin because they had all studied it in school.

Rome never imposed Latin on conquered peoples. Like English today, Latin carried prestige, and people wanted to learn it. The modern descendants of Latin—French, Italian, Spanish, Portuguese, and Romanian—are known collectively as the Romance languages, from the politico-geographical term *Romania*, which was used as early as the fourth century A.D. as a name for the Roman Empire. By that time, Latin was spoken daily, alongside various native languages, from one end of the Mediterranean basin to the other. The Romance languages are derived (directly descended) from Latin, and they are cognate with (related to) English.

The English language derives not from Latin but from the Germanic family of languages, by way of Anglo-Saxon. English is, however, cognate with Latin, for both languages descend from a common ancestor spoken as early as 4000 B.C. Linguists have been able to reconstruct important parts of this common ancestor (called Proto-Indo-European), even though no written evidence of it survives. Between 50 and 75 percent of English vocabulary, moreover, is derived from Latin or Greek. As you learn Latin vocabulary, you will also learn many English derivatives, which will help you remember the meanings of the Latin words (and will also help you expand your English vocabulary).

The reading selections in this book will introduce you to many writers of Latin, both famous and anonymous, over the long span of Latin dominance, and even into its decline, when it remained the language of the educated classes. You will find some background information about these authors in the chapters themselves, and a chronological table in Appendix E.[1]

Latin Alphabet and Pronunciation Guide

The Latin alphabet is the same as ours, except that Latin has no *j* or *w*. You will rarely encounter *k*, and *y* and *z* appear only in words borrowed from Greek. Two letters, *i* and *u*, serve as both vowels and consonants, as described below.

The chief difference of pronunciation between English and Latin lies in the concept of vowel length. When we speak of vowels in English as being long or short, we refer primarily to a qualitative difference of sound: "sat" (short *a*) and "state" (long *a*), for example, contain two very different *a* sounds. Measurement of speech by testing equipment proves that English long vowels do take longer to pronounce than short ones, for we pronounce them not as pure, single sounds but as diphthongs: the *a* in "state," for example, shades into an *e* sound before the *t*.

The qualitative differences between short and long vowels in Latin are much more subtle. Quantitative difference—length itself, the time it takes to utter a sound—is a more important contrastive tool. Modern Italian preserves this feature: in *amare*, for example, the two *a*'s have the same sound, but the second takes longer to pronounce. For speakers of English, consonants can illustrate the phenomenon better than vowels. Say aloud "bitter" and "nighttime": the *t*'s in the two words have the same sound, but take longer to pronounce in the second word.

In Latin, vowel length is phonemic. This means that two words can be spelled exactly alike and be differentiated solely by whether a vowel is long or short:

[1] For additional information, see *The Oxford Classical Dictionary*, 2d ed. (Oxford, 1970); E. J. Kenney and W. V. Clausen, eds. *The Cambridge History of Classical Literature*, vol. 2, *Latin Literature* (Cambridge, 1982); Michael Grant, *History of Rome* (New York, 1978); L. R. Palmer, *The Latin Language* (London, 1961); W. D. Elcock, *The Romance Languages*, 2d ed. (London, 1975).

Long	Short
ōs mouth	**ŏs** bone
vēnit he (she/it) came	**vĕnit** he (she/it) is coming
māla apples	**măla** bad things

Latin textbooks and dictionaries normally mark only long vowels, as in the three words on the left above, with a long mark (called a macron). The sign ˘, called a breve (short), can be used to mark short vowels.

It is necessary to learn vowel length as part of each Latin word, for the word's accent depends on it, and the rhythms of all classical Latin poetry are based not on the stress accent of words (as in English), but on patterns determined in part by vowel lengths. Vowel length is not as difficult to learn as you might think: the vowels in Latin words are more often short than long, so you need only note long vowels in learning any Latin word.

First let us examine how individual letters are pronounced. The English words used to illustrate are only approximations, of course. Try to keep each Latin vowel a pure, single sound as you pronounce it. Long vowels should actually take longer to pronounce than short ones.[2] There are no silent letters in Latin: every letter is pronounced.

Vowels

Long	Short
ā as in *father*: **mā́ter**, **clā́rus**	**ă** as in *about*: **páter**, **áger**
ē as in *hey*, or as *a* in *fate*: **tē**, **pēs**, **accḗpit**	**ĕ** as in *fed*: **mel**, **pétere**
ī as in *marine*, or as *e* in *equal*: **amīcus**, **spīrā́re**	**ĭ** as in *fit*: **cápitis**, **bíbit**
ō as in *focus*: **cṓgō**, **bōs**	**ŏ** as in *soft*: **lócus**, **bónus**
ū as in *rude*, or as *oo* in *brood*: **inclū́dō**, **fū́gī**	**ŭ** as in *put*: **ápud**, **ténuit**

ȳ̆ as *ew* in *lewd*: **Cȳ́mē**, **mystḗrium**

Diphthongs

A diphthong consists of two vowels pronounced together as a single sound. Diphthongs are always long by nature: they never have a long mark over them, since there is no possibility that they will be short. Latin has six diphthongs:

ae as *ai* in *aisle*, or the long *i* in *high*: **saévus**, **amī́cae** (**ae** becomes *e* in English derivatives: **aéquus**, equal; **aetérnus**, eternal)

[2] Phoneticians distinguish between tense vowels (which we call long) and nontense, or lax, vowels (which we call short). Syllables are also called long or short in this book (as in most Latin texts). A syllable is long if it contains a long, or tense, vowel, or a diphthong; a syllable containing a short vowel may be lengthened by its position (i.e., if it is followed by two or more consonants). For further discussion, see M. Halle and S. J. Keyser, *English Stress: Its Form, Its Growth, and Its Role in Verse* (New York, 1971); N. Chomsky and M. Halle, *Sound Pattern of English* (New York, 1968).

au as *ou* in *loud*, or as *ow* in *how*: **caúda**, **laúdō**

ei as in *eight*: **déin**, **deínde**, **eíus**

eu as Latin **e** plus **u** pronounced quickly together, or as Latin **e** plus English *oo* as in *food*: only in **neúter**, **neu**, **heu**, **seu**, **ceu**, and in words borrowed from Greek. Elsewhere **e** and following **u** are pronounced in separate syllables: **mé–us**, **aú–re–us**.

oe as *oi* in *oil*: **coepísse**, **foédus**, **poénae** (but **o** and following long **ē** are pronounced in separate syllables: **po–ḗ–ta**, **co–ḗ–gī**)

ui as Latin **u** plus **i** pronounced quickly together: only in **huic**, **cui**, **hui**, and **huíus** and **cuíus** (pronounced *húy–yus*, *cúy–yus*: see the pronunciation of the semiconsonant **i** below). Elsewhere the two letters are pronounced in separate syllables: **rú–it**, **ex–plí–cu–it**, **má–nu–ī**, **fú–it**.

Consonants

Latin consonants are pronounced as in English, with the following exceptions:

b before **s** and **t**, like *p*: **urbs** (*urps*), **obtúndō** (*optundo*)

c always hard, as in *cat*; never soft, as in *city*: **cádō**, **círcum**, **conclū́dō**, **Cícerō**, **Caésar** (compare German *Kaiser*)

g always hard, as in *girl*; never soft as in *ginger*: **gígnō**, **grā́tia**, **fíngō**, **sígnum**, **rígidus**

h lightly aspirated, as in *history*: **históría**, **haec**, **míhi**

i before a vowel, usually a semiconsonant, pronounced like an initial *y*, as in *yes*. Between two vowels within a word, it represents a double **i**, to be pronounced like *y–y* in *toy yacht*: **māíor**, **eíus**, **cuíus**, pronounced *may–yor, ey–yus, cuy–yus.* (This semiconsonantal **i** becomes a *j* in English derivatives: **iustítia**, justice; **coniúnctiō**, conjunction.)

n before **c** or **q**, and before **g**, as *nc* in *uncle*, and as *ng* in *anger*: **víncula**, **relínquō**, **fíngō**

q always followed by **u** and pronounced *kw*, as in *liquid*: **quóque**, **quīcúmque**, **équus**, **áqua**

r trilled (like Italian): **spērā́re**, **revértere**, **virṓrum**

s always voiceless, as in *sister*; never voiced, as in *tease*: **sed**, **míserīs**, **caúsa**

t like *t* in *tight*; never like *sh*, as in *mention*: **patiéntia**, **rátiō**, **coniúnctiō**, **pótuit**

v like *w*, as in *wine*: **vī́num**, **vólvō**. This is the semiconsonantal form of **u**, and in texts it is often printed as **u**: **uī́num**, **uóluō**. Latin has no sound corresponding to English *v* as in *vine*.

x, a double consonant, the equivalent of *cs* or *gs*, and always voiceless, like *ks*, as in *express*; never voiced, like *gz*, as in *exist*: **fī́xī**, **exémplum**, **dī́xit**

ch, **ph**, and **th** appear chiefly in words borrowed from Greek, where each represents a single letter. Pronounce each as described above for the simple consonants, **c**, **p**, or **t** plus **h**, then try to pronounce them quickly together (they developed their modern values well after the classical period):

ch as *k* plus *h*, as in *look here*; never as in *church*: **charácter**, **mắchina**, **púlcher**

ph as *p* plus *h*, as in *clap hands*; never as in *philosophy*: **triúmphus**, **phantásia**, **philosóphia**

th as *t* plus *h*, as in *not here*; never as in *myth*: **theắtrum**, **thēsaúrus**, **mȳ́thos**

Double Consonants

In English, a double consonant within a word merely signals that the preceding vowel is short: bitten; bite; matter; mate—there is no difference in the sound of the *t*'s. In Latin, as in Italian, double consonants are pronounced individually, as we pronounce them in adjoining words: not true; bus service. Double consonants, in effect, are similar to long vowels, in that they take a longer time to pronounce—and in fact, there was a short-lived movement around 100 B.C. to write long vowels double!

Syllables and Word Accent

1. A Latin word has as many syllables as it has vowels or diphthongs:

aes	1
quis	1
át–que	2
scrīp–sís–se	3
dī–li–gén–ti–a	5

2. Two adjacent vowels, or a vowel and a diphthong, are separated:

de–ō–rum **sa–pi–en–ti–ae** **ō–ti–um** **ma–nu–um**

3. A single consonant belongs with the vowel or diphthong that follows (**ch**, **ph**, **th**, and **qu** count as single consonants):

nú–me–rus **naú–ta** **phi–ló–so–phus** **é–qui–dem** **thē–saú–rus**

4. When two or more consonants follow a vowel or diphthong, the last consonant goes with the syllable that follows:

ma–gís–ter **púl–cher** **sánc–tus** **ex–saé–vi–ō**

But if the last consonant is **l** or **r**, the preceding consonant goes with it:

pá–trem **púl–chra** **tém–plum**

5. A syllable containing a long vowel or a diphthong is said to be *long by nature.* A syllable containing a short vowel followed by two consonants is said to be *long by position.* Otherwise, the syllable is short.

6. Latin accent is governed by the length of the penultimate syllable.[3] The last syllable in a word is called the "ultima" (from **ultima syllaba**). The word "penult" (from **paene**, "almost," and **ultima syllaba**) denotes the next-to-last syllable. The antepenult (from **ante**, "before," and **paene ultima syllaba**) is the third syllable from the end.

Words of only one syllable are accented:

mṓs **bṓs** **rḗx** **séd**

In words of two syllables, the accent goes on the first:

múl–tās **pó–test** **lí–ber**

In words of three or more syllables, the accent goes on the antepenult unless the penult is long, in which case the accent falls on the penult:

dó–mi–nus	**po–tú–i–mus**	**mā́–tri–bus**	**res–pón–de–ō**
dū–xḗ–runt	**au–dī́–mus**	**ma–gís–ter**	**res–pón–dī**

Scrībenda

Pronunciation

A. Long and short vowels—say each pair aloud, emphasizing the contrast between the marked vowels:

cădit	cāsus
vĕnit	vēnit
vĭdet	vīdit
mŏvet	mōvit
mŭndus	mūnus

B. Long and short vowels—contrast the long and short vowels within each word as you pronounce it:

a	ămāmus	iānuă	părāvit	grātiă
e	tĕnērĕ	cētĕra	fēcĕrit	

[3] This is also true of a large class of English nouns: "One of the most surprising discoveries of Chomsky and Halle (1968) was that in a large class of English words the stress contour was totally predictable; that is, given the sequence of consonants and vowels that compose the word, the location of the stress can be determined automatically. This discovery was so surprising because textbooks had for many years specifically denied this fact and, moreover, because the rule that was postulated to assign the stress did not resemble that of any Germanic language but rather was all but identical with the stress rule of Classical Latin." (Halle and Keyser, p. 3)

i	fīlĭus	ĭnĭmīcus	mīsĭt	
o	mŏdō	mŏneō	sŏmnō	sŏrōrem
u	dūcimŭs	ūnŭs	mūrŭs	

C. Single and double consonants—while observing vowel length, emphasize the difference between the single and double consonant of each pair as you pronounce the words:

teris	terrīs
ager	agger
sitis	mittimus
oculus	occāsiō
stilus	stella
posuit	posset

D. Syllabification and accent—divide into syllables and mark the position of the word's accent:

habuisset	capita
misericordiā	nostrōs
quaererent	aut
adventus	agricolārum
dēmōnstrāvit	cognoscere

E. Although the rules of pronunciation apply to all of Latin, they really come into their own in classical Latin poetry, which is based on various metrical patterns of alternating long and short syllables. Applying all the rules you have learned here about pronunciation, syllable division, and accent, mark the long and short syllables of the following poetic stanzas. Read each one aloud several times, until it feels natural and you can hear a rhythm of long and short syllables.

Pronounce every letter distinctly (including the double consonants), and remember to take more time to pronounce the long vowels.[4]

1. Nunc est bibendum, nunc pede līberō
   pulsanda tellūs, nunc Saliāribus
   ornāre pulvīnar deōrum
   tempus erat dapibus, sodālēs.
   (Horace, Odes *1.37.1–4)*
2. Vidēs ut alta stet nive candidum
   Sōracte, nec iam sustineant onus
   silvae labōrantēs, gelūque
   flūmina constiterint acūtō.
   (Horace, Odes *1.9.1–4)*
3. Vēlōx amoenum saepe Lucrētilem
   mūtat Lycaeō Faunus et igneam
   dēfendit aestātem capellīs
   usque meīs pluviōsque ventōs.
   (Horace, Odes *1.17.1–4)*

[4] For further examples, consult Stephen G. Daitz, *Pronunciation of Classical Latin: A Practical Guide* (Guilford, Conn., 1984).

Word Order

Latin, like English and every other language, has several ways to express meaning in a sentence. For our comparison between Latin and English, two are especially important: form, or inflection, and word order.

Inflection

In "the man's dog" and "I saw him," the relationship between words is expressed by form: the *'s* shows that the dog belongs to the man, and the form *him* indicates the direct object of the verb. Only pronouns change their form to distinguish subject (he, they) from object (him, them). Nouns, in addition to the possessive form, distinguish between singular and plural: book/books, computer/computers (except for a few that do not change: series, moose). Adjectives modifying nouns do not change their form at all: a sophisticated computer, several sophisticated computers; a long series, three long series.

Word Order

English follows regular patterns of word order, which thus becomes an important key to meaning. In "The dog is biting that child," the subject is "the dog" just because it precedes the verb, and "that child" is the direct object simply because it follows the verb. Exchanging the positions of "dog" and "child" produces a completely different meaning. So, too, we expect adjectives to come before the nouns to which they refer. In "The cold winter made travel difficult," we know that "cold" refers to "winter"; but in "That winter cold weather came early," "cold" by its position refers to "weather."

Latin is a much more highly inflected language than English. That is, individual Latin words have many more variable forms by which grammatical functions and meaning are expressed. The inflected endings of Latin nouns, pronouns, adjectives, and verbs indicate with great precision their roles in a sentence. To distinguish possible meanings of the verb form *sing*, we must add a noun or subject pronoun—"I sing badly, but you sing beautifully"—or else, in writing, an exclamation point, "Sing!" (and we still need a context to tell us whether the speaker is addressing one singer or a whole choir). Latin makes it all perfectly clear: the corresponding forms are **cantō**, "I sing," **cantās**, "you sing," and **cantā** (singular) or **cantāte** (plural), "Sing!" Latin, as a result, is far less dependent upon word order to convey meaning, and enjoys great freedom to arrange words so as to show the relative importance of ideas in a sentence.

Obviously, therefore, you must memorize these inflectional patterns so that you can quickly identify each word ending. This will take time and effort, but essentially it is a mechanical task. Your greater challenge, and greatest source of pleasure and satisfaction, will come in learning to read *latīnē*, "Latinly"—to take the words in their order of appearance and construct the complete thought from an order of presentation that is normally very different from English. Doing it successfully often requires juggling parts of several incomplete phrases until matching or related elements appear. Try to resist the (very natural) temptation to tear the Latin sentence down and reconstruct it into a more familiar form by hunting down first the subject, then the verb, then . . . , as if you were searching for pieces in a jigsaw puzzle.

In fact, it is possible to describe a typical pattern of word order in a Latin sentence:

The subject and its modifiers usually stand first or near the beginning.

Next comes the indirect object of the verb, and then the direct object, along with any modifiers.

The verb stands last, preceded by any adverbs or adverbial phrases that modify it.

The beginning and the end of the sentence are the positions of greatest emphasis. Thus, if the verb is to be especially stressed, it can be placed at the beginning, and the subject postponed. Any word receives emphasis simply by being placed in an unusual position. Either (or even both) of two words that normally stand together, such as a noun and its adjective, will acquire emphasis by being separated. Certain words regularly stand first or second in a clause; these will be noted as they are introduced.

Latin writers did magnificent things with their language, exploiting in a remarkable variety of ways the possibilities offered by free word order. Throughout this book, you will be introduced to some of these possibilities.

I

The Verbal System

A verb denotes an action—sing, laugh, work—or a state of being or becoming: we exist; flowers are blooming. In English, we add a noun or pronoun to indicate the subject of the verb: I sing; you laugh; it works. In each tense, the verb form itself does not usually change. Thus, the past tense of "sing" is "sang" for all persons, singular and plural: I sang, you sang, he (she/it) sang, we sang, you sang, they sang. Similarly, the future tense is "will sing" for all persons, singular and plural. The one exception is the third person singular of the present tense:

I sing	we sing
you sing	you sing
he (she/it) sings	they sing

To indicate when the action takes place, we may change the stem of the verb (I sang), use an auxiliary verb (I shall sing, you will love), or add an ending (I loved). We add other auxiliary forms to convey possibility (he may sing), exhortation (let's sing; don't love), necessity (you must sing), and so on. The passive voice, too, requires auxiliary verb forms (a hymn was being sung; we have been loved).

Latin can convey all this information in a single inflected form:

amō	I love, I do love
amāvī	I have loved
amābit	he will love
amābantur	they used to be loved

To describe a verb form fully, we must identify the four kinds of information it conveys:

1. subject: person and number (e.g., second person plural)
2. mood: indicative, subjunctive, or imperative
3. tense: present, past, and future are the basic divisions
4. voice: active or passive

1. The subject of a verb indicates, in the active voice, who or what is performing the action. In the passive voice the subject is the person or thing to whom something is being done. Latin offers the same choices of person (first, second, or third) and number (singular or plural) as English (Greek, by contrast, has in addition a dual number for a "you" or "they" defined as two persons.)

2. "Mood" is a misleading term. It does not refer to one's feelings or frame of mind, but rather to the mode or manner in which the action of the verb is represented. Statements of fact ("He loves her") or direct questions ("Does he love her?") are presented in the indicative mood. The subjunctive mood, which is almost extinct in English, is used very widely in Latin to express possibility, wish, and other concepts not regarded as fact, and also for purely formal syntactical reasons. The imperative mood expresses a command ("Come!" "Sit!" "Don't tell me!"). The infinitive, expressed in English with "to" ("to sing"; "to love"), is sometimes referred to as a mood.

3. The indicative mood in Latin has six tenses: present, imperfect, future, perfect, pluperfect (or past perfect), and future perfect. The subjunctive mood has four tenses: present, imperfect, perfect, and pluperfect. The imperative mood has two tenses: present and future. The infinitive occurs in the present, perfect, and future tenses.

4. The subject of a verb in the active voice is the person or thing performing the action. A transitive verb takes a direct object: "I sang a song"; "We loved the poet." The action need not have a direct object: "I sang often." An intransitive verb is incapable of taking a direct object: "He walks"; "We exist." If the verb is in the passive voice, its action is being performed on its subject ("The poet was loved") instead of on its object, as in the active voice.

5. We can also consider the aspect of a verb: is the action regarded as incomplete (still continuing, repeated, or open-ended), or is it definitely over and done with, finished? All Latin tenses are organized into two broad systems, according to whether the action is viewed as incomplete (the present system) or completed (the perfect system, so called from Latin **perfectus**, "completed," "finished").

Principal Parts of the Verb

Every Latin verb belongs to one of four conjugations, or verbal families, identified by the ending of its present active infinitive. The infinitive is the second of the principal parts, which appear in the vocabulary entry for a verb. When you learn a verb, you must memorize all its principal parts; this is not so difficult as it may seem, since the principal parts of most verbs do follow certain patterns, which you will learn to recognize. Most verbs, such as the verb meaning "to love," have four principal parts:

1. **amō**, first person singular, present tense, indicative mood, active voice: "I love," "I do love"
2. **amāre**, infinitive, present tense, active voice: "to save"
3. **amāvī**, first person singular, perfect tense, indicative mood, active voice: "I loved," "I have loved"
4. **amātus**, participle, perfect tense, passive voice: "loved," "beloved"

The first principal part provides the form for the first person singular of the present active indicative (**amō**), which, as you will learn, is not always evident from the information provided by the infinitive.

The present infinitive ending (-**āre**) of the second principal part (**amāre**) tells you that this verb belongs to the first conjugation.[1] The present tense of the infinitive provides the stem of the present, future, and imperfect tenses of the verb.

The third principal part, the first person singular of the perfect active indicative (**amāvī**), provides the stem for the perfect, pluperfect, and future perfect tenses of the verb.

The fourth principal part, the perfect passive participle (**amātus**), is the basis for the perfect passive system (which you will learn in a later chapter), and provides the stem for several other important verb forms. This participle also functions as a verbal adjective. You will learn to use some of these verbal adjectives in the next chapter.

Throughout this book, you will use the same model verb for each conjugation as you learn new verb forms. To interpret a verb form, work outward from the stem of the verb (**amā**-), where its kernel of meaning ("love") resides. Once you have identified the stem of the verb, you must identify the tense markers and personal endings that have been added to it. When you join these parts together to produce all the forms of any one tense, you are said to conjugate the verb. In conjugating a verb, you must abide by certain inflectional patterns. The patterns for some tenses apply to all four conjugations; others, to only two conjugations. Watch for these patterns so that you can construct your own mental map of the verbal system.

The Present System of Tenses

In Latin, verbs in the present tense, the imperfect tense, and the future tense are based on the present stem of the verb. These three tenses are therefore referred to as the present system of the verb. You will first learn the present and future tenses, in the indicative mood and active voice.

[1] The second, third, and fourth conjugations are also identified by their present active infinitive endings (-**ēre**, -**ĕre**, -**īre**), as you will see.

Our starting point is the second principal part, the present active infinitive. It is called infinitive because, though it does show time and voice, it is not limited by person or number, and therefore is thought of as infinite, unlimited. It merely indicates the action or state of being, without specifying who or what is doing, acting, or being, or even that it is happening—just as the English infinitives "to love" and "to sing" indicate these actions but do not specify that anyone in fact does love or is singing.

The present infinitive shows to which of the four conjugations a verb belongs. It also provides the present stem, to which you will add the tense markers and personal endings, producing a finite verb, a verb that has a subject, tense, and voice: "I love"; "you will sing." Beginning, then, with the present active infinitive (**amāre**), identify the stem (**amā**-) and add the tense markers and personal endings. For the active voice in the present system of tenses, the personal endings of all four conjugations are:

	SINGULAR	PLURAL
First person	-**ō** or -**m**, I	-**mus**, we
Second person	-**s**, you	-**tis**, you
Third person	-**t**, he (she/it)	-**nt**, they

Notice the different endings for singular and plural "you." In English, we often seem to need such phrases as "you two" or "you all" to make clear that more than one person is being addressed.

Present Indicative Active

First conjugation: ***amāre****, "to love."* The present active infinitive of the first conjugation ends in -**āre**. Dropping the -**re** leaves the stem, **amā**-, with the long -**ā**- characteristic of first conjugation verbs. To conjugate such verbs in the present indicative, simply add the personal endings directly to the stem:

ENDINGS		
-**ō**	**amō**	I love, do love, am loving
-**s**	**amās**	you (s.) love, do love, are loving
-**t**	**amat**	he (she/it) loves, does love, is loving
-**mus**	**amāmus**	we love, do love, are loving
-**tis**	**amātis**	you (pl.) love, do love, are loving
-**nt**	**amant**	they love, do love, are loving

Notice that:

1. In the first conjugation, the first person singular does not retain the final -**ā**- of the stem. If it did, the form would be ***amāō**;[2] in speaking,

[2] An asterisk (*) preceding a Latin form marks it as hypothetical: although it may once have existed, it does not appear in any surviving Latin writing.

however, that second -**a**- would merge with the personal ending -**ō**, producing **amō**. (You will use the first person ending -**m** in other verb forms, beginning in Chapter III.)

2. The long vowel of the stem shortens before final -**t** and -**nt** (the endings of the third person singular and plural): **amat**, **amant**. This is a general rule for third person active endings in all tenses.

3. Latin has only one form for the present tense, whereas English offers three: the simple present "I love," the present progressive "I am loving," and the present intensive or emphatic "I do love." Since any of these three translations would be correct in strictly grammatical terms, you must rely on context or word order to guide your choice when you translate from Latin to English.

Second conjugation: **tenēre**, *"to hold."* The second conjugation is characterized by a long -**ē**- in the verb stem, and by a present active infinitive ending in -**ēre**. Verbs of this conjugation retain the final -**ē**- of the stem throughout all forms of all tenses in the present system, including the first person singular. Again, to form the present indicative active, add the personal endings directly to the stem:

-ō	**teneō**	I hold, am holding, do hold
-s	**tenēs**	you (s.) hold, are holding, do hold
-t	**tenet**	he (she/it) holds, is holding, does hold
-mus	**tenēmus**	we hold, are holding, do hold
-tis	**tenētis**	you (pl.) hold, are holding, do hold
-nt	**tenent**	they hold, are holding, do hold

Notice that in the first person singular, **teneō**, the long -**ē**- of the stem has become short before the personal ending, -**ō**. This illustrates another general pattern that will be very useful to know: a vowel before another vowel is usually short.

Future Indicative Active

For the first and second conjugations, the sign of the future tense is -**bi**-, which is affixed to the present stem of the verb, and to which the personal endings are then added:

-bi+ō	amā**bō**, I shall love	tenē**bō**, I shall hold
-bi+s	amā**bis**, you (s.) will love	tenē**bis**, you will hold
-bi+t	amā**bit**, he (she/it) will love	tenē**bit**, he (she/it) will hold
-bi+mus	amā**bimus**, we shall love	tenē**bimus**, we shall hold
-bi+tis	amā**bitis**, you (pl.) will love	tenē**bitis**, you will hold
-bi+nt	amā**bunt**, they will love	tenē**bunt**, they will hold

Notice that the first person singular ending **-ō** absorbs the **-i-** of the future tense marker (compare the present tense of the first conjugation), and that the **-i-** in the third person plural changes to **-u-** before the personal ending, **-nt**. This phenomenon, too, you will encounter again.

Scrībenda

First Conjugation Verbs

amō, amāre, amāvī, amātus love
cantō, cantāre, cantāvī, cantātus sing
cōgitō, cōgitāre, cōgitāvī, cōgitātus think
optō, optāre, optāvī, optātus want; wish

Second Conjugation Verbs

moneō, monēre, monuī, monitus warn; advise
teneō, tenēre, tenuī, tentus hold
videō, vidēre, vīdī, vīsus see

Other

tē you (s.; direct object)
mē me (direct object)
sī if
nōn not
cūr adv., why?

A. Conjugate the following verbs:
1. cōgitō (present tense)
2. videō (present tense)
3. cantō (future tense)
4. moneō (future tense)

B. Translate the following sentences into English:
1. Cantās. Nōn cantābis.
2. Sī cantābunt, cantāre optābimus.
3. Monēbis mē sī male cantābō. (**male**, adv., badly)
4. Videt mē. Vidēbō tē. Tē vidēre optāmus.
5. Cōgitant. Cōgitābunt. Cōgitāre nōn optābitis.
6. Tē amō. Mē nōn amās. Cūr mē vidēre nōn optās?

The Perfect System of Tenses

Like the present system, the perfect system contains three tenses in the indicative mood: the perfect, the pluperfect (or past perfect), and the future perfect, all formed on the perfect stem. To obtain the perfect stem, drop the personal ending from the third principal part, which is the first person singular of the perfect indicative active. Here are the principal parts of your first two model verbs:

First conjugation	**amō, amāre, amāvī, amātus**
Second conjugation	**teneō, tenēre, tenuī, tentus**

Dropping the personal ending, **-ī**, from **amāvī** and **tenuī**, you obtain the perfect stem: **amāv-**, **tenu-**. You are now ready to conjugate the active tenses of the perfect system.

Perfect Indicative Active

This tense has its own set of personal endings, which are added directly to the perfect stem. The personal endings for the present system are shown at the right for comparison; it is easy to see that all forms except the first person singular share common elements:

	Perfect Tense	Present System
	SINGULAR	
First person	**-ī**	**-ō** or **-m**
Second person	**-istī**	**-s**
Third person	**-it**	**-t**
	PLURAL	
First person	**-imus**	**-mus**
Second person	**-istis**	**-tis**
Third person	**-ērunt**	**-nt**

Now, add these endings to the perfect stem:

First Conjugation	Second Conjugation
amāv**ī**, I loved, have loved, did love	tenu**ī**, I held, have held, did hold
amāv**istī**, you loved (etc.)	tenu**istī**, you held (etc.)
amāv**it**, he (she/it) loved	tenu**it**, he (she/it) held
amāv**imus**, we loved	tenu**imus**, we held
amāv**istis**, you loved	tenu**istis**, you held
amāv**ērunt**, they loved	tenu**ērunt**, they held

The Latin perfect tense denotes either the English simple, or historical, perfect ("I loved"; "I held"), the present perfect ("I have loved"; "I have held"), or the emphatic perfect ("I did love"; "I did hold"). The simple perfect denotes a completed action that took place at some time in the past:

Catullus loved Clodia. Catullus Clōdiam **amāvit**.

The present perfect indicates a completed action the result or effect of which is still felt in the present:

Catullus has long loved Clodia (and he still loves her now.)
Catullus Clōdiam diū **amāvit**.

The emphatic perfect is in the past also, but focuses on the doing more than on when it was done:

Catullus did love Clodia (although he sometimes was very angry with her).
Catullus Clōdiam **amāvit**.

Latin uses the same form, the perfect indicative active, in all these senses. As with the choices for translating the present terms, so too with the perfect, the context usually suggests which is appropriate.

> **Vēnī, vīdī, vīcī**. "I came, I saw, I conquered," is the usual rendering of Julius Caesar's famous report, to preserve the fearful symmetry of the Latin. In fact, though, "I have come, I have seen, I have conquered" would better convey Caesar's thought: I have conquered the enemy (who is now subdued).

Imperative

The present active imperative expresses a simple command:

Think! Hold me! Love me! Don't sing!

English must rely on context to distinguish whether one person is being addressed, or more than one. In Latin, however, the ending of the verb indicates whether the command is being directed to one person (you, s.) or to more than one person (you, pl.):

you, s.	Cōgitā!	Tenē mē!	Amā mē!
you, pl.	Cōgitāte!	Tenēte mē!	Amāte mē!

The singular imperative is the same form as the present stem: **cōgitā**; **amā**; **tenē**. No ending is added. To form the plural imperative, add **-te** to the present stem: **cōgitāte**; **amāte**; **tenēte**.

A negative imperative, or prohibition, is expressed by the imperative forms of the irregular verb **nōlō**, "be unwilling" (Chapter VI), together with a present infinitive:

you, s.	Nōlī mē amāre!	Nōlī mē tenēre!
you, pl.	Nōlīte mē amāre!	Nōlīte mē tenēre!
	Don't love me!	Don't hold me!

Scrībenda

A. Conjugate **cōgitō** and **videō** in the perfect tense.

B. Form the imperative, singular and plural, of the following verbs:

cantāre videre optāre monēre

C. Translate:

1. Cantāvistī. Nōn cantāvistis. Cantābitis. Cantātis.
2. Vīdit mē. Mē videt. Vidēte. Vidē.

3. Tē vīdistī. Mē vidēre nōn optāvistis.
4. Cōgitāvērunt. Cōgitābunt. Cōgitāre nōn optāvimus.
5. Amā. Amat. Amāte. Amābit. Amāvit. Amābunt. Amāvērunt.
6. Tenēs. Tenēbis. Tenētis. Tenuistī. Tenuistis.
7. Optat. Optāvit. Optāmus. Optāvimus. Optābimus.
8. Amābō tē, cūr mē vidēre nōn optāvistī?
9. Cūr mē vidēre nōn optāvistis?
10. Nōlī mē vidēre. Vidē. Nōlīte vidēre.
11. Monēs. Monē. Monētis. Monēte. Monuit. Monuī.

Verba tenenda must know

First Conjugation Verbs

amō, **amāre**, **amāvī**, **amātus** love
amābō tē please
cantō, **cantāre**, **cantāvī**, **cantātus** sing
captō, **captāre**, **captāvī**, **captātus** try to seize; catch; capture
cōgitō, **cōgitāre**, **cōgitāvī**, **cōgitātus** think; plan
errō, **errāre**, **errāvī**, **errātus** wander; make a mistake
optō, **optāre**, **optāvī**, **optātus** desire; wish (for); want
parō, **parāre**, **parāvī**, **parātus** prepare; provide
spērō, **spērāre**, **spērāvī**, **spērātus** hope (for)
spīrō, **spīrāre**, **spīrāvī**, **spīrātus** breathe

Second Conjugation Verbs

moneō, **monēre**, **monuī**, **monitus** warn; advise; remind
mordeō, **mordēre**, **momordī**, **morsus** bite; sting
teneō, **tenēre**, **tenuī**, **tentus** hold; grasp
timeō, **timēre**, **timuī**, — fear; be afraid (of)
videō, **vidēre**, **vīdī**, **vīsus** see; understand (what has been seen)

Irregular Verbs

dō, **dăre**, **dĕdī**, **dătus** give
nōlī (2nd pers. s.), **nōlīte** (2nd pers. pl.), *with infinitive* don't . . . (negative command)

Other

cūr, adverb why
nōn, adverb not
-ne (interrogative enclitic; attaches to the first word of its sentence, indicating that a question is being asked; does not translate as a separate word)
saepe, adverb often

Notanda

cōgitāre has much the same sense as its English derivative "cogitate"—ponder, reflect upon, form a plan. The suffix **-tor** added to a verb stem indicates a doer of its action; accordingly, **cōgitātor** would be the perfect Latin name to coin for Rodin's famous sculpture *The Thinker.*

optāre can also mean "choose, select." "Opt for" seems to have entered English indirectly, however, as a translation of the French *opter pour.* Compare the English noun "option."

parāre the motto of the United States Coast Guard is *Semper Parātus,* "Always Prepared." Compare the English verb "prepare."

spērāre means "to hope for": the preposition "for" is contained in the meaning of the verb, which takes a direct object in the accusative case: **victōriam spērāmus**, "We are hoping for a victory." You may translate similarly **optāre** and **timēre**, and many other verbs, when alternate meanings make the construction clear: "to wish for" or "to desire"; "to be afraid of" or "to fear."

tenēre often has the sense of "hold fast," literally or metaphorically. What is a "tenet" in English? Compare English "detain," "retain," "tentative," "tenable."

videō is only the first of many Latin forms you will encounter that have been adopted unchanged into English. (If you start a list, it will grow quickly.) The basic meaning of **videō** is "see" or "look at," and this meaning is frequently extended to mean "perceive," and hence "understand."

dō, dăre, dĕdī, dătus this verb is irregular. Its present infinitive has a short **-a-**, and the present stem therefore has a short **-a-** except in the second person singular, where the **-a-** is lengthened: **dō**, **dās**, **dăt**, **dămus**, **dătis**, **dănt**. The future tense retains the short **-a-** throughout: **dăbō**, **dăbis**, and so on.

-ne the interrogative enclitic functions like the inverted question mark in Spanish, to signal that a question is coming. (Enclitic means "leaning on" something else: it has no independent existence.) **-ne** attaches to the first word of its sentence to indicate that a question is being asked, and is translated by the English question mark (?). Consequently, **timēsne** translates "Are you afraid?" (The punctuation marks you see in Latin texts are usually modern editorial additions, and are not found in the original manuscripts.)

Ante legenda

A. Translate the following forms:

1. cantās; cantābis; nōlīte cantāre; cantābō; cantāvī; cantāte.
2. timent; timē; timuit; timēbunt; timuērunt; timēbimus.
3. momordistī; mordēbis; mordēbunt; mordent; momordimus; nōlī mē mordēre.
4. vidēbimus; vidēte; vidēbunt; vīdit; vidēre; vidē; vidērunt.
5. spīrāre; spērāre; spīrā; spērat; spīrāvistī; spīrātis.
6. cōgitāre; cōgitās; cōgitāvistī; cōgitā; cōgitāvērunt.

B. Translate; then change each form to the plural, retaining the same person and tense: cantō; vidēs; spīrat; spērāvit; momordī; optābis; monē; dō; dedistī; nōlī.

C. Translate; then change to the future tense, retaining the same person and number: cantās; cantāvērunt; optātis; momordimus; mordent; spērāvit; vīdit; dās.

D. Translate; then change to the perfect tense, retaining the same person and number: vidēmus; optābunt; dat; tenēmus; timet; cantās; captātis; monētis; amant.

E. Form the singular and plural imperatives of: cōgitō; moneō; spērō; teneō.

F. Form the singular and plural negative imperatives of the verbs in Exercise E.

G. Translate the following into Latin:

1. He is singing.
2. She wants to sing.
3. Will they sing?
4. We see.
5. They understand.
6. You (s.) are making a mistake.
7. You (pl.) will wander.

H. Translate the following into English:

1. Saepe cantat. Saepe cantāte. Saepe cantāvistis.
2. Nōlī cantāre. Optāsne cantāre? Cūr cantāvit?
3. Timentne mē? Cūr mē timuērunt? (**mē**, pronoun, me)
4. Saepe mē vidēs.
5. Nōn errābunt. Nōlī errāre. Errātisne? Saepe errāvimus.
6. Spīrā. Spērā. Nōlīte spērāre.
7. Monē mē sī errō. Saepe tē monuimus. (**sī**, conjunction, if; **tē**, pronoun, you [s.])
8. Saepe cantāmus. Numquam errābimus. (**numquam**, adverb, never)
9. "Vīdī mē in aquā." "Tē vīdistī sed nōn vīdistī." (**in aquā**, in the water; **sed**, conjunction, but)

II

Nouns, Adjectives, and Adverbs

A noun names a person, place, thing, or abstract concept: physicist, laboratory, chalk, relativity; judge, courtroom, gavel, justice. An adjective describes a noun: a *good* speech, a *wise* judge. An adverb describes an adjective, a verb, or another adverb: a *very* good speech, to speak *quickly,* to speak *very quickly.*

Cases

In Latin, virtually every noun or adjective is expressed in a precise form, called a case, that indicates by its ending how the word functions grammatically in the sentence. Latin has six cases:

1. The nominative case indicates the subject of the verb or the predicate nominative. A predicate nominative is a noun or adjective that is equated with the subject by a copula, or linking verb (the most common linking verbs are "be," "seem," and "become"):

Bestia timet.	*The animal* is afraid. (subject)
Bestia **magna** est.	The animal is *large.* (predicate nominative adjective)
Ursa **bestia** est.	The bear is *an animal.* (predicate nominative noun)

2. The genitive case defines a relationship between two nouns, such as possession, object of a verbal idea, or part of a collective whole. Ordinarily the noun in the genitive follows the noun to which it is related. The most usual translation in English is "of":

dentēs **bestiae**	the teeth *of the animal; the animal's* teeth (the animal possesses the teeth)
timor **bestiārum**	fear *of animals* (the animals are the object of fear)
ūna **bestiārum**	one *of the animals* (a portion or part of the animals)

3. The dative case identifies the person or thing affected indirectly by a verb, that is, the person or thing in reference to whom or to which the action of the verb takes place:

Cibum **bestiae** dat.	She is giving *the animal* food. (or *to the animal*)
Cibum **bestiae** optat.	He wants food *for the animal.*
Poētae cantābimus.	We will sing *for the poet.* (or *to the poet*)

4. The accusative case marks the direct object of a verb. It is also used after certain prepositions, especially prepositions indicating motion toward something (e.g., **ad**, toward; **in**, into):

Puer **bestiam** vīdit.	The boy saw *an animal.*
Puer **ad bestiam** cucurrit.	The boy ran *toward the animal.*
Bestia **in silvam** cucurrit.	The animal ran *into the forest.*

5. The ablative case describes in some way a verbal action or state.

Carmen **ā poētā** cantum est.	The song was sung *by the poet.*
Daniēl spīnam **ex pede** leōnis extraxit.	Daniel removed a thorn *from* the lion's *paw.*
Terrā marīque metuēbantur.	They were feared *on land and sea.*
Illud **cum timōre et horrōre** dēlīberō.	*With fear and trembling* I ponder that.
Eō ipsō tempore gallus cecinit.	*At that very moment* the cock crowed.

The ablative case is frequently translated into English with a preposition such as "by," "from," "on," "with," "at." Some of these uses require a preposition in Latin also. The most common use of the ablative case in Latin shows by what means or instrument something is done. This ablative, consequently, is known as the *ablative of means or instrument*:

Vinculīs bestiam tenet.	He is restraining the animal *with chains.*
Bestia **dentibus** mordet.	The animal bites *with (its) teeth.*

6. The vocative case is used to address a person or thing directly, and is often introduced by an exclamatory word such as **Ō**:

Ō, **magister**, dīc mihi dē stellīs!	*Teacher*, tell me about the stars!
Virī, quid vidētis?	*Men*, what do you see?
Quid optātis, **puerī**?	What do you want, *boys*?

With one exception (see "Nouns: Second Declension," below), the form of the vocative is the same as that of the nominative case, and therefore is not included in most paradigms.

Gender

Every Latin noun has a grammatical gender—masculine, feminine, or neuter—which frequently has nothing to do with natural gender. The feminine noun **invidia** means "envy" or "spite," emotions not confined to females. **Bestia** is a feminine noun too, but the beast it designates may be either male or female. In **vir**, "man," on the other hand, natural and grammatical gender coincide: masculine. The nearest equivalent in English is the convention by which boats and cars, which have no natural gender, are sometimes referred to as feminine. The gender of a Latin noun is an important part of its vocabulary entry.

Declensions

Virtually all Latin nouns and adjectives belong to one of five formal groups called declensions. A declension is a pattern of case endings distinguished by the final letter of a noun stem and by its genitive singular form. "Declension" can also refer to the act of declining or inflecting a noun and its modifiers, that is, of systematically changing the case and number of a noun or adjective to the different cases. As you will learn in the course of this book, the five declensions of Latin nouns are characterized by the following:

Declension	Stem Characteristics	Genitive Singular Ending
First	**a**	**-ae**
Second	**o**	**-ī**
Third	**i** or consonant	**-is**
Fourth	**u**	**-ūs**
Fifth	**ē**	**-ēī**

Latin adjectives belong either to the first and second or else to the third of these declensions, as you will see later.

In dictionaries and vocabulary lists, nouns are listed in the nominative case (**bestia**). The genitive case (**bestiae**) is also given, as are the gender and the meaning or meanings. In learning a noun, you must always learn thoroughly its nominative and genitive forms and its gender, in addition to its meaning. A typical vocabulary listing is **bestia**, **bestiae**,[1] *f*, "beast, wild animal."

The genitive (**bestiae**) contains the stem of the noun. The stem cannot always be determined from the nominative form; it is obtained by dropping the genitive case ending (-**ae**). To this stem the various case endings are added.

Nouns: First Declension

The first declension is characterized by the letter -**a**-, which is found in every case ending except the dative and ablative plural, (-**īs**). In order to

[1] When forms are readily predictable from the nominative case, the genitive form is usually abbreviated, e.g., **bestia**, -**ae**, *f*.

decline this noun, drop the genitive singular ending (-**ae**) and add the appropriate case ending to the stem (**besti**-):

Case	Endings	**bestia, bestiae**, *f, animal*	Translation
		SINGULAR	
Nom.	**-a**	besti**a**	An *animal* bit him.
Gen.	**-ae**	besti**ae**	The *animal's* teeth are sharp. (*of the animal*)
Dat.	**-ae**	besti**ae**	Give the animal food. (*to the animal*)
Acc.	**-am**	besti**am**	We see *the animal*.
Abl.	**-ā**	besti**ā**	She was bitten *by an animal*.
Voc.	**-a**	besti**a**	*Animal*, stop biting!
		PLURAL	
Nom.	**-ae**	besti**ae**	The *animals* bit him.
Gen.	**-ārum**	besti**ārum**	The *animals'* teeth are sharp. (*of the animals*)
Dat.	**-īs**	besti**īs**	Give *the animals* food. (*to the animals*)
Acc.	**-ās**	besti**ās**	We see *the animals*.
Abl.	**-īs**	besti**īs**	She was bitten *by animals*.
Voc.	**-ae**	besti**ae**	You will be punished, *animals*!

Most nouns of the first declension are feminine, but there are some important exceptions, such as **nauta**, **-ae**, *m*, "sailor," **agricola**, **-ae**, *m*, "farmer," and **poēta**, **-ae**, *m*, "poet." The first declension contains no neuter nouns.

Nouns: Second Declension

Case	Endings M.	Endings N.	**dominus, dominī**, *m, master*	**ager, agrī**, *m, field*	**puer, puerī**, *m, boy*	**dōnum, dōnī**, *n, gift*
				SINGULAR		
Nom.	**-us**, —	**-um**	domin**us**	ager	puer	dōn**um**
Gen.	**-ī**	**-ī**	domin**ī**	agr**ī**	puer**ī**	dōn**ī**
Dat.	**-ō**	**-ō**	domin**ō**	agr**ō**	puer**ō**	dōn**ō**
Acc.	**-um**	**-um**	domin**um**	agr**um**	puer**um**	dōn**um**
Abl.	**-ō**	**-ō**	domin**ō**	agr**ō**	puer**ō**	dōn**ō**
Voc.	**-e**, —	**-um**	domin**e**	ager	puer	dōn**um**

			PLURAL			
Nom.	-ī	-a	dominī	agrī	puerī	dōna
Gen.	-ōrum	-ōrum	dominōrum	agrōrum	puerōrum	dōnōrum
Dat.	-īs	-īs	dominīs	agrīs	puerīs	dōnīs
Acc.	-ōs	-a	dominōs	agrōs	puerōs	dōna
Abl.	-īs	-īs	dominīs	agrīs	puerīs	dōnīs
Voc.	-ī	-a	dominī	agrī	puerī	dōna

Again, to find the stem, drop the ending of the genitive singular (in this declension, **-ī**), and then add the case endings to the stem. Observe the following points:

1. The neuter endings differ from the masculine endings only in the nominative and vocative singular and plural, and in the accusative plural.

2. The difference between **puer** and **ager** shows why you must learn both the nominative and the genitive forms of each noun. The nominative **puer** contains the stem as it appears in the genitive, **puer-**. The stem of **ager**, however, is **agr-**, without the **-e** found in the nominative singular. **Ager** is more typical than **puer** of the **-er** group nouns of the second declension. Another example is **liber**, **librī**, *m*, "book." English derivatives are often helpful for remembering whether or not the **-e-** is present (e.g., puerile, agriculture, library).

3. Singular nouns of the second declension that end in **-us** or **-ius** in the nominative case are the exception wherein the vocative does not have the same form as the nominative. For second declension nouns ending in **-us**, the singular vocative ending is **-e**, as in **Domine!** For nouns ending in **-ius** (e.g., **fīlius**, "son"), the vocative **-e** contracts with the **-i-** of the stem (***fīlie**) to produce a long **-ī** (**fīlī**). **Meus**, "my," which would become an unpronounceable ***mee** according to the rule, contracts its stem with the ending and becomes **mī**: **Ō mī fīlī!** "Oh, my son!"

4. Nearly all second declension nouns are masculine or neuter, but there are a few feminine nouns of the second declension. Various kinds of trees, for example, such as the elm (**ulmus**, **-ī**) and the pine (**pīnus**, **-ī**), are feminine, as are the words for home (**domus**, **-ī**) and for ground or soil (**humus**, **-ī**). They are declined like second declension masculine nouns.

A Note on Translation

A thousand years ago, the English language had a similar system of cases and inflections. We have lost most of them, however, and now must depend almost entirely on word order to express the connections between parts of a sentence: DOG BITES BOY and BOY BITES DOG—only one might be newsworthy. Compare some of the possibilities in Latin, where each of the two nouns carries its functional marker in its case ending:

Bestia puerum mordet.
Puerum mordet bestia.
Mordet puerum bestia.

Since the subject, **bestia**, is in the nominative case, and the object, **puerum**, is in the accusative case, each version of the sentence means essentially the same thing: "The animal is biting the boy." The emphasis, however, is different in each instance.

But wait a minute. Why "*the* animal," "*the* boy"? Where did "the" come from? Perhaps you noticed that in the illustrations of case uses, the English versions sometimes had "the," sometimes "a" or "an," or even no article at all. Latin has no definite article ("the") and no indefinite article ("a," "an"). Therefore, in the absence of any defining context, we might just as well have rendered this sentence, "An animal is biting a boy." Sometimes, too, no article is needed: **Bestiās nōn timeō**, "I am not afraid of animals." The principle is the same as in choosing among the possible translations for a verb: look to the context for guidance.

Scrībenda

First declension nouns

agricola, **agricolae**, *m* farmer
bestia, **bestiae**, *f* animal
nauta, **nautae**, *m* sailor
poēta, **poētae**, *m* poet
stella, **stellae**, *f* star

Second declension nouns

ager, **agrī**, *m* field
caelum, **caelī**, *n* sky
dominus, **dominī**, *m* master; ruler
dōnum, **dōnī**, *n* gift
puer, **puerī**, *m* boy
servus, **servī**, *m* slave; servant

A. Decline the following nouns: stella; servus; ager; caelum.

B. Identify all possible cases for the following forms:

bestiae	bestiam	bestiā	bestiīs
agricola	agricolīs	agricolās	agricolārum
nautae	nautārum	nautam	nautīs
dominō	dominīs	dominōs	dominōrum
agrī	agrum	agrōs	agrīs
puerō	puerum	puerōrum	puerīs
dōna	dōnum	dōnīs	dōnōrum

C. Translate:

1. Videō puerum. Puer cantat. Puerō cantat. Puerī cantant.
2. Nautae cōgitant. Cōgitā, nauta. Cōgitābit nauta.
3. Puer poētam videt. Puerī, poētam vidēte.
   Vidē, poēta puerō cantat.
4. Agricola dōna dat. Dōna puerōrum captāvit agricola.
5. Agricola poētae cantāre optat. Agricolaene poēta cantāvit?

Adjectives: First and Second Declension

An adjective describes (modifies) a noun or pronoun: a *good* horse, a *bad* man, a *tall* tree, we are *happy*. An adjective has no gender of its own; the declined endings on an adjective indicate the gender, case, and number of the noun or pronoun that the adjective is modifying. For this reason, an adjective of the first and second declension appears in dictionaries and vocabulary lists with endings -**us**, -**a**, -**um**: **bonus**, -**a**, -**um**, good; **magnus**, **a**, **um**, large, great. The nominative ending -**a** indicates that, when this adjective modifies a feminine noun, it takes endings of the first declension: **magna bestia.** The nominative endings -**us**, -**um** indicate that the adjective takes endings of the second declension when it modifies a masculine or neuter noun: **servus bonus**; **magnum dōnum**.

Words such as **poēta**, **nauta** and **agricola**, which are masculine even though they belong to the first declension, will be modified by adjectives with masculine endings: **magnus poēta**; **nauta bonus**; **agricola bonus**. Conversely, feminine nouns of the second declension, such as **pīnus**, the pine tree, and **ulmus**, the elm tree, will be modified by adjectives with feminine endings: **magna pīnus**; **magna ulmus**. When we modify the nouns below, then, with the adjective **bonus**, **bona**, **bonum**, "good," the endings of the adjectives reflect the gender, number, and case of the nouns they modify.

The most usual position for the adjective is immediately after the noun it modifies, but generally the more emphatic word precedes. Consequently, adjectives denoting size (a "large" or "small" tree), quantity ("one" or "many" trees) or interrogative adjectives ("which" tree?) will tend to precede the noun.

viae bonae (nom. pl.)	good roads
viam bonam (acc. s.)	a good road
poētās bonōs (acc. pl.)	good poets
humus bona (nom. s.)	good soil
dōnōrum bonōrum (gen. pl.)	of good gifts
ager bonus (nom. s.)	a good field

Some adjectives, following the pattern of the second declension -**er** nouns (**puer**, **ager**), end in -**er** in the masculine nominative singular:

līber, lībera, līberum	free
miser, misera, miserum	unhappy, wretched
pulcher, pulchra, pulchrum	beautiful, handsome
noster, nostra, nostrum	our
vester, vestra, vestrum	your (pl.)

Observe that the last three adjectives in this group have no -**e**- before the -**r**- in the feminine and neuter forms, and that the first two adjectives retain the -**e**- throughout. The stems of these adjectives vary in the same way that the stems of nouns vary (compare **ager** and **puer**). The best way to determine whether the adjective retains the -**e**- is to refer to the feminine nominative singular form. Thus, the stem of **līber** is **līber**- (from **lībera**), retaining the -**e**-, and the stem of **pulcher** is **pulchr**-. In learning these adjectives you must therefore pay particular attention to the feminine and neuter forms. English derivatives are also helpful here, for they are usually formed from the stem, and so will indicate whether the -**e**- is retained in the declined Latin forms: liberal, pulchritude, miserable.

Sometimes the noun itself is omitted, and the adjective is used as a noun; it is then called a substantive adjective. In such cases, the gender and number of the adjective will indicate the basic attributes of the missing noun, which can often be supplied from the context:

Dominus servīs **bona** dabunt.	The master will give *good gifts* to the slaves.
Virī malī sunt; puer **malōs** timet.	The men are evil; the boy fears *the evil men*.

When the reference is not so clear, you can translate the substantive adjective as "man" if it is masculine, "woman" if feminine, or "thing" if neuter.

Magnus mē videt.	*The great man* sees me.
Misera bestiam timet.	*The poor woman* fears the animal.
Dominus **magna** optābit.	The master will want *great things*.

Adverbs: Formation

Adverbs are regularly formed from adjectives of the first and second declensions by adding -**ē** to the stem:

clārus, -a, -um, bright; clear	**clārē**, brightly, clearly
līber, -a, -um, free	**līberē**, freely
pulcher, -chra, -chrum, beautiful	**pulchrē**, beautifully

Some of the most common adverbs are irregular:

bonus, -a, -um, good	**benĕ**, well (note the short -**e**)
malus, -a, -um, bad	**malĕ**, badly

Adverbs formed from adjectives of the third declension will be discussed in Chapter XI. Irregular adverbs, and various other adverbs that are not derived from adjectives, will be listed separately in the vocabulary.

Verba tenenda

First Declension Nouns

amīca, -**ae**, *f* girlfriend, sweetheart	**agricola**, -**ae**, *m* farmer
bestia, -**ae**, *f* wild animal, beast	**nauta**, -**ae**, *m* sailor
fīlia, -**ae**, *f* daughter	**poēta**, -**ae**, *m* poet

learn vocab

invidia, **-ae**, *f* envy, jealousy; ill will, spite
puella, **-ae**, *f* girl; daughter; sweetheart
stella, **-ae**, *f* star
via, **viae**, *f* way, road, path; journey

Second Declension Nouns

amīcus, **-ī**, *m* friend
dominus, **-ī**, *m* master; ruler
fīlius, **fīliī**, *m* son
numerus, **-ī**, *m* number
servus, **-ī**, *m* slave, servant

ager, **agrī**, *m* field
liber, **-brī**, *m* book
magister, **-trī**, *m* teacher; master
puer, **puerī**, *m* boy; child; slave
vir, **virī**, *m* man (i.e., a male human being)

auxilium, **-iī**, *n* help, aid, assistance
caelum, **-ī**, *n* sky; weather
dōnum, **-ī**, *n* gift, present
verbum, **-ī**, *n* word
vinculum, **-ī**, *n* chain

First and Second Declension Adjectives

amātus, **-a**, **-um** loved, beloved
bonus, **-a**, **-um** good
clārus, **-a**, **-um** clear; bright; famous
datus, **-a**, **-um** given
magnus, **-a**, **-um** large, big, great
malus, **-a**, **-um** bad
meus, **-a**, **-um** my
parvus, **-a**, **-um** small, little
tuus, **-a**, **-um** your (s.: i.e., belonging to one person)
vīsus, **-a**, **-um** seen

līber, **lībera**, **līberum** free
miser, **misera**, **miserum** unhappy, wretched, miserable
noster, **-tra**, **-trum** our
pulcher, **-chra**, **-chrum** beautiful, handsome
vester, **-tra**, **-trum** your (pl.: i.e., belonging to more than one person)

Other

mē, pron. (acc./abl.) me
tē, pron. (acc./abl.) you, s.

in, prep., (+ abl.) in, on, inside; (+ acc.) into, against

dum, conj. while, as long as
et, conj. and
et . . . et both . . . and
sed, conj. but

Notanda

amīca and **amīcus** are both substantive forms of the adjective **amīcus**, **-a**, **-um**, "friendly." Note that the usages are not parallel: the feminine form has been restricted to a specific kind of female friend.

agricola is a compound: the verb **colō** means "to tend," "to cultivate," and so an **agricola** is one who tends the field, a farmer. As **agri-** shows, compounds are normally formed from the stem.

nauta and **poēta** are both borrowings from Greek, occupational names that the Romans adopted comparatively late.

dominus and **magister** can both mean "master," but in different senses. A **dominus** is the master of the house (**domus**), and by extension is the ruler of a people. A **magister**, a "master" or "commander" (from **magis**, adv., "more") directs a group of people engaged in a specific activity—most often, learning. (A **minister**, by contrast, from the adverb **minus**, "less," is a servant or attendant.)

Although **puer** can refer to a child of either sex, its diminutive form **puella** is the usual word for "girl."

dōnum is related to **dō**, **dare**; from **dōnum** in turn is formed the first conjugation verb **dōnāre**, "to give as a present," "to bestow."

vinculum can refer to anything used to tie or bind—even metaphorically: for example, the bonds of friendship, **vincula amīcitiae**.

amātus, **datus**, and **vīsus** are the fourth principal parts (the perfect passive participles) of the verbs **amō**, **dō**, and **videō**. The English derivative "data" is taken directly from the Latin neuter plural form of the adjective **datus**, meaning "the things given." A visa (shortened from Latin **carta vīsa**) indicates that a government has seen and approved the passport bearing its stamp.

magnus means "great" in the figurative as well as the physical sense: "noble," "lofty," "important."

liber, "book," and **līber**, "free" the noun has a short -**i**-; the adjective, a long -**ī**-. Be sure to distinguish them in speaking.

tuus and **vester** are both possessive adjectives meaning "your." The choice depends on the number of possessors, not on whether what is possessed is singular or plural: **tuōs librōs videō**, "I see your books," speaking to one person; **vestrum dōnum parābit**, "she will prepare your gift," with two or more people sharing one gift.

in with the ablative case expresses stationary position, the place where someone or something is, or where something happens; **in** followed by the accusative case denotes motion toward—sometimes in a hostile sense. (Most Latin prepositions govern only one case.)

et, "and" is sometimes used for emphasis, adverbially, as in Julius Caesar's dying words to his friend-turned-assassin, *Et tu, Brūte?*—"Even you, Brutus?" or "You also, Brutus?" When **et** is repeated in a series, and seems to occur once too often to make sense, it is probably being used with the meaning "both . . . and," as in *Et Brūtum et Cassium vīdit*, "He saw both Brutus and Cassius."

Ante legenda

A. Translate the following phrases; then decline them in Latin in the singular and in the plural:

amīcus bonus	magnus ager
magna stella	fīlius vester
vir līber	

B. Modify each of the following nouns with the adjective **tuus**, **-a**, **-um**, and translate the new phrase into English:

dōnum
poēta
puer
fīlius
bestia
invidia
liber
magister

C. Identify the case and number of the following phrases; if more than one case is possible, identify all possible cases:

poētae clarī
vinculī malī
nautīs bonīs
invidiā tuā
amīcās nostrās
amīcō tuō
agricolā bonō
vincula mea
dōnīs tuīs
servōrum malōrum
amīcōs vestrōs
amīcae meae
puerōrum bonōrum
agricolae bonō

D. Fill in the appropriate form of the adjective indicated, and translate the entire sentence:

1. (Magnus, -a, -um) bestia _____ momordit (parvus, -a, -um) _______ puerum.
2. Puer bestiam (miser, -a, -um) _______ (magnus, -a, -um) ______ vinculīs captāvit.
3. Poēta (pulcher, -chra, -chrum) _______ amīcae (amātus, -a, -um) ______ cantābit.
4. Magister (bonus, -a, -um) _____ fīliō (noster, -tra, -trum) ______ (magnus, -a, -um) ______ auxilium līberē dabit.
5. Nōlī spērāre auxilium (meus, -a, -um) _____.
6. Poēta (clārus, -a, -um) ______ dē stellīs (clārus, -a, -um) ______ in caelō cōgitat. (**dē** + abl., about, concerning)

E. Translate:

1. Servus cantat. Servus magna cantat. Servō cantābō. Servīs pulchra cantāvimus.
2. Poētae clārī puerīs cantāvērunt. Poētae magna amīcīs nostrīs cantābunt.
3. Agricola bestiam videt. Agricolam bestia vīdit.
4. Puer magnam bestiam timēbit. Bonus parvam bestiam nōn timuit. Bonae mala timēmus.
5. Vidēs numerum bestiārum, sed nōn timēs.
6. Bestia, nōlī mē mordēre! Bestia, servum mordē! Servī, bestiās vidēte! Servum bestia momordit.
7. Invidia malum poētam mordet; bonum nōn mordēbit.
8. Poēta cantāvit, "Dum spīrō, spērō!"
9. Dōnum vestrum fīliō meō dabō.
10. Amīcī tuī, mī fīlī, mala cōgitant.

F. Translate into Latin:

1. Do you see the stars in the sky?
2. The poet did not see stars in the sky. He saw animals.

3. The small animal wanted to bite the large animal.
4. I have seen your (pl.) beautiful gifts.
5. They sang clearly for the poet.

Legenda

Bestiae in caelō

Callisto, a nymph, was a companion of the huntress-goddess Diana, but was cruelly changed into a bear. Her son grew up to be a hunter. When he encountered this bear in the forest, his natural instinct was to kill it. But the gods intervened and changed them both into the constellations we now know as the Big Dipper and the Little Dipper—Ursa Maior ("bigger bear") and Ursa Minor ("smaller bear").

See notes for words marked with an asterisk (*).

PUER: Ō magister, vidēsne stellās in caelō?

MAGISTER: Videō. Nam* stellae nautīs viās bonās dant. Sī stellās nōn vident, nautae errābunt.

2: **nam** (conj.), for (introducing explanation); For, you see

The constellation Ursa Maior. The Big Dipper consists of the seven stars in the tail, hips, and waist.

PUER: Vidēsne illās* stellās in caelō?

MAGISTER: Nōn stellās videō, sed bestiās. Vidē, bestia parva magnam mordēre et captāre spērat. Aliās* stellās nōn tōtum annum* in caelō vidēmus, sed illae bestiae semper* circum polum* errant. Nautae viās tenēbunt sī illās bestiās vidēbunt.

PUER: Cūr parva bestia magnam bestiam captāre optat?

MAGISTER: Ōlim* parva bestia vēnātor* fuit*. Fuit et fīlius bestiae magnae, sed hoc factum* nōn vīdit. Ūnō diē* magnam bestiam in agrō vīdit. Optāvit vēnātor bestiam necāre*. Deī* timuērunt. Fīlium igitur* et mātrem* in caelum mōvērunt*. Nunc* illās bestiās in caelō vidēmus, ubi* circum polum errant.

4, 6, 7, 13: **illī**, **illae**, **illa** (pl. adj.), those
6: **aliās** (acc. fem. pl. adj.), other
tōtum annum, throughout the year
7: **semper** (adv.), always
7, 14: **circum polum**, around the Celestial North Pole
10: **ōlim** (adv.), once upon a time
10, 12: **vēnātor** (nom. masc. s.), hunter
10: **fuit** (perfect tense), he (she/it) was
11: **hoc factum** (acc.), this fact
ūnō diē (abl. showing time when), one day
12: **necō**, **necāre**, **necāvī**, **necātus**, kill
deī (nom. masc. pl.), the gods
igitur (conj.), therefore
13: **mātrem** (acc. fem. sing.), mother
nunc (adv.), now
13, 14: **moveō**, **movēre**, **mōvī**, **mōtus**, move
14: **ubi** (adv.), where

III

Third and Fourth Conjugations; Special Adjectives; *Sum* and *Possum*; Ablative Case (1)

Third and Fourth Conjugation Verbs

As with the first two conjugations, the present active infinitive indicates which conjugation a verb belongs to, and contains the present stem of the verb:

		Infinitive Ending	Stem
First conjugation	**amāre**	**-āre**	**amā-**
Second conjugation	**tenēre**	**-ēre**	**tenē-**
Third conjugation	**dūcere**	**-ere**	**dūce-**
Fourth conjugation	**audīre**	**-īre**	**audī-**

The only difference between infinitives of the second and the third conjugations is in the length of the stem vowel. It is a very important difference, however, because the short **-ĕ-** of third conjugation verb stem changes (weakens) to **-ĭ-** in the present tense, and even seems to disappear completely in the future tense. You may find it simpler, therefore, to think of the present stem of third conjugation verbs as shortened, ending in a consonant (**dūc-**), and to treat the vowel that follows as part of the conjugated ending.

Fourth conjugation verbs, on the other hand, retain the long **-ī-** of the stem throughout the conjugation, in all tenses.

Present Indicative Active

	THIRD CONJUGATION	FOURTH CONJUGATION	COMPARE
Infinitive	**dūcere**, *to lead*	**audīre**, *to hear*	**tenēre,** *to hold*
	SINGULAR		
First person	dūcō	audiō	teneō
Second person	dūcis	audīs	tenēs
Third person	dūcit	audit	tenet
	PLURAL		
First person	dūcimus	audīmus	tenēmus
Second person	dūcitis	audītis	tenētis
Third person	dūcunt	audiunt	tenent

Observe that:

1. In the first person singular of the third conjugation, the stem vowel has been absorbed into the personal ending **-ō** (compare ***amaō**, ***amābiō**, ***tenēbiō**).

2. In the third person plural, the vowel preceding the ending changes from **-i-** to **-u-** (compare **-bunt** in the first and second conjugation future).

3. The difference between **-ĭ-** (a reduced form of **-ĕ-**) and **-ī-** in the stem vowels of third and fourth conjugation verbs produces a different pattern of accent: **dū́cĭmus**, **dū́cĭtis**, accenting the antepenult; but **audī́mus**, **audī́tis**, with the accent on the penult.

Another group of verbs, a subgroup of the third conjugation, shares features of both the third and fourth conjugations: their infinitives end in **-ĕre**, but they are conjugated like verbs of the fourth conjugation. To identify a verb as a member of this hybrid class, you must see its first two principal parts:

THIRD CONJUGATION -IŌ VERBS	
capiō, **capere**, *to seize*	**fugiō**, **fugere**, *to flee; avoid*
SINGULAR	
cap**iō**	fug**iō**
capis	fugis
capit	fugit
PLURAL	
capimus	fugimus
capitis	fugitis
cap**iu**nt	fug**iu**nt

Note that the **-iō** verbs of the third conjugation add **-ĭ-** to the shortened, consonant stem (**cap-**, **fug-**) throughout, and consequently look like fourth conjugation verbs, except that the **-i-** in third conjugation **-iō** verbs is short.

Future Indicative Active

In all forms except the first person singular, the future tense marker for the third and fourth conjugations, including the third conjugation **-iō** verbs, is **-ē-**. This **-ē-** is added directly to the present stem. For the first person singular, however, the future tense marker is **-a-**, followed by the first person singular ending **-m**. (Note that any vowel before final **-m**, **-t**, or **-nt** is short.)

ENDINGS	THIRD AND FOURTH CONJUGATIONS			COMPARE	
	dūc-	**cap-i-**	**audī-**	amā-	tenē-
		SINGULAR		SINGULAR	
-am	dūc**am**	capi**am**	audi**am**	amābō	tenēbō
-ēs	dūc**ēs**	capi**ēs**	audi**ēs**	amābis	tenēbis
-et	dūc**et**	capi**et**	audi**et**	amābit	tenēbit
		PLURAL		PLURAL	
-ēmus	dūc**ēmus**	capi**ēmus**	audi**ēmus**	amābimus	tenēbimus
-ētis	dūc**ētis**	capi**ētis**	audi**ētis**	amābitis	tenēbitis
-ent	dūc**ent**	capi**ent**	audi**ent**	amābunt	tenēbunt

Some of these new forms look just like the present indicative of second conjugation verbs: compare, for example, **tenēs** (present) and **dūcēs** (future). In order to identify any given form correctly, you must always know first what conjugation the verb belongs to.

Perfect Indicative Active

All four conjugations use the same personal endings for the perfect indicative active:

	SINGULAR	PLURAL
First person	**-ī**	**-imus**
Second person	**-istī**	**-istis**
Third person	**-it**	**-ērunt**

These special endings are added to the perfect stem, found by dropping the **-i** from the third principal part. Here are the principal parts for the model verbs of the third and fourth conjugations:

Third conjugation	**dūcō**, **dūcere**, **dūxī**, **ductus**
Third **-iō** hybrids	**capiō**, **capere**, **cēpī**, **captus**
Fourth conjugation	**audiō**, **audīre**, **audīvī**, **audītus**

By combining the perfect stems and endings we obtain:

THIRD CONJUGATION		THIRD CONJUGATION -iō	
		SINGULAR	
dūxī	I led, have led, did lead	**cēpī**	I seized. . .
dūxistī	you led (etc.)	**cēpistī**	
dūxit	he (she/it) led	**cēpit**	
		PLURAL	
dūximus	we led	**cēpimus**	
dūxistis	you led	**cēpistis**	
dūxērunt	they led	**cēpērunt**	

FOURTH CONJUGATION

audīvī	I heard. . .
audīvistī	
audīvit	
audīvimus	
audīvistis	
audīvērunt	

Formation of the Perfect Stem

Examine once more the principal parts of our model verbs for each conjugation. Compare the third principal part, which contains the perfect stem, to the present stem as seen in the second principal part:

amō, amāre, **amāvī**, amātus
teneō, tenēre, **tenuī**, tentus
dūcō, dūcere, **dūxi**, ductus
capiō, capere, **cēpī**, captus
audiō, audīre, **audīvī**, audītus

The boldface forms seem to have nothing in common except the final -**ī**, and the -**v**- of **amāvī** and **audīvī**. Can we discover any rules for predicting the perfect stem of a verb? Yes and no. Although you must indeed memorize their principal parts individually, the many apparent variations you will encounter actually reduce to four patterns:

1. -**vī** (-**uī**) is added to the present stem.[1] This is the characteristic Latin perfect, seen in most first, second, and fourth conjugation verbs:

[1] The -**u**- seen in most second conjugation perfects is identical to the -**v**- of the first and fourth conjunctions, but in the second conjunction (**tenuī**) the stem vowel -**ē**- is dropped before the -**uī**. The distinction between **u** and **v** is merely a convention of printing, and depends on whether a vowel or a consonant precedes. Both will appear as **u** in printed texts that do not differentiate the two functions of the semivowel **u**/**v**.

First conjugation	amāre, amā**vī**
Second conjugation	tenēre, ten**uī**
Fourth conjugation	audīre, audī**vī**

2. The root vowel (not the stem vowel) of the present infinitive lengthens:

vĭdēre, v**ī**dī
fŭgere, f**ū**gī
vĕnīre, v**ē**nī

If it is a short -**ă**-, it changes to a long -**ē**-:

căpere, c**ē**pī
făcere, f**ē**cī
ăgere, **ē**gī

3. -**sī** is added to the present stem, sometimes triggering further changes:

iubēre, ius**sī** (**iub-sī*)	dūcere, dū**xī** (**dūc-sī*)[2]
mittere, mī**sī** (**mitt-sī*)	sentiō, sēn**sī** (**sent-si*)

Here **mīsī** and **sēnsī** show compensatory lengthening in the root vowel.

4. The root reduplicates; if the root vowel is -**a**-, it changes to -**e**-:

mordēre, **mo**mordī
currere, **cu**currī
dare, **de**dī (**dadedi*)

Imperative

The singular imperative of the fourth conjugation is the same as its present stem, that is, the present active infinitive less -**re**. Regular and -**iō** verbs of the third conjugation add an -**e** to the shortened (consonant) stem:

		COMPARE
Scrībe!	Write!	**Amā**!
Fuge mala!	Avoid evil!	**Tenē**!
Audī me!	Listen to me!	**Cōgitā**!

Four third conjugation verbs (and only four!) are an exception to this rule; they drop the stem vowel, -**e**, as well:

Dīc!	Speak!	**Fac**!	Do!
Dūc!	Lead!	**Fer**![3]	Bring!

The plural imperative forms of the third conjugation add -**ite** to the stem; fourth conjugation verbs add -**te**:

[2] Remember that **x** is a double consonant.
[3] See Chapter XII for discussion of this irregular verb.

		COMPARE
Amīcī, **fugite** mala!	Friends, avoid evil!	**Amāte**!
Puerī, **audīte** mē!	Children, listen to me!	**Tenēte**!
Dūcite!	Lead on!	**Cōgitāte**!

The negative imperatives are formed with **nōlī** or **nōlīte** plus the present infinitive:

Nōlī mē tangere!	Don't touch me!
Nōlīte fugere, puerī!	Don't run away, children!

Special Adjectives

Nine common adjectives of the first and second declensions have irregular genitive and dative singular endings: in these nine adjectives the genitive singular of all genders ends in **-īus**, and the dative singular of all genders ends in **-ī**. Plural forms of these adjectives are declined just like **magnus**, **-a**, **-um**:

sōlus, **-a**, **-um**, *alone, only*

	SINGULAR			PLURAL		
	M.	F.	N.	M.	F.	N.
Nom.	sōlus	sōla	sōlum	sōli	sōlae	sōla
Gen.	sōl**īus**	sōl**īus**	sōl**īus**	sōlōrum	sōlārum	sōlōrum
Dat.	sōl**ī**	sōl**ī**	sōl**ī**	sōlīs	sōlīs	sōlīs
Acc.	sōlum	sōlam	sōlum	sōlōs	sōlās	sōla
Abl.	sōlō	sōlā	sōlō	sōlīs	sōlīs	sōlīs

Arranged in the order given below, these nine adjectives form an acronym, **ūnus nauta**, which makes them easy to remember:

U	ūnus, ūna, ūnum	one
N	nūllus, nūlla, nūllum	no, none (the negative form of **ūllus**)
U	ūllus, ūlla, ūllum	any
S	sōlus, sōla, sōlum	alone, only
N	neuter, neutra, neutrum	neither (of two: the negative form of **uter**)
A	alius, alia, aliud	other; another (pl., some)
U	uter, utra, utrum	which one (of two)
T	tōtus, tōta, tōtum	whole, entire
A	alter, altera, alterum	the other (of two); the second

Observe that:

1. The neuter nominative and accusative singular of **alius** ends in **-d**, **aliud**.

2. **Uter** and **neuter** follow the pattern of **ager**, **pulcher**, and the like, inserting an **-e-** in the masculine nominative singular. The English derivative "neutral" contains the stem, without that **-e-**.

Scrībenda

Third Conjugation Verbs

agō, agere, ēgī, actus do, make; lead, drive; act; spend (of time)
grātiās agere thank (+ dative)
vītam agere live, spend one's life
dūcō, dūcere, dūxī, ductus lead, guide
mittō, mittere, mīsī, missus send, let go
petō, petere, petīvī, petītus seek; ask (for)
vīvō, vīvere, vīxī, vīctus live

Third Conjugation -**iō** *Verbs*

capiō, capere, cēpī, captus take, seize
faciō, facere, fēcī, factus do; make
fugiō, fugere, fūgī, fugitūrus flee, run away (from); avoid

Fourth Conjugation Verbs

audiō, audīre, audīvī, audītus hear, listen to
sentiō, sentīre, sēnsī, sēnsus perceive, sense, feel
veniō, venīre, vēnī, ventus come
inveniō, invenīre, invēnī, inventus come upon, discover

Special Adjectives

alius, alia, aliud other; another
aliī, aliae, alia some
alter, altera, alterum the other (of two); the second
neuter, neutra, neutrum neither (of two)
nūllus, -a, -um no, none
sōlus, -a, -um alone, only
tōtus, -a, -um whole, entire
ūllus, -a, -um any
ūnus, -a, -um one, single
uter, utra, utrum which one (of two)

A. Conjugate in the tense indicated, translating each form:

vīvō (present)
dūcō (perfect)
mittō (future)
fugiō (perfect)
inveniō (future)
sentiō (present)

B. For each form, identify the conjugation, translate, and then change to the future tense, retaining the same person and number:

agis
dūcō
vīvit
capis
mittunt
capitis
agitis
vīvimus
facit
faciunt
fugitis
fugiō
audit
audīmus
inveniunt

C. Translate; then change to the perfect tense, retaining the same person and number:

aget
fugit
venīs
vīvēmus
timet
timent
vidēmus
sentient
audiō
agō
capis

D. Translate each form; then give its singular and plural imperatives:
ēgistī parāmus sentiō veniam dūcunt

E. Identify the person, number, and tense of each underlined verb; then substitute each form and translate the entire sentences into English:

1. Poētam clārum audīvī (audī, audiēmus, audiam).
2. Verba poētae audiet (audīvit).
3. Servōs miserōs audīte (audiētis).
4. Vītam bonam aget (age, ēgit).
5. Bestiam vinculō dūcam (dūc, dūxī).
6. Bestia mē fugit (fūgit, fugiet).
7. Magistrō vestrō gratiās agitis (agētis, ēgistis).
8. Magnum auxilium inveniet (invenit, invēnit, invēnistī).
9. Dominus mē miserum facit (fēcit, faciet).
10. Magna dōna petit (petet, petīvit) tua amīca.

F. Give the Latin for:

no books (nom.)
neither star (abl.)
other men (gen.)
the other daughter (dat.)
the entire field (gen.)
another gift (acc.)
one farmer alone (dat.)

G. Decline, in all cases, in the singular only:

only the teacher
one friend
any beast
other aid

H. Translate the following sentences into English:

1. Neuter nauta stellās ūllās vīdit.
2. Ūnam bestiam parvam nōn timuī.
3. Dominus sōlus amīcōs nūllōs inveniet.
4. Vidēsne ūllās stellās? Ūnam sōlam videō.
5. Virī miserī et terram aliam et caelum aliud petunt. Ūnam invenient, sed nōn alterum.

Sum and *Possum*: Present, Future, and Perfect Indicative

Since *being* and *being able*—I am, I can—are basic human concepts, forms of these verbs occur very frequently. In Latin, the two verbs are related, and so their forms can be learned together. The forms are irregular. Study the principal parts and the two paradigms carefully:

sum, esse, fui, futūrus, *be, exist*
possum, posse, potuī, ——, *be able, can*

PRESENT INDICATIVE

		SINGULAR	
sum	I am, I exist	**possum**	I am able, I can
es	you are (etc.)	**potes**	you are able (etc.)
est	he (she/it) is	**potest**	he (she/it) is able
		PLURAL	
sumus	we are	**possumus**	we are able
estis	you are	**potestis**	you are able
sunt	they are	**possunt**	they are able

The present infinitive of **sum** is **esse**, and its stem is **es**-. Thus, the three forms that begin with **es**- are regular. The perfect system of **sum** is formed on a different stem (compare English: I am, I was, I have been).

Possum is a compound of **sum** and the adjective **potis**, **pote**, "able," and so "I am able" is a literal translation of **possum**. You might expect its infinitive to be **potesse**, and in fact that form does appear frequently in early Latin, especially Plautus; but **posse** is regular in classical Latin. The -**t**- of the root changes to -**s**- before present-tense forms of **sum** beginning with **s**-:**pot-se* becomes **posse**. But otherwise the -**t**- is retained: **potes**.

In the future tense of **sum**, the stem **es**- has changed to **er**-.[4] Note the vowels in the first person singular and third person plural endings, and compare them to the pattern for first and second conjugation verbs: -**bō** and -**bunt**.

FUTURE INDICATIVE

		SINGULAR	
erō	I shall be	pot**erō**	I shall be able
eris	you will be	pot**eris**	you will be able
erit	he (she/it) will be	pot**erit**	he (she/it) will be able
		PLURAL	
erimus	we shall be	pot**erimus**	we shall be able
eritis	you will be	pot**eritis**	you will be able
erunt	they will be	pot**erunt**	they will be able

The formation of the perfect tense is regular:

PERFECT INDICATIVE

		SINGULAR	
fu**ī**	I was, I have been	potu**ī**	I was able, I have been able, I could
fu**istī**	you were (etc.)	potu**istī**	you were able (etc.)
fu**it**	he (she/it) was	potu**it**	he (she/it) was able
		PLURAL	
fu**imus**	we were	potu**imus**	we were able
fu**istis**	you were	potu**istis**	you were able
fu**ērunt**	they were	potu**ērunt**	they were able

[4] Between vowels, -**s**- regularly changed to -**r**- in Latin. This phenomenon, called "rhotacism" after the name of the Greek letter for *r*, occurs in many languages, including English: compare "was" and (originally pronounced in two syllables) "were."

Predicate Nominative

Cōgitō, ergō sum. "I think, therefore I am." Thus the seventeenth-century French philosopher René Descartes formulated his principle that thinking proves existence. Here, in its sense of "exist," **sum** makes a complete predicate, and needs no noun or adjective to complete the sense.

Suppose we wanted to say instead, in a fit of wishful thinking, **cōgitō, ergō poēta sum**. I think, and that makes me something—what? Most often, a form of **esse** serves to connect the subject with a predicate noun or adjective also in the nominative case, rather like a sign of equality in mathematics; then it is called a connecting verb, or *copula*:

Poēta **agricola** est.	The poet is *a farmer*.
Poēta **clārus** est.	The poet is *famous*.
Nostrī **agricolae** sunt.	Our men are *farmers*.

A noun or adjective that describes or defines the subject may stand in the predicate with forms of **esse** or verbs with meanings such as "to become," "to be named," "to be called," "to appear." Since it refers back through the linking verb to the subject, this predicated noun or adjective will agree with that subject in case (nominative), number, and gender (unless the predicate noun is of a different gender from that of the subject).

The predicate adjective is a special use. More often an adjective is *attributive*: it simply attends its noun, whatever its role (and thus its case) in the sentence, whether in the subject, or in a prepositional phrase, or as the direct object, and so on. The following pair of sentences illustrates the distinction.

Sunt virī clārī.	(predicate noun with attributive adjective)
Virī clārī sunt.	(predicate adjective)

When it means "exist," the form of **esse** normally comes first in the sentence for emphasis: the first sentence means, "There are famous men," "Famous men do exist." The second sentence isn't interested in the fact of their existence—that is taken for granted—but is concerned with describing a quality of these men: they are famous.

Complementary Infinitive

Posse is an excellent example of a verb whose meaning is not complete in itself. **Possum**, "I can." You can *what*? "I can *come*," **venīre possum**. (Don't feel obliged to translate "I am able to come"—always try to make your English version sound natural.) Many verbs require an infinitive of some other verb to complete the meaning of the subject's action. For some verbs, such as **possum**, this is always true; others can also take a direct object or another construction. Consider the following sentences:

Servus dōna optat.	The slave wants gifts.
Servus dōna vidēre optat.	The slave wants to see the gifts.

In the first example, the main verb, **optat**, takes a direct object, **dōna**; in the second example, **vidēre** completes the action of the main verb, and itself governs the direct object.

Similarly, the second conjugation verb **dēbeō** can mean "owe," and take a direct object, for example, "money," **pecūniam**; but it can also take a complementary infinitive, and mean "be bound or obliged (to do something)":

Fīliae meae grātiās **agere dēbēs**.	You *ought to thank* my daughter.
Nōn dēbuistī librum magistrī **capere**.	You *should not have snatched* the teacher's book.

Observe that the English version of the second example does not contain an infinitive form: you can translate the Latin verb's sense of obligation with "should" or "must," just like an auxiliary verb in English. Note also that English, lacking a simple past form of "ought," transfers the tense of the Latin **dēbuistī** to the complementary infinitive.

If the complementary infinitive is **esse**, a predicate noun or adjective is likely to follow it. In that case, the predicate noun or adjective takes the case, number, and (if an adjective) gender of the subject of the main verb:

Poēta noster **clārus esse** incipit.	Our poet is beginning *to be famous*.
Puer **nauta esse** optat.	The boy wants *to be a sailor*.

Scrībenda

A. Conjugate:

sum in the present singular	**possum** in the perfect plural
sum in the future plural	**possum** in the future singular

B. Identify the following forms; then change each to the plural of the form given, retaining the same person and tense:

es	sum	potes
potuit	poterō	est
erit	fuistī	potuī

C. Identify and translate the following forms; then change them to the present tense, retaining the same person and number:

potuērunt	poterunt	fuimus
poteris	erunt	potuistis
poterimus	fuērunt	poterit

D. Fill in the appropriate Latin word, and then translate the sentence:

1. Poētam clārum audīre nōn (we were able).
2. Nūllum auxilium possumus (hope for).
3. Servī miserī (free) esse optant.
4. Fīlius vester vir pulcher (will be).
5. Sōla (to live) nōn timēbō.
6. Magnum numerum stellārum vidēre (you [s.] can).
7. Et nauta et magister amīcī fīliae meae (are).

The Ablative Case

Latin uses the ablative case for three different groups of concepts. Prepositions introduce some ablative constructions; for others the case form alone conveys the meaning. The various uses overlap, and a single idea can often be viewed—and hence expressed—in more than one way. The important thing is to remember the following three major categories of ablatives. As you meet each new use of the ablative, try to analyze how it fits into one of the three categories:

Separation. The "taking away" or "from" use is what some would call the true ablative, since the word is a combination of **ab**, "from," and **lātus**, "taken." After words of depriving, freeing, or lacking, ablative of separation can be expressed by the ablative alone or with a preposition:

Sum lībera **cūrīs**.	I am free *of (from) care(s)*.
Bestiam **vinculīs** līberābō.	I will free the beast *from its chains*.

The prepositions **ā** (**ab**), **dē**, **ē** (**ex**), all meaning "from," and the preposition **sine**, "without," regularly govern an ablative of separation:[5]

ab agrō	from the field	ex librīs	from the books
ā magistrō	from the teacher	dē caelō	down from the sky
ē numerō	from out of the number	sine amīcīs	without friends

Location. The second category of ablatives expresses location, in place or time, either by the ablative alone or following the preposition **in**, which when used with the ablative means "in" or "on":

in agrīs	in the fields
in viā	on the road

Sociative-Instrumental: "With" or "By." The third and largest group consists of a variety of uses, each with its own name. All these uses in one way or another describe the person, thing, or behavior associated with the action. Here are three members of this group:

1. Ablative of accompaniment: The preposition **cum**, "with," always introduces nouns or pronouns that indicate the person in whose company something is done:

Cum fīliā meā veniam.	I shall come *with my daughter*.
Magistrum **cum amīcō tuō** vīdimus.	We saw the teacher *with your friend*.

Cum is frequently attached to the end of personal pronoun forms:

Venīte **mēcum**, puerī!	Come *with me*, boys.
Pax **vōbīscum**.	(May) peace (be) *with you*.

[5] Before a word beginning with a vowel, the forms **ab** and **ex** are used to avoid hiatus, the clumsy gap that occurs between a word ending with a vowel and a word beginning with a vowel. English similarly adds the letter "n" to the indefinite article to avoid hiatus, e.g., "an animal." Before a word beginning with a consonant, either form (**ā** or **ab**, **ē** or **ex**) is used.

2. Ablative of manner: The ablative of manner directly modifies the verb, answering the question "How?": How did he speak? "With anger," "angrily," **cum irā**. For native English speakers, this is the most clearly adverbial use of the ablative. The ablative of manner is introduced by the preposition **cum**: **Cum irā** bestiam cēpit, "*With anger* [angrily] he seized the animal." When the noun is modified, the **cum** will frequently be omitted, or else placed between the noun and its modifier: **Magnā cum irā** bestiam cēpit, "*With great anger* [very angrily] he seized the animal." Here, the **cum** can be omitted (unlike that of the ablative of accompaniment), and the meaning will be the same: **Magnā irā** bestiam cēpit, "With great anger he seized the animal." Thus:

Poētam **cum invidiā** audīvī.	I listened *with envy* (enviously) to the poet.
Magnā (**cum**) **cūrā** audīvī.	I listened *with great care* (very carefully).

3. Ablative of means or instrument: The instrument with which or by means of which you do something is expressed by the ablative case alone, without any preposition:

Bestiam **vinculīs** tenēbunt.	They will hold the beast *with chains* (by means of chains).
Auxiliō puerōrum dōnum pulchrum faciēmus.	*With the help* of the boys, we shall make a handsome gift.

The instrument can be a concrete, physical object (**vinculīs**) or an abstract idea (**auxiliō**), but usually it will not be a person: for persons, the Romans would normally use the ablative of agent, or the preposition **per** with the accusative case—both of which we will encounter in a later chapter.

Scrībenda

A. What Latin prepositions are used to express:

1. ablative of accompaniment?
2. ablative of means?
3. ablative of separation?
4. ablative of manner? When can the ablative of manner omit its preposition?

B. Translate each sentence, and explain the underlined constructions:

1. Petam librum ā magistrō.
2. Auxiliō vestrō, amīcī meī, bona parāre poterimus.
3. Vinculīs magnīs bestiam tenēre nōn potest.
4. Bestia ab agrō fūgit cum servō.
5. Sine tuō auxiliō spērāre nōn possumus.
6. Dominō nostrō dōnum magnā cum cūrā faciam. (**cūra**, **-ae**, *f*, care)
7. Nōlīte poētam clārum cum invidiā audīre.
8. In agrō poēta cum agricolā cantābit.
9. Nautae viam stellīs in caelō invenient.

Verba tenenda

Verbs

accipiō, accipere, accēpī, acceptus take, accept, receive
adveniō, advenīre, advēnī, adventus come to, arrive at
agō, agere, ēgī, actus do, make; lead, drive; act; spend (of time)
age come!; hey!
agedum come, now!
grātiās agere (+ dative) thank
appellō, appellāre, appellāvī, appellātus address, speak to; call, name
audiō, audīre, audīvī, audītus hear, listen to
bibō, bibere, bibī, —— drink, imbibe
cadō, cadere, cecidī, cāsus fall (down)
capiō, capere, cēpī, captus take, seize
dēbeō, dēbēre, dēbuī, dēbitus owe; be bound or obliged (to do something)
dīcō, dīcere, dīxī, dictus say, speak
dūcō, dūcere, dūxī, ductus lead, conduct, guide; consider
faciō, facere, fēcī, factus do, make
fugiō, fugere, fūgī, fugitūrus flee, run away (from); avoid
incipiō, incipere, incēpī, inceptus begin, start
inveniō, invenīre, invēnī, inventus come upon, discover, find
legō, legere, lēgī, lectus choose; gather; select; read
mittō, mittere, mīsī, missus send; let go
nesciō, nescīre, nescīvī, nescītus not to know
occidō, occidere, occidī, occāsus fall (down); perish, die
petō, petere, petīvī, petītus seek, ask (for)
possum, posse, potuī, —— be able
pulsō, pulsāre, pulsāvī, pulsātus strike repeatedly; knock
respondeō, respondēre, respondī, respōnsus reply (to), answer
sciō, scīre, scīvī, scītus know, understand, perceive
sentiō, sentīre, sēnsī, sēnsus perceive, sense, feel
sum, esse, fuī, futūrus be, exist
veniō, venīre, vēnī, ventus come
vīvō, vīvere, vīxī, vīctus live

Nouns

convīva, -ae, *m* or *f* guest, dinner or drinking companion
cūra, -ae, *f* care, concern, worry
grātia, -ae, *f* favor, charm, friendship, gratitude
iānua, -ae, *f* door
lingua, -ae, *f* tongue, language
terra, -ae, *f* earth, ground, land; country
vīta, -ae, *f* life

Pronouns

ego (nominative sing.) I
nōs (nominative or accusative pl.) we, us
tū (nominative sing.) you
quid (interrogative, nominative or accusative *n* sing.) what?
quis (interrogative, nominative *m* or *f* sing.) who?

Adjectives

alius, alia, aliud other, another
alter, altera, alterum the other (of two), the second
ēbrius, -a, -um drunk, inebriated
Latīnus, -a, -um Latin
neuter, neutra, neutrum neither (of two)
nūllus, nūlla, nūllum no, none
salvus, -a, -um safe, sound, unharmed
sōlus, sōla, sōlum alone; only
tōtus, tōta, tōtum whole, entire
ūllus, ūlla, ūllum any
ūnus, ūna, ūnum one
uter, utra, utrum which one (of two)

Adverbs

hīc here, in this place
iam already, now
ibi there, in that place
tum then, at that time
ubi (interrogative) where?
ubi (relative) where, when

Conjunctions

quod because
sī if

Prepositions

ā, ab (+ ablative) from, away from
cum (+ ablative) with
sine (+ ablative) without

Notanda

For **agō** the *Oxford Latin Dictionary* lists forty-four definitions, and very many idiomatic uses, including: **quid agis?** "How are you?" "How do you do?"; **vītam agere**, "to live, spend one's life"; **grātiās agere**, "to thank" (+ dative; literally, "to give thanks to"); **causam agere**, "to plead a case."

appellō, a technical term in Roman law for appealing to a higher legal authority, gives us "appellate" court.

The present stem of **cadō** has a short **-a-**, which in its compounds becomes short **-i-**: **cadō, occidō**; compare **capiō** and **faciō** and their compounds. But note the long **-ā-** of its fourth principal part, **cāsus**, making up for the lost **-d** of the stem (see above, Formation of the Perfect Stem, page 38, under type number 3 for other examples of compensatory stem lengthening). Compare also the perfect stem of **cādo** (**cecidī**) and of its compound **occidō** (**occidī**): the reduplication does not necessarily continue in compounds.

capiō and **captō**: what is the difference between them? **captō** belongs to a group of first conjugation verbs derived from other verbs; the suffix **-tō** (or **-itō**) properly denotes intensive or repeated action, and verbs formed with this suffix are called *frequentative* verbs. (Often, however, this nuance has faded before the classical period.) **cantō**, derived from **canō, canere**, "sing," belongs to another such pair. In each pair of this sort, the first conjugation (**-to**) verb is more likely to have survived in the Romance languages, because its forms are so regular: thus, from **cantāre**, Italian *cantare*, Spanish *cantar*, French *chanter*.

faciō shares with **agō** the semantic field "do; make." Lewis and Short's *Latin Dictionary* (Oxford, 1879 [Impression of 1966]) distinguishes them thus: "[**agō**] To drive at something, to pursue a course of action, i.e., to make something an object of action; either in the most general sense, like the English *do*, . . . for every kind of mental or physical employment; or, in a more restricted sense, *to exhibit in external action*, *to act* or *perform*, *to deliver* or *pronounce*, etc., so that after the act is completed nothing remains permanent, e.g. a *speech*, *dance*, *play*, etc. (while *facere*, 'to make,' . . . denotes the production of an object which continues to exist after the act is completed)."

In the many compounds of **capiō** and **faciō**, the **-a-** of the present stem changes to **-i-**: **accipiō**, **efficiō**, and so on.

fugiō can take a direct object (to avoid or run away from something), or be used absolutely, without any object (to flee, run away).

incipiō is a compound: **in** + **capiō**, "take in [hand]," that is "begin." It may be used intransitively ("The play is beginning"), or take either a direct object or a complementary infinitive.

mittō has many compounds, whose meanings correspond, generally, to their English derivatives (e.g., **admittō**, **committō**, **omittō**, **permittō**). Note the lengthening of the root vowel in the third principal part, explained above under Formation of the Perfect Stem; similarly, **sēnsī**, **vēnī**, and **fūgī**.

petō is classed as a third conjugation verb, but its last two principal parts have fourth conjugation forms. When **petō** means "request, ask for," the person to whom the request is addressed is expressed by the preposition **ab**, with the ablative case: **auxilium ā magistrō petam**, "I shall seek help from the teacher," "I shall ask the teacher for help."

possum has no fourth principal part. The fourth principal part of **sum** is **futūrus**, **-a**, **-um**, which is the future active participle and means "about to be."

respondeō may take an (indirect) object in the dative case: **puer magistrō respondit**, "the child answered (replied to) the teacher."

alius . . . **alius**: when repeated two or more times, **alius** . . . **alius** means "one . . . another," or, in the plural, "some . . . others." A sentence with two different forms of **alius** in it requires translating each twice: **Aliī aliud clamābant**, "Some were shouting one thing; some were shouting another." When not repeated, it can also mean "different": **Aliī, Lyde, nunc sunt morēs**, "Customs are different now, Lydus" (Plautus, *Bacchides* 437). The genitive singular, **alīus**, is usually replaced by **alterīus**.

alter ego, literally "another I," in its original Latin can refer only to a male. If your alter ego is female, how would you refer to her in Latin?

ubi: distinguish its interrogative use (**ubi es?** "Where are you?") from the relative, often paired with an adverb of place or time (**hīc sum**, **ubi mē vidēs**. "I am here where you see me.")

cum: the preposition is often attached as an enclitic to the pronoun it governs: **Mēcum vēnit**. "He came with me." **Tēcum erimus**. "We shall be with you."

Ante legenda

A. Identify the conjugation (first, second, third, or fourth) of each of the verbs in *Verba tenenda* p. 48.

B. Translate into English:

1. Agricola vītam bonam in agrīs ēgit (aget / agit).
2. Poētae dōna amīcīs bonīs mittent (mīsērunt / mittunt).
3. Utram bestiam in caelō petēmus (petimus / petīvimus)?
4. Puerī, vincula capite! Vincula magna sunt; tenēre nōn potuimus.
5. Malōs fugere nōn potest. Malās fugere dēbuit. Bonī mala fugient.
6. Nūllam bestiam malam in agrum alterīus mitte.
7. Fac dōna amīcīs tuīs. Facite dōna amīcīs vestrīs.
8. Amīca, tē tōtam mēcum esse optō.
9. Poētīs sōlīs librōs nostrōs dare dēbēmus.
10. Aliī amīcōs spērant, aliī nōn; aliī miserī esse petunt, aliī nōn.
11. Linguā Latīnā cantāre nōn potuērunt.
12. Respondē virō linguā Latīnā. Respondēte verbīs servī linguā Latīnā.
13. Amīcus meus ēbrius est quod nimium bibit. (**nimium**, adv., excessively) Quid facere dēbeō? Nesciō. Sī bibet, cadet. Iam bibit et cadit, quod ēbrius est. Iam bibit et cecidit, sed nōn occidit.
14. Magnās grātiās agō quod salvus advēnī. Grātiās ēgit quod salvus advēnit. Grātiās aget sī salvus adveniet.
15. Pulsāvimus iānuam. Nūllus respondit. Alteramne iānuam pulsābimus? Sī fīlius vester iānuam adveniet, quid dīcere dēbēbimus?

C. Translate into Latin:

1. Come (s.) with me; then you will be able to find the servant.
2. Listen (pl.) to your master carefully! Speak with great care!
3. The farmers will not be able to perceive the sailors' envy.
4. We ought to lead no wild animal with (by means of) chains.
5. Some people will understand my words, others will not.

Legenda

Scenes from Roman Comedy (1)

The oldest works of Latin literature to survive intact are the comedies of Plautus (ca. 254–184 B.C.) and Terence (died 159 B.C.). Their plays continued to be very popular at Rome, and were studied in school and revived on stage well into the Middle Ages. Twenty-one[6] plays by Plautus, and six by Terence, survive.

The Roman comedies of Plautus and Terence were themselves based on Greek "New Comedy"; their settings and characters are Greek, with Roman touches slipped in. The strongly conventional comic tradition inherited from the Greeks called for stock characters—the clever slave (**servus**

[6] Only fragments remain of one of these plays, Plautus' *Vīdulāria* ("The Travelling Bag").

callidus), the irascible father, the lovesick young man (**adulescēns**), the sweet young call girl (who usually proves, in the nick of time, to be a wellborn lady)—and endless comic complexities mounted on a simple plot that often includes a case of mistaken identity and a recognition scene. The stage setting is almost invariably a street in Athens, with a row of houses which the characters go in and out of and several corners suitable for eavesdropping. Plautus, especially, loved slapstick buffoonery and extravagant language; Terence's plays are more decorous, and thus were more popular in the Middle Ages.

Only eight of Plautus' plays were known throughout most of the Middle Ages, until twelve more were rediscovered in 1429. By that time, the early Italian humanists were writing comedies in Latin, chiefly for reading rather than performance. The rediscovery of Plautus, plus the invention of printing in the fifteenth century, stimulated stage performances and printed editions of the ancient comedies (Terence first in 1470, Plautus first in 1472), followed by a great wave of comedies written in Italian. The Italian drama, in turn, influenced comic playwrights in northern European countries during the sixteenth and seventeenth centuries. From Shakespeare and Molière down to Giraudoux and P. G. Wodehouse (whose hero Bertie Wooster is a hapless **adulescēns**, attended by a clever **servus**, his butler Jeeves), the traditions of Roman comedy have continued to shape Western literature. Can you identify any of these ancient stereotypes in modern film and TV situation comedies?

Language. The dialogue of Roman comedy comes as close to everyday spoken Latin as we can hope to get. Characteristic of colloquial speech are the short, disconnected, or incomplete sentences and elliptical phrases, the frequent use of personal and demonstrative pronouns—probably accompanied on stage by pointing, a battery of exclamations and oaths (several are listed below), and slang. Use your imagination in translating to find modern idioms, colloquial expressions that are equivalent to the Latin, not merely literal translations of it. Sometimes the English will be nothing like the Latin: **tē amābō**, literally "I will love you," regularly introduces a request, and therefore means "please." Sometimes, Latin and English idioms nearly coincide: **quid ita?** is an elliptical expression corresponding to "How so?" i.e., "Why do you say that?" **Periī** and **occidī**, literally "I have perished, died," turn easily into "I'm dead! I'm ruined!" Invocations of various gods are used as casual oaths roughly equivalent in meaning and gravity to "Oh, my gosh!" or perhaps "Great Scot!" Various monosyllables reflect the sounds one makes as an utterance of despair (**vae! heu!**) or disgust (**vah!**) or surprise (**hem!**).

I. A Stranger in Town

When people from different countries meet, they may not understand each other's language—a problem seldom addressed in classical literature. In this scene from *Poenulus* ("The Carthaginian"), Plautus turns the

Tragic and comic masks. Mosaic from Pompeii.

problem into a source of humor. Hanno, an elderly Carthaginian gentleman traveling in search of his lost daughters, has come to Calydon, an ancient city in western Greece. He approaches the young man Agorastocles and his wily slave Milphio to make inquiry. This play was produced within a decade or so after the Second Punic War (218–202 B.C.), in which Rome defeated her fearsome enemy Hannibal, the great Carthaginian general, and won control of the Western Mediterranean.

HANNO: Hōs * puerōs appellābō Pūnicē*; sī respondēbunt, Pūnicā * linguā pergam * dīcere; sī nōn, tum aliā linguā appellābō.

MILPHIO [*to Agorastocles*]: Quid dīcis tū? Optāsne mē hunc * Pūnicē * appellāre?

AGORASTOCLES: Scīsne linguam Pūnicam * ?

MIL: Nūllus Poenus * est Poenior * quam ego.*

1: **hōs** (adjective), these (agrees with **puerōs**)
1, 14: **Pūnice** (adverb), in the Punic language
1, 5: **Pūnicus**, **-a**, **-um**, Carthaginian (adjective)
2: **pergō**, **-ere**, **perrexī**, **perrectus**, proceed, continue

AGOR.: Hunc* ergō* appellā.
MIL. [*to Hanno*]: Quis es? Quid optās? Unde* es?
HAN.: Annobynmytthymballebechaedreanech.*
AGOR.: Quid dīcit?
MIL.: Dīcit, "Hanno sum Carthāgine,* Mytthumballis* fīlius."
HAN.: Avō.*
MIL.: Salūtat.*
AGOR.: Salūtā* hunc* Pūnicē.
MIL.: Avō dīcit tibi.*
HAN.: Meharbocca.*
MIL.: Istud* est tua cūra, non mea!
AGOR.: Quid dīcit?
MIL.: Misera est bucca* eius*: fortasse* medicos* nōs esse cōgitāt.

II. Three scenes from Plautus' Mostellaria, *"The Haunted House"*

1. Callidamates, accompanied by his girl-friend, Delphium, is en route from one party to another at the home of his friend Philolaches.

CALLIDAMATES: Audī: age, venīre ad Philolachem* optō.
Ib-ib-ibi bibēmus et convīvēmus* et nōs
hilarō ingeniō* ac-ac-accipiet.
DELPHIUM: Nōsne accipiet sī tū, sī tū . . .
CALLI.: C-c-cōgitāsne mē m-m-madēre*?

3, 7, 14: **hunc** (demonstrative pronoun, acc. *m* sing.), this man
6: **Poenus**, **-ī**, *m* Carthaginian (noun)
Poenior quam ego, "more a Carthaginian than I"
7: **ergō** (adverb), therefore, then
8: **unde** (adverb), from where?
9: (This line is either gibberish or a phonetic reproduction of the lost Carthaginian language; similarly, l. 16)
11: **Carthāgine**, from Carthage
Mytthumballis, "of Mytthymballis"
12, 15: **avō** (meaning unknown; Latin **avē** would mean "hello")
13, 14: **salūtō**, **-āre**, **-āvī**, **-ātus**, greet
15: **tibi** (pronoun, dative sing.), to you
17: **istud** (pronoun, nominative *n* sing.), that (thing, or fact)
19: **bucca**, **-ae**, *f* cheek; mouth
eius (possessive pronoun), of him (i.e., his)
fortasse (adverb), perhaps
medicus, **-ī**, *m* doctor

1, 15: **ad Philolachem**, to Philolaches' house
2: **convīvō**, **-ere**, **-vīxī**, ——, eat together, eat with
3: **hilarus**, **-a**, **-um**, cheerful; **ingenium**, **-ī**, *n* disposition;
hilarō ingeniō, cheerfully [what sort of ablative?]
5, 6: **madeō**, **-ēre**, **-uī**, ——, be wet (with drink) [use modern slang equivalent]

Mask of Silenus. Mosaic from Pompeii.

Delph.: Tūne mādes * ? potesne astāre * ? cadēsne?
Calli.: N-nōn sī t-tū mē t-tenēbis.
Delph.: Agedum * : astā *.
Calli.: Sine *, sine * cadere mē.
Delph.: Nōn sinam *. Sī cadēs, nōn cadēs nisi * cadam tēcum.
Calli.: Sī cadēmus, aliusne nōs tollet * ?

6, 8: **astō**, **-āre**, **astitī**, ——, stand upright
8: **agedum**, come on!
9, 10: **sinō**, **-ere**, **sīvī**, **situs**, allow, let, permit
10: **nisi** (conjunction), if . . . not; unless
11: **tollō**, **-ere**, **sustulī**, **sublātus**, pick up, lift

DELPH.: Age; nunc* advēnimus . . .
CALLI.: Ubi nunc* advēnimus?
DELPH.: Nescīs?
CALLI.: Iam sciō. Advēnimus ad Philolachem*.
DELPH.: Euge*! Hīc nunc* sumus.
CALLI.: Dormiam* ego iam.

2. As soon as Callidamates arrives at Philolaches' house, he falls into a deep, drunken sleep. Suddenly the slave Tranio hurries in to warn his master, Philolaches, of his father's imminent return from a trip.

PHILOLACHES: Eccum*! Tranio ā portū* advenit.
TRANIO: Philolachēs!
PHILO.: Quid est?
TRAN.: Et ego et tū . . .
PHILO.: Quid et ego et tū?
TRAN.: Occidimus.
PHILO.: Quid ita*?
TRAN.: Pater* advenit.
PHILO.: Ah, quid ego audiō?
TRAN.: Pater*, dīcō, advenit.
PHILO.: Ubi est?
TRAN.: In portū* iam est.
PHILO.: Quis id* dīcit? Quis vīdit?
TRAN.: Ego, dīcō, vīdī.
PHILO.: Vae, mihi*. Occidam, sī tū vēra* dīcis. Quid ego agam?
TRAN.: Tuōs amīcōs fugere iubē*.
PHILO.: Callidamatēs! Callidamatēs, vigilā*!
CALLIDAMATES: Vigilō.* Bibere optō.
DELPHIUM: Callidamatēs, vigilā*! Pater* Philolachis* advenit.
CALLI.: Euge*!
PHILO.: Age, edepol*, vigilā*; pater* advenit.

12, 13, 16: **nunc** (adverb), now
16: **euge**, bravo! well done!
17: **dormiō**, **-ire**, **-īvī**, **-ītus**, (go to) sleep

1: **Eccum**, Look who's here!
ā portū, from the harbor
7: **quid ita**, how so? (**ita**, thus, so)
8, 10, etc.: **pater** (nom. sing. *m*), father
12: **in portū** (abl.), in the harbor
13: **id** (acc. sing. *n*), that, it
15: **vae, mihi**, woe is me! (literally "to or for me," dative of personal pronoun)
vērus, **-a**, **-um**, true
16, 23: **iubeō**, **-ēre**, **iussī**, **iussus**, order
18, 19, etc.: **vigilō**, **-āre**, **-āvī**, **ātus**, wake up, be awake
20: **Philolachis** gen. sing.
21: **Euge!** Splendid!
22: **edepol**, by Pollux! (Pollux was a Roman god.)

CALLI.: Tuusne pater* advenit? Iubē* abīre rursum*

PHILO.: Quid ego agam? Pater* iam mē inveniet miserum, ēbrium, et domum* plēnam* convīvārum.

3. The father, Theopropides, soon arrives, before evidence of the party can be removed. Tranio saves the day by persuading the father that the house is haunted.

THEOPROPIDES: Magnās grātiās agō Neptūnō*, quod et vīvō
et salvus advēnī domum*.
Hīc est iānua. Pulsābō. Heus*, ecquis* hīc est?
[*Tranio approaches from the street*]
TRANIO: Quis nostram iānuam pulsat?
THEO.: Meus servus hīc est Tranio.
TRAN.: Ō, Theopropidēs, ere*, salve*:
salvum tē vidēre gaudeō*.
THEO.: Quid est? Ubi pulsāvī, nūllus respondit neque* iānuam reclūsit*.
TRAN.: Eho*, tūne tetigistī* nostram iānuam?
THEO.: Quō modo* pulsāre potuī nisi* tetigī*?
TRAN.: Tetigistīne*?
THEO.: Tetigī*, dīcō, et pulsāvī.
TRAN.: Vah.
THEO.: Quid est?
TRAN.: Nōn possum dīcere quam* indignum factum* fēcistī et malum.
THEO.: Quid iam?
TRAN.: Venī, Venī atquē* fuge ab iānuā!
Occidistī hercle. Fuge ad* mē!
Et tange* quoque* terram!

23: **abīre rursum**, to go away again
25: **domus**, -ī, *f* house, home
plēnus, -**a**, -**um**, full (of, + gen.)

1: **Neptūnus**, -ī, *m* Neptune, god of the sea
2: **domum**, "(to) home"
3: **heus**, hey!
ecquis, anyone
6: **erus**, -ī, *m* master
salvē (imperative of **salveō**, be well), hello!, greetings!
7: **gaudeō**, -**ēre**, **gāvīsus**, ——, rejoice, be happy
8: **neque**, and . . . not, nor
recludō, -**ere**, **reclūsī**, **reclūsus**, open
9: **eho** (interjection) Hey!
9, 10, etc.: **tangō**, -**ere**, **tetigī**, **tactus**, touch
tange . . . **terram**: touching the ground was apparently intended to avert evil
10: **quō modo**, how? (lit., in what way?)
nisi, if . . . not; unless
15: **quam indignum factum** (*n* acc.), how shameful a deed
17: **atque**, and, and also
18: **ad** (prep. + acc.), to, toward
19: **quoque**, also

Probanda I–III

In this and subsequent review sections, you will find the answers in the key that follows. For the best results, write out the answers to the review questions, and then compare your answers with those given in the key.

A. Identify the mood (indicative, imperative), person (first, second, third), number (singular or plural), and tense of the following verbs. Translate all forms; list the infinitive for all the verbs.

cantās	est	mōvit	petētis	sentīs	potuit
cantāte	sumus	occidistī	petite	sentiētis	fugimus
cōgitāvit	fuistī	cecidit	petīvistis	cēpit	fūgimus
cōgitābit	dās	occidet	nescit	incipiēs	fugiēmus
errat	spīrās	ēgit	nescīvit	accēpit	fuge
errāmus	spērat	aget	esse	potuistī	dīc
erimus	movet	age	sēnsit	potes	dīxī

B. Translate the following sentences into English:

1. Convīva neuter ēbrius est.
2. Salvus ego adveniam.
3. Cūram magistrī accēpit puer.
4. Bestiae in caelō, alia parva, alia magna, errant.
5. Bestiae in caelō sunt.
6. Narcissus puerum pulchrum vīdit.
7. Servus sōlus iānuam nostram advenīre dēbēbit.
8. Ego cadam sed nōn occidam.
9. Virōne miserō dīcētis?
10. Virī clārī in tuā terrā sunt.
11. In librō meō erunt verba poētārum.
12. Stellae nautās dūcent.
13. Agēsne vītam sine amīcīs? Agēsne virō grātiās?

C. List three verbs that govern a complementary infinitive.

D. Translate the following phrases, identify the case, and then change to the singular, retaining the original case:

1. nūllōrum puerōrum
2. virīs clārīs
3. verba tua
4. dōnīs magnīs
5. agricolīs sōlīs
6. agrī nostrī
7. cūrae parvae
8. fīliārum vestrārum

Probanda I–III: Key

A. **cantās**: indicative; second sing.; present; "you are singing"; **cantāre**.
cantāte: imperative; second pl.; "sing!" **cantāre**.
cōgitāvit: indic.; third sing.; perfect; "he thought/planned"; **cōgitāre**.
cōgitābit: indic.; third sing.; future; "he will think/plan"; **cōgitāre**.

errat: indic.; third sing.; present; "he is wandering"; **errāre**.
errāmus: indic.; first pl.; present; "we wander"; **errāre**.
erimus: indic.; first pl.; future; "we will be"; **esse**.
est: indic.; third sing.; present; "he is"; **esse**.
sumus: indic.; first pl.; present; "we are"; **esse**.
fuistī: indic.; second sing.; perfect; "you have been"; **esse**.
dās: indic.; second sing.; present; "you give/are giving"; **dare**.
spīrās: indic.; second sing.; present; "you are breathing"; **spīrāre**.
spērat: indic.; third sing.; present; "he is hoping"; **spērāre**.
movet: indic.; third sing.; present; "he is moving"; **movēre**.
mōvit: indic.; third sing.; perfect; "he has moved"; **movēre**.
occidistī: indic.; second sing.; perfect; "you have fallen/perished"; **occidere**.
cecidit: indic.; third sing.; perfect; "he has fallen"; **cadere**.
occidet: indic.; third sing.; future; "he will fall/perish"; **occidere**.
ēgit: indic.; third sing.; perfect; "he has done/led/driven"; **agere**.
aget: indic.; third sing.; future; "he will do/lead/drive"; **agere**.
age: imperative; second sing.; "do/lead/drive!"; "come!" (colloquial); **agere**.
petētis: indic.; second pl.; future; "you will do/lead/drive"; **petere**.
petite: imperative; second pl.; "seek/ask!"; **petere**.
petīvistis: indic.; second pl.; perfect; "you have sought/asked"; **petere**.
nescit: indic.; third sing.; present; "he does not know"; **nescīre**.
nescīvit: indic.; third sing.; perfect; "he did not know"; **nescīre**.
esse: infinitive; present; "to be"; **esse**.
sēnsit: indic.; third sing.; perfect; "he felt/sensed"; **sentīre**.
sentīs: indic.; second sing.; present; "you feel/sense"; **sentīre**.
sentiētis: indic.; second pl.; future; "you will feel/sense"; **sentīre**.
cēpit: indic.; third sing.; perfect; "he has seized"; **capere**.
incipiēs: indic.; second sing.; future; "you will begin"; **incipere**.
accēpit: indic.; third sing.; perfect; "he accepted/received"; **accipere**.
potuistī: indic.; second sing.; perfect; "you have been able"; **posse**.
potes: indic.; second sing.; present; "you are able"; **posse**.
potuit: indic.; third sing.; perfect; "he was/has been able"; **posse**.
fugimus: indic.; first pl.; present; "we are fleeing"; **fugere**.
fūgimus: indic.; first pl.; perfect; "we fled/have fled"; **fugere**.
fugiēmus: indic.; first pl.; future; "we shall flee"; **fugere**.
fuge: imperative; second sing.; "flee!" **fugere**.
dīc: imperative; second sing.; "speak!" **dīcere**.
dīxī: indic.; first sing.; "I have spoken/I spoke"; **dīcere**.

B.
1. Neither dinner guest is drunk.
2. I shall arrive safe.
3. The child welcomed (accepted) the teacher's care.
4. Animals, one small, the other large, are wandering in the sky.
5. Animals are in the sky. (There are animals in the sky.)
6. Narcissus saw a beautiful boy.
7. Only the servant (the servant alone) will be obligated to come to our door.
8. I shall fall but I shall not perish.

9. Will you speak to the poor man?
10. Famous men are in your land. (There are famous men in your land.)
11. The poets' words will be in my book.
12. The stars will guide the sailors.
13. Will you spend your life without friends?
    Will you thank the man?

C. possum; debeō; optō.

D.
1. no children (genitive); nūllīus puerī
2. famous men (dative or ablative); virō clārō
3. your words (nominative or accusative); verbum tuum
4. large gifts (dative or ablative); dōnō magnō
5. the farmers alone (dative or ablative); agricolae sōlī or agricolā sōlō
6. our fields (nominative); ager noster
7. small concerns/cares (nominative); cūra parva
8. your (pl.) daughters (genitive); fīliae vestrae

IV

Subjunctive Mood (1); Jussive and Purpose Clauses; Dative Case (1)

The Subjunctive Mood

All of the verb forms used so far have been in either the indicative or the imperative mood, making statements or asking questions about matters of fact, or issuing commands:

Pater iānuam **pulsat**.	Father *is knocking* at the door.
Quis iānuam **pulsāvit**?	Who *knocked* at the door?
Nōlī iānuam pulsāre!	*Don't* knock at the door!

Now you will meet the first two (of four) tenses of the subjunctive mood, and begin to learn its various uses. Like the indicative, the subjunctive mood is used in both independent (main) clauses and dependent (subordinate) clauses.

Subjunctive verb forms appear on every page of any Latin text. In English, however, the subjunctive mood persists only in a few fixed constructions and formulaic phrases:

God save the Queen!
If I were you, I'd stay home.
So be it.

English uses auxiliary verbs (*may*, *should*, etc.) or different constructions altogether to express shades of meaning conveyed in Latin by a verb form in the subjunctive mood.

"Mood," you recall, refers not to one's feelings or frame of mind, but to the "mode" or manner (**modus**) with which the speaker colors the verb. The indicative mood in Latin indicates that the speaker views his or her statement as objective reality. **Pater iānuam pulsāvit**. Here the speaker considers it a fact that someone did knock at the door. The imperative mood is a simple command: **Iānuam pulsā**! The subjunctive mood of the verb, by contrast, performs a variety of functions, including some once handled by other verb forms now extinct (and so in its versatility is rather like the ablative case of the noun). Broadly speaking, the subjunctive conveys nuances other than simple statements of fact. There are many possible ways to translate a verb in the subjunctive mood, but no general translation can be given with the subjunctive forms out of context.

Present Subjunctive Active

The present stems of first, second, and fourth conjugation verbs, as you have already learned, are obtained by dropping **-re** from the present active infinitive. The present stem of these verbs actually consists of the root of the verb (**am-**, **ten-**, or **aud-**) plus the long vowels **-ā-**, **-ē-**, or **-ī-**, respectively. The third conjugation has a consonant stem identical with its root and is obtained by dropping **-ere** from its present active infinitive; to this root a short **-i-** or **-u-** is added when the verb is conjugated in the present indicative.

The present subjunctive in Latin is formed as follows:

1. by replacing final long **-ā-** with long **-ē-** in the first conjugation;
2. by adding a long **-ā-** to the present stem of verbs of the second, third **-iō**, and fourth conjugation verbs—long vowels of the present stem of the second and fourth conjugations are shortened before the characteristic subjunctive vowel;
3. by adding a long **-ā-** to the present (consonant) stem of regular third conjugation verbs.
4. Note that the first person singular of the present subjunctive in all conjugations is **-m**;
5. here, as elsewhere, a long vowel is shortened before final **-m**, **-t**, or **-nt**.

amāre	**tenēre**	**dūcere**	**capere**	**audīre**
am~~ā~~ + ē	tenē + ā	dūc~~e~~ + ā	capi + ā	audī + ā
		SINGULAR		
am**em**	tene**am**	dūc**am**	capi**am**	audi**am**
am**ēs**	tene**ās**	dūc**ās**	capi**ās**	audi**ās**
am**et**	tene**at**	dūc**at**	capi**at**	audi**at**
		PLURAL		
am**ēmus**	tene**āmus**	dūc**āmus**	capi**āmus**	audi**āmus**
am**ētis**	tene**ātis**	dūc**ātis**	capi**ātis**	audi**ātis**
am**ent**	tene**ant**	dūc**ant**	capi**ant**	audi**ant**

Present Subjunctive of **sum** and **possum**

For **sum**, **esse** personal endings added to the subjunctive stem, **si-**, provide the present active subjunctive. For **possum**, **posse** the element **pot-**

changes to **pos**- throughout the present subjunctive, since it always precedes an -**s**- (**pot**- + **sim**, etc.), and is prefixed to the present subjunctive forms of **sum**:

esse	**posse**
SINGULAR	
sim	pos**sim**
sīs	pos**sīs**
sit	pos**sit**
PLURAL	
sīmus	pos**sīmus**
sītis	pos**sītis**
sint	pos**sint**

Independent Uses of the Subjunctive: Jussive/Hortatory

The jussive (from **jussus**, "ordered") or hortatory subjunctive in an independent clause (that is, where the subjunctive verb is the main verb of the sentence) expresses the speaker's will by conveying a command or exhortation, or—with the negative **nē**—a prohibition. In the first person, it indicates the speaker's urging of himself, or self-exhortation (hence "hortatory," from **hortārī**, "to encourage").

Semper **parātī sīmus**.	*Let us* always *be prepared.*
Vīvāmus, mea Lesbia, atque **amēmus**.	*Let us live*, my Lesbia, and *let us love*. (Catullus 5.1)
Nē **timeam**.	*Let me* not *be afraid.*

The English word "let" in this construction is idiomatic: it does not mean "allow." In the second and third person the jussive subjunctive expresses commands or prohibitions:

Bonus **sīs**.	*Be* good.
Nē **timeās**.	Don't *be afraid.*
Poēta **cantet**.	*Let* the poet *sing.*

In the second person forms, however, Latin frequently replaces the subjunctive with a verb in the imperative mood. The two constructions are similar in meaning, the main difference being that the subject of the second person jussive subjunctive tends to be indefinite:

vidēte!	Look!	**videātis**!	Look!
nōlī timēre!	Don't be afraid!	**nē timeās**!	Don't be afraid!
venī!	Come!	**veniās**!	Come!

Dependent Uses of the Subjunctive: Purpose Clauses

The man is coming to see his son.
The man is coming in order to see his son.
The man is coming so that he may see his son.[1]

These three sentences are identical in meaning. The first two represent the way we normally express purpose in English: with an infinitive. The third sentence corresponds to the way the Romans expressed purpose.

Latin does not use an infinitive to express purpose. Instead, the most common way to express purpose is by a subordinate clause, with its verb in the subjunctive, introduced by **ut**, "in order that, so that, to," or, if the purpose is negative, by **nē**, "in order not to, so that . . . not, in order that . . . not." This subjunctive verb expresses the intent or purpose of the man (the subject of the sentence), namely, to see his son.

Vir venit **ut** fīlium **videat**.	The man is coming *to see* his son.
Fīlius fugit **nē** virum **videat**.	The son is fleeing *so that* he *will not* (*so as not to*) *see* the man.

In the above examples, the subject of the subjunctive verb is the same as the subject of the main verb (the man in the first example, the son in the second). Sometimes the subject of the subordinate verb will change:

Fugiāmus nē **vir** nōs **videat**.	Let's run away so that *the man* won't *see* us.
Tenēbō tē nē **cadās**.	I will hold you so that *you* won't *fall*.

In both these examples, the change of personal ending marks a clear change of subject. Sometimes the subordinate clause will also contain its own subject, e.g., **vir** in the first of these examples. If there is no indication of a change of subject, assume that both verbs have the same subject.

Scrībenda

A. Conjugate each verb in the present tense, subjunctive mood:

faciō	sciō	spērō
audiō	possum	petō
agō	dō	sum

B. Translate the following sentences:

1. Nē timeāmus.
2. Veniant. Nē veniātis. Venīte. Veniāmus.

[1] The English auxiliary verb "may" is sometimes confusing, because it has several possible meanings. It can indicate permission ("you may sing"), a wish ("may you sing beautifully"), or contingency (in clauses of purpose, result, concession, etc.)—which is its function here. "Might" was originally the past tense of "may," but its meaning has broadened in current usage.

3. Cadam. Nē cadās. Tēne mē nē cadam.
4. Pater veniat. Nē pater veniat. Pater venit ut nōs videat.
5. Fugiāmus nē nōs videant.
6. Venit Callidamatēs ut amīcum videat.
7. Amīca puerō auxilium dat nē puer cadat. Puerō auxilium det.
8. Advenimus ut amīcum nostrum vidēre possīmus.
9. Pūnicā linguā dīcit vir. Servus Pūnicā linguā dīcet. Pūnicā linguā dīcat.
10. Appellābō virum linguā Pūnicā ut mihi respondēre possit. (**mihi**, to me)
11. Linguā nostrā nōs appellet ut respondeāmus.

Imperfect Subjunctive Active

The imperfect subjunctive is regularly used in subordinate clauses following a main verb in a past tense. It indicates action contemporaneous with or subsequent to (and therefore incomplete—**imperfectus**—in relation to) the time of the main verb. The formation of this tense is easy: for all four conjugations and **sum** and **possum**, simply add the personal endings to the present active infinitive.

amāre	**tenēre**	**dūcere**	**audīre**	**capere**
		SINGULAR		
amāre**m**	tenēre**m**	dūcere**m**	audīre**m**	capere**m**
amārē**s**	tenērē**s**	dūcerē**s**	audīrē**s**	caperē**s**
amāre**t**	tenēre**t**	dūcere**t**	audīre**t**	capere**t**
		PLURAL		
amārē**mus**	tenērē**mus**	dūcerē**mus**	audīrē**mus**	caperē**mus**
amārē**tis**	tenērē**tis**	dūcerē**tis**	audīrē**tis**	caperē**tis**
amāre**nt**	tenēre**nt**	dūcere**nt**	audīre**nt**	capere**nt**

esse		**posse**	
SING.	PL.	SING.	PL.
essem	essēmus	possem	possēmus
essēs	essētis	possēs	possētis
esset	essent	posset	possent

If we take the earlier examples of purpose clauses and put the main verb in the perfect tense, we get the following:

Vir **vēnit** ut fīlium **vidēret**.	The man *came to see* his son.
Fīlius **fūgit** nē virum **vidēret**.	The son *fled* so that he *would* not (*might* not, so as not to) *see* the man.
Tē **tenuī** nē **caderēs**.	I *held* you so that *you would* not *fall*.

These shifts of tense in the subjunctive verb follow the shift of tense in the main verb, in keeping with what is called the rule of "sequence of tenses." In the above examples the changes followed this pattern:

MAIN CLAUSE	SUBORDINATE CLAUSE
Present Indicative	Present Subjunctive
Perfect Indicative	Imperfect Subjunctive

For the present you need not learn the rule of sequence of tenses beyond recognizing that the subordinate clause will have a verb in the present subjunctive when the main clause has its verb in the present or future tense, and that the subordinate clause will have a verb in the imperfect subjunctive when the main clause has its verb in a past tense. You will learn the rule of sequence of tenses in full after the remaining tenses of the indicative and subjunctive have been introduced.

Scrībenda

Verbs

cēdō, cēdere, cessī, cessus go, depart
dēmōnstrō, -āre, -āvī, -ātus show, point out
habeō, habēre, habuī, habitus have, hold
iubeō, iubēre, iussī, iussus order, command
pōnō, pōnere, posuī, positus put, place
quaerō, quaerere, quaesīvī, quaesītus seek; **quaerere** (+ accusative) **ab** (+ ablative), to ask someone (abl.) for something (accus.)

Nouns

causa, -ae, *f* cause, reason
pecūnia, -ae, *f* money

Adverb

numquam never

A. Conjugate each verb in the tense and number indicated:

1. Imperfect subjunctive, singular: mittō; possum; cōgitō; timeō; veniō
2. Imperfect subjunctive, plural: iubeō; cadō; sentiō; agō.

B. Identify each form, and change it to the present indicative, retaining the person and number of the form given:

mordeāmus	sit	quaesīvistī
mittet	possim	inveniātis
posset	pōneret	monuistis
scīrēmus	dīcam	dedistī
capiēs	agās	dabis
habeant	potuērunt	erunt

C. Translate each sentence, and explain the syntax of the underlined forms:

1. Servus virum Pūnicum appellāre incipiat.
2. Cantēmus ut bestiae nōs audiant et cēdant.
3. Puerī cantāvērunt ut bestiae audīrent atque timērent.
4. Servōs audiāmus. Servī audiēmus. Nē servī nōs audiant.
5. Servī pecūniam numquam habēmus.
6. Nē servī ā filiīs tuīs pecūniam quaerant.
7. Nōn causam ā tē quaeram. Nē causam ā tē quaeram.

8. Fīlius fūgit nē occideret.
9. Fīlius et amīcus fugiunt nē occidant.
10. Puer ab iānuā fugiet ut salvus sit.
11. Ab iānuā fūgērunt et in agrōs cessērunt.
12. Amābō tē, et ego et tū in agrōs cēdāmus.
13. Vīvant et ament.
14. Vīvunt et amant.
15. Vīvimus ut amēmus.
16. Vīvāmus et amēmus.
17. Bibāmus et convīvāmus. (**convīvō**, **convīvere**, dine together)
18. Vēnit ut cum amīcīs biberet.
19. Sī servus vēra dīcet, puer occidet. (**vērus**, **-a**, **-um**, true)
20. Servus nōn vēra dixit nē puer occideret.
21. Nē pater veniat. Venī, pater.
22. Amīcī, fugiāmus. Amīcus fugiat. Amīce, fuge. Amīcī fugient.
23. Librōs legēmus. Librum tuum legāmus. Da puerō librum ut legat.

> Nōn amō tē, Sabidī, nec possum dīcere quārē*:
> Hoc* tantum possum dīcere, nōn amō tē.
>
> *Martial, I.32*
>
> (**quārē**, "why"; **hoc tantum**, "this much" or "only this." In the seventeenth-century English version by Thomas Brown, "Sabidius" becomes "Dr. Fell.")

The Dative Case

The dative case indicates the person (most often) or thing indirectly affected by the verbal action. Although the preposition "to" or "for" will usually express the relationship in English, in Latin the dative is never used after a preposition.

Most often met is the dative marking the indirect object of a transitive verb. This chapter also introduces representatives from a second cluster of dative constructions that describe various less explicit relationships. In each, the dative designates a person (or thing) somehow interested in the verbal action, in reference to whom, or for whose benefit or harm, advantage or disadvantage, the action is carried out or the state of affairs exists. The same capacious definition covers the dative following certain compound verbs and verbs that English regards as transitive ("obey," for example) but Latin analyzes as intransitive ("be obedient to"), and after adjectives denoting a quality that affects the person or thing named in the dative ("unfriendly to someone," "suitable for something"). Those categories you will study later.

Since the dative is often used with pronouns, it will be convenient to learn the dative forms of the first and second person singular of the personal pronouns; you already know the others listed here:

	First Person	Second Person
Nom.	egŏ̄	tū
Dat.	**mihĭ̄**	**tibĭ̄**
Acc.	mē	tē
Abl.	mē	tē

Dative of Indirect Object. Its name **datīvus** (from **datus**, "having been given," the fourth principal part of **dō**) associates this case with giving and receiving. It is used after verbs meaning "give, show, tell," and the like.

Stellae viam **nautīs** dēmōnstrābunt.	The stars will show the way *to/for the sailors*.
Librum pulchrum **tibi** invēnī.	I've found a beautiful book *for you*.
Magister dōnum **poētae** dedit.	The teacher gave a gift *to the poet*.
Amīcō cantat.	She is singing *to/for her friend*.
Servus **Pūnicō** dīxit.	The slave spoke *to the Carthaginian*.

The last two examples show that no direct object need be expressed, although in both instances one is latent in the verb: singing implies a song; speaking, words. Nor must "to" or "for" always introduce the indirect object in English; the first sentence, for example, could just as well be rendered, "The stars will show the sailors the way," and the third, "The teacher gave the poet a gift." In translating from English to Latin, you must analyze the underlying structure carefully to distinguish between direct and indirect objects.

Dative of Possession. The most specific in the second cluster of dative constructions sketched above is the dative of possession. The dative with any form of the verb **esse** can indicate possession:

Sunt **agricolae** multī servī.	*The farmer* has many slaves. (Literally, there are for the farmer many slaves.)
Liber est **magistrō**.	*The teacher* has a book. (Literally, a book exists for the teacher.)
Miserae sunt nūllī amīcī.	*The poor woman* has no friends. (Literally, for the poor woman there are no friends.)

This construction emphasizes the existence of the thing possessed, and suggests that the possession exists for the benefit of the person named in the dative case. The genitive of possession and the possessive adjectives **meus**, **tuus**, **noster**, **vester**, by contrast, emphasize the possessor.

Liber est **magistrō**. Liber est **mihi**.	The teacher has a *book*. I have a *book*.	Dative emphasizes the thing possessed.
Liber **magistrī** est.	The book belongs to the *teacher*; it is the *teacher's* book.	Genitive or possessive adjective emphasizes the possessor.
Liber **meus** est.	The book belongs to *me*, is *mine*; it is *my* book.	

Dative of Reference. Also called the dative of advantage, the dative of reference is an "umbrella term" comprising several barely distinguishable constructions. Each denotes the person (or thing) who has some kind of indirect interest in the action: it is performed for his benefit—or the opposite, to his disadvantage or harm—or he simply has an opinion about it. This construction differs from the preceding in that it qualifies an action or idea, whereas dative of possession denotes a specific relationship (possession) between the subject and the dative. The word in the dative of reference is often a personal pronoun.

Bestiam **agricolīs** captāvimus, nōn **tibi**.	We captured the beast for the *farmers'* benefit, not *yours*.
Vae **mihi**!	Alas *for me*!
Quid **tibi** petis?	What do you seek *for yourself*?
Neuter **mihi** vītam bene ēgit.	Neither, *in my opinion*, lived well.

Dative of Purpose and Double Dative. The dative of a thing may indicate the purpose it is meant to serve.

Librum **dōnō** quaerō.	I am looking for a book (for the purpose of) *as a gift*.

Here the dative **dōnō** expresses the function or purpose—with regard to this particular situation—of the book, whereas the accusative **librum** marks the book as the object of the verbal action (seeking).

The dative of purpose is often accompanied by a dative of reference. The use of these two datives together is called the "double dative" construction. The verb is usually a form of **esse**.

Servi sunt **magnō auxiliō** (purpose) **agricolae** (reference).	The slaves are (function as) *a great help* (with reference) *to the farmer*.
Liber **dōnō poētae** erit.	The book will be (serve as) *a gift* (with reference) *to the poet*.
Librum **dōnō amīcae** quaerō.	I'm looking for a book (to serve) *as a gift* (with reference to) *for a friend*.

Obviously a literal English translation of this construction would be clumsy. In fact, the Latin is more precise than English, which is content to treat the two nouns as equivalents (slaves = help; book = gift). Latin conveys the functional relationship between the two nouns more precisely by specifying one (**auxiliō**, **dōnō**) as a dative of purpose.

Verba tenenda

Verbs

adsum, **adesse**, **adfuī**, —— be present, be at hand; + dative: assist, aid, give assistance to

ambulō, **-āre**, **-āvī**, **-ātus** walk, take a walk

cēdō, **cēdere**, **cessī**, **cessus** go, move, yield; withdraw, depart; + dative: submit to, yield to, grant
cognoscō, **cognoscere**, **cognōvī**, **cognitus** learn, become acquainted with; (in the perfect tense: know)
dēmonstrō, **-āre**, **-āvī**, **-ātus** show, point out, indicate, demonstrate
dēsum, **dēesse**, **dēfuī**, —— be absent, be lacking, fail
habeō, **habēre**, **habuī**, **habitus** have, hold; consider, regard
iubeō, **iubēre**, **iussī**, **iussus** order, command
noscō, **noscere**, **nōvī**, **nōtus** learn, become acquainted with; (in the perfect tense: know)
pōnō, **pōnere**, **posuī**, **positus** put, place
quaerō, **quaerere**, **quaesīvī**, **quaesītus** seek, look for, ask
salveō, **salvēre**, ——, —— be well, be in good health
salvē (s.) or **salvēte** (pl.) hello!
supersum, **superesse**, **superfuī**, —— remain, exist still, survive; be in abundance
vocō, **-āre**, **-āvī**, **-ātus** call, summon

Nouns

animus, **-ī**, *m* soul, mind; pl.: courage, high spirits
aqua, **-ae**, *f* water
causa, **-ae**, *f* cause, reason; case (in court)
cibus, **-ī**, *m* food
cōnsilium,, **-iī**, *n* advice; plan; judgment
fēmina, **-ae**, *f* woman
pecūnia, **-ae**, *f* money
satis, *n* (indeclinable) enough

Adjectives

cēterī, **-ae**, **-a** (pl. only) the other, the rest (of)
ignōtus, **-a**, **-um** unknown
insānus, **-a**, **-um** of unsound mind; raving; insane
molestus, **-a**, **-um** annoying, irksome
multus, **-a**, **-um** many, much
sānus, **-a**, **-um** sound, whole, healthy (physically or mentally)
satis (indeclinable) enough

Adverbs

bene well
certē certainly, undoubtedly
hodiē today
numquam never
nunc now
satis enough
sīc thus, in this way
sōlum only
umquam ever

Conjunctions

atque or **ac** and, and also, and even
aut, **aut** . . . **aut** or; (in pairs) either . . . or
nam for (confirms or explains a preceding statement)
nisi unless, if not (negative form of **sī**); except
ut (+ subjunctive mood) in order that, in order to
ut (+ indicative mood) as; when

nē (+ subjunctive) in order not to, in order that . . . not

nec or **neque**, **nec** . . . **nec** or **neque** . . . **neque** and not, also not; (in pairs) neither . . . nor

Prepositions

ad (+ accusative) to, toward, near

ante (+ accusative) before, in front of

dē (+ ablative) from, down from; about, concerning

NOTANDA

ambulō seems to have been a colloquial word: much used by Plautus and Terence, it appears in later literature chiefly in informal contexts, such as letters, and then very frequently in the Bible. There the word often has a metaphorical sense, "live," e.g., Romans 13:13, **honestē ambulēmus**, or 4 Kings 21:22, **et nōn ambulāvit in viā Dominī**.

cēdō has several compounds, such as **accēdō**, "approach," and **recēdō**, "go back, withdraw." This verb family is a fertile source of English derivatives formed on both the present and perfect stems, **cēd-** and **cess-**.

cognoscō and **noscō** are essentially interchangeable. In the tenses of the perfect system, both mean "know": I have learned = I know. The **g-** of the root, present in **cognoscō** and **ignōtus**, has been lost from the simple verb.

The short **-a-** of **habeō** changes to **-i-** in compounds: **exhibeō**, **adhibeō**.

iubeō takes an accusative + infinitive construction: **iussit mē dīcere**, "he ordered me to speak." The noun or pronoun in the accusative is the subject of the infinitive, and the whole phrase is the direct object of **iubeō**.

quaerō means "seek" in two senses: (1) search for, look for (seek to obtain); (2) ask, inquire (seek to learn). Note that although it belongs to the third conjugation, its last two principal parts have fourth conjugation forms (cf. **petō**). As with **petō**, you seek something from someone, using **ab**, **dē**, or **ex** + ablative: **pecūniam ex meō amīcō quaeram**, "I shall seek money from my friend."

causa in legal contexts, means "lawsuit, case." Its meaning has been diluted to "thing" in its Romance descendants, Italian and Spanish *cosa*, French *chose*.

The prefix **con-** in **cōnsilium** comes from **cum**, and so the word carries the sense of consulting with someone else or debating with oneself. **cōnsilium capere** means "to form a plan, resolve, decide." English "council" and "counsel" both derive from this word.

ceterae fēminae, "the rest of the women, the remaining women": the "of" is part of the adjective, and is not followed by a noun in the genitive case.

satis functions as a noun, adjective or adverb. As a noun or adjective it is indeclinable; adjectives modifying the noun take singular neuter endings.

The opposite of **sānus**, "well," is **insānus**, but its meaning is restricted to mental ill health. From **insānus** is formed a 4th conjugation verb, **insāniō**. (When used as a prefix, **in** can mean "not," as here and in **i**(**n**)**gnotus** above, or have the force of the preposition, "in, on, into.")

certē can be used to answer "yes" to a question: **certē sciō**, "I know for certain, I'm sure."

hodiē, from **hōc diē**, "on this day," is an ablative expressing time when. It persists in Italian *oggi*, Spanish *hoy*, and French *aujourd'hui*.

nunc can only refer to present time, whereas **iam** may also refer to the past ("already") or the future ("soon").

sīc too is used for affirmative replies; from it come the Italian and Spanish words for "yes."

atque (**ac**) adds emphasis or weight to whatever follows, often strengthening or correcting the previous term: **magnus atque clārus poēta**, "a great *and also* famous poet."

In compounds, **ad** often assimilates: **accipiō**, **afficiō**, **appōnō**; before -**q**- the -**d**- may change to -**c**-: **acquirō** from **ad** + **quaerō**.

Ante legenda

A. Translate, and explain the syntax of all verb forms and all dative constructions:

1. Veniēsne ut librum tuum mihi dēmōnstrēs?
2. Advēnī ut librum tibi darem.
3. Dominus mē iussit dōnum fēminae quaerere hodiē.
4. Caelum tōtum auxiliō nautīs est.
5. Pecūniā agricolīs miserīs adsīmus.
6. Nē tibi cōnsilium dēsit, nec supersit tibi cūra.
7. Servī miserī dominō malō cēdere dēbuērunt, (1) ut salvī essent; (2) nē occiderent.
8. Aquam hīc pōne ut bestiae bibere possint; nē cibus dēsit.
9. Et fēminae alterī et cēterīs virīs pecūniam dēbētis.
10. Cōnsilium vestrum erit magnō auxiliō mihi.
11. Ceterōs tuōs librōs hodiē lege.
12. Multōs librōs magnōs legere potest puer.
13. Vae mihi, amīca est fīliō meō!
14. Mihi eris magnae cūrae.
15. Bestiae in agrōs cēdant. Tibi cēdō. Mihi cēdās.

B. Translate into Latin:

1. Let's sing for your (pl.) friends.
2. She gave gifts to good poets.
3. The stars are a great help to sailors.
4. We thanked the teacher so that he would not be unhappy.
5. I couldn't send the book to your (s.) son for you.

Legenda

Scenes from Roman Comedy (2): The Menaechmī

Plautus' *Menaechmi* is a comedy of errors. Menaechmus of Syracuse (a Greek city on the coast of Sicily) has come to Epidamnus (a Greek city on the coast of Asia Minor) with his slave Messenio, in the course of searching for his long-lost twin brother, also named Menaechmus (of Epidamnus). Menaechmus of Syracuse is mistaken for his brother by the latter's cook, mistress, wife, and parasite. The two brothers finally meet and the puzzle is solved.

This play has long been a favorite of adapters and imitators. Shakespeare, who closely modeled his *Comedy of Errors* on it, introduced a number of additional complications, including a second set of twins. The musical by Rodgers and Hart, *The Boys from Syracuse*, in turn, is based on Shakespeare's version of Plautus's play.

A Note on Proper Names in Roman Comedy. The names assigned to characters in Roman comedies are often a source of humor in themselves. They may convey the stereotype represented by a character: Erotium, the prostitute, is named after Eros, the Greek personification of love, and the cook's name, Cylindrus, suggests the rotund shape associated with his profession. Very often the names, particularly in Plautus, cannot be translated literally, because they are a strange conglomeration of pieces of Greek and/or Latin words, hinting all kinds of things about the characters to whom they are assigned. Thus, Philematium, "precious kiss," is the girl-friend of Philolaches, "fond of chance," and Callidamates is "he who subdues by beauty," or "lady-killer."

Among English dramatists, one of the most skillful inventors of significant or "speaking" names was Ben Jonson in the sixteenth century: his plays are crowded with such characters as Wellbred, Morose, Sir Epicure Mammon, Sir Amorous La-Foole, and Sir Diaphanous Silkworm. Other examples are Shakespeare's Mistress Quickly, Pistol, and Shallow, and, in eighteenth-century Restoration comedy, Richard Sheridan's Joseph Surface, Lady Sneerwell, and Mrs. Candour.

1. Erotium, the mistress of Menaechmus of Epidamnus, is instructing the cook, Cylindrus, to buy food and prepare a meal for Menaechmus and his parasite, Peniculus.

EROTIUM: Habēsne pecūniam ut cibum emās*?
CYLINDRUS: Habeō.
EROT.: Cibus sit tribus* satis: neque dēsit neque supersit.
CYL.: Cuiusmodī* hīc convīvae erunt?

1: **emō**, **-ere**, **ēmī**, **emptus**, buy, purchase
3: **tribus** (dat. pl.), for three people
4: **cuiusmodī**, of what sort?

Banquet scene. Wall painting from Pompeii.

EROT.: Ego et Menaechmus * et parasītus * Menaechmī *.
CYL.: Decem * convīvīs prandium * parābō; nam parasītum * quasi * octo * convīvās habeō.

2. Cylindrus goes off to the market. In the meantime, Menaechmus of Syracuse has just arrived in Epidamnus. He is wary of this town, for his slave Messenio has warned him that Epidamnus is filled with informers

5: **Menaechmus**, -ī, *m* a proper name
parasītus, -ī, *m* parasite, free-loader (originally *parasītus* meant "dinner guest")
6: **decem** (indeclinable), ten
prandium, -iī, *n* meal (esp. lunch)
quasi, as if
octo (indeclinable), eight

and conniving prostitutes. Cylindrus, returning from the market, sees Menaechmus of Syracuse and Messenio outside Erotium's house and assumes that the guests have arrived before the meal is ready.

Cylindrus: Bene ēmī** atque bonum prandium** ante convīvās pōnam.
Sed ecce* Menaechmum** videō. Vae tergō* meō!
Iam convīvae ambulant ante iānuam.
Appellābō. Menaechme, salvē.
Menaechmus: Et tū salvē, quisquis* es.
Cyl.: Ubi convīvae ceterī sunt?
Men.: Quōs* tū convīvās quaeris?
Cyl.: Parasītum** tuum.
Men.: Meum parasītum?
Cyl. [aside]: Certē insānus est vir.
Messenio [*to Menaechmus*]: Sīc tibi dīxī, sunt hīc sycophantae* multī.
Men. [*to Cylindrus*]: Insānus es tū, certe sciō.
Nam mihi molestus es virō ignōtō, quisquis* es.
Cyl.: Cylindrus ego sum: nōnne nōvistī nōmen* meum?
Men.: Sīve* tu Cylindrus es sīve* Coriendrus* es,
ego tē nōn nōvī, neque nōvisse* optō.
Cyl.: Est tibi nōmen* "Menaechmus."
Men.: Quasi** sānus dīcis; sed nōvistīne mē?
Cyl.: Quid quaeris? Nam amīcam habēs eram* meam Erōtium.
Men.: Neque hercle* amīcam ūllam habeō neque tē sciō.
Cyl.: Mēne nescīs? Ego tibi saepe cyathissō*!
Men.: Tūne saepe mihi cyathissās*? Sed nisi hodiē
tē numquam vīdī neque Epidamnum* advēnī!
Cyl. [*aside*]: Certē insānit. Sed saepe est ridiculus*
ubi uxor* nōn adest.
[*aloud*]: Quid dīcis tū? Satisne tribus** emī**?
Nunc cibum ad Vulcānī* violentiam pōnam et Erōtium vocābō.

** see passage 1 above
2: **ecce**, look!
tergum, -ī, *n* back, backside
5, 13: **quisquis** (nom. *m/f* sing.), whoever
7: **quōs** (interrogative adj. acc. *m* pl.), which?
11: **sycophanta**, **-ae**, *m* informer, spy (literally, "fig-informer," one who informed on those who smuggled figs)
14, 17: **nōmen** (nom./acc. *n* sing.), name
15: **sīve** . . . **sīve**, whether . . . or
Coriendrus, -ī, *m*: the cook's "alternate name" is a play on two words, **coriandrum** (a spice used in cooking), and **corium** (leather, often signifying a leather whip). What is Menaechmus suggesting in his pun?
16: **nōvisse** perfect infinitive of **noscō**, to know
19: **era**, **-ae**, *f* mistress
20: **hercle** (exclamation), By Hercules!
21, 22: **cyathissō**, **-āre**, ladle out wine (a transliterated Greek word)
23: **Epidamnus**, -ī, *f* Epidamnus; **Epidamnum**, "to (the city) Epidamnus"
24: **ridiculus**, **-a**, **-um**, funny, absurd (from **rideō**, laugh)
25: **uxor** (nom. *f* sing.), wife
27: **Vulcānī violentiam**, the violence of Vulcan i.e., fire, or the stove. (Vulcan was the god of fire)

3. The cook enters the house and summons Erotium, who comes out and seductively invites Menaechmus of Syracuse to lunch—thinking, of course, that he is Menaechmus of Epidamnus.

EROTIUM: Animule * mī,* agedum,* hīc accumbe *. Tē ūnum
Venus * mē optāvit magnificāre *.
MENAECHMUS: Certē haec * fēmina aut insāna aut ēbria est.
Nam virum ignōtum tam familiāriter * appellat.
MESSENIO: Sīc tibi dīxī: Nōlī fēminam audīre.
Folia * nunc cadunt; mox * arborēs * in tē cadent.
Nam sīc sunt hīc fēminae.
Sed ego fēminam appellem. Heus, fēmina, tibi dīcō.
EROT.: Quid est?
MES.: Ubi tū hunc * virum nōvistī?
EROT.: Ibidem * ubi mē nōvit: in Epidamnō.
MES.: In Epidamnō? Sed numquam nisi hodiē hīc adfuit.
EROT.: Vah! Dēliciās facis *. Mī Menaechme, tē amābō,
venī intrō * !
MEN.: Rectē edepol * appellat mē fēmina.
MES.: Oboluit * marsuppium * tuum.
MEN.: Et edepol * tū mē monuistī rectē. *
Nōlī timēre. Accipe nunc marsuppium * meum ut sciam:
amatne mē aut marsuppium * meum?
EROT.: Cēdāmus intrō * ut prandeāmus. *
MEN.: Bene vocās, tamen * grātia * est.
EROT.: Cūr * igitur * mē tibi prandium * * parāre iussistī?

** see passage 1
1: **animulus**, -ī, *m* sweetheart (the diminutive ending **-ulus** indicates affection)
1, 13: **mī**, vocative of meus
agedum, come on
accumbō, **-ere**, **-cubuī**, **-cubitus**, lie down, recline (for the purpose of dining)
2: **Venus**, goddess of love
magnificō, **-āre**, **-āvī**, **-atus**, exalt, glorify
3: **haec** (demonstrative adjective, nom. *f* sing.), this
4: **tam familiāriter**, so intimately
6: **folium**, **-iī**, *n* leaf
mox (adverb), soon
arborēs (nom. *f* pl.), trees
10: **hunc** (demonstrative adjective, acc. *m* sing.), this
11: **ibidem** (adverb), in the same place
13: **dēliciās facis**, you're joking, playing tricks
14, 20: **intrō** (adverb), inside
15, 17: **rectē** (adverb), correctly
15, 17: **edepol** (exclamation), By Pollux!
16: **oboleō**, **-ēre**, **-uī**, emit a smell, scent
16, 18, 19: **marsuppium**, **-iī**, *n* wallet, purse
20: **prandeō**, **-ēre**, **prandī**, **prānsum**, eat lunch (cf. **prandium**, Scene 1)
21: **tamen** (adverb), however, nevertheless
grātia est, no, thank you
22: **cūr** (adverb), why?
igitur (conjunction), therefore

MEN.: Egone tē iussī?
EROT.: Certē, tibi et parasītō** tuō.
MEN.: Meō parasītō**? Certē fēmina nōn sāna est.

Erotium goes on to describe Peniculus, the parasite, as the man who had accompanied Menaechmus when he brought her a dress he had stolen from his wife. The confusion mounts . . . .

V

Indicative Mood (2); Subjunctive Mood (2); Conditions; Potential Subjunctive

Indicative Mood (2)

The remaining tenses in the indicative mood are the imperfect, pluperfect, and future perfect tenses.

Imperfect Indicative

For all conjugations, the sign of the imperfect tense in the indicative mood is -**bā**-, affixed to the present stem and followed by the personal endings:

Endings	**amāre**	**tenēre**	**dūcere**	**capere**	**audīre**
			SINGULAR		
-bam	amā**bam**	tenē**bam**	dūcē**bam**	capiē**bam**	audiē**bam**
-bās	amā**bās**	tenē**bās**	dūcē**bās**	capiē**bās**	audiē**bās**
-bat	amā**bat**	tenē**bat**	dūcē**bat**	capiē**bat**	audiē**bat**
			PLURAL		
-bāmus	amā**bāmus**	tenē**bāmus**	dūcē**bāmus**	capiē**bāmus**	audiē**bāmus**
-bātis	amā**bātis**	tenē**bātis**	dūcē**bātis**	capiē**bātis**	audiē**bātis**
-bant	amā**bant**	tenē**bant**	dūcē**bant**	capiē**bant**	audiē**bant**

Observe that:

1. In the first person singular, the personal ending is -**m**, in all conjugations.

2. The vowel immediately preceding the -**bā**- is always long, even in the third conjugation, which adds an -**ē**- to the shortened stem (**dūc-ē-bā**-).

3. All -**iō** verbs (that is, fourth conjugation verbs and -**iō** verbs of the third conjugation) add a long -**ē**- to the stem. In fourth conjugation verbs the -**ī**- of the stem is shortened before the -**ē**-. Third conjugation verbs add an -**i**- to the shortened stem before the -**ē**-.

Meaning of the Imperfect. The imperfect tense indicates a past action that is in some way incomplete (from **imperfectus**, not completed). This very general definition covers an interesting variety of ideas in English. Most often the imperfect denotes an action or state that continued or occurred habitually or repeatedly in the past:

audiēbāmus	We were listening, kept listening (continuing for an unspecified length of time).
	We used to listen (habitually, not referring to a particular incident or time).

The imperfect is appropriate for description, especially of mental states—thoughts, feelings, or emotions—because it is often not possible to determine clearly when they begin or end:

Multa dōna semper **optābat**.	He always *wanted* many gifts.

And, because it expresses continuation over time, the imperfect can convey the effort to do something, or the beginning of an action:

Puer poētam **audiēbat**.	The boy *was listening* to (was trying to hear) the poet.
Convīvae ad Philolachem **adveniēbant**.	The dinner-companions *were coming to* (were about to arrive at, were just beginning to reach) Philolaches' house.

Depending on the context, then, a Latin imperfect tense form can be rendered by any of these English phrases:

was/were —ing	tried to —
used to —	began to —
kept —ing	would —
continued to —	

Imperfect Indicative of ***sum, possum****.* The imperfect indicative of the verb **sum**, **esse** is indicated by the tense marker -**ā**- (compare the imperfect tense marker -**bā**- for regular verbs in the indicative mood), which is affixed to the stem **er**-.[1] The imperfect indicative, accordingly, of **esse** is formed by adding personal endings to **erā**-. The imperfect indicative of **possum**, **posse** consists of the element **pot**- plus the entire imperfect indicative form of **esse**. Note that after the letter -**a**- the first person singular ending is -**m**.

esse		**posse**	
	SINGULAR		SINGULAR
eram	I was, used to be	pot**eram**	I was/used to be able, could
erās	You were, used to be	pot**erās**	You were/used to be able, could
erat	He (she/it) was, used to be	pot**erat**	He (she/it) was/used to be able, could

[1] Regarding the stem **er**-, see the discussion of rhotacism on page 43.

	PLURAL		PLURAL
erāmus	We were, used to be	pot**erāmus**	We were/used to be able, could
erātis	You were, used to be	pot**erātis**	You were/used to be able, could
erant	They were, used to be	pot**erant**	They were/used to be able, could

If **eram** and **fuī** both can be translated "I was," what is the difference between the imperfect and the perfect tenses? It may help to compare them, respectively, to movies and snapshots. Latin uses the imperfect tense in narrative to describe an action that is habitual or still in progress, unfinished, or a continuing condition, state of affairs, or mental state. The perfect tense, like a still photograph, merely records the action or state of affairs as a completed fact.

Poēta cantāre nōn **poterat**.	The poet was not able to sing.	(The imperfect describes a condition continuing over an unspecified period of time)
Poēta cantāre nōn **potuit**.	The poet was not able to sing.	(The perfect reports his incapacity at a past point in time)

The two tenses are often used together, combining description or continuing action (imperfect) with a single discrete event (perfect):

> The sky was blue and all was calm, when suddenly there came a flash of lightning.
>
> While I was walking in the woods, a bear attacked me.

Sometimes the perfect tense carries a special overtone of finality, of something being over and done with:

Pulcher **erat**.	He was handsome (a continuing state in past time).
Pulcher **fuit**.	He *was* handsome [but no longer is].
Fuit agricola; iam poēta est.	He *was* a farmer; now he is a poet.

Pluperfect and Future Perfect Indicative Active

The two remaining tenses of the indicative mood are the *pluperfect* (or past perfect) and the *future perfect*. Both appear chiefly in the subordinate clause of a compound sentence, accompanying a main verb in another tense; that is, their actions are usually relative.

The Formation of the Pluperfect and Future Perfect Indicative. In all conjugations these two tenses are formed, like the perfect tense, by adding the appropriate endings to the perfect stem (**amāv**-, **tenu**-, **dūx**-, **cēp**-, **audīv**-). The pluperfect consists of the perfect stem plus -**erā**- plus the personal endings. The future perfect indicative consists of the perfect stem plus -**eri**- plus personal endings. Note that the first person singular ending of the future perfect indicative is -**ō**, whereas the first person singular ending of the pluperfect indicative is **-m**. Observe also that, while the pluperfect indicative endings are identical with the imperfect indicative forms of **esse**, the future perfect indicative endings differ from future indicative forms of **esse** in the third person plural (compare **erunt**, "they will be").

In the indicative mood of the active voice, then, the three tenses of the perfect system of all verbs, including **esse** and **posse**, will follow the model provided by **amāre**:

PERFECT	PLUPERFECT	FUTURE PERFECT
I have loved I loved I did love	I had loved	I shall have loved
	SINGULAR	
amāvī	amāv**eram**	amāv**erō**
amāvistī	amāv**erās**	amāv**eris**
amāvit	amāv**erat**	amāv**erit**
	PLURAL	
amāvimus	amāv**erāmus**	amāv**erimus**
amāvistis	amāv**erātis**	amāv**eritis**
amāvērunt	amāv**erant**	amāv**erint**

The Meaning of the Pluperfect and Future Perfect Indicative. The pluperfect tense (from **plus quam perfectum**, "more than completed") refers to an event already completed at some time in the past, previous to another past action. English regularly uses the auxiliary verb "had" to translate the pluperfect tense.

By the time the dinner guests arrived, Cylindrus had prepared a good meal. (The preparation of the meal was completed before the dinner guests arrived.)

The future perfect tense describes an action that will have been completed at some time in the future. It is most often used in temporal or conditional subordinate clauses. Consider these two sentences:

If you prepare a good meal (when you have prepared a good meal), I shall summon the dinner guests.

If you take my purse (if you will have taken my purse), I shall attend the dinner in safety.

In each sentence, both actions ("prepare, summon"; "take, be") lie in the future, but the first must take place—be completed—before the second can occur: in both, a future act will be completed in the future before the dinner guests can be summoned or Menaechmus can feel safe. Note that English idiom calls for the simple present, "prepare," "take," in the subordinate clause. Latin, always careful to specify the temporal relationship between two verbs precisely, requires in both cases the future perfect, the equivalent of our seldom-used "will have prepared" or "will have taken":

Sī bonum prandium parāveris, convīvās vocābō.

Sī meum marsuppium cēperis, salvus convīva erō.

Subjunctive Mood (2)

The subjunctive mood in Latin comprises four tenses. You have already learned the present and imperfect subjunctive; the remaining two tenses of the subjunctive mood are the perfect and the pluperfect. There is no future subjunctive and no future perfect subjunctive, for the future in its meaning approaches the subjunctive. (In early Latin the future and the subjunctive are sometimes used interchangeably.) As in other tenses, these tenses of the subjunctive cannot be translated out of context.

Perfect and Pluperfect Subjunctive Active

The perfect active subjunctive adds -**eri**- plus personal endings to the perfect stem. The only difference between the future perfect active indicative endings and the perfect active subjunctive endings occurs in the first person singular, where the future perfect subjunctive adds the personal ending -**m** (**amāverim**) (compare **amāverō**, "I shall have loved"). For the remaining forms, only the context of the verb will determine whether it is perfect subjunctive or future perfect indicative.

The pluperfect active subjunctive is formed by adding -**isse**- plus the personal endings to the perfect active stem. The first person plural ending is -**m**: **amāv-isse-m**; **tenu-isse-m**; **dūx-isse-m**; **cēp-isse-m**.[2] The perfect and pluperfect active subjunctive of all verbs follow these models of **amāre** and **esse**:

PERFECT		PLUPERFECT	
	SINGULAR		
amāv**erim**	fu**erim**	amāv**issem**	fu**issem**
amāv**eris**	fu**eris**	amāv**issēs**	fu**issēs**
amāv**erit**	fu**erit**	amāv**isset**	fu**isset**
	PLURAL		
amāv**erimus**	fu**erimus**	amāv**issēmus**	fu**issēmus**
amāv**eritis**	fu**eritis**	amāv**issētis**	fu**issētis**
amāv**erint**	fu**erint**	amāv**issent**	fu**issent**

The Synopsis

You have now learned the entire active system of all Latin verbs. A useful way to study and review these forms is to write a *synopsis* (from Greek, "a

[2] The perfect active stem plus -**isse** (**amāvisse**, **tenuisse**, etc.) is in fact the perfect active infinitive ("to have saved," "to have held," etc.). The formation of the pluperfect subjunctive by the addition of personal endings to the perfect infinitive is analogous to the formation of the imperfect subjunctive in which personal endings are added to the present active infinitive.

general view") of a verb, in a specified person and number. Here, for example, is a synopsis of **capiō** in the second person singular:

capiō, capere, cēpī, captus

	INDICATIVE	
Present	capis	you seize, are seizing
Imperfect	capiēbās	you were seizing, used to seize
Future	capiēs	you will seize
Perfect	cēpistī	you seized, have seized, did seize
Pluperfect	cēperās	you had seized
Future perfect	cēperis	you will have seized
	SUBJUNCTIVE	
Present	capiās	(Translation depends on context.)
Imperfect	caperēs	
Perfect	cēperis	
Pluperfect	cēpissēs	

Test yourself frequently with verb synopses: you will find them an efficient and helpful method of study.

Scrībenda

A. Identify each form, listing all possibilities:

habērem	habuerō	habuerim	habeam
cantāverint	cantārent	cantābunt	cantābant
dūcam	dūxerim	dūxissem	dūcēbam
accipit	accipiat	accipiet	accēperat
momordistī	momorderitis	mordeātis	momordissēs

B. Write a complete synopsis (ten forms) of each verb in the person specified:

dare:	Third person singular	cōgitāre:	Second person singular
vidēre:	Second person plural	noscere:	Third person plural
sentīre:	First person plural	posse:	First person singular

C. Change from the indicative mood to the subjunctive, retaining the person, number, and tense of the original. (Example, scīs: sciās)

1. vēnī; veniēbās; advenit; invēnistī.
2. audīmus; audīvimus; audīverās; audiēbam.
3. potes; poterant; potuit; poterāmus.
4. agō; ēgistis; agēbātis; ēgeram.
5. fugit; fūgit; fugiēbat; fūgerat.
6. noscimus; nōvimus; noscēbam; nōveram.
7. quaeris; quaesīvistis; quaerēbātis; quaesīverās.

Conditions

A conditional sentence contains two basic clauses, an "if" clause, stating a condition (called the *protasis*), and a conclusion (called the *apodosis*): If A, then B. The protasis is a dependent clause, introduced in Latin by **sī**, "if," or **nisi**, "if . . . not," "unless." The apodosis—the main clause—states what is, was, will be, would be, or would have been true if the condition expressed in the protasis is, was, or will be, fulfilled. Latin expresses the several possible combinations of these two parts of a conditional sentence very precisely, more so than English does even at its best. (Although English too has rules for expressing each type of condition, current usage is often careless.)

Conditional sentences in Latin can be grouped into three main categories: *General*, *Ideal*, and *Contrary-to-Fact* conditions, according to the nature of the protasis. Study the following examples, and learn the name and characteristics of each type of condition. Be careful to translate conditions according to the logical categories described. (You may find it both interesting and helpful to examine conditional sentences as you read in English, too; analyze and label the types you encounter.)

A. General: simple or general conditions of fact—present, future, or past. In a general condition, "if" actually means "whenever," as in examples 1 and 3. Nothing is implied as to whether or not the condition is, has been, or will be, fulfilled.

Protasis ("if" clause): indicative; *Apodosis*: any appropriate form (indicative, imperative, independent subjunctive)

1. *Present*: Sī auxilium optāmus, tē vocāmus. If we want help, we call you.
2. *Future*: Sī auxilium optābitis, mē vocāte. If you (will) want help, call me.
3. *Past*: Sī auxilium optābant, mē vocābant. If they wanted help, they called (used to call) me.

B. Ideal: hypothetical, imagined circumstances in future time; often called "should–would" conditions. Compared with a general condition referring to the future, an ideal condition is more tentative, and implies doubt that the condition will be fulfilled.[3]

Present subjunctive in both clauses

4. Sī auxilium optēmus, tē vocēmus. If we should (were to) want help [it is not likely that we will in fact want help], we would call you.

C. Contrary-to-Fact: unreal or impossible of fulfillment, in present or past time.

[3] Many textbooks refer to Ideal Conditions as Future–Less–Vivid Conditions, and to General Conditions in the future tense as Future–More–Vivid Conditions.

Present time: imperfect subjunctive in both clauses
Past time: pluperfect subjunctive in both clauses

5. *Present*: Sī auxilium optārēs, mē vocārēs. If you wanted (were now wanting) help [but you do not], you would call (would be calling) me [but you are not].
6. *Present*: Sī mē vocārēs, venīrem. If you were [now] calling me [but you are not], I would be coming [but I am not].
7. *Past*: Sī auxilium optāvissem, tē vocāvissem. If I had wanted help [but I did not], I would have called you [but I did not].
8. *Past*: Nōn tē vocāvissem nisi auxilium optāvissem. I wouldn't have called you [but I did] if I had not wanted help [but I did].

D. In addition to these clear-cut categories, "mixed" conditions occur; they should cause no difficulty, however, since they obey the dictates of logic and common sense. Example 9 combines an Ideal condition in the protasis with an imperative in the apodosis, and the final example illustrates the mixing of tenses in a contrary-to-fact condition.

9. Sī auxilium optēs, vocā mē. If you should want help, call me.
10. Nisi tē vocāvissem, nōn salva essem. If I hadn't called you, I wouldn't be safe [now].

Potential Subjunctive

The subjunctive may be used independently to express the opinion of the speaker as an opinion, and hence will tend to be in the first person ("I should think . . ."), or in an imaginary second person ("you would have thought . . ."), although it does occur in the third person ("someone may say . . ."). Since it conveys the opinion of the speaker, it is most commonly used with verbs of saying, thinking, or wishing.

The tenses used in the potential subjunctive will be a source of confusion unless one understands how the tenses differ in each mood. Only the indicative mood expresses a period of time directly and uniformly. The imperative mood of necessity refers to the future (even though Latin does have separate future imperative forms in addition to its present imperative forms). The tenses of the subjunctive are always relative to something else: in dependent clauses (discussed more fully in the next chapter) they are relative to the tense of the main verb. In independent clauses, they are relative to the time of the speaker.

The potential subjunctive in the present or perfect tense expresses the opinion of the speaker with regard to present or future time, without clear distinction. (The negative is expressed by **nōn**.)

Dīcam/Dīxerim . . .	I would say . . .
Crēdās/crēdideris . . .	You would think . . .
Fāmam tuam nōn optem/optāverim.	I would not want your reputation.

The potential subjunctive in the imperfect tense expresses the opinion of the speaker in the past. (The negative is expressed by **nōn**.)

Dīcerem . . .	I would have said . . .
Crēderēs . . .	You would have thought . . .
Fāmam tuam nōn optārem.	I would not have wanted your reputation.

Scrībenda

A. Identify each condition, and translate the sentence.

1. Nisi salvus es, miser sum.
2. Nisi salvus sīs, miser sim.
3. Sī salva fuisset, nōn timuissēmus.
4. Sī convīva ēbrius erat, ambulāre nōn poterat.
5. Sī convīva ēbrius esset, ambulāre nōn posset.
6. Sī convīva ambulāre nōn poterit, fīlius timēbit.
7. Sī sāna sim, bona sōla optem.
8. Sī fēmina vocābit, nōlī respondēre.
9. Sī cūrās meās habērēs, tuās mitterēs.
10. Tibi cantārem sī poēta essem.
11. Aliud sānus nōn audiam (audīrem).

B. Identify each condition, and translate into Latin.

1. If you should call, I would come.
2. If he calls, I will come.
3. If she had asked for help, I would have come.
4. If I called, they came.
5. If I were living alone, I would ask for help.
6. If he drinks, he falls down.
7. In my right mind (**sānus**), I would not have listened to another person.

Verba tenenda

Verbs

cēlō, -āre, -āvī, -ātus conceal, hide, keep secret
cēnseō, -ēre, cēnsuī, cēnsus estimate, assess, judge
cōgō, -ere, coēgī, coāctus compel, force; collect, bring together
commendō, -āre, -āvī, -ātus entrust
crēdō, -ere, crēdidī, crēditus (+ dat.), believe, trust; think
cūro, -āre, -āvī, -ātus care for, attend to, take care of
dēlīberō, -āre, -āvī, -ātus consider carefully, deliberate
distrahō, -ere, -traxī, -tractus tear into pieces, divide; perplex
extrahō, -ere, -traxī, -tractus drag out; release; extricate
iaciō, -ere, iēcī, iactus throw, hurl
impendeō, -ēre, ——, —— hang over, threaten, be imminent
laudō, -āre, -āvī, -ātus praise
maneō, -ēre, mānsī, mānsus remain, stay, await
remaneō, -ēre, remānsī, remānsus remain, stay behind

trahō, **trahere**, **traxī**, **tractus** drag, draw, pull
valeō, **-ēre**, **valuī**, **valitūrus** be strong, be well
valē! **valēte**! goodbye! (literally, "fare well!")

Nouns

audācia, **-ae**, *f* courage, boldness, daring
equus, **-ī**, *m* horse
fortūna, **-ae**, *f* fortune, luck
modus, **-ī**, *m* manner, method, way; measure, limit
nihil or **nīl**, *n* (indeclinable), nothing
nuptiae, **-ārum**, *f* pl. marriage, wedding
remedium, **-iī**, *n* remedy, cure; solution
sententia, **-ae**, *f* opinion, way of thinking

Adjectives

aequus, **-a**, **-um** equal, even, fair
  aequum est it is right, fair, just
incertus, **-a**, **-um** uncertain, doubtful
integer, **-gra**, **-grum** untouched, unimpaired, whole, fresh
  in (**ad**) **integrum** to a former or original state
invītus, **-a**, **-um** unwilling, reluctant
quantus, **-a**, **-um** how great, how large, how much
saevus, **-a**, **-um** raging, cruel, savage
tantus, **-a**, **-um** so great, so large
  tantus . . . **quantus** as great (large) . . . as
timidus, **-a**, **-um** timid, fearful
quot (indeclinable), how many?
tot (indeclinable), so many
  tot . . . **quot** as many . . . as

Adverbs

ergō therefore, consequently
etiam also, even
  nōn sōlum . . . **sed etiam** not only . . . but also
nōnne (interrogative particle) affirmative answer expected
num (interrogative particle) negative answer expected
simul at the same time, together

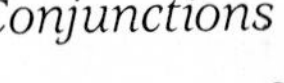

Conjunctions

enim (postpositive) for, indeed, for indeed, truly
-que (enclitic) and

Preposition

ē, **ex** (+ ablative) from, out of

Notanda

cōgō is a compound of **con** (from **cum**) + **agō**; the prefix adds the idea of bringing together. With a complementary infinitive it means "compel," "force (to do something)."

crēdō usually behaves as a transitive verb, "to have trust/belief (in)," and takes an object in the dative case: **crēde mihi**; **tibi crēdō**.

dēlīberō contains the notion of weighing, from **lībra**, "scales, balance." We put one idea, course of action, etc., in each pan of the scales to see which carries more weight.

The prefix **dis**- (as in **distrahō**) means "in different directions, apart." Thus "distract" implies a splintering of attention, not simply a shift from one focus to another. Distinguish from "detract."

iaciō and its compounds follow the stem-vowel pattern already met in **capiō** and **faciō**. Its compounds lose the initial semi-consonantal **i**- in tenses formed on the present stem: e.g., **coniciō**, "throw together" (**coni~~a~~ciō**).

The essence of **impendeō** is continuing, uncompleted action, and therefore only tenses formed on the present stem are found.

fortūna, by itself, is neutral—the luck of the draw. The context, or a modifying adjective, will tell you whether it is **bona** or **mala**.

modus often carries a coloring of "moderation, restraint": the proper limit, due measure, the right way.

nihil, **nīl**: since **h** was always very weakly pronounced, it readily dropped out between two like vowels; the two short -**i**-'s combine to form -**ī**-. (For the same reason you will often see **mī** for **mihi**.)

The different meanings of **sententia** are preserved in our "sentence," which may mean either a complete thought or a penalty handed down by a judge.

aequus as a military term describes land which is level, flat, and so gives no advantage to either side in battle. In the idiom **aequum est**, "it is right," the neuter **aequum** is in agreement with a substantive infinitive, that is, an infinitive used as a neuter noun. **Aequum est hīc manēre**, "It is right to remain here."

The negative prefix **in**- appears in the three adjectives **incertus**, **integer**, and **invītus**.

"Integer" (the root **teg**- comes from **tangō**, "touch") is used as a noun in mathematics, the noun it originally modified having been discarded. (What gender was that noun?) All other derivatives are formed from the stem: integral, integrity, integrate.

quantus and **tantus** often appear together as correlatives, as do **tot** and **quot**: **Nūllās cūrās umquam vīdī *tantās*, *quantae* nunc sunt**. "Never have I seen *such great* concerns *as* now exist."

nōnne and **num** correspond to interrogative phrases in English; respectively, "you're going to class, *aren't you*?" (expecting an affirmative answer) and "you aren't leaving, *are you*?" (expecting a negative answer).

enim normally comes second in the sentence, and hence is said to be postpositive. It confirms and explains a preceding statement; **enimvērō** (a compound of **enim** + **vērō**, "truly, indeed"), "certainly," usually stands first, and emphasizes what follows.

The enclitic conjunction -**que**, "and," translates before the word to which it is affixed: **poēta cantat puer*que* audit**, "the poet is singing *and* the child is listening."

ex may be used before words beginning with either a vowel or a consonant, **ē** only before a consonant.

Ante legenda

Translate:

1. Et tuam et meam terram cēlat ūnum caelum.
2. Aequum est verba tua audīre.
3. Aequō animō tibi dīcerem.
4. Nōnne fortūna tua meaque aequa est?
5. Num tanta mala impendent?
6. Sī tanta mala impendērent, nōn hīc manērem.
7. Ā tuā terrā cēdāmus ut tanta mala fugiāmus.
8. Tanta quanta dīxistī dēlīberābō.
9. Quot viae ad vītam bonam sunt virō integrō?
10. Sunt tot viae quot virī bonī.
11. Valēte! Vītam meam in terrā incertā agam.
12. Manē in nostrā terrā nē vītam sine amīcīs agās.
13. Sī fortūna saeva mihi sit, auxilium tuum petam.
14. Sī fortūna saeva mihi esset, auxilium tuum peterem.
15. Sī fortūna bona mihi fuisset, alium vitae modum nōn petīvissem.
16. Sententia tua mē distrahit. (distrahat)
17. Nōn tē audīrem sī sententia tua mē distraheret.
18. Fortūna bona mē in terram aliam dūcet.
19. Tanta audācia erat tibi remediō malōrum. Audācia esset tibi remediō malōrum.
20. Timidōs virōs nōn laudābam sī modum vitae bonum cēnsēre optābam.
21. Simul dat Fortūna et cūram et remedium.
22. Cōgitō, ergō sum.
23. Nōnne meam sententiam laudās? Coēgit mē laudāre tē.
24. Invītus tua verba audiō. Tua sententia cōgitāre mē cōgit.
25. In equō magnō veniet ut timidōs virōs ā terrā saevā dūcat.

Legenda

Scenes from Roman Comedy (3): Phormiō; Pamphilus

Terence's *Phormiō* (first produced in 161 B.C.) is named for its central character, a clever parasite who manipulates the lively and complex plot. Terence's plays contain many pithy sayings that passed into folk wisdom; can you spot a maxim in each of these scenes?

1. Antipho ("talk back"), a young man, has fallen in love with Phanium, a girl who has no dowry and, apparently, no family—both, serious obstacles to a proper marriage. Nevertheless, Phormio has concocted a scheme enabling Antipho to marry Phanium during his father's absence. In this scene, Antipho's slave Geta, who should have been guarding his young master more effectively, anticipates big trouble when Antipho's father returns and learns about the marriage.

GETA [*talking to himself*]: Nihil eris, Geta, nisi iam cōnsilium tibi
celeriter* invēneris: tē nunc imparātum* tanta impendent mala.
Nunc fugerēs aut tē extraherēs sī viam aut modum scīrēs.
Nam nōn potes cēlāre nostram diūtius* audāciam.
Erus* adest, et ubi audīverit, quod* remedium inveniam īrācundiae*?
Heu mē miserum*! Antipho mē excruciat.*
Nisi eum* cūrāvissem, ego mihi vīdissem* atque hinc* fūgissem.

ANTIPHO [*having overheard the last*]: Geta! Quid est malum?
Cūr fugere parās? Dīc!

GE.: Tuum patrem* vīdī.

ANTI.: Occidī! Quid agam? Egone nunc remedium inveniam miser?
Sī meae fortūnae mē ā tē distrahant, Phanium, nūlla vīta mē maneat.

GE.: Ergō advigilāre* dēbēs, Antipho: fortēs* fortūna adiuvat*.
Nam sī pater sēnserit tē timidum esse, crēdet tē commerēre* culpam.

ANTI.: Sed nōn possum aliud facere. Vae mihi, Geta, quid agam?

GE.: Nunc mea verba audī. Sī pater verba saeva dīcet, respondē,
"aliī mē coēgērunt invītum nuptiās facere." Tenēs? Sed venit pater!

ANTI.: Nōn possum adesse.

GE.: Quid agis? Cūr fugis, Antipho? Manē!

Anti.: Mē nōvī et culpam meam. Phanium et vītam meam tibi commendō. Valē!

[*Fugit Antipho*]

2: **celeriter** (adverb), quickly
imparātus, **-a**, **-um**, unprepared
4: **diūtius** (adverb), for a longer time, any longer
5: **erus**, **-ī**, *m* master
quod (interrog. adjective, acc. *n* sing.), what? (modifying **remedium**)
6: **īrācundia**, **-ae**, *f* wrath, rage (genitive after **remedium**)
7: **Heu**, Alas!
mē miserum, accusative of exclamation: "poor me!"
excruciō, **-āre**, **-āvī**, **-ātus**, torment, torture; vex, harass
8: **eum** (pronoun, acc. *m* sing.), him
vīdissem, here = **prōvīdissem**, "I would have looked out for"
hinc (adverb), from here
11: **patrem** (acc. *m* sing.), father
15: **advigilō**, **-āre**, **-āvī**, **-ātus**, be on guard, watch out
fortēs (acc. pl.), brave [men]
adiuvō, **-āre**, **adiūvī**, **adiūtus**, help, favor
16: **commereō**, **-ēre**, **-uī**, **-itus**, deserve fully

From the Phormio *by Terence: Demipho consults his advisers about how to handle his son's marriage. From a ninth-century manuscript (Vat. lat. 3868, vol. 82v), one of a series illustrating the plays of Terence. The original is in full color.*

2. Antipho's father, Demipho, is—of course—extremely upset about his son's marriage, but he cannot remove Phanium from his house without violating her rights as a free citizen. He therefore calls upon his friends Hegio, Cratīnus, and Crīto for some legal advice. The medieval illustration above depicts this scene.

DEMIPHO: Quantā mē cūrā afficit* fīlius! Quam* mē impedīvit* nuptiīs!
Neque ad mē venit ut saltem* sciam eius* sententiam dē nuptiīs.
Sī ad mē veniat, sententiam noscere possim.
[*to his friends*] Vidētis, virī, meam difficultātem*.
Quid agō? Dīc, Hegio.
HEGIO: Ego? Cratīnus, cēnseō, prīmum* dīcere dēbet.

1: **afficiō**, **-ere**, affect, afflict
quam (exclamatory adverb), how [greatly]
impediō, **-īre**, entangle, embarrass, hinder
2: **saltem** (adverb), at least
eius (pronoun, gen. *m* sing.), of him, his
5: **difficultātem** (acc. *f* sing.), difficulty
7: **prīmum** (adverb), first

Dem.: Dīc, Cratīne.
Cratinus: Mēne rogās*?
Dem.: Tē.
Cra.: Ahem, sī meam sententiam scīre optās, ego sīc respondeō:
quod* tē absente* fīlius ēgit, restituere* in integrum aequum est
et bonum. Dīxī.
Dem.: Dīc nunc, Hegio.
Heg.: Sedula* sunt verba Cratīnī. Vērum ita est*,
"quot hominēs*, tot sententiae." Sīc ego crēdō:
nuptiae sī lēgitimae* erant, rescindere* nōn potes.
Et sī incipiās, malum faciās.
Dem.: Dīc, Crīto.
Crīto: Sīc ego cēnseō: amplius* dēlīberāre dēbēmus. Rēs* magna est.
Cra.: Num optās plūs* quaerere?
Dem.: Fēcistis bene. Sī incertus dūdum* eram, nunc incertior sum multō*!

Medieval Drama

Of plays and their authors after Terence, we have only fragments and names. Strangely, the creative period of Roman comedy had ended by the first century B.C. Popular entertainment subsequently favored vulgar farces and mime, which were rather like vaudeville sketches. The only other ancient Latin plays extant are several tragedies on Greek mythical themes written by Seneca the Younger in the first century A.D. The plays of Plautus and Terence continued to be read, however, and they were studied in schools and explicated by grammarians for centuries: a detailed commentary on Terence's plays by Aelius Donatus, St. Jerome's teacher in the mid-fourth century, survives.

Remarkably little is known about the survival of staged drama throughout most of the Middle Ages, although scraps of evidence suggest that it did survive. The illustrated manuscripts of Terence's plays that were copied in the ninth and tenth centuries prove that Terence was still being read, and they also preserve much older traditions of costumes and staging. Six playlets written in the latter part of the tenth century by the nun

9: **rogō**, **-āre**, ask
12: **quod** (relative pronoun, acc. *n* sing.), [that] which
tē absente, "with you absent" ("in your absence")
restituō, **-ere**, restore
15: **sedulus**, **-a**, **-um**, careful, painstaking
vērum ita est, "thus it is true"
16: **hominēs** (nom. *m* pl.), men (human beings)
17: **lēgitimus**, **-a**, **-um**, lawful, legal
rescindō, **-ere**, break up, annul
20: **amplius** (adverb), further, at greater length
rēs (nom. *f* sing.), thing, situation, problem
21: **plūs** (acc. *n* sing.), more
22: **dūdum** (adverb), previously
incertior sum multō, "I am much more uncertain"

Hrotsvitha of Gandersheim in Germany confirm Terence's persistent popularity: her plays, which feature young women resisting, succumbing to, or being redeemed from sin, form a unique bridge between the ancient Roman plays and medieval religious and secular drama.

It is to the church itself that we owe the eventual revival of dramatic performances. Liturgical drama began perhaps as early as the ninth century, with reenactments of the story of the Resurrection. Secular dramatic literature reappears in the twelfth century with a group of twenty anonymous works, written in northern France. Scholars are still puzzling over their ancestry. One link with the ancient comedies is clear enough: Terence's *Andria* includes three characters whose names (Pamphilus, Gliscerium and Birria) turn up as the title of the shortest of these twelfth century works.

"Pamphilus, Gliscerium et Birria"

Pamphilus sets out on horseback, accompanied by his servant Birria, to look for his **amīca** Gliscerium ("sweet little thing"). After they find her in Paris, the three of them stop at a tiny inn for the night. Birria (like Erotium's cook in the *Menaechmi*) is sent out to buy and prepare food. After an ample meal of spit-roasted chicken, boiled fish, assorted fruit and nuts, and plenty of wine, Pamphilus and Gliscerium go off to snuggle in bed, while Birria has to sleep on the ground outdoors, next to the fire. Gliscerium questions Pamphilus about his intentions.

Birriae caelum tegimen,* culcitra* terra fuit.
Dum Vulcānus* terga* cūrat, altera pars* potuit scīre hiemem*.
Et miser ante iānuam philosophātur equus*.
Gliscerium incerta quaerit
causam principiumque* viae. Pamphilus
"Cēlās," dīcit, "in tē causam integram;
Tu causa es principiumque* viae."
Gliscerium: "Cūr* mē dērīdēs,* Pamphile?
Digna* tibī causa viae nōn esse possum.
Pamphilus: "Num dubitās*? Nōnne tē amō?
Est ergō evangelium, quod tibi dicō.*"

1: **tegimen** (nom. *n* sing.), covering
culcitra, **-ae**, *f* mattress
2: **Vulcānus**, -ī, *m* Vulcan, god of fire, and thus "fire"
tergum, -ī, *n* (often used in pl.), back
pars (nom. *f* sing.), part
hiemem (acc. *f* sing.), winter
3: **philosophātur equus**, "the horse philosophizes"
5, 7: **principium**, **-iī**, *n* origin, beginning
8: **cūr** (adverb), why?
dērīdeō, **-ēre**, **-rīsī**, **-rīsus**, mock, make fun of
9: **dignus**, **-a**, **-um**, worthy, worthwhile; deserving
10: **dubitō**, **-āre**, **-āvī**, **-ātus**, doubt
11: "What (**quod**) I say to you is the gospel truth (**evangelium**)."

VI

Pronouns (1); Questions: Direct, Indirect, Deliberative; Sequence of Tenses; *Volō, Nōlō, Mālō*

Relative Pronouns

In Latin, as in English, a sentence can be simple or complex. A simple sentence consists of an independent clause:

Nōlī fēminam audīre.	Don't listen to the woman.
Folia nunc cadunt.	Now the leaves are falling.

Simple sentences can be compounded, with each clause retaining its independence:

Folia nunc cadunt, sed mox arborēs in tē cadent.
Now the leaves are falling, but soon the trees will fall on you.

Independent clauses will often be subordinated in order to show a more complex relationship between clauses, such as purpose, condition, temporal sequence, etc. A relative pronoun is used to subordinate an adjectival clause:

Nōlī fēminam **quae tē vocat** audīre.
Don't listen to the woman *who is calling you*.
Arborēs in tē, **cui fēmina nunc dīcit**, mox cadent.
On you, *to whom the woman is now speaking*, trees will soon be falling.

The relative pronoun agrees in number and gender with its antecedent—the noun to which the pronoun refers, or, literally, the noun which "goes (**cēdō**) before (**ante**)" the pronoun. The case, however, of the relative pronoun is determined by its grammatical function within its own clause. In the first example above, **quae** refers back to **fēminam**, and therefore the feminine singular of the relative pronoun is used; **quae** is the subject of the clause **quae tē vocat**, however, and therefore the nominative case of the relative pronoun is used. In the second example, **cui** refers back to its masculine singular antecedent **tē**, but it is dative because, in its own clause, it is the indirect object of **dīcit**.

Learn the forms of the relative pronoun[1]:

qui, quae, quod
who, which

	Singular			Plural		
	M.	F.	N.	M.	F.	N.
Nom.	quī	quae	quod	quī	quae	quae
Gen.	cuius	cuius	cuius	quōrum	quārum	quōrum
Dat.	cui	cui	cui	quibus	quibus	quibus
Acc.	quem	quam	quod	quōs	quās	quae
Abl.	quō	quā	quō	quibus	quibus	quibus

Sometimes the relative pronoun at the beginning of one sentence refers back to something in the previous sentence:

Folia nunc cadunt; mox arborēs in tē cadent. **Quae** saepe tibi dixī: nam sīc sunt fēminae.
Now the leaves are falling; soon the trees will fall on you. I have often said *these things* (lit., "which") to you. For women are like that.

Menaechmum et parasītum, quī ambulant ante iānuam, vocābō. **Quibus** bonum prandium parāvī.
I shall call Menaechmus and the parasite, who are strolling in front of the door. I have prepared a nice lunch *for them* (lit., "for whom").

Scrībenda

A. Identify all possible meanings of the following forms: quī; cui; cuius; quā; quae; quibus; quem; quō.

B. Identify the antecedent of the relative pronoun, and then translate the entire sentence into English:

1. Fēmina erat causa cūrae quam sentīs.
2. Quid quaerēbās ā librīs quōs legēbās?
3. Da mihi cōnsilium quod mē salvum faciet.
4. Remedium mihi dedit fēmina quod numquam petīveram.
5. Remedia cūrārum cēterārum spērābat quās sēnserat.

C. Indicate the case, number and gender for the Latin equivalent of the underlined pronoun:

1. Have you met the woman who is the cause of my concern?
2. Did you speak to the woman whom I mentioned?
3. Do they want the advice which we are giving?
4. Are you the person whom I spoke to yesterday?
5. Do you understand the words which you are writing?
6. The road (on) which you are traveling is long and arduous.

[1] Compare these endings to those of **sōlus**, -**a**, -**um**, especially in the genitive and dative singular.

7. Roman women whose husbands were senators were themselves powerful.
8. The woman whose children you met is a good friend of mine.
9. The cook prepared a meal for those guests which you invited.

D. Supply the relative pronoun in Latin; the antecedent is underlined:

1. Sententiam respondēbat Cratīnus, (who) verba sedula semper dīcēbat. (**sedulus**, **-a**, **-um**, careful)
2. Sedula erant verba Cratīnī, (who) sententiam dīxit.
3. Fīlius, (whose) amīcī sunt ēbriī, timet.
4. Servus, (to whom) fīlium meum commendāvī, nuptiās cēlāre nōn potest.
5. Vir (whom) vidēbis auxilium petet.
6. Arborēs in tē, in (whom) folia cecidērunt, nunc cadunt. (**arborēs**, nom. *f* pl., trees; **folium**, -ī, *n* leaf)
7. Arborēs in tē, (who) fēminam audīs, cadent.
8. Tanta tē impendent mala, (which) fugere nōn poteris.

Questions

Direct Questions

In English, direct questions can be introduced by an interrogative word or by inverting word order, so that the working verb precedes the subject; Whom do you see? contains both an inversion of word order and an interrogative. Latin questions, unlike those in English, are not distinguished by the order of words. Latin questions are introduced by interrogative pronouns, adjectives, or adverbs.

Interrogative Pronouns, Adjectives, and Adverbs. The plural forms of the interrogative pronoun are the same as the relative pronoun. In the singular, the interrogative pronoun is the same except for the nominative masculine and feminine, **quis**, and the nominative and accusative neuter, **quid**.

quis, **quid**
who, what

	Singular		Plural		
	M. and F.	N.	M.	F.	N.
Nom.	**quis**	**quid**	quī	quae	quae
Gen.	cuius	cuius	quōrum	quārum	quōrum
Dat.	cui	cui	quibus	quibus	quibus
Acc.	quem	**quid**	quōs	quās	quae
Abl.	quō	quō	quibus	quibus	quibus

An interrogative pronoun asks who? or what? By definition, it cannot have an antecedent: if we knew the answer, we wouldn't ask the question!

Quis prandium parāvit? — *Who* prepared lunch?
Quibus prandium antepōnam? — *To whom* shall I serve lunch?
Cuius marsuppium mihi commendāvistī? — *Whose* purse did you entrust to me?

The interrogative adjective is identical in form to the relative pronoun (**quī**, **quae**, **quod**):

Quem cibum parābō? — *What meal* shall I prepare?
Quae fēmina tē vocat? — *What woman* is calling you?
Dē quō fīliō quaesīvistī? — *Which son* did you ask about?

Among interrogative adverbs, you already know the enclitic **-ne**, which appears only as a particle attached to the end of the first word in a question: **Habēsne trēs nummōs**? Do you have three cents? **Nōnne** anticipates the answer "yes": **Nōnne trēs nummōs habēs**? You do have three cents, don't you? **Num** anticipates the answer "no": **Num trēs nummōs habēs**? You don't have three cents, do you? When **num** introduces an indirect question (discussed later in this chapter), on the other hand, it simply means "if" or "whether."

An, "can it be that," can introduce a direct or indirect question: **An mē amat**? "Does she love me?" It can also be the second part of a double question: **Amatne mē an marsuppium meum**? Does she love me or my purse? **Utrum**, "which of two," can also be paired with **an** for a double question: **Utrum mē amat an marsuppium meum**? Does she love me or my purse? (The question asks, "Which of these two alternatives is correct?")

Quandō asks "when": **Quandō tē vidēbō**, "When will I see you?" You have already learned **unde**, "from where": **Unde venit Menaechmus**? "Where is Menaechmus coming from?" and **ubi**?, "where": **Ubi sunt convīvae ceterī**? "Where are the other guests?"

The question, "how," meaning "to what degree," is asked by **quam**: **Quam male vīvit**? "How badly does he live?" **Quō modo** asks "in what way": **Quō modo prandium parābimus**? "How shall we prepare the meal?"

cūr, **quārē**, or **quam ob rem** (sometimes spelled as one word, **quamobrem**) can all be translated as "why": **Cūr tē tam familiāriter appellat**? "Why does she address you so intimately?"

Scrībenda

A. From the following list, identify all possible relative pronouns, interrogative pronouns, and interrogative adjectives:

quem	quōs	quae	quā
quās	cui	quam	quibus
quid	quis	quī	quod
cuius	quōrum	quō	quārum

B. Identify the pronoun or adjective (relative or interrogative) in each of the following sentences, and translate the entire sentence:

1. Cui cibum parābō?
2. Quid parās?

3. Cibus quem parāvistī erat bonus.
4. Femina quae tē vocat mala est.
5. Quis tē vocat?
6. Quam fēminam vocāvistī?
7. Dē quō quaesīvistī?
8. Fēmina dē quā quaesīvistī advēnit.
9. Quō modo fēminam vocābō?
10. Ubi est servus cui convīva dīxit?

Indirect Questions

An indirect question reports the substance of a direct question, adapted to the form of the sentence in which it is subordinated. The verb of an indirect question is always in the subjunctive, regardless whether it was indicative or subjunctive in its direct form.[2] An indirect question, like a direct question, always begins with an interrogative word or the enclitic **-ne**. If the main verb of the sentence is in the present or future tense, the subordinated verb is in the present tense. If the main verb is in a past tense, the subordinated verb is in the imperfect or pluperfect tense.

Direct:	Quid dīxit Hanno? What did Hanno say?
Indirect:	Milphio petīvit **quid dīxisset Hanno**. Milphio asked *what Hanno had said.*
Direct:	Quid est amor? What is love?
Indirect:	Nunc sciō **quid sit amor**. Now I know *what love is.*
Direct:	Quis iānuam pulsat? Who is knocking at the door?
Indirect:	Servus petet **quis iānuam pulset**. The slave will ask *who is knocking at the door.*
Direct:	Cūr iānuam pulsābis? Why will you knock at the door?
Indirect:	Petunt **cūr iānuam pulsātūrus sīs**. They are asking *why you are going to knock at the door.* Petīvērunt **cūr iānuam pulsātūrī essētis**. They asked *why you were going to knock at the door.*

Future Active Participle. In the last example, the direct question is in the future tense. Since there is no future tense in the subjunctive, the futurity of the original question is indicated by the use of the future active participle plus the appropriate form of the verb **esse**. The future active participle is a verbal adjective, formed from the stem of the fourth principal part of the verb, to which is added **-ūrus**, **-a**, **-um**. It indicates the action of the verb from which it is formed, in the future tense and active voice, and translates "about to (do something)" or "going to (do some-

[2] It is consequently impossible to know with certainty whether the original question was indicative or subjunctive (deliberative).

thing)." Accordingly, the future active participle of **pulsō, pulsāre, pulsāvī, pulsātus** is **pulsātūrus, -a, -um**, "about to knock" or "going to knock." As an adjective, however, it must agree with the noun it modifies in case, number and gender. "The woman (who is) about to knock," therefore, in the nominative case, is **fēmina pulsātūra**. Finally, like most Latin adjectives, these verbal adjectives are sometimes used in place of a noun. Thus, "I spoke to the woman (who was) about to knock" would be **pulsātūrae dīxī**.

Sequence of Tenses. As we have already seen in the discussion of the potential subjunctive in Chapter V, the tenses of the subjunctive express not a uniform period of time, but time in relation to something else. In a dependent clause (e.g., indirect questions and purpose clauses), the tense of the subjunctive is always relative to the tense of the main verb of the sentence.

In order to understand this relationship, we must first distinguish between *primary* and *secondary* tenses of Latin verbs. The primary tenses in Latin are the present tense, the future tense, and the future perfect tense.[3] The secondary tenses are the past tenses: the imperfect tense, the perfect tense, and the pluperfect tense. The rule of sequence of tenses, which applies to all subjunctive verbs in dependent clauses,[4] can be summarized as follows:

> If the verb of the main clause is in a primary tense, the verb in a dependent clause will be in the present or perfect subjunctive.
>
> If the verb of the main clause is in a secondary tense, the verb in a dependent clause will be in the imperfect or pluperfect subjunctive.

In primary sequence of tenses the present subjunctive in the subordinate clause indicates that the action there is occurring at the same time as or later than (i.e., future with respect to) the time of the action of the main clause. In secondary sequence of tenses this relationship is indicated by the imperfect subjunctive.

In primary sequence the perfect subjunctive in the subordinate clause indicates that the action there occurred prior to (i.e., past with respect to) the time of the action of the main clause. In secondary sequence this relationship is indicated by the pluperfect subjunctive.

A simple chart to outline the above rules would look like this:

VERB OF MAIN CLAUSE	VERB(S) OF SUBORDINATE CLAUSE(S)	
	CONTEMPORANEOUS OR FUTURE ACTION	PRIOR ACTION
Primary tense	present subjunctive	perfect subjunctive
Secondary tense	imperfect subjunctive	pluperfect subjunctive

[3] To this list should be added the "present perfect" aspect of the perfect tense. Latin, you will recall, expresses both the present perfect ("I have sung") and the historical perfect ("I sang") with the same verb form. To avoid confusion, however, the present perfect has been omitted from the discussion that follows.

[4] The only exception, as will be seen in Chapter IX, is in result clauses.

Sequence of Tenses in Indirect Questions. The above rules apply to indirect questions, which are always expressed in subordinate clauses with subjunctive verbs. In order to distinguish between an original question which was in the present tense and one which was in the future tense, however, Latin additionally indicates that the original question was in the future tense with a compound verb consisting of the future active participle plus a conjugated form of the verb **esse** (in the present subjunctive for primary sequence, and in the imperfect subjunctive for secondary sequence).

The following chart shows how the tense of the original (direct) question is modified when it is subordinated. Conversely, the tense of the indirect question indicates whether the original question was in a present, past or future tense.

1. Original (direct) question in the present tense:

	Quid faciunt?	What are they doing?

Indirect question:

	PRIMARY SEQUENCE	
Present	Petit quid faciant.	He asks what they are doing.
Future	Petet quid faciant.	He will ask what they are doing.
Future Perfect	Petīverit quid faciant.	He will have asked what they are doing.
	SECONDARY SEQUENCE	
Imperfect	Petēbat quid facerent.	He used to ask what they were doing.
Perfect	Petīvit quid facerent.	He asked what they were doing.
Pluperfect	Petīverat quid facerent.	He had asked what they were doing.

2. Original (direct) question in a past tense:

	Quid faciēbant?	What were they doing? (imperfect)
	Quid fēcērunt?	What did they do? (perfect)
	Quid fēcerant?	What had they done? (pluperfect)

Indirect question:

	PRIMARY SEQUENCE	
Present	Petit quid fēcerint.	He asks what they did/have done.
Future	Petet quid fēcerint.	He will ask what they did/have done.
Future Perfect	Petīverit quid fēcerint.	He will have asked what they did/have done.
	SECONDARY SEQUENCE	
Imperfect	Petēbat quid fēcissent.	He used to ask what they had done.

Perfect	Petīvit quid fēcissent.	He asked what they had done.
Pluperfect	Petīverat quid fēcissent.	He had asked what they had done.

3. Original (direct) question in a future tense:

Quid facient?	What will they do?
Quid factūrī sunt?	What will they do?/What are they about to do?

Indirect question:

	PRIMARY SEQUENCE	
Present	Petit quid factūrī sint.	He asks what they will do.
Future	Petet quid factūrī sint.	He will ask what they will do.
Future Perfect	Petīverit quid factūrī sint.	He will have asked what they will do.

	SECONDARY SEQUENCE	
Imperfect	Petēbat quid factūrī essent.	He used to ask what they would do.
Perfect	Petīvit quid factūrī essent.	He asked what they would do.
Pluperfect	Petīverat quid factūrī essent.	He had asked what they would do.

Scrībenda

A. Form the future active participle of the following verbs, and then translate the participle:

faciō	audiō	cantō	valeō
capiō	mordeō	dūcō	vīvō
sum		quaerō	

B. Translate the following:

1. Captūrus est.
2. Quaesītūra est.
3. Cantātūrae dīxī.
4. Bestiam puerum morsūram cēpī.
5. Virō iānuam pulsātūrō dīxit servus.

C. Indicate whether the underlined words are relative pronouns, interrogative pronouns, or interrogative adjectives:

1. Quem cibum parāvistī?
2. Quid parāvistī?
3. Cibus quem parāvistī erat bonus.
4. Fēmina quae tibi dīxit mala parābat.
5. Quae fēmina tibi dīxit? (two possibilities)
6. Quis tibi dīxit?
7. Scīsne cui dīxeris?

8. Ā quibus servīs pecūniam petēbant?
9. Cuius pecūniam petam?
10. Quōrum pecūniam petis?

D. Subordinate the direct question to the verbs that follow, modifying the verb of the original direct question as required by the rule of sequence of tenses. Translate the new sentence into English.

For example: Subordinate **Quis tē vocat**? to **sciō**; **scīvī**:

Answer: **Sciō quis te vocet**, I know who is calling you.
Scīvī quis tē vocāret, I knew who was calling you.

1. Ā quō vīrō quaerēbās? Scīsne? Scīvistīne?
2. Quam fēminam vocābis? Petimus. Petēbāmus.
3. Quid agam? Nesciō. Nesciēbam.
4. Quandō tē vidēbō? Dīc mihi. Nōverantne?
5. Amatne mē an marsuppium meum? Nesciēbātis. Nescīvistis.
6. Quis sententiam dīxit? Scīsne? Scīvistīne?
7. Quam fēminam vidēbimus? Servus petit. Servus petīvit.
8. Quō modo prandium parābō? Nesciō. Nescīvī.

E. Change the indirect question to a direct question:

1. Scīsne quis iānuam pulset?
2. Petit quis iānuam pulsāverit.
3. Petīvit quem virum vidērēs.
4. Dīcam quō modo cibum parāre dēbeās.
5. Dīcēbam quō modo cibum parātūrus essem.
6. Quaesīvit cūr tibi dīcere dēbēret.
7. Nesciō quis sit neque cūr vēnerit.
8. Nesciēbam ubi essent convīvae ceterī.
9. Dīc mihi quid quaerās.

Deliberative Subjunctive

In questions implying doubt, indignation, or the impossibility of something being done, the main verb of the sentence is in the subjunctive mood. The negative is **nōn**. This is called a deliberative subjunctive; it is a rhetorical question, a question that does not really seek a direct answer. It is as if the speaker were deliberating aloud about what is happening now or in the future (present subjunctive) or about what happened in the past (imperfect subjunctive):

Quid **agam**?	What *am I* to do?
Quis nōn **timeat**?	Who *would*n't *be frightened*?
Quid **faciāmus**?	What *are we to do*?
Quid **agerem**?	What *was I to do*?
Quid **dīcerem**?	What *was I to say*?

Irregular Verbs: *volō, nōlō, mālō*

The irregular third conjugation verb **volō**, "I want, I wish, I am willing," has a separate negative form **nōlō** (**nē** + **volō**), "I do not want, I do not wish, I am unwilling," and a separate comparative form **mālō** (**magis** + **volō**), "I prefer, I want A more than B." All the irregularities occur in the present tense; the other tenses follow the principles you have already learned. **Volō** and **mālō** have no imperative forms; you have already learned the imperative of **nōlō** (**nōlī**, **nōlīte**) in Chapter I. Study the following forms:

volō, **velle**, **voluī**, *want, be willing*
nōlō, **nōlle**, **nōluī**, *not want, be unwilling*
mālō, **mālle**, **māluī**, *prefer, want A more than B*

Indicative			Subjunctive		
			PRESENT		
volō	nōlō	mālō	velim[5]	nōlim	mālim
vīs	nōn vīs	māvīs	velīs	nōlīs	mālīs
vult	nōn vult	māvult	velit	nōlit	mālit
volumus	nōlumus	mālumus	velīmus	nōlīmus	mālīmus
vultis	nōn vultis	māvultis	velītis	nōlītis	mālītis
volunt	nōlunt	mālunt	velint	nōlint	mālint
			IMPERFECT		
volēbam	nōlēbam	mālēbam	vellem	nōllem	māllem
volēbās	nōlēbās	mālēbās	vellēs	nōllēs	māllēs
volēbat	nōlēbat	mālēbat	vellet	nōllet	māllet
etc.			etc.		
	FUTURE				
volam	nōlam	mālam	——		
volēs	nōlēs	mālēs			
volet	nōlet	mālet			
etc.					
			PERFECT		
voluī	nōluī	māluī	voluerim	nōluerim	māluerim
voluistī	nōluistī	māluistī	volueris	nōlueris	mālueris
voluit	nōluit	māluit	voluerit	nōluerit	māluerit
etc.					
			PLUPERFECT		
volueram	nōlueram	mālueram	voluissem	nōluissem	māluissem
voluerās	nōluerās	māluerās	voluissēs	nōluissēs	māluissēs
voluerat	nōluerat	māluerat	voluisset	nōluisset	māluisset
etc.					

[5] Note that the present stem of the indicative comes from the first principal part of the verb (**vol**-), whereas the present stem of the subjunctive (**vel**-) comes from the infinitive.

	FUTURE PERFECT		
voluerō	nōluerō	māluerō	——
volueris	nōlueris	mālueris	
voluerit	nōluerit	māluerit	
etc.			
	IMPERATIVE		
——	nōlī	——	
——	nōlīte	——	

Scrībenda

A. Identify the person, number, tense, and mood of the following forms of **volō**, and then change them to the corresponding forms of **mālō** and **nōlō**:

vult	vīs	voluerō
velīs	voluistis	voluissēmus
voluērunt	volunt	velint
volēs	voluerim	

B. Write a complete synopsis in the active voice of **volō**: third person singular; **mālō**: second person singular; and **nōlō**: second person plural.

C. Translate the following sentences into English:

1. Servus vult fīliī nuptiās cēlāre.
2. Servus māllet nuptiās cēlāre sī posset.
3. Pater fīlium ex nuptiīs extrahere velit sī aequum sit.
4. Quid fīlius faceret?
5. Fīlius nescit quid factūrus sit.
6. Potestne pater esse aequus si fīlium ex nuptiīs extrahit?
7. Aequumne sit fīlium extrahere?
8. Nescīmus utrum extrahere fīlium sit aequum.
9. Saepe quaerō an fortūna umquam sit aequa.
10. Petīvistī an fortūna nostra umquam esset (fuisset) alia.
11. Nunc sciō cūr cōnsilium dare voluerit.
12. Nunc cōnsilium quod dare vīs audīre mālumus.

D. Translate into Latin:

1. Do you know to whom you are speaking?
2. If you (s.) could escape, would you?
3. If we should conceal the marriage, who would praise us?
4. The Roman people will judge whom we ought to believe.
5. If I had asked what you were doing, would you have told me?

> Nūper* erat medicus*, nunc est vispillo* Diaulus*:
> [id] quod vispillo facit, fēcerat et medicus.
>
> *Martial I.47*
>
> nūper (adverb), recently
> medicus, ī, *m* doctor
> vispillo (nom. *m* sing.), undertaker (for the poor)
> Diaulus, ī, *m* a proper name

Verba tenenda

Verbs

agitō, **-āre**, **-āvī**, **-ātus** set in motion, disturb
  agitō mēcum I consider, I deliberate
āmittō, **-ere**, **āmīsī**, **āmissus** send away, lose
dēclāmō, **-āre**, **-āvī**, **-ātus** speak as an orator, make a speech, declaim
disputō, **-āre**, **-āvī**, **-ātus** dispute, argue
discō, **-ere**, **didicī**, —— learn
doceō, **-ēre**, **docuī**, **doctus** teach
exerceō, **-ēre**, **-uī**, **-itus** exercise, train
floreō, **-ēre**, **-uī**, —— flourish, be prosperous, be distinguished
formō, **-āre**, **-āvī**, **-ātus** give form to, shape, fashion
gerō, **-ere**, **gessī**, **gestus** do, accomplish, carry, bring
imbuō, **-ere**, **imbuī**, **imbūtus** moisten; dye; stain; give initial instruction, introduce (to)
impleō, **-ēre**, **-ēvī**, **-ētus** fill
instituō, **-ere**, **instituī**, **institūtus** establish; teach, instruct
labōrō, **-āre**, **-āvī**, **-ātus** labor, take pains, exert oneself
lūdō, **-ere**, **lūsī**, **lūsus** play, play at a game, make sport of
mālō, **mālle**, **māluī**, —— prefer
meminī, **meminisse** (defective verb), remember
mūtō, **-āre**, **-āvī**, **-ātus** change
nōlō, **nōlle**, **nōluī**, —— be unwilling
ostendō, **-ere**, **ostendī**, **ostentus** show, reveal
prōpōnō, **-ere**, **-posuī**, **-positus** propose, state a proposition, set before the mind
rogō, **-āre**, **-āvī**, **-ātus** ask
scrībō, **-ere**, **scrīpsī**, **scrīptus** write
sedeō, **-ēre**, **sēdī**, **sessus** sit, continue sitting, sit down
servō, **-āre**, **-āvī**, **-ātus** save, preserve, protect
solvō, **-ere**, **solvī**, **solūtus** loosen, set free, relax, weaken; dissolve
sonō, **-āre**, **sonuī**, **sonitus** make a sound
volō, **velle**, **voluī**, —— want, be willing

canticum, **-ī** *n* song, monody
dēliciae, **-ārum** *f* pl., delight, pleasure; luxuries; indulgence
deus, **-ī** *m* nom. pl.: **dī** god
discipula, **-ae** *f* student
discipulus, **-ī** *m* student
dīvitiae, **-ārum** *f* pl., wealth, riches
elementum, **-ī** *n* element; first principle; pl., alphabet
ēloquentia, **-ae** *f* eloquence; art of persuasive speech
exemplum, **-ī** *n* pattern, example
fābula, **-ae** *f* fictitious tale; story, fable
fāma, **-ae** *f* reputation, rumor
infantia, **-ae** *f* infancy
līberī, **-ōrum** *m* pl., children
littera, **-ae** *f* letter (of the alphabet); pl., letter; literature
lūdus, **-ī** *m* play, game; elementary school
memoria, **-ae** *f* memory
  memoriā tenēre to remember ("to hold by means of the memory")
mundus, **-iī** *m* universe, world
nātūra, **-ae** *f* nature

opprobrium, -**iī** *n* reproach, disgrace, scandal, dishonor
paedagōgus, -**ī** *m* child-attendant; paedagogue
sapientia, -**ae** *f* wisdom; philosophy
schola, -**ae** *f* learned conversation; a place for learned conversation, school
sonus, -**ī** *m* sound
studium, -**iī** *n* enthusiasm, interest, study
vicīnus, -**ī** *m* neighbor
vitium, -**iī** *n* fault, defect, imperfection, vice

Pronouns

quī, **quae**, **quod** (relative) who, which
quis, **quid** (interrogative) who? what?

Adjectives

quī, **quae**, **quod** (interrogative) which?
dignus, -**a**, -**um** (+ ablative) worthy (of)
fictus, -**a**, -**um** false, fictitious
honestus, -**a**, -**um** honorable, distinguished
  inhonestus, -**a**, -**um** dishonorable, disgraceful
pudīcus, -**a**, -**um** bashful, modest, chaste
  impudīcus, -**a**, -**um** unchaste, immodest
pūrus, -**a**, -**um** pure, clean, honest, unstained

Adverbs

antequam before
deinde then, next
male badly
mox soon
quam (exclamatory) how greatly, how much, how
quandō since, because

Interrogative Adverbs and Phrases

an? or can it be that?
  -**ne** . . . **an** whether . . . or
  utrum . . . **an** (whether) . . . or?
cūr why?
quam how? to what degree?
quam ob rem why?
quandō? when?
quārē why?
quō modo how?
unde from where?
num (introducing indirect question) whether, if (introducing direct question, anticipates a negative answer)

Conjunctions

seu or if
  seu . . . **seu** whether . . . or

Notanda

The defective verb **meminī** has no present stem, and no fourth principal part. The first principal part is a perfect active form, and the second principal part is a perfect active infinitive; they translate, "I remember," "to remember." (Compare the perfect active forms of **noscō**, which translate "I know," etc.)

An ostentatious person is one who likes to show (**ostendō**) himself off. The English suffix "-ible" (or "-able" in verbs derived from first conjugation Latin verbs) indicates ability. Hence "ostensible" means "capable of being shown."

What is the connection between "solve" or "solution" and **solvō** "loosen"?

sonō means making the sound (**sonus**) appropriate to the subject of this verb: **equus sonat** therefore means "the horse neighs," whereas **iānua sonat** means something like "the door squeaks" or "the door slams."

dēliciae and **dīvitiae** occur mainly in plural form. **dēliciae** (from **dēliciō**, "entice, allure from the right way") are pleasures that delight and charm, but sometimes suggest luxuriousness, which tends to have a negative connotation.

The feminine form of **deus** (**dea**, **-ae**) is regular in the nominative plural, whereas the masculine plural form can be either **dī** or **deī**. The dative plural of either gender is usually **dīs**, but the forms **diīs**, **deīs** and the feminine **deābus** are found.

A **discipulus** (feminine, **discipula**) is one who learns (**discō**). (Note the reduplicated perfect stem: **didicī**.) A **doctor** is one who has already been taught (**doceō**, **doctus**) and now is the teacher. **Docēre** governs a double accusative, one of the person taught and one of the thing taught: **magister *discipulum elementa* docēbit**, "the teacher will teach *the student the alphabet*."

dīvitiae derives from the third declension adjective **dīves**, **dīvitis**, "rich."

The abbreviation "e.g." is short for **exemplī grātiā**, "for the sake of an example."

The root of **fābula**, **fāma** and **infantia** is found in the deponent verb **fārī**, "to speak." (An infant is one who cannot yet speak.)

līberī (from **līber**, "free") is sometimes used instead of **puerī**. It rarely occurs in the singular.

littera refers to a single letter of the alphabet; the verb **legō**, "read" actually means "gather, collect." Reading is the act of "collecting" individual letters. A "letter" to someone is "**litterae**"; **epistola**, **-ae**, *f* (cf. English "epistle") is another word for "letter." "Literature" is also **litterae**.

The word for school is **schola** (cf. English "scholar") or **lūdus** (which also means "play, game," from **lūdō**). When we "allude" to something, then, we are literally making a playful reference to it.

Do not confuse **vīta**, "life" (note the long -ī-), and **vĭtia**.

The prefix **in-** in **inhonestus** and **impudīcus** negates, but it is the preposition **in** in **impleō** and **instituō**.

seu and **sīve** are alternate spellings of the same word, a compound of **sī**, "if," and **-ve**, an enclitic form of **vel**, "or."

Ante legenda

Translate:

1. Pater meus mē in ludum Rōmānum mittere māvult.
2. Sciō cūr mē in aliam scholam mittere nōlit.

3. Maluit mē puerum in scholā Rōmānā discere ut mē digna scīrem.
4. Pater, quī paedagōgus meus etiam fuit, mē pudīcum ab opprobriō servāvit.
5. Paedagōgus meus exemplīs docuit quid fugere dēbērem.
6. Nunc agitō mēcum quid mē honestum factūrum sit.
7. Mēcum agitō an faciam ego tanta mala quanta facit vicīnus meus.
8. Vitia vicīnī fugere vellem. (velim)
9. Sī possem, vitia fugere vellem. Sī potuissem, vitia tua fūgissem.
10. Agitet puer cum animō nōn sōlum sententiās virōrum clārōrum, sed etiam verba singula quae dīcunt. (**singulī**, **ae**, **a**, individual)
11. Nec impudīca verba nec cantica mundī discat discipulus.
12. Imbuāmus linguam līberōrum verbīs bonīs pulchrīsque.
13. Meminī unde dīcere didicissem.
14. Puer sonāre sonum quem audīverat labōrāvit.
15. Puer sonum quem audiverat memoriā tenuit.
16. Poēta in fābulā impudīca deōrum exemplō puerō prōpōnit. (prōposuit; prōpōnere potuit.)
17. Quis verba tē digna dīcere possit? (potest)
18. Nescīmus quam bene dictūrus sīs.

Legenda

Education at Rome (1)

Roman children were traditionally trained by their mother until age seven, at which time the father assumed personal responsibility for his son's education. This meant, ideally, that the father taught his son reading, writing, physical "manliness," moral and social conduct, and the laws of the state. This practice persisted into Imperial times, when Latin schools became the more common method of education. In the Roman elementary school (**lūdus**), the teacher (**lūdī magister**) offered a basic education in reading, writing, and arithmetic for boys and girls from seven to eleven years of age. Boys between the ages of twelve to fifteen (girls usually married by age fourteen, and therefore seldom extended their formal education beyond the elementary level) then went on to a **grammaticus**, who taught grammar, literature, and general subjects as preparation for their final schooling, in rhetoric.

Romans adopted the Greek practice of assigning **paedagōgī** (child attendants) to their children. Basically, the **paedagōgus** was responsible for taking the child to and from school, but he often had the additional responsibility of helping the child with school work. The **paedagōgus** sometimes acquired a good education himself. The classic example of this was the slave Remmius Palaemon, in the mid first century A.D.: as a result of sitting in on lessons, he became so skilled that eventually he set up his own school and became one of the best known grammarians in Rome.[6]

1. The poet Horace (Quintus Horatius Flaccus, 65 B.C.–8 B.C.) was the son of a former slave.[7] Despite his limited means, Horace's father was determined that his son should receive an excellent education. Consequently, the family moved to Rome to enroll the boy in school there. Unable to provide his son with a **paedagōgus**, Horace's father took on that role himself—thus assuming, in effect, the station which he had already transcended. In the following passage, based on *Satires* I.4 and I.6, Horace acknowledges his indebtedness to his father, while simultaneously treating with gentle humor himself and his simple origins. His father's **exempla** (examples) recall the practice of using **exempla** as an educational device at every level of education in antiquity. Horace's father uses them to illustrate a pattern of behavior which the boy should avoid. At the most advanced level of education, the student would encounter them as historical analogies in his study of rhetoric.

Sī pūrus vīvō et cārus * amīcīs, causa fuit pater meus, quī nōluit mē in Flāviī * lūdum mittere. Mē puerum in lūdum Rōmānum mittere māluit ut discerem artēs * dignās fīliō equitis * atque senātōris *. Paedagōgus incorruptissimus * mihi erat pater. Quid aliud dīcam? Mē pudīcum ab opprobriō servāvit et docuit quid mē exemplīs fugere vellet. Nam dīcēbat "Nōnne vidēs quam male vīvat Albiī * fīlius? Est magnum exemplum quod tē discere volō nē patriam rem * āmittere velis," et "Mihi satis est sī vītam fāmamque tuam servāre possum." Sīc mē formābat puerum exemplīs verbīsque, seu iubēbat seu vetābat * mē aliquid * facere. Etiam nunc, ubi lectulus * aut porticus * mē cēpit, nōn dēsum mihi: labrīs compressīs *

1, 11: **cārus**, **-a**, **-um** (+ dative) dear (to), precious
2: **Flāvius**, **-iī** *m* the name of a schoolmaster, whose school was out in the provinces, and therefore inferior
3: **artēs** (acc. *f* pl.) the (liberal) arts
equitis (gen. *m* sing.) of an equestrian. The **equitēs** were the merchant class of Rome.
senātōris (gen. *m* sing.) of a senator. The senatorial class was the most elite.
4: **incorruptissimus**, **-a**, **-um** exceedingly upright, utterly incapable of corruption
6: **Albius**, **-iī** *m* a proper name; Albius was probably a neighbor or a well-known Roman
7: **patriam rem** (acc. *f* sing.) "your inheritance"
9: **vetō**, **-āre**, **-uī**, **-itus**, forbid
aliquid (acc. *n* sing.) anything
10: **lectulus**, **-ī** *m* bed, couch, reading-couch
porticus (nom. *f* sing.) arcade, public colonnade. The distinction here is whether he was at home reading (on his reading-couch) examples of good or bad behavior, or whether he was wandering in the public colonnade, where he could observe the conduct of others directly.

[6] S. F. Bonner, *Education in Ancient Rome: from the Elder Cato to the Younger Pliny* (Berkeley, 1977), 37–46.

[7] His father was a **lībertīnus**, a freedman.

mēcum agitō quid mē amīcīs cārum* faciat, atque quō modo melius* vīvam, an faciam ego umquam tanta mala quanta facit vicīnus meus. Est mihi vitium parvum, cēdō, sed cui sit malō*?

2. A famous teacher of rhetoric and a practicing advocate was Quintilian (Marcus Fabius Quintiliānus, c. A.D. 40–c. A.D. 100). In about A.D. 88, Quintilian retired from these activities in order to write several works, including his best-known work, the *Institūtiō Ōrātōria*, which he intended to be useful to "intelligent young men" (**bonae mentis iuvenēs**). Quintilian's *Institūtiō Ōrātōria* covers the training of an orator from infancy to adulthood. It survived the Middle Ages only in fragments. In 1416, in a filthy dungeon in St. Gall, Switzerland, the Italian humanist Poggio discovered a dusty, dirty, but complete text. His discovery led to the humanist philosophy of education, and secured Quintilian's place in the history of education as the earliest advocate of a child-centered education.[8] The following passages are based on the first book of the *Institūtio Ōrātōria*.

2a. In this passage, Quintilian discusses the question of whether to teach the child at home or at school. He of course prefers the latter, but for surprising reasons.

Nōs sumus quī infantiam dēliciīs solvimus. Quid nōn adultus* volet quī in purpurīs* repit*? Palātum* līberōrum nostrōrum antequam lābra* instituimus. Gaudēmus* sī verba callida* dīcunt līberī. Nostrās amīcās, nostrōs concubīnōs* vident, nostra multa impudīca vident, ex quibus venit cōnsuētūdo*, deinde nātūra. Miserī nōndum* cognoscunt vitia quae discunt. Ergō nōn accipiunt mala ex scholīs sed in scholās mala gerunt.

2b. As soon as the boy has learned to read and write, says Quintilian, he should be sent to the **grammaticus**, the teacher of literature and languages. Here he will learn the arts of writing well and speaking correctly. He will learn simultaneously how to read the poets correctly, and then how to interpret them, but he must also study history, music, astronomy, and philosophy.

10: **lābrīs compressīs** (ablative) "with my lips pressed firmly together"
labrum, -ī *n* lip
11: **melius** (adverb) better
13: **cui sit malō** what kind of datives is Horace using here?

1: **adultus, -a, -um** (when) grown up
2: **purpura, -ae** *f* purple (carpet) (symbolizing wealth, luxury)
repō, -ere, repsī, reptus creep, crawl
palātum, -ī *n* the palate (the organ of taste)
lābrum, -ī *n* lip
3: **gaudeō, -ēre, gāvīsus sum, ——** rejoice, be happy
callidus, -a, -um clever
4: **concubīnus, -ī** *m* bedfellow
5: **cōnsuētūdo** (nom. *f* sing.) habit, custom
nōndum (adverb) not yet

[8] G. Kennedy, *Quintilian* (New York, 1969), pp. 140–141.

A schoolroom scene. The two seated students unroll their papyrus-rolls, while a third student is scolded by the schoolmaster for arriving late.

Alius puer ā Graecō, alius ā Latīnō grammaticō incipiet. Nec poētās legere satis est. Agitet cum animō nōn sōlum historiās* sed etiam verba singula* quae legit. Nec poētās discipulus intellegat nisi dē metrīs* rhythmīsque* discat, nec sī stellārum aut philosophiae ignarus* sit.

3. The historian Cornelius Tacitus (c. A.D. 56–115) also expressed strong opinions on education in his dramatic *Dialogus*, a discussion concerning the decline of Roman oratory. Like Quintilian, he finds fault with the parents' tendency to be overly indulgent of their children and with their failure to teach "goodness and self-control." All too often, says Tacitus in *Dialogus* 29, the children are handed over to "some silly little Greek serving maid," whose foolish chatter becomes the basic model for the child.

Nunc puerum Graecae ancillae* damus, quae animum tenerum* fābulīs imbuit, nec cūrāmus quid puerō aut dīcat aut faciat ancilla*. Nam Rōmānīs est gladiātōrum* equōrumque studium multum; sciō paucōs* quī dē aliō umquam dīcunt.

4. St. Jerome (Eusebius Hieronymus, A.D. 348–420), was one of the most important scholars of the early church. Among his major accomplishments was a revision of the Latin version of the Bible, resulting in what we now know as the Vulgate Bible. In 386 he left Rome for a monastic life in

2: **historia**, **-ae** *f* narrative, story; history
3: **singulī**, **-ae**, **-a** individual
metrum, **-ī** *n* meter
4: **rhythmus**, **-ī** *m* rhythm
ignārus, **-a**, **-um** (+ genitive) unaware (of)

1, 2: **ancilla**, **-ae** *f* maidservant
tener, **tenera**, **tenerum** delicate, young
3: **gladiātōrum** (gen. *m* pl.) "for gladiators"
paucī, **paucae**, **pauca** (pl. adj.) few

Writing implements. On the left is a circular wooden or metal case, with a lid, containing six books or volumes (**volumina**) *rolled up and labelled. Below this lies a* **stylus** *and inkstand. In the center is a* **calamus,** *a reed pen. Next to the case of books is a* **tabella** *or* **tabula,** *here joined by a hinge. Pinned to the wall above this is a single* **tabella;** *both were frequently covered with wax. A book containing several* **tabellae,** *called a* **cōdex** *or* **caudex,** *lies open beside the single* **tabella.** *In front of the* **cōdex** *are single volumes in their cases. Four volumes lie open on the right; the title of one of them is attached to the papyrus itself, the other is attached to the* **umbilicus** *or cylinder of wood in its center. (From a drawing in Gell's* Pompeiana.)

Bethlehem, from where he corresponded extensively. In this letter to a former disciple, he outlines a proper Christian education for a baby daughter. Three hundred years earlier Quintilian recommended these same techniques for teaching the alphabet and writing.

Sīc animam* instituāmus quae futūra est templum* Dominī. Nihil aliud discat audīre, nihil dīcere nisi id* quod ad timōrem Deī* agit. Impudīca verba nōn intellegat, cantica mundī ignōret*, teneram* linguam psalmīs* imbuāmus. Fac litterās vel* buxeās* vel eburneās* quibus

1: **anima**, **-ae** *f* soul, breath of life
templum, **-ī** *n* temple
2: **id** (pronoun, nom. *n* sing., antecedent of **quod**), "that (thing)"
ad timōrem Deī "to(ward) fear of God"
3: **ignōrō**, **-āre**, **-āvī**, **-ātus** not know, be unacquainted with
tener, **tenera**, **tenerum** delicate, young
4: **psalmus**, **-ī** *m* psalm
4, 7: **vel** or
vel . . . **vel** either . . . or
buxeus, **-a**, **-um** of box-wood
eburneus, **-a**, **-um** of ivory

nōmina* dās. Discipula lūdat in litterīs ut lūdus doceat. Discat canticum quod ordinem* litterārum docet. Ubi incēperit stilum* in cērā* dūcere, vel* dūc manum* discipulae vel in tabellā* sculpā* elementa ut per* sulcōs* vestigia* trahat. . . . Habeat sociās* quibus invidet* et quārum laus* nostram discipulam mordēbit.

(After Epistula *107)*

5. St. Augustine (Aurēlius Augustīnus, A.D. 354–430), born in Northwest Africa, taught rhetoric at Carthage, Rome and Milan. After a series of conversions, beginning with his conversion at age nineteen to "Philosophy," Augustine rediscovered Christianity, the "Divine Philosophy," in 386, at the age of thirty-two. His autobiographical *Confessions*, a vivid account of his life to A.D. 388, reveals a keen psychologist recording his own changing outlook. In the first book of his *Confessions* Augustine describes the process of acquiring speech and the difficulties children encounter in the elementary stages of education. In the last passage he criticizes the use of Terence's plays to educate the young. Notice Augustine's style: he addresses God directly, asks endless questions, and puts his entire discussion on an intimate level.

5a. Nōnne ab infantiā vēnī in pueritiam*? Et meminī unde dīcere didicissem. Nōn enim docēbant mē aliī, sed ego animō quem mihi Deus dederat, sonum sonāre quod audiveram labōrābam. Tum mēcum agitābam ubi aliquid* appellābant et memoriā tenēbam sonum quem sonābant. Ita verba quae in variīs sententiīs ponēbant paulātim* colligēbam* et signīs* ostendēbam quid dīcere vellem, et semper vidēbam ad parentēs* ut nūtum* eōrum* vidērem.

5: **nōmina** (acc. *n* pl.), names (of letters)
6: **ordinem** (acc. *m* sing.) "order" (arrangement)
stilus, **-ī** *m* pointed writing instrument
cēra, **-ae** *f* wax
7: **manum** (acc. *m* sing.) hand
tabella, **-ae** *f* tablet. Students did their lessons on a wax-coated tablet with a **stilus**, a sharp instrument. To erase, they reversed the **stilus**, which was flat at the other end, to smooth out the wax. (See figure opposite.)
sculpō, **-āre**, **-āvī**, **-ātus** carve, engrave, form
per (prep. + acc.) through
8: **sulcus**, **-ī** *m* furrow (made by a plough)
vestigium, **-ī** *n* track, trace
socia, **-ae** *f* companion
invideō, **-ēre**, **invīdī**, **invīsus** (+ dative) feel envy for, look with envy (at someone)
9: **laus** (nom. *f* sing.) praise

1: **pueritia**, **-ae** *f* boyhood, childhood
4: **aliquid** (acc. *n* sing.) something, anything
5: **paulātim** (adverb) little by little
colligō, **-ere**, **collēgī**, **collectus** collect
6: **signum**, **-ī** *n* sign
7: **parentēs** (acc. *m* pl.) parents
vidēbam ad parentēs: "I looked toward my parents"
nūtum (acc. *m* sing.) nod (of approval)
eōrum (pronoun, gen. *m* pl.) of them, their

5b. Deus, Deus meus, quās* ibi miseriās* invēnī, ubi rectē vīvere* mihi prōpōnēbant, et obtemperāre* monēbant ut in hōc mundō flōrērem et fictās dīvitiās acciperem. Inde mē in scholam dedērunt ut discerem litterās in quibus quid bonī* esset nōn vīdī miser.

5c. Et tamen docent fīliōs vestrōs hās fābulās* et dīcunt, "hinc verba discētis, hinc adquirētis* ēloquentiam ut sententiās ostendātis persuādeātisque.*" Sed vidē quid doceat Terentius: indūcit* puerum quī prōpōnit sibi* exemplō Iōvis* impudīca et dīcit, "Egone homunciō* nōn faciam idem* quod fēcit tantus deus?"

1: **quās** (exclamatory adjective) agreeing with **miseriās** "what miseries!"
miseria, -ae *f* misery
rectē vīvere: here the infinitive is used as a verbal noun, the direct object of **prōpōnēbant**.
rectē (adverb) correctly
2: **obtemperō, -āre, -āvī, -ātus** comply, obey
4: **quid bonī** "what good" (literally, "what of good")

1: **fābulās** note that **docēre** can take two accusatives: "to teach someone (acc.) something (acc.)"
2: **adquirō, -ere, -quisīvī, -quisītus** gain, acquire
3: **persuādeō, -ēre, -suāsī, -suāsus** persuade, be persuasive
indūcō, -ere, -dūxī, -ductus introduce
4: **sibi** (dat. *m* sing.) to himself
sibi exemplō is a double dative
Iōvis (gen. *m* sing.) of Jupiter
homunciō (nom. *m* sing.) a mere mortal, a little man
5: **idem** (*n* acc. sing.) the same thing

Probanda IV–VI

A. Write complete synopses of the following verbs in the active voice, and translate the indicative forms:

veniō, first pers. sing. — cōgō, first pers. pl.
errō, second pers. sing. — sum, second pers. pl.
timeō, third pers. sing. — fugiō, third pers. pl.

B. Identify all possible subjunctive constructions in the following sentences, and translate the sentence according to the subjunctive construction you identify.

1. Quid ageret?
2. Aequumne sit fīlium ex nuptiīs extrahere?
3. Tūne tantā ēloquentiā dīcere possis?
4. Semper amēmus.
5. Cadāmus.
6. Fugiāmus nē nōs videant.
7. Nē fugiāmus.
8. Nōn fugiāmus.

9. Nōn fugerēmus.
10. Rōmānī timeant nisi Caesar veniat.
11. Rōmānī timērent nisi Caesar venīret.
12. Rōmānī timuissent nisi Caesar vēnisset.
13. Sī occidat, multī multa timeant.
14. Nisi occidisset, Rōmānī nōn timuissent.
15. Rōmānī nōn timērent.
16. Sī occident, multī timēbunt.
17. Scīsne cūr occiderit?
18. Nescīvērunt quōmodo occidisset.
19. Rogābunt multīne virī fēminaeque timeant.

C. Explain the use of the dative case in the following sentences:
1. Sī parva vitia habeam, cui sit malō?
2. Iam cōnsilium mihi inveniam.
3. Virō integrō sunt multae viae ad vītam bonam.
4. Nunc esset audācia remediō malōrum.
5. Sī fortūna saeva esset mihi, tua verba dēlīberārem.
6. Simul nōbīs dat Fortūna et cūram et remedium cūrae.

D. Sequence of tenses:
1. To what clauses does the rule of sequence of tenses apply?
2. What verbs govern primary sequence?
3. What verbs govern secondary sequence?
4. What tenses are found in subordinate clauses which follow primary sequence?
5. What tenses are found in subordinate clauses which follow secondary sequence?
6. Change the tense of the underlined verbs as indicated, and then make all other necessary changes in the rest of the sentence, in keeping with the rule of sequence of tenses:
   a. Ā tuā terrā cēdāmus ut tanta mala fugiāmus. (change to: present indicative; future indicative; future perfect; pluperfect indicative; imperfect indicative; historical perfect)
   b. Nescīvit cūr iānuam pulsārem. (change to present indicative; future; imperfect indicative)
   c. Puerī nōn vident quam male vīctūrus sit fīlius Albiī. (change to imperfect indicative; present subjunctive, jussive; imperfect subjunctive, potential)

E. Give the proper forms of the relative or interrogative pronoun:
1. **Whom** do you see?
2. **What men** do you see?
3. **What women** do you see?
4. **What** do you see?
5. **What things** do you see?
6. **To what person** did you speak?
7. **Whose** hat is this? (*f* sing.)
8. **Whose** home is that? (*f* pl.)
9. Do you know **who** did this?
10. The man **who** did this is my friend.

11. The thing **which** you want is not here.
12. I know **what** you want.
13. I know **who** called you.
14. I know the man **who** called you.

Probanda III–VI: Key

A. Synopses and translations:

veniō	errās	timet	cōgimus	estis	fugiunt
veniēbam	errābās	timēbat	cōgēbāmus	erātis	fugiēbant
veniam	errābis	timēbit	cōgēmus	eritis	fugient
vēnī	errāvistī	timuit	coēgimus	fuistis	fūgērunt
vēneram	errāverās	timuerat	coēgerāmus	fuerātis	fūgerant
vēnerō	errāveris	timuerit	coēgerimus	fueritis	fūgerint
veniam	errēs	timeat	cōgāmus	sītis	fugiant
venīrem	errārēs	timēret	cōgerēmus	essētis	fugerent
vēnerim	errāveris	timuerit	coēgerimus	fueritis	fūgerint
vēnissem	errāvissēs	timuisset	coēgissēmus	fuissētis	fūgissent

Translations:

veniō I come; I used to come; I shall come; I came; I had come; I will have come.

errō you wander; you used to wander; you will wander; you wandered; you had wandered; you will have wandered.

timeō he fears; he used to fear; he will fear; he feared; he had feared; he will have feared.

cōgō we compel; we used to compel; we shall compel; we compelled; we had compelled; we shall have compelled.

sum you are; you were; you will be; you have been; you had been; you will have been.

fugiō they flee; they used to flee; they will flee; they fled; they had fled; they will have fled.

B.
1. What was he to do? (deliberative)
2. Could it be right to remove the son from (his) marriage? (deliberative)
3. Would you be able to speak with such (great) eloquence? (deliberative)
4. Jussive: Let us always love. Potential: We may aways love.
5. Jussive: Let us fall. Potential: We may fall.
6. Jussive: Let's run away so that they will not see us. (**videant**, purpose) Potential: We may run away so that they will not see us. (**videant**, purpose)
7. Jussive: Let's not run away.
8. Potential: We may not run away.
9. Potential: We would not have fled/run away.
10. Ideal condition, present subj.: If Caesar should not come/If Caesar were not to come, the Romans would be afraid.
11. Present contrary-to-fact condition, imperfect subj.: The Romans would be afraid if Caesar were not coming.
12. Past contrary-to-fact condition, pluperfect subj.: The Romans would have been afraid if Caesar had not come.
13. Ideal condition, present subj.: If he should perish/Were he to perish, many people would fear many things.

14. Past contrary-to-fact, pluperfect subj.: If he had not perished, the Romans would not have been afraid.
15. Potential subj., imperfect tense: The Romans would not have been afraid.
16. Simple future condition, future indicative: If he perishes, many people will be afraid.
17. Indirect question: Do you know why he perished?
18. Indirect question: They did not know how he had perished.
19. Indirect question: They will ask whether many men and women are afraid.

C. 1. **cui**: dative of reference; **malō**: dative of purpose (double dative)
2. **mihi**: indirect object or reference ("for me")
3. **virō integrō**: dat. of possession
4. **remediō**: dat. of purpose
5. **mihi**: dat. of possession
6. **nōbīs**: indirect object ("to us")

D. 1. all dependent clauses whose verbs are in the subjunctive mood (except result clauses, to be learned later).
2. present, future, (present perfect), future perfect.
3. imperfect, (historical) perfect, pluperfect.
4. present subjunctive (including future active participle + present subjunctive of **esse**); perfect subjunctive.
5. imperfect subjunctive (including future active participle + imperfect subjunctive of **esse**); pluperfect subjunctive.
6. a. cēdimus . . . fugiāmus
cēdēmus . . . fugiāmus
cesserimus . . . fugiāmus
cesserāmus . . . fugerēmus
cēdēbāmus . . . fugerēmus
cessimus . . . fugerēmus

b. Nescit . . . pulsem
Nesciet . . . pulsem
Nesciēbat . . . pulsārem

c. nōn vidēbant . . . vīctūrus esset [**vīctūrus**, from **vīvō**]
nē videant . . . vīctūrus sit
nōn vidērent . . . vīctūrus esset

E. 1. quem; 2. quōs; 3. quās; 4. quid; 5. quae; 6. cui; 7. cuius; 8. quārum; 9. quis; 10. quī; 11. quod; 12. quid; 13. quis; 14. quī.

VII

Genitive Case (1); Pronouns (2); Indirect Statement

Uses of the Genitive Case

The main function of the genitive case is to indicate the relationship between two nouns. The most common relationship is one of possession:

> Sedula sunt verba **Cratīnī**.
> *Cratinus'* words are cautious.
>
> Palātum **līberōrum nostrōrum** antequam lābra instituimus.
> We train the palate *of our children* before we train their lips.

Other frequently encountered relationships are the partitive, objective, and descriptive genitives.

Partitive Genitive. The genitive can indicate that one thing is a part of some individual thing or grouping of things. The word in the genitive will then denote the larger whole, of which the other noun forms a part:

Pars **cōnsiliī tuī** erat bona.	Part *of your advice* was good.
Neuter **puerōrum** venit.	Neither *of the boys* is coming.

This is called the partitive genitive, or genitive of the whole. It is frequently used with neuter words, such as **quid**, "what," **satis**, "enough," **plus**, "more," **parum**, "too little," **nihil**, "nothing," **nimis**, "too much," to the extent that they express quantity or degree:

Quid novī est?	What's new? (lit.: what of new is there?)
satis sapientiae:	enough (of) wisdom
plūs pecūniae:	more (of) money
parum sapientiae:	too little (of) wisdom

Objective Genitive. Nouns containing verbal ideas, such as care, enthusiasm, or remedy, frequently govern another noun that is the direct object of the verbal idea: **cūra agrī**, care of the field; **studium litterārum**, enthusiasm for (of) literature, **remedium cūrārum**, a remedy for (of) cares. Notice that a smooth English translation often requires the preposition "for" rather than "of," although sometimes either preposition is appropriate. Conversely, when translating English into Latin, be careful not to confuse the objective genitive with the dative of indirect object. Compare the following sentences, where the verbal idea of planning in the second example governs **bellī**.

Cōnsilium **tibi** nunc petis.	Now you are seeking a plan *for yourself.* (dative, indirect object)
Cōnsilium **bellī** nunc petis.	Now you are seeking a plan *for (of) war.* (genitive, objective)

In the following passage, **cūra** governs both **cibī** and **bonī**:

Tibi est magna cūra **cibī**, non **bonī**.	You have a great concern *for (of) food*, not *for what is good.*

You will see many more examples of the objective genitive with nouns of the third and fourth declensions.

Descriptive Genitive. A noun in the genitive case and modified by an adjective can describe a quality in another noun:

Vir **multae fāmae**	A man *of much fame*
Fēmina **magnae prōvidentiae**	A woman *of great foresight*
Bestia **cuius modī**	An animal *of what kind*, i.e., what kind of animal?

Since this genitive describes a quality, it is frequently known as a "genitive of quality." The genitive of quality tends to be confined to expressions of measure or number, or to phrases like **cuius modī** ("of what kind"). This genitive cannot be used with a noun that does not have a modifier.

Personal Pronouns

As in English, a personal pronoun (I, you, he, etc.) can be used in place of a common or proper noun. In Latin, the nominative forms are used only for emphasis, since the ending of the verb indicates the subject of the sentence. In their declined forms, however, personal pronouns cannot be omitted without a loss of information. You have already learned some of the singular forms of the first and second person pronouns. Here are the remaining forms:

FIRST PERSON

	SINGULAR		PLURAL	
Nom.	**ego**	I	**nōs**	we
Gen.	**meī**	of me, mine	**nostrum/nostrī**	of us, our
Dat.	**mihĭ**	to/for me	**nōbīs**	to/for us
Acc.	**mē**	me	**nōs**	us
Abl.	**mē**	by/with me	**nōbīs**	by/with us

SECOND PERSON

	SINGULAR		PLURAL	
Nom.	**tū**	you	**vōs**	you
Gen.	**tuī**	of you, your	**vestrum/vestrī**	of you/your
Dat.	**tibĭ**	to/for you	**vōbīs**	to/for you
Acc.	**tē**	you	**vōs**	you
Abl.	**tē**	by/with you	**vōbīs**	by/with you

The genitive plural of the first and second person pronouns has two forms, one for the partitive genitive (ūnus **nostrum**, "one *of us*," quis **vestrum**? "which *of you?*"), the other for the objective genitive (cūra **nostrī**, "concern *for us*," timor **vestrī**, "fear *of you*"). In order to indicate possession for the first and second persons, you must use the adjectives **meus**, **tuus**, **noster**, and **vester**, which you already know. When they modify a noun that expresses a verbal idea, these possessive adjectives can also represent the subject of that verbal idea, as in **mea cūra** vestrī, "the concern that *I* feel for you," or **tuus** timor nostrī, "the fear that *you* feel for us."[1]

Reflexive Pronouns

When the declined forms of the personal pronouns refer back to the subject of the verb, they are called reflexive pronouns:

Nihil eris nisi **tibi** cōnsilium invēner**is**.
You will be nothing, unless *you* discover a plan *for yourself*.
Nisi tē cūrāvissem, hinc nunc **mē** conicer**em**.
If I had not been attending to you, *I* would now be getting *myself* out of here.

Compare the following, where the personal pronoun is not reflexive:

Nunc magna **tē** impendent mala.	Now great misfortunes are threatening *you*.
Quam **mē** impedīvit nuptiīs!	How greatly he embarrassed *me* with his marriage!

The reflexive pronoun for the third person has no nominative form, and uses the same forms for the singular and plural:

[1] For a discussion of the subjective genitive, see Chapter XVII.

Nom.	——	
Gen.	**suī**	of himself, herself, itself, themselves
Dat.	**sibi**	to/for himself, herself, itself, themselves
Acc.	**sē**	himself, herself, itself, themselves
Abl.	**sē**	by/with himself, herself, itself, themselves

The third person reflexive possessive adjective is **suus**, **-a**, **-um**, "his," "her," "its," "their":

Quam **sē** impedīvit **suīs** nuptiīs!	How greatly he embarrassed himself (**sē**) with his (**suīs**) marriage!

is, ea, id. When the third person pronoun is not reflexive, however, Latin uses instead the demonstrative pronoun **is**, **ea**, **id**, "this" or "that," which would then translate "he, she, it." These pronouns are also used as demonstrative adjectives: **is vir**, "this/that man"; **ea fēmina**, "this/that woman"; **id donum**, "this/that gift." Learn the forms of **is**, **ea**, **id**:[2]

THIRD PERSON

	M.	F.	N.	
		SINGULAR		
Nom.	is	ea	id	he, she, it
Gen.	eius	eius	eius	his, hers, its; of him, of her, of it
Dat.	eī	eī	eī	to/for him, her, it
Acc.	eum	eam	id	him, her, it
Abl.	eō	eā	eō	by/with him, her, it
		PLURAL		
Nom.	eī/iī	eae	ea	they
Gen.	eōrum	eārum	eōrum	of them, their
Dat.	eīs	eīs	eīs	to/for them
Acc.	eōs	eās	ea	them
Abl.	eīs	eīs	eīs	by/with them

Examples:

Cratīnus dīxit **suam** sententiam.	Cratinus has given *his own* opinion.
Cratīnus dīxit **eam** sententiam.	Cratinus has given *this* (or *that*) opinion.
Dēmipho quaesīvit **eius** sententiam.	Demipho asked *his* (Cratinus') opinion.
Is mē impedīvit **suīs** nuptiīs.	*He* embarrassed me with *his* marriage.
Is fīlius mē impedīvit.	*This* son embarrassed me.
Is quī venit est meus fīlius.	*That person* who is coming is my son.
Eum quī tē impedīvit cognōvī.	I know *that person* who embarrassed you.
Id quod fēcistī mē impedīvit.	*That thing* which you did embarrassed me.

[2] Compare the endings of **sōlus**, **-a**, **-um**, p. 40.

Scrībenda

A. Supply the appropriate Latin pronouns in the following sentences:

1. She will come with him.
2. I told them (*m* pl.) what they (*m* pl.) wanted to know.
3. They (*f* pl.) will call you (pl.)
4. We will give it to him.
5. Where is that man whom you (sing.) visited?
6. She will entrust them (*n*) to you (pl.).
7. He embarrassed them (*f*) with his (own) marriage.
8. He gave his (own) money to her friends.
9. The father gave his (son's) case to his (own) lawyers.
10. The lawyers gave their (own) opinions. The father repeated their words.

B. Translate the following sentences, and then supply the appropriately declined pronoun in place of the underlined noun:

1. Fāma flōret.
2. Da mihi exemplum.
3. Multās dēliciās ā nātūrā petīvimus.
4. In lūdō elementa discāmus.
5. In lūdō elementa discēbam.
6. Canticum magistrī discēs.
7. Magistrō dōna dēmus.
8. Sententiam ā mē quaesīvit.
9. Cantica fēminārum erant pulchra.
10. Cantica erant pulchra.
11. Fēminae erant pulchrae.

Indirect Statement

In Chapter VI you encountered indirect questions, which are a form of indirect discourse. Even more common than indirect questions are indirect statements. An indirect statement occurs when one person reports his own or someone else's statement or idea:

Direct:	Albius' son does not behave properly.
Indirect:	My father says that Albius' son does not behave properly.
Direct:	I am concerned about your reputation.
Indirect:	My father said that he was concerned about my reputation.

An indirect statement will follow expressions of saying, thinking, believing, or perceiving. In English we normally subordinate an indirect statement with the word "that." Classical Latin never uses such a word. In Latin, the subject of the indirect statement (along with all its modifiers) becomes accusative, and the verb of the indirect statement becomes an infinitive:

Direct:	Fīlius Albiī male vīvit.
Indirect:	Pater meus dīcit **fīlium** Albiī male **vīvere**.
Direct:	Cūrō fāmam tuam.
Indirect:	Pater meus dīxit **sē** fāmam meam **curāre**.

Perfect and Future Active Infinitives. In the above examples, the infinitives are in the present tense and in the active voice (**vīvere**; **cūrāre**). Latin infinitives also occur in the perfect tense, active voice, and in the future tense, active voice. The stem for the perfect active infinitive is found in the third principal part of the verb (**cantāv-**, **momord-**, **mīs-**, etc.), to which is added **-isse**:

cantāv-isse	Scīs **mē** bene **cantāvisse**. You know that *I sang* well.
momord-isse	Crēdō **bestiam** eōs **momordisse**. I think *the animal bit* them.
mīs-isse	Dīcit **sē** litterās **mīsisse**. He says that *he sent* the letter.

To form the future active infinitive, we turn again to the future active participle. As we saw in Chapter VI, we form the future active participle by taking the fourth principal part of the verb (**cantātus**, **morsus**, **missus**), from which we drop the final **-us** and add **-ūrus**, **-a**, **-um**:

cantāt-ūrus, **-a**, **-um**, about to sing, going to sing
mors-ūrus, **-a**, **-um**, about to bite, going to bite
miss-ūrus, **-a**, **-um**, about to send, going to send

Once we have the future active participle, we add the present infinitive of the verb **sum**, **esse**, and the combination of these two words gives us the future active infinitive:

cantātūrus esse, cantātūra esse, cantātūrum esse
morsūrus esse, morsūra esse, morsūrum esse
missūrus esse, missūra esse, missūrum esse

As you can see, the participial portion of this infinitive, like all participles, is essentially a verbal adjective and therefore, like all adjectives, will have to agree in gender, number and case with whatever it modifies. When the participle is part of the infinitive in indirect statement, the participle will have to agree in case, number, and gender with the accusative subject of the infinitive:

Scīs **eam** bene **cantātūram esse**.	You know that *she will sing* well.
Crēdō **bestiās** nōs **morsūrās esse**.	I believe that *the animals will bite* us.
Dīcit **sē** litterās **missūrum esse**.	He says that *he will send* the letter.

Finally, our translation of the tense of the infinitive in indirect statement will be determined by the tense of the verb (of saying, thinking, etc.) that subordinates the indirect statement. The present infinitive in indirect statement refers to time that is the same as the time of the subordinating verb. In other words, if the subordinating verb is in a past tense, a present infinitive in the indirect statement will translate into that same past tense. If the subordinating verb is in the future tense, the present infinitive in the indirect statement indicates an action that will also take place at the same future time as the subordinating verb:

Direct Statement
Cūrō.

Dīcit sē cūrāre.	He says he is concerned.
Dīcēbat sē cūrāre.	He used to say he was concerned.
Dīcet sē cūrāre.	He will say that he is concerned. (i.e., he will be concerned when he [will] say so.)
Dīxit sē cūrāre.	He said that he was concerned.

The perfect infinitive in indirect statement refers to action which occurred prior to the time of the subordinating verb:

Direct Statement
Male vīxit, or
Male vīvēbat.

Dīcis eum male vīxisse.	You say he has lived badly.
Dīcēbās eum male vīxisse.	You used to say he had lived badly.
Dīcēs eum male vīxisse.	You will say he has lived badly.
Dīxistī eum male vīxisse.	You said he had lived badly.

The future active infinitive in indirect statement refers to action occurring after the time of (i.e., future with respect to) the subordinating verb:

Direct Statement
Male vīvet.

Nescīs eum male vīctūrum esse.	You do not know that he will live badly.
Nesciēbās eum male vīctūrum esse.	You did not know that he was going to live badly. (ongoing unawareness)
Nescīvistī eum male vīctūrum esse.	You did not know that he was going to live badly.
Nesciēs eum male vīctūrum esse.	You will not know that he is going to live badly.

Observe the difference in meaning when the reflexive pronoun, **sē**, is used instead of the third person personal pronoun, **is**, **ea**, **id**:

Cicerō dīcit **sē** cūrāre.	Cicero says that he (Cicero) is concerned.
Cicerō dīcit **eum** cūrāre.	Cicero says that he (someone else) is concerned.

Subordinate Clauses in Indirect Statement

When an indirect statement contains a subordinate clause, the verb of the subordinate clause is in the subjunctive, even if it was in the indicative in the original, direct statement. If the verb of the original subordinate clause was in the future tense, in indirect statement the future sense is conveyed by the future active participle plus the appropriate tense of **esse** in the subjunctive. The rule of sequence of tenses determines the tense of the verb in the subordinate clause.

Direct:	Id est magnum exemplum **quod** tē discere **volō**. It is the great example *which I want* you to learn.
Indirect:	Pater dīcēbat id esse magnum exemplum **quod** mē discere **vellet**. Father used to say that it was the great example *which he wanted* me to learn.
Direct:	Līberī nōndum cognoscunt vitia **quae discunt**. The children do not yet recognize the faults *which they are learning*.
Indirect:	Sēnsit līberōs nōndum cognoscere vitia **quae discerent**. He perceived that the children did not yet recognize the faults *which they were learning*.
Direct:	Nōs sumus eī **quī** infantiam dēliciīs **solvēmus**. We are the ones *who will weaken* (their) infancy with pleasure.
Indirect:	Crēdit nōs esse eōs **quī** infantiam dēliciīs **solūtūrī sīmus**. He believes that we are the ones *who will weaken* their infancy with pleasure.

Scrībenda

A. Change the following sentences to indirect statement, governed by the verb indicated. Then translate the new sentence, showing the change in meaning dictated by the change of tense.

1. Cūrābō fāmam tuam. Dīcit. Dīcēbam.
2. Rōmānīs est equōrum studium multum. Scīs. Scīvistī.
3. Puerum ancillae Graecae, quae animum eius fābulīs imbuet, datis. (**ancilla, -ae,** *f* slave) Dīcit. Dīxit.
4. Multa impudīca videt puer ex quibus venit natūra. Crēdunt. Crēdidērunt.
5. Ego animō quem Deus mihi dedit sonāre ea quae audīveram labōrāvī. Memoriā teneō. Memoriā tenēbam.
6. Tum memoriā tenēbam sonum quem sonābant. Dīcō. Dīcit.
7. Tum incipiēbam discere litterās in quibus quid bonī esset nōn nōveram. Scrībet. Scrībit.

B. Translate the following sentences, and then change them from indirect statement to direct statement:

1. Puer dīcit sē factūrum esse id quod fēcerit tantus deus.
2. Magistrī crēdidērunt fābulās Graecās verba et ēloquentiam doctūrās esse.
3. Crēdimus discipulōs stellās et philosophiam discere dēbēre ut poētās intellegant.
4. Crēdēbat discipulōs aut ā Graecō aut ā Latīnō grammaticō discere incipere dēbēre.
5. Dīxit discipulam in litterīs lūdere dēbēre ut eam lūdus docēret.
6. Scrīpsit Augustīnus sē nescīvisse quid bonī esset in litterīs.
7. Nōn crēdit Horātius poēta vitium suum aliīs malō futūrum esse.

C. Translate the following sentences into Latin:

1. By my example you will learn to be a student worthy of your teacher.
2. The teacher says that I will be a worthy student.
3. The teacher believed games would teach the children.
4. You (sing.) say you want to teach me by your example.
5. I believe they did not want to teach a child of that kind.

Verba tenenda

Verbs

āvertō, **-ere**, **āvertī**, **āversus** turn (something) away from; avert, hinder
claudō, **-ere**, **clausī**, **clausus** close, shut
conclūdō, **-ere**, **conclūsī**, **conclūsus** shut up closely, confine
contemnō, **-ere**, **contempsī**, **contemptus** value little, despise, disdain
crescō, **-ere**, **crēvī**, **crētus** grow, increase in size
decet, **decēre**, **decuit**, —— (impersonal verb) (it) is becoming, fitting, suitable, proper
exclūdō, **-ere**, **exclūsī**, **exclūsus** shut out, remove, put out
plantō, **-āre**, **-āvī**, **-ātus** plant, set
probō, **-āre**, **-āvī**, **-ātus** approve, find acceptable
prōficiō, **prōficere**, **prōfēcī**, **prōfectus** advance, make progress, accomplish
prōfundō, **-ere**, **prōfūdī**, **prōfūsus** pour out, pour forth; cause to flow
prōveniō, **prōvenīre**, **prōvēnī**, **prōventus** come forth
putō, **-āre**, **-āvī**, **-ātus** think
soleō, **-ēre**, **solitus sum** (+ complementary infinitive) be accustomed
tolerō, **-āre**, **-āvī**, **-ātus** tolerate, endure
vertō, **-ere**, **vertī**, **versus** turn, turn around

Nouns

benevolentia, **-ae** *f* good will, favor
decōrum, **-ī** *n* propriety, fitness
glōria, **-ae** *f* glory
grammaticus, **-ī** *m* teacher of grammar and literature
ingenium, **-iī** *n* natural ability, talent, genius
lētum, **-ī** *n* death
negōtium, **-iī** *n* business, employment; labor
oculus, **-ī** *m* eye
officium, **-iī** *n* duty, responsibility; office
ōtium, **-iī** *n* leisure, peace
patria, **-ae** *f* fatherland, native land
persōna, **-ae** *f* personage, character; a mask
philosophus, **-ī** *m* philosopher
planta, **-ae** *f* sprout, shoot, slip of a plant
populus, **-ī** *m* (collective noun) the people, nation
parum (indeclinable) a little, too little, not enough

Pronouns

is, **ea**, **id** he, she, it; this or that person or thing
sē (reflexive, sing. or pl.) himself, herself, themselves

Adjectives

adultus, **-a**, **-um** grown, adult
decōrus, **-a**, **-um** becoming, fitting, proper
indecōrus, **-a**, **-um** unbecoming, disgraceful, shameful
iustus, **-a**, **-um** just, equitable, lawful
perversus, **-a**, **-um** not right; turned the wrong way, distorted
plēnus, **-a**, **-um** (+ abl.) filled (with); full
poēticus, **-a**, **-um** poetic; after the manner of poets
pūblicus, **-a**, **-um** public (as opposed to private)
sevērus, **-a**, **-um** strict, stern
suus, **-a**, **-um** (reflexive) his own, her own, their own

Adverbs

autem however, but
contrā in opposition, in turn, in return
parum too little

Prepositions

contrā (+ accusative) against, contrary to
prō (+ ablative) for, in behalf of; before, in front of

NOTANDA

āvertō and **perversus**, **-a**, **-um** are both compounds of the verb **vertō**, "turn." **Vertō** is transitive in Latin, whereas in English, "turn" can be either transitive or intransitive. To say in Latin, "I turned toward my friend," you will have to use a reflexive pronoun: **Vertī *mē* ad amīcum meum**.

The diphthong **-au-** in the basic verb **claudō**, "close, shut," becomes **-ū-** in the compounds **conclūdō** and **exclūdō**, but is retained in the noun **claustrum**, an "enclosure," which in medieval Latin means a monastery or cloister.

"Increase" is derived from **crescō**.

soleō always takes (or implies) a complementary infinitive. The third principal part is **solitus sum**; like **audeō** in the next chapter, **soleō** uses passive forms in the perfect tenses, even though the perfect forms translate as active. (These verbs, known as "semi-deponents," will be discussed in Chapter XVI; regular passive verbs will be discussed in Chapter X.)

benevolentia literally means "wishing well," hence "good will," from **bene** + **volō**.

decōrum—propriety—was an important matter to Romans. A lack of decorum (**indecōrum**) was a matter of shame or disgust. The English adjective "decent" is related to the impersonal verb **decet**, which is another way of saying **decōrum est**.

officium means a helpful act or service which fulfills an obligation. It can mean "duty" on a personal or civic level, or even one's position of employment and post; cf. English "office."

The most basic sense of **ōtium** is free time, unoccupied with business or work, but the connotation of this word is positive. (English "otiose," by contrast, tends to have a negative connotation.) The opposite is **negōtium**, literally, an absence of free time, and hence, work, business, employment; cf. English derivatives "negotiate, negotiable."

populus is a community of people; the plural means more than one community of people, e.g., the "peoples of the world." Closely related is the adjective **pūblicus**, signifying something belonging to the people as a community.

The abbreviation "i.e." is short for **id est**, "that is (to say)" or "in other words."

The adverb **parum** is sometimes used as an indeclinable neuter noun and sometimes as an adverb. As a noun, it will govern the partitive genitive: **Parum pecūniae habeō**, "I don't have enough money," or "I have too little (of) money." Its sense is the opposite of **satis**.

contrā can be an adverb or a preposition, both indicating opposition. "Contradict" comes from **contrā dīcere**, "to speak against."

The preposition **prō** has been adopted directly into the English expression, "pro and con" (from **contrā**), i.e., "for and against." Its meaning "in behalf of" is a development of its more basic meaning, "in front of, before" which is usually its sense when it is compounded with other words (**prō-fundō**, **prō-faciō**, **prō-veniō**).

Ante legenda

Translate:

1. Ā negōtiō nōs āvertāmus ut ad ōtium fugiāmus.
2. Tē ā negōtiō āvertere dēbēs.
3. Putāvī vōs ad ōtium fugitūrōs esse.
4. Putō eōs ad ōtium fūgisse.
5. Dīxit sē ad ōtium fugere dēbēre.
6. Eī quī sē ā negotiīs āvertunt ōtiumque petunt officia sua contemnunt.
7. Vir clārus ostendit sē vītam prō patriā prōfundere velle.
8. Contrā cōnsilium amīcōrum suōrum, dīxit sē fugere sine opprobriō suō nōn posse.
9. Quis nostrum sē ā suō officiō āvertat?
10. Cūra puerōrum dūcat magistrum bonum nē virī perversī futūrī sint.
11. Nihil bonī umquam erit mihi.
12. Quid benevolentiae sēnsit?

Ancient Italy

Map of Ancient Italy.

13. Nōbīscum nunc agitābimus dē eō quod appellāmus decōrum.
14. Rōmānī docuērunt id quod decēret honestum esse.
15. Eōs virōs iustōs esse audīvimus.
16. Is vir scrīpsit sē puerum litterās Latīnās amāvisse.
17. Augustīnus crēdidit puerōs dēbēre fābulās poēticās et legere et scrībere, sed nōn memoriā tenēre.
18. Dīxit sē errāvisse quia eās fābulās māllet.

Legenda

Education at Rome (2)

1. For Romans and their successors, Cicero was the model of an educated man. Not only had he mastered the art of rhetoric, which enabled him to pursue a brilliant political career and even to write handbooks on the subject, but he also made ethical philosophy acceptable to Romans by writing a number of philosophic dialogues modelled on those of his Greek predecessors Plato and Aristotle and, near his own time, the Stoic philosopher Panaetius. Cicero's *De officiis* ("Concerning Moral Responsibilities") is addressed to his young son, to whom Cicero attempts to convey his own values. In the first two passages, he is concerned with ethical values; in the third passage, Cicero discusses rhetorical decorum.

1a. Multī autem et sunt et fuērunt quī sē ā negōtiīs publicīs removēre * ad ōtiumque perfugere* solent ut tranquillitatem animī* petant; in eīs erant clārī philosophī et virī sevērī quī populī mōrēs* tolerāre nōn potuērunt. Eīs forsitan * quī doctrīnae * sē dedērunt et eīs quī in morbō * fuērunt concēdere* dēbēmus. Sī autem nūlla sit causa, sī contemnere sē dīcant sua officia, id vitiō esse putō. Nam dīcunt sē glōriam contemnere et prō nihilō * putāre; vidēmus autem eōs nōn glōriam sed molestiās * repulsārum * quasi opprobrium timēre.

(*After* Dē officiīs *1.21.69–71*)

1b. Callicratidas *, quī Lacedaemoniōs * dūcēbat, ostendit sē vītam prōfundere prō patriā velle sed glōriae iactūram * nē minimam quidem * accipere velle. Nam contrā cōnsilium eōrum quī cum Atheniēnsibus * dīmicāre * nōlēbant, dīxit Lacedaemoniōs * classem aliam * parāre posse, sed sē fugere sine suō opprobriō nōn posse.

(*After* Dē officiīs *1.24.84*)

1: **removeō, -ēre, -mōvī, -mōtus** remove
2: **perfugiō, -ere, -fūgī, ——** (+ **ad**) take refuge (in)
tranquillitātem animī "calmness of soul" (necessary for philosophic contemplation)
3: **mōrēs** (acc. *m* pl.) habits, customs; (collectively) character
4: **forsitan** (adverb) perhaps
doctrīna, -ae *f* science, erudition, learning
morbus, -ī *m* sickness, illness, disease
5: **concēdō, -ere** (+ dative) excuse, grant pardon to, be lenient to
7: **nihilō** (ablative) nothing
prō nihilō: "worth nothing"
molestia, -ae *f* trouble, annoyance
8: **repulsa, -ae** *f* defeat (in an election)

1: **Callicratidas** (nom. *m* sing.) the name of a Spartan leader
1, 4: **Lacedaemoniī, -ōrum** *m* Spartans
2: **iactūra, -ae** *f* loss
nē minimam quidem "not even the smallest (loss)"
3: **Atheniēnsibus** (abl. *m* pl.) Athenians
4: **dīmicō, -āre** fight
classem aliam another fleet of ships (if the Spartans should lose their own in battle)

1c. Nunc nōbīscum agitēmus dē eō quod Latīnā linguā appellāmus decōrum. Ab honestō id sēparāre* nōn possumus, nam quod decet, honestum est, et quod honestum est, decet. Et poētae id sīc dēfīnīre* solent: sī persōna* dīceret aliquid* sē dignum, id decēret. Sed sī Aeacus* aut Mīnos* dīceret, "Ōderint* dum timeant"* aut "nātīs sepulchrō* ipse est pater," indecōrum esset, quod eōs fuisse iustōs accēpimus*. Sed ubi Atreus* eās sententiās dīcit, omnēs* plaudunt*; est enim digna persōnā ōrātiō*.

(*After* Dē officiīs *1.27.93ff.*)

Under the Empire, many well-to-do Romans continued to educate their children at home, hiring tutors when the children were ready to learn grammar and literature. When the boys (girls rarely) were ready to study rhetoric, however, they had to pursue studies outside the home. A Latin rhetorician was chosen for his mastery and for his discipline of pupils, but much consideration was also directed toward the morals he would impart to his students.

2. Pliny the Younger (Gaius Plinius Caecilius Secundus, c. A.D. 61–112) had a successful political and administrative career at Rome. He is known to us through the nine books of letters he exchanged with his friends and through a tenth book of official letters to the emperor Trajan. In this letter, he agrees to investigate schools of rhetoric to find a suitable teacher for the nephews of his friend, Junius Mauricus, since their father was no longer alive. The respectful silence of the students when Pliny enters the classroom shows they have learned the proper behavior.

Officium iūcundum* ā mē quaesīvistī. Nam beneficiō* tuō in scholam redeō*; sedeō inter iuvenēs* ut solēbam. Proximē*, ubi intrāvī*, con-

2: **sēparō**, **-āre** separate
3: **dēfīniō**, **-īre**, **-īvī**, **-ītus** define
4: **persōna** a character on stage
aliquid (acc. *n* sing.) something
Aeacus, **-ī** *m* and **Mīnos** (nom. *m* sing.) were judges in the underworld
5: **ōdī**, **ōdisse** hate;
ōderint (jussive subjunctive) "let them hate"
dum + subjunctive (**timeant**) "provided that," "Let them hate, provided that they (also) fear"
sepulchrum, **-ī** *n* tomb
nātīs sepulchrō (double dative) "the father himself (**ipse**) is a tomb for his children"
6: **accēpimus**: "we have received (implied: with our ears)," and hence the idiomatic meaning here is "we have heard"
7: **Atreus**, **-ī** *m* tyrannical king of Mycenae, murdered the children of his brother Thyestes and then served them to their father.
omnēs (nom. *m* pl.) all, everyone
plaudō, **-ere** applaud
8: **ōrātiō** (nom. *f* sing.) speech

1: **iūcundus**, **-a**, **-um** pleasant
beneficium, **-iī** *n* favor, benefit
2: **redeō**, **redīre**, **redīvī**, **reditus** return
inter iuvenēs "among the young men"
proximē (adverb) recently
intrō, **-āre**, **-āvī**, **-ātus** enter

ticuērunt* Quod nōn dīcerem nisi vellem tē spērāre fīliōs frātris tuī* probē* discere posse. Mox* quid dē quōque* magistrō sentiam epistulā* scrībam. Dēbeō enim tibi, dēbeō memoriae frātris tuī* studium meum.

(*After* Epistulae *2.18*)

3. For Tacitus, the ideal education would be similar to that of Cicero. Tacitus attributes Cicero's eloquence to a wealth of learning, a multitude of accomplishments, and a knowledge that is universal.

Quondam* multī labōrābant nōn ut in rhētorum* scholīs dēclāmārent, nec ut fictīs contrōversiīs* linguam et vōcem* exercērent, sed ut animum implērent eīs artibus* in quibus dē bonīs ac malīs, dē honestō et inhonestō, dē iustō et iniustō disputārent. Quae est enim māteria* quam ōrātor* agitāre et dē quā dīcere dēbet.

(*After* Dialogus *31*)

4. Cicero, like any great figure, was also criticized—sometimes with tongue in cheek: Juvenal, for example, observes that all schoolboys long to be a Cicero. Cicero's genius for eloquence, however, proved, Juvenal argues, to be his undoing. In the so-called "Philippics," Cicero attempted repeatedly to have Mark Antony declared a public enemy. As soon as Antony gained power (in 43 B.C.), he had Cicero arrested and killed, completing his revenge in the way Juvenal here describes. It would have been far safer, concludes Juvenal, to have written bad poetry, rather than these orations (in which Cicero's declamation was, in fact, probably at its best).

Ēloquium* aut fāmam Cicerōnis* incipit
optāre et tōtīs Quinquātribus* optat
bonus discipulus. . . .

3: **conticescō, -ere, conticuī, ——** become silent
3, 5: **frātris tuī** (gen. *m* sing.) "of your brother"
4: **probē** (adverb) properly
mox (adverb) soon
dē quōque "concerning each (**magistrō**)"
epistula, -ae *f* letter

1: **quondam** (adverb) formerly (Tacitus is looking back to Cicero's time)
rhētorum (gen. *m* pl.) of rhetoricians
2: **controversia, -ae** *f* debate
vōcem (acc. *f* sing.) voice
3: **eīs artibus** (abl. *f* pl.) "with those skills"
4: **māteria, -ae** *f* subject-matter
5: **ōrātor** (nom. *m* sing.) orator

1: **ēloquium, -iī** *n* eloquence
Cicerō, -ōnis *m* Cicero
2: **Quinquātribus**: The **Quinquātria** was the five-day festal period, beginning March 19, in which Minerva, goddess of skilled labor, was honored. It was also a school holiday, after which the school year began. (Compare our Labor Day ritual.)
tōtīs Quinquātribus: "throughout his holiday"

Ēloquiō * sed perīvit ōrātor * quem ingenium lētō dedit.
Ingeniō manus * et cervix * caesa est * ; nec umquam
sanguine * causidicī * maduērunt * rostra * pusillī *.
"Ō fortūnātam nātam mē cōnsule * Rōmam!"
Antoniī * gladiōs * potuisset contemnere sī ea verba
sōla dīxisset. Ridenda * poēmata scrībere mālō
quam tē *, dīvīna Philippica, cum tuā cōnspicuā * fāmā.

(After Satire *X.114–125)*

4. St. Augustine's opinion of Cicero was also ambivalent: he admired the man's eloquence, but questioned his intentions.

Ego puer legēbam librōs dē ēloquentiā, in quā florēre cupiēbam; invēnī librum, Hortensium nōmine *, cuiusdam Cicerōnis *, cuius linguam ferē omnēs mīrantur *, animum nōn ita. Cuius liber mūtāvit affectum * meum; quam ardēbam *, Deus meus, quam ardēbam * revolāre * ā terrēnīs * ad tē, et nesciēbam quid agerēs mēcum! Apud tē * est enim sapientia. Amor * autem sapientiae nōmen * Graecum habet philosophiam,* quō is liber mē accendēbat *.

(After Confessions *III.4)*

4: **ēloquiō**: "for eloquence" (dat.) (parallel to **ingeniō**, line 6)
perīvit ōrātor: "the speaker (**ōrātor**) perished"
5–6: **Ingeniō . . . pusillī** "for genius his hands (**manus**) and also his neck (**cervix**) was severed (**caesa est**); yet the speaker's platform (**rostra**) has never been drenched (**maduērunt**) by the blood (**sanguine**) of a petty advocate (**causidicī . . . pusillī**)." When Cicero was murdered, his head and hands were cut off and posted on the rostra, as ordered by Antony.
7: **mē consule** (ablative) "with me [being] consul." The line is taken from a poem written by Cicero, referring to his dispersal of the conspirators around Catiline during Cicero's consulship (63 B.C.): "How fortunate was Rome when I was consul." Juvenal ridicules Cicero's boast by immediately alluding to Cicero's mortal enemy, Mark Antony, who once cited these lines in derision, and to Cicero's death.
8: **Antonius**, **-iī** *m* Mark Antony
gladius, **-iī** *m* sword
potuisset . . . dīxisset what kind of condition is Juvenal using here?
9–10: **ridenda poēmata scrībere mālō quam tē** "I prefer to write poems worthy of ridicule (**ridenda**) rather than (**quam**) you (**tē**), divine Philippic."
10: **cōnspicuus**, **-a**, **-um** distinguished, illustrious, attracting attention

2: **Hortensium nōmine** "*Hortensius* by name." This work of Cicero, which urged the study of philosophy, is now lost.
cuiusdam Cicerōnis "of a certain Cicero"
3: **ferē omnēs mīrantur** "almost all men admire"
affectum (acc. *m* sing.) state of mind
4: **quam ardēbam** "how I burned"
revolō, **-āre** fly back, return on wings
4–5: **terrēnus**, **-a**, **-um** having to do with the earth
5: **apud tē** "with you," "in your presence," "in your power"
6: **amor** (nom. *m* sing.) love (antecedent of **quō**, line 7)
nōmen (acc. *n* sing.) name
philosophia, **-ae** *f* philosophy (in Greek, this means "love of wisdom")
7: **accendō**, **-ere** set aflame

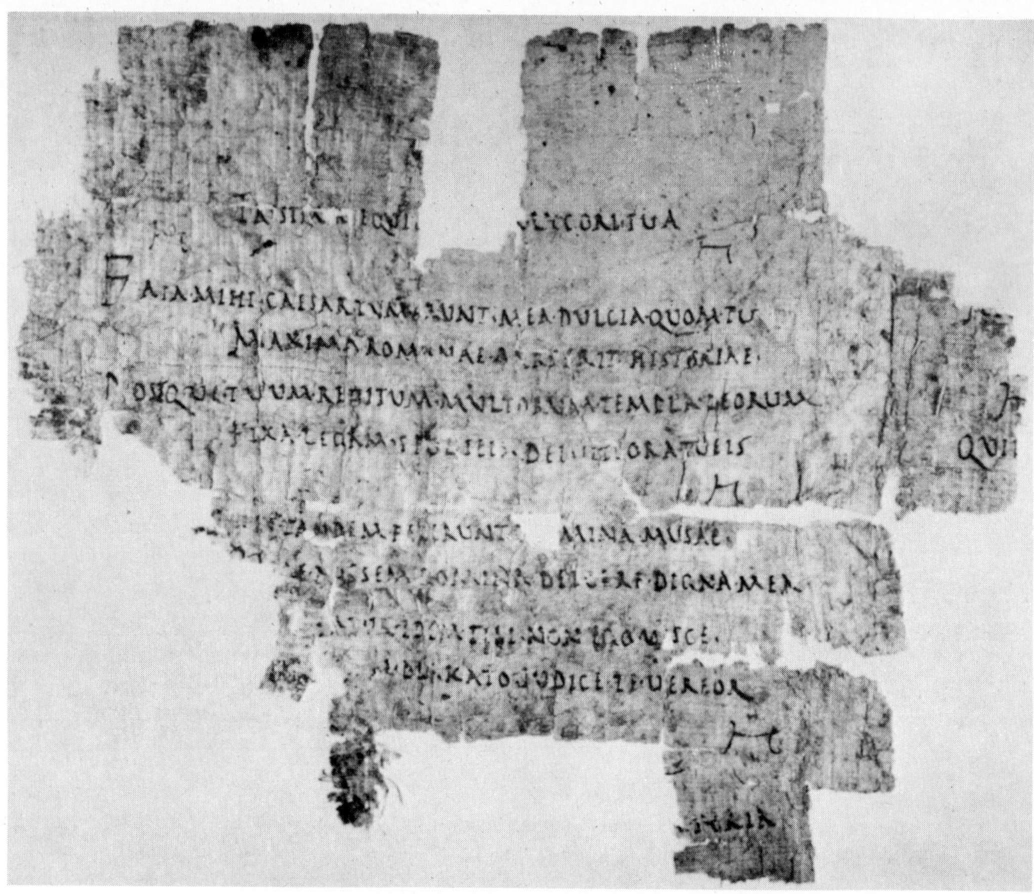

Papyrus from the first century B.C., *discovered at Qaṣr Ibrîm, Egypt in 1978, thought to contain probably unknown poetry of the Roman poet Gallus. Gallus, after being appointed governor of Egypt, had let his political ambitions get out of hand. He was recalled to Rome, committed suicide, and suffered a* **damnatio memoriae:** *all his work was ordered destroyed, and his name was not to be mentioned. Prior to this discovery, only one line of Gallus's poetry was known. Lines 2 through 5 read,* **Fata mihi, Caesar, tum erunt mea dulcia, quom tu/ maxima Romanae pars eri[s] historiae/ postque tuum reditum multorum templa deorum/ fixa legam spolieis deivitiora tueis:** *"My fate will then be sweet to me, Caesar, when you will be the greatest part of history, and after your return I will read (of) the temples of the gods, richer (from) having been adorned with your trophies." See R. D. Anderson, P. J. Parsons, and R. G. M. Nisbet,* Journal of Roman Studies, *LXIX (1979), 125–155.*

Third Declension (1); *eō, īre*; Constructions of Place and Time

Third Declension Nouns: Regular

Nouns of the third declension exhibit a number of different endings in the nominative singular. We must therefore turn to the genitive to find the proper stem. The gender of nouns in this declension, moreover, can be masculine, feminine, or neuter. It is particularly important to memorize the gender as well as the nominative and genitive forms of these nouns.

Third declension endings are as follows:

	SINGULAR		PLURAL	
	M. AND F.	N.	M. AND F.	N.
Nom.	——	——	**-ēs**	**-a**
Gen.	**-is**	**-is**	**-um**	**-um**
Dat.	**-ī**	**-ī**	**-ibus**	**-ibus**
Acc.	**-em**	——	**-ēs**	**-a**
Abl.	**-e**	**-e**	**-ibus**	**-ibus**

As in the second declension, the nominative and the accusative forms of the neuter are the same. In all other cases, the neuter endings are the same as the masculine and feminine endings. Here are some examples of third declension nouns:

	dux, **duc-is** *m* *leader*	**lībertās**, **lībertāt-is** *f* *freedom*	**homō**, **homin-is** *m* or *f* *human being*	**tempus**, **tempor-is** *n* *time*
Nom.	dux	lībertās	homō	tempus
Gen.	ducis	lībertātis	hominis	temporis
Dat.	ducī	lībertātī	hominī	temporī
Acc.	ducem	lībertātem	hominem	tempus
Abl.	duce	lībertāte	homine	tempore

Nom.	ducēs	lībertātēs	hominēs	tempora
Gen.	ducum	lībertātum	hominum	temporum
Dat.	ducibus	lībertātibus	hominibus	temporibus
Acc.	ducēs	lībertātēs	hominēs	tempora
Abl.	ducibus	lībertātibus	hominibus	temporibus

There is no easy way to recognize the gender of most third declension nouns other than the obvious rule that words denoting human beings are masculine or feminine according to their meaning.[1] A few fairly reliable indicators, however, are as follows:

1. Nouns ending in the nominative **-tor**, genitive **-tōris** (e.g., **amātor**, **scrīptor**, **ōrātor**), are usually masculine. (But do not confuse this with **-or**, **-ŏris**, as in **arbor**, **arboris**, *f*, or **marmor**, **marmoris**, *n*.)

2. Nouns ending in **-tās**, **-tātis** (**lībertās**, **vēritās**), in **-tūs**, **-tūtis** (**virtūs**, **senectūs**), in **-tūdō**, **-tūdinis** (**multitūdo**, **pulchritūdō**), and in **-tiō**, **-tiōnis** (**ōrātiō**, **nātiō**) are feminine.

3. Nouns ending in **-ŭs** in the nominative singular (**tempus**, **corpus**, **genus**), in **-e** (**mare**), in **-al** (**animal**), and in **-ar** (**exemplar**) are neuter.

The adjectives which modify these nouns agree in case, number and gender. There are also third declension adjectives which have similar endings; the adjectives you have learned thus far, however, all belong to the first and second declensions, and therefore retain their first and second declension endings: **magna lībertās**; **magnus dux**; **tempus longum**.

Scrībenda

arbor, **arboris** *f* tree
dux, **ducis** *m* leader
homō, **hominis** *m* or *f* human being, person
lībertās, **-tātis** *f* freedom
ōrātiō, **-tiōnis** *f* speech
ōrātor, **-tōris** *m* speaker
tempus, **temporis** *n* time

A. Decline the following in the singular and plural:

tempus multum
arbor magna
dux noster
ōrātiō longa

B. Identify the case and number of the following. When there is more than one possibility, identify all possible cases:

dux	arboris	tempus
ducum	arboribus	temporum
ducem	arborēs	tempora
ducī	arborum	tempore
duce	arborem	temporī

[1] The gender of words like **homō**, which can be masculine or feminine, is sometimes listed in dictionaries as "c.," meaning "common gender."

homō	lībertātum	ōrātiōnēs
homine	lībertātem	ōrātiōnī
hominī	lībertātis	ōrātiōne
hominibus	lībertātibus	ōrātiōnem
hominum	lībertātī	ōrātiō

c. Identify the case of the following nouns, and then add the proper ending to the adjective that follows:

tempora long____	ōrātiō me____
miser____ hominēs	tu____ lībertātem
vestr____ ducibus	ōrātiōne long____
ōrātiōnī su____	pulchr____ arborem

Irregular Verb: *eō, īre, iī* (*īvī*), *itum*, "Go"

The irregular verb **eō**, **īre**, denotes every kind of motion by animate or inanimate objects: "go," "walk," "ride," "sail," "fly," "move," etc. It is very common in Latin, by itself and also in compounds. Study carefully the forms of this verb.

INDICATIVE

SINGULAR

Pres.	*Imperf.*	*Fut.*	*Perf.*	*Plpf.*	*F.Perf.*
eō	ībam	ībō	iī	ieram	ierō
īs	ībās	ībis	īstī	ierās	ieris
it	ībat	ībit	iit	ierat	ierit

PLURAL

īmus	ībāmus	ībimus	iimus	ierāmus	ierimus
ītis	ībātis	ībitis	īstis	ierātis	ieritis
eunt	ībant	ībunt	iērunt	ierant	ierint

SUBJUNCTIVE

SINGULAR

eam	īrem	ierim	īssem
eās	īrēs	ieris	īssēs
eat	īret	ierit	īsset

PLURAL

eāmus	īrēmus	ierimus	īssēmus
eātis	īrētis	ieritis	īssētis
eant	īrent	ierint	īssent

IMPERATIVE		INFINITIVES	
sing.	ī	*pres.*	īre
pl.	īte	*perf.*	īsse
		fut.	itūrus esse

FUTURE PARTICIPLE

itūrus, -a, -um

Observe the following:

1. **i**- is the normal stem. Before -**a**, -**o**, and -**u** the stem becomes **e**- (**eō**, **eunt**, **eam**).

2. The imperfect has no -**ē**- before -**ba**- (**ībam**; compare **audiēbam**).

3. The future is formed, like first and second conjugation verbs, by adding -**bi**- to the stem.

4. The stem of the perfect is **i**- (or, less usual, **īv**-). The perfect system is regular except for the fact that **ii**- before **s** contracts to **ī**-: hence **iisse** becomes **īsse**, and **iistī** becomes **īstī**. When the alternative perfect stem is used, the indicative forms are **īvī** (perfect), **īveram** (pluperfect), and **īverō** (future perfect); the subjunctive forms become **īverim** (perfect) and **īvissem** (pluperfect).

Eō, **īre** frequently appears in compound verbs as well as independently. In compounds, the irregularities of the uncompounded form persist. Hence the future of **pereō**, "perish," will be **perībō**, and the imperfect will be **perībam**, etc.

Learn the following compounds of **eō**, **īre**:

ab	**abeō**, **abīre**, **abiī**, **abitum**,	go away, depart
ad	**adeō**, **adīre**, **adiī**, **aditum**,	approach
ambo	**ambiō**, **ambīre**, **ambiī**, **ambitum**,	go around, visit, solicit
in	**ineō**, **inīre**, **iniī**, **initum**,	enter
per	**pereō**, **perīre**, **periī**, **peritum**,	perish, pass away, be destroyed
praeter	**praetereō**, -**īre**, -**iī**, -**itum**,	pass by, omit
pro	**prōdeō**, **prōdīre**, **prōdiī**, -**itum**,	go forth
re	**redeō**, **redīre**, **rediī**, **reditum**,	return

Constructions of Place and Time

Place constructions. You have already learned the use of certain prepositions governing the accusative or ablative case to indicate place constructions. By way of review, they are:

1. Place where: **in** + ablative:

   In Italiā vīvit.
   He lives *in Italy*.

   Deus puerōs quasi plantās **in hortō** ecclēsiae plantāvit.
   God has placed children like plants *in the garden* of the church.

2. Place to which: **in** or **ad** + accusative:

   Ad Italiam vēnit.
   He came *to Italy*.

   In Italiam vēnērunt.
   They came *into Italy*.

The Roman Forum was the chief public square and center of Roman life.

Multī **ad ōtium** fugiunt.
Many take flight *to inactivity.*

3. Place from which: **ab**, **dē**, or **ex** + ablative:

Ab Italiā abībunt.
They will leave (*from*) *Italy.*
Multī sē **ē negōtiīs pūblicīs** exclūsērunt.
Many have removed themselves *from public affairs.*

There are, however, certain special constructions for names of cities, towns, small islands, **domus** and **rūs**:

1. Locative case: A special form, called the *locative* case, is used for the names of cities, towns, small islands, **domus**, *f*, "home," and **rūs, rūris**, *n*, "countryside," to indicate place where.[2] The locative case, for first and second declension nouns, has the same form as the genitive in the singular (Rōmae, "in" or "at Rome"; Corinthī, "in" or "at Corinth"), and the ablative in the plural (Athēnīs, "in" or "at Athens"; Delphīs, "in" or "at Delphi"; Syrācūsīs, "in" or "at Syracuse"). Third declension nouns use the dative in the singular (Carthāginī, "in" or "at Carthage") and the dative (or ablative) in the plural (Trallibus, "in" or "at Tralles").

[2] Perhaps the most convenient way to deal with **domus** and **rūs** is to treat them as adverbs of place; to home or to the countryside: **domum**, **rūs**; from home or from the countryside: **domō**, **rūre**; at home or in the countryside: **domī**, **rūrī**.

Rōmae vīvit.
He lives *at Rome.*

Domī numquam labōrāmus.
We never work *at home.*

Athēnīs docēbat.
He used to teach *in Athens.*

2. Place to which: accusative without a preposition:

Rōmam redeāmus.
Let us return *to Rome.*

Rūs nunc ībō.
Now I shall go *to the countryside.*

Domum adeō.
I am going (to) *home.*

3. Place from which: ablative without preposition:

Rōmā vēnit.
She came *from Rome.*

Rūre rediit.
He returned *from the countryside.*

Magister **Athēnīs** Rōmam prōdībat.
The teacher was going *from Athens* to Rome.

Time Constructions. The ablative case specifies a given point within a larger period of time, whereas the accusative case designates how long over an unbroken period of time something happened or was happening.

1. Time when or within which: ablative without a preposition:

Ūnō annō redībit.
He will return *within one year.*

Eō tempore abbās puerōs verberābat.
At that time the abbot used to beat the children.

Ūnā hōrā veniet.
He will come *at one o'clock.* (or: He will come *within one hour.*)

2. Duration of time: accusative without a preposition:

Ūnum annum sē quaerēbat cūr puerī nōn prōficerent.
For (throughout) one year he kept asking himself why the children were not making progress.

Paucās hōrās ad ōtium fugiāmus.
Let us escape *for a few hours* to inactivity.

Paucōs annōs nōs ē negotiīs pūblicīs removeāmus.
Let us remove ourselves *for a few years* from public affairs.

Scrībenda

A. Give the future active participle for each of the following compounds of **eō** and translate each participle:

abeō	redeō
prōdeō	adeō

B. Write synopses for the following verbs, and translate each indicative form:

1. **eō**, second person singular
2. **abeō**, second person plural
3. **pereō**, third person singular
4. **prōdeō**, third person plural
5. **redeō**, first person plural

C. Translate the following sentences:

1. Perībō. Periī. Perībam. Pereās.
2. Dux ad eum adit (adiit).
3. Homō dīxit sē peritūrum esse.
4. Scīsne cūr lībertās perierit?
5. Rogāvit num lībertās peritūra esset.
6. Redībis domum cum hominibus ceterīs.
7. Hominēs aliī Rōmam Athēnīs redībunt.
8. Ea est arbor quae in hominēs cadet.
9. Adiērunt ad ducem ut auxilium peterent.
10. Longum erit id tempus ubi nōn erō.
11. Ībam in Viā Sacrā et ad mē adiit is homō. (**Via Sacra**, The Sacred Way)
12. Ībat domō servus. Ībat rūs servus. Ībat rūre servus.
13. Athēnīs servī multa mala faciēbant, Rōmae numquam.
14. Malīs temporibus agricolae Rōmam rūre abiērunt.
15. Romae vīvō; ibi vītam meam agō; hīc est nūlla vīta mihi.

D. Translate into Latin:

1. I judged that those things were evil.
2. If I had known those things are evil, I would have turned you away from them.
3. Do you (pl.) know what games the children prefer?
4. We pointed out their bad habits so that you (s.) would avoid them.
5. He believed he could change his own bad habits if he observed theirs.

Verba tenenda

Verbs

abeō, **abīre**, **abiī** (**abīvī**), **abitum** go away (from)

adeō, **adīre**, **adiī** (**adīvī**), **aditum** go to, approach

ambiō, **ambīre**, **ambiī** (**ambīvī**), **ambitum** go about, solicit

cōnstituō, **-ere**, **cōnstituī**, **cōnstitūtus** decide, place, establish

eō, **īre**, **iī** (**īvī**), **itum** go

gerō, **-ere**, **gessī**, **gestus** bear, carry; do, carry out, accomplish; wear
  sē gerere behave, conduct oneself
  mōrem gerere (+ dat.) comply with the wishes (of someone in the dative)

ineō, **inīre**, **iniī** (**inīvī**), **initum** enter

insum, **inesse**, **infuī** (**in** + **sum**) be in, be contained in

pereō, **perīre**, **periī** (**perīvī**), **peritum** perish, pass away, be destroyed

praetereō, **praeterīre**, **peraeteriī** (**-īvī**), **praeteritum** pass by, omit

prodeō, **prodīre**, **prodiī** (**-īvī**), **proditum** go forth

redeō, **redīre**, **rediī** (**-īvī**),

reditum return, go back
removeō, -**ēre**, -**mōvī**, -**mōtus** remove
studeō, **ēre**, **studuī**, —— (+ dat.) be zealous, be eager for
vītō, -**āre**, -**āvi**, -**ātus** avoid

Nouns

annus, -ī *m* year
arbor, **arboris** *f* tree
Athēnae, -**ārum** *f* Athens
audītor, **audītōris** *m* listener
brevitās, **brevitātis** *f* brevity, conciseness
cōnsul, **cōnsulis** *m* consul
corpus, **corporis** *n* body; substance
dēfensiō, **dēfensiōnis** *f* a defending, defense
dux, **ducis** *m* leader, general
factum, **factī** *n* deed, fact
genus, **generis** *n* race, stock, sort, species, gender
hōra, **hōrae** *f* hour
homō, **hominis** *m* or *f* human being
iniūria, -**ae** *f* harm, injury
Ītalia, -**ae** *f* Italy
iūs, **iūris** *n* right, law, justice (that which is binding by its nature)
lex, **lēgis** *f* a bill which has become law; law
lībertās, -**tātis** *f* freedom
mōs, **mōris** *m* custom, habit; pl., character; customs, habits
multitūdō, **multitūdinis** *f* multitude
narrātiō, **narrātiōnis** *f* a relating, a narrative; (in rhetorical sense) a separate section of a speech
nōmen, **nōminis** *n* name; appellation; noun
opīniō, **opīniōnis** *f* opinion
ōrātiō, **ōrātiōnis** *f* speech
ōrātor, **ōrātōris** *m* speaker, orator
pater, **patris** *m* father
probābilitās, -**tātis** *f* probability
Rōma, -**ae** *f* Rome
rūs, **rūris** *n* countryside
tempus, **temporis** *n* time
vēritās, **vēritātis** *f* truth
virtūs, **virtūtis** *f* virtue, manliness, excellence
vulgus, **vulgī** *n* the great mass, the multitude, the people

Adjectives

certus, -**a**, -**um** certain, sure
longus, -**a**, -**um** long, lengthy; far
medius, -**a**, -**um** middle, the middle of
novus, -**a**, -**um** new; recent; unusual; strange
opportūnus, -**a**, -**um** (with ad + acc.) fit, suitable (for)
Rōmānus, -**a**, -**um** Roman

Adverbs

domī "at home"
domum "to home"
domō "from home"
item just so, in like manner, likewise
rūs "to the countryside"
rūrī "in the countryside"
rūre "from the countryside"

Notanda

gerō (like **agō**) has a wide range of meanings (and in fact the two verbs sometimes overlap). As a rule, however, the root meaning, "bear," "carry on," "endure," can usually be extracted from most of the idiomatic expressions in which this verb is found.

studeō, "be eager for," suggests that "students" are enthusiastic about the subjects they "study." This verb cannot take a direct object, since it is intransitive. Whereas English has "I am studying Latin literature," Latin has **litterīs Latīnīs studeō**, "I am eager *for* Latin literature."

Do not confuse the various forms of **vītō**, **vītāre**, "avoid," **vīta**, "life," and **vitium**, "fault."

Nouns denoting abstract qualities—e.g., brevity, freedom, probability, truth, virtue, etc.—tend to be feminine: **brevitās**, **lībertās**, **probābilitās**, **virtūs**, **vēritās**.

iūs and **lex** both mean "law"; **lex** is usually limited to the context of institutional legal authority. **ius** can be limited to this same meaning, or it can be used in a broader, ethical sense to connote what is right, good, or just. English derivatives reflect this distinction: compare "just, justice, injustice, injury (**iniūria**)" and "legal, legality, legislate, illegal," etc.

"Rural" refers to the countryside (**rūs**).

"Temporary" will help you remember the stem of **tempus**. Cicero's famous lament, "**Ō tempora, Ō mōrēs**!" ("Oh, the times, Oh, the customs") still rings true. **Mōs** in the plural means "customs, habits"; the sum of one's habits define one's character, and therefore the plural also means "character." (**Tempora** and **morēs** are not nominative or vocative, but accusative of exclamation in the above quotation.)

vulgus means the general public; it can also refer to a particular multitude. The verb **vulgō**, **-āre**, "make available to the multitude" frequently suggests promiscuity.

Latin uses the adjective **medius**, "the middle (of)," to express what English perceives as a noun: **in mediō forō**, "in the middle of the forum."

Rōmānus, **-a**, **-um** is frequently used substantively (**Rōmānus**, **-ī**, *m*; **Rōmāna**, **-ae**, *f*), "a Roman man, a Roman woman."

Ante legenda

A. Translate the following sentences:

1. Quae pars ōrātiōnis est nōmen? (**nōmen**, noun)
2. Genera nōminis quot sunt?
3. Numerī nōminum quī sunt?
4. Cuius generis sunt patriae nostrae lēgēs?
5. Cuius est generis dux vester? Quid est eius nōmen?
6. Aliī in eō librō invenient multa quae ego nōn dīxī; aliī erunt quī contrā sentient.
7. Eī viam sōlam quam iniērunt probant.
8. In narrātiōne brevitās inesse dēbet.
9. Brevitās inerit sī narrātiō incipiet unde dēbet.
10. Ōrātōris officium est dē eīs posse dīcere quae populus mōribus et lēgibus cōnstituit.
11. Eō tempore iniūriam patriae fēcit cōnsulum stultitia. (**stultitia**, **-ae**, *f*, stupidity)
12. Decetne nōmine mōribus tuīs dignō tē appellāre?
13. Bestia vincula nōn gereret sī ea removēre posset.
14. Gere mōrem mihi. Audeāsne mihi mōrem gerere?

15. Id quod audītōrēs audīre volunt nōn praeterībit ōrātor.
16. Perīvit ōrātor quem ingenium lētō dedit.

B. Translate Ovid's account of Phaethon's visit to his father's house:

Ūnō tempore puer adiit domum parentis*, quī erat Sōl.*
Ibi vīdit deās quae hominum bestiārumque facta regunt*:
Positae* spatiīs* aequālibus* Hōrae eō domō inerant;
et Vēr* novum corōnam* Aestāsque* spīcea* serta* gerēbat.
Sōl* oculīs puerum vīdit, "Quae" que "viae tibi causa est?" dīxit.

(*After* Metamorphoses *2. 26ff.*)

Legenda

Education at Rome (3)

We can gain much insight into methods of education in antiquity by reading the textbooks through which Latin was taught. Most of the evidence surviving today comes from sources as late as the fourth to sixth centuries A.D.

1. Among the foremost grammarians of the fourth century was Aelius Donatus, who numbered among his pupils the future St. Jerome. Medieval grammarians wrote commentaries on Donatus's longer and more advanced Latin grammar, the *Ars Maior*. His *Ars Minor*, however, a beginner's textbook, remained the child's introduction to Latin throughout the Middle Ages. In the following selection he explains, in question and answer form, the eight parts of speech. (Notice that Donatus does not include adjectives, for he considers them a part of the noun group.)

Partēs* ōrātiōnis quot sunt? Octo*. Quae? Nōmen*, prōnōmen, verbum, adverbium, participium, coniunctiō, praepositiō, interiectiō.*

Dē Nōmine: Nōmen quid est? Pars* ōrātiōnis quae cāsū* corpus pro-

1: **parēns, parentis** *m* father
1, 5: **Sōl, Sōlis** *m* the Sun
2: **regō, -ere, rexī, rectus** rule, guide, direct
3: **positus, -a, -um** placed
spatium, -iī *n* space
aequālibus (adj., abl. *n* pl.) equal
4: **Vēr, vēris** *n* Spring
corōna, ae *f* crown
Aestās, aestātis *f* Summer
spīceus, -a, -um consisting of ears of grain
serta, ōrum *n* pl. wreaths

1, 3: **pars, partis** *f* part
1: **octo** (indeclinable) eight
1–2: **Nōmen . . . interiectiō**: Try to identify the English equivalents of these parts of speech.
3: **cāsū** (abl. *m* sing.) case

priē* commūniterque* significat*. Genera nōminis quot sunt? Quattuor* Quae? Masculīnum, ut is magister; fēminīnum, ut ea Mūsa; neutrum, ut id scamnum*; commūne*, ut is et ea sacerdos*. Numerī nōminum quot sunt? Duo* Quī? Singulāris*, ut is magister; plurālis*, ut iī magistrī.

(Ars Donatī Grammaticī *1,2)*

2. Priscian, a sixth-century grammarian and teacher in Constantinople (formerly Byzantium), wrote an advanced Latin grammar that became the second basic textbook for the Latin Middle Ages. He also wrote a word-by-word explication of the first twelve lines of Vergil's *Aeneid*, which had long been a standard school text. In this passage, Priscian is explaining the *Aeneid*'s famous opening words, **arma virumque canō**:

"Virum," quae pars** ōrātiōnis est? Nōmen. Quid est nōmen? Pars** ōrātiōnis quae commūnem* vel propriam* quālitātem significat**. Cuius est generis? Masculīnī. Unde id possumus scīre? Tam* ā nātūrā eius quod significat**, quam* ā terminātiōne* et declinātiōne*. Cuius est cāsūs* "virum"? Accusatīvī singulāris**. . . . Virtūtem hinc multī dērīvāre* volunt. . . . "-que" quae pars ōrātiōnis est? Coniunctiō. Quid est coniunctiō? Pars ōrātiōnis quae cōnectit* ordinatque* sententiam. . . .

(Partitiōnes XII Vers. Aen., *21–26)*

3. Gaius Suetonius Tranquillus (born c. A.D. 69) is best known for his *Dē vītā Caesārum* (*The Lives of the Caesars*). Another of his important works, *Dē Virīs Illustribus*, consists of biographies of Roman literary men. In the following excerpt from the section of this work known as the *Dē grammaticīs et rhētoribus*, Suetonius gives us information about Marcus Antonius Gnipho, a first-century B.C. teacher of rhetoric, who first taught in the home of the young Julius Caesar, about 89 B.C.

3–4: **propriē commūniterque** (adverbs) "individually and generally." Donatus is distinguishing proper and common nouns.
4: **significō, -āre** indicate
quattuor (indeclinable) four
6: **scamnum, -ī** *n* bench
commūne (adj., nom. *n* sing.) common (like **masculīnum** and **fēminīnum**, agreeing with **genus**, understood from **genera**)
sacerdos, -dōtis *m* or *f* priest, priestess
7: **duo** two
singulāris, plurālis (adj., nom. *m* sing., agreeing with **numerus**, understood from **numerī**) "singular . . . plural"

** (see notes on passage 1)
2: **commūnem** (adj., acc. *f* sing.) common, general
proprius, -a, -um individual, one's own (not common with others)
3–4: **tam . . . quam** as much . . . as
4: **terminātiō, -iōnis** *f* ending, termination
dēclinātiō, -iōnis *f* declension
cāsūs (gen. *m* sing.) case
5: **dērīvō, -āre** derive
7: **cōnectō, -ere, cōnexuī, cōnexus** tie, bind, fasten, connect
ordinō, -āre arrange, order, set in order

M. Antonius Gnipho erat vir cui ingenium magnum fuisse dīcunt. Docuit primum* in domō* Dīvī Iuliī* puerī adhuc*, deinde in suā prīvātā* domō*. Sīc docuit rhētoricam artem*: cotidiē* praecepta* ēloquentiae trādēbat*, sed nōn dēclamābat nisi nundinīs*. Scholam eius clārōs virōs frequentāvisse* dīcunt, in quibus esset M. Cicerō. Scrīpsit multa sed nōn longam vītam ēgit. Aliī dīcunt eum duo* tantum* volumina* dē Latīnō sermōne* relīquisse*: nam cetera scrīpta* in quibus eius nōmen inveniāmus discipulōrum eius esse.

4. The poet Lucretius (c. 99–55 B.C.) wrote a lengthy poem entitled *Dē rērum nātūrā* (*Concerning the Nature of Things*), in which he attempted to explain the physical theory of the philosopher Epicurus. Realizing that most Romans would find the philosophy of Epicurus rather dry, Lucretius used poetry rather than prose as his medium. He compared his use of poetry to a doctor sweetening medicine with honey. A century later, Quintilian cited Lucretius' vivid metaphor:

Lucrētius poēta dīxit medicōs*, sī vellent puerīs absinthia* taetra* dare, prius* poculōrum* circum ōrās* contingere* mellis* dulcī* flavōque liquōre* ut puerōrum animōs imprōvidōs* lūdificārent*, et ut biberent amārum* absinthiī* laticem.* Ergō philosophiam suam "suāviloquentī carmine*" expōnere* voluit, et "quasi* mūsaeō* dulcī contingere melle.*"

2: **prīmum** (adverb) first
1, 2: **domō** (abl. *f* sing.) house, home
2: **Dīvus Iulius** "Divine Julius," a reference to Julius Caesar, who was deified after his death
adhuc (adverb) while still, yet
2–3: **prīvātus**, **-a**, **-um** private (it was unusual to teach in one's own home)
3: **rhētoricam artem** "the art of rhetoric"
cotidiē (adverb) every day, daily
praeceptum, **-ī** *n* maxim, rule, precept
4: **trādō**, **-ere**, **trādidī**, **trāditus** hand over, transmit, hand down; deliver by teaching
nundinīs "on market days" (held every eighth day—"within a nine-day period")
5: **frequentō**, **-āre** visit or make use of frequently; frequent
6: **duo** (acc. *n* pl.) two
tantum (adverb) only
6–7: **volumen**, **-inis** *n* volume
7: **sermō**, **-ōnis** *m* ordinary speech, conversation
relinquō, **-ere**, **relīquī**, **relictus** leave behind, abandon
scrīpta (acc. *n* pl.) writings
1: **medicus**, **-ī** *m* doctor
1, 4, 7: **absinthium**, **-ī** *n* wormwood, absinth (medicine used to purge worms)
absinthiī multum "Much (of) absinth" (what kind of genitive?)
1: **taeter**, **-tra**, **-trum** foul, loathsome
2: **prius** (adverb) first, in advance
poculum, **-ī** *n* cup
ōra, **-ae** *f* edge, rim
contingō, **-ere** touch on all sides
2, 7: **mel**, **mellis** *n* honey
parum mellis "too little (of) honey"

Liber autem meus, sī parum mellis* et absinthiī* multum habeat, salūbris* erit etiamsī* nōn dulcis*. Aliī autem hīc invenient multa quae nōn ego docuī; aliī erunt quī contrā sentient quia, ut eadem* doceāmus, dīversās* viās iniimus atque in suam viam quisque* dūcit discipulōs* suōs. Eī autem probant quālemcumque* iniērunt viam*, nec facile* inculcātās* puerīs suāsiōnēs* mutāveris.

(*After* Institutiōnēs Ōrātiōnēs *III.1.4–5)*

5. While still a young man, Cicero wrote his first technical treatise on the art of rhetoric, the *Dē Inventiōne*. In the following selection from this treatise, Cicero discusses the need to be **brevis**, brief and to the point—a goal we still labor to achieve.

In narrātiōne quae causae* expositiōnem* habet et brevitās et probābilitās inesse dēbent. Brevitās inerit sī narrātiō incipiet unde dēbet et sī nōn ab ultimā* parte factī incipiet cuius satis erit summam* dīxisse. Is putat sē breviter* dīcere quī ita dīcit: "Adīvī ad aedēs* eius. Puerum* vocāvī. Respondit. Quaesīvī dominum. Domī negāvit* esse." Is tamen ōrātor quia satis est dīxisse "domī negāvit* esse," est factōrum multitūdine longus. Quārē ōrātor eō in genere vitet brevitātis imitātiōnem*, id est, tam* nōn necessāria* quam* verbōrum multitūdinem.

(*After* Dē inventiōne *I.20.25)*

2–3: **dulcī flavōque liquōre** "with sweet, golden fluid"
3: **imprōvidus, -a, -um** without foresight, improvident
lūdificō, -āre treat as a plaything, trifle with
4: **amārum absinthiī laticem** "the bitter, liquid absinth"
4–5: **suāviloquentī carmine** "with sweetly-speaking song"
expōnō, -ere explain, set forth
5–6: **quasi . . . melle** "to touch [his philosophic poem], as it were, with the sweet honey of the Muse (**mūsaeō**)."
8: **salūbris** (nom. *m* sing.) healthful, wholesome
etiamsī (conjunction) even if
dulcis (nom. *m* sing.) sweet
9: **eadem** (acc. *n* pl.) the same things
10: **dīversus, -a, -um** different
10: **quisque dūcit discipulōs (in suam viam)**: "Each person leads his followers onto his own path"
11: **quālemcumque viam**: "whatsoever path"
facile (adverb) easily
11–12: **inculcātās puerīs suāsiōnēs**: "beliefs which were crammed into them when they were young (**puerīs**)"

1: **causa, -ae** *f* (here) lawsuit, legal case
expositiō, -iōnis *f* (in a speech) a setting forth, exposition
3: **ultimus, -a, -um** most distant
ab ultimā parte "from the most distant part"
summa, -ae *f* substance, essence
4: **breviter** (adverb) briefly
aedēs, aedum *f* pl. house, dwelling
puer a household slave
5, 6: **negō, -āre** say . . . not, deny; the implied subject of **esse** is **eum**.
7: **imitātiō, -iōnis** *f* imitation
8: **tam . . . quam** as much . . . as
necessārius, -a, -um unavoidable, indispensable, necessary

6. One of the most influential books on speaking and writing ever produced in the western world was the *Rhētorica Ad Herennium*, a treatise known to medieval writers as the *Rhētorica nova* (*The New Rhetoric*). It was mistakenly attributed to Cicero, whose *Dē inventiōne* was called *Rhētorica vetus* (*The Old Rhetoric*). The following passages are adapted from this book.

6a. The first selection defines the orator's task and the three basic kinds of speeches. Passages 6b and 6c describe some of the "tricks of the trade."

Ōrātōris officium est dē eīs posse dīcere quae populus mōribus et lēgibus constituit, cum assēnsiōne* audītōrum quoad* facere poterit. Tria* genera sunt causārum quae recipere* dēbet ōrātor: dēmonstrātīvum*, dēlīberātīvum*, iūdiciāle*. Dēmonstrātīvum* est quod certam persōnam aut laudat aut vituperat*. Dēliberātīvum* est quod cōnsultat* et quod habet in sē suāsiōnem* et dissuāsiōnem*. In controversiā* constituimus iūdiciāle*, quod habet in sē accusātiōnem* aut petitiōnem* cum dēfensiōne.

6b. **Dūbitātiō**, "Indecision," occurs when:

Ōrātor quaerit utrum* dē duōbus* dīcat, id est: "Eō tempore iniūriam patriae fēcit* cōnsulum—seu stultitiam* seu malitiam* dīcere dēbeō." Item: "Tū id dīcere audēs, homō omnium mortalium*—nam quō nōmine moribus dignō tuīs tē appellem?"

6c. **Dissolūtum**, "Asyndeton," occurs when:

Ōrātor coniunctiōnēs verbōrum ē mediō removet, id est: "gere morem parentī*, placē* amīcīs, cēde lēgibus." Item: "Dēscende* in inte-

2: **assēnsiō, -iōnis** *f* agreement
quoad (adverb) as far as, as much as
3: **tria** (acc. *n* pl.) three
recipiō, -ere, -cēpi, -ceptus to treat
3–4: **dēmōnstrātīvum [genus]** "demonstrative," aimed at praising or censuring.
4, 5: **dēliberātīvum [genus]** "deliberative," a speech weighing many sides of an issue.
4, 7: **iūdiciāle [genus]** "judicial," a speech containing accusation or defense.
5: **vituperō, -āre** blame, censure, find fault with
cōnsultō, -āre reflect, deliberate, take counsel
6: **suāsiō, -iōnis** *f* advice, counselling, persuasion
dissuāsiō, -iōnis *f* advising to the contrary, dissuasion
controversia, -ae *f* contention, dispute
7: **accūsātiō, -iōnis** *f* complaint, accusation, indictment
petitiō, -iōnis *f* attack; a request; a laying claim to anything
10: **utrum dē duōbus** "which of two things (he should say, **dicat**)"
11: **fēcit** the subject is the **stultitia** or **malitia** (of the consuls) (understood from what follows)
stultitia, -ae *f* stupidity
malitia, -ae *f* evil intent, malice; cunning
12: **omnium mortālium** (partitive gen. pl.) "of all mortal beings"
16: **parēns, parentis** *m* parent
placeō, -ēre (+ dative) be pleasing to someone, please
dēscendō, -ere go down, lower oneself
16–17: **integer, integra, integrum** whole, "complete"

gram * dēfensiōnem, nōlī quicquam * negāre, da * servōs tuōs in quaestiōnem *, studē vēritātem invenīre." Id genus et acrimōniam * habet in sē et vehementissimum * est et ad brevitātem accommodat *.

6d. **Praecīsiō** *, "Aposiopesis," occurs when:

Ōrātor dīcere incēpit sed dicta * inchoāta relinquit *, id est: "Mihi tēcum par certātiō * nōn est, quod populus Rōmānus mē—nōlō dīcere, nē hominēs mē arroganter * dīcere putent; tē autem saepe opprobriō dignum putāvit *."

17: **quicquam** (accus. *n* sing.) anything
17–18: **da servōs tuōs in quaestiōnem** "turn in your servants for questioning"
18: **acrimōnia, -ae** *f* sharpness, pungency, "animation"
19: **vehementissimus, -a, -um** having great force, very forceful
19: **accommodō, -āre** (with **ad** + acc.) be suitable for
20: **praecīsiō** "aposiopesis," a sudden pause by the speaker, as if unable to continue.
21: **dicta inchoāta relinquit** "He leaves his statement without completing it" (literally, **dicta inchoāta**, "words begun")
22: **par certātiō** "an equal contest"
23: **arroganter** (adverb) with presumption, arrogantly
24: **putāvit** the subject is **populus**

IX

Pronouns (3): Demonstrative and Intensive; Subjunctive Mood: Result, Characteristic

Demonstrative and Intensive Pronouns

A demonstrative pronoun points out a person or thing for special attention.[1] You have already learned the demonstrative pronoun **is**, **ea**, **id** (he, she, it, this/that), which, like all demonstrative pronouns, can also be used as an adjective (e.g., **is vir**, "this/that man"). **Is**, **ea**, **id**, as a demonstrative, is relatively weak, usually not much stronger than the English article, "the." To make a more pointed reference to something near the speaker (near in time, place, or thought), Latin uses **hic**, **haec**, **hoc**, "this." To indicate something at a distance, Latin uses **ille**, **illa**, **illud**, "that." To contrast two different persons or things, **hic** can mean "the latter" (which would be nearer in time or space) when paired with **ille**, "the former" (the more distant in time or space). **Iste**, **ista**, **istud**, this/that . . . of yours (i.e., with which I do not associate myself), makes a pointed reference, but frequently implies antagonism or contempt. **Īdem**, **eadem**, **idem** means "the same," and sometimes translates better into English as an adverbial phrase.

Ille vir suam sententiam dīxit.	That man gave his own opinion.
Hic **idem** fēcit.	*So* did this man. (This man did likewise.)
Illa **eandem** sententiam dīxit.	That woman gave the *same* opinion (*this* opinion *also*).
Iste fīlius mē impedīvit.	*That* son *of yours* embarrassed me.
Pater fīliō dīcere vult, sed **hīc illum** fugit.	The father wants to speak to the son, but *the latter* is avoiding the *former*.
Eōdem tempore domō abībam.	At *the same* (or *that very*) time I was leaving home.

[1] Hence demonstrative pronouns and adjectives are sometimes called "deictic," which means "pointing" or "indicating."

***Hic**, this, the latter; **ille**, that, the former*:

	SINGULAR					
	M.	F.	N.	M.	F.	N.
Nom.	hic	haec	hoc	ille	illa	illud
Gen.	huius	huius	huius	illīus	illīus	illīus
Dat.	huic	huic	huic	illī	illī	illī
Acc.	hunc	hanc	hoc	illum	illam	illud
Abl.	hōc	hāc	hōc	illō	illā	illō
	PLURAL					
Nom.	hī	hae	haec	illī	illae	illa
Gen.	hōrum	hārum	hōrum	illōrum	illārum	illōrum
Dat.	hīs	hīs	hīs	illīs	illīs	illīs
Acc.	hōs	hās	haec	illōs	illās	illa
Abl.	hīs	hīs	hīs	illīs	illīs	illīs

If you examine these paradigms carefully, you will see that the plural endings are those of the first and second declensions. The only exception in the plural is the neuter nominative and accusative, **haec**. The ending -**c** in **hic**, **haec**, **hoc** is a remnant of the demonstrative enclitic -**ce**, which is still found in **ecce**, "Look!"[2] For the singular endings, compare the declension of **solus**, -**a**, -**um** in Chapter II.

***Iste**, this, that, that of yours.* **Iste** follows the declension of **ille**:

	SINGULAR			PLURAL		
	M.	F.	N.	M.	F.	N.
Nom.	iste	ista	istud	istī	istae	ista
Gen.	istīus	istīus	istīus	istōrum	istārum	istōrum
Dat.	istī	istī	istī	istīs	istīs	istīs
Acc.	istum	istam	istud	istōs	istās	ista
Abl.	istō	istā	istō	istīs	istīs	istīs

Iste can be used as a somewhat stronger form of the weak demonstrative, **is**, or as an equivalent of **ille**. More often, however, it conveys hostility, which is best expressed in English as "of yours." (English, unfortunately, is limited here; the expression "of yours" is not intended to show possession.) Compare the following:

Ea tē vocat.	*She* is calling you.
Haec tē vocat.	*This woman* is calling you.
Illa tē vocat.	*That woman* is calling you.
Ista tē vocat.	*That woman of yours* is calling you.

[2] The final -**e** of this enclitic has been dropped from the singular forms; the plural forms (with the exception of the neuter plural) have also dropped the final -**c**. The -**i**- in the nominative masculine singular is short in early Latin, long in the Classical period; -**o**- in the neuter nominative and accusative singular is frequently lengthened in poetry.

Illud marsuppium oboluit.	*That* purse gave off an odor.
Istud marsuppium huic fēminae oboluit.	*That* purse *of yours* emitted an odor to this woman.

***Idem**, the same.* **Īdem**, **eadem**, **idem** follows the declension of **is**, **ea**, **id**, to which is added the indeclinable suffix **-dem**. The exceptions are: the masculine singular nominative, where the -**s**- has dropped out;[3] the neuter singular nominative and accusative, where one -**d**- has dropped out; the accusative singular masculine and feminine, and the genitive plural in all genders, where the -**m**- has changed to -**n**- (compare **hunc**, **hanc**).

	Singular			Plural		
	M.	F.	N.	M.	F.	N.
Nom.	īdem	eadem	idem	eīdem	eaedem	eadem
Gen.	eiusdem	eiusdem	eiusdem	eōrundem	eārundem	eōrundem
Dat.	eīdem	eīdem	eīdem	eīsdem	eīsdem	eīsdem
Acc.	eundem	eandem	idem	eōsdem	eāsdem	eadem
Abl.	eōdem	eādem	eōdem	eīsdem	eīsdem	eīsdem

Īdem or **is** emphasizes a person or thing already named:

Nōs sumus **eī** quī infantiam dēliciīs solvēmus.
We are *the ones* who will weaken their infancy with pleasure.

Nōs sumus **eīdem** quī infantiam solvēmus.
We are *the same ones* who will weaken their infancy.

Īdem meaning "the same" often occurs where English would use an adverb or adverbial phrase, such as "also, too, yet, at the same time":

Ōrātiō tua splendida et grandis et **eadem** facēta erit.
Your oration will be brilliant, lofty, and witty *too*.

Ipse. The intensive adjective **ipse**, **ipsa**, **ipsum**, can be translated "the very . . ." or "himself, herself, itself" or "themselves." Its main purpose is to emphasize the person or thing it refers to, and its translation varies to the extent necessary to achieve that end. It occurs with any of the other pronouns or with a noun for the sake of emphasis. It can also be used alone as an emphatic pronoun.

The nominative is **ipse**, **ipsa**, **ipsum**; the genitive singular is **ipsīus** and the dative is **ipsī** for all genders. The accusative and ablative singular, and all plural endings are those of the first and second declension.

Ipse mihi dixit.
He (and no one else) spoke to me.

Ipsī haec nōvistī.
You (as distinct from anyone else) know these things.

Ipsum vīdī Rōmae.
I saw *him* (that very person) at Rome.

Eā ipsā hōrā Rōmam adiērunt.
At that very hour (and not at some other time) they approached Rome.

[3] Observe the compensatory lengthening of **i**- in the masculine singular **īdem** (whereas the neuter singular is **idem**).

Hoc est **genus ipsum** ōrātiōnis quod Cicero **ipse** disserēbat.
This is *the very kind* of speech which Cicero *himself* was discussing.

The intensive **ipse** should not be confused with the reflexive **sē**. **Ipse** is sometimes used, however, to emphasize the reflexive relationship, with the nominative laying stress on the subject, and the other cases laying stress upon the object:

Puer **ipse** in aquā sē vīdit. (nominative)
The boy *himself* (**ipse**) saw himself (**sē**) in the water. (**sē** is reflexive)

Puer sē **ipsum** in aquā vīdit. (accusative)
The boy saw *himself* (his very own self) (**sē ipsum**) in the water.

Scrībenda

A. Decline **ipse**.

B. Add the correct endings to the demonstrative adjectives in the following phrases, and then translate the entire phrase:

dux ill____	arbor ill____	tempus ____dem
ducī h____	arbore h____	temporis h____
nautae ill____	lībertātum ips____	tibi ips____
virī h____	ōrātiōnēs ist____	ducibus ____dem

C. Translate the following sentences into English:

1. Illa dīcit sē hunc virum nōvisse.
2. Ista dīcit eum sē ipsam nōvisse.
3. Īdem negat sē ipsam nōvisse.
4. Certē iste nōn sānus est.
5. Putāmus illam sānam nōn esse.
6. Illae stellae quās in caelō vidēs bestiae sunt.
7. Haec bestia parva illam magnam mordēbit.
8. Bestiae in caelō nautās quī illās vident dūcent.
9. Hōs linguā Pūnicā appellābō.
10. Vīsne mē hunc appellāre?
11. Rogāvit mē num Pūnicōs ipsōs appellātūrus essem.
12. Hunc eundem appellā.
13. Istud est tua cūra.
14. Fīlius petīvit quis patrem ipsum vīdisset. Fīlius patrem fugiet nē hic illum videat.
15. Ego homuncio id nōn facerem? Ego vērō illud fēcī. (**homuncio = homo parvus**)

The Subjunctive Mood

Clauses of Result

When a subordinate clause shows the result of an action or quality in the main clause, the verb of the subordinate clause is in the subjunctive mood and is introduced by **ut**. Negative result clauses are introduced by **ut nōn** or by **ut** and some negative word, such as **nihil**, **numquam**, or **nēmō**. Clauses of result are frequently preceded in the main clause by certain adjectives or adverbs of degree. The most usual adjectives are **tantus**, **-a**, **-um**, "so great"; **tālis**, **tāle**, "of such a sort"; and **tot**, "so many." The most usual adverbs are **sīc**, "in this way"; **ita**, "so," "in such a way"; **adeō**, "so far"; and **tam** (with adjectives and adverbs), "so":

> Augustīnus crēdidit sē **tam** nimis plōrāvisse Didōnis mortem **ut** animum suum **neglexerit.**
> Augustine believed he had *so* excessively lamented the death of Dido *that* [as a result of his sorrow] *he neglected* his own soul.
>
> **Ita** respondit **ut nēmō** eius sententiam vēram noscere **potuerit**.
> He answered *in such a way that* [as a result of the way he answered] *no one was able* to learn his true opinion.
>
> Nēmō est **tam** stultus **ut** hoc **faciat**.
> No one is so stupid *as to do* this. (i.e., so stupid that, as a result of his stupidity, he would do this.)
>
> **Ita** vītam ēgit **ut** nōs eum **probāverimus**.
> He lived his life *in such a way* that we approved of him.

Tenses in Result Clauses. The rule of sequence of tenses applies to result clauses in primary sequence. After secondary tenses, however, the perfect subjunctive tends to be used rather than the imperfect tense, for the perfect tense emphasizes the finality of the result, whereas the imperfect tense would imply that the action was ongoing. Compare the following examples:

> Tam nimis plōrāvit Dīdōnis mortem ut animum suum neglexerit. (perfect tense)
>
> Tam nimis plōrāvit Dīdōnis mortem ut animum suum neglegeret. (imperfect)

In the first example, we have an account of something which happened in the past, but is now completed. The second example, in the imperfect tense, emphasizes the contemporaneity of Augustine's neglect of his soul. Either could be correct, depending on the context, but the former is more usual in a result clause.

Result Clauses versus Purpose Clauses. It is not unusual to confuse result clauses and purpose clauses. They look alike when they are in the affirmative, since both are introduced by **ut**. Result clauses, however, are usually signaled in advance by adjectives and adverbs of degree, as mentioned earlier. When the clauses are negative, on the other hand, there is no confusion, for negative purpose clauses are always introduced by **nē**, which replaces **ut**. Negative result clauses retain **ut** and use in addition a separate negating word. Finally, the sequence of tenses in result clauses will sometimes differ from the sequence required in purpose clauses.

> Result: **Tam** celeriter vēnit **ut** fugere **nōn potuerimus**.
> He came *so* quickly *that* we *were unable* to escape.

Here **tam** signals that a result clause will follow; the negative result is indicated by **ut** and **nōn**, and the verb in the result clause is in the perfect subjunctive.

Purpose: Celeriter vēnit **nē** fugere **possēmus**.
He came quickly *so that* we *would not be able* to escape.

Here the negative purpose clause is introduced by **nē**, and the verb in the purpose clause is in the imperfect subjunctive, following secondary sequence after the past tense of **vēnit**.

Result: Servus dabit **tam** bonum consilium **ut** fīlius fugiat.
The servant will give *such* good advice *that* the son will escape.

Purpose: Servus dabit bonum consilium **ut** fīlius fugiat.
The servant will give good advice *so that* the son will escape.

Here the only difference in the Latin is the use of the adverb **tam** to anticipate result.

Relative Clauses of Result and of Purpose. Result clauses and purpose clauses are sometimes introduced by a relative pronoun (**quī**, **quae**, **quod**) or by a relative adverb (**ubi**, **unde**, **quō**, etc.) instead of by **ut**. The antecedent of the relative word is expressed or implied in the main clause. In this case, the relative pronoun or adverb is equivalent in meaning to **ut** and the equivalent form of the implied demonstrative pronoun (**ut is**, **ut ea**, **ut id**) or adverb (**ut ibi**, **ut inde**, **ut eō**, etc.):

Tam celeriter vēnit **quem** (**ut eum**) fugere nōn potuerimus.
He came so quickly *that* we were unable to escape *him*.

Domum adīit ubi (**ut ibi**) salvus esset.
He went home *where* he would be safe/He went home *so that* he would be safe *there*.

Relative Clauses of Characteristic

Relative clauses of characteristic are closely related to relative clauses of result. Instead of showing a result anticipated by an adjective or adverb of degree (**tam**, **ita**, **adeō**, **tālis**, **tantus**, etc.), however, a relative clause of characteristic[4] indicates a tendency or likely result of a category or characteristic of the antecedent. The antecedent, in turn, tends to be undefined, frequently a general, an interrogative, or a negative expression:

General: **Nōn est quae** tibi placeat.
She is not the sort (of woman) *who* would be pleasing to you.

Sunt quī sē sōlōs ament.
There are people (of such a kind) *who* love only themselves.

Multī et sunt et fuērunt quī sē ā negōtiīs publicīs remōverint ad otiumque perfūgerint.
There are and have been many men (of the sort) *who* have withdrawn from public affairs and taken refuge in retirement.

[4] Also called "generic relative clause." "Generic" comes from **genus**, **generis**, *n.*

Interrogative: **Quid est quod** tibi placeat?
What (sort of thing) *is there which* would be pleasing to you?

Negative: **Nēmō est quī** tibi placeat.
There is no one (of such a sort) *who* would be pleasing to you.

Implicit in all these examples is an expression such as "of such a sort as to," "of such a kind that," "the kind who or which." The result expressed in the subjunctive follows from the general characteristics of the kind of thing or person implied. Observe, by contrast, how the meaning changes when the verb in the relative clause is in the indicative mood:

Nēmō est quī tibi placet.	No one (actually) exists who pleases you.
Ea nōn est quae tibi placet.	She is not the (real, existing) woman who pleases you.

Here we see most sharply delineated the difference between the indicative mood, which conveys actual fact, and the subjunctive mood, which conveys something other than simple fact.

Scrībenda

A. Translate the following sentences:

1. Ille linguā Pūnicā dīcit.
2. Ille est quī bona numquam dīcat.
3. Quis est quī hāc linguā dīcat?
4. Nēmō est quī linguā istā dīcat.
5. Īdem est quī ea ipsa dīxit.
6. Quid pater docet?
7. Quid est quod pater doceat?
8. Sunt quī fīliōs suōs domī docēre mālint.
9. Pater est qui fīlium suum doceat.
10. Ipse fīlium docet.
11. Nullam linguam nesciō.
12. Nulla lingua est quam nesciam.
13. Linguam tuam tam bene didicit ut tuā et suā dīcere possit.
14. Linguam tuam tam bene didicit quī tuā et suā dīcere possit.
15. Linguam vestram bene didicimus ut vestrā et nostrā dīcere possēmus.

B. Translate the following sentences into English. Explain why the underlined verb is in the subjunctive mood, and indicate what kind of subjunctive (i.e., result clause, relative clause of characteristic, purpose clause, contrary-to-fact condition, etc.) it is:

1. Tam celeriter fūgit ut pater eum nōn vīderit.
2. Celeriter fūgit nē pater eum vidēret.
3. Tam ēbrius est ut ambulāre nōn possit.
4. Eadem fēmina Menaechmum tam familiāriter appellāvit ut servus timuerit. (**familiāriter**, adv., intimately)
5. Menaechmus marsuppium cēlāvit ut sciret utrum ea fēmina amāret.
6. Ille discipulus linguam Latīnam ita didicit ut et illā et suā linguā dīcere potuerit.

7. Ita ōrātor dīcat ut ex eō quod dīxerit, id quod nōn dīxerit intellegāmus. (**intellegō, -ere, -lēxī, -lectus**, understand)
8. Multōs imitātiō brevitātis tam captat ut sē breviter dīxisse putent. (**imitātiō, -iōnis**, *f*, imitation)
9. Tantum erat eius ingenium ut ōrātōrēs clārī scholam eius frequentāverint. (**frequentō, -āre**, visit)
10. Natūra nōs sīc fēcit ut vēritātem vidēre studeāmus.
11. Natūra nōs fēcit ut vēritātem vidēre studērēmus.

D. Translate into Latin:

1. This man's speech was so long that no one listened.
2. At that time the speaker decided to pass over the things we did not want to hear so that we would be willing to listen to him for many hours.
3. She believed her son would tell his father the truth. The former, however, was so afraid of the latter that he ran away from home.
4. In the countryside and at Rome, fathers prefer to teach their sons by example.
5. He was the sort of man who could teach good habits by example.

Verba tenenda

Verbs

absum, abesse, āfuī, āfutūrus be absent
addō, addere, addidī, additus bring to, add to
ardeō, ardēre, arsī, arsus be on fire, burn
convertō, -ere, -vertī, -versus turn around, reverse
dēdūcō, -ere, dēdūxī, dēductus lead away, lead down
fleō, flēre, flēvī, flētus weep, weep over
fluō, fluere, fluxī, fluctus flow
fundō, -ere, fūdī, fūsus pour, pour out; shed
incendō, -ere, incendī, incēnsus set fire to, kindle; burn; arouse
līberō, -āre, -āvī, -ātus (with or without **ab** + abl.) free (from), liberate
mōnstrō, -āre, -āvī, -ātus show, point out, indicate
opprimō, -ere, oppressī, oppressus overwhelm, oppress
pervertō, -ere, -vertī, -versus overturn, overthrow, subvert
praecēdō, -ere, -cessī, -cessus go before, precede
premō, -ere, pressī, pressus hold fast, bear down, press
reddō, reddere, reddidī, redditus give back, restore, return
reprimō, -ere, -pressī, -pressus press back, check, curb, restrain
scindō, -ere, scidī, scissus cut, tear, split
stō, stāre, stetī, stātus stand upright, stand firm, remain
subdō, subdere, subdidī, subditus put under, place under; subject, subdue
superō, -āre, -āvī, -ātus conquer, overcome
trādō, trādere, trādidī, trāditus hand over, transmit, deliver; report; betray

Nouns

amor, **amōris** *m* love
bōs, **bovis** (gen. pl: **boum** dat. and abl. pl: **bōbus** or **būbus**) *m* or *f* cow, cattle
cauda, **-ae** *f* tail
Cācus, **-ī** *m* a proper name
Dēianīra, **-ae** *f* a proper name (the wife of Hercules)
dolor, **dolōris** *m* pain, grief
flamma, **-ae** *f* flame, blaze
fluvius, **fluviī** *m* river
frōns, **frontis** *f* forehead, brow
grex, **gregis** *m* flock, herd
Herculēs, **-is** *m* proper name
ignis, **-is** *m* fire
Iūnō, **Iūnōnis** *f* Juno (queen of the gods, wife of Jupiter)
Iuppiter, **Iovis** *m* Jupiter (ruler of the gods)
labor, **labōris** *m* labor, toil
membrum, **-ī** *n* limb
mōnstrum, **-ī** *n* monster, wonder, omen
nēmo, **nēminis** *m* or *f* nobody
pars, **partis** *f* part; direction
pulchritūdo, **-tūdinis** *f* beauty
pyra, **-ae** *f* funeral pyre
sanguis, **sanguinis** *m* blood, gore
sopor, **sopōris** *m* sleep, drowsiness
spēlunca, **-ae** *f* cave
vestigium, **vestigiī** *n* footprint; pl., tracks
vestis, **vestis** *f* clothing, cloak
vīnum, **-ī** *n* wine
vox, **vōcis** *f* voice, sound, cry

Demonstrative Pronouns and Adjectives

hic, **haec**, **hoc** this (man, woman, thing); the latter
īdem, **eadem**, **idem** the same
ille, **illa**, **illud** that (man, woman, thing); the former
iste, **ista**, **istud** that (man, woman, thing) of yours
ipse, **ipsa**, **ipsum** himself, herself, itself; the very

Adjectives

altus, **-a**, **-um** high, lofty; deep, profound
dīvīnus, **-a**, **-um** of or belonging to a divinity, divine
dūrus, **-a**, **-um** hard, harsh, rough; stern
falsus, **-a**, **-um** deceptive, feigned, false
fessus, **-a**, **-um** exhausted
Herculeus, **-a**, **-um** of Hercules
hūmānus, **-a**, **-um** of a human being; human
ignārus, **-a**, **-um** not knowing; unaware
nescius, **-a**, **-um** not knowing; unaware
saucius, **-a**, **-um** wounded
varius, **-a**, **-um** varied
vērus, **-a**, **-um** true

Adverbs

adeō so, so far, to such a degree
ita so, thus, in this way, in that way, to such a degree; as follows
ōlim formerly, once, once upon a time
prope near, nearly
sīc so, thus, in this way, in that way, to such a degree; as follows
tam (modifying an adjective or adverb) so

Conjunction

postquam after

Prepositions

inter (+ acc.) amid, among, between
prae (+ acc.) before, in front of
prope (+ acc.) near
trāns (+ acc.) across

Notanda

addō, **reddō**, **subdō** and **trādō** are all compounds of **dō**, **dare**. Note that these compounded forms are regular third conjugation verbs, and that the perfect stem is reduplicated (**addidī**, **reddidī**, etc.; compare **dedī**).

fluō, "flow," describes the motion of a **fluvius**, a "river" or body of flowing water.

stō, **stāre** is a first conjugation verb, but **stetī**, its third principal part, is irregular.

Iovis, the genitive of **Iuppiter**, is the source of the English exclamation, "By Jove!" Notice that the nominative case is spelled with two *p*'s, not one, as in the English equivalent.

nēmō (declined **nēmō**, **nēminis**, **nēminī**, **nēminem**, **nēmine**) can be masculine or feminine. The genitive **nūllīus** and the ablative **nūllō** or **nūllā** are frequently used instead of the declined forms of this noun.

Compare the abstract nouns **pulchritūdo** and **vēritās** (Chapter VIII) with the related adjectives **pulcher**, **-chra**, **-chrum** and **vērus**, **-a**, **-um**.

altus can refer to height or depth; hence the ocean and the sky can both be described by this adjective.

hūmānus means "having to do with human beings" (cf. **homō**). Hence Terence's famous maxim, "**Homō sum; putō nihil hūmānum mihi aliēnum**."

ignārus and **nescius** both mean "ignorant," not in the sense of "stupid," but in the more literal sense of not knowing, being uninformed.

Do not confuse the adverb **adeō** with the first person singular of the verb **adeō**—although the form is the same, the context will tell you whether it is a finite verb or an adverb.

The abbreviation commonly found in footnotes, **ibid.**, is short for **ibidem**, a combination of **ibi**, "there," and **idem**, "the same." Hence its meaning, "in the same place," indicating that the same reference is being cited as in the previous footnote in which a person or thing was mentioned.

The adverb **tam** modifies an adjective or adverb; it is not used alone. Additionally, **tam** is used in comparisons, frequently correlated with **quam**, "as . . . as": **tam cāra mihi est vīta mea quam tua** [**est tibi**]. "My life is as precious to me as yours [is to you]."

The conjunction **postquam**, "after," like **ubi**, "when," is followed by a verb in the indicative mood, usually in the perfect tense, even if the sense is in the pluperfect tense: **Postquam haec prōfēcī, populus mihi grātiās ēgit**, "After I [had] accomplished these things, the people thanked me." When the present tense follows, it will tend to be the "historical present," that is, the present tense used to give a lively account of past events: **Ubi haec prōficiō, populus mihi gratiās agit**, "When I accomplish[ed] these things, the people thank[ed] me."

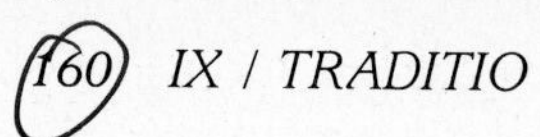

Ante legenda

Translate:

1. Trādunt Herculem in illum locum quī futūrus esset Rōma bovēs ēgisse.
2. Trāns fluvium bovēs eāsdem ēgit.
3. Postquam trāns fluvium illās ēgit, fessus erat.
4. Tam fessus erat ut sopor eum superāverit.
5. Adeō fessus erat quem sopor superāverit.
6. Nēmō est quem fessum sopor nōn superet.
7. Sopor sīc eum oppressit ut nōn sēnserit pastōrem istum bovēs dēdūcere.
8. Pastor iste est quī bovēs dēdūcat.
9. Sīc populum eius locī līberāvit istīus pastōris timōre.
10. Fāma, quae vērīs addere falsa semper amat, praecessit ad illam fēminam.
11. Fāma huic dīxit virum eius amōrem fēminae alterīus sentīre. (**vir**, husband)
12. Haec fāma illam tam terruit ut virō vestem mīserit.
13. Illī vestem mīsit ut vir sibi amōrem reddere vellet.
14. Fēmina servō ignārō quid trādat vestem dat.
15. Tantus erat dolor ut tolerāre nōn potuerit.
16. Iuppiter constituit sē līberātūrum esse partem suī fīliī dīvīnam ab hūmānā parte.
17. Tantus erat ignis pyrae ut nūllum sonum alium audīre possem.
18. Sine membrīs hūmānīs flōrēre incēpit Herculēs, quem pater deōrum in stellam novam mutāvit.
19. Postquam ille flammās istās tolerāvit, pater ipse eum in caelō posuit.
20. Poēta Homērus trādit Herculem nōn in caelō sed apud inferōs esse. Sunt autem quī dīcant nōn esse eundem Herculem apud inferōs, sed eius īdōlum. (**Homērus**, -**ī**, *m*, the poet Homer; **apud inferōs**, "in the Underworld"; **īdōlum**, -**ī**, *n*, image, apparition)

Legenda

Mythology (1): The Story of Hercules

The importance of Greek myth in Roman thought and literature cannot be overstated. Romans recognized most of the Greek gods, whom they sometimes equated with native Latin gods. For example, the Roman equivalent of Zeus, the supreme deity of the Greek pantheon, was Jupiter. Juno became the Roman equivalent of Hera, Venus the equivalent of Aphrodite, Mars the equivalent of Ares, and Ceres the equivalent of Demeter. As early

Hercules killing the centaur Nessus. Detail on a jar found in a seventh century B.C. *Athenian grave.*

as the sixth century B.C. we find Greek thinkers pondering the philosophical implications of their myths, and by the time of the Roman Empire the psychological and philosophical significance of these myths had become a major reason for their continuing appeal and popularity.

Greco-Roman gods have been explained as cosmic symbols, as allegories, or as distortions of historical fact. As cosmic symbols, the gods represent the union or conflict of the elementary powers of the universe. As allegories, the myths are merely the expression of moral and philosophical ideas. The Alexandrian philosopher, Euhemerus (third century B.C.), claimed the gods were once mortal but had made such important contributions to civilization that they were deified after their deaths. During the Roman Empire, the Roman Senate decreed deification for deceased emperors, and Roman writers, conversely, presented the gods as metaphors for their rulers or their rulers as embodiments of the gods. Mythology was integral to natural science, morality, and world history, with the result that its influence in the western world continued, despite the rising influence of Christianity, throughout the Middle Ages and into the Renaissance.

A good example of Greco-Roman myth and its evolution can be found in the story of Hercules—or Herakles, as the Greeks called him—the hero who became a god. He was particularly important in Italy, so much so that by Vergil's time it was difficult to find a place in that country in which the god was not honored. In Greece he had been honored for his strength and bravery, but his hot temper, his gluttony, and his lust made him a somewhat ambiguous figure. During the Alexandrian period the dominant features of the Herakles myth were his accomplishment of wondrous deeds and his travels to exotic lands. In his Roman setting, however, Hercules takes on a new seriousness. By conquering evil and extending the borders of the civilized world,[5] he improved the human condition. He therefore is viewed at Rome as a symbol of Stoic **virtūs**.

The myth of Hercules, briefly, is one of continuous struggle, usually with wild creatures and monsters which hinder the spread of civilization. While still an infant, he strangled the serpents Juno had sent to destroy him in his crib. Most of his famous labors (the canonical number was twelve, although the number varied in later accounts—in the fourteenth century, Boccaccio could list thirty-one) involve the slaying or capture of monsters, and his most spectacular achievement was the successful descent into and return from Hades, the land of the dead. This great hero was finally destroyed when his jealous wife, Deianira, attempted to win back her errant husband's love with the cloak of the centaur, Nessus. The cloak contained a deadly poison rather than a love potion, as Deianira mistakenly believed.

Roman tradition claimed Hercules' presence, before the coming of Aeneas, at the future site of Rome. Here he tamed the powerful monster-

[5] J. G. Winter, "The Myth of Hercules at Rome," *Roman History and Mythology* (New York, 1910); G. K. Galinsky, *The Herakles Theme* (Totowa, New Jersey, 1972); W. Burkert, *Structure and History in Greek Mythology and Ritual* (Berkeley, 1979).

shepherd Cacus,[6] the terror of that region prior to Hercules' arrival. Hercules was returning from his contest with Geryon, leading Geryon's cattle (Hercules' prize from that contest), when he encountered and defeated Cacus and thus opened the possibility of civilization in that region. In the *Aeneid*, Vergil makes Hercules a role model for Aeneas and Augustus, since all three have a divine mission to bring peace and order to a world in chaos.

1. The historian Livy (59/64 B.C.–A.D. 17/12) gives the following account of Hercules' confrontation with Cacus.

Trādunt Herculem ōlim in eum locum quī Rōma futūra esset bovēs pulchrās ēgisse. Postquam trāns Tiberim* prae sē gregem ēgit, tam fessus erat ut ipse prope fluvium prōcubuerit.* Mox Herculem cibō vīnōque gravātum* sopor sīc oppressit ut ille nōn sēnserit Cācum, pastōrem eius locī, adīsse ad bovēs pulchrās; quārum pulchritūdo sīc Cācum cēpit ut eās habēre vellet. Cacus eās bovēs āvertit nē ipsa vestigia dominum in spēluncam dēdūcerent, et bovēs caudīs in spēluncam traxit. Hercules ad prīmam aurōram* gregem perlustrāvit* oculīs et partem abesse sēnsit. Adīvit ad proximam* spēluncam ut invenīret num eō* vestigia dūcerent. Haec vestigia forās* dūcere vīdit.

Herculēs, confūsus* atque incertus animī,* ex locō istō molestō agere gregem incēpit. Sed bovēs quās Herculēs agēbat dēsīderium* illārum relictārum* sēnsērunt, et, ut bovēs solent, mugīvērunt*; relictae* bovēs ita respondērunt ex spēluncā ut Herculem converterent. Hunc Cācus fugere nōn potuit. Sīc Herculēs eius locī populum līberāvit istīus pastōris ā timōre.

(After Livy, Ab urbe condita, *1.7)*

2. Hercules met a painful death when he put on a cloak sent by his wife, Deianira. Deianira had been deceived by the dying Centaur, Nessus, into thinking that the cloak was steeped in a love potion which would win back

2: **Tiber, Tiberis** *m* the river Tiber, which flows through Rome;
Tiberim, acc. sing.
3: **prōcumbō, -ere, -cubuī, -cubitus** fall forward; sink down
4: **gravātus, -a, -um** heavy, weighted down
8: **aurōra, -ae** *f* dawn, daybreak
perlustrō, -āre wander all through, view all over
9: **proximus, -a, -um** near-by, very close
eō (adverb) there, in that place
10: **forās** (adverb) away, outwards
11: **confūsus atque incertus animī** "confused and uncertain in his mind"
(**animī** is locative)
12: **dēsīderium, -ī** *n* desire, longing
12–13: **relicitus, -a, -um** left behind, remaining
dēsīderium relictārum "a longing for the cattle left behind"
13: **mugiō, -īre, -īvī, -ītus** low, bellow, "moo"

[6] "Cacus" comes from the Greek word meaning "evil, bad"; hence in this story Hercules can be seen as "Virtue" conquering evil.

her husband's love. It had, however, been imbued with a deadly poison. At his death, according to Ovid's account, Hercules was transformed into a heavenly constellation.

Herculēs vōta* Iōvī parābat ubi Fāma, quae vērīs addere falsa semper amat et ē minimō* sua per mendācia* crescit, praecessit ad Dēianīrae aurēs*. Huic dīxit Fāma Herculem, virum eius, fēminae alterīus amōrem sentīre. Quae fāma adeō illam terruit ut multās lacrimās* fūderit. Mox deinde sēcum agitat, "Cūr ego fleō? Altera illa nondum* thalamōs* tenet meōs. Iniūriam istī inveniām."

In partēs animus variās abiit: cōnstituit tandem* vestem, quam centaurus* saevus ōlim suō sanguine imbuerat, mittere ut vīrēs* redderet amōrī. Servōque ignārō quid trādat, nescia ipsa dolōrem suum trādit, et servum dōna dare virō iubet. Accipit vestem nescius hērōs*.

Venēnō* vestis celeriter incaluērunt* Herculea membra. Dum potuit suā gemitum* virtūte repressit, sed tantus erat dolor ut tolerāre nōn potuerit implēveritque suīs vōcibus Oetam*. Nec potuit vestem ā membrīs scindere lētiferam*. Nēquīquam* plōrat* dolōrem, altamque per Oetam* saucius errat. Arborēs tandem magnās struit* in pyram subditque flammam.

Quae dum contemptōrem* petēbat suum, Iuppiter constituit sē līberātūrum esse dīvīnam suī fīliī partem ā parte hūmānā. Utque serpēns* quī posuit pellem* senectam* et luxuriāre* solet flōrēreque pelle* novā, sīc ubi hūmāna exuit* membra, parte dīvīnā floruit incēpitque

1: **vōtum**, **-ī** *n* prayer, offering
2: **minimus**, **-a**, **-um** very small
mendācium, **-ī** *n* lie, falsehood
3: **auris**, **-is** *f* ear
4: **lacrima**, **-ae** *f* tear
5: **nōndum** (adverb) not yet
5–6: **thalamus**, **-ī** *m* bedroom; marriage (s. or pl.)
7: **tandem** (adverb) finally
7–8: **centaurus**, **-ī** *m* centaur (mythical creature, half-man and half-beast)
8: **vīrēs** (acc. *f* pl.) strength
10: **hērōs** (nom. *m* sing.) hero
11: **venēnum**, **-ī** *n* poison
incalescō, **-ere**, **incaluī** grow warm or hot
12: **gemitum** (acc. *m* sing.) moan, groan, complaint
13, 14–15: **Oeta**, **-ae** *f* Mt. Oeta (mountain in central Greece)
14: **lētifer**, **-fera**, **-ferum** deadly
nēquīquam (adverb) in vain
plōrō, **-āre** lament; weep over, bewail
15: **struō**, **-ere**, **struxī**, **structus** pile up, construct
17: **contemptor**, **-tōris** *m* one who puts small value upon something; a despiser, scorner
18–19: **serpēns**, **serpentis** *m* serpent
19: **pellis**, **-is** *f* skin
senectus, **-a**, **-um** old, aged
luxuriō, **-āre** be wanton or luxuriant, revel, indulge to excess
20: **exuō**, **-ere**, **exuī**, **exūtus** strip off, uncover, cast off

crescere et dignus esse augustā* gravitāte*. Tum pater deōrum fīlium suum, stellam novam, in caelō posuit.

(After Ovid, Metamorphoses *9.136ff.)*

3. For the philosopher and playwright Lucius Annaeus Seneca (c. A.D. 1–65), Hercules is the ultimate Stoic saint, the embodiment of **virtūs**. Hercules' **virtūs** is exemplified by the fortitude with which he endured the labors imposed (often unjustly) upon him as well as by the manner in which he confronted his own monstrous death. In the following passage from Seneca's tragedy *Hercules Oetaeus*, the fiery death of the hero is described by Philoctetes, who had ignited the funeral pyre at the request of Hercules:

Caucasum* aut Pindum* aut Athon*
ardēre crēdās:
nūllus erat sonus, tantus sonāvit ignis.
Tȳphōn* in illā positus* pyrā ingemuisset* ipse.
Inter vapōrēs* positus* et flammae minīs*
immōtus*, inconcussus*, in neutrum latus*
vertit membra; nōbīs addidit
animum ministrīs*. Stupet* vulgus;
vix* habent flammae fidem*,
tam placida* frōns est, tanta māiestās* virō.

(After Hercules Oetaeus *1729ff.)*

4. The Italian writer and poet Giovanni Boccaccio (1313–1375) reportedly devoted the last twenty-five years of his life to compiling the *Genealogy of the Gods*, which was to become "the chief link between the mythology of the Middle Ages and the Renaissance."[7] Here Boccaccio counts the death

21: **augustus**, **-a**, **-um** majestic, venerable, worthy of honor
gravitās, **-tātis** *f* weight, heaviness; seriousness

1: **Caucasus** and **Pindus** are mountain ranges in southern Soviet Union and central Greece, respectively; **Athos** is a mountain in northeastern Greece.
4: **Tȳphōn**, **-ōnis** *m* a giant whom Jupiter struck with lightning and buried under Mt. Aetna (in Sicily)
4, 5: **positus**, **-a**, **-um** placed
4: **ingemō**, **-ere**, **-uī**, **-itus** groan aloud, wail
5: **vapor**, **-ōris** *m* vapor, steam, smoke
minae, **-ārum** *f* pl. threats
6: **immōtus**, **-a**, **-um** unmoved
inconcussus, **-a**, **-um** unshaken
latus, **lateris** *n* side, flank
8: **minister**, **-strī** *m* attendant, helper
nōbīs ministrīs (dative) "(to) us, his assistants"
stupeō, **-ēre**, **-uī** be stunned, benumbed; gaze with wonder at something
9: **vix** (adverb) hardly, scarcely
fidem (acc. *f* sing.) confidence
10: **placidus**, **-a**, **-um** calm, peaceful, placid
māiestās, **-tātis** *f* majesty, grandeur, dignity

[7] Jean Seznec, *The Survival of the Pagan Gods: the mythological tradition and its place in Renaissance humanism and art*, translated by B. F. Sessions (Princeton, 1953) 220.

of Cacus as the seventeenth labor, out of a total of thirty-one, and records the death and apotheosis of Hercules:

Septiōdecimō labōre* Cācum fūrem* Herculēs interēmit*. . . . Trīgēsimumprīmum* labōrem superāre nōn potuit. Nam postquam cetera superāvit mōnstra, illum superāvit fīliae Eurytī* amor. Dēianira autem meminit mūnera* quae ā Nessō centaurō ōlim accēperat; ipsa crēdēbat vērum esse id quod ille centaurus moritūrus* dīxerat. Ut Herculis amōrem revocāret*, mīsit illī clam* centaurī vestem, quam Herculēs induit*. Sīc sūdor* resolvit* sanguinem venēnātum* per* porōs* quōs amplificāverat* calor* ut in praecordia* flueret sanguis: eumque in dolōrem adeō intolerābilem* incendit ut morī* cōnstitueret. Ille cōnstruxit* in* Oetā monte* pyram, et sagittās* et pharētram* dedit Philoctētī.* Tum in pyram cōnscendit* Philoctētemque eam incendere iussit; et sīc fessam animam exhalāvit.* Hunc Seneca in tragoediā* *Herculis Oetaeī* in caelum Iovem accēpisse dīcit. Tum Iuppiter eum et Iūnōnem conciliāvit* et eī despōnsāvit* Hēbem* iuventūtis* deam et Iūnōnis fīliam. Homērus autem in Odysseā dīcit Ulyssem eum apud inferōs* vīdīsse. Dīcit tamen nōn eum quem vidēbat Ulyssēs Herculem vērum esse sed eius īdōlum*.

(Genealogiae deōrum gentilium, *13.1)*

1: **septiōdecimō labōre** "in the seventeenth labor"
fur, fūris *m* thief
interimō, -ere, -emi, -emptus destroy, kill
1–2: **trīgēsimumprimus, -a, -um** thirty-first
3: **Eurytus, -ī** *m* Eurytus
4: **mūnus, -eris** *n* gift, offering
5: **moritūrus, -a, -um** about to die
6: **revocō, re- + vocō, -are** recall
clam (adverb) secretly
induō, -ere, induī, indūtus put on (clothing)
7: **sūdor, -ōris** *m* sweat
resolvō, -ere, -solvī, -solūtus loosen, relax, open
venēnātus, -a, -um poisoned
per (prep. + acc.) through
porus, -ī *m* passage, channel in the body
7–8: **amplificō, -āre** enlarge, make wide
8: **calor, -ōris** *m* warmth, heat
praecordia, -orum *n* pl. internal organs
9: **intolerabilem** (acc. *m* sing. adj.) intolerable
morī (infinitive) "to die"
construō, -ere, -struxī, -structus construct, build
9–10: **in Oetā monte** "on Mt. Oeta"
10: **sagitta, -ae** *f* arrow
pharētra, -ae *f* quiver
10, 11: **Philoctētēs, -is** *m* a proper name (Hercules' friend and the narrator of passage 3.)
11: **cōnscendō, -ere, cōnscendī, cōnscēnsus** ascend, climb
12: **exhalō, -āre** exhale; breathe out one's life; expire
tragoedia, -ae *f* tragedy
13: **conciliō, -āre** reconcile
13–14: **despōnsō, -āre** betroth
14: **Hēbem** (acc. *f* sing.) Hebe
iuventūs, -tūtis *f* youth
15: **apud inferōs** "among the dead," "in the Underworld"
16: **īdōlum, -ī** *n* image, apparition

Probanda VII–IX

A. Translate the following verbs. Then, retaining the person and number of the original, write a synopsis of each verb.
Example: **abīs**, you are going away.

INDICATIVE

Present	abīs
Imperfect	abībās
Future	abībis
Perfect	abīstī (alternative form: abīvistī)
Pluperfect	abierās (abīverās)
Future Perfect	abieris (abīveris)

SUBJUNCTIVE

Present	abeās
Imperfect	abīrēs
Perfect	abieris (abīveris)
Pluperfect	abīssēs (abīvissēs)

adimus	superant	prōdit	funditis
venit	flēmus	crescō	discimus
reddunt	putās	decet	vertit
stās	trāditis	premunt	gerimus
pereō	student	scindit	constituit

B. Identify the case(s) and number(s) of each noun and then translate.
Example: **vestibus**, dative or ablative plural; to/for or by/with cloaks.

temporis	populō	sopōrī	brevitās
arborum	generis	patriae	virtūtum
cōnsulis	boum	lēgēs	multitūdo
labōre	mōrēs	oculīs	vulgus
sanguis	ōtiī	amōrī	ignis

C. Add to the nouns of the preceding exercise the appropriate form of the following demonstrative or relative adjectives: **hic**, **ille**, **iste**, **ipse**, **is**, **īdem**, **quī**.
Example: **vestibus**: hīs/hīs; illīs/illīs; istīs/istīs; ipsīs/ipsīs; eīs/eīs; eīsdem/eīsdem; quibus/quibus.

D. Translate the following sentences into Latin.

1. They say (**trādō**, **-ere**) that Hercules, who was a man of great virtue, at one time came to Rome with a herd of beautiful cattle.
2. Many people thought that Jupiter did the thing that was fitting.
3. The Romans said they would return (**redeō**) home so that they themselves would restore (**reddō**) their native land.
4. I myself will comply (**gerō** + appropriate construction) with you (s.) if you will comply with me.
5. You (pl.) know that we will comply (**gerō** + appropriate construction) with you if you will comply with us and our friends.

6. I do not know how he will behave (**gerō** + appropriate construction) in this office.
7. After we had carried out (**gerō** + appropriate construction) our responsibilities, we freed ourselves from work and went to the countryside.
8. The Roman people established their own laws and customs; the gods established their human rights.
9. One of you (pl.) will want to turn us away, but our friends will not turn away from us.
10. So (**adeō**) decorous was her speech that she left Rome and went (**adeō**) home filled with glory.

Probanda VII–IX: Key

A.

we approach	*he comes*	*they give back*	*you (s.) stand*
adīmus	venit	reddunt	stās
adībāmus	veniēbat	reddēbant	stābās
adībimus	veniet	reddent	stābis
adiimus (adīvimus)	vēnit	reddidērunt	stetistī
adierāmus (adīverāmus)	vēnerat	reddiderant	steterās
adierimus (adīverimus)	vēnerit	reddiderint	steteris
adeāmus	veniat	reddeant	stēs
adīrēmus	venīret	redderent	stārēs
adierimus (adīverimus)	vēnerit	reddiderint	steteris
adīssēmus (adīvissēmus)	vēnisset	reddidissent	stetissēs

I am dying	*they overcome*	*we weep*	*you (s.) think*
pereō	superant	flēmus	putās
perībam	superābant	flēbāmus	putābās
perībō	superābunt	flēbimus	putābis
periī (perīvī)	suberāvērunt	flēvimus	putāvistī
perieram (perīveram)	superāverant	flēverāmus	putāverās
perierō (perīverō)	superāverint	flēverimus	putāveris
peream	superent	fleāmus	putēs
perīrem	superārent	flērēmus	putārēs
perieris (perīveris)	superāverint	flēverimus	putāveris
perissem (perīvissem)	superāvissent	flēvissēmus	putāvissēs

you (pl.) transmit, hand over	*they are eager*	*he goes forth*	*I am growing*
trāditis	student	prōdit	crescō
trādēbātis	studēbant	prōdībat	crescēbam
trādētis	studēbunt	prōdībit	crescam
trādidistis	studuērunt	prōdiit (prōdīvit)	crēvī
trādiderātis	studuerant	prōdierat (prōdīverat)	crēveram
trādideritis	studuerint	prōdierit (prōdīverit)	crēverō

15.25/16 A

Quizzes to make up: #8, #10

Quiz #11
Latin 1
Section 16129
23 Apr 1990

name deven desai

I. Conjugate eō, īre in the second person singular

ACTIVE INDICATIVE:

PRESENT īs

IMPERFECT ībās

FUTURE ībis

PERFECT īstī

PLUPERFECT ierās

FUTURE PERFECT ieris

In this conjugation, whenever an initial "i" is followed

ACTIVE SUBJUNCTIVE:

PRESENT	eās
IMPERFECT	īrēs
PERFECT	~~īerās~~ ieris
PLUPERFECT	~~ī~~ ~~ī~~ īssēs

immediately of vowel, the initial "i" is short. ("It" might help you remember —)

II. Decline dux, ducis in all cases, singular and plural. Include long marks.

	singular	plural
nom.	dux	ducēs
gen.	ducis	ducum
dat.	ducī	ducibus
acc.	ducem	ducēs
abl.	duce	ducibus
voc.	dux	ducēs

trādātis	studeant	prōdeat	crescam
trāderētis	studērent	prōdīret	crescerem
trādideritis	studuerint	prōdierit (prōdīverit)	crēverim
trādidissētis	studuissent	prōdīsset (prōdivesset)	crēvissem

it is fitting	*they press*	*he splits*	*you (pl.) pour*
decet	premunt	scindit	funditis
decēbat	premēbant	scindēbat	fundēbātis
decēbit	prement	scindet	fundētis
decuit	pressērunt	scidit	fūdistis
decuerat	presserant	sciderat	fūderātis
decuerit	presserint	sciderit	fūderitis
deceat	premant	scindat	fundātis
decēret	premerent	scinderet	funderētis
decuerit	presserint	sciderit	fūderitis
decuisset	pressissent	scidisset	fūdissētis

we learn	*he turns*	*we carry*	*he decides*
discimus	vertit	gerimus	cōnstituit
discēbāmus	vertēbat	gerēbāmus	cōnstituēbat
discēmus	vertet	gerēmus	cōnstituet
didicimus	vertit	gessimus	cōnstituit
didicerāmus	verterat	gesserāmus	cōnstituerat
didicerimus	verterit	gesserimus	cōnstituerit
discāmus	vertat	gerāmus	cōnstituat
discerēmus	verteret	gererēmus	cōnstitueret
didicerimus	verterit	gesserimus	cōnstituerit
didicissēmus	vertisset	gessissēmus	cōnstituisset

B. temporis, gen. s., of time
arborum, gen. pl., of trees
cōnsulis, gen. s., of the consul
labōre, abl. s., by/with work
sanguis, nom. s., blood
populō, dat. or abl. s., to/for or by/with the people
generis, gen. s., of the kind or race
boum, gen. pl., of the cattle
mōrēs, nom. or acc. pl., customs or character
ōtiī, gen. s., of peace or leisure
sopōrī, dat. s., to/for sleep
patriae, gen. s. or nom. pl., of the native land or native lands
lēgēs, nom. or acc. pl., laws
oculīs, dat. or abl. pl., to/for or by/with eyes
amōrī, dat. s., to/for love
brevitās, nom. s., brevity
virtūtum, gen. pl., of virtues

multitūdo, nom. s., multitude
vulgus, nom. or acc. s., the common people, the great multitude of common people
ignis, nom. or gen. s., fire, of the fire

C. temporis: huius; illīus, istīus; ipsīus; eius; eiusdem; cuius
arborum: hārum; illārum; istārum; ipsārum; eārum; eārundem; quārum
cōnsulis: huius, illīus; istīus; ipsīus; eius; eiusdem; cuius
labōre: hōc; illō; istō; ipsō; eō; eōdem; quō
sanguis: hic; ille; iste; ipse; is; īdem; quī
populō: huic/hōc; illī/illō; istī/istō; ipsī/ipsō; eī/eō; eīdem/eōdem; cui/quō
generis: huius; illīus; istīus; ipsīus; eius; eiusdem; cuius
boum (*m* or *f*): hārum/hōrum; illārum/illōrum; istārum/istōrum; ipsārum/ipsōrum; eārum/eōrum; eārundem/eōrundem; quārum/quōrum
mōrēs: hī/hōs; illī/illōs; istī/istōs; ipsī/ipsōs; eī/eōs; eīdem/eōsdem; quī/quōs
ōtiī: huius; illīus; istīus; ipsīus; eius; eiusdem; cuius
sopōrī: huic; illī; istī; ipsī; eī; eīdem; cui
patriae: huius/hae; illīus/illae; istīus/istae; ipsīus/ipsae; eius/eae; eiusdem/eaedem; cuius/quae
lēgēs: hae/hās; illae/illās; istae/istās; ipsae/ipsās; eae/eās; eaedem/eāsdem; quae/quās
oculīs: hīs/hīs; illīs/illīs; istīs/istīs; ipsīs/ipsīs; eīs/eīs; eīsdem/eīsdem; quibus/quibus
amōrī: huic; illī; istī; ipsī; eī; eīdem; cui
brevitās: haec; illa; ista; ipsa; ea; eadem; quae
virtūtum: hārum; illārum; istārum; ipsārum; eārum; eārundem; quārum
multitūdo: haec; illa; ista; ipsa; ea; eadem; quae
vulgus: hoc/hoc; illud/illud; istud/istud; ipsum/ipsum; id/id; idem/idem; quod/quod
ignis: hic/huius; ille/illīus; iste/istīus; ipse/ipsīus; is/eius; idem/eiusdem; quī/cuius

D.
1. Trādunt Herculem, virum magnae virtūtis, ūnō tempore Rōmam cum suō grege pulchrārum boum advēnisse.
2. Multī putāvērunt Iovem fēcisse id quod decēret (or: id quod decorum esset).
3. Rōmānī dīxērunt sē domum reditūrōs esse ut ipsī patriam suam redderent.
4. Ego ipse tibi mōrem geram sī tū mihi mōrem gerēs.
5. Scītis nōs vōbīs mōrem gessūrōs esse sī vōs nōbīs mōrem gessūrī sitis.
6. Nesciō quō modo in hōc officiō sē gessūrus sit.
7. Postquam officia nostra gessimus, nōs ā negōtiō līberāvimus et rūs adiimus.
8. Populus Rōmānus suās lēgēs mōrēsque cōnstituit, sed dī eōrum iūra cōnstituērunt.
9. Ūnus vestrum nōs āvertere volet, sed amīcī nostrī sē ā nōbīs nōn āvertent.
10. Adeō decora erat eius ōrātiō (or: Eius ōrātiō adeō decēbat) ut Rōmā abīret et domum adīret glōriā (or: glōriae) plēna.

Passive Voice; Ablative Case (2)

Passive Voice

In Latin, as in English, verbs have an active voice and a passive voice. When the voice of a verb is active, the subject of the verb is the agent, that is, the person or thing doing or responsible for the action of the verb. In the sentence, **Dēianīra vestem trādit**, Deianira is the person who hands over the deadly garment, and hence the subject of the active verb **trādit**. The same action can be expressed in the passive voice: **Vestis ā Dēianīrā trāditur**, "The garment is being handed over by Deianira." When the verb is passive, the thing that was the object of the active verb (the garment) becomes the subject of the passive verb, and the agent—the person handing over the garment (Deianira)—must be expressed by the ablative case.

Present Passive System

Thus far you have learned only the active personal endings of verbs. The passive endings for tenses formed on the present stem are:

PERSON	SINGULAR	PLURAL
First	**-r**	**-mur**
Second	**-ris**, **-re**	**-minī**
Third	**-tur**	**-ntur**

The imperative passive endings for tenses formed on the present stem are -**re** for the second person singular, and -**minī** for the second person plural.

If we add these endings to our model verbs, we get:

INDICATIVE

PRESENT

amor	teneor	dūcor	capior	audior
amāris/ amāre	tenēris/ tenēre	dūceris/ dūcere	caperis/ capere	audīris/ audīre
amātur	tenētur	dūcitur	capitur	audītur

amāmur	tenēmur	dūcimur	capimur	audīmur
amāminī	tenēminī	dūciminī	capiminī	audīminī
amantur	tenentur	dūcuntur	capiuntur	audiuntur
		IMPERFECT		
amābar	tenēbar	dūcēbar	capiēbar	audiēbar
amābāris/ amābāre	tenēbāris/ tenēbāre	dūcēbāris/ dūcēbāre	capiēbāris/ capiēbāre	audiēbāris/ audiēbāre
amābātur	tenēbātur	dūcēbātur	capiēbātur	audiēbātur
amābāmur	tenēbāmur	dūcēbāmur	capiēbāmur	audiēbāmur
amābāminī	tenēbāminī	dūcēbāminī	capiēbāminī	audiēbāminī
amābantur	tenēbantur	dūcēbantur	capiēbantur	audiēbantur
		FUTURE		
amābor	tenēbor	dūcar	capiar	audiar
amāberis/ amābere	tenēberis/ tenēbere	dūcēris/ dūcēre	capiēris/ capiēre	audiēris/ audiēre
amābitur	tenēbitur	dūcētur	capiētur	audiētur
amābimur	tenēbimur	dūcēmur	capiēmur	audiēmur
amābiminī	tenēbiminī	dūcēminī	capiēminī	audiēminī
amābuntur	tenēbuntur	dūcentur	capientur	audientur

SUBJUNCTIVE

		PRESENT		
amer	tenear	dūcar	capiar	audiar
amēris/ amēre	teneāris/ teneāre	dūcāris/ dūcāre	capiāris/ capiāre	audiāris/ audiāre
amētur	teneātur	dūcātur	capiātur	audiātur
amēmur	teneāmur	dūcāmur	capiāmur	audiāmur
amēminī	teneāminī	dūcāminī	capiāminī	audiāminī
amentur	teneantur	dūcantur	capiantur	audiantur
		IMPERFECT		
amārer	tenērer	dūcerer	caperer	audīrer
amārēris/ amārēre	tenērēris/ tenērēre	dūcerēris/ dūcerēre	caperēris/ caperēre	audīrēris/ audīrēre
amārētur	tenērētur	dūcerētur	caperētur	audīrētur
amārēmur	tenērēmur	dūcerēmur	caperēmur	audīrēmur
amārēminī	tenērēminī	dūcerēminī	caperēminī	audīrēminī
amārentur	tenērentur	dūcerentur	caperentur	audīrentur
		IMPERATIVE		
amāre	tenēre	dūcere	capere	audīre
amāminī	tenēminī	dūciminī	capiminī	audīminī

The first person singular passive indicative forms translate "I am being loved, held, led, seized, or heard," "I was being loved, held, led, seized, or heard," and "I shall be loved, held, led, seized, or heard," respectively. As in the active voice, the passive subjunctive forms cannot be translated out of context. Observe that:

1. In the present and future indicative tenses, the first person singular ending -**r** is added to the entire first person singular active form: **amō** + -**r**; **amābō** + -**r**. The vowel that precedes final -**r** or -**ntur** is short.

2. The second person singular ending -**ris** is sometimes replaced by an alternate ending, -**re**, which can be confused with the present active infinitive (**amāre** for **amāris**; **tenēre** for **tenēris**; **dūcere** for **dūceris**; **capere** for **caperis**; **audīre** for **audīris**). In such cases, context alone will determine whether it is an infinitive or a finite verb. Note that -**re** can also be the singular passive imperative ending.

3. The short vowel -**i**- before -**r**- becomes short -**e**-, both in the -**bi**- sign of the future (**amāberis**) and in the present stem of the third declension verbs (**dūceris**; **caperis**). As a result, the only difference between the present **dūceris** and the future **dūcēris** is the length of the -**e**- (the future tense has a long -**ē**-). The future tense of third conjugation -**iō** verbs should cause no difficulty, however, since the future has an -**i**- before the -**ē**-: **capiēris**: "you will be captured."

4. Every ending except the second person plural (-**minī**) contains an -**r**.

Ablative of Personal Agent. The person or thing doing or responsible for the action of the passive verb is indicated by the ablative case. If a person (or a thing personified) is responsible for the action, the ablative of personal agent, always introduced by the preposition **ā** or **ab**, must be used:

Vestis **ā Dēianīrā** trādētur.	The garment will be handed over *by Deianira*.
Bovēs āvertuntur **ā Cācō**.	The cattle are being turned away *by Cacus*.

As you already know, the means or instrument by which the action is accomplished is expressed by the ablative of means, which never takes a preposition:

Cibō vīnōque opprimitur.	He is being overcome *by (means of) food and wine*.
Pulchritūdine boum capiēbātur.	He was captivated by *the beauty* of the cattle.
Bovēs **ā Cācō** caudīs trahēbantur.	The cattle were being dragged *by Cacus* (agent) *by means of their tails* (instrument).

Perfect Passive System

The perfect passive forms of all verbs consist of the fourth principal part of the verb plus the appropriate form of the verb **sum**, **esse**. The fourth principal part of the verb is in fact the perfect passive participle. You have already encountered the future active participle in Chapter V. There you learned that a participle is a verbal adjective, which means that it has voice and tense, like all verbs, and that, like all adjectives, it agrees in case, number and gender with the noun or pronoun it modifies. Consider the fourth principal parts of our model verbs:

DECLENSION	PARTICIPLE	TRANSLATION
First	**amātus**, **-a**, **-um**	loved (in a state of having been loved)
Second	**tentus**, **-a**, **-um**	held (in a state of having been held)
Third	**ductus**, **-a**, **-um**	led (in a state of having been led)
Third -iō	**captus**, **-a**, **-um**	seized (in a state of having been seized)
Fourth	**audītus**, **-a**, **-um**	heard (in a state of having been heard)

The voice of each of these participles is passive, and the tense is past. When the present tense of **sum** is added to any of these participles, the Latin says that someone or something is in a state of having been loved, held, led, seized, or heard, and therefore the Latin is actually saying that someone or something has been loved, held, led, seized or heard:

amātus est	he has been loved
tentum est	it has been held
ductī sunt	they (*m*) have been led
capta sunt	they (*n*) have been seized
audītae sumus	we (*f*) have been heard

Observe how the participles agree in number and gender with the subject of the verb. The perfect passive system of **amō** is formed, then, as follows:

INDICATIVE	SUBJUNCTIVE
PERFECT	
amātus sum	amātus sim
amātus es	amātus sīs
amātus est	amātus sit
amātī sumus	amātī sīmus
amātī estis	amātī sītis
amātī sunt	amātī sint
PLUPERFECT	
amātus eram	amātus essem
amātus erās	amātus essēs
amātus erat	amātus esset
amātī erāmus	amātī essēmus
amātī erātis	amātī essētis
amātī erant	amātī essent
FUTURE PERFECT	
amātus erō	——
amātus eris	
amātus erit	
amātī erimus	
amātī eritis	
amātī erunt	

The first person singular passive indicative in the perfect, pluperfect, and future perfect translates, respectively, "I have been/was loved," "I had been loved," and "I shall have been loved." The perfect and pluperfect passive subjunctive, like other tenses of the subjunctive, cannot be translated out of context.

Passive Infinitives

Infinitives, too, can be active or passive. The present passive infinitive of first, second, and fourth conjugation verbs is formed by changing the final **-e** of the present active infinitive to a long **-ī**:

Present Active Infinitive	Present Passive Infinitive
amāre, to love	**amārī**, to be loved
tenēre, to hold	**tenērī**, to be held
audīre, to hear	**audīrī**, to be heard

The present passive infinitive of third conjugation verbs, including third **-iō** verbs, is formed by replacing the entire **-ere** ending of the present active infinitive with a long **-ī**:

Present Active Infinitive	Present Passive Infinitive
dūcere, to lead	**dūcī**, to be led
capere, to seize	**capī**, to be seized
trādere, to hand over	**trādī**, to be handed over
agere, to do, make	**agī**, to be done, be made

The perfect passive infinitive for all conjugations consists of the perfect passive participle and the infinitive **esse**:

Perfect Active Infinitive	Perfect Passive Infinitive
amāvisse, to have loved	**amātus**, **-a**, **-um esse**, to have been loved
tenuisse, to have held	**tentus**, **-a**, **-um esse**, to have been held
dūxisse, to have led	**ductus**, **-a**, **-um esse**, to have been led
cēpisse, to have seized	**captus**, **-a**, **-um esse**, to have been seized
audīvisse, to have heard	**audītus**, **-a**, **-um esse**, to have been heard

Ablatives of Separation, Agent, Source, and Cause

As you learned in Chapter III, "ablative" can mean "the taking away" case. Accordingly, one of the main functions of this case is to signify separation. Closely related to the ablative of separation is the ablative of agent, which you have just learned, and the ablatives of source and cause, which are described below. These four categories are frequently referred to as the "true" ablative, or the "ablative proper."

Ablative of Source. The ablative of source signifies the source from which anything is derived. It is usually introduced by a preposition:

> Nōn accipiunt mala **ex scholīs**.
> They don't acquire bad habits *at/from school(s)*. (Source)
> Periit **ab amōre**.
> She died of *love*. (Love here is seen as the source of her destruction.)

Words denoting birth or origin—the best example is **nātus**, which is actually a perfect participle meaning "having been born"—often govern the ablative of source, with or without a preposition:

Iōve nātus	the son *of Jupiter* (literally, born *from Jupiter*)
Ex mē nātus nōn est.	He is not *my* son (literally, He was not born *from me*).

The material of which something consists is indicated by the closely related ablative of material, usually introduced by a preposition.

> Templum **dē marmore** pōnam.
> I shall build a temple of *marble*. (Material)
> Valvae erant **ex aurō atque ebore** perfectae.
> The doors were finely made *of gold and ivory*. (Material)

Ablative of Cause. The ablative of cause, expressed with or without a preposition, conveys the motive or emotion of the person acting:

Amōre periit.	She died *because of love*.
Ardeō **dolōre et īra**.	I am aflame *with* (i.e., because of) *pain and anger*.
Ex suīs factīs saucius erat.	He was wounded *because of his own deeds*.

As you can see, some of these ablatives overlap. Source and cause are often difficult to distinguish, as in the sentence, "she died of love," where it is a question of interpretation whether love was the source or the cause of her destruction. Cause is also frequently confused with the more common ablative of means or instrument. In such a case, you will have to decide which makes the most sense in context: did she die because of love or by means of love, or was her death the outgrowth of that love? In an example such as this, the best translation might reflect more than one of these possibilities.

Scrībenda

A. Identify the following forms and translate all but the subjunctive forms:

1. reprimeris / reprimēris / reprimāre / reprimī / repressus / repressus es / repressus essēs

1. reprimeris	repressus
reprimēris	repressus es
reprimāre	repressus essēs
reprimī	

2. geritur — gestae
   gerētur — gesta sunt
   gerātur — gestus sit
   gerī
3. conclūduntur — conclūditur
   conclūsī sunt — conclūdī
   conclūsae sunt — conclūsus esse
   conclūsus est
4. mutāmur — mutātī
   mutēmur — mutātī sunt
   mutārī — mutāta erō
   mutāre

B. Write a synopsis of each of the following in the passive voice only; translate the indicative forms:

fundō: third person sing.
trahō: second person sing.
līberō: third person sing.
fleō: first person pl.
vertō: second person pl.
sentiō: third person pl.

C. Translate the following sentences into English:

1. Ita studēte ut nōn lingua exerceātur sed ut animus sapientiā impleātur.
2. Animus eius illō librō mutātus est.
3. Dīcitur virōs clārōs docuisse.
4. Virī clārī ad eius scholam vēnisse dīcuntur.
5. Illī librī nōn ab illō sed ab illīus discipulīs scrīptī sunt.
6. Multa hīc invenientur quae nōn ā mē sed ab aliīs trādita sunt.
7. Brevitās inerit sī narratiōnis initium sūmētur unde sūmī dēbet. (**sūmo**, **-ere**, **sumpsī**, **sumptus**, take up, assume)
8. Brevitās falsa ab ōrātōre vitētur.
9. Ōrātōris officium est dē eīs posse dīcere quae mōribus et lēgibus cōnstitūta sunt.
10. Puerī quasī in hortō plantātī sunt ut crescerent.
11. Sīc arbor plantāta est ut crescere nōn possit.
12. Vestis servō ā Dēianīrā trādita est.
13. Herculēs sopōre sīc oppressus est ut bovēs ā Cācō āvertī nōn sēnserit.
14. Vestigia versa esse vidēbantur.
15. Cācus pulchritūdine boum adeō captus est ut in spēluncam eās trāxerit.
16. Pyram ascendit incendīque iussit. (**ascendō**, **-ere**, **ascendī**, **ascēnsus**, climb, ascend)
17. Decet Herculem flērī. Decet Herculem flēre.

D. Translate the following sentences into Latin:

1. At that time, the cattle were being led across the river.
2. The cattle had been led by their tails so that they would not be found by Hercules.
3. Will the Roman people be moved by her speech?
4. Hercules was not the kind of person who would be overcome by pain.
5. The slave who carried Deianira's gift was killed by his wounded master.

Verba tenenda

Verbs

colō, **-ere**, **coluī**, **cultus** cultivate; inhabit; cherish; worship
comedō, **-ere**, **comēdī**, **comēsus** eat up, consume; waste
contineō, **-ēre**, **-uī**, **-tentus** hold together, enclose, contain, limit, retain
dēsinō, **-ere**, **dēsiī** (or **dēsīvī**), **dēsitum** (+ infinitive) cease, desist, stop; end, terminate
egeō, **-ēre**, **eguī**, —— (+ abl.) need, lack, be without
excēdō, **-ere**, **excessī**, **excessus** go from, depart
expellō, **-ere**, **expulī**, **expulsus** throw out, expel
fingō, **-ere**, **finxī**, **fictus** form, fashion; imagine
gignō, **-ere**, **genuī**, **genitus** bring forth, produce, beget; passive: be born, arise
interficiō, **-ere**, **-fēcī**, **-fectus** kill
locō, **-āre**, **-āvī**, **-ātus** place, set, arrange
noceō, **-ēre**, **nocuī**, **nocitus** (+ dat.) do harm to
pellō, **-ere**, **pepulī**, **pulsus** push, hurl, drive out
perficiō, **-ere**, **-fēcī**, **fectus** accomplish, complete, do thoroughly, perfect
prōsum, **prōdesse**, **prōfuī**, **prōfutūrus** (+ dat.) be useful to, do good to, benefit
pugnō, **-āre**, **-āvī**, **-ātus** fight
rapiō, **-ere**, **rapuī**, **raptus** seize and carry off, carry off by force; snatch
regō, **-ere**, **rexī**, **rectus** guide, direct, rule, manage
relinquō, **-ere**, **relīquī**, **relictus** leave, abandon, leave behind
tollō, **-ere**, **sustulī**, **sublātus** lift, elevate; destroy
vincō, **-ere**, **vīcī**, **victus** conquer, subdue

Nouns

āēr, **āeris** *m* air
aetās, **aetātis** *f* time of life, age; lifetime of a human being; a generation, an age
anima, **-ae** *f* breath of life; soul
arma, **-ōrum** *n* pl. weapons
beneficium, **-ī** *n* kindness, favor, benefit
cīvitās, **-tātis** *f* state, the body politic
cōgitātiō, **-tiōnis** *f* thinking, thought
figūra, **-ae** *f* form, image; symbol
forma, **-ae** *f* form, shape
honor, **-ōris** *m* honor, esteem; public office
locus, **-ī** *m* (in plural, becomes neuter: **loca**, **-ōrum**) place
locī, **locōrum** *m* pl. passages (in literature)
lux, **lūcis** *f* light of the sun and other heavenly bodies; daylight, light
mīles, **mīlitis** *m* soldier
nātus, **-ī** *m* son
opus, **operis** *n* work, labor
patrimōnium, **-iī** *n* an estate inherited from a father; inheritance
pax, **pācis** *f* peace
perīculum, **-ī** *n* danger
potentia, **-ae** *f* might, force, power
ratiō, **-iōnis** *f* reckoning, account, calculation; reason, reasoning; system
  ratiōnem reddere give an account
sōl, **sōlis** *m* the sun

Adjectives

aeternus, **-a**, **-um** eternal, without any beginning or end
aliēnus, **-a**, **-um** belonging to someone else; foreign
aliēnus ā + abl. different from
antīquus, **-a**, **-um** old, ancient, former
cunctus, **-a**, **-um** all, all together, entire
impius, **-a**, **-um** irreverent, impious
rectus, **-a**, **-um** straight; right, correct
superbus, **-a**, **-um** haughty, proud
vīvus, **-a**, **-um** alive, living

Adverbs

idcircō on that account, for that reason, therefore
lībenter willingly, gladly
quidem indeed (gives emphasis, usually by contrasting one thing with another) **nē . . . quidem** not even, not . . . either
quoque also, too
sīcut as, as if, just as

Conjunctions

quia (+ indicative or subjunctive) because
vel perhaps; or
vel . . . vel either . . . or
igitur therefore

Prepositions

per (+ acc.) through
apud (+ acc.) at, near; among; at the house of; in the presence of

Notanda

"Cult" and "culture" come from **colō**, as does **agricola**, "a cultivator of the fields."

dēsinō + an infinitive means "stop [doing something]": **Numquam tē amāre dēsinam**; "I will never stop loving you."

Note that **expellō**, a compound of **pellō**, does not have a reduplicated stem for the perfect tense: **expulī** versus **pepulī**. Note as well the English derivatives "impulsive," "repulsive," from the fourth principal part of the verb.

The passive forms of **habeō** can mean "be held," but the meaning "consider," "regard," is particularly common in the passive: **Ista facta impia esse habentur**; "Those deeds are considered irreverent."

The third and fourth principal parts of **tollō** are taken from another verb (**sufferō**). **tollō** can mean "lift up, raise" or "destroy."

The passive forms of **videō** sometimes mean "be seen," but just as often mean "seem," as in **intellegere vidētur**, "he seems to understand." In this construction, the dative of reference is used to indicate who is doing the seeing or thinking: **Mihi intellegere vidētur**; "I think he understands"; literally, "He seems to me to understand."

Caesar's famous words, **vēnī**, **vīdī**, **vīcī**, will help you remember the third principal part of **vincō**. The fourth principal part looks very much like that of **vīvō**, but the long **ī** in **vīvō**, **vīctus** marks the difference.

The word for air, **āēr**, comes directly from Greek. Although its gender is masculine, in early Greek as well as in early Latin it is sometimes feminine. It sometimes has Greek case endings (genitive **āeros** instead of **āeris**, accusative singular **āera** instead of **āerem**). **Āēr** is properly the lower atmosphere, as opposed to **aether**, the pure upper air.

anima is essentially the air that is breathed, and thence comes to mean the breath of life, life itself, and sometimes the non-material part of a being (the soul). The masculine noun **animus** usually signifies the mind as the seat of consciousness, thought, or will.

opus has come directly into English, as a singular noun meaning "a work or composition." The Latin word means the work to be done, a particular piece of work, or work in general. The phrase **opus est** means "there is a need" to someone (in the dative) of something (ablative of separation): **Opus est mihi pecūniā**, "I need money." **Egeō** also governs an ablative of separation: **Egēs pecūniā**, "You need money."

Do not confuse **sōl**, **sōlis**, sun, with the adjective **sōlus**, **-a**, **-um** (or with the noun **sŏlum**, **-ī**, *n* soil—note the short **-ŏ-**).

When **aliēnus**, **-a**, **-um** means "different" or "separate from," it also governs an ablative of separation: **Adeōne aliēnus ā sānitāte videor?**, "Do I seem so far removed from sanity?" **aes aliēnum** literally means "someone else's money (**aes**)," a euphemism for "debt."

rectus is the fourth principal part of **regō**, "guide, direct, rule." Compare our term "ruler" to denote a straight edge used to draw lines.

A person who is **superbus** is full of haughty self-esteem, of excessive pride. The last of the Etruscan kings, deposed in the sixth century B.C. is believed to have had this as his **cognōmen**: Lucius Tarquinius Superbus.

sīcut can be paired with a correlative or another adverb: ***Sicut* caelum dīs, *ita* terra generī hūmānō data est**, "*Just as* heaven has been given to the gods, *so* earth has been given to the human race." With the subjunctive it can mean "just as if": **Sīcut ā suīs audīrī aut vidērī possent**. "Just as if they were able to be heard or seen by their own (people)."

apud is equivalent to the French *chez*, "at the house of," "in the presence of."

The preposition **per** sometimes means "through the instrumentality or agency of," as in **mihi per alium sententiam suam ostendit**, "through the agency of another, he revealed to me his own opinion." As a prefix, **per** adds the idea of "through" (**percurrō**, "run through"), or of thoroughness or completion (**perficiō**), or of upset (**pervertō**).

Ante legenda

Translate:

1. Deus ille fuit quī invēnit id quod nunc sapientia appellātur.
2. Hāc aetāte impiā, nēmō est quī vītam hūmānam tollere in lūcem possit.
3. Illā aetāte, vīta hūmāna ab ūnō virō dīvīnō sublāta est.
4. Cui nunc nocērent ista mōnstra sī ab Hercule nōn victa essent?
5. Mīles armīs philosophusque verbīs cūrās perīculaque ex animīs nostrīs expellit.
6. Haec igitur perīcula cuncta ab illīs expulsa sunt.
7. Nōnne decēbit hunc hominem in numerō deōrum locārī?
8. Virī bonī beneficiīs in caelum famā populīque voluntāte sublātī sunt. (**beneficiīs**: ablative of cause; **voluntās**, **-tātis** *f*, will, choice)
9. Apud Aegyptiōs Herculēs multās aetātēs cultus est. (**Aegyptius**, **-a**, **-um**, Egyptian)
10. Opus est honōrēs petere ut beneficia cīvitātī perficiāmus. Opus est honōrēs petere ut beneficia cīvitātī perficiantur.
11. Apud philosophōs Herculēs est sīcut figūra animae nostrae quī reprimit id quod corporī noceat.
12. Ille Iōve nātus, quī perīcula cuncta superāvit, ā philosophīs antiquīs aut corporis anima aut Sōlis lux esse fingitur.
13. Hercules dē vitiīs ad virtūtem animōs dūcere habēbātur.
14. Sunt quī beneficia deōrum sīcut patrimōnium suum regant. Ab eīs beneficia deōrum quasi patrimōnium regentur.
15. Sī cōnsilium meum vīs, ā dīs* ipsīs cōnstituitur
quid nōbīs prōfutūrum sit.
Dīs* est homō cārior* quam* sibi. Nōs animōrum
. . . caecā* magnāque cupīdine* ductī
coniugium* petimus natōsque.
Dī* autem sōlī nōvērunt quī puerī quālisque*
futūra sit uxor*. . . .
Ōrāre dēbēs, "Mihi sit mēns* sāna in corpore sānō."
Quaere animum quī timōre egeat,
quī spatium vītae extrēmum* sīcut dōnum nātūrae
habeat, quī nōn amōrem sed Herculis labōrēs mālit.

1, 3, 6: **dīs**, **dī**: from **deus**
3: "**homō** is dearer (**cārior**) to **dīs** than (**quam**) to **sibi**."
4: **caecus**, **-a**, **-um** blind
cupīdo, **cupīdinis** *f* desire
5: **coniugium**, **-ī** *n* marriage
6–7: **quālis uxor** (nom. *f*) "what sort of wife"
8: **mēns**, **mentis** *f* the mind
10: **extrēmus**, **-a**, **-um** last, final

Mōnstrō* quod ipse tibi possīs dare:
Est ūna per virtūtem via ad vītam tranquillam*. Nōs tē,
nōs facimus, Fortūna, deamque in caelō locāmus.

(After Juvenal Satire *X.346–366)*

Legenda

Mythology (2): Hercules in Roman Religion and Philosophy

1. Questions about the origins and nature of the gods are often raised in Roman philosophical and poetic works. In the following passage, taken from his didactic poem about the philosophy of Epicurus, the poet Lucretius compares the deeds of Hercules with the accomplishments of Epicurus, and argues that the latter had made the greater contribution to humanity. (The complex word order in this passage is very close to Lucretius' original arrangement.)

Deus ille fuit, deus
quī prīmus* vītae ratiōnem invēnit eam quae
nunc appellātur sapientia, quīque per artem*
fluctibus* ē tantīs vītam tantīsque tenēbrīs*
in tam tranquillā* et tam clārā lūce locāvit.
Confer* enim dīvīna aliōrum antīqua inventa*.
Nam Cerēs* dīcitur frugēs* Līberque* liquōrem*
vītigenum* hominibus instituisse:
sed tamen sine hīs poterat vīta manēre,
ut fāma est aliōs etiam nunc vīvere hominēs. . . .
Herculis antistāre* autem sī facta putābis,
longē ā ratiōne vērā gerēris. . . .
Illa mōnstra ab eō sī nōn victa essent, cui vīva nocērent?

12: **mōnstrō** this is the verb, not the noun.
13: **tranquillus, -a, -um** peaceful, tranquil. (Observe how the order of **ūna per virtūtem via** mimics the meaning.)

2: **prīmus, -a, -um** first
3: **ars, artis** *f* skill, science
4: **fluctibus** (abl. *m* pl.) flood, surge; commotion
tenēbrae, -ārum *f* darkness
5: **tranquillus, -a, -um** quiet, still, calm
6: **confer** (imperative) "Compare"
inventa, -ōrum *n* pl. from **inveniō**
7: **Cerēs, Cerēris** *f* Ceres, goddess of grain
frugēs, -um *f* pl. fruits of the earth
Līber, Līberī *m* Liber, an old Italian deity who presided over planting and the harvest, later identified with Dionysus/Bacchus, god of wine.
liquor, -ōris *m* fluidity, fluid
8: **vītigenus, -a, -um** produced from vines
11: **antistō, -āre** be superior, excel

A group of philosophers engage in a lively discussion. Mosaic from Pompeii.

Illīs bestiīs nunc terra scatit*
per loca quae nōs vitāre possumus.
Sed nisi purgātum* est pectus*, quanta perīcula,
quantae cūrae in nōs quantīque timōrēs insinuābunt*.
Haec igitur quī cuncta ex animō
expulerit dictīs, nōn armīs, nōnne decēbit
hunc hominem locārī in deōrum numerō?

(After Lucretius, Dē rērum nātūrā *5.8ff.)*

14: **scatō, -ere** + abl. abound with, swarm with
16: **purgō, -āre** cleanse, purge, free oneself from
pectus, pectoris *n* the breast; the seat of emotions; the mind
17: **insinuō, -āre** wind or steal into, penetrate

2. In Cicero's philosophical dialogue on the nature of the gods (*Dē nātūrā deōrum*), Balbus, presenting the Stoic position, asserts that the gods were once mortal but became gods because of their good deeds.

Beneficiīs* bonī virī in caelum famā ac voluntāte* sublātī sunt. Hinc* Herculēs, hinc Līber, hinc etiam Rōmulus*, quī post mortem* dī sunt habitī. Aliā ex ratiōne multitūdo deōrum, qui fābulās poētīs suppeditāvērunt,* hominum vītam superstitiōne* implēvērunt. Nam antīqua haec opīniō Graeciam implēvit: victum esse Caelum* ā fīliō Sāturnō*, victumque esse Sāturnum* ipsum ā fīliō Iove.

Sāturnum* autem eum esse voluērunt quī cursum* et conversiōnem* spatiōrum* ac temporum* continēret. Hic deus Graecē id ipsum nōmen habet, nam Chronos* dīcitur, id est spatium* temporis. "Sāturnus" autem est appellātus quod saturārētur* annīs. Ex sē enim nātōs comēdisse fingitur, quia cōnsumit* aetās temporum spatia* annīsque praeteritīs* insaturābiliter* explētur. Victus esse ā Iove quī ā poētīs "pater deōrum hominumque" dīcitur.

(*After* Dē nātūrā deōrum, *II.62ff.*)

3. The Academic philosopher, Cotta, representing the Academic or skeptical school of thought, now refutes the arguments of Balbus:

Intellegō nōs frugēs* Cererem vīnumque Līberum appellāre solēre, sed quem tam insānum esse putās quī illud quod comedat deum esse crēdat? Nam quōs ab hominibus deōs factōs esse dīcis, sī tū reddēs ratiōnem quō modo id fierī* potuerit aut cūr fierī* dēsīverit*, ego discam

1: **beneficiīs** ablative of cause
voluntās, -**tātis** *f* will, choice
hinc (adv.) from here, hence, (**sublātī sunt** is implied.)
2: **Rōmulus**, -ī *m* founder of Rome
post mortem "after death"
3: **suppeditō**, -**āre**, -**āvī**, -**ātus** supply in abundance
4: **superstitiō**, -**iōnis** *f* superstition, excessive fear of the gods
5: **Caelum**, -ī *n* the sky, personified (the Greek *Ouranos*)
5, 6, etc.: **Sāturnus**, -ī *m* Saturn, equivalent of the Greek god *Chronos* (Time) and father of Jupiter.
7: **cursum** (acc. *m* sing.) passage
7–8: **conversiō**, -**iōnis** *f* a turning round; a periodic return.
cursum . . . temporum "the cyclic courses of the times and seasons"
8, 11: **spatium**, -**iī** *n* space
9: **Chronos** see note above on Saturnus
10: **saturō**, -**āre** fill, satisfy, satiate. Balbus gives a "false etymology"—the -**ā**- in **Sāturnus** is long, whereas in this verb and its derivatives it is short—but etymological speculation such as this, however faulty, is widespread throughout classical and medieval times.
quod . . . saturārētur, subjunctive to indicate that this is the reasoning not of the speaker but of the sources he is citing.
11: **cōnsūmō**, -**ere**, -**sumpsī**, -**sumptus** consume, use up
11–12: **prateritus**, -**a**, -**um** (perfect passive participle of **praetereō**) past, gone by
12: **insaturābiliter** (adv.) insatiably

1: **frugēs**, **um** *f* pl. fruits of the earth, crops
4: **fierī** (passive infinitive of **faciō**) "to be done," "to happen"
dēsīverit from **dēsinō**

lībenter. Nōn quidem videō quō modo ille Herculēs in caelum ex illā pyrā vēnerit; quem tamen Homērus apud inferōs* vidērī facit ab Ulixe* sīcut aliōs quī excesserant ā vītā.

Quem quidem Herculem colāmus scīre velim. Eī quī reconditās* litterās indāgant* nōbīs trādunt multōs Herculēs fuisse, et antīquissimum* fuisse Iove nātum—sed Iove antīquissimō*, nam Iovēs quoque multōs in antīquīs Graecōrum litterīs invenimus. [*He names six different Hercules.*] Atque in multīs cīvitātibus potest intellegī virōrum bonōrum memoriam honōre deōrum immortālium* consecrātam* esse ut virtūs populī cresceret. Alabandēnsēs* quidem sanctius* quam quemquam deōrum ceterōrum* Alabandum* colunt, ā quō est urbs illa condita*; apud quōs nōn inurbānē* Stratonīcus* cuidam* molestō Alabandēnsī quī Alabandum deum esse confirmābat et Herculem deum esse negābat, "ergō" respondit, "mihi Alabandus tibi Herculēs sit irātus*."

Sunt quī dīcant optimē* nōbīs deōs prōvidēre*, sed multōs hominēs deōrum beneficia pervertere; multōs patrimōnia pervertere, sed nōn ob eam causam eōs beneficium ā patribus nūllum habēre. Quis istud negat, et quae est similitūdo* in collātiōne* istā? Nec enim Herculī nocēre Deianīra voluit cum* eī vestem sanguine Centaurī imbūtam daret. Multī enim et cum* nocēre vellent prōfuērunt, et cum* prōdesse vellent nocuērunt.

(After Dē nātūrā deōrum *III. 42, 50, 70ff.)*

4. The Neo-Platonist Ambrosius Theodosius Macrobius is perhaps best known for his *Sāturnālia* (c. A.D. 430), whose central theme is Vergilian criticism. The Neo-Platonists believed that all pagan gods are the manifestation of one divine power (in the following passage, the Sun). While there is no evidence of Christian ideology in the works of Macrobius, his

6: **inferī**, **-ōrum** *m* pl. the dead
Ulixe (abl. *m* sing.) Ulysses (Odysseus) hero of Homer's epic poem, *The Odyssey*.
8: **reconditus**, **-a**, **-um** concealed, obscure; profound
9: **indāgō**, **-āre** trace out, search, explore
9, 10: **antīquissimus**, **-a**, **-um** most ancient
13: **immortālium** (adj., gen. *m* pl.) immortal
consecrō, **-āre**, **-āvī**, **-ātus** dedicate, consecrate, make immortal
14, 16: **Alabandēnsēs**, **-is** *m* inhabitant of Alabanda
14–15: **sanctius quam quemquam deōrum ceterōrum** "more reverently than any of the other gods"
15: **Alabandus**, **-ī** *m* (name of person after whom the city was named)
condō, **-ere**, **condidī**, **conditus** found, establish
16: **inurbānē** (adv.) inelegantly, without wit
Stratonīcus, **-ī** *m* a proper name
cuidam (pronoun, dat. *m* sing.) to a certain person
18: **irātus** (+ dat.) angered with
19: **optimē** (adv.) very well
prōvideō (+ dat.) look out for
22: **similitūdo**, **-inis** *f* likeness, resemblance; analogy
collātio, **-iōnis** *f* comparison
23–24: **cum** + subjunctive "when" (showing the circumstances rather than the actual time of an event)

syncretistic argument enables its holder to profess monotheism while practicing polytheism.

Nec Herculēs ā substantiā sōlis* aliēnus est: Herculēs enim ea est sōlis potentia quae hūmānō generī virtūtem sīcut deōrum ostendit. Nec Alcmēnā* nātus sōlus Herculēs appellātus est: post multōs aliōs ille dignus erat hōc nōmine quia virtūtem regit. . . . Aegyptiī autem eum ultrā* memoriam, quae apud illōs retrō* longa est, quasi sine initiō colunt. Ipse prō caelō pugnāvit et Gigantēs* interfēcisse crēditur. Gigantēs autem quid aliud* fuisse crēdimus quam* hominum impiam gentem* quae deōs negāvit et sīc deōs pellere dē caelō voluit? Hōrum pedēs* in dracōnum* volūmina* dēsinēbant, quod significat* nihil eōs rectum, nihil superum* cōgitāvisse, sed tōtīus vītae eōrum gradūs* in inferna* dēdūcere. Ab hīs sōl poenās dēbitās vī* pestiferī calōris* exēgit*. Et vērē Herculem sōlem esse vel* ex nōmine clāret*. *Herakles* enim quid aliud est nisi *heras*,* id est āeris, *kleos**? Quae alia āeris glōria est nisi sōlis illūminātiō*?

(*After* Sāturnālia, *I.20.6–10*)

5. During the Renaissance, writers interpreted the Hercules myth as a moral allegory. Coluccio Salutati (d. 1406), wrote a lengthy exegesis of Hercules' adventures, *Dē labōribus Herculis*, in which he treats Hercules as the embodiment of the abstract idea of virtue, and his adventures as representing the struggle of virtue to overcome the forces opposing it. This kind of elaborate allegorical analysis, which often seems far-fetched to a modern reader, was a highly developed literary technique made popular by Christian theologians from the fourth century on.

1: **substantia sōlis** "the essence of the sun"
3: **Alcmēna, -ae** *f* Alcmena, the mother of Hercules
4: **ultrā** + acc. beyond
5: **retrō** (adv.) backwards, back
retrō longa est "goes far back in time"
6: **Gigās, Gigantis** *m* Giant (the Giants were the fabled sons of Earth and Tartarus, with snakes for legs)
7: **aliud . . . quam** other . . . than
gēns, gentis *f* race, tribe
8: **pēs, pĕdis** *m* foot
dracō, dracōnis *m* serpent, dragon
9: **volūmen, volūminis** *n* roll, coil
significō, -āre mean, signify
superus, -a, -um lofty
10: **gradūs** (nom. *m* pl.) steps, pace
in inferna "into the underworld"
11: **vī pestiferī calōris** "by the destructive power of its heat"
exigō, -ere, exēgī, exactus exact, demand
12: **vel ex nōmine clāret** "perhaps even from his name it is clear that" (+ acc. subject and infin. verb)
12–13: ***heras kleos*** "the glory of the air" (Macrobius' explanation of the Greek name *Herakles*.)
13: **illūminātiō, -iōnis** *f* light, a lighting up

Salutati follows the ancient and medieval theory of human physiology—still believed at that time—according to which four chief fluids or "humours" rule the body, namely blood, phlegm, choler, and melancholy or black choler. These humours, according to their relative proportions in an individual, determine one's physical and mental qualities and disposition.

5a. Herculēs autem, quī figūra est animae nostrae, . . . reptat* ad anguēs* et ipsōs manibus* interficit. Nam anima hūmōrēs* et spīritūs* regit reprimitque et sīc mūtat illa quae corpus mortiferē* invadent* ut nōn sōlum dēsinant nocēre sed etiam incipiant esse vītae hominis salūtāria*. Unde illōs anguēs* dīcitur interfēcisse quia ea quae nocēre incēperant mūtāta sunt in instrūmenta* salūtis*. Nam poētae circulatiōnem* hūmōrum* et spīrituum per anguēs* finxērunt ut revolūtōs* atque tortuōsōs*. Sed Herculēs animā potentiīsque et operibus suīs interfēcit anguēs*.

5b. Dē Cācī fābulā, quī ab Hercule interfectus est, historia* et varia et obscūra* est. Allēgoriam* igitur quam deus suggerit* disserāmus*.

Herculēs dē occāsū*, hoc est vitiīs, ad ortum*, hoc est virtūtem, dūcit Geryonis* gregēs, id est affectūs* corporeōs et sēnsibilēs, quōs poētae per bovēs finxērunt. Sunt enim affectūs* quasi bestiae: sī ponantur sub iugum*, hominem (hoc est ratiōnem) ad vitae cultūram*, sīcut bes-

1: **reptō, -āre** crawl, creep
1, 5, 9: **anguis, -is** *m* serpent, snake
2: **manibus** (abl. pl.) "with his hands"
2, 7: **hūmor, hūmōris** *m* moisture
2, 7: **spīritūs** (acc. *m* pl.); **spīrituum** (gen. *m* pl.) moisture
3: **mortiferē** (adv.) fatally
invadō, -ere attack
4–5: **salūtārius, -a, -um** (+ gen.) salutary, beneficial (for)
6: **instrumentum, -ī** *n* instrument, means
salūs, salūtis *f* health, safety, salvation
6–7: **circulātio, -iōnis** *f* circulation
7: **revolūtus, -a, -um** turned back on itself
8: **tortuōsus, -a, -um** twisted

1: **historia, -ae** *f* history
2: **obscūrus, -a, -um** dark, obscure, hidden
allēgoria, -ae *f* allegory (i.e., what is said is different from what is meant—the relationship between the two is based upon the resemblance between them.)
suggerō (sub + gerō) suggest
disserō, -ere discuss, talk about
3: **dē occāsū** "from [the land of] the setting (sun)," i.e., from the west (where Geryon, whose cattle Hercules had won, lived)
ad ortum "to [the land of] the rising (sun)," i.e., to the east
4: **Geryon, -onis** *m* Geryon, mythic king in the far west; in some accounts, a herdsman in the Underworld (which was located in the distant "West").
4, 5, 19: **affectūs** (nom. or acc. *m* pl.) feeling, inclination
affectūs corporeōs et sēnsibilēs "physical and emotional inclinations"
6: **iugum, -ī** *n* yoke

tiae ad cultūram* agrōrum, adiuvent*. Fīlius autem Vulcānī*, Cācus, sīcut cantāvit Vergilius*,

> *Quattuor ā stabulīs praestantī corpore taurōs
> āvertit, totidem formā superante iuvencās.
> Atque hōs, nē qua forent pedibus vestīgia rectīs,
> caudā in spēluncam tractōs versīsque viārum
> indiciīs raptōs saxō occultābat opācō.
>
> (Aeneid *8.207–211)*

Cācus autem figūram complexiōnis* obtinet*, quae ā praevalenti* hūmōre appellātur, id est colericae*, quae respondet ignī, sīcut sanguinea* āerī respondet, flegmatica* aquae, et melancholica* terrae. Īrācundōs* enim crēdimus esse colericōs*, levēs* sanguineās*, pigrōs* flegmaticōs*, sed obstinātōs* esse melancholicōs* putāmus.

Rapit autem Cācus bovēs, id est affectūs* nostrōs, dē custōdiā* Herculis, id est virtūtis, et caudā retrōversim* suam dēdūcit in spēluncam. Sīcut enim via virtūtis est recta, sīc vitiōrum est retrōgrada* et oblīqua*.

6, 7: **cultūra**, **-ae** *f* cultivation (+ objective genitive)
7: **adiuvō**, **-āre** help, assist
Vulcānus, **ī**, *m* Vulcan, god of fire and father of Cacus
8: **Vergilius**, **-ī** *m* the poet Vergil. This is the original Latin of the *Aeneid*: "He stole from their enclosure four bulls of outstanding physique and an equal number of overwhelmingly beautiful heifers. And in order to avoid direct tracks, he dragged them by the tail into his cave; reversing the direction of their path, he concealed the booty in his dark cave."
14 **complexiō**, **-iōnis** *f* physical constitution
obtineō, **-ēre** demonstrate, embody
praevalentī humōre (abl. sing.) "the prevailing humor"
15, 17: **colericus**, **-a**, **-um** touchy, irritably impatient, bilious; **colericae** (**complexiōnis**)
15–16, 17: **sanguineus**, **-a**, **-um** bloody, blood-thirsty
16, 18: **flegmaticus**, **-a**, **-um** phlegmatic, not easily excited
16, 18: **melancholicus**, **-a**, **-um** melancholic
16–17: **īrācundus**, **-a**, **-um** prone to anger, irascible
17: **levēs** (adj., acc. *f* pl.) light, trivial, capricious
piger, **pigra**, **pigrum** slow, lazy, sluggish
18: **obstinātus**, **-a**, **-um** determined, stubborn
19: **custōdia**, **-ae** *f* protection
20: **retrōversim** (adv.) backwards
21: **retrōgradus**, **-a**, **-um** (modifying **via**) going backward
oblīquus, **-a**, **-um** not direct, sideways, oblique

XI

Third Declension (2); Participles; Dative of Agent; Ablative Absolute

Third Declension I–Stem Nouns

Some nouns of the third declension have a characteristic **-i-** in the genitive plural. The accusative plural masculine and feminine can be either **-īs** or **-ēs**. The neuter nominative and accusative plural is **-ia**. These **i**-*stem nouns* fall into one of the following categories:

1. Parisyllabic[1] masculine or feminine nouns ending in **-is** (nom.) and **-is** (gen.), or in **-ēs** (nom.) and **-is** (gen.):

cīv**is**, cīv**is** *m* citizen
ign**is**, ign**is** *m* fire
nūb**ēs**, nūb**is** *f* cloud
aed**ēs**, aed**is** *f* room, temple; pl., dwelling, house

2. Masculine or feminine nouns whose nominative ends in **-s** or **-x** and which have a stem ending in two consonants:

pa**rs**, pa**rt**is *f* part, direction
a**rs**, a**rt**is *f* skill, trade, art
no**x**, no**ct**is *f* night
dē**ns**, de**nt**is *m* tooth
gē**ns**, ge**nt**is *f* race, family, nation

3. Neuter nouns ending in **-al**, **-ar**, or **-e**. The nominative singular of **i**-stem neuter nouns ending in **-al** or **-ar** is the same as the stem; the endings in the declined cases are added directly to the nominative singular neuter form:

[1] Parisyllabic means having an equal number of syllables in both the nominative and the genitive singular. (Compare **pater**, **patris**, which is parisyllabic but is not an **i**-stem because the nominative ending is not **-is** or **-es**. **Mīles**, **mīlitis**, has the right endings but is not parisyllabic. Consequently neither noun is an **i**-stem.)

anim**al**, animālis *n* animal
exempl**ar**, exemplāris *n* copy, pattern, example
mar**e**, maris *n* the sea

The ablative singular of neuter **i**-stem nouns is **-ī**, whereas masculine and feminine **i**-stems usually have the regular **-e** ending in the ablative.

PARISYLLABICS

	cīvis, cīvis *m* *citizen*		**aedēs, aedis** *f* *temple*	
	SINGULAR	PLURAL	SINGULAR	PLURAL
Nom.	cīvis	cīvēs	aedēs	aedēs
Gen.	cīvis	cīv**ium**	aedis	aed**ium**
Dat.	cīvī	cīvibus	aedī	aedibus
Acc.	cīvem	cīvēs (-īs)	aedem	aedēs (-īs)
Abl.	cīve	cīvibus	aede	aedibus

TWO CONSONANTS

	pars, partis *f* *part*		**dēns, dentis** *m* *tooth*	
Nom.	pars	partēs	dēns	dentēs
Gen.	partis	part**ium**	dentis	dent**ium**
Dat.	partī	partibus	dentī	dentibus
Acc.	partem	partēs (-īs)	dentem	dentēs (-īs)
Abl.	parte	partibus	dente	dentibus

	NEUTER IN -E, -AL, -AR		IRREGULAR	
	animal, animālis *n* *animal*		**vīs, vīs** *f* *force*	
Nom.	animal	animāl**ia**	vīs	vīrēs
Gen.	animālis	animāl**ium**	vīs *[2]	vīr**ium**
Dat.	animālī	animālibus	vī *	vīribus
Acc.	animal	animālia	vim	vīrēs (-īs)
Abl.	animāl**ī**	animālibus	**vī**	vīribus

Third Declension Adjectives

Adjectives belonging to the third declension can have one (**sapiēns**, *m, f* or *n*, "wise"), two (**dulcis**, *m* or *f*, **dulce**, *n* "sweet"), or three endings (**celer**, *m*, **celeris**, *f* **celere**, *n* "swift") in the nominative singular. Aside from their differences in the nominative singular, however, third declension adjectives decline in the same way as third declension **i**-stem nouns, except for the ablative singular. The ablative singular of third declension adjectives is always **-ī**. Adjectives of one ending are listed in dictionaries

[2] The genitive and dative singular of **vīs** are marked with an asterisk to indicate that they occur only rarely.

with their nominative and genitive singular endings (e.g., **sapiēns**; **-ntis**):[3] here the genitive singular provides the stem: **sapient-**. Adjectives of two or three endings are listed by the nominative endings (**dulcis**, **-e**; **celer**, **celeris**, **celere**) and the feminine nominative singular provides the stem.

ADJECTIVES OF THREE ENDINGS

celer, **celeris**, **celere** *swift*

	SINGULAR			PLURAL		
	M.	F.	N.	M.	F.	N.
Nom.	celer	celeris	celere	celerēs	celerēs	celeria
Gen.	celeris	celeris	celeris	celerium	celerium	celerium
Dat.	celerī	celerī	celerī	celeribus	celeribus	celeribus
Acc.	celerem	celerem	celere	celerēs (-īs)	celerēs (-īs)	celeria
Abl.	celerī	celerī	celerī	celeribus	celeribus	celeribus

ADJECTIVES OF TWO ENDINGS

dulcis, **dulce** *sweet*

	SINGULAR		PLURAL	
	M. OR F.	N.	M. OR F.	N.
Nom.	dulcis	dulce	dulcēs	dulcia
Gen.	dulcis	dulcis	dulcium	dulcium
Dat.	dulcī	dulcī	dulcibus	dulcibus
Acc.	dulcem	dulce	dulcēs (-īs)	dulcia
Abl.	dulcī	dulcī	dulcibus	dulcibus

ADJECTIVES OF ONE ENDING

sapiēns; **sapientis** *wise, knowing*

	SINGULAR		PLURAL	
	M. OR F.	N.	M. OR F.	N.
Nom.	sapiēns	sapiēns	sapientēs	sapientia
Gen.	sapientis	sapientis	sapientium	sapientium
Dat.	sapientī	sapientī	sapientibus	sapientibus
Acc.	sapientem	sapiēns	sapientēs (-īs)	sapientia
Abl.	sapientī	sapientī	sapientibus	sapientibus

Adverbs from Third Declension Adjectives. Adverbs are normally formed from third declension adjectives by the addition of **-iter** to the stem of the adjective: **celeriter**, "swiftly"; **dulciter**, "sweetly." If the stem ends in **-nt**, only **-er** is added to the stem: **sapienter**, "wisely."

[3] **sapiēns**; **-ntis**: Most dictionaries do not include a semicolon. In this text the semicolon has been added to indicate that this is an adjective of one ending. Another way to identify these adjectives is the absence of a separate listing of a neuter form.

Scrībenda

Nouns

aedēs, -is *f* building for habitation; temple; pl., dwelling for people
animal, animālis *n* animal
ars, artis *f* skill, trade, art
cīvis, cīvis *m* or *f* citizen
dēns, dentis *m* tooth
exemplar, exemplāris *n* example, pattern
mare, maris *n* the sea
mors, mortis *f* death
nox, noctis *f* night
nūbēs, nūbis *f* cloud
pars, partis *f* part, direction
senex, senis *m* old man (note that this noun is not an **i**-stem)
vīs, vīs *f* force, energy, violence; pl. **vīrēs, vīrium** physical strength

Adjectives

acer, acris, acre sharp, pointed, piercing; keen
brevis, breve brief, short, concise
celer, celeris, celere swift, fleet, quick
dulcis, dulce sweet, pleasant, charming
fēlix; fēlīcis (gen.) fruitful; lucky, happy, fortunate
fortis, forte brave, strong
inēlegāns; inēlegantis (gen.) tasteless, inelegant
iūdiciālis, iūdiciāle judicial
omnis, omne every; pl., all
potēns; potentis (gen.) powerful, able
sapiēns; sapientis (gen.) wise, knowing

A. Decline the following (singular and plural):
celer ignis
dux fortis
magna aedēs
illud animal
eadem pars
senex sapiēns

B. Identify all possible cases of the following:

cīve	pars	animal
cīvis	partī	animālia
cīvibus	parte	animālī
cīvēs	partium	animālibus

C. Identify the case and translate each of the following:

vīs magna	vīrium eārum
virīs magnīs	virōrum eōrundem
vīribus magnīs	vī magnā
vīrīs magnās	vī magnae

D. Change the following to the case and number indicated:
lībertās dulcis: gen. pl.; dat. sing.
tempus celere: nom. pl.; abl. sing.
animal saevum: gen. pl.; dat. pl.

homō sapiēns: accus. sing.; accus. pl.
ōrātiō brevis: gen. pl.; nom. pl.

E. Change the following adjectives to adverbs and translate the adverb you have formed:

fēlix	iūdiciālis
potēns	saevus
inēlegāns	acer
fortis	brevis

F. Translate the following sentences into good English:

1. Memoria cīvium bonōrum ā nōbīs saepe laudābitur.
2. Ōrātor facta nostra cīvibus cīvitātis illīus ostendit.
3. Cīvitātī facta ista ostendet.
4. Cīvēs mōnstrum tollere voluērunt.
5. Vīsne vīrēs eōrum vincere? Velim vim istīus vincere.
6. Quī vir tam sapiēns est ut vīrēs virī istīus habēre nōn velit?
7. Dulce est prō cīvitāte bene facere.
8. Vīvit dulciter quī sapienter vītam agat.
9. Per urbem celeriter it fāma; fāmā celerī mors nuntiābātur.
10. Celere mōnstrum fūgit nē vincerētur.
11. Verba ipsa sunt mihi dulcia; dulce erat verbum dictum ā tē.
12. Nōn omnia animālia vim maris timent.
13. Ceterī cīvēs vocātī sunt ut cīvitātī auxilium darent.
14. Ūnā nocte pars cīvium celeriter ab urbe discessit.
15. Eā nocte urbs ā cīvibus relicta est.
16. Nēmō in urbe mānsit nisi illī senēs sapientēs.
17. Dux potēns ad urbem adiit nē saevē perīrent eīdem senēs.
18. Fēlīcēs vīdērunt dūcem fortem ad urbem adīre.
19. Senibus factum dūcis esse exemplar decorī vidēbātur.

Present Active Participles

Many third declension adjectives of one ending are actually present active participles. **Sapiēns**, for example, comes from the verb **sapiō**, **sapīre**, "to know," and hence it means "knowing," or "wise." As we have seen before, participles are verbal adjectives. In Chapter VI we saw how future active participles function (e.g., **captūrus**, **-a**, **-um**, "about to seize"). In Chapter X we learned how to use perfect passive participles (e.g., **captus**, **-a**, **-um**, "having been captured"). Latin has two other participles, the present active participle and the future passive participle.

The present active participle of the first and second conjugations is formed by adding **-ns** (nom.), **-ntis** (gen.) to the present stem of the verb:[4]

[4] Note that a vowel before **-ns** is regularly long, whereas before **-nt** or **-nd** the vowel is regularly short; hence **amāns**, but **amăntis**; **dūcēns**, but **dūcĕntis**.

amāre: amā + -ns, -ntis = **amāns**, **amantis**, loving
tenēre: tenē + -ns, -ntis = **tenēns**, **tenentis**, holding

Third conjugation verbs add **-ēns**, **-entis** to the shortened present (consonant) stem of the verb. The irregular verbs **volō**, **nōlō**, **mālō** follow this pattern, taking their stem from the first principle part of the verb:

dūcere: dūc + -ēns, -entis = **dūcēns**, **ducentis**, leading
velle: vol + -ēns, -entis = **volēns**, **volentis**, willing
nōlle: nōl + -ēns, -entis = **nōlēns**, **nolentis**, unwilling
mālle: māl + -ēns, -entis = **mālēns**, **malentis**, preferring

Third **-iō** and fourth conjugation verbs retain an **-i-** before these endings. Think of these verbs as taking their stems from the first principle part of the verb (**audiō**, **capiō**) and adding **-ēns**, **entis**:

capiō: capi + -ēns, -entis = **capiēns**, **capientis**, seizing
audiō: audi + -ēns, -entis = **audiēns**, **audientis**, hearing

The present participle of the irregular verbs **eō**, **īre** and its compounds is **iēns**, **euntis**. The verb **sum**, **esse** has no present active participle, but its compounds are based on the hypothetical form ***ēns**, ***entis**:

abeō: ab + iēns, euntis = **abiēns**, **abeuntis**, going away
absum: abs + ēns, entis = **absēns**, **absentis**, being absent

Present active participles are declined as third declension adjectives of one ending (compare **sapiēns**). The ablative singular of present participles, however, is **-ī** only when the adjectival force predominates, that is, when the participle is used strictly as an adjective: **ā virō *dīcentī***, "by the *speaking* man." When the verbal force predominates, as in an ablative absolute construction (discussed below), or if the participle is used as a noun, the ablative singular is **-e**: **ā *dīcente* haec inventa sunt**, "these things were discovered by the *speaker*." In the second example, **dīcente** is viewed as a verbal noun, and hence declines like a third declension noun.

Future Passive Participles

The future passive participle is formed from the same stem as the present active participle; to this stem is added **-ndus**, **-nda**, **-ndum**, which is declined like **magnus**, **-a**, **-um**. As its name suggests, the future passive participle indicates that something is about to be done or deserves to be done:

amandus, **-a**, **-um**: about to be loved
tenendus, **-a**, **-um**: about to be held
dūcendus, **-a**, **-um**: about to be led
capiendus, **-a**, **-um**: about to be seized
audiendus, **-a**, **-um**: about to be heard

The future passive participle takes on the added meaning of propriety, obligation, or necessity, particularly when combined with the verb **esse**. This construction (the future passive participle and some form of the verb **esse**) is called the *passive periphrastic*, which means "a roundabout way of speaking." To indicate the agent in this construction, Latin uses the dative of agent: **Haec verba *tibi* legenda sunt**. Recall the ablative of agent, which is used with other forms of passive verbs: the ablative of agent is governed by the preposition **ā**, **ab**, (e.g. **Urbs ā *dūce* capta est**). The dative, by contrast, is never governed by a preposition.

Haec verba **tibi** legenda sunt.	You must read those words. (literally, "These words must be read *by you*.")
Patria **nōbīs** amanda est.	We must love our country. (literally: "The country must be loved *by us*.")
Vir saevus **animālī** mordendus erat.	The cruel man deserved to be/had to be bitten *by the animal*.
Carmen cantandum **tibi** erit.	You will have to sing the song. (literally: "The song will have to be sung *by you*.")

Translation of Participles. In translating participles, you must decide from the context whether they are temporal, conditional, causal or concessive:

Haec **agēns**, servus cantat. *Doing* these things, the slave sings.

Temporal:	*When/While* he does these things,
Conditional:	*If* he does these things,
Causal:	*Because/Since* he does these things,
Concessive:	*Although* he does these things,

Sometimes the best translation is a relative clause: "The slave who does these things is singing." In your translation, you will also have to determine the tense of the participle in relation to the tense of the main verb. A present participle takes place at the same time as the main verb; if the main verb is past or future, the translation of the present participle should reflect the fact that its action also takes place, respectively, in the past or in the future, at the same time that the action of the main verb is taking place. So, too, a perfect participle indicates that the action of the participle occurred before the time of the main verb. A future participle indicates something that is done after the time of the main verb:

Present Participle (contemporaneous with main verb):
Hercules, gregem **agēns**, cantat/cantāvit/cantābit.
Hercules, *leading* his herd, is singing/sang/will sing.

If the main verb is in the present tense (**cantat**), then the appropriate translation might be "because he is leading his herd, Hercules is singing"; if the main verb is in the perfect tense (**cantāvit**), a better translation (depending of course on context in all these cases) might be "when Hercules was leading his herd, he sang." And if the main verb is in the future tense (**cantābit**), an appropriate translation might be "if Hercules is leading his herd, he will be singing." The same range of choices apply to the past and future participles. Translate the following examples into good English, putting the main verb first into the present tense, then into the perfect tense, and finally into the future tense.

Past Participle (prior to main verb):

Bovēs in spēluncam **tractae** mugiunt/mugīvērunt/mugient.

The cattle, *having been dragged* into the cave, are lowing/lowed/will low.

Future Participle (takes place after main verb):

Virō vestem **nocitūram** dat/dedit/dabit.

She gives/gave/will give an *about-to-do-harm* garment to her husband.

Hercules suscipit/suscēpit/suscipiet dolōrem nōn **tolerandum**.

Hercules is undergoing/underwent/will undergo *not-to-be-tolerated* pain.

Attendant Circumstances and Ablative Absolute

In Chapter III, we divided the ablative case into three groups. Of these groups, the third consists of constructions that can be translated "with" or "by," and is frequently categorized as "sociative-instrumental" uses of the ablative. Each of these constructions in one way or another describes the person, thing, or behavior associated with the action of the sentence. Included in this group are the ablative of accompaniment, the ablative of means or instrument, and the ablative of manner.

Another construction in this category is the ablative of attendant circumstances. As you might guess, "attendant circumstances" covers a lot of territory. Without specifying the relationship as precisely as the other constructions in this group, this ablative nevertheless describes some thing or circumstance that accompanies the verbal action. **Cum** is used or omitted by the same rule that governs its use with the ablative of manner.

(**Cum**) **stellīs clārīs** in caelō, servī dominum malum fūgērunt.
With the stars bright (*With bright stars*) in the sky, the slaves ran away from the bad master.

Here, the "bright stars" do not provide the means which enable the slaves to run away, nor are the stars the cause of their fleeing. In fact, the logical connection is rather vague. Thanks perhaps to its very vagueness, the ablative of attendant circumstances finds widespread use in Latin. Particularly characteristic is a development of this construction called the "ablative absolute." "Absolute"[5] means simply that the noun or pronoun in

[5] "Cut" (**solūtus**) "off" (**ab**) from the rest of the sentence.

the ablative, as well as its modifier(s), is not referred to elsewhere in the sentence: that is, the ablative phrase is syntactically independent and could be removed without damaging the structure of the sentence.

Typically, an ablative absolute consists of a noun and a participle, both in the ablative case:

> **Stellīs vīsīs**, nautae gaudent.
> *The stars have been seen*, the sailors rejoice. (Better English: "After seeing the stars," or "Because they have seen the stars," or "When they have seen the stars.")

When the main verb of the clause is some form of **esse**, which does not have a present or perfect participle in Latin, the ablative absolute consists of a noun plus an adjective or noun plus a noun phrase, with some form of the verb **esse** understood:

> **Cicerōne cōnsule**, magnum erat perīculum Rōmae.
> *When Cicero was consul*, the danger at Rome was great.
> **Stellīs clārīs**, servī fugient.
> *When the stars are bright*, the servants will run away.

In translating an ablative absolute, you must try to decide what logical relationship the ablative phrase bears to the rest of the sentence. Usually the most natural way to express it in English is by a subordinate clause, not a prepositional phrase; hence, you must choose a conjunction—when, since, although, after, if—and, if no participle is expressed, supply a form of "to be." The context usually suggests the appropriate choices. Here again is the "bright stars" example:

> Stellīs in caelō clārīs, servī dominum malum fūgērunt.

First, note that **stellīs clārīs** (with its modifying phrase **in caelō**) has no grammatical connection with either the subject (**servī**) or the object (**dominum**) of the sentence. Next, consider what logical connections between **stellīs clārīs** and the main clause are possible. Finally, you must decide what the tense of the verb in the ablative absolute will be.

To get the correct tense of the participle or the understood verb "to be" in the ablative absolute, you must consider the tense of the verb in the main clause:

Stellīs in caelō **vīsīs** (the *stars* in the sky *having been seen*),

> Servī fugiunt/fugient.
> When they *have seen* the stars in the sky, the servants run away/will run away.
>
> Servī fugiēbant/fūgērunt.
> When they *had seen* the stars in the sky, the servants began to run away/ran away.

Good English will frequently require that you change the passive voice of the Latin to the active voice. This is why we have changed the rather rigid translation, "the stars having been seen" to the active voice.

In translating from English to Latin, another problem arises: there is no present passive participle or perfect active participle in Latin. In order to express some ideas in the ablative absolute, therefore, it is sometimes necessary to change an active construction to passive, and vice versa:

Bōbus āmissīs, Herculēs discēdere incēpit.
Because he had lost his cattle (literally, "his cattle having been lost"), Hercules began to depart.

Finally, any of the participles can be used in an ablative absolute construction, provided of course that they do not refer to anything or anyone in the main clause of the sentence:

Hercule **discessūrō**, bovēs mugīvērunt.
When Hercules *was about to depart*, the cattle lowed.

Hercule **discēdente**, bovēs mugīvērunt.
When Hercules *was departing*, the cattle lowed.

Bōbus **inveniendīs**, Hercules nōn discēdet.
Since the cattle *must be found* (Since *he must find* the cattle) Hercules will not depart.

Scrībenda

A. Form all four participles of each of the following verbs, and translate each participle.

Example:

	Active	*Passive*
Present	agēns, agentis, "doing"	——
Perfect	——	actus, -a, -um, "done"
Future	actūrus, -a, -um, "about to do"	agendus, -a, -um, "to be done"

līberō	faciō
locō	incipiō
doceō	audiō
maneō	veniō
āvertō	adeō
fundō	adsum
relinquō	volō

B. Translate and identify the underlined participles:

1. Ea pars narrātiōnis expositiōnem continentis erit brevis. (**expositiō**, **-iōnis** *f*, the setting forth)
2. Haec pars tibi breviter dīcenda erit.
3. Ea pars ā tē breviter dicta erit.
4. Tū eam partem dīcēns brevis eris.
5. Tē dīcente, haec pars brevis erit.
6. Multī sē brevēs fuisse putantēs longī fuērunt.
7. Sīc est discipula magistrō exercenda.
8. Omnēs suōs discipulōs exercitūrus erat.
9. Discipulae ā magistrō sīc exercitae ingenium laudandum est.
10. Paedagōgus vitiīs opprobriīsque egēns tibi quaerendus est.
11. Sīc nox discipulam nostram inveniat labōrantem.

12. Errōrēs docentis semper inveniunt discipulī.
13. Fluviusne diū errāns in agrō umquam in mare fluet?
14. Sunt quī viam erranti mōnstrāre nōn possint.
15. Nesciō quae fuerit lingua Deī mundum creantis et dīcentis, "tū es fīlius meus amātus"; nōndum enim erant linguae.
16. Servus miser Herculem auxilium petentem mortemque optantem ipse vidēns nihil facere potuit.
17. Nōn timenda est mors; et dolōrēs et labōrēs tolerandī sunt.
18. Et virō mortem nōn timentī sunt dolōrēs et labōrēs tolerandī.
19. Sāturnō victō, Iuppiter pater deōrum hominumque appellārī incēpit.
20. Veste acceptā, Herculēs periit.
21. Neque hercle tuam amīcam vīdī neque tibi haec dīcentī respondēbō. (**hercle**, By Hercules!)
22. Vincēmus, deō volente.
23. Dīcendum est; deus ille fuit quī vītae ratiōnem invēnit eam quae nunc appellātur sapientia.

C. Translate the following sentences into Latin, using the grammatical construction indicated for the underlined portion of the English sentence:

Ablative Absolute:

1. When the citizens had been summoned, the speaker revealed these things.
2. After they had heard the speaker, the citizens were sent home.
3. When the other animals were about to flee, the horse began to neigh. (neigh, **vōcem sonare**)
4. Since part of the citizens are departing, the city will soon be abandoned.

Passive Periphrastic:

1. We must not listen to the words of poets.
2. Art must not be revealed by art.
3. You must fear the sea.

Verba tenenda

Verbs

augeō, **-ēre**, **auxī**, **auctus** increase, augment, strengthen

canō, **-ere**, **cecinī**, **cantus** sing, sing of, prophesy

iactō, **-āre**, **-āvī**, **-ātus** toss, throw, hurl, scatter; mention, discuss; **sē iāctāre** to boast

intellegō, **-ere**, **-lexī**, **-lectus** understand

memorō, **-āre**, **-āvī**, **-ātus** recall to mind, remind of, recount, narrate, mention

mereō, **-ēre**, **meruī**, **meritus** deserve, be worthy of

nuntiō, **-āre**, **-āvī**, **-ātus** announce

pacō, **-āre**, **-āvī**, **-ātus** pacify, make peaceful

praesum, **praeesse**, **praefuī**, —— (+ dat.) be before; preside over, have charge of

recipiō, **-ere**, **-cēpī**, **-ceptus** take back, recover, accept

subiciō, **-ere**, **subiēcī**, **subiectus** subject, bring or place under, set below

sumō, **-ere**, **sumpsī**, **sumptus** take, take up, lay hold of, assume

turbō, **-āre**, **-āvī**, **-ātus** disturb, upset, discompose

Nouns

aedēs, **-is** *f* building for habitation; temple; pl., dwelling for men
animal, **-ālis** *n* animal
ara, **arae** *f* altar
ars, **artis** *f* skill, trade, art
bellum, **-ī** *n* war
caput, **capitis** *n* head
cīvis, **-is** *m* or *f* citizen
cor, **cordis** *n* heart
dēns, **dentis** *m* tooth
exemplar, **-lāris** *n* example, pattern
fīnis, **-is** *f* boundary, limit, border, end
forum, **-ī** *n* public market place
gēns, **gentis** *f* a race; a clan; kind, class
imperium, **-iī** *n* an order, command; power of command; authority; dominion, empire
imāgo, **imāginis** *f* an image, likeness, copy, statue; ghost
intellegentia, **-ae** *f* understanding, knowledge, perception
īra, **īrae** *f* anger, wrath
laus, **laudis** *f* praise
mare, **maris** *n* the sea
mēns, **mentis** *f* the mind
mēnsis, **-is** *m* month
mors, **mortis** *f* death
nātiō, **-iōnis** *f* a people, a nation; the birth of a child
nox, **noctis** *f* night
nūbēs, **nūbis** *f* cloud
orbis, **-is** *m* round surface: sphere; circle, ring;
orbis terrārum the world
pēs, **pĕdis** *m* foot
prīnceps, **prīncipis** *m* the chief; head person; the first member of the Senate; the ruler, emperor
prīncipium, **-iī** *n* beginning, commencement
prōvincia, **-ae** *f* a province; territory governed by Rome
rex, **rēgis** *m* king
scriptor, **-tōris** *m* writer, author
senex, **senis** *m* old man
silentium, **-iī** *n* stillness, freedom from disturbance; silence
urbs, **urbis** *f* city
victōria, **-ae** *f* victory
vīs, **vīs** *f* force, energy, violence; **vīrēs**, **vīrium** pl. physical strength

Pronouns

nescioquis (*m* and *f*), **nescioquid** (*n*) someone (I know not whom), something (I know not what)

Adjectives

acer, **acris**, **acre** sharp, pointed, piercing; keen
adversus, **-a**, **-um** turned face to face; opposite, contrary
augustus, **-a**, **-um** majestic, august, worthy of honor
brevis, **-e** brief, short, concise
celer, **celeris**, **celere** swift, fleet, quick
cīvīlis, **-e** of or pertaining to citizens; civic, civil
commūnis, **-e** common, public, general
dīvus, **-a**, **-um** divine
dulcis, **-e** sweet, pleasant, charming
ēlegāns; **ēlegantis** (gen.) luxurious, fastidious; fine, neat, elegant
fēlix; **fēlīcis** (gen.) fruitful; lucky, happy, fortunate
fortis, **-e** brave, strong
immortālis, **-e** immortal

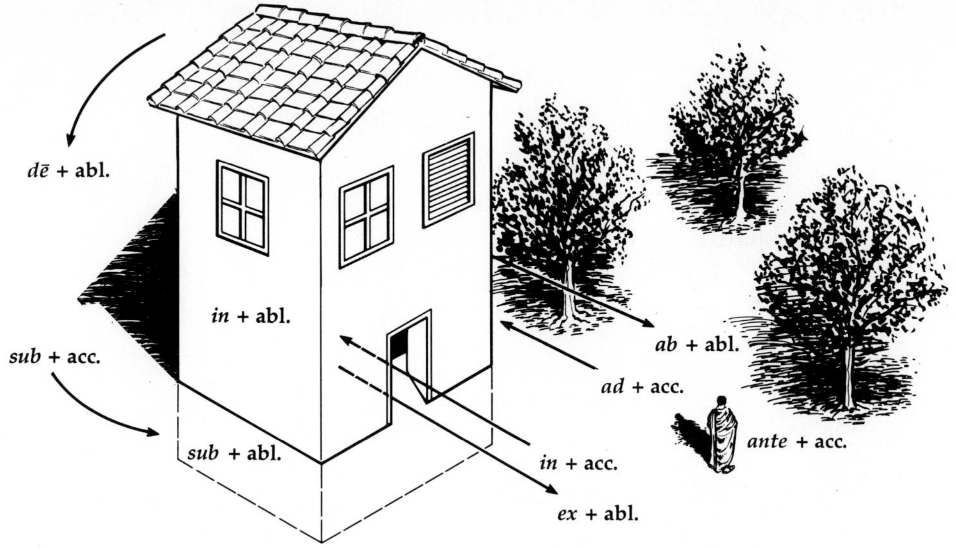

Prepositions expressing motion and location.

inēlegāns; **inēlegantis** (gen.) tasteless, inelegant
iūdiciālis, **-e** judicial
memor; **memoris** (gen.) mindful (of); remembering
mortālis, **-e** mortal, subject to death
obscūrus, **-a**, **-um** dark, shady, obscure, hidden
omnis, **-e** all, every
potēns; **potentis** (gen.) powerful, able
prosperus, **-a**, **-um** favorable, fortunate, prosperous
quālis, **-e** of what sort
sapiēns; **sapientis** (gen.) wise, knowing
superus, **-a**, **-um** situated above, upper; heavenly
superī, **-ōrum** *m* pl. the gods

Adverbs

circum around, about
cito quickly
diū for a long time
inde from that place, from that time
procul at a distance
scīlicet of course, evidently; it is evident

Prepositions

circum (+ acc.) around, about
ob (+ acc.) on account of, because of
post (+ acc.) after
sub (+ acc.) under, below, beneath (with verb showing motion toward)
sub (+ abl.) underneath, below, beneath (showing place where)

Notanda

Praesum, **praeesse** literally means "be before" (**prae**); a person in command would stand in front of his troops, and consequently the meaning "be in charge" or "in command." **praesēns** is the present active participle of this verb; the English adjective "present" derives from this participle.

aedēs is originally a simple building to be inhabited by the gods. In the plural it can signify a dwelling-place for mortals, as a collection of several apartments.

Skill in producing any material thing is **ars**; our twentieth-century romanticized notion of "art" as opposed to "skill" was not current in antiquity.

gēns and **nātiō** both have root meanings relating to birth. Both can be translated "race" or "nation," but **gēns** tends to refer to blood ties, and in that sense to the peoples of the world. **Nātiō** has more nationalistic overtones, and frequently implies a backward, uncivilized people.

imperium means "a command," "the authority or right of command," and, especially after the Augustan period, "dominion" or "empire." An **imperātor** was a general or commander (compare **imperāre**, "to command"); after Augustus the emperor was called **imperātor** or **prīnceps**, "the first man" in the Senate on the Censor's list, and hence the most distinguished.

mare can mean the sea in a general sense, or a particular sea: when Romans speak of **mare nostrum**, they mean the Mediterranean. The expression **terrā marīque** (or **et terrā et marī**) means "on land and sea" or "by land and sea."

A **mēnsis** is the measure of the period of time between two new moons (a lunar month); it can also denote a solar or zodiacal month.

orbis denotes a circular shape, and hence occurs in idioms reflecting perceptions in antiquity: **orbis terrārum** conveys a notion of the circularity of the world; the Zodiac is **orbis signōrum**; the Milky Way is **orbis lacteus**; a mirror is a **nitidus orbis**; **orbis volvitur in annōs** reflects the notion of things that return in a period of time; an **orbis doctrīnae** is an encyclopedia.

prīncipium, like **prīnceps**, derives from the adjective **prīmus**, "first." The famous opening words of the Gospel according to St. John, **In prīncipiō erat verbum**, are illuminated in the manuscript facsimile shown on page 203.

The irregular noun **vīs** in the singular means "force" or "power," "potency." This can be mental strength or vigor (**vīs illa dīvīna**), or with a hostile connotation, "violence." The plural indicates an accumulation of potency, and hence "strength," including military strength (troops). Compare the English word "vise," denoting a device which forcibly holds an object in place.

The indefinite pronoun **nescioquis**, **nescioquid** is declined like the interrogative pronoun **quis**, **quid**.

Do not confuse the adjectives **acer**, "keen, sharp," and **acerbus**, "bitter."

The adjective **augustus**, "majestic," is closely related to the verb **augēre**, "to increase." The title "Augustus," by which he is now more commonly known, was given to the emperor Octavian in 27 B.C. after he had consolidated his power in the Roman empire. His wife Livia subsequently became known as "Augusta." Roman poets sometimes toyed amusingly with the name.

Cīvīlis is the adjective derived from **cīvis**; the **cīvitās** (note again that the abstract substantive is feminine) is the collective body of **cīvēs**.

The opposite of **commūnis** is **proprius**, "belonging to one"; "community" and "common" derive from **commūnis**.

mortālis means "subject to **mors**," whereas the prefix **im-** in **immortālis** negates that limitation. The negating prefix remains **in-** before a vowel, as in **inēlegāns**.

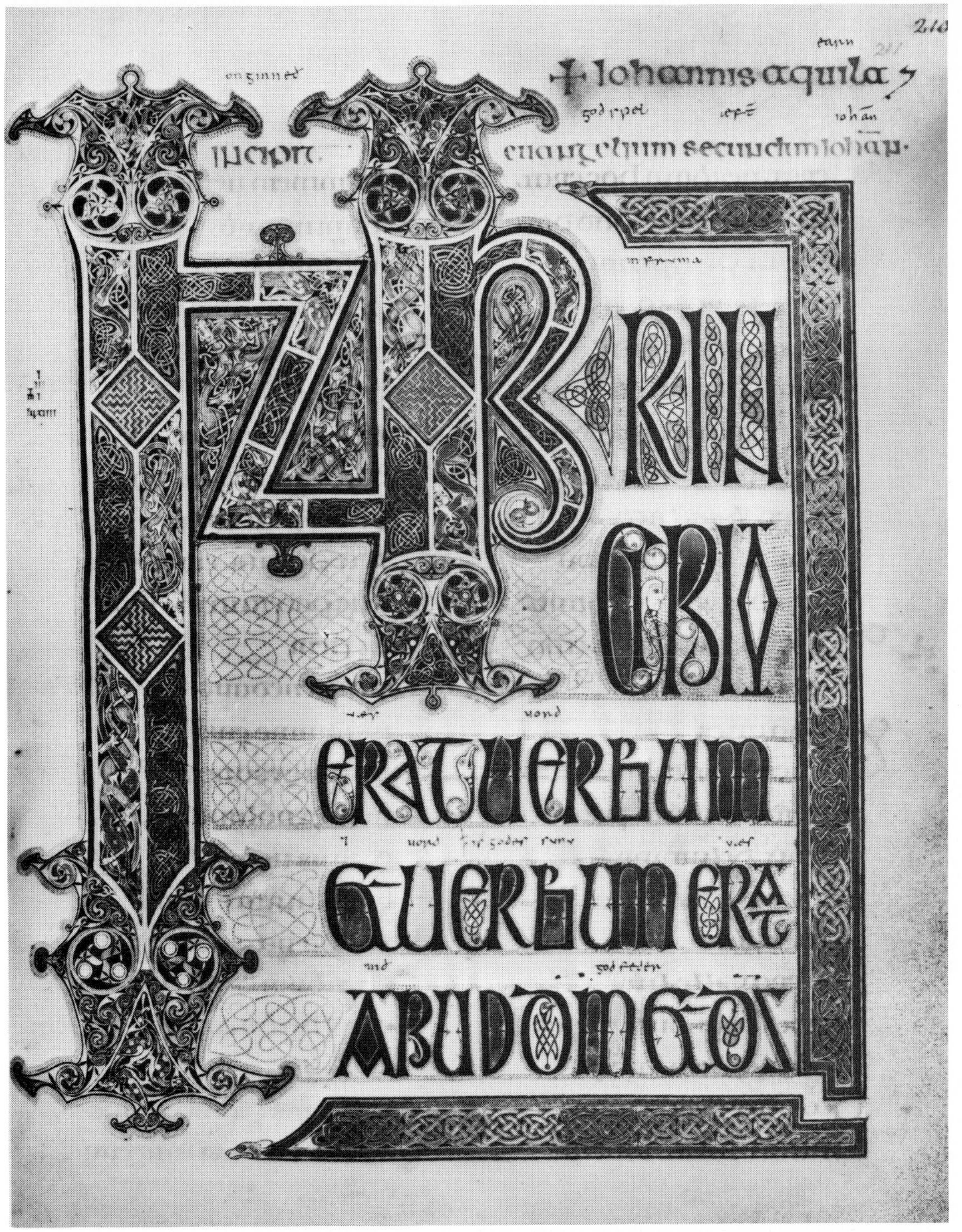

The beginning of the Latin Vulgate version of the Gospel of St. John reads: IN PRINCIPIO erat verbum et verbum erat apud d(eu)m et d(eu)s (erat verbum), *"In the beginning was the word, and the word was with God, and the word was God." From the Lindisfarne Gospels, named after the monastery in England where this manuscript was made about* A.D. *700. The script is a mixture of square and rounded letters, as seen here in the letters A and a, or D and d.*

Northern constellations, including the twelve signs of the zodiac. Albrecht Dürer, 1515.

Omnis means "every" in the singular, "all" in the plural. Compare the adjective **tōtus**, which refers not to every individual person or thing, but to the entirety. **Omnis homō**, "every human being," **omnēs hominēs**, "all (individual) human beings" vs. **tōtus homō**, "the entire (whole) human being."

potēns is the present active participle of **possum**; **potentia** is the abstract noun embodying the idea of ability or power. **Impotēns**, by contrast, means "lacking in ability to control (oneself)," hence, "wild," "out of control."

circum can be an adverb: ***Circum* ambulāvērunt**, "They walked *around*," or a preposition: ***Circum templum* ambulāvērunt**, "They walked *around the temple*."

deinde was used to denote succession in place ("from that place," "next") or time ("and after that," "afterwards," "then"). It is synonymous with **inde**.
The English expression "for a long time" is expressed not by **tempus longum**, but by the adverb **diū**.

Ante legenda

Translate:

1. Arma virumque canō. Arma factaque virī ā poētā canuntur (canta sunt). Arma factaque virī poētae canenda sunt. Poēta arma virumque canēns multōs hominēs mōvit.
2. Tē pugnāre decet terrā, Messalla,* marīque,
   ut domus hostīlēs* exuviās* ostendat:
   Mē tenent victum formōsae* vincla* puellae.
   (Tibullus I.1.53–55)

   (**Messalla**, **-ae** *m*, Messalla Corvinus, patron of the poet, Tibullus; **hostīlis**, **-e**, hostile; **exuviae**, **-ārum** *f* pl., booty, spoils; **formōsus**, **-a**, **-um**, beautiful; **vincla** = **vincula**)
3. Nōmine audītō, rex Herculem in aedēs accēpit.
4. Eō tempore, poēta cecinit faciendam esse aram quam ōlim gēns Rōmāna cultūra esset.
5. Eōs cīvēs ā quibus pater meus interfectus est vīcī bellō.
6. Bella civilia terrā marīque saepe mihi gerenda erant.
7. Imperium mihi et absentī et praesentī ā populō datum nōn recēpī.
8. Bellīs prosperē gestīs, Rōmam rediī.
9. Ter, mē prīncipe, pax per tōtum imperium populī Rōmānī victoriīs facta est. (**ter**, three times)
10. Nautae Rōmānī ad gentēs fīnēsque quōs numquam vīderant, mē prīncipe, adiērunt.
11. Ā prīncipiō rēgēs urbem Rōmam habuērunt.
12. Lībertāte ā Brūtō institūtā, multōs post annōs arma Antōniī vīcit Augustus, quī omnia fessa bellīs cīvīlibus sub imperium suum accēpit. (**Brūtus**, **-ī** *m*, Lucius Brutus, first consul of the Roman Republic; **Antōnius**, **-ī** *m*, Mark Antony, opponent of Augustus)
13. Fuērunt quī crēderent mēnsem Septembrem appellandam esse mēnsem Augustī. Aliī cēnsuērunt tōtum tempus eius vītae aetātem Augustam appellandam esse. (**September**, **-bris** *m*, the seventh month of the Roman year: March is the first month.)
14. Nuntiātum est hominem vēnisse verba nova dīcentem.
15. Herculī ille verba nova dīcēns homō esse vidētur. Illī videntī hic homo esse vīsus est.
16. Illī quaerentī cuius nātiōnis esset hic homō Graecē respondit.
17. Ex omnibus superīs, quālis deus erit iste?

18. Dīvus Claudius ex hōc tempore deus faciendus est. (**Claudius**, -**ī** *m*, Claudius, the Roman emperor)

19. Vīve memor mortis.

20. Nunc est bibendum, nunc pede līberō pulsanda terra [est]. (Horace, *Odes* I.37.1–2)

Legenda

Mythology (3): Hercules as Exemplum

1. The exclamations **mehercle** and **hercle**, so familiar in Roman comedy, reflect Hercules' early popularity in Italy. In his great epic, the *Aeneid*, Vergil makes Hercules an **exemplum** for Aeneas. Both have come in exile (**profugus**) to Italy, and by their deeds here they improve the condition of the inhabitants. Hercules and Aeneas, moreover, are both compelled by Juno to undergo enormous **labōrēs**. The opening lines of the *Aeneid* reflect some of these parallels.

Arma virumque canō, Troiae * quī prīmus * ab orīs *
[ad] Ītaliam fātō profugus * . . . vēnit;
multum * ille et terrīs * iactātus [est] et altō *
vī super[ōr]um saevae memorem Iūnōnis ob īram. . . .
Mūsa, mihi causās memorā . . .
quid dolēns * rēgīna * de[ōr]um . . .
insignem * pietāte * virum tot adīre labōrēs
impulerit. Tantaene animīs caelestibus * [sunt] īrae?

(*After* Aeneid *I.1–10)*

2. One of the very early religious rituals at Rome was the one held annually at the **ara maxima** in honor of Hercules. In the following passage, the historian Livy tells how king Evander, after Hercules had defeated Cacus, dedicated this altar to Hercules at the future site of Rome.

Evander tum profugus * ex Peloponnēsō * regēbat ea loca. Is Evander, vidēns pastōrēs * circa Herculem causāque audītā, quaesīvit quī vir ille

1: **Troiae ab orīs** "from the sea-coast of Troy"
prīmus, -**a**, -**um** first
2: **fātō profugus** "exiled by fate"
3: **multum** (adv.) much
terrīs et altō (abl.) "on land and on the deep (sea)"
6: **doleō**, -**ēre** (+ acc.) grieve, grieve at
rēgīna, -**ae** *f* queen
7: **insignis**, -**e** distinguished
pietās, **pietātis** *f* piety, reverence
8: **caelestis**, -**e** heavenly

1: **profugus**, -**ī** *m* an exile
Peloponnēsus, -**ī** *f* Peloponnesus (the southern part of Greece)
2: **pastōr**, -**ōris** *m* shepherd

esset. Ubi nōmen patremque ac patriam accēpit, "Iove nāte, Herculēs, Salvē," dīxit. "Tē mihi māter auctūrum esse superōrum numerum cecinit, nōsque aram hīc factūrōs esse quam gēns Rōmāna ōlim in terrīs maximam * vocātūra tuōque rītū * cultūra sit."

(After Livy, Ab urbe conditā, *1.7.8–10)*

3. In the *Aeneid*, Vergil indicates that Augustus is heir to the great civilizing tradition of Hercules. When Aeneas descends to the underworld and sees the parade of future Roman heroes, his father Anchises points out the shade of Augustus and says of him "Not even Hercules traversed so much of the earth" (**nec vērō Alcīdēs tantum tēllūris obīvit**, *Aeneid* VI.801). Whether Augustus actively elicited praise from his contemporaries is often debated. In his autobiography, the *Res Gestae Dīvī Augustī* (literally, "The Achievements of the Divine Augustus"), however, which he wrote when he was seventy-six years old, Augustus reveals that he did envision himself as a great pacifier and civilizer. The following are based on excerpts from the *Res Gestae*:

1. Quī parentem * meum interfēcērunt, eōs in exilium * expulī et posteā * vīcī bis * bellō.

2. Bella terrā et marī cīvīlia externaque * tōtō in orbe terrārum saepe gessī, victorque omnibus veniam * petentibus cīvibus pepercī *. Externās * gentēs, sī tūtō * hoc facere potuī, servāre quam * tollere māluī*.

3. Dictātūram * et absentī et praesentī * mihi dēlātam * et ā populō et ā senātū * M. Marcellō * et L. Arruntiō cōnsulibus nōn recēpī. Cōnsulātum * tum * annuum * et perpetuum mihi dēlātum * nōn recēpī.

5–6: **maximus**, **-a**, **-um** the greatest
6: **rītū** (abl. *m* sing.) religious ceremony

1: **parēns**, **parentis** *m* parent (here a reference to Julius Caesar, who had legally adopted Augustus as his son and heir)
exilium, **-ī** *n* exile
posteā (adv.) afterwards
2, 14: **bis** (adv.) twice
3, 4: **externus**, **-a**, **-um** foreign
4: **venia**, **-ae** *f* forgiveness, pardon
parcō, **-ere**, **pepercī**, **parsūrus** (+ dat.) be sparing to, spare
5: **tūtō** (adv.) safely, in safety
māluī . . . **quam**: "I preferred to (**servāre**) rather than to (**tollere**)"
6: **dictātūra**, **-ae** *f* dictatorship
praesēns; **praesentis** (gen.) at hand, present, in person
6, 8: **dēlātus**, **-a**, **-um** offered
7: **senātū** (abl. *m* sing.) the senate
M. Marcellō et L. Arruntiō cōnsulibus: the names of each year's two consuls are regularly used in the ablative absolute to date events in Latin historical writing. Translate: "during the consulship of Marcus Marcellus and Lucius Arruntius"
7–8: **cōnsulātum anuum** (acc. *m* sing.) "the office of consul (a one-year office) that recurs every year"
8, 9: **tum** then

4. Rēbus* in eīs provinciīs prosperē gestīs*, Rōmam rediī; tum* aram Pācis Augustae* senātus* prō* reditū meō* cōnsacrāre* ad Campum* Martium, et in eā anniversarium sacrificium* faciendum esse cēnsuit.

5. Iānum Quirīnum* clausum esse māiōrēs* nostrī voluērunt cum* per tōtum imperium populī Rōmānī terrā marīque esset facta victoriīs pax; ā conditā* urbe bis* sōlum clausum erat, sed ter* mē prīncipe senātus* claudendum esse cēnsuit.

6. Mare pacāvī ā praedōnibus*.

7. Omnium provinciārum populī Rōmānī quibus fīnitimae* fuērunt gentēs quae nōn parērent* imperiō nostrō fīnēs auxī. Galliās* et Hispānās* prōvinciās, item Germāniam* pacāvī. Alpēs* pacāvī. Classis* mea usque ad* fīnēs Cimbrōrum* nāvigāvit*, quō locō neque terrā neque marī ūllus Rōmānus ante id tempus adīverat. Meō iussū et auspiciō* ductī sunt duo exercitūs* eōdem ferē* tempore in Aethiopiam* et in Arabiam*.

(After Augustus, Rēs Gestae *2, 3, 5, 12, 13, 25, 26)*

9: **rēbus . . . gestīs** (ablative absolute) "since affairs in those provinces had been successfully arranged"
10: **Augustus, -a, -um** (adj.) of Augustus
10, 14: **senātus** (nom. *m* sing.) the senate
10: **prō reditū meō** "in thanks for my (safe) return"
cōnsacrō, -āre, -āvi, -ātus consecrate
10–11: **Campus Martius** "The field of Mars" (a place of assembly for the Roman people). The Ara Pacis, whose reliefs are among the most important products of Augustan art, was constructed in the Campus Martius in Rome. The Monument, reconstructed with most of its surviving sculptures, is now located near its original site.
11: **anniversārium sacrificium** (acc. *n* sing.) an annual sacrifice
12: **Iānus Quirīnus** the temple of Janus (Janus was an old Italian deity whose temple doors stood open in time of war, and were closed in time of peace.)
māiōrēs, -um *m* pl. ancestors .
cum + subjunctive "whenever"
14: **condō, -ere, condidī, conditus** found, establish; **ā conditā urbe**: "from the time when the city (Rome) was founded"
ter (adv.) three times
16: **praedō, -ōnis** *m* robber, pirate
17: **fīnitimus, -a, -um** neighboring
18: **pareō, -ēre, paruī** (+ dat.) be obedient to, obey
Gallius, -a, -um Gallic
Hispānus, -a, -um Spanish
19: **Germānia, -ae** *f* Germany
Alpēs, -ium *f* the high mountains of Switzerland (unknown to the Romans, in their entirety, until the time of Augustus)
classis, -is *f* fleet
19–20: **usque ad** all the way to
20: **Cimbrī, -ōrum** *m* a people of northern Germany
nāvigō, -āre, -āvī, -ātus sail
21: **meō iussū et auspiciō** "at my command and under my auspices"
22: **duo exercitūs** (nom. *m* pl.) two armies
ferē (adv.) almost
Aethiopia, -ae *f* Ethiopia
Arabia, -ae *f* Arabia

The famous statue of Augustus found at Porta Prima depicts him as an **imperātor,** *but the scenes on his breastplate depict the restoration of peace.*

4. Augustus tried to maintain at least the appearance of a republic. In his *Res Gestae* he says, "In my sixth and seventh consulships, after I had extinguished civil wars, and at a time when with universal consent I was in complete control of affairs, I transferred the republic from my power to the dominion of the senate and people of Rome." The date of this supposed transfer of power was 28–27 B.C.—which was in fact only a few years after the beginning of his long reign. After his death in A.D. 14 he was succeeded by his stepson, the dour Tiberius, who was followed in turn by the mad Caligula, then by the eccentric Claudius, and finally by Claudius' stepson, Nero, who proved to be the last of the Julio-Claudian emperors.

The historian Tacitus, with the benefit of hindsight, depicted Augustus not as a republican but as the first of the emperors. Tacitus clearly considers rule by emperors no great improvement over that of Rome's early kings.

Urbem Rōmam ā principiō rēgēs habuērunt. Lībertātem et cōnsulātum* L. Brūtus* instituit. Dictātūrae* ad tempus* sumptae nōn diū valuērunt. Nōn Cinnae*, nōn Sullae* longa erat dominātiō*; et Pompei* Crassique* potentia celeriter in Caesārem*, Lepidī* atque Antōniī* arma in Augustum cessērunt, quī cuncta discordiīs* cīvīlibus fessa nōmine prīncipis sub imperium accēpit. Sed veteris* populī Rōmānī prospera vel adversa ā clārīs scriptōribus memorāta sunt. Nōn dēfuērunt decōra ingenia quae tempora Augustī dīcerent, dōnec* crescente adūlātiōne* dēterrērentur*. Tiberiī* Gāiīque* et Claudiī* ac Nerōnis* rēs gestae*, flōren-

1–2: **cōnsulātum** (acc. *m* sing.) the office of consul

2: **Lūcius Iūnius Brūtus** consul in 509 B.C.; possibly ancestor of Marcus Brutus, assassin of Julius Caesar)

dictātūra, **-ae** *f* dictatorship; the office of a dictator

ad tempus "for a temporary crisis"

3: **Lūcius Cornēlius Cinna** (consul 87, 85, 84 B.C.)

Lūcius Cornēlius Sulla (consul 88 B.C., dictator 81–79 B.C.)

dominātiō, **-iōnis** *f* rule, dominion

Gnaeus Pompeius Magnus ("Pompey") (106–48 B.C.): Roman General; consul 70 B.C.

4: **Marcus Licinius Crassus** (consul 70 B.C.)

Gāius Jūlius Caesar: Roman General; (consul 59 B.C.; dictator 48–44; assassinated in 44 B.C.)

Marcus Aemilius Lepidus (consul 46 B.C.)

Marcus Antōnius ("Mark Antony") (83–30 B.C.)

5: **discordia**, **-ae** *f* discord

6: **vetus**, **veteris** (adj.) ancient, of long standing

8: **dōnec** (conj.) + subjunctive until

adūlātiō, **-iōnis** *f* flattery

crescente adūlātiōne is what kind of ablative?

8–9: **dēterreō**, **-ēre**, **-uī**, **-itus** frighten off, deter

9, 12: **Tiberius** (emperor A.D. 14–37)

Gāius ("Caligula") (emperor A.D. 37–41)

Claudius (emperor A.D. 41–54)

Nerō, **Nerōnis** (emperor A.D. 54–68)

rēs gestae (nom. *f* pl.) accomplishments

tibus ipsīs, ob timōrem falsae erant; postquam illī periērunt, recentibus odiīs* scriptae sunt. Inde cōnsilium mihi est pauca dē Augustō trādere, tum Tiberiī* prīncipātum* et cetera, sine īrā et studiō*, quōrum causās procul habeō.

(After Tacitus, Annales *I.1)*

5. The biographer Gaius Tranquillus Suetonius (b. A.D. 69), a contemporary of Tacitus, had access to the imperial archives. Among his works are *Dē vītā Caesārum Librī* (*Lives of the Caesars*). In his *Life of Augustus*, Suetonius depicts the Roman Senate deliberating, at the time of Augustus' death, the proper way to conduct his funeral:

Alii cēnsuērunt fūnus* triumphālī portā* dūcendum esse, praecēdente Victōriā, canentibus nēniam* līberīs; aliī fuērunt quī cēnsērent exsequiārum diē* pōnendōs esse ānulōs* aureōs* ferreōsque* sūmendōs esse. Fuit et quī crēderet appellātiōnem* mēnsis Augustī in Septembrem* mūtandam esse quod Augustus hōc* genitus*, illō* dēfunctus* esset; alius cēnsuit omne tempus ā prīmō* diē nātālī ad exitum* eius saeculum* Augustum appellandum esse. Nec dēfuit vir quī sē imāginem* cremātī Augustī euntem* in caelum vīdisse iūrāret*.

(After Suetonius, Dīvus Augustus, *100)*

6. Among the works attributed to Seneca, who was also the teacher and adviser of the emperor Nero, is the satirical *Apocolocyntōsis Dīvī Claudiī* ("The Pumpkinification of Claudius"). The satire, written shortly after the death of the Emperor Claudius, describes Claudius' death and subsequent attempt to join the company of the gods. Hercules is persuaded to represent Claudius before the tribunal of the gods and, by promising bribes, almost persuades them. Augustus, however, who is now one of the gods, has the final speech, in which he argues successfully against Claudius' ad-

10–11: **recentibus odiīs** "under the irritation of a recent hatred"
12: **prīncipātum** (acc. *m* sing.) reign, sovereignty
studium, **-ī** *n* here, "partiality"

1: **fūnus**, **fūneris** *n* funeral procession
porta triumphālis an archway at the beginning of the triumphal procession from the Campus Martius
2: **nēnia**, **-ae** *f* a song sung at a funeral, a dirge
2–3: **exsequiārum diē** "on the day of the funeral procession"
ānulus, **-ī** *n* ring
aureus, **-a**, **-um** made of gold
ferreus, **-a**, **-um** made of iron
4: **appellātiō**, **-iōnis** *f* name, title
September, **-bris** *m* the seventh month of the Roman year (counting from March)
5: **hōc** . . . **illō** [**diē**] "on this day . . . on that day"
genitus [**esset**] "he was conceived"
dēfunctus esset "he died"
6: **ā prīmō diē nātālī ad exitum** "from his first birthday to his death"
saeculum, **-ī** *n* century, generation, age
7: **imāginem cremātī Augustī euntem** "the likeness of Augustus after he had been cremated going" (**euntem** is the present participle of **eō**, **īre**, go)
8: **iūrō**, **-āre** swear, take an oath, affirm on oath

mission to their ranks. In the following passage Claudius' arrival is being announced to Jupiter:

6a. Nuntiātur Iōvī vēnisse hominem nescioquid minantem*: assiduē* eum caput movēre et pedem dextrum trahere. Nuntius* dīxit sē* quaesisse cuius nātiōnis esset*: respondisse eum nescioquid turbātō sonō et vōce confūsā*; nōn intellegere sē* linguam eius; eum nec Graecum esse nec Rōmānum nec ūllīus gentis nōtae. Tum Iuppiter iubet Herculem, quī per tōtum orbem terrārum errāverat et nōvisse vidēbatur omnēs nātiōnēs, īre et quaerere quōrum hominum esset*.

Herculēs autem, quī nōn omnia mōnstra timuerit, hunc vidēns turbātus est. Herculī dīligenter* videntī vīsus est quasi homō esse. Accessit ergō et, quod facillimum* fuit Graecō, quaesīvit Graecē cuius nātiōnis esset*. Claudius, gaudēns* esse illīc* philologōs* hominēs, spērat futūrum esse historiīs* suīs locum. Ergō et ipse Homēricō* versū Caesārem sē esse respondit.

(After Apocolocyntosis *5)*

6b. Claudius finally persuades Hercules to be his advocate before the gods. In the following passages the gods are discussing Claudius' petition for deification, and the gods Janus and Diespiter argue, respectively, against and for the deification:

Dīc nōbīs quālem deum istum esse velis. Epicūrēus* deus nōn potest esse: dolet* enim nec sibi nec aliīs. Stōicus? Quōmodo potest rotundus* esse, ut dīcit Varrō? Est nescioquid in illō Stōicī deī*, iam videō: nec cor nec caput habet. Sī mē Hercule ā Sāturnō* petīvisset hoc beneficium cuius mēnsem tōtum annum celebrāvit*, Sāturnālicius prīnceps*, nōn recēpisset illud, nēdum* ab Iove, quem damnāvit incestī*.

1: **nescioquid minantem** threatening something
assiduē (adv.) continuously; Claudius had visible physical handicaps, which are mercilessly exploited in this satiric work.
2: **nuntius**, **-ī** *m* messenger
2, 4: **sē** the subject of this clause of the indirect statement is the messenger, implied in **nuntiātur**.
3, 7, 10–11: **quōrum hominum esset** the standard questions asked of a stranger, from Homer on, were "Who are you? What is your nationality? (**cuius nātiōnis es?**) Who are your parents? Where is your home?"
4: **confūsus**, **-a**, **-um** confused, disturbed
9: **dīligenter** (adv.) carefully
10: **facillimus**, **-a**, **-um** very easy
11: **gaudeō**, **-ēre** delight in, rejoice
illīc (adv.) in that place
philologus, **-a**, **-um** learned, literary
12: **historia**, **-ae** *f* history (Claudius had written several long historical works.)
Homēricō versū (abl.) "in Homeric verse"

1: **Epicūrēus**, **-a**, **-um** of Epicurus. The Epicurean "Blessed and Incorruptible Power" has no trouble itself nor causes trouble to another. The implication is that Claudius fails to qualify on both accounts.
2: **doleō**, **-ēre**, **-uī**, **-itus** feel pain, suffer, grieve
rotundus, **-a**, **-um** round, globular. Varro apparently burlesqued the Stoic **vir perfectus** as being **tōtus teres atque rotundus** (**teres**, smooth, graceful)
3: **nescioquid** . . . **Stōicī deī** "something of a Stoic god" (partitive genitive)

Iānus* pater multa disertē*, quod in forō vīvēbat, dīxit. "Ōlim" dīxit, "magna rēs* erat deus fierī*: iam fāmam mīmum* fēcistis. Ergō nē videar in persōnam, nōn in rem*, dīcere sententiam, post* hunc diem* nēmō* mortālis deus fīat*."

Diespiter, quī nummulāriolus* fuerat, cēnset haec: "Claudius et dīvum Augustum sanguine contingit* nec minus* dīvam Augustam* aviam* suam, quam ipse deam esse iussit, longēque omnēs mortālēs sapientiā praecēdit; sitque* ē rēpūblicā sī ūnus nostrum cum Rōmulō possit "ferventia* vapa vorāre." Cēnseō igitur dīvum Claudium ex hōc diē* deum esse faciendum ita ut* ante eum quī optimō iūre factus sit* eamque* rem ad metamorphōsēs Ovidiī esse adiciendam*."

(After Apocolocyntōsis *8–9)*

Augustus has the final say in the debate, however; he persuades the other gods not to admit Claudius, who then goes to the underworld, where he becomes a servant to his mad nephew, Caligula.

4: **Sāturnus**, -ī *m* the saturnalia held in honor of Saturnus (a Roman agricultural god equated with the Greek god Chronos, who is Time personified; compare Father Time) was celebrated over a period of several days beginning December 17th (compare our Christmas holidays).

5: **celebrō**, **-āre** celebrate
cuius . . . celebrāvit: "even if he celebrated Saturnus' month . . ."
Sāturnālicius prīnceps "a (true) Saturnalian prince"

6: **nēdum** "even less"
damnāvit incestī "he charged with incest." Jupiter and Juno were brother and sister as well as husband and wife. Claudius' marriage to his niece was considered incestuous.

7: **Iānus**, -ī *m* Janus, the Italian god of beginnings, was also called Janus Quirinus. The doors of his temple in the Roman Forum stood open in time of war, and were closed in time of peace. He was represented with a face on the front and another face on the back of his head.
disertē (adv.) eloquently

8: **rēs** (nom. *f* sing.) thing, situation
rem (acc. *f* sing.)
fierī (passive infinitive of **facio**) to be made, become
mīmus, -ī *m* mime, farce

9: **post hunc diem** "after today"

10: **nēmō mortālis deus fīat** "let no mortal become a god."
Diespiter, -**tris** *m* a deity sometimes identified as Pluto (Dīs), ruler of the underworld

11: **nummulāriolus**, -ī *m* money-lender

12: **contingō**, **-ere**, **-tīgi**, **-tactus** touch
minus (adv.) less
Augusta, **-ae** *f* Livia, the wife of Augustus

13: **avia**, **-ae** *f* grandmother

14: **sitque ē rēpūblicā** "and it would be a good thing for the republic"

15: **ferventia vapa vorāre** (a nonsensical quotation from some unknown poet) "to devour boiled turnips"
ex hōc diē "from this day forth"

16: **ut ante eum optimō iūre factus sit** "with all the appurtenances in as full a degree as any other before him" (tr. W. H. D. Rouse, Seneca, *Apocolocyntosis* [London/Cambridge, 1961], p. 389).

16–17: **Eamque rem ad metamorphōsēs Ovidiī esse adiciendam** "and that a note to that effect should be added to Ovid's *Metamorphoses*. (Ovid's lengthy poem relates the history of the universe in terms of the transformation of various beings into all sorts of things, including gods.)

Fourth Declension; Indefinite Pronouns; *Ferō*; *Cum*-Clauses

Fourth Declension

The stem of fourth declension nouns ends in -**u**-. Masculine and feminine nouns add -**s** to form the nominative. The nominative singular of fourth declension neuter nouns consists of the stem alone, with the final -**u** lengthened:

	versus, versūs, *m* *row, line*	**manus, manūs,** *f* *hand*	**cornū, cornūs,** *n* *horn*
		SINGULAR	
Nom.	versus	manus	cornū
Gen.	versūs	manūs	cornūs
Dat.	versuī	manuī	cornū
Acc.	versum	manum	cornū
Abl.	versū	manū	cornū
		PLURAL	
Nom.	versūs	manūs	cornua
Gen.	versuum	manuum	cornuum
Dat.	versibus	manibus	cornibus
Acc.	versūs	manūs	cornua
Abl.	versibus	manibus	cornibus

Observe that:

1. The characteristic -**u**- of this declension is retained in all endings except the dative and ablative plural, where -**ubus** usually becomes -**ibus**. (You will find examples in some authors, however, of the ending -**ubus**.)

2. The neuter ending in the dative singular is the stem alone, unlike the masculine and feminine forms which add -**i**.

3. Most nouns of the fourth declension are masculine. There are only four neuter nouns in this declension: **cornū**, "horn," **genū**, "knee," **pecū** (usually in the plural **pecua**), "flocks, herds," and **verū**, "spit," "javelin."

4. The main feminine nouns are **manus** and **domus**. **Domus** has both second and fourth declension endings:

	SINGULAR	PLURAL
Nom.	domus	domūs
Gen.	domūs	domuum
Dat.	domuī	domibus
Acc.	domum	domōs (domūs)
Abl.	domō (domū)	domibus
Loc.	domī	

The form **domī** is locative and means "at home"; the ablative singular **domō** and the accusative plural **domōs** are more common than their fourth declension equivalents, but all these forms do occur.

5. Nouns of the fourth declension are frequently formed from the fourth principal part of verbs:

versus, **-ūs**	row; line of verse	**vertere**	to turn
cursus, **-ūs**	course, journey	**currere**	to run
exitus, **-ūs**	departure	**exīre**	to depart
adventus, **-ūs**	arrival	**advenīre**	to arrive
exercitus, **-ūs**	army	**exercēre**	to exercise, to train
cāsus, **-ūs**	accident, chance	**cadere**	to fall

Indefinite Pronouns and Adjectives

An indefinite pronoun or adjective designates some person or thing, but not which one:

Someone will regret this.
Some people derive **virtūs** from the word **vir**.
Don't deny *anything*.

Most Latin indefinites are formed from the relative **quī** or the interrogative **quis**, to which a suffix or prefix has been added; in each case, this root word—not the suffix or prefix—is declined (the suffix or prefix is indeclinable):

1. **aliquis**, **aliquid**: someone, anyone, something, anything (**ali** + **quis**, **quid**). After **sī**, **nisi**, **num**, **nē**, and after a relative pronoun, the prefix **ali-** is dropped, leaving the appropriately declined form of **quis**, **quid**:[1]

[1] A popular mnemonic verse runs as follows:
'After **sī**, **nisi**, **num**, and **nē**,
All your "**ali**'s" go away.'

Aliquis hoc fēcit.	*Someone* did this.
Num **quis** hoc faciat?	Would *anyone* do this?
Sī **quid** fēcit,	If he did *anything*,

The adjectival form of **aliquis** is **aliquī**, **aliqua**, **aliquod**, which follows the declension of the relative **quī**, **quae**, **quod** except in the nominative singular feminine and in the neuter nominative and accusative plural, all of which are **aliqua**:

Aliqua animālia mē terrent.	*Some* animals terrify me.
Sī **qua** animālia tē terrent,	If *some* animals terrify you,
Aliqua puella hoc sciet.	*Some* girl will know this.
Sī **qua** puella hoc scit,	If *any* girl knows this,

2. **nesciōquis**, **nesciōquid**, someone [or other], something [or other] (**nesciō** + **quis**, **quid**: "I know not who/what thing"). Often this indefinite pronoun is separated into two words (**nesciō quis**, **nesciō quid**) but the meaning remains the same:

Nesciō quid consiliī contrā nōs facit.	He is making *some sort* of plan against us.
Ego **nesciōquem** vulnerāvī.	I wounded **someone**.

3. **quisquam**, **quidquam** or **quicquam**, anyone at all, anything at all (**quis**, **quid** + **quam**). It is used mainly after negatives (expressed or implied):

Nōlī **cuiquam** crēdere.	Don't believe in *anyone*.
Num **quisquam** mē vērē amet?	Does *anyone* truly love me?

4. **quīvīs**, **quaevīs**, **quidvīs**, whoever you will, whatever you please; hence, anyone, anything (**quī**, **quae**, **quid** + **vīs** [from **volō**]). **Quodvis** is the form of the neuter adjective.

5. **quīdam**, **quaedam**, **quiddam**, a certain person/thing; someone, something (**quī**, **quae**, **quid/quod** + **-dam**). **Quoddam** is the form of the neuter adjective.[2] As in English, the speaker may have a specific person or thing in mind.

The relative **quī** is the root word of the masculine and feminine pronouns **quīvīs**, **quaevīs**, and **quīdam**, **quaedam**, and also of the neuter adjectives **quodvīs** and **quoddam**. The interrogative **quid**, by contrast, is the root word of the neuter pronouns **quidvīs** and **quiddam**.

6. **quicumque**, **quaecumque**, **quodcumque**, whoever, whatever. This is an indefinite relative formed by the addition of the adverb **-cumque** to a relative pronoun. Only the part of the word from the relative pronoun is declined (**cuiuscumque**, **cuicumque**, etc.).

7. **quisquis**, **quidquid** or **quicquid**, whoever, whatever. Both parts are declined, but the only forms in regular use are the nominative singular, the accusative neuter singular, and the ablative singular (**quōquō**).

[2] Do not confuse the pronoun **quīdam** with the conjunction **quidem**, "indeed."

8. **quisque, quaeque, quidque**, each person, each thing. **quodque** is the neuter adjective.

9. **uterque, utraque, utrumque**, each of two.

The distributive pronouns/adjectives **quisque** and **uterque** are often grouped with indefinite pronouns, since they are frequently used in a general sense. Compare the difference between the pronoun **quisque**, "each one," and the adjective **omnis**, "every."

Quisque sibi sōlī crēdit.	Each person (in a general sense) trusts himself alone.
Tyrannus omnis sibi sōlī crēdit.	Every tyrant (every individual tyrant) trusts himself alone.

Scrībenda

A. Identify all possible cases of the following phrases:

manus magna	versus longus
manūs magnās	versūs longī
manuum dulcium	cornū tuō
manus dulcis	cornū tuum
domūs nostrae	exitū nostrō
domuī nostrae	exitūs nostrōs
domō dulcī	

B. Decline the following:

aliquis
aliquī versus
aliquod cornu
quaeque manus
quīdam cursus

C. Translate the following sentences.

1. Tibi grātiās agimus, quisquis es.
2. Quīdam sōlam probant quamcumque iniērunt viam.
3. Num quemquam deōrum colunt?
4. Nōmina ostendunt quae vīs sit in quōque deō.
5. Bovēs quāsdam amor quīdam sīc mōvit ut sonum sonuērunt.
6. Quisque vestrum habet suam opiniōnem.
7. Nōlī quicquam negāre.
8. Sī persōna quid sē dignum dīceret, id decōrum esset.
9. Sīc mē formābat puerum exemplīs verbīsque, seu mālēbat seu nōlēbat mē aliquid facere.
10. Mox quid dē quōque magistrō sentiam scrībam.
11. Nūllus eris, Geta, nisi quid cōnsiliī celeriter invēneris.
12. Cōgēbar memoriā tenēre Aenēae nesciōcuius errōrēs. (**Aenēas**, **-ae** *m*, Aeneas; **error**, **errōris** *m*, a wandering)
13. Sī quid volō, scrībam ipse.
14. Invēneram librum cuiusdam Cicerōnis.

Irregular Verb: *ferō, ferre, tulī, lātus*

Ferō is a very common Latin verb. Its basic meaning is "carry." It also means "bring," "bear," "endure," and "relate" or "tell" (in the sense of conveying information).

Indicative		Subjunctive	
ACTIVE	PASSIVE	ACTIVE	PASSIVE
	PRESENT		
ferō	feror	feram	ferar
fers	ferris	ferās	ferāris
fert	fertur	ferat	ferātur
ferimus	ferimur	ferāmus	ferāmur
fertis	feriminī	ferātis	ferāminī
ferunt	feruntur	ferant	ferantur
	IMPERFECT		
ferēbam	ferēbar	ferrem	ferrer
ferēbās	ferēbāris	ferrēs	ferrēris
(etc.)			
	FUTURE		
feram	ferar	——	——
ferēs	ferēris		
(etc.)			
	PERFECT		
tulī	lātus sum	tulerim	lātus sim
tulistī	lātus es	tuleris	lātus sīs
(etc.)			
	PLUPERFECT		
tuleram	lātus eram	tulissem	lātus essem
tulerās	lātus erās	tulissēs	lātus essēs
(etc.)			
	FUTURE PERFECT		
tulerō	lātus erō	——	——
tuleris	lātus eris	——	——
(etc.)			

Imperative

SINGULAR		PLURAL	
fer	carry! endure!	ferte	carry! endure!

INFINITIVES

	ACTIVE	PASSIVE
Present	ferre to carry/endure	ferrī to be carried/endured
Perfect	tulisse to have carried/endured	lātus esse to have been carried/endured
Future	latūrus esse to be about to carry/endure	[lātum īrī to be about to be carried/endured]

PARTICIPLES

Present Active	ferēns, ferentis carrying/enduring	——
Perfect Passive	——	lātus, -a, -um having been carried/endured
Future	lātūrus, -a, -um about to carry/endure	ferendus, -a, -um about to be carried/endured

Observe that:

1. In the present stem, the second and third singular active and passive, the second plural active, and the passive and active infinitives lack a connecting vowel[3] between the stem **fer**- and the personal or infinitive ending.

2. The perfect active stem, **tul**-, comes from the verb **tollere** (the reduplicated form **tetulī** is found in Plautus), as does the perfect passive stem (***tlātus**).

3. The imperative **fer**, **ferte** is irregular. Compare the other three irregular imperatives, **dūc**, **dīc**, **fac**, which you learned in Chapter III.

The following compounds of **ferō** are very common:

ad	**afferō**, **afferre**, **attulī**, **allātus**, bring, convey to
ab	**auferō**, **auffere**, **abstulī**, **ablātus**, carry away
cum	**conferō**, **conferre**, **contulī**, **collātus**, bring together, compare **conferre** + reflexive (**tē confers**; **sē confert**, etc.), take oneself, go
dē	**dēferō**, **dēferre**, **dētulī**, **dēlātus**, bring away, bring down; remove; report
dis	**differō**, **differre**, **distulī**, **dīlātus**, carry in different directions; scatter; postpone; differ
ex	**efferō**, **efferre**, **extulī**, **ēlātus**, carry out; bring forth
in	**inferō**, **inferre**, **intulī**, **illātus**, carry into; inflict upon (+ dat.)
ob	**offerō**, **offerre**, **obtulī**, **oblātus**, bring to (+ dat.); present, offer
re	**referō**, **referre**, **retulī**, **relātus**, bring back, report **referre** + reflexive, to return, withdraw
sub	**sufferō**, **sufferre**, **sustulī**, **sublātus**, endure, suffer

[3] Also called a "thematic vowel" (-**i**- or -**u**- in Latin; -**e**- or -**o**- in Indo-European), as in **dūc-i-s**, **dūc-u-nt**. **Ferō** is one of the few "athematic" verbs in Latin, i.e., the personal endings are added directly to the root (compare **es-t**, **es-tis**).

Cum-Clauses

Frequently you will encounter **cum** as a subordinating conjunction, meaning "since/because," "although," or "when." The verb in the clause it introduces will be either indicative or subjunctive, depending on the meaning of **cum**.

1. *Cum + Indicative*: **Cum** meaning "when" governs the indicative if the clause defines or identifies the time at which the action of the main clause takes place:

> Animus, **cum adest**, nōn appāret.
> *When the soul is present*, it is not visible.
>
> Longum illud tempus **cum nōn erō** mē movet.
> That long period of time *when I will not exist* disturbs me.

2. *Cum + Indicative, "whenever"*: **Cum** is also used with the indicative to identify a general time:

> Hoc nōbīs magnum vitium est: **cum amāmus**, tum perīmus.
> This is our great flaw: *whenever we love*, we perish.

3. *Cum + Subjunctive*: **Cum** with the subjunctive can be translated "when," "because," or "although." This **cum** is more subjective than the temporal or general **cum**; it denotes the reason something happened (cause) or the circumstances under which it happened, or it allows some concession to the event.

> **Cum haec dīxissem**, omnēs tacuērunt.
> *When I had said these things*, everyone fell silent. (Circumstance)
>
> Deī sunt habitī **cum aeternī essent**.
> They were considered gods *because they were immortal*. (Cause)
>
> Animus, **cum adsit**, nōn tamen apparet.
> *Although the soul is present*, it is not visible. (Concession)

Frequently the causal and circumstantial **cum** overlap in meaning. For example, in the first sentence **cum . . . dīxissem** could also be interpreted, depending on the context, as causal: "because I had said (these things)." The use of **tamen**, "nevertheless," in the third example rules out the possibility that this **cum** could be causal or circumstantial. This gives us one guideline in translating **cum**-clauses: when **tamen** appears in the main clause, the **cum**-clause is usually concessive.

Scrībenda

A. Write a complete synopsis of **auferō** in the third person singular and translate all the indicative forms.

B. Identify the following forms:

ablātus	abstulit	auferendus
offerrī	illātus esse	adlatūrus

attulit offerēns obtulisse
dīlātus esse dēferendus differs

C. Translate the following sentences, and then change the ablative absolute to a **cum**-clause:

1. Hīs dictīs, discessit.
2. Mē redeunte, senātus populusque Rōmānus deīs grātiās ēgērunt.
3. Pāce victōriīs factā, Iānus Quirīnus clausus est. (**Iānus Quirīnus**, the temple of Janus)
4. Vitiīs aliōrum vīsīs, sapientēs factī sumus.
5. Animō absente, nihil vīvere potest.

D. Translate the following sentences. If the sentence contains a **cum**-clause, identify it as temporal, general, causal, circumstantial or concessive.

1. Cum Herculem cibō vīnōque gravātum sopor oppressisset, Cācus bovēs in spēluncam traxit. (**gravō**, **-āre**, **-āvī**, **-ātus**, make heavy)
2. Cācus, cum āvertere bovēs vellet, tamen nōverat vestigia quaerentem dominum ad spēluncam dēductūra esse.
3. Cum bovēs sonum sonuissent, reddita inclusārum boum vox Herculem convertit.
4. Cum parentēs meī appellābant aliquid et cum, id dicentēs, corpus ad aliquid movēbant, vidēbam et memoriā tenēbam hoc esse eius nōmen. (**parēns**, **-ntis** *m* or *f*, parent)
5. Crēdō Graecīs puerīs Vergilium esse amārum cum eum sīc discere cōgantur ut ego Homērum discere coactus sum. (**amārus**, **-a**, **-um**, unpleasant)
6. Cum constituissem scrībere ad tē aliquid hōc tempore, ab eō incipere voluī quod aetātī tuae aptum esset.
7. Cum multa sint in philosophiā et gravia et ūtilia ā philosophīs agitāta, referam ea quae dē officiīs trādita ab illīs sunt. (**ūtilis**, **-e**, useful)
8. Cum sumus negotiīs cūrīsque vacuī, tum studēmus aliquid novī vidēre, audīre, discere.
9. Multōs imitātiō brevitātis dēcipit ut, cum sē brevēs putent esse, longī sint. (**dēcipiō**, **-ere**, deceive; **imitātiō**, **-iōnis** *f*, imitation)
10. Augustum cum Hercule conferam.
11. Cum frūgēs Cererem vīnumque Līberum vocēmus quem tam insānum esse putās quī illud quod comedat deum esse crēdat? (**quī** = **ut is**, **frūgēs**, **-um** *f* pl., fruits of the earth, grain)
12. Stratonīcus cum quīdam molestus Alabandum deum esse dīceret et Herculem esse negāret, "ergō" inquit "mihi Alabandus, tibi Herculēs sit irātus." (**Stratonīcus**, **-ī** *m* and **Alabandus**, **-ī** *m* are proper names; **irātus**, **-a**, **-um** + dat., angry with, at)
13. Nōn Herculī nocēre Dēianīra voluit cum eī vestem dedit. Multī enim prōfuērunt cum obesse vellent, et offuērunt cum prōdesse vellent. (**obsum**, **obesse**, **offuī**, **offutūrus** + dat., injure, harm)
14. Confer dīvīna aliōrum antīqua reperta.
15. Dubitātiō est cum quaerere videātur ōrātor utrum dīcat. (**dubitātiō**, **-ōnis** *f*, hesitation)
16. Dictātūram et absentī et praesentī mihi oblātam nōn recēpī. (**dictātūra**, **-ae** *f*, dictatorship)

E. Translate the following sentences from English to Latin. When a word is followed by a double asterisk (**), use **ferō** or the appropriate compound of **ferō**.

1. Give me strength to go** to Athens.
2. A certain man had to endure** great pain.
3. The horn of plenty was snatched by Hercules from the head of a god. (plenty, **copia**, **-ae** *f*)
4. Each person said he would endure** great pain for his country.
5. He does not give money to someone unless he expects to receive something.
6. Don't give anyone anything you want for yourself.

Verba tenenda

Verbs

afferō, **afferre**, **attulī**, **allātus** bring near, bring to; report

appareō, **-ēre**, **apparuī**, **apparitus** become visible, appear, come into sight

auferō, **auferre**, **abstulī**, **ablātus** take away, carry off, remove

conferō, **conferre**, **contulī**, **collātus** bring together, compare
sē conferre go, betake oneself

cupiō, **-ere**, **-īvī**, **-ītus** long for, desire, wish

currō, **-ere**, **cucurrī**, **cursus** run, hasten

dēferō, **dēferre**, **dētulī**, **dēlātus** bring down, bring, deliver

differō, **differre**, **distulī**, **dilātus** carry in different directions; scatter, disperse; postpone; differ

discēdō, **-ere**, **-cessī**, **-cessus** divide, separate; depart, leave

efferō, **efferre**, **extulī**, **ēlātus** bring out, carry out; set forth; publish; proclaim

ferō, **ferre**, **tulī**, **lātus** bring, carry, bear, report

imprimō, **-ere**, **impressī**, **impressus** press into, stamp, imprint; impress, influence

inferō, **inferre**, **intulī**, **illātus** carry in, bring in;
+ dat. inflict upon; attack

offerō, **offerre**, **obtulī**, **oblātus** present, show, bring forward, offer

oppōnō, **-ere**, **opposuī**, **oppositus** set against; oppose

pandō, **-ere**, **pandī**, **passus** spread, spread out, unfold, expand, extend

prōcēdō, **-ere**, **-cessī**, **-cessus** go forward, forth; proceed; advance

referō, **referre**, **retulī**, **relātus** carry back, bring back; report

sufferō, **sufferre**, **sustulī**, **sublātus** carry under; bear; support, sustain; undergo, suffer

surgō, **-ere**, **surrexī**, **surrectus** raise, lift; rise, arise, get up

volvō, **-ere**, **volvī**, **volūtus** (active) roll, turn over; (passive) revolve

Nouns

actus, **-ūs** *m* motion, performance, act
affectus, **-ūs** *m* a state of body and of mind, produced by some outside influence: affection, mood, disposition
astrum, **-ī** *n* star, constellation
bracchium, **-iī** *n* arm
cāsus, **-ūs** *m* a falling, a falling down; accident; misfortune
cornū, **cornūs** *n* horn
cursus, **-ūs** *m* a running, a course, a passage
domus, **-ūs** (also **domus**, **-ī**) *f* home
exercitus, **-ūs** *m* army, troops
exitus, **-ūs** *m* departure
genū, **genūs** *n* knee
intellectus, **-ūs** *m* intellect, perception
iuvenis, **-is** (gen. pl., **iuvenum**) *m* young man
lūmen, **lūminis** *n* light; pl., eyes
manus, **-ūs** *f* hand; band of men
mōtus, **-ūs** *m* motion, movement; emotion
occāsus, **-ūs** *m* a fall; a setting
ortus, **-ūs** *m* a rising; rise, beginning, origin
reditus, **-ūs** *m* a returning; return
sēnsus, **-ūs** *m* sense, feeling
sīdus, **sīderis** *n* constellation; star
signum, **-ī** *n* sign, mark; constellation
versus, **-ūs** *m* a furrow; a line; a line of writing; a verse
virgo, **virginis** *f* maiden; unmarried girl; the constellation Virgo
vīsus, **-ūs** *m* a seeing; a looking; sight; the thing seen: appearance
voluntās, **-tātis** *f* free will, choice

Indefinite and distributive pronouns

aliquis, **aliquid** someone, something; anyone, anything
quīcumque, **quaecumque**, **quodcumque** whoever, whatever
quīdam, **quaedam**, **quiddam** (neuter adj.: **quoddam**) someone, something; a certain person, a certain thing
quisquam, **quidquam** (or **quicquam**) anyone, anything (used mainly after implied or expressed negative)
quisque, **quaeque**, **quidque** (neuter adj.: **quodque**) each person, each thing (properly, of more than two persons or things)
quisquis, **quidquid** whoever, whatever
quīvīs, **quaevīs**, **quidvīs** (neuter adj.: **quodvīs**) anyone, anything
uterque, **utraque**, **utrumque** each person, each thing (of two)

Adjectives

caelestis, **-e** having to do with the heavens, heavenly
corporālis, **-e** having to do with the body; physical, corporal
cupidus, **-a**, **-um** (+ gen.) desirous (of); longing, eager (for)
ingēns; **ingentis** (gen.) huge, enormous, large
nātūrālis, **-e** natural, in keeping with nature
paucī, **-ae**, **-a** (pl.) few, a few
proprius, **-a**, **-um** special, particular, one's own
tardus, **-a**, **-um** slow, sluggish; late

Conjunctions

at but, but indeed
cum + indicative when (temporal); whenever (general)
cum + subjunctive when (circumstantial), since, because, although

Adverbs

nātūrāliter naturally
tam . . . **quam** as much . . . as; as well . . . as
nōn tam . . . **quam** not so much . . . as
vērō in truth; in fact; certainly; (as corroborating adversative): but in truth, but in fact; however

Notanda

There are several Latin words meaning "star" and "constellation": **astrum** comes from the verb meaning "strew," since the stars were "strewn over the vault of heaven." **Sīdus** is more often a collection of stars, and hence a constellation, and can be used in the singular as a collective noun or in the plural as a constellation. **Stella** is usually a single star, a comet or meteor, or even the sun.

Cursus is a running on foot, horse, chariot, ship, etc.; it can also be a fixed path (e.g., **sōlis cursus**, the path of the sun). During the Roman Empire the **cursus publicī** were a series of relay stations set up for the speedy transmission of information. What is **vītae cursus**? **verbōrum cursus**? **honōrum cursus**?

Contrary to the principle that parisyllabic nouns of the third declension are **i**-stems (and hence end in -**ium** in the genitive plural) the noun **iuvenis** in the genitive plural is **iuvenum**, and therefore not an **i**-stem noun.

lūmen is not only light, a source of light, or a lamp, but also the light of the eye, and hence the eye itself; and by extension it comes to mean (particularly in poetry) the light of life or life itself.

occāsus and **ortus** can mean the setting and the rising, respectively, of the sun (compare "Occident," the West: the land of the setting sun, and "Orient," the East: the land of the rising sun).

The adjective **paucī**, **paucae**, **pauca** rarely occurs in the singular. As a noun, **paucī** sometimes has the sense of "the few" or the "select few" (as opposed to the multitude). The neuter **pauca** sometimes means "a few words" (**verba** is implied).

Ante legenda

Translate

1. Tūne novum sīdus caelō post mortem daberis?
2. Iam Scorpius bracchia ad sē confert magnamque partem caelī tibi relinquit. (**Scorpius**, **-ī** *m*, the constellation Scorpio)
3. Surgit clārum sīdus ex omnī caelō signa alia expellēns.
4. Quoddam sīdus tam clārum est ut surgēns ē caelō alia sīdera expellat. Cum sīdus illud surgit, sīdera alia ē caelō fugiunt. Cum illud surgat, alia fugere videntur.
5. Tam clārum erat sīdus ut differret omnia alia fulgentia in caelō. Quaecumque fulgēbant illō dilāta sunt. (**fulgeō**, **-ēre**, shine)
6. Cuiusdam sīderis et ortum et occāsum ūnā horā vidēmus quibusdam noctibus.
7.

   Omnia quī magnī dispexit lūmina mundī,
      quī stellārum ortūs invēnit atque occāsus
   Īdem mē ille Conōn caelestī in lūmine vīdit . . .
      fulgentem clārē.

   (Catullus 66.1–9)

   (**dispiciō**, **-ere**, **dispexī**, **dispectus**, see with an effort; discern; investigate; **Conōn**, **-ōnis** *m*, an astronomer of the third century B.C., who discovered the constellation "Coma Berenices")

8.

   Cēnābis bene, mī Fabulle, apud mē . . .
   sī tēcum attuleris bonam atque magnam
   cēnam, nōn sine candidā puellā
   et vinō. . . .
   Haec sī, dīcō, attuleris, cēnābis bene.

   (Catullus 13)

   (**cēnō**, **-āre**, dine; **Fabullus**, **-ī** *m*, a proper name; **candidus**, **-a**, **-um**, beautiful)

9.

   Vīvāmus, mea Lesbia, atque amēmus. . . .
   Sōlēs occidere et redīre possunt:
   Nōbīs cum semel occidit brevis lux,
   nox est perpetua ūna dormienda.

   (Catullus 5.1–6)

   (**Lesbia**, **-ae** *f*, Lesbia, the poetic name of Catullus' mistress; **dormiō**, **-īre**, sleep)

10.

    Quaecumque hominēs bene cuiquam aut dīcere possunt
       aut facere, haec ā tē dictaque factaque sunt.

    (Catullus 76)

11.

Bella es, nōvimus, et puella, vērum est,
  et dīvēs, quis enim potest negāre?
Sed cum tē nimium, Fabulla, laudās,
  nec dīvēs nec bella nec puella es.

(Martial I.64)

(**bellus**, **-a**, **-um**, beautiful; **dīvēs**, **dīvitis** [adj.], rich; **Fabulla**, **-ae** *f*, a proper name; **nimium** [adv.], excessively)

12.

Quem recitās meus est, ō Fīdentīne, libellus;
  sed male cum recitās, incipit esse tuus.

(Martial I.38)

(**recitō**, **-āre**, read aloud; **Fīdentīnus**, **-ī** *m*, a proper name; **libellus**, **-ī** *m*, (little) book)

13. Aliquis refert quendam vēnisse. Fertur Iōvī quendam novum vēnisse.

14. Sī rex aliēnus vim urbī vestrae inferet, prīnceps auxilium mittet. Sī quī rex vim urbī inferret, quid auxiliī prīnceps mitteret? Sī quod auxilium mīsisset, vīs urbī ā rege nōn illāta esset.

15. Cum quīdam crēdant corpora caelestia affectūs mōtūsque suōs imprimere, stellae vītam eōrum regere videntur.

16. Cum nōn crēdidisset corpora caelestia hominēs imprimere, mōtibus stellārum tamen studuit.

17. Nunc canere incipiam quō sīdere agricolae terra vertenda sit. *(After Vergil,* Georgics *I.1)*

18. Hīs versibus discēs quō sidere terra tibi vertenda sit.

Legenda

Mythology (4): Astrology and Astronomy

When Hercules became a god, he acquired his own constellation in the heavens. There is some uncertainty as to which constellation was supposed to be Hercules—some writers identify the **Herculeum sīdus** as the constellation Leo, the Nemean lion whose skin Hercules wore after defeating the creature. In late antiquity, however, the constellation of Hercules was identified as **Engonasin** ("The Kneeling Figure"), and astronomers now call this constellation, "Hercules." (Hercules is thought to be kneeling in exhaustion after his labors.)

The constellations had long been a subject of widespread interest, particularly in agricultural and pastoral societies. Astrology, the so-called science of the influence of heavenly bodies upon human life, emerged in the Greek world, and during the first century A.D. spread rapidly through the Roman world.

The Roman attitude toward astrology was very mixed. Emperors from Augustus to Alexander Severus consulted astrologers. The poet Juvenal satirized them. As a philosopher, Cicero fulminated against astrology, but as a rhetorician, he subscribed to its principles. The Stoic philosopher Seneca was a firm believer. Ptolemy, the greatest astronomer of the ancient world, became a convert to astrology and its most famous spokesman. Joined with an almost universal acceptance of astrology was an enormous distrust of its commercial practitioners, who were considered mere charlatans. As early as Augustus, laws against "**Chaldaeī**" and "**mathēmaticī**" were passed. Tacitus called them "a source of danger for the powerful, and of deception for the ambitious—a race of men which in our state will ever be shunned—and retained" (**genus hominum potentibus infīdum, spērantibus fallax, quod in cīvitāte nostrā et vetābitur semper et retinābitur**, *Historiae* I.22).

When the church attained a position of prominence, it virulently attacked astrology. It forbade Christians to participate in any divinatory acts, and rejected as fatalistic the belief in the stars as the arbiters of human destiny. In the fourth century, Augustine formulated the church doctrine that diabolic aid is involved in astrological predictions. Isidore of Seville in the seventh century is said to have done more than any other writer "to fasten upon the Middle Ages the patristic condemnation of astrology."[4] At the same time, Isidore established a distinction between astronomy (**nātūrālis astrologia**) and astrology (**superstitiōsa astrologia**), the latter being the science practiced by **mathēmaticī**. The church did not have to deal again directly with astrologers until the thirteenth century, but an ongoing acceptance of this "science" can be easily detected throughout these centuries. During the Carolingian period (mid-eighth through tenth centuries), for example, we find attempts being made to Christianize signs of the Zodiac.[5]

During the twelfth century, the study of astrology suddenly became widespread and was legitimized within the Church, after translators such as Adelard of Bath (born c. 1100) made astronomy and geometry available to the west by translating works on Arabic science such as Albumasar's *Introductorium in Astronomiam* into Latin. These translations did much to make astrology acceptable to the Church and to render it credible as a science, for now Latin astrologers could make predictions based on calculating the position of the planets, whereas previously they had been unable to do this correctly and had had to rely on such devices as the numerical value of the letters of a name or other superstitious plays on numbers.

Arabic astrology also lessened the dependence on fate. Whereas Ptolemy's *Tetrabiblos* confined itself to judicial astrology (prediction of the future according to the stars at birth), Arabic astrology minimized the importance of judicial astrology and emphasized **interrogātiōnēs**—

[4] Thomas O. Wedel, *The Mediaeval Attitude Toward Astrology* (New Haven, 1920), p. 27.
[5] Jean Seznec, *The Survival of the Pagan Gods*, p. 50*ff*.

The signs of the zodiac superimposed on the parts of the body they were thought to control. From a fifteenth century French Book of Hours of the Duc de Berry.

(questions regarding the discovery of a thief, lost treasure, the trustworthiness of a friend, the dowry of a prospective bride, etc.)—and **ēlectiōnēs**, the determination of the propitious moment for undertaking any act of daily life. This latter form of astrology led to the development of medical astrology. Arabic astrology was considered superior to the rival doctrine of judicial astrology, as it did not attempt to predict the future itself and thus avoided the fatalism of Ptolemy's astrology. It was therefore welcomed by Christian scientists of the thirteenth century, such as Roger Bacon (c. 1214–1294). Thomas Aquinas (c. 1225–1274), a contemporary of Bacon, faced with the difficulty of providing a compromise between the early church and the new astrology, found the solution in a passage in Augustine, who had allowed that the stars have influence but that the human will remains inviolate.

Ever since Juvenal poets had satirized astrologers. The Italian poet and scholar Petrarch (1304–1374) continued this tradition, and his friend Coluccio Salutati denounced astrology as an empty science and a vain art, but no astronomer of note until the time of Kepler (1571–1630) dared to question the reality of astrology. Even Galileo (1564–1642) wrote horoscopes for the Medicean court. So long as the cosmology of Aristotle, with its doctrine of the prime mover, and the geocentric astronomy of Ptolemy held sway, refutation of astrology was impossible. With the emergence of the new astronomy of Copernicus (1473–1543), which showed that the earth and planets moved around the sun, the refutation of astrology should no longer have been necessary. The humanists of the Renaissance, however, saw no contradiction between astrology and the sciences. Their eventual rebellion against the tyranny of the stars was for moral reasons: "Humanist pride in a new concept of man's worth rose in opposition to astrology even before new methods of observation and reckoning had advanced far enough to condemn it."[6]

1. Aratus (third century B.C.) was a Greek poet best known to us today for his astronomical poem *Phaenomena*, in which he versifies the theories of the fourth century astronomer Eudoxus. Aratus' poem achieved immediate fame and remained popular among Greeks and Romans throughout antiquity. Portions of Latin translations of Aratus' poem (called **Arātēa**) by Cicero, by the emperor Tiberius' nephew Germanicus, and by the fourth century A.D. poet Avien(i)us, still survive. The following excerpts, taken from Cicero's **Arātēa**, show the procession of constellations moving through the night sky. We see the rising of Virgo (also known as **Iustitia**, Justice), followed by Sirius (the Dog), and then by the Ship, and finally by the Claws of Scorpio. The appearance of Scorpio (usually associated with Mars, the god of war) reminds the poet of the story of Orion, the hunter, whose constellation appears to be fleeing the attack of the ferocious scorpion.

[6] Seznec, p. 60.

Nicolaus Copernicus with a figure showing the earth revolving around the sun.

Nōn pauca ē caelō dēpellēns* signa* repentē*
surgit pandēns clāra lūmina Virgo. . . .
Inde pedēs Canis* ostendit iam posteriōrēs*,
et post ipse trahit clārō cum lūmine Puppim* . . .
et cum iam tōtō prōcessit corpore Virgo,
haec medium ostendit . . . mālum*.
At cum prōcēdunt obscūrō corpore Chēlae*
. . . surgit ille . . . Nixus*
. . . cuius nocte occāsum atque ortum vīdimus ūnā*
saepe. . . .
Cum vērō vīs vehemēns* surgit Nepae*
. . . errat per terrās fāma haec:
Ōrīon* quondam* manibus violāsse* Diānam*
dīcitur, excelsīs* errāns in collibus* āmēns*. . . .
Ille ferās vēcors* āmentī corde necābat,
rēgis ornāre* epulās* cupiēns. . . .
At vērō*, pedibus subitō* percussa* Diānae
insula* discessit . . .
et caecās lustrāvit* lūce lacūnās*.
Ē quibus ingentī surrexit cum corpore prae sē

1: **dēpellō**, **-ere** drive away
signum, **-ī** *n* constellation, star
repentē (adv.) suddenly
3: **canis**, **-is** *m* or *f* dog; the constellation Sirius
posterior, **-e** rear
4: **puppis**, **-is** *f* ship; the constellation Argo
(**puppim**: acc.)
6: **mālus**, **-ī** *m* beam, pole; the staff held by Virgo (sometimes represented as a staff of grain)
7: **Chēlae**, **-arum** *f* the claws of Scorpio (also known as the constellation **Lībra**)
8: **Nixus** the Kneeler (Greek: *Engonasin*) (i.e., Hercules)
9: **ūnā** (adv.) at the same time
11: **vehemēns**, **-ntis** violent, furious
11, 24: **Nepa**, **-ae** *f* the constellation Scorpio
13: **Ōrīon**, **-iōnis** *m* the constellation Orion
quondam (adv.) once, at one time
violā(vi)sse, from **violō**, **-āre** violate, injure, dishonor
13, 17: **Diāna**, **-ae** *f* goddess of the hunt
14: **excelsus**, **-a**, **-um** high, lofty
collis, **-is** *m* hill
āmēns; **āmentis** (gen.) senseless, mad
15: **vēcors**, **vēcordis** mad, insane, senseless
16: **ornō**, **-āre** furnish, equip, adorn
epulae, **-ārum** *f* pl. banquet, feast
17: **at vērō** but
subitō (adv.) sudden
percūdō, **-ere**, **-cūdī**, **-cussus** strike, break through (by Diana's kick)
18: **insula**, **-ae** *f* island (where he was hunting)
19: **lustrō**, **-āre** wander over, purify, illuminate
lacūna, **-ae** *f* hole, pit, pool (a hole where water accumulates)

scorpius* . . . praeportāns* flēbile acūmen*:
hic vēnantem* perculit* ictū* . . .
mortiferum* in vēnās fundēns vīrus*.
Quārē, cum magnīs sē Nepa* lūcibus effert,
Ōrīon fugiēns commendat corpora terrīs.

(After Cicero, Arātēa, *379–435)*

2. Early in Augustus' reign poets began predicting the apotheosis of the new emperor. In Vergil's *Georgics*, published shortly after Augustus had defeated Antony and become the sole ruler of the empire, the constellations are said to be making room in the heavens for Augustus' constellation (**sīdus**), Libra, the "Scales (of Justice)," referred to here as the "Claws" (**Chēlae**). The constellation Scorpio is drawing in his "pursuing claws" (**chēlās sequentēs**), leaving a space between himself and the constellation Virgo (**Ērigonē**). Libra is the sign under which Augustus was born (September 23, 63 B.C.).

Anne* novum tardīs sīdus tē mēnsibus addēs
quā [viā] locus Ērigonēn* inter Chēlāsque sequentēs
panditur (ipse tibī iam bracchia contrahit ardēns
Scorpius et caelī iustā plūs* parte relīquit)?

(Vergil, Georgics *I.32.35)*

3. During the reigns of Augustus and Tiberius, a relatively obscure poet named Marcus Manilius wrote a lengthy poem on astrology, the *Astronomica*. The poem is an instructional book, in dactylic hexameters, explaining all the minutiae (how to determine one's horoscope, how to interpret all the various possible arrangements of the various signs of the zodiac, etc.). Here Manilius explains that different constellations govern each part of the human body and determine not only how long a person will live but even the quality of one's life from the moment of birth.

Accipe dīvīsās* hominis per sīdera partēs
singulaque* imperiīs propriīs parentia* membra,
in quibus praecipuās* tōtō dē corpore vīrēs

21: **scorpius**, -ī *m* scorpion
praeportō, **-āre** carry in front of, before
flēbile acūmen "a sting that brings mourning or tears"
22: **vēnantem** the hunter (the person hunting)
percellō, **-ere**, **-culī**, **-culsus** beat down, destroy
ictus, **-ūs** *m* blow, stroke, sting
23: **mortiferum in vēnās fundēns virus** "by pouring his death-bearing poison (**vīrus**) in the veins (**vēnās**)"

1: **anne** (conj.), **an** + enclitic **-ne**)
2: **Ērigonēn** (acc. *f* sing., after **inter**)
4: **plūs** (acc. *n* sing.) (+ abl.) more than (**iustā parte**)

1: **dīvīsus**, **-a**, **-um** distributed
2: **singulī**, **-ae**, **-a** single, individual
pareō, **-ēre** + dat. be obedient to
3: **praecipuus**, **-a**, **-um** particular, special

exercent. Ariēs* caput est . . . sortītus*;
pulcherrima colla* [est sortītus]
Taurus*, et in Geminīs* aequālī* bracchia sorte*
scrībuntur cōnexa* umerīs, pectusque* locātum*
sub Cancrō* est, laterum* regnum scapulaeque* Leōnis,
Virginis in propriam dēscendunt* īlia* sortem*,
Lībra regit clūnēs*, et Scorpius inguine* gaudet*,
Centaurō* femora* accēdunt*, Capricornus* utrīsque
imperitat* genibus, crūrum* fundentis Aquārī*
arbitrium* est, Piscēsque* pedum sibi* iūra reposcunt*.

(After Manilius, Astronomica *2.453–465)*

4. The satiric poet Juvenal (born c. A.D. 50–65) was sharply critical of astrologers and of Romans who trusted in them. In the following passage, the speaker is explaining his decision to emigrate from Rome, where he feels out of place:

Quid Rōmae faciam? Mentīrī* nesciō; librum,
sī malus est, nequeō* laudāre et poscere*; mōtūs

4: **Ariēs, Ariĕtis** *m* the Ram
5: **Ariēs est sortitus** + acc. "Aries has been alotted (the head)"
5: **collum**, -ī *n* neck
pulcherrima colla (acc. *n* pl.) very handsome neck
6: **Taurus**, -ī *m* the Bull
Geminī, **-ōrum** *m* Gemini, the Twins
aequālis, **-e** equal
6, 9: **sors**, **sortis** *f* lot, fate
6–7: **in Geminīs scrībuntur**: "are assigned to the ranks of the Twins."
aequālī sorte i.e., one arm to each Twin
7: **cōnectō**, **-ere**, **-nexuī**, **-nexus** + dat. connect to, link to
pectus, **pectoris** *n* chest, breast
7–8: **locātum sub** "dependent on"
8: **Cancer**, **-crī** *m* the Crab
latus, **lateris** *n* side, lungs
scapulae, **-ārum** *f* pl. shoulder blades
laterum regnum scapulae que Leōnis: "the lungs and the shoulders are the Lion's realm."
9: **dēscendō**, **-ere** come down
īliā, **-ōrum** *n* pl. belly: "the belly comes down to the lot (**sortem**) of the Maiden"
10: **clūnis**, **-is** *f* buttock
inguen, **-inis** *n* groin
gaudeō, **-ēre** (+ abl.) rejoice in
11: **Centaurō accēdunt** "(they) yield to the Centaur"
femur, **-oris** *n* thigh
Capricornus, -ī *m* Capricorn
12: **imperitō**, **-āre** + dat. give orders to
crūs, **crūris** *n* leg, shin
Aquārius, -ī *m* Aquarius, the Water-carrier
13: **arbitrium**, -ī *n* decision, judgment
Piscēs, **-ium** *m* pl. the Fishes
sibi iura reposcunt (+ gen.) "they claim their right over"

1: **mentīrī** (present infinitive) "to tell a lie"
2: **nequeō**, **-īre** = nōn possum
poscō, **-ere** ask for (a copy)

astrōrum ignōrō; fūnus* prōmittere* patris
nec volō, nec possum; rānārum* viscera* numquam
inspexī*

(Juv. 3.41–44)

5. Thomas Aquinas (1225–1274) faced the difficulty of forging a compromise between the early church and the new astrology. A passage in Augustine's *Dē cīvitāte Deī* gave the solution: stars have influence but the human will remains inviolate. Medieval astrology and Arabian **ēlectiōnēs** easily squared with this doctrine. Aquinas argued that the human intellect and will are not corporeal, and hence they escape that influence which the stars necessarily exert over matter. Indirectly there is an influence, however, since both intellect and will are intimately connected with corporeal organs.

Spirituālēs substantiae* quae caelestia corpora movent in corporālia quidem agunt mediantibus* caelestibus corporibus, sed in intellectum* hūmānum agunt immediatē*, illūminandō*. Voluntātem autem hūmānum mūtāre nōn possunt.

Dīcendum est multitūdinem hominum dūcī passiōnibus* suīs, quae sint mōtūs sēnsitīvī*, quās imprimere possint corpora caelestia. Paucī autem sunt sapientēs, quī huius modī passiōnibus* resistant*. Et ergō astrologī* ut in plūribus* vēra possunt praedīcere*, et maximē in commūnī*. Nōn autem in speciālī*, quia nihil prohibet* aliquem hominem per līberum arbitrium* passiōnibus* resistere*. Unde ipsī astrologī dīcunt sapientem hominem dominārī* astrīs, inquantum* scīlicet dominārī* suīs passiōnibus.

(After Thomas Aquinas, Summa Theologiae, *Ia.115.4)*

3: **fūnus, -eris** *n* funeral, death
prōmittō, -ere promise (i.e., foretell)
4: **rāna, -ae** *f* frog
viscera, -ōrum *n* inner organs
5: **inspiciō, -ere, inspexī, inspectus** inspect, examine (one frequent practice of Roman soothsayers was to inspect the entrails of animals, here of frogs.)

1: **spirituālēs substantiae** "the immaterial substances"
2: **mediō, -āre, -āvī, -ātus** be in the middle, act as agent
intellectus, -ūs *m* perception
3: **immediatē** (adv.) directly
illūminandō "by way of illumination"
5, 7, etc.: **passiō, -iōnis** *f* passion, emotion
6: **sensitīvus, -a, -um** of the senses
7, 10: **resistō, -ere** (+ dat.) oppose, resist
8: **astrologus, -ī** *m* astrologer
in plūribus "in the majority of cases"
praedīcō, -ere, -dixī, -dictus foretell, predict
8–9: **maximē in commūnī** "especially in a general sense"
9: **in speciālī** "in particular cases"
prohibeō, -ēre, prohibuī, prohibitus prevent
10: **arbitrium, -ī** *n* judgment
11: **dominārī** (pres. infin.) + abl. or dat."he is master over"
inquantum "inasmuch as"

6. Nicholas Copernicus (1473–1543), the great Polish astronomer and founder of modern astronomy, entitled his epochal work on the circular motions of heavenly bodies *Dē revolutiōnibus orbium caelestium*. With the publication of this work, the earth resumes its place among the ranks of the planets instead of being a unique object around which the other heavenly bodies revolve.

Iam quidem dēmonstrātum est terram quoque globī* formam habēre; videndum esse cēnseō an etiam forma terrae et mōtus sint idem, et quem partem mundī obtineat* terra, sine quibus nōn possumus invenīre certam apparentium in caelō ratiōnem. Multī auctōrēs* in mediō mundī terram quiescere* tam certē habent ut inopīnābile* putent sīve etiam ridiculum* contrārium* sentīre. Sī tamen attentius* rem* consīderēmus*, vidēbitur haec quaestiō* nōndum* absolūta* et idcircō* minimē* esse contemnenda*. Omnis enim quae vidētur secundum locum* mūtātiō* aut est propter* reī spectātae* mōtum, aut videntis, aut certē dispārem* utriusque mūtātiōnem. Nam inter mōta aequāliter* ad eadem nōn percipitur* mōtus, inter vīsum dīcō* et vidēns. Terra autem est unde caelestis ille circuitus* aspicitur* et vīsuī nostrō rēprōdūcitur*. Sī igitur mōtus aliquis terrae dēputētur*, mōtus ipse, in omnibus quae extrīnsecus* sunt, īdem apparēbit, sed ad partem oppositam tamquam praete-

1: **globus**, -ī *m* a round body, a sphere
3: **obtineō**, **-ere**, **-tinui**, **-tentus** hold, occupy
4: **auctor**, **-ōris** *m* author, writer
5: **quiescō**, **-ere**, **quiēvī**, **quiētus** be at rest, be quiet
inopīnābilis, **-e** inconceivable
6: **rīdiculus**, **-a**, **-um** ridiculous
contrārius, **-a**, **-um** opposite
attentius (adv.) more attentively; carefully, closely
rem (acc. *f* sing.) the matter, thing
6–7: **consīderō**, **-āre**, **-āvī**, **-ātus** inspect, examine
7: **quaestiō**, **-iōnis** *f* investigation
nōndum not yet
absolūtus, **-a**, **-um** brought to a conclusion, complete
idcircō (adv.) therefore, on that account
minimē (adv.) least of all, by no means
8: **contemnō**, **-āre**, **-āvī**, **-ātus** scorn, disdain
secundum locum "in respect to position"
8–9: **mūtātiō**, **-iōnis** *f* changing, alteration
9: **propter** (prep. + acc.) on account of
reī spectātae (gen. *f* sing.) "of the thing observed"
9–10: **dispār**, **dispāris** different, unequal
10: **aequāliter** (adv.) equally
11: **percipiō**, **-ere**, **-cēpī**, **-ceptus** perceive
dīcō "I mean"
12: **circuitus**, **-ūs** *m* from **circum-eō**
aspiciō, **-ere**, **aspexī**, **aspectus** behold, look at
rēprōdūcō, **-ere**, **-dūxī**, **-ductus** lead forth again; (+ dat.) "into **visui nostro**"
13: **dēputō**, **-āre**, **-āvī**, **-ātus** consider. Note the polite, almost apologetic tone of the mixed condition.
13–14: **extrīnsecus** (adv.) on the outside, from without

reuntia apparēbit. Tālis est revolūtiō * quotīdiāna * imprīmīs *. Haec enim tōtum mundum vidētur capere, praeterquam * terram quaeque circā * ipsam sunt. Atquī * sī caelum nihil dē hōc mōtū habēre concesseris, sī quī sēriō * animadvertat *, inveniet terram vērō ab occāsū in ortum volvī.

Cumque caelum, quod continet et cēlat omnia,[7] commūnis omnium locus sit, nōn statim * apparet cūr nōn magis * contentō quam continentī, magis * locātō quam locantī mōtus attribuātur *. Erant sānē * huius sententiae * philosophī Pythagoricī * et apud Cicerōnem, in mediō mundī terram videntēs. Existimābant * enim stellās obiectū * terrae occidere, eāsque cēdente terrā surgere.

(After N. Copernicus, Dē revolūtiōnibus *I.5)*

15: **revolūtiō, -iōnis** *f* a revolving
quotīdiānus every day, daily, usual
imprīmīs (adv.) especially, particularly
praeterquam (adv.) beyond, besides, except
16: **circā** (prep. + acc.) around
17: **atquī** and yet
18: **sēriō** (adv.) in earnest, seriously
animadvertō, -ere turn one's attention toward, notice
20: **statim** (adv.) firmly, immediately
20–21: **magis . . . quam** "more ——— than ———"
21: **attribuō, -ere, -uī, -ūtus** (+ dat.) assign to
sānē (adv.) indeed, by all means
21–22: **huius sententiae** "of this opinion"
22: **philosophī Pythagoricī** followers of Pythagoras, a Greek philosopher from Samos, about 550 B.C. The reference here is to a conversation in Cicero's *Dē rēpūblicā*, where a philosophic discussion takes place out in space, from the vantage point of the Milky Way, far from Earth.
23: **existimō, -āre** think, suppose
obiectus, -ūs *m* (from **obiciō**) a casting in the way, appearance;
obiectū terrae "when the earth blocked the view (of the stars)"

[7] Copernicus believes the universe is enclosed by the celestial sphere, which he calls **caelum**. In later Latin the diphthongs -**ae**- and -**oe**- change to -**ē**-. **Caelum** could therefore be spelled **cēlum** or **coelum**, and consequently Copernicus mistakenly assumes **cēlum** is derived from **cēlāre**, "conceal, cover."

Probanda X–XII

A. Translate each of the following verbs into English. Then, retaining the person and number of the original verb, write a synopsis of this verb in the passive voice only. Translate the present passive form into English: Example: **reddunt**. They give back;

INDICATIVE

Present	redduntur, they are being given back;
Imperfect	reddēbantur;
Future	reddentur;
Perfect	redditī sunt;
Pluperfect	redditī erant;
Future Perfect	redditī erunt;

	SUBJUNCTIVE
Present	reddantur;
Imperfect	redderentur;
Perfect	redditī sint;
Pluperfect	redditī essent.

VERBS:

iactās	gerimus	offertis	interficimus
regimus	ferimus	sūmis	colunt
trāditis	tollunt	relinquit	meret
imprimit	sufferunt	vincō	confers
fundit	accipit	refert	subicimus
vertis	intellegit	servātis	augēt

B. Supply and translate the present, perfect and future active infinitives and the present and perfect passive infinitives for each of the following verbs:
Example: **vertō**

	ACTIVE	PASSIVE
Present	vertere, to turn	vertī, to be turned
Perfect	vertisse, to have turned	versus esse, to have been turned
Future	versūrus esse, to be about to turn	

VERBS:

reddō	iactō
tollō	accipiō
sufferō	gerō
conferō	mereō
relinquō	fundō

C. Supply and translate all the participles for the above verbs.
Example: **vertō**

	ACTIVE	PASSIVE
Present	vertēns; -ntis, turning	——
Perfect	——	versus, -a, -um, turned
Future	versūrus, -a, -um, about to turn	vertendus, -a, -um, about to be turned

D. Translate the following sentences, and then reconstruct the statement in the passive voice, omitting the verb **dēbēre** and instead using the passive periphrastic to express necessity:
Example: Pecūniam reddere dēbent.
Translation: They ought to give back the money.
With Passive Periphrastic: Pecūnia eīs reddenda est.

1. Librōs tollere dēbēbit.
2. Tē et mē conferre dēbēs.
3. Iuvenis eam relinquere dēbēbit.
4. Mea verba accipere dēbētis.
5. Omnia haec bona merēre dēbēbāmus.

E. Identify the case of the following phrases, which are all in the singular. Then translate the phrase, and change it to the same case in the plural:

1. cīvī omnī
2. cīvitāte omnī
3. lūcis dulcis
4. mīlēs fortis
5. cor dūrum
6. opus ingēns
7. ignī tollentī
8. vī quādam
9. noctis cuiusdam
10. urbem quamvīs
11. affectūs potentis
12. cornūs ingentis
13. vīs āmissae
14. domuī impiō
15. iuvene relictō
16. casūs cunctī
17. mundō tōtī
18. versū brevī
19. manūs alicuius
20. lūmen dulce

Probanda, X–XII: Key

A. Synopses:

iactās, you (s.) are tossing; iactāris/iactāre, you (s.) are being tossed; iactābāris/iactābāre; iactāberis/iactābere; iactātus es; iactātus erās; iactātus eris; iactēris/iactēre; iactārēris/iactārēre; iactātus sis; iactātus essēs.

regimus, we are ruling; regimur, we are being ruled; regēbāmur; regēmur; rectī sumus; rectī erāmus; rectī erimus; regāmur; regerēmur; rectī sīmus; rectī essēmus.

trāditis, you (pl.) are handing over; trādiminī, you (pl.) are being handed over; trādēbāminī; trādēminī; trāditī estis; trāditī erātis; trāditī eritis; trādāminī; trāderēminī; trāditī sītis; trāditī essētis.

imprimit, he influences; imprimitur, he is being influenced; imprimēbātur; imprimētur; impressus est; impressus erat; impressus erit; imprimātur; imprimerētur; impressus sit; impressus esset.

fundit, it is pouring; funditur, it is being poured; fundēbātur; fundētur; fūsum est; fūsum erat; fūsum erit; fundātur; funderētur; fūsum sit; fūsum esset.

vertis, you (s.) are turning; verteris/vertere, you (s.) are being turned; vertēbāris/vertēbāre; vertēris/vertēre; versus es; versus erās; versus eris; vertāris/vertāre; verterēris/verterēre; versus sīs; versus essēs.

gerimus, we are carrying/doing; gerimur, we are being brought/carried; gerēbāmur; gerēmur; gestī sumus; gestī erāmus; gestī erimus; gerāmur; gererēmur; gestī sīmus; gestī essēmus.

ferimus, we bear/endure/bring; ferimur, we are borne/brought; ferēbāmur; ferēmur; lātī sumus; lātī erāmus; lātī erimus; ferāmur; ferrēmur; lātī sīmus; lātī essēmus.
tollunt, they are lifting/destroying; tolluntur, they are being lifted/destroyed; tollēbantur; tollentur; sublātī sunt; sublātī erant; sublātī erunt; tollantur; tollerentur; sublātī sint; sublātī essent.
sufferunt, they are supporting; sufferuntur, they are being supported; sufferantur; sufferentur; sublātī sunt; sublātī erant; sublātī erunt; sufferāntur; sufferrentur; sublātī sint; sublātī essent.
accipit, he is receiving/hearing; accipitur, he is being received (welcomed)/heard; accipiēbatur; accipiētur; acceptus est; acceptus erat; acceptus erit; accipiātur; acciperētur; acceptus sit; acceptus esset.
intellegit, he understands; intellegitur, he is understood; intellegēbātur; intellegētur; intellectus est; intellectus erat; intellectus erit; intellegātur; intellegerētur; intellectus sit; intellectus esset.
offertis, you (pl.) are presenting/offering; offeriminī, you are being presented; offerēbāminī; offerēminī; oblātī estis; oblātī eratis; oblātī eritis; offerāminī; offerrēminī; oblātī sītis; oblātī essētis.
sūmis, you (s.) are taking; sumeris/sumere, you are being taken; sumēbāris/sumēbāre; sumēris/sumēre; sumptus es; sumptus erās; sumptus eris; sumāris/sumāre; sumerēris/sumerēre; sumptus sis; sumptus essēs.
relinquit, he is abandoning/leaving; relinquitur, he is being abandoned; relinquēbātur; relinquētur; relictus est; relictus erat; relictus erit; relinquātur; relinquerētur; relictus sit; relictus esset.
vincō, I am conquering; vincor, I am being conquered; vincēbar; vincar; victus sum; victus eram; victus erō; vincar; vincerer; victus sim; victus essem.
refert, he reports; refertur, he is being reported; referēbātur; referētur; relātus est; relātus erat; relātus erit; referātur; referrētur; relātus sit; relātus esset.
servātis, you (pl.) are saving; servāminī, you are being saved; servābāminī; servābiminī; servātī estis; servātī erātis; servātī eritis; servēminī; servārēminī; servātī sītis; servātī essētis.
interficimus, we are killing; interficimur, we are being killed; interficiēbāmur; interficiēmur; interfectī sumus; interfectī erāmus; interfectī erimus; interficiāmur; interficerēmur; interfectī sīmus; interfectī essēmus.
colunt, they worship/cultivate; coluntur, they are being worshipped/cultivated; colēbantur; colentur; cultī sunt; cultī erant; cultī erunt; colantur; colerentur; cultī sint; cultī essent.
meret, he deserves; merētur, he is deserved; merēbātur; merēbitur; meritus est; meritus erat; meritus erit; mereātur; mererētur; meritus sit; meritus esset.
confers, you (s.) are comparing; conferris/conferre, you (s.) are being compared; conferēbāris/conferēbāre; collātus es; collātus erās; collātus eris; conferāris/conferāre; conferrēris/conferrēre; collātus sīs; collātus essēs.

subicimus, we are subjecting; subicimur, we are being subjected; subiciēbāmur; subiciēmur; subiectī sumus; subiectī erāmus; subiectī erimus; subiciāmur; subicerēmur; subiectī sīmus; subiectī essēmus.
auget, he is increasing/augmenting; augētur, he is being increased/augmented; augēbātur; augēbitur; auctus est; auctus erat; auctus erit; augeātur; augērētur; auctus sit; auctus esset.

B. Infinitives:
reddō: reddere, to give back; reddidisse, to have given back; redditūrus esse, to be about to give back; reddī, to be given back; redditus esse, to have been given back.
tollō: tollere, to lift/destroy; sustulisse, to have lifted/destroyed; sublātūrus esse, to be about to lift/destroy; tollī, to be lifted/destroyed; sublātus esse, to have been lifted.
sufferō: sufferre, to support/suffer; sustulisse, to have supported/suffered; sublātūrus esse, to be about to support/suffer; sufferrī, to be supported; sublātus esse, to have been supported.
conferō: conferre, to compare/collect; contulisse, to have compared/collected; collātūrus esse, to be about to compare/collect; conferri, to be compared/collected; collātus esse, to have been compared/collected.
relinquō: relinquere, to abandon; reliquisse, to have abandoned; relictūrus esse, to be about to abandon; relinquī, to be abandoned; relictus esse, to have been abandoned.
iactō: iactāre, to toss; iactāvisse, to have tossed; iactātūrus esse, to be about to toss; iactārī, to be tossed; iactātus esse, to have been tossed.
accipiō: accipere, to receive; accēpisse, to have received; acceptūrus esse, to be about to receive; accipī, to be received; acceptus esse, to have been received.
gerō: gerere, to do/carry; gessisse, to have done/carried; gestūrus esse, to be about to do/carry; gerī, to be carried; gestus esse, to have been carried.
mereō: merere, to deserve; meruisse, to have deserved; meritūrus esse, to be about to deserve; merērī, to be deserved; meritus esse, to have been deserved.
fundō: fundere, to pour; fūdisse, to have poured; fusūrus esse, to be about to pour; fundī, to be poured; fūsus esse, to have been poured.

C. Participles:
reddō: reddēns, -ntis, giving back; redditūrus, about to give back; redditus, given back; reddendus, about to be given back.
tollō: tollēns, -ntis, lifting/destroying; sublātūrus, about to lift/destroy; sublātus, lifted/destroyed; tollendus, about to be lifted/destroyed.
sufferō: sufferēns, -ntis, supporting; sublātūrus, about to support; sublātus, supported; sufferendus, about to be supported.
conferō: conferēns, -ntis, comparing; collātūrus, about to compare; collātus, compared; conferendus, about to be compared.
relinquō: relinquēns, -ntis, abandoning; relictūrus, about to abandon; relictus, abandoned; relinquendus, about to be abandoned.

iactō: iactāns, -ntis, tossing; iactātūrus, about to toss; iactātus, tossed; iactandus, about to be tossed.
accipiō: accipiēns, -ntis, receiving; acceptūrus, about to receive; acceptus, received; accipiendus, about to be received.
gerō: gerēns, -ntis, carrying/doing; gessūrus, about to carry/do; gestus, carried/done; gerendus, about to be carried/done.
mereō: merēns, -ntis, deserving; meritūrus, about to deserve; meritus, deserved; merendus, about to be deserved.
fundō: fundēns, -ntis, pouring; fūsūrus, about to pour; fūsus, poured; fundendus, about to be poured.

D. Passive Periphrastic.

1. He will have to destroy the books.
   Librī eī tollendī erunt.
2. You (s.) ought to compare yourself and me.
   Tū et ego tibi conferendī sumus.
3. The young man will have to leave her behind/abandon her.
   Ea iuvenī relinquenda erit.
4. You (pl.) ought to hear my words.
   Mea verba vōbīs accipienda sunt.
5. We had to earn/deserve all these good things.
   Omnia haec bona nōbīs merenda erant.

E. Third Declension.

1. cīvī omnī: dat.; to/for every citizen; cīvibus omnibus.
2. cīvitāte omnī: abl.; by/with every city-state; cīvitātibus omnibus.
3. lūcis dulcis: gen.; of the sweet light; lūcum dulcium.
4. mīlēs fortis: nom.; brave soldier; mīlitēs fortēs.
5. cor dūrum: nom./acc.; hard heart; corda dūra.
6. opus ingēns: nom./acc.; huge work; opera ingentia.
7. ignī tollentī: dat.; to/for destructive fire; ignibus tollentibus.
8. vī quādam: abl.; by/with a certain force; vīribus quibusdam.
9. noctis cuiusdam: gen.; of a certain night; noctium quārundam.
10. urbem quamvīs: acc.; whatever city; urbēs quāsvīs.
11. affectūs potentis: gen.; of a powerful mood/disposition; affectuum potentium.
12. cornūs ingentis: gen.; of a huge horn, cornuum ingentium.
13. vīs āmissae: gen.; of lost power; vīrium āmissārum.
14. domuī impiō: dat.; to/for the irreverent home; domibus impiīs.
15. iuvene relictō: abl. absolute; since/when/although the young man is/was abandoned; iuvenibus relictīs. ("By the young man" would require the preposition **ab**, and "with the young man" would require the preposition **cum**.)
16. cāsūs cunctī: gen.; of every misfortune; casuum cunctōrum.
17. mundō tōtī: dat.; to/for the entire universe; mundīs tōtīs.
18. versū brevī: abl.; by/with a short line of verse; versibus brevibus.
19. manūs alicuius: gen.; of some hand; manuum aliquārum.
20. lūmen dulce: nom./acc.; sweet light; lūmina dulcia.

Comparison of Adjectives and Adverbs; Indirect Commands

Comparison of Adjectives and Adverbs

An adjective or adverb occurs in the positive degree ("good," "well"), the comparative degree ("better"), or in the superlative degree ("best"). The adjectives and adverbs learned in the previous chapters were all in the positive degree, which merely ascribes some quality or condition to the entity it modifies:

Insānus est iste vir.
That man is *crazy*.

Saepe est **rīdiculus** ubi uxor nōn adest.
He is often *amusing* when his wife is not present.

Comparative Degree

Comparative adjectives and adverbs indicate that this quality or condition is greater in one entity than in another. The second element in the comparison is introduced by the adverb **quam**, "than," and is in the same case as the first element in the comparison:

Tū quidem es **insānior quam ego**.
You are certainly *crazier than I*.

Sciō nūllum Poenum **Poeniōrem quam tuum servum**.
I know no Carthaginian *more Carthaginian than your slave*.

Sometimes, instead of **quam**, Latin uses the ablative of comparison. Here, the second element of the comparison is put into the ablative case, and the resultant ablative form can be translated "than ———":

Tū quidem es insānior **mē**.
You are certainly crazier *than I*.

Sciō nūllum Poenum Poeniōrem **tuō servō**.
I know no Carthaginian more Carthaginian *than your slave*.

Additionally, the ablative of degree of difference is used in comparisons to show by how much one thing exceeds another:

Tū quidem es **multō** insānior quam ego.
You are certainly *much* (literally, by much) more crazy than I.

Vīsne scīre **quantō** sim Poenior quam ille?
Do you want to know *how much* (literally, by how much) more Carthaginian I am than he?

When the second element in the comparison is omitted, the comparative form can be translated as "rather ———," "too ———":

Rīdiculior est ubi uxor nōn adest.
He is *rather funny/too funny* when his wife is not present.

Brevior erat ōrātor hīs respondēns.
The speaker was *rather brief/too brief* in his response to these things.

Ōrātiō **multō brevior** vidēbātur.
The speech seemed *much too short* (literally, too short by much).

Formation of Comparative Adjectives. The comparative adjective is formed by adding **-ior** (*m* and *f*) or **-ius** (*n*) to the stem of the positive adjective:

POSITIVE	STEM	COMPARATIVE
dulcis, dulce	**dulc-**	**dulcior**, **dulcius**, sweeter, rather sweet
sapiēns	**sapient-**	**sapientior**, **sapientius**, wiser, rather wise
acer, acris, acre	**acr-**	**acrior**, **acrius**, sharper, rather sharp
insānus, -a, -um	**insān-**	**insānior**, **insānius**, more foolish, rather foolish

The comparative degree of **dulcis**, **dulce** is declined as follows:

SINGULAR		PLURAL	
M. AND F.	N.	M. AND F.	N.
dulcior	dulcius	dulciōrēs	dulciōra
dulciōris	dulciōris	dulciōrum	dulciōrum
dulciōrī	dulciōrī	dulciōribus	dulciōribus
dulciōrem	dulcius	dulciōrēs	dulciōra
dulciōre	dulciōre	dulciōribus	dulciōribus

The entire nominative masculine/feminine singular form of the comparative adjective serves as the stem of the declined comparative form (**dulciōr-**), with the exception of the neuter nominative and accusative singular form (**dulcius**). Comparative adjectives are declined for the most part like third declension adjectives of two endings (**dulcis**, **-e**), but unlike all other third declension adjectives, they are not **i**-stems and lack the characteristic **-ī-** in the ablative singular, the genitive plural, and the nominative/accusative neuter plural endings.[1]

[1] Comparative adjectives with ablative singular **-ī** and accusative plural **-īs** are sometimes found in later and earlier periods, but not in the classical period.

Superlative Degree

The superlative degree in English is indicated by "very," "the most," or by the suffix "-est" ("largest," "happiest," "sweetest"):

Saepe est **rīdiculissimus** ubi uxor nōn adest.
He is often *very amusing* when his wife is not present.

Dulcissima sunt tua verba.
Your words are *very sweet*.

Poenissimus omnium hominum sum.[2]
I am the "*Carthaginianest*" (most Carthaginian) of all men.

When a superlative adjective or adverb is introduced by **quam**, the meaning of the phrase is "as——as possible":

Quam rīdiculissimus est.
He is *as funny as possible*.

Quam dulcissimē dīxit ille.
He spoke *as sweetly as possible*.

Formation of Superlative Adjectives. The superlative adjective is formed by adding -**issimus**, -**a**, -**um** to the stem of the positive adjective:

dulcis, -e	**dulcissimus**, -**a**, -**um**, very sweet, most sweet, sweetest
brevis, -e	**brevissimus**, -**a**, -**um**, very brief, most brief, briefest
insānus, -a, -um	**insānissimus**, -**a**, -**um**, very crazy, most crazy, craziest
rīdiculus, -a, -um	**rīdiculissimus**, -**a**, -**um**, very funny, most funny, funniest

There are two exceptions to the above rules:

1. Adjectives ending in -**er** in the masculine nominative of the positive degree form the superlative by adding -**rimus**, -**a**, -**um** to the entire masculine nominative form:

Positive Degree	Superlative Degree
miser, misera, miserum	**miserrimus**, -**a**, -**um**, very unhappy, most unhappy, unhappiest
acer, acris, acre	**acerrimus**, -**a**, -**um**, very sharp, most sharp, sharpest

2. Six third declension adjectives ending in -**lis** in the masculine and feminine add -**limus**, -**a**, -**um** to the stem of the adjective:

facilis, -**e**, easy	**facillimus**, -**a**, -**um**, very easy, most easy, easiest
difficilis, -**e**, difficult	**difficillimus**, -**a**, -**um**, very difficult, most difficult
similis, -**e**, similar	**simillimus**, -**a**, -**um**, very similar, most similar
dissimilis, -**e**, unlike	**dissimillimus**, -**a**, -**um**, very different, most unlike
gracilis, -**e**, thin, slender	**gracillimus**, -**a**, -**um**, very slender, thinnest
humilis, -**e**, humble, low	**humillimus**, -**a**, -**um**, lowest, most humble, very humble

Other third declension adjectives ending in -**lis** are regular.

[2] In this example, the superlative **Poenissimus** is governing the partitive genitive **omnium hominum**. A superlative adjective frequently will govern a partitive genitive.

Formation of Comparative and Superlative Adverbs

Comparative Adverbs. The neuter nominative/accusative singular of the comparative adjective is used as the comparative adverb:

Vox eius **dulcius** sonābat.	Her voice rang out *rather sweetly.*
Omnia haec **facilius** fēcit.	He did all these things *too easily.*

Superlative Adverbs. Adverbs of the superlative degree are formed by adding **-ē** to the superlative stem:

Vox eius **dulcissimē** sonābat.	Her voice rang out *most sweetly.*
Omnia haec **facillimē** fecit.	He did all these things *very easily.*

Scrībenda

A. Decline the following, in the singular and plural:

ēlegantior, ēlegantius
celerior, celerius
pulchrior, pulchrius

B. For each of the following, supply the comparative and superlative adjectives and adverbs. Translate each new form:

brevis	dulcis	pulcher
altus	ignārus	obscūrus
iudiciālis	dexter	turpis
dīves	vetus	fēlix
acer	celer	amāns
sapiēns	potēns	

C. Translate the following sentences:

1. Quid est dulcius quam domum redīre?
2. Quam dulce est redīre!
3. Eius verba sunt dulciōra quam tua.
4. Dulcius dīcit poēta quam tū.
5. Verba quam dulcissima dīcēmus.
6. Tum mihi dulcissimum spectāculum erat equus armīs plēnus et Trōia incēnsa. (**spectāculum**, -ī *n*, show, spectacle)
7. Puerī dē virīs fortissimīs interfectīs legentēs gaudēbāmus. (**gaudeō**, **-ēre**, rejoice, take delight)
8. Ego puer Latīnās litterās, quae certiōrēs erant quam Graecae, legere mālēbam.
9. Sī facta Herculis graviōra quam Epicūrī putās, ā ratiōne vērā longius multō ferris. Longissimē ā ratiōne vērā ferēris.
10. Augustus auctōritāte quam imperiō facilius regēbat. Augustō erat dulcior auctōritās imperiō. (**auctōritās**, **-tātis** *f*, authority, influence)
11. Augustior erat Herculēs post mortem. Quam augustissimus erat Herculēs cum deus esset factus.

12. Longissima est Aegyptiōrum memoria. Multō longior est nostrā. Quam dissimillima est nostra memoria. Novissima sōlum memorāmus.
13. Vulcānī fīlius erat Cācus, sīcut ēlegantissimē cecinit Vergilius. Num quis umquam ēlegantius cecinit quam Vergilius? (**Vergilius**, **-ī** *m*, Vergil [the poet])
14. Celeriter medicāmen tibi quaere. Celerrimē medicāmen bibe. Quam celerrima erit medicāminis vīs. (**medicāmen**, **-inis** *n*, medicine, poison, antidote)

Indirect Commands (Jussive Noun Clauses)

Direct commands, as we have seen, can be expressed by the imperative mood (**Vidēte!** Look! **Nōlī timēre.** Don't be afraid.) or by the subjunctive mood (**Bonus sis.** Be good. **Nē timeās.** Don't be afraid.). An indirect command is introduced by **ut** (**nē** negative) and its verb is always in the subjunctive mood. In fact, indirect commands have the same construction as purpose clauses. The only way to distinguish an indirect command from a purpose clause is by the verb that introduces the subordinate clause. Most verbs that indicate or imply a command or request, such as **petō**, **quaerō**, **moneō**, can introduce an indirect command.[3] Words like **dīcō** can also introduce an indirect command. Compare the following:

DIRECT COMMANDS

Hoc fac.
Do this thing.

Amīcī, fugiāmus.
Friends, let us flee.

Nōlī fēminam audīre.
Don't listen to the woman.

Pecūniam hanc cape et cibum eme.
Take this money and buy the food.

INDIRECT COMMANDS

Mihi dīxit **ut hoc facerem**.
He told me *to do this thing*.

Amīcōs monēs **ut fugiant**.
You are warning your friends *to flee*.

Servus dominum monuit **nē fēminam audīret**.
The slave advised his master *not to listen to the woman*.

Dominus mihi dixit **ut pecūniam caperem et cibus emerem**.
The master told me *to take the money and purchase food*.

Compare the following purpose clause with the indirect command in the sentence above:

Dominus mihi pecūniam dedit **ut cibum emerem**.
The master gave me money *to purchase food*.

[3] The notable exceptions here are **iubeō** and its opposite, **vetō**, "forbid," both of which govern the accusative subject plus infinitive verb construction.

Observe again the tendency of English to use an infinitive ("he advised him *not to listen*"; "he told me *to take the money*") where Latin uses a finite verb in the subjunctive ("eum monuit **nē audīret**"; "mihi dīxit **ut pecūniam caperem**").

The entire indirect command is viewed as the object of the verb of commanding, and therefore indirect commands are frequently called jussive noun clauses.[4] A noun clause, as you will see in later chapters, can be the object or the subject of the main verb. Observe the way a noun clause can replace a single noun:

I told him a story. ("a story" is the direct object.)
I told him to listen to my story.
(The entire clause of the indirect command—that he listen to my story—is the direct object of the verb of command.)

You must distinguish between a purpose clause and a jussive noun clause in order to comprehend the correct meaning of a sentence. The context will usually help you determine whether the sentence contains a jussive or a purpose clause. After verbs of advising, commanding, or urging, however, there is seldom ambiguity.

Scrībenda

cōgō, **cōgere**, **coēgī**, **coactus** compel (governs either double accusative + infinitive or **ut** + subjunctive: **coēgī eum hoc facere** or **coēgī eum ut hoc faceret**: "I compelled him to do this thing.")

imperō, **-āre**, **-āvī**, **-ātus** (+ dat.) order, command

ōrō, **-āre**, **-āvī**, **-ātus** ask, beg, pray

rogō, **-āre**, **-āvī**, **-ātus** ask

suādeō, **suādēre**, **suāsī**, **suāsus** (+ dat.) advise, urge, persuade

A. Translate the following sentences:

1. Monēbō patrem ut medicāmen bibat quam celerrimē. (**medicāmen**, **-inis** *n*, medicine, poison, antidote)
2. Monuit patrem nē cibum ante medicāmen acciperet.
3. Magister discipulīs imperavit nē in suum errōrem dūcerentur.
4. Mihi suāsit nē quicquam negārem.
5. Pater mē monuit nē indecōra facerem.
6. Ōrās quid faciam. Ōrās ut turpiōra faciam. Ōrās nē turpissima faciam.
7. Servō suadēbāmus ut aliquid cōnsiliī celeriter invenīret.
8. Cōget eōs discipulōs errōrēs Aenēae cuiusdam discere. Coactī sunt eī discipulī ut errōrēs discerent.
9. Boum inclūsārum vox suāsit ut Herculēs celeriter redīret. (**inclūdō**, **-ere**, **-clūsī**, **-clūsus**, shut in, confine)
10. Rogat nōs ut brevēs simus.
11. Centaurus Dēianīrae suāsit ut vestem Herculī daret.
12. Moneāmus patrem nē sē salvum esse crēdat.

[4] "Jussive" is from **iubeō**, "order," "command."

13. Nōbīs dīxit terram volvī.
14. Suāsit nē crēderēmus terram nōn volvī.
15. Monet puerōs nē fāmam cupiant.
16. Poēta rogātus est cūr nōn Rōmae esset.
17. Poēta rogātus est ut Rōmam adīret.
18. Petam ā poētā ut Rōmā discēdat.

B. Translate the following sentences into Latin:

1. Someone will ask you to leave Rome.
2. They will urge us to return to Athens as quickly as possible.
3. These men advised those men to leave very quickly.
4. For a long time we told him not to do it.
5. We told him this so that he would bring us assistance.

Verba tenenda

Verbs

afficiō, **-ere**, **-fēcī**, **-fectus** exert an influence on, influence, affect

agnoscō, **-ere**, **-nōvī**, **-nitus** recognize, acknowledge, acknowledge as one's own

aperiō, **-īre**, **aperuī**, **apertus** uncover, lay bare, disclose

dēficiō, **-ere**, **-fēcī**, **-fectus** desert, fail, forsake; grow faint, disappear

dēpōnō, **-ere**, **-posuī**, **-positus** set down, put down, lay aside; deposit

dispōnō, **-ere**, **-posuī**, **-positus** distribute, arrange, place here and there

ēdō, **-ere**, **ēdidī**, **ēditus** give out, put forth, bring forth

ēripiō, **-ere**, **ēripuī**, **ēreptus** snatch out, tear out, take away

excipiō, **-ere**, **-cēpī**, **-ceptus** take out; except, make an exception of; catch, capture

expōnō, **-ere**, **-posuī**, **-positus** put out, expose, explain

fīniō, **-īre**, **-īvī**, **-ītus** limit, enclose within boundaries; finish, end, terminate

imperō, **-āre**, **-āvī**, **-ātus** (+ dat.) order, command

impōno, **-ere**, **-posuī**, **-positus** place upon, set upon; (+ dat.) impose upon

inquam, **inquis**, **inquit** (defective **-iō** verb) I say, you say, he (she/it) says

mandō, **-āre**, **-āvī**, **-ātus** order, command, give a command

misceō, **-ēre**, **miscuī**, **mixtus** mingle, intermingle, unite, mix

negō, **-āre**, **-āvī**, **-ātus** deny; say no; (with acc. + infinitive) say that . . . not

ōdī, **ōdisse**, **ōsus** (defective verb) hate, despise

ōrō, **-āre**, **-āvī**, **-ātus** ask, pray, beg, plead

rīdeō, **-ēre**, **rīsī**, **rīsus** laugh, laugh at

spectō, **-āre**, **-āvī**, **-ātus** look at, behold, observe

suādeō, **-ēre**, **suāsī**, **suāsus** (+ dat.) advise, urge, persuade

subeō, **-īre**, **-īvī**, **-itum** (**sub** + **eō**) come or go under, approach, undergo, submit to

ūrō, **-ere**, **ussī**, **ustus** burn

Nouns

coniunx, coniugis *m* or *f* spouse; husband or wife
cupīdō, -inis *f* or *m* desire, longing; the god of love (Cupid)
frāter, frātris *m* brother
gaudium, -iī *n* joy, delight
lacrima, -ae *f* tear
māter, mātris *f* mother
metus, -ūs *m* fear, dread
mulier, mulieris *f* woman, female, wife
mūnus, mūneris *n* function, duty, gift, offering
osculum, -ī *n* kiss
pietās, pietātis *f* reverence, piety, devotion
potestās, -tātis *f* ability, power
senectūs, -tūtis *f* old age
soror, sorōris *f* sister
thalamus, -ī *m* an inner room; bedchamber; marriage bed
uxor, uxōris *f* wife, spouse

Adjectives

aptus, -a, -um (+ dat.) fit (for), suitable, proper
bellus, -a, -um pretty, handsome, charming
cārus, -a, -um dear, precious, expensive
crūdēlis, -e cruel, hard, unmerciful
difficilis, -e difficult
dissimilis, -e (+ dat.) dissimilar, different
dīversus, -a, -um turned different ways, diverse; contrary, opposite
facilis, -e easy
formōsus, -a, -um beautiful, lovely
gracilis, -e slender
gravis, -e heavy, weighty, serious, important
humilis, -e humble, lowly, poor
infīnītus, -a, -um unlimited, boundless, infinite
levis, -e light (in weight), slight, trivial
nātālis, -e having to do with one's birth
pār; pāris (gen.) (+ dat. or gen.) equal (to)
prīmus, -a, -um first
similis, -e (+ dat. or gen.) similar, like
tālis, -e of such a sort, of such a kind
  tālis . . . quālis (correlative) of such a sort . . . as
tristis, -e sad, gloomy, unhappy
vīcīnus, -a, -um neighboring, near; (+ dat.) near (to)

Adverbs

adhūc to this place, thus far; until now; yet
difficile with difficulty
facile easily
forte by chance, by accident
prōtinus straightway, immediately
quam (exclamatory): how ——!; (interrogative): how?; (with comparisons): than; (with superlatives): as . . . as possible
semper always
tandem at last, finally

Notanda

afficiō and **dēficiō** are compounds of **faciō**. The first consonant of the verb to which the prefix **ad** is affixed duplicates (as in **afficiō**), whereas if the prefix is **ā** (**ab**) it will be a long **ā-** (as in **āmittō**), or a diphthong (as in **auferō**).

Compounds of **pōnō, pōnere**, "put or place" include **dēpōnō, dispōnō, expōnō** and **impōnō**.

Adjectives whose English equivalents are followed by "to" or "for" will frequently govern the dative case in Latin, as do both **aptus**, "suitable for," and **cārus**, "dear to."

formōsus means "full of **forma** (form, shape, beauty)." Do not confuse the adjective **bellus, -a, -um** with the word for war, **bellum**.

The adjectives **pār** and **similis** (as well as their opposites, **dispār, dissimilis**) govern the dative case: **Fīlia matrī similis est**, "The daughter is like her mother"; **Numquam erat bellum pār eī quod, Hannibāle dūce, Carthāginiēnsēs cum populō Rōmānō gesserant**, "There was never a war equal to the one which the Carthaginians had waged with the Roman people under Hannibal's leadership." **Pār** and **similis** can also govern the genitive, particularly when used as nouns. **Fīlia *matris similis* est** could have the same translation as the example above, but the sense would be "The daughter is her mother's *likeness*." **Numquam erat bellum *pār eius*** would have the sense, "Never was a war *the equivalent of that one*."

The endings of a number of adverbs which are irregular in the positive degree are the same as the neuter singular of the corresponding adjective: **facile, difficile, sōlum, vērum**. These forms are sometimes referred to as *cognate accusatives*, which means that the adjectival root is modifying an object which is not expressed as a noun but is part of the verb. In the expression, **hoc tē moneō**, "I warn you (of) *this*," **hoc** is an inner accusative modifying "warning," which is not a separate noun but is implied in the verb, **moneō**, "I give warning."

The adverb **forte** comes from the noun **fors, fortis**, "chance" or "luck," and is identical with the ablative form of that noun; hence its meaning, "by chance." Do not confuse this adverb with **fortiter**, "strongly," "bravely," from **fortis**.

Note the wide range of meaning possible in **quam**. In addition to the four possibilities mentioned in the vocabulary list, remember that **quam** can also be the accusative feminine singular relative pronoun.

The adverb **semper** is popular in a great many mottoes, as in **Semper Fidēlis** (motto of the United States Marine Corps), **Semper Parātus** (motto of the Boy Scouts and the United States Coast Guard).

Ante legenda

Translate:

1. Quaerō ut mē vocēs. Quaeram ut ā tē vocer. Mandābō ut vocer. Mandāvī ut vocārer. Haec fēcī ut vocārer.
2. Petīvit ut eius manus sibi darētur. Petīvit ut ea suum manum tenēret.
3. Petō ut tē spectem mihi cum vēnerit ista hōra tristis.
4. Sī tēcum sim cum vēnerit hōra tristissima, quaeram ut tē spectem et tuum manum teneam.

5. Mulier mea dīcit nūllī sē nūbere mālle quam mē. Negāvit sē ūllī nūbere mālle quam mē. Ea quam celerrimē mē nūbere māvult (mālit). (**nūbō, -ere, nūpsī, nūptus** + dat., marry)
6. Multō mihi es formōsior quam illa [est]. Multō formōsior es. Tū es formōsissima. Tū es quam formōsissima.
7. Illa prīma suīs miserum mē cēpit oculīs cārīs. Prīma mē miserrimum cēpit. Mē miseriōrem omnibus hominibus aliīs cēpit.
8. Cupīdō mē, numquam ante cupidum, impositīs pedibus caput meum pressit et imperāvit ut nūllō cōnsiliō vīverem.
9. Cupīdō impudīcior est aliīs dīs. Impudīcissimus est omnium deōrum. Quam impudīcissimus est ille deus.
10. Ille deus ōrābit ut et ego et tū nūllō cōnsiliō vivāmus. Pedibus suīs caput meum premit et mē tenet ut nūllō cōnsiliō vīvam.
11. Senectūs est similis mortī. Rogat an senectūs sit similior mortis an infantiae. Rogat ut nōs cōnstituāmus.
12. Num quid molestius est quam rūrī vītam agere? Nunc vīs mē cōgit ut rūrī molestō vītam agam. Quis rūrī vītam miserrimam agere mālit?
13. Dulcius urbe quid sit? Urbs dulcior rūre est. Urbs dulcior quam rūs semper erit, sed nunc ego cōgor ut ab urbe rūs discēdam.
14. Monuit eum nē tristis esset.
15. Ego tē docēbō puellam istam ōdisse. Mihi sōlī docendus eris. Moneō ut discās.
16. Monuit ut dē actibus puellae nostrae molestiōribus adsiduē cōgitārēmus. (**adsiduē**, adv., continuously)
17. Sī bene cantāre nōn potest, quaere ab eā ut cantet. Pete ut quam saepissimē cantet.
18. Prōdest haec facere sī sānissima esse vīs.

Legenda

The Roman Experience (I): Latin Love Poetry

Omnia vincit Amor: et nōs cēdāmus Amōrī.

Vergil, Eclogue *10.69*

"A Slave of Love." For Catullus (c. 84–c. 54 B.C.) and his successors, writing Latin poetry becomes an intensely personal experience. Catullus and his friends write about their own joy, sorrow, friendship, anger—personal

experiences which formerly had been considered too intimate for poetry. In doing so, they experiment with different meters and genres, and in the process develop what becomes a new literary genre, known now as Latin Love Elegy.[5]

The poet's focus is usually his or her beloved, although other themes are often interwoven. Catullus calls his beloved "Lesbia," after the Greek poetess Sappho, who came from the island of Lesbos. The other elegiac poets also give their beloved a fictitious name: Tibullus' mistress is "Delia," Propertius' is "Cynthia," and Ovid's is "Corinna." Similarly, the Latin poetess Sulpicia calls her sweetheart "Cerinthus."

In Catullus' elegies we see three major themes: one is his rocky relationship with his mistress, Lesbia, seen in the first two poems. Another is his sorrow over the death of his brother. In some of his elegies he weaves these two very different themes together to profound effect. A third important theme in Catullus' poems is friendship, indicated in the third poem by some rather coarse teasing.

1. Nūllī sē dīcit mulier mea nūbere * mālle
   quam mihi, nōn sī sē Iuppiter ipse petat.
dīcit: sed mulier cupidō quod dīcit amantī
   in ventō et rapidā * scrībere oportet * aquā.

(Catullus 70)

2. Dīcēbās quondam * sōlum tē nōsse * Catullum,
   Lesbia, nec prae mē velle tenēre Iovem.
dīlexī * tum tē nōn tantum * ut vulgus amīcam,
   sed pater ut nātōs dīligit * et generōs *.
nunc tē cognōvī: quārē etsī * impēnsius * ūror
   multō mī * tamen es vīlior * et levior.

1: **nūbō**, **-ere**, **nūpsī**, **nūptus** marry, wed
4: **rapidus**, **-a**, **-um** swift, rapid
oportet (+ infinitive) "it is fitting"

1: **quondam** (adv.) once, formerly
nōsse = **nōvisse**
3, 4: **dīligō**, **-ere**, **dīlexī**, **dīlectus** love, esteem
3: **tantum** (adv.) so much, so greatly
4: **gener**, **generī** *m* son-in-law or grandson-in-law
5: **etsī** even if; although
impēnsus, **-a**, **um** expensive; (adv.), at great cost
6: **mī** = **mihi**
vīlis, **-e** of small price or value; cheap

[5] Latin Love Elegy is written in elegiac couplets, which consist of alternating lines of dactylic hexameter (–⏕|–⏕|–⏕|–⏕|–◡◡|–⏓) and dactylic pentameter (–⏕|–⏕|–||–◡◡|–◡◡|⏓). The poems in this section, unless otherwise indicated, are in meter.

Lady musician entertains her friends. Painting from Stabiae.

"quī * potis est * ?" inquis. quod amantem iniūria tālis
cōgit amāre magis *, sed bene velle minus *.

(Catullus 72)

3. Nōlī admīrārī *, quārē . . . fēmina nūlla,
Rūfe *, velit [tēcum cubāre *] . . .

7: **quī** (adv.) how?
potis est "it is possible"
8: **magis** (adv.) more
minus (adv.) less

1, 8: **admīrārī** (infinitive) "to wonder"
2: **Rūfus**, **-ī** *m* a proper name
2, 6: **cubō**, **cubāre**, **cubuī**, **cubitus** lie down, recline

laedit* tē quaedam mala fābula, quā tibi fertur
valle* sub ālārum* trux* habitāre* caper*.
hunc metuunt* omnēs. neque mīrum*: nam mala valdē* est
bestia, nec quīcum* bella puella cubet*.
quārē aut crūdēlem nāsōrum* interfice pestem*
aut admīrārī* dēsine cūr fugiunt.

(Catullus 69)

Latin Love Elegy flourishes in the Augustan period, most prominently in the works of Tibullus (c. 55/48–19 B.C.), Propertius (c. 54/47–c. 2 B.C.), and Ovid (43 B.C.–A.D. 17). Here the conventions of the genre become set: the helplessness of the lover; the **paraclausithyron**, or the lament of the lover to the closed door (keeping him outside of his mistress' house); the **recūsātiō** or the poet's "refusal" to write poems glorifying war, usually accompanied by his reasons for devoting himself to Love's service. Tibullus interweaves into his poetry his need to live a simple life in the country, and his strong opposition to war:

4. Tē bellāre* decet terrā, Messalla*, marīque,
ut domus hostīlēs* praeferat* exuviās*:
mē retinent* vinctum* formōsae vincla* puellae,
et sedeō dūrās iānitor* ante forēs*.
nōn ego laudārī cūrō, mea Dēlia*; tēcum
dum modo* sim, quaesō* segnis* inersque* vocer.

3: **laedō, ere, laesī, laesus** wound, injure
4: **vallēs, -is** *f* valley, hollow
āla, -ae *f* the wing of a bird; (hence, the armpit of a human being)
trux, trūcis (adj.) fierce, savage, grim
habitō, -āre inhabit, dwell in
caper, caprī *m* a he-goat
5: **metuō, -ere, -uī, -ūtus** fear, dread
mīrus, -a, -um surprising, strange
valdē (adv.) powerfully, exceedingly
6: **quīcum = cum quō**
7: **nāsus, -ī** *m* the nose
pestis, -is *f* pestilence, plague, disease

1: **bellō, -āre** wage war
Messalla, -ae *m* Valerius Messalla Corvinus, Tibullus' patron
2: **hostīlis, -e** belonging to the enemy
praeferō, praeferre exhibit, show
exuviae, -ārum *f* pl. spoils, booty (lit., that which is stripped from the body)
3: **retineō, -ēre** hold back, retain
vinciō, -ere, vinxī, vinctus bind, fetter
vincla = vincula
4: **iānitor, iānitōris** *m* door-keeper
foris, -is *f* door; pl., two leaves of a door
5, 9: **Dēlia, -ae** *f* Delia (Tibullus' mistress)
6: **dum modo** + subjunctive provided that, on the provision that
quaesō = quaerō: (quaerō [ut] . . . vocer)
segnis, -e lazy
iners, inertis inactive

te spectem, suprēma * mihi cum vēnerit hōra,
  et teneam moriēns * dēficiente manū.
flēbis et * arsūrō positum mē, Dēlia *, lectō *,
  tristibus et * lacrimīs oscula mixta dabis.

(Tibullus I.1.53–60)

5. The speaker in Propertius' elegies depicts the power his mistress "Cynthia" exercises over him:

Cynthia prīma suīs miserum mē cēpit ocellīs *,
  contactum * nullīs ante cupīdinibus.
tum mihi cōnstantis * dēiēcit * lūmina fastūs *
  et caput impositīs pressit Amor pedibus,
dōnec * mē docuit castās * ōdisse puellās,
  improbus *, et nūllō vīvere cōnsiliō.
et mihi iam tōtō furor * hic nōn dēficit annō,
  cum tamen adversōs cōgor habēre deōs.

(Propertius I.1.1–8)

6. Sulpicia, who lived during the time of Augustus, is the earliest Roman poetess whose work has survived. She was a member of the circle of poets whose patron was Valerius Messalla Corvinus. (Tibullus was also a member of this circle.) Although only six short elegies (a total of forty lines) by Sulpicia survive, they have led at least one scholar to call her the "one true successor" of Catullus.[6] Her poems, like those of Catullus, have simplicity and a lack of pretension.

The name of her sweetheart, "Cerinthus," in Greek means "bee-bread," which is the pollen collected and converted by honeybees. The modern sense of his name could be something like "Honey."

Invīsus * nātālis * adest, quī rūrī molestō
  et sine Cērinthō tristis agendus erit.

7: **suprēmus, -a, -um** last, final
8: **moriēns** (pres. act. participle) "dying"
9–10: **et . . . et**: the conjunctions are delayed for metrical and rhetorical reasons; the natural order would be **et flēbis . . . et tristibus**
9: **lectus, -ī** *m* couch, bed

1: **ocellus, -ī** *m* (little) eye; (the diminutive makes this a term of endearment: "her sweet little eyes")
2: **contingō, -ere, contīgī, contactus** touch (on all sides), be in contact with
3: **cōnstāns, constantis** firm, unchangeable, fixed
dēiciō, -ere, dēiēci, dēiectus cast down
fastus, -ūs *m* scornful contempt, disdain; pride
cōnstantis fastūs descriptive genitive
5: **dōnec** (conj.) until
castus, -a, -um morally pure, chaste, unpolluted
6: **improbus, -a, -um** morally bad; wicked, shameless
7: **furor, furōris** *m* madness, fury, relentless desire

1: **invīsus, -a, -um** hated, hateful, detested
nātālis [diēs] *m* birthday

[6] G. Luck, *The Latin Love Elegy* (London, 1959), p. 60.

dulcius urbe quid est? an villa * sit apta puellae
atque Ārrētīnō * frīgidus * amnis * agrō?
iam, nimium * Messalla * meī studiōse *, quiescās *;
nōn tempestivae * saepe, propinque *, viae.
hīc animum sēnsūsque meōs abducta * relinquō,
arbitriō * quam vīs nōn sinit esse meō.

(Pseudo-Tibullus [Tibullus IV.3])

7. The most light-hearted of the Augustan elegiac poets was Ovid, as we see from the very opening of his *Amōrēs*, where he gives an ingenious reason for his refusal to write poems glorifying war:

Arma gravī numerō violentaque * bella parābam
ēdere, māteriā * conveniente * modīs.
pār erat inferior * versus; rīsisse Cupīdō
dīcitur atque ūnum surripuisse * pedem.
lūnāvitque * genū * sinuōsum * fortiter arcum *
'quod' que 'canās, vātēs *, accipe' dīxit 'opus'.
mē miserum! certās habuit puer ille sagittās *:
ūror et * in vacuō * pectore * regnat * Amor.

3: **villa, -ae** *f* country house, farm
4: **Ārrētīnus, -a, -um** of the town Aretium, in Etruria
frīgidus, -a, -um cold, chilly
amnis, -is *m* river
5: **nimium** (adv.) excessively
Messalla, -ae *m* Valerius Messala Corvinus
studiōsus, -a, -um (+ gen) zealous, devoted to
quiescō, -ere, quiēvī, quiētus rest, keep quiet. The jussive subjunctive here suggests a polite request: "please don't be troubled."
6: **tempestīvus, -a, -um** seasonable, timely, early
propinquus, -ī *m* relation, kindred
7: **abducō, -ere, -duxī, -ductus** lead away, seduce, alienate
8: **arbitrium, -ī** *n* judgment, decision
arbitriō meō (abl.) acting in accordance with my own judgment (i.e., preference)

1: **violentus, -a, -um** violent
2: **māteria, -ae** *f* subject
conveniēns, -ntis agreeing
3: **inferus, -a, -um** low, below
4: **surripiō, -ere, -uī, -reptus** snatch away. Here Ovid jokes about his verse form: the elegiac couplet is unsuited for heroic subjects since it has lost a metrical foot to Cupid. (The first line of the couplet has six feet, the second line has five feet.)
5: **lūnō, -āre** to bend like a half-moon
genū, genūs *n* knee
sinuōsus, -a, -um bent
arcus, -ūs *m* bow
6: **vātēs, -is** *m* seer; poet
7: **sagitta, -ae** *f* arrow
8: **ūror et = et uror** see 4, 9–10.
vacuus, -a, -um empty
pectus, -oris *n* breast
regnō, -āre, -āvī, -ātus rule, reign

Pompeii: A girl with tablet and pen.

sex * mihi surgat opus numerīs, in quinque * resīdat *
ferrea * ; cum vestrīs bella valēte modīs.

(Ovid, Amōrēs *I.1)*

8. Many Roman poets wrote didactic poems, intended to give instruction in some subject: Vergil's *Georgics* give instruction in the art of farming; Manilius' *Astronomica* give instruction in astrology. Ovid also writes di-

9: **sex** (indecl.) six
quinque (indecl.) five
resīdō, -ere, resēdī, —— settle
10: **ferreus, -a, -um** made of iron; hard, unfeeling

dactic poems, but his instructions are in the art of love. His *Ars Amatōria* teaches how to win love, while his *Remedia Amōris* teaches how to get out of a love affair. In the following passage, he gives some advice (intended, he assures us, for women as well as for men) on how to cure one's passion, using himself and his own recent recovery as a model to follow:

tū mihi, quī, quod amās, aegrē * dēdiscis * amāre
    nec potes et vellēs posse, docendus eris.
saepe refer tēcum scelerātae * facta puellae
    et pōne ante oculōs omnia damna * tuōs.
prōfuit adsiduē * vitiīs insistere * amīcae,
    idque mihī factum saepe salūbre * fuit.
"quam mala" dīcēbam "nostrae sunt crūra * puellae"
    (nec tamen, ut vērē confiteāmur *, erant);
"bracchia quam nōn sunt nostrae formōsa puellae"
    (et tamen, ut vērē confiteāmur *, erant) .
"quam brevis est" (nec erat), "quam multum * poscit amantem";
    haec odiō * vēnit * maxima * causa meō.
et mala sunt vīcīna bonīs:
"turgida,*" sī plēna est, sī fusca * est, "nigra *" vocētur;
    in gracilī "maciēs *" crīmen * habēri potest.
quīn etiam *, quācumque caret * tua fēmina dōte *
    hanc moveat *, blandīs * usque precāre * sonīs.

1: **aegrē** (adv.) uncomfortably, with displeasure, reluctantly
dēdiscō, -ere, dēdidicī, —— unlearn, forget
3: **scelerātus, -a, -um** wicked, harmful, vicious
4: **damnum, -ī** *n* injury, damage, hurt
5: **adsiduē** (adv.) continuously
insistō, -ere (+ dat.) dwell upon
6: **salūbris, -e** healthful
7: **crūrum, -ī** *n* leg
8, 10: **ut vērē confiteāmur** "to tell the truth"
11: **multum** (adv.) much
12: **odium, -ī** *n* hatred, loathing
haec vēnit "This came, the greatest reason for my loathing."
maximus, -a, -um the largest, the greatest
15: **turgidus, -a, -um** swollen, fat
fuscus, -a, -um dark, swarthy (of complexion)
niger, nigra, nigrum black
16: **maciēs, maciēī,** *f* leanness, thinness
crīmen, crīminis *n* fault
17: **quīn etiam** and furthermore
careō, -ēre, caruī, caritūrus (+ abl.) be without, lack
dōs, dōtis *f* dowry, endowment; talent, quality
hanc moveat "let her set this (quality she lacks) in motion." (in lines 19ff., some examples are given.)
18: **blandus, -a, -um** flattering
precāre "entreat her (with **blandīs sonīs**)."

sī male dentāta * est, narrā *, quod rīdeat, illī;
mollibus est oculīs *, quod fleat illa, refer.
prōderit et subitō *, cum sē nōn finxerit ūllī,
ad dominam celerēs māne * tulisse pedēs:
improvīsus * ades: dēprendēs * tūtus inermem *;
infēlix * vitiīs excidet * illa suīs.

(Ovid, Remedia Amōris, *297–344)*

9. A few centuries later, we find that Latin Love Elegy is still a vital literary form, as in the following poem of Decimus Magnus Ausonius (d. ca. A.D. 395). Ausonius, whose literary and political life was centered in France, left a moving tribute to his wife and their life together.

Uxor, vīvāmusque * ut vīximus et teneāmus
nōmina quae prīmō sumpsimus in thalamō;
nec [sē] ferat ūlla diēs ut commūtēmur * in aevō *,
quīn * tibi sim iuvenis tūque puella mihi.
Nestore * sim quamvīs * prōvectior * aemulaque * annīs
vincās Cūmānam * tū quoque Dēiphobēn *,
nōs ignōrēmus * quid sit matūra * senectūs:
scīre aevī * meritum, nōn numerāre * decet.

(Ausonius, Epigrammata *40)*

19: **dentātus, -a, -um** toothed, having teeth
narrō, -āre, -āvī, -ātus tell a story
20: [Sī] **mollibus oculīs est** "If she has watery eyes"
21: **subitō** (adv.) suddenly, unexpectedly
22: **māne** (adv.) early in the morning
23: **imprōvīsus, -a, -um** unexpected
dēprendō, -ere, dēprendī, dēprēnsus catch, surprise
inermis, -e unarmed, unprepared (here, with makeup, etc.)
24: **infēlix, infēlīcis** unhappy, unlucky
excidō, -ere, excidī fall, be lost, perish

1: **vīvāmusque . . . et teneāmus = et vīvāmus . . . et teneāmus**
3: **commūtō, -āre, -āvī, -ātus** change
3, 8: **aevum, -ī** *n* time
4: **quīn** but that
5: **Nestor, -oris** *m* the aged patriarch who accompanied the Greeks to Troy
quamvīs + subjunctive although
prōvectus, -a, -um advanced, protracted
aemula, -ae *f* rival
Cūmānam Dēiphobēn (acc.) the Cumaean Sibyl; Dēiphobe is the name given to the Sibyl at Cumae in book VI of the *Aeneid*. The Sibyl was a female prophet, usually depicted as very old.
7: **ignōrō, -āre** be ignorant of
matūrus, -a, -um mature, ripe
8: **numerō, -āre** count, reckon

XIV

Fifth Declension; *Fīō*; Gerund and Gerundive; Supine

Fifth Declension Nouns

The fifth (and final) declension is characterized by the letter **-ē-**. Most nouns in this declension are feminine; the one important exception is **diēs**, "day," which is regularly masculine.[1]

One very important fifth declension word you have already encountered in previous chapters is **rēs**. Literally, **rēs** means "thing," and can refer to some abstract thing or something more concrete, such as a lawsuit, one's personal property, or even the state itself, the **rēs pūblica** (from which we get "republic").

	rēs, rēī, *f* *thing*	**diēs, diēī**, *m* *day*
	SINGULAR	
Nom.	rēs	diēs
Gen.	rēī	diēī
Dat.	rēī	diēī
Acc.	rem	diem
Abl.	rē	diē
	PLURAL	
Nom.	rēs	diēs
Gen.	rērum	diērum
Dat.	rēbus	diēbus
Acc.	rēs	diēs
Abl.	rēbus	diēbus

[1] You will sometimes see it as feminine, however: e.g., **diēs īrae**, **diēs illa**, "the day of wrath, that day." For the purposes of this text, we will consistently treat **diēs** as masculine.

Irregular Verb: *fīō, fierī, factus sum*

The present passive forms of **faciō**, **facere** are not usually used in Latin. Instead, the present passive voice is normally supplied by the verb **fīō**, **fīěrī**, meaning "become, be made," or "happen." The perfect tenses of **fīō**, conversely, are supplied by the perfect passive forms of **faciō**.

Lux facta est.	Light was made, or Light came into being.
Puer senex factus erat.	The child had become an old man.

The only new forms for this verb are those based on the present stem of **fīō**, but note the long -**ī**- of the stem, even before another vowel, except when followed by -**ěr**-, as in **fīěrī**, and in the imperfect subjunctive:

Indicative			Subjunctive	
PRESENT	IMPF.	FUTURE	PRESENT	IMPF.
fīō	fīēbam	fīam	fīam	fierem
fīs	fīēbās	fīēs	fīās	fierēs
fit	fīēbat	fīet	fīat	fieret
fīmus	fīēbāmus	fīēmus	fīāmus	fierēmus
fītis	fīēbātis	fīētis	fīātis	fierētis
fīunt	fīēbant	fīent	fīant	fierent

	Infinitives	Participles
Present	fierī	——
Perfect	factus esse	factus, -a, -um
Future	——	faciendus, -a, -um

Consider the following examples of **fīō**, **fierī**. Notice that, like the verb **esse**, **fīō** cannot take a direct object but instead takes a predicate noun or adjective:

Ōlim magna rēs erat deum **fierī**.
It was once an important matter *to be made* a god.

Post hunc diem nēmō mortālis deus **fīat**.
After today let no mortal *become* a god.

Tum illud quod **fit** nātūrāliter agitur.
Then the thing that *happens* is done naturally.

Et Deus dīxit, "**Fīat** lux," et lux **facta est**.
And God said, "*Let there be* light," and light came *into being*.

Brevis esse labōrō: obscūrus **fīō**.
I labor to be brief [and to the point]: [but instead] I *become* obscure.

Scrībenda

rēs, rēī *f* thing
diēs, diēī *m* day
spēs, spēī *f* hope

A. Decline the following:
rēs pūblica
diēs quisque
spēs omnis

B. Write a complete synopsis of **fīō** in the third person plural, including participles and infinitives.

C. Translate the following:

1. Rērum gestārum dīvī Augustī exemplar hīc compositum est.
2. Hīs rēbus gestīs, Rōmam rediī.
3. Nē videar in persōnam, nōn in rem, dīcere sententiam, post hunc diem nēmō mortālis deus fīat.
4. Imperāvit deus ut post hunc diem nēmō mortālis deus fieret.
5. Ibi multa fīēbant quae tū fierī volēbās.
6. Ōdī et amō; quārē* id faciam fortasse* requīris*.
   Nesciō, sed [id] fierī sentiō et excrucior*.
   (Catullus 85)
   (**quārē** = quā rē, why?; **fortasse** (adv.), perhaps; **requīrō**, **-ere**, ask, inquire; **excruciō**, **-āre**, torment, torture)
7. Sī tū reddās ratiōnem quā rē id fierī potuerit aut cūr fierī dēsīverit, ego discam lībenter. (**dēsīverit**, from **dēsinō**)

Gerunds and Gerundives

As you have seen in earlier chapters, the infinitive is sometimes used as a noun:

Bene **dīcere** est difficile. *Speaking* well is difficult.

Dīcere here functions as a neuter noun in the nominative or accusative case. A separate form, called a *gerund*, is used when declined forms of a verbal noun are needed.

Gen.	*dīcendī* amor, a love of speaking
Dat.	aptum *dīcendō*, suitable for speaking
Acc.	ad *dīcendum*, for/toward speaking
Abl.	*dīcendō* suasit, he persuaded by speaking

You will recognize the gerund as being identical in appearance with the neuter singular future passive participle, which, as you learned in Chapter

XI, is a verbal adjective. A gerund, by contrast, is a verbal *noun*, neuter gender, of the second declension. It is always active in meaning, and occurs only in the singular genitive, dative, accusative and ablative cases. The gerund of the irregular verb **eō**, "go," is **eundī**, **eundō**, **eundum**, **eundō**. The irregular verbs **sum**, **possum**, **volō**, **nōlō**, and **mālō** have no gerunds. Consider the following examples:

> Haec sunt bene **dīcendī** praecepta.
> These are rules (**praecepta**) *for speaking* well. (objective genitive)
>
> Multī solent quaerere an **scrībendō** an **legendō** an **dīcendō** conferātur **vīs dīcendī**.
> Many people are inclined to ask whether true eloquence (**vīs dīcendī**, "the power of speaking") is acquired *by writing* or *by reading* or *by speaking*.
>
> Nox **ā nocendō** appellāta est, quod oculīs noceat.
> **Nox** is named *from "harming,"* because it is harmful to the eyes. (Isidore, *Etymologiae* V.31)
>
> **Pulsandō** paene confrēgī hās forēs.
> I almost broke these doors *with knocking*.

A gerundive construction consists of a future passive participle (called a "gerundive") and the noun it modifies. A gerundive is a verbal adjective, is always passive in meaning, and occurs in all cases, singular and plural.

Consider the gerund, **dīcendī**. It is common for a gerund, when it takes an object, to become adjectival and modify its object, thus becoming a gerundive construction. Thus, "a love of speaking words," (**verba**) **dīcendī amor** may become **verbōrum dīcendōrum amor**. A very literal translation of this phrase back into English, "a love of words to-be-spoken," will not readily reveal the underlying action or intention of the Latin. The best solution (in order to arrive at a satisfactory meaning) is to convert a gerundive construction back into a gerund-plus-direct-object before translating it into English:

Gerundive:	hīs foribus pulsandīs, by these doors to-be-struck
Gerund:	hās forēs pulsandō, by striking these doors
Gerundive:	aptum vītae agendae, suitable for life to-be-spent
Gerund:	aptum vītam agendō, suitable for spending (one's) life

Gerund and Gerundive Used to Express Purpose

The preposition **ad** followed by a gerund or gerundive in the accusative case indicates purpose, as does the genitive of the gerund or gerundive followed by the ablative **causā**:

Gerund:	Diū labōrāvimus **ad** bene **dīcendum**. Diū labōrāvimus bene **dīcendī causā**. We worked for a long time *in order to speak* well.
Gerundive:	Diū labōrāvimus **ad verba** bene **dīcenda**. Diū labōrāvimus **verbōrum** bene **dīcendōrum causā**. We worked for a long time *in order to speak words* well.

The Supine

Another way to express purpose is with the accusative of the *supine*. The supine is a verbal noun of the fourth declension, formed from the fourth principal part of the verb. It occurs only in the accusative and ablative singular.

The accusative supine is used only with verbs of motion to express purpose. It may take an object in the proper case:

Cūr nōn intrō eō prandium **parātum**?
Why don't I go inside *to prepare* the meal?

Vēnērunt animālia **vīsum**.
They came *to see* the animals.

The supine is used in the ablative only with a few adjectives or nouns which denote ease or difficulty (**facilis**, **difficilis**), wonder or admiration (**mīrābilis**), right or wrong (**fās**, **nefās**), or need (**opus**).[2]

Deus dixit, "Fīat lux" et, **mīrābile dictū**, facta est lux.
God said, "Let there be light," and, *wonder of wonders* (*wonderful to tell*) light came into being.

Nefās est hoc **crēditū**.
It is *wrong to believe* this.

Fās est hoc **dictū**.
It is *right to say* this.

Tālia **vīsū opus** est.
Such things *must be seen* (literally, "there is a *need to see* such things").

Scrībenda

A. Form the gerund of the following verbs:

dūcō	audiō	gaudeō
fugiō	eō	ferō

B. Translate the following:

1. Bene scrībere est difficile. Cupidus erat bene scrībendī. Celeriter scrībendō nōn bene scrībēs.
2. Librōrum scrībendōrum causā diū labōrāvit. Ad bene scrībendum labōrat. Ad librōs scrībendōs diū labōrābis.
3. Verba ōrātōrum bonōrum discendō bene dīcere optat.
4. M. Tullius stilum vocat "magistrum dīcendī." (**stilus**, **-ī**, *m*, pen)
5. Omnēs puerī vim dīcendī valēre volunt. Quis est quī sciat quae semper sint dīcenda?
6. Nōbīs copia verbōrum paranda est; id autem fit bonīs litterīs legendīs atque audiendīs. (**cōpia**, **-ae**, *f*, supply)

[2] The ablative supine may originally have been a dative of purpose, which early was confused with the ablative, and thus now retains the ablative ending rather than the dative ending, although it retains its purposive force, i.e., "to" or "for" the doing of something.

7. Verba poētae audiendī causā Rōmam vēnimus. Ad verba poētae audienda Rōmam veniēbāmus. Rōmam eāmus ut verba poētae audiāmus. Rōmamne adīstī poētam audītum?
8. Difficile est poētam audīre. Fās est dictū haec ferenda esse. Opus est poētam audītū.
9. Hīc veniās ut spectāculum videās. (**spectāculum**, **-ī**, *n*, show, theatrical entertainment)
10. Venī ad spectāculum videndum. Venīte spectāculī videndī causā.
11. Vēnistis spectāculum vīsum. Spectāculum vīsū nōn est facile.

C. Translate the following into Latin:

1. She will not escape her father's power by going to Rome.
2. By giving the daughter to a friend, the mother was able to conceal the truth. (Use a gerundive.)
3. It seemed more difficult to laugh than to cry.
4. In reading this book you will find nothing difficult to understand.
5. Let him go home to see his mother. (Write four different versions, using first the supine, then the gerund, then the gerundive, and finally a purpose clause.)

Verba tenenda

Verbs

clāmō, **-āre**, **-āvī**, **-ātus** shout, cry out

cernō, **-ere**, **crēvī**, **crētus** separate; distinguish (visually), perceive, discern

concēdō, **-ere**, **-cessī**, **-cessus** grant, yield; go, depart

dēmittō, **-ere**, **-mīsī**, **-missus** send down, let down, drop, lower

dubitō, **-āre**, **-āvī**, **-ātus** doubt, be uncertain; (+ infinitive) hesitate

fīō, **fierī**, **factus sum** become, be made, happen

gaudeō, **-ēre**, **gāvīsus sum** rejoice; (+ abl.) take pleasure in

invideō, **-ēre**, **-vīdī**, **-vīsus** envy, look askance at; begrudge something (acc.) to someone (dat.)

permittō, **-ere**, **-mīsī**, **-missus** surrender; commit; allow, grant, permit

pervideō, **-ēre**, **-vīdī**, **-vīsus** look over, survey, examine

poscō, **-ere**, **poposcī**, —— ask urgently for, beg, request; demand; summon

taceō, **-ēre**, **tacuī**, **tacitus** be silent, be still

tangō, **-ere**, **tetigī**, **tactus** touch, handle; strike; border on or be contiguous to

Nouns

canis, **-is** (gen. pl. **canum**) *m* or *f* dog

cōpia, **-ae** *f* abundance, wealth, power; supply; pl., troops

diēs, **-ēī** *m* day

faciēs, **-ēī** *f* face

fās (indeclinable neuter noun) that which is right or permissible by divine law; that which is right; an obligation

iter, **itineris** *n* a going, journey; walk, way, path, road

nefās (indeclinable neuter noun), that which is contrary to divine law, sinful, unlawful; sin, crime
rēs, **rēī** *f* thing, matter, event; property; situation
rēs pūblica commonwealth, republic
silva, **-ae** *f* a wood, forest, woodland
sors, **sortis** *f* lot, share, chance, fortune
umbra, **-ae** *f* shade, shadow
ūsus, **-ūs** *m* use, exercise, practice; need, necessity

Adjectives

dubius, **-a**, **-um** doubtful, uncertain
mollis, **-e** soft, flexible, tender, gentle
sacer, **sacra**, **sacrum** sacred, holy; cursed
suāvis, **-e** sweet, pleasant, agreeable

Adverb

quō where, to what place

Notanda

cernere properly means "to separate," either physically or mentally. Frequently the "separating" is done with the eyes, and hence the verb means to distinguish, perceive, discern. It is frequently used as a synonym for **videō**. Note that the perfect stem begins **cr-**. **Crescō**, "increase," has the same third and fourth principal parts as **cernō** (**crēvī**, **crētus**).

poscō often is equivalent in meaning to **petō** or **quaerō**, and can also be followed by the accusative of the object plus the ablative of the person of whom something is being asked. This verb can also govern two accusatives to the same effect: **Ab eō pecūniam poscimus** or **Eum pecūniam poscimus** both mean "We are asking him (urgently) for money." When this verb takes no object, it can mean "beg": **Improbus es cum poscis** (Juvenal): "You are disgraceful when you beg."

Note that **canis**, like **iuvenis** (Chapter XII) is not an **i**-stem, even though it is a parisyllabic third declension noun.

Fās carries religious connotation as the dictates of divine law, as opposed to human law. The opposite is **nefās**.

Iter, **itineris** (compare English "itinerary," "itinerant") is the act of travelling (from **eō**, **īre**, **iī**/**īvī**, **itum**), whether on a short or long journey. **Iter facere** therefore means "to make a journey" or "to travel."

A **sors** can be anything used to determine chance. **Sors** is properly the lot that is cast, but comes to mean the casting of lots, the result of the casting, and even destiny or fate itself.

The adjective **sacer** means consecrated to a divinity, and consequently means either "holy, sacred," or, conversely, dedicated to a divinity for destruction, hence "accursed, wicked." In the ancient Roman Laws of the Twelve Tables, one punishment named for a number of crimes is **Sacer estō**: "Let that person be **sacer**," which meant that that person could be killed with impunity, since he was now accursed and consequently deprived of ordinary human rights.

Ante legenda

Translate:

1. Urbem quae appellant Rōmam putāvī huic urbī nostrae similem esse.
2. Sīc magnās urbēs cum parvīs compōnere solēbam, sīcut animālia magna parvīs similia esse nōveram. (**compōnō**, **-ere**, compare)
3. In hāc urbe lībertātem invenīre spērābam. Hīc lībertātis spem invēnī. Ad hanc urbem vēnī spem inventum. Hīc vēnī ad spem inveniendam. Magnum iter fēcit speī inveniendae causā.
4. In hāc urbe servus factus est līber. In hanc urbem iter fēcit ut līber fieret. Ibi erat lībertās facilis inventū. Tibi est facilis inventū, mihi difficilis.
5. Num haec erat causa Rōmam videndī? Iter fecit Rōmam videndī causā. Et ego iter faciam Rōmae videndae causā.
6. Rōmae iuvenem vīdī quī mē līberum fēcit. Omnī diē mūnera suāvissima huic dabō quī mihi petentī bonum rēsponsum dedit.
7. Umquamne ego patriōs fīnēs longō post tempore vidēbō? (**patrius**, **-a**, **-um**, ancestral, native; **post**, adv., afterwards)
8. Ingenium molle atque facētum Vergiliō concessērunt gaudentēs rūre Camēnae. (**facētus**, **-a**, **-um**, elegant; fine; **Camēnae**, **-ārum**, *f* pl., the Roman Muses)
9. Hoc sapientī molliter est ferendum.
10. Ille aquam poposcit ad manūs lavandōs. Aquam ad manūs poposcit. (**lavō**, **-āre**, wash, clean)
11. Stābat dux silentium manū poscēns.
12. Cum nūlla sint salva bellō, pācem tē poscimus omnēs.
13. Nōs nē nunc quidem cernimus ea quae vidēmus.
14. Omnia sīc aperiam ut ea cernere oculīs videāminī.
15. Nox erat . . . cum tacet omnis ager.
16.

    Quam sīdera multa, cum tacet nox,
    furtīvōs hominum vident amōrēs,
    tam tē bāsia multa bāsiāre
    insānō satis est . . . Catullō.
    (Catullus 5.7–10)

    (**furtīvus**, **-a**, **-um**, stolen; **bāsia** = **oscula**; **bāsiō**, **-āre**, to kiss)
17. Avāritia puellās malās fēcit canemque posuit ad iānuam custōdiendam. Cōpiā pecūniae datā, canis ipse tacēbit. (**avāritia**, **-ae**, *f*, greed; **custōdiō**, **-īre**, guard, protect)
18. Dubiī inter spem metumque āmissōs sociōs quaerēbant. (**inter**, prep. + acc., between)
19. Quid dubitās? Nunc tempus [est] equōs, nunc poscere currūs. (**currus**, **-ūs**, *m*, war-chariot)

20. Dubitāmusne virtūtem ostendere factīs? Virtūtem ostendēmus hostēs ē terrā expellendō. (**hostis**, **-is**, *m*, enemy)

21. Utrum taceam an praedīcam? Tacendō dīcere vidēberis. Ad dīcendum et ad tacendum tū habēs portisculum. (**portisculus**, **-ī**, *m*, a truncheon or hammer with which the master of the rowers beat out the time; here, "control")

Legenda

The Roman Experience (2): Poets and Patrons

The development of poetry and drama at Rome was largely dependent upon literary patronage, since writers received little or nothing in the way of royalties from their works. In the early period of Rome, writers sometimes benefitted from generous bequests. Writers of the Augustan period benefitted more immediately from the economic assistance given them by literary patrons, who frequently provided the channel through which the work reached the public, as well as the financial means of pursuing this art. The most famous literary circles during the Augustan period are those that formed around Maecenas (his circle included the poets Horace, Propertius and Vergil) and around Messalla Corvinus (his included the poets Tibullus and Sulpicia). Augustus' successors followed his example of literary patronage only to a limited degree, as the complaints of Martial make evident, although there was a minor renaissance of Latin poetry under the emperor Nero, stemming from his support.

1. Vergil's earliest known poetry is a book of ten pastoral poems, known as the *Eclogues* or *Bucolica*. Pastoral poetry depicts an idealized countryside; its inhabitants are shepherds who sing poetic song, often in formalized competitions. Harsh political realities intrude upon the world of Vergil's shepherd-poets, however. The redistribution of land in 41 B.C. to returning war veterans causes the displacement of the young shepherd, Meliboeus, whose misfortune is contrasted with the good fortune of the elderly shepherd, Tityrus, whose land has been restored to him.

The meter is dactylic hexameter.

MELIBOEUS: Tītyre *, tū patulae * recubāns * sub tegmine * fāgī *
silvestrem * tenuī * mūsam * meditāris * avēnā * :
nōs patriae fīnēs et dulcia linquimus * arva * ;
nōs patriam fugimus: tū, Tītyre, lentus * in umbrā

1, 6, etc.: **Meliboeus**, **-ī** *m* the name of the younger shepherd
1, 4, 16: **Tītyrus**, **-ī** *m* the name of the elder shepherd
1: **patulus**, **-a**, **-um** spread out, extended
recubō, **-āre** recline
tegmen, **tegminis** *n* cover, covering
fāgus, **-ī** *f* beech

Fifth century manuscript of Vergil's First Eclogue shows Meliboeus meeting Tityrus under the shade of the spreading beech tree. The first two lines read, **Tityre tū patul(a)e recubāns sub tegmine fāgī/ silvestrem tenuī mūsam meditāris avēnā.** *(Cod. Vat. Lat. 3867)*

formōsam resonāre * docēs Amaryllida * silvās.
TITYRUS: Ō Meliboee *, deus nōbīs haec ōtia fēcit.

2: **silvestris**, **-e** wooded, overgrown with woods
tenuis, **-e** thin, delicate
mūsa, **-ae** *f* muse; song
meditāris (second pers. sing.) "you exercise, practice"
avēna, **-ae** *f* pipe (a reed pipe)
3: **linquō**, **-ere**, **līquī**, **lictus** leave, abandon
arvum, **-ī** *n* ploughed fields
4, 23: **lentus**, **-a**, **-um** leisurely, without haste
5: **resonō**, **-āre** resound, echo
Amaryllida (acc. *f* sing.) Amaryllis. The song Tityrus sings is "**Formōsa** [**est**] **Amaryllis**."

namque * erit ille mihī semper deus, illius aram
saepe tener * nostrīs ab ovīlibus * imbuet agnus*.
ille meās errāre bovēs, ut cernis, et ipsum
lūdere quae vellem calamō * permīsit agresti*.
Mel: Nōn equidem * invideō, mīror * magis * ; undique * tōtīs
usque adeō * turbātur * agrīs. ēn *, ipse capellās *
prōtinus * aeger * agō. . . .
Saepe malum hoc nōbīs, sī mēns nōn laeva * fuisset,
dē caelō tactās meminī praedīcere * quercus*.
sed tamen iste deus quī sit, dā, Tītyre, nōbīs.
Tit: Urbem quam dīcunt Rōmam, Meliboee, putāvī
stultus * ego huic nostrae similem, quō saepe solēmus
pastōrēs ovium * tenerōs * dēpellere * fētūs *.
sīc canibus catulōs * similēs, sīc mātribus haedōs *
nō[ve]ram, sīc parvīs compōnere * magna solēbam.
vērum * haec tantum * aliās inter caput extulit urbēs
quantum lenta * solent inter vīburna * cupressī *.
Mel: Et quae tanta fuit Rōmam tibi causa videndī?
Tit: Lībertās . . . longō post * tempore vēnit. . . .

7: **namque** (conj.) for indeed
8, 19: **tener, tenera, tenerum** of tender age; young
8: **ovīle**, **-is** *n* sheepfold
agnus, **-ī** *m* lamb
10: **calamus**, **-ī** *m* reed pipe
agrestis, **-e** rustic, rural
11: **equidem** = "ego quidem"
mīror (first pers. sing.) "I marvel"
magis (adv.) more
undique (adv.) in all directions, everywhere
12: **usque adeō** (adv.) continuously
turbātur (impersonal) "there is disruption"
12, 35, 38: **ēn** (exclamation) "look!" "see!"
capella, **-ae** *f* goat
13: **prōtinus** immediately
aeger, aegra, aegrum sick
14: **laevus, -a, -um** on the left side; of ill omen
15: **praedico, -ere** foretell, predict
quercus, **-ūs** *f* oak
18: **stultus, -a, -um** stupid
19: **ovis, ovis** *f* sheep
dēpellō, -ere drive down (to market)
fētus, **-ūs** *m* offspring
20: **catulus**, **-ī** *m* puppy
haedus, **-ī** *m* goat
21: **compōnō, -ere** compare
22: **vērum** (adv.) but
22–23: **tantum** . . . **quantum** (adv.) as much . . . as
23: **lentus, -a, -um** pliant, flexible
vīburnum, **-ī** *n* Viburnum is a short shrub, contrasting with the tall cypress (**cupressus**, -ī, *f*).
25, 35: **post** (adv.) afterwards

hīc illum vīdī iuvenem, Meliboee, quotannīs *
bīs sēnōs * cui nostra diēs altāria * fūmant *.
hīc mihi respōnsum * prīmus dedit ille petentī:
"pascite * ut ante * bovēs, puerī, . . ."
Mel: Fortūnāte * senex, ergō tua rūra manēbunt.
et tibi magna satis [erunt], . . .
fortūnāte senex, hīc inter flūmina * nōta
et fontēs * sacrōs frīgus * captābis opācum *.
....
At nōs hinc . . . ībimus . . .
En * umquam patriōs * longō post * tempore fīnēs
[vidēbō]? . . .
impius haec tam culta * novālia * mīles habēbit,
barbarus * hās segetēs *! ēn *, quō discordia * cīvēs
prōdūxit * miserōs: hīs nōs cōnsēvimus * agrōs!

(From Eclogue *I.1–72)*

2. The poet Horace had been introduced to his patron, Maecenas, by Vergil. Such introductions were precious, as the following encounter suggests: here an ambitious but unknown poet makes a clumsy but amusing attempt to win from Horace an introduction to Maecenas. The meter of the *Satires* is dactylic hexameter; this adaptation is not in meter.

Ībam forte Viā Sacrā,* sīcut meus est mōs,
nescioquid cōgitāns nūgārum *, tōtus in illīs.

26: **quotannīs** (adv.) every year
27: **bīs sēnōs** twice six; "for twelve (days)" (accus. showing duration of time).
altāria, -ium *n* pl. altars
fūmō, -āre smoke, give off smoke or steam
28: **respōnsum, -ī** *n* reply
29: **pascō, -ere** feed
ante (adv.) previously
30: **fortūnātus, -a, -um** blessed, fortunate
32: **flūmen, -inis** *n* river, stream
33: **fōns, fontis** *m* fountain
frīgus, frīgoris *n* coldness, chill
opācus, -a, -um shaded, shady
35: **patrius, -a, -um** ancestral, native
37: **cultus** from **colō**
novālia, -ium *n* pl. crop-land which has been left fallow
haec tam culta novālia "this land, so carefully cultivated"
38: **barbarus, -ī** *m* foreigner, stranger
seges, segetis *f* field of growing grain
discordia, -ae *f* discord, dissension
39: **prōdūcō, -ere, -dūxī, -ductus** lead
cōnserō, -ere, cōnsēvī, cōnsitum sow or plant with something

1: **Viā Sacrā** (abl.) "on the Via Sacra," the principal street in Rome
2: **nūgae, -ārum** *f* pl. trifles
nescioquid nūgārum "some trifle or another"

accurrit* quīdam nōtus mihi nōmine sōlum,
raptāque manū quaesīvit 'quid agis, dulcissime rērum?'
'suāviter*, ut nunc est,' inquam, 'et cupiō omnia quae vīs.'
cum nōn discēderet, 'num quid vīs?' quaesīvī. at ille
'nōveris nōs' inquit; 'doctī sumus'. Ego miserē discēdere
quaerēns, illī quidlibet* garrientī* et vīcōs* urbemque
laudantī nihil respondēbam. 'Miserē cupis' inquit 'abīre;
iamdūdum* videō: sed nihil agis; usque* tenēbō;
persequar* hinc quō nunc iter est tibi.' 'nōn opus
est tē circumagī*: quendam volō vīsere* nōn tibi nōtum:
trāns Tiberim* longē cubat* is, prope Caesāris* hortōs*.'
'Nihil habeō quod agam et nōn sum piger*: usque sequar tē*.'
Dēmittō auriculās, ut inīquae mentis asellus,
cum gravius dorsō subiit onus*. Incipit ille:
'Num quis mē scrībere celerius possit versūs?
Aut membra movēre mollius? Ego cantō quod et Hermogenēs*
invideat.' Interpellandī* locus hīc erat: "est tibi māter,
cognātī*, quibus tē salvō est opus*?' 'Nēmō: nōn mihi
quisquam: omnēs composuī*.' Fēlīcēs! Nunc ego supersum.
Confice*; namque instat fātum mihi* triste, quod

3: **accurrō** (**ad** + **currō**) run up to
5: **suāviter, ut nunc est** "very well, thank you, as things go"
8: **quidlibet** (*n* acc.) anything whatsoever
garriō, -īre chatter, talk
vīcus, -ī *m* row of houses, street (the point is, the unwelcome intruder was chattering at random)
10: **iamdūdum** (adv.) long since, for a long time now
usque (adv.) constantly, continuously
11: **persequar** "I shall follow"
11–12: **nōn opus est tē circumagī** "there is no need for you to be dragged around"
12: **vīsō, -ere** go to see, visit
13: **Tiberim** (acc.) the river Tiber
cubō, -āre lie down, lie sick, be sick
Caesar, Caesāris *m* Julius Caesar's estate on the Janiculum was left in his will to be a public park.
hortus, -ī *m* garden
14: **piger, pigra, pigrum** lazy, inactive
usque sequar tē "I'll follow you all the way over there"
15–16: **dēmittō auriculās . . . subiit onus** "I felt like a badly treated donkey whose ears drop down when he is given too heavy a load."
18: **Hermogenēs** In attempting to ingratiate himself, the intruder makes a serious mistake when he brags about his singing ability. Horace elsewhere has made it clear how much he dislikes verses written rapidly and in great profusion; Horace has a particularly low opinion of Hermogenes' singing and dancing.
19: **interpellō, -āre** interrupt by speaking
20: **cognātus, -ī** *m* relative (**quibus** is dat. of possession)
tē salvō est opus **opus** here governs the ablative **tē salvō**
21: **omnēs composuī** "I've buried them all"
22: **confice** "Finish me off too"
instat fātum mihi "a prediction hanging over me draws near fulfillment."
instō + dat. approach, threaten

Sabella anus * puerō cecinit dīvīnā mōtā urnā * :
"hunc neque dīra * venēna * nec hosticus * auferet ēnsis *,
nec laterum * dolor aut tussis *, nec tarda * podagra * ;
garrulus * hunc quandō * cōnsūmet cumque * : loquācēs *,
sī sapiat *, vītet, simul atque adolēverit aetās *."
Vēnerāmus ad Vestae *, quartā * iam parte diēī
praeteritā *, et cāsū tum respondēre * vadātō *
dēbēbat; quod nisi fēcisset, dīxit sē perditūrum * esse lītem *.
'Sī mē amās' inquit 'paulum hīc ades *.' 'Inteream * sī
aut valeō stāre aut nōvī cīvīlia iūra; et properō * quō scīs.'
'Dubius * sum quid faciam' inquit, tēne * relinquam an rem.'
'Mē, sōdēs *.' 'Nōn faciam' inquit et praecēdere incēpit.
Ego, ut contendere * dūrum est cum victōre, sequor *.

[The intruder now begins prying into Horace's friendship with Maecenas. Horace refuses to answer. The intruder then offers to be Horace's hatchet-man within Maecenas' circle in return for an introduction. After other unsuccessful attempts to free himself from this boorish intruder, Horace is finally rescued by the intruder's opponent in the lawsuit; the opponent asks Horace to serve as a witness against him, and Horace agrees.]

23: **Sabella anus** (nom.) an aged Sabine woman (who gave predictions, like the Cumaean Sibyl). Horace now recalls her prediction that he would be talked to death.
dīvīnā mōtā urnā (ablative absolute) "shaking the lots in her urn" until one of them fell out.
24: **dīrus, -a, -um** dread, dire
venēnum, -ī *n* poison, medicine
hosticus ēnsis an enemy's sword
25: **latus, lateris** *n* the side; the lungs
tussis, -is *f* a cough
tardus, -a, -um "which makes one move slowly"
podagra, -ae *f* gout in the feet
26: **garrulus, -a, -um** talkative
quandō . . . cumque at some time or other
loquax, loquācis (adj.) talkative, chattering, loquacious
27: **sapiō, -ere** have good taste, be wise
simul atque adolēverit aetās "as soon as he has become an adult"
28: **ad Vestae** "to the temple of Vesta"
28–29: **quartā parte . . . praeteritā** (ablative absolute) about nine o'clock
29: **respondēre** to appear in court
vadātō (ablative) "under bond"
30: **perdō, -ere, perdidī, perditus** lose utterly
līs, lītis *f* lawsuit
31: **paulum hīc ades** "be present in court as my supporting friend and adviser"
inteream "I'll be darned (if)" (literally, "May I perish [if]")
32: **properō, -āre** hasten, hurry
33: **dubius, -a, -um** doubtful, unsure
tēne = tē + -ne
34: **sōdēs = sī audēs** "please"
35: **contendō, -ere** fight, contend
sequor "I follow"

    Cāsū vēnit obvius illī
adversārius * et 'quō tū *, turpissime?' magnā
clāmat vōce, et rapit illum in iūs * : clāmor * erat utrimque,
undique concursus *. Sīc mē servāvit Apollo *.

(After Satire *9)*

36–37: **cāsū vēnit obvius illī adversārius** "by chance his opponent (in the lawsuit) came to meet him"

37: **quō tū** = **quō tū** [**curris**]?

38: **in iūs** into court

38–39: **clāmor utrimque**, **undique concursus** "there is shouting on both sides, and from everywhere there is a flocking together"

39: **Apollō**, **-inis** *m* Apollo, the guardian of poetry and poets

Irregular Comparisons; Dative Case (2): Summary of Uses

Comparison of Irregular Adjectives and Adverbs

Irregular Adjectives. Many of the more common adjectives have irregular forms in the comparative and superlative degrees. It is best to memorize these irregular forms, although English derivatives will help to recognize them:

POSITIVE	COMPARATIVE	SUPERLATIVE
bonus, -a, -um good	**melior, melius** better	**optimus, -a, -um** best
malus, -a, -um bad	**pēior, pēius**[1] worse	**pessimus, -a, -um** worst
magnus, -a, -um large, great	**māior, māius**[1] larger, greater	**maximus, -a, -um** greatest
parvus, -a, -um small	**minor, minus** smaller	**minimus, -a, -um** smallest
multus, -a, -um much	——, **plūs** more	**plūrimus, -a, -um** most
[**prae, pro**] in front of	**prior, prius** former	**prīmus, -a, -um** first
superus, -a, -um above	**superior, superius** higher	**summus, -a, -um** highest **suprēmus, -a, -um** last

Plūs is the only one of the above forms whose declension is irregular. In the singular it is a neuter noun, and is frequently followed by a partitive

[1] You will find that many texts mark the **-e-** in **peior** and the **-a-** in **maior** with a circumflex (^) or even list it as short. These vowels are originally short, but are lengthened before the following consonant **-i-**; they are pronounced **pey-yor** (**pêior**) and **may-yor** (**mâior**). The **-e-** and **-a-** in words derived from these adjectives are usually long (**maiestas**, "majesty, grandeur"; **peiurium**, "false oath, perjury").

genitive: **plūs sapientiae**, "More wisdom." The plural is declined like other comparative adjectives, except that the genitive plural ends in **-ium**:

	SINGULAR NOUN	PLURAL ADJECTIVE	
	N.	M. AND F.	N.
Nom.	plūs	plūrēs	plūra
Gen.	plūris	plūrium	plūrium
Dat.	——	plūribus	plūribus
Acc.	plūs	plūrēs	plūra
Abl.	plūre	plūribus	plūribus

Irregular Adverbs. The adverbs derived from these irregular adjectives are also irregular, particularly in the positive degree. The comparative forms, with the exception of **magis**, are regular, as are the superlative forms, with the exception of **prīmō/prīmum** and **plūrimum:**

POSITIVE	COMPARATIVE	SUPERLATIVE
bene well	**melius** better	**optimē** best
male badly	**pēius** worse	**pessimē** worst
magnopere greatly	**magis** more	**maximē** most, especially
parum little, not much	**minus** less	**minimē** least
multum much	**plūs** more	**plūrimum** most, very much
[prō]	**prius** before, earlier	**prīmō/prīmum** at first in the first place

Observe that:

1. **Prior, prius** has no positive degree. The superlative adverbs **prīmō** and **prīmum** can be used interchangeably.

2. **Superus** has two superlatives, one referring to height (**summus**) and one to time (**suprēmus**).

3. **Plūs** tends to be used with numerical expressions or with expressions of quantity, e.g., **plūs annīs decem**, "more than ten years," as opposed to **magis**, e.g., **magis ambitiō quam avāritia animōs hominum exercēbat**, "Ambition used to arouse men's hearts more than avarice."

Scrībenda

A. Modify the following nouns with the appropriate form of the positive, comparative, and superlative degree of the adjectives indicated:

1. malus: rēs (nom. pl.)
   diēs (nom. sing.)
   exitū

2. multus: manūs (acc. pl.)
versuum
animālibus
3. parvus: versūs (gen. sing.)
cornū (abl. sing.)
cornū (acc. sing.)
4. magnus: artī
dente
animālis
marī (abl.)
vim

B. Translate the following sentences:

1. Num quis mē scrībere plūrēs aut celerius possit versūs?
2. Quis tē plūra scrībere potest?
3. Illa vērō tē plūs ingeniī ostendit.
4. Auctōritāte magis quam imperiō regēbat. (**auctōritās**, **-tātis**, *f*, authority, power)
5. Ursa māior ursam minōrem fugiendō nautās domum dūcit. (**ursa**, **-ae**, *f*, she-bear)
6. In plūrimīs cīvitātibus intellegī potest virōrum bonōrum memoriam cōnsecrātam esse ut lībentius prō suīs cīvibus perīculum adīrent virī fortēs. (**cōnsecrātus**, **-a**, **-um**, immortalized; **lībentius** (adv.), more willingly)
7. Sunt quī dīcant nōn optimē deōs nōbīs auxilium dare.
8. Corporis vīrēs māiōrēs pecudibus quam hominibus datae sunt. (**pecus**, **-udis**, *f*, cattle)
9. Prīmas litterās, cum legere et scrībere et numerāre discerem, nōn minus onerōsās habēbam quam omnēs Graecās, sed meliōrēs, quia certiōrēs erant. (**numerō**, **-āre**, count; **onerōsus**, **-a**, **-um**, burdensome)
10. Astrologī in plūribus vēra possunt praedīcere et maximē in rē commūnī.
11. Ē plūribus cīvitātibus facta est ūna rēs pūblica.
12. Māiōrēs nostrī nōn prohibuērunt dolōrem sed eum fīniērunt.
13. Optimum modum inter pietātem et ratiōnem ostendēs dolōrem sentiendō et opprimendō.
14. Minus pietātis ostendās dolōre gravissimō quam dolōre opprimendō.
15. Dolōrem quam maximē opprimendō pietātem ostendimus.
16. Graecī rēs levissimās prō maximīs semper habuērunt.

Special Verbs Governing the Dative Case

Some verbs by their very meaning are incapable of governing a direct object. Perhaps the most obvious examples of these "intransitive verbs" are, in both English and Latin, verbs of coming and going. Some intransitive verbs can, however, govern an indirect object. In previous chapters you have encountered intransitive Latin verbs which govern an indirect object, for example:

> Discipulus **litterīs Graecīs studet**.
> The student *is eager for/is studying Greek literature*.
> Lux **oculīs nocet**.
> Light *is harmful to the eyes*.
> Cīvitās nostra **ceterīs praestat**.
> Our state *is superior to the others*.

By emphasizing the meanings of intransitive Latin verbs which make most evident their inability to take a direct object, you will find yourself using the dative case quite naturally with these verbs.[2] The more abbreviated English equivalents of some of these verbs can be misleading. **Lux oculīs nocet**, for example, can be translated "Light harms the eyes," leading you to expect **oculōs** in Latin instead of **oculīs**. It is therefore wise to emphasize the English phrasing that clearly conveys the intransitive nature of the verb; the final translation of course should be in smooth English.

crēdō, **-ere**, **crēdidī**, **crēditus** believe in, trust (in)
Crēdimus vōbīs. We believe (in) you.

faveō, **-ēre**, **fāvī**, **fautus** be favorable to, favor
Favent nōbīs. They favor us/are favorably inclined toward us.

ignoscō, **-ere**, **ignōvī**, **ignōtus** be forgiving to, forgive
Mihi ignosce! Forgive me!

imperō, **-āre**, **-āvī**, **-ātus** (+ indirect command) give orders to, command
Illīs imperāverat ut hoc facerent. He had ordered them to do this thing.

noceō, **-ēre**, **nocuī**, **nocitūrus** be harmful to, harm
Tua amīcitia mihi nocēbit. Your friendship will hurt me.

parco, **-ere**, **pepercī**, **parsūrus** be sparing to, spare
Parce mihi! Spare me!

pareō, **-ēre**, **paruī**, **paritus** be obedient to, obey
Tuō parentī parēre dēbēs. You ought to obey your parent.

placeō, **-ēre**, **placuī**, **placitus** be pleasing to
Omnia haec tibi placent. All these things are pleasing to you/please you.

serviō, **-īre**, **-īvī**, **-ītus** be a servant to, serve
Cui serviēs? Whom will you serve?[3]

studeō, **-ēre**, **studuī**, —— be eager for, study
Philosophiae studeāmus. Let's study philosophy.

[2] Verbs which regularly govern the dative case are those which signify to favor, help, please, trust, and the opposites of these. Verbs meaning to believe, command, obey, serve, resist, envy, threaten, pardon, and spare also take the dative.

[3] Do not confuse **servīre**, to "serve," with **servāre**, "to save."

suādeō, **-ēre**, **suāsī**, **suāsus** or **persuādeō**, **-ēre**, etc. (+ indirect command) make "sweet" to, persuade
Tibi suādēbō ut hoc faciās. I will persuade you to do this thing.

Dative with Compound Verbs

Frequently verbs which, in their simple form (e.g., **currō**, **cubō**, **pōnō**), indicate an indirect relationship by means of a prepositional phrase will govern the dative case when compounded with a prepositional prefix. This occurs with both intransitive and transitive verbs:

INTRANSITIVE VERBS: **CURRŌ**, **CUBŌ**

1. **currō** + **ob**
   Equī **ob urbem** cucurrērunt.
   The horses ran *toward the city*.
2. **occurrō** run toward, run to meet
   Occurrit dulcis aqua **marī acerbō**.
   The sweet water runs to meet *the bitter sea*.
3. **cubō** lie down
   In lectō cubat.
   He is lying *on the bed*.
4. **incubō** lie on
   Condit opēs alius **dēfessōque incubat aurō**.
   Another buries his wealth and *broods over worn-out gold*. (literally, "lies on")

TRANSITIVE VERBS: **PŌNŌ** AND ITS COMPOUNDS

5. **pōnō** + **sub**
   Pōne mē **sub currū** Sōlis.
   Put me *under the chariot* of the Sun.
6. **suppōnō** place under
   Sī dēmās bracchia cancrō et cetera **suppōnās terrae**, dē parte sepultā scorpius exībit.
   If you take the arms away from a crab and *place* the rest (of it) *under the ground*, from the buried part will come a scorpion.
7. **pōnō** + **in**
   Cibum **in mensam** pōnet.
   He will place the food *on the table*.
8. **impōnō** place upon
   Ēripe, nāte, fugam, fīnemque **impōne labōrī**.
   Take flight, my son, and *put* an end *to your toil*.
9. **postpōnō** place after, treat as if of secondary importance
   Vōs ausa est **nātīs suīs postpōnere**.
   She dared to *treat* you *as inferior to her own children*.

10. **compōnō** place with, compare
Sīc **parvīs compōnere** magna solēbam.
Thus I was accustomed to *compare* great things *with small things*.

The dative case with a compound verb is usually an alternative to repeating the preposition and its object: **occurrit ob mare** (example 2), **incubat in aurō** (4), **suppōnās sub terrā** (6), **fīnem impōne in labōrem** (8), and **compōnere cum parvīs** (10) would also be correct grammatically. For reasons of clarity, style, meter or rhetorical effect, however, the authors have chosen to employ instead the dative construction.

Finally, the dative with compound verbs is most common when the prepositions prefixed to the verb are **ad**, **ante**, **cum** [**con-**], **in**, **inter**, **ob**, **post**, **prae**, **prō**, **sub**, **super**, and, occasionally, **circum**.

Summary: Uses of the Dative Case

Now that you have learned the major uses of the dative case, a brief summary of these uses may be helpful. The dative case is used primarily to express an indirect object; the more idiomatic uses express possession, agent, reference, and purpose.[4]

1. The dative of the indirect object may occur with any transitive verb whose meaning allows:

Dō **tibi** librum.
I am giving *you* a book.

Litterās **mihi** fēmina reddet.
The woman will return the letter *to me*.

Illī quidlibet garrientī nihil respondēbam.
I gave no response *to him* as he chattered on about anything whatsoever.

2. The dative of the indirect object may occur with any intransitive verb whose meaning allows:

Mihi ignosce!
Forgive *me*!

Nōbīs imperābunt ut haec faciāmus.
They will order *us* to do these things.

3. The dative of the indirect object frequently occurs with compound verbs as an alternative to a prepositional phrase:

Pecūniam **amīcitiae** praeposuit.
She preferred money *to friendship*.

Terrīs nātūra circumfūdit Ōceanum.
Nature caused Ocean to surround *the land*.

[4] You will find it helpful to refer back to Chapter IV for a more extensive discussion of some of these uses.

Ōrāvit ut Caesar **sōlitūdinī** subvenīret.
She asked that Caesar bring aid *to her solitude.*

4. The dative occurs with any form of the verb **esse** to indicate possession:

Dīxit **fēminīs probīs** esse nōn aliud sōlācium.
She said that *decent women* have no other consolation.

Quibus est nūlla lībertās, sunt nūllae opēs.
Those who have no freedom have no wealth.

5. The dative of agent occurs with the gerundive (passive periphrastic) construction to denote the person who must perform the action:

Haec **nōbīs** facienda erant.
We had to do these things.

Invīsus nātālis **mihi** agendus rurī molestō erit.
I shall have to spend my hated birthday in the dreadful countryside.

6. The dative of reference or interest, also known as the dative of advantage or the dative of disadvantage, often depends not on any particular word, but on the general meaning of the sentence. It can be used in almost any circumstance to designate a person who is interested in or somehow involved in the situation:

Laudāvit **mihi** frātrem.
He praised my brother *out of regard for me.*

Nec sē ferat ūlla diēs quīn **tibi** sim iuvenis tūque puella **mihi**.
And never come the day when I am not a youth *to you* and you are not a young girl *to me.*

Tōtum hōc studium **mihi** mors abstulit.
Death has taken all this enthusiasm *from me.* ("*As for me,* death has taken away . . .") (dative of disadvantage)

7. The dative of purpose expresses the purpose which a person or thing serves. It is frequently used in connection with the dative of reference. (When the two are used together, they are referred to as the double dative construction.)

Ea rēs mihi **summae voluptātī** erat.
That business gave me *the greatest pleasure.*

Illī nōbīs **auxiliō** vēnērunt.
They came *to help* us.

8. The dative, finally, is used with many adjectives which denote fitness, nearness, likeness, service, inclination and their opposites:[5]

Quisque **sibi cārus** est.
Each person is *dear to himself.*

Ille vidētur **pār** esse **deō**.
That man seems to be *equal to a god.*

An villa sit **apta puellae**?
Could a farmhouse be *suitable for a young lady*?

[5] The English equivalents of these adjectives tend to be followed by "to" or "for." Cf. J. Mountford, *Bradley's Arnold Latin Prose Composition* (London, 1958), 146.

Scrībenda

A. Translate the following sentences:

1. Crēde tibi. Crēdite mihi vestram pecūniam. Crēdō vōs hoc numquam esse factūrōs.
2. Dīc nōbīs ubi sīs futūrus.
3. Quam tē lībenter videō, vix mihi ipse crēdēns mē Bīthȳnōs campōs līquisse. (**vix** (adv.), scarcely; **Bīthȳnus**, **-a**, **-um**, of Bithynia, a country in northwest Asia Minor; **campus**, **-ī**, *m*, field, plain; **linquō**, **-ere**, **līquī**, ——, leave, abandon)
4. Et mihi discendī et tibi docendī tempus dabitur.
5. Semper vōs vōbīs ignoscitis.
6. Quisquis es, faveās nostrīsque labōribus adsīs!
7. Sī quisquam est quī sē bonīs quam plūrimīs placēre et minimē multīs nocēre studeat, scīte, mē esse quem petās.
8. Rōmāne, hae tibi erunt artēs, pācī impōnere mōrem et parcere subiectīs.
9. Id faciendum est nōbīs quod parentēs imperant. (**parēns**, **-ntis**, *m* or *f*, parent)
10. Cui dōnō lepidum novum libellum? (**libellus**, **-ī**, *m* (diminutive of **liber**), little book; **lepidus**, **-a**, **-um**, charming; **dōnō**, **-āre**, give)
11. Nec tibi castaneae, mē coniuge, nec tibi dēerunt arbuteī fētūs: omnis tibi serviet arbor. (**castanea**, **-ae**, *f*, chestnut; **arbuteus**, **-a**, **-um**, of the strawberry tree; **fētus**, **fētūs**, *m*, offspring)
12. Nōn ego Graecīs servītum mātribus ībō. (**servītum** is here the supine of **serviō**)
13. Habē tibi quālecumque est hoc libellum.

B. Translate the following sentences into Latin:

1. For me, nothing is sweeter than understanding very difficult things.
2. Do you know what our ancestors believed was the highest good?
3. A less able person, although he receives less praise, will work more to receive it.
4. We will serve the state better if we become very good citizens.
5. When writing the last poem in his book, the poet decided that more than a very small part of his work would survive.

Verba tenenda

Verbs

caveō, **-ēre**, **cāvī**, **cautus** be on guard, take heed; beware

faveō, **-ēre**, **fāvī**, **fautus** (+ dat.) be favorable toward; favor, protect

dēfendō, **-ere**, **dēfendī**, **dēfensus** ward off, protect, defend

ignoscō, **-ere**, **-nōvī**, **-notus** (+ dat.) forgive

inscrībō, **-ere**, **inscrīpsī**, **inscriptus** write in or upon

inspiciō, **-ere**, **-spexi**, **-spectus** inspect, examine

intrō, **-āre**, **-āvī**, **-ātus** go into, walk into

notō, **-āre**, **-āvī**, **-ātus** mark, indicate, denote; pay attention to

parcō, **-ere**, **pepercī**, **parsūrus** (+ dat.) be sparing to; spare

pareō, **-ēre**, **paruī**, **paritus** (+ dat.) be obedient to; obey, comply with

pendeō, **-ēre**, **pependī**, —— be suspended, hang; be weighed

persuādeō, **-ēre**, **persuāsī**, **persuāsus** (+ dat.) win over by talking, persuade
pingō, **-ere**, **pinxī**, **pictus** paint, embroider, adorn; represent pictorially
placeō, **-ēre**, **placuī**, **placitus** (+ dat.) be pleasing to, please
praestō, **-stāre**, **praestitī**, **praestitus** (+ dat.) (intransitive): stand in front of, stand out, be superior; (transitive): show, exhibit
serviō, **-īre**, **servīvī** (-iī), **-ītus** (+ dat.) be a servant to; serve

Nouns

amīcitia, **-ae** *f* friendship
hospes, **hospitis** *m* guest, visitor
inscriptiō, **-iōnis** *f* inscription, title
lībertīnus, **-ī** *m* freedman
līmen, **līminis** *n* threshold, edge
pictor, **-tōris** *m* painter
plūs, **plūris** *n* more
proelium, **-iī** *n* battle, combat
saxum, **-ī** *n* large stone, rock
unda, **-ae** *f* wave; pl., the sea; waves
voluptās, **-tātis** *f* satisfaction, enjoyment, pleasure
vōtum, **-ī** *n* solemn promise, vow, prayer

Adjectives

aureus, **-a**, **-um** of gold, golden
beātus, **-a**, **-um** fortunate, blessed
dīves; **dīvitis** (gen.) wealthy, rich, sumptuous, costly
māior, **māius** larger, greater
maximus, **-a**, **-um** greatest
melior, **melius** better
minor, **minus** smaller
minimus, **-a**, **-um** smallest
optimus, **-a**, **-um** best
pauper; **pauperis** (gen.) poor, not wealthy; of small means
pēior, **pēius** worse
pessimus, **-a**, **-um** worst
plūrimus, **-a**, **-um** most
prīmus, **-a**, **-um** first
prior, **prius** former
sinister, **-tra**, **-trum** left, on the left side; of bad omen
summus, **-a**, **-um** highest
suprēmus, **-a**, **-um** last
ūber; **ūberis** (gen.) full, fruitful, fertile, plentiful

Adverbs

dēnique finally, at last; and then
diūtius, **diūtissimē** for a longer time, for a very long time
hinc from here, from this place
illīc from there, from that place
magis more
magnopere greatly
minus less
multum much
paene almost
paulātim little by little
plūrimum most, very much
plūs more
prīmō, **prīmum** at first, in the first place
quemadmodum how, in what way
super up above

Notanda

An "inscription" usually means something that has been written into a piece of stone, as opposed to things which are written on a wall; the latter are called "graffiti" (from the Greek verb **graphein**, "to write"). Many graffiti from antiquity can still be seen today, particularly at places like Pompeii, which was buried and thus preserved by a volcanic explosion in A.D. 79.

pendeō, the intransitive form of the verb meaning "hang," is a second conjugation verb. A transitive form, **pendō**, **-ere**, **pependī**, **pēnsus**, belongs to the third conjugation. The intransitive form has no fourth principal part.

The **Pictī** or Picts of Britain were so named by the Romans because of their practice of tattooing or "painting" themselves. An embroidered fabric will also be called **pictus**.

"Libertine," the English derivative of **lībertīnus** (**lībertīna**, *f*), means a person free of moral restraint or control.

Something that is "subliminal" is "below the **līmen**," the threshold, of consciousness.

The opposite of **sinister** is **dexter**. The English derivative "sinister" reflects the Greek method of interpreting omens, that what happens on the left is unfavorable. Although the Roman method of observation interprets omens on the left as favorable, the negative connotation of **sinister** is common in Latin literature.

Ūber as an adjective means "rich," "fertile." As a noun it means "breast" or "udder" of an animal, a source of milk or nourishment, hence its adjectival meaning.

Ante legenda

Translation:

1. Sibyllam in ampullā pendēre vīdī. (**Sibylla**, **-ae**, *f*, the Sibyl; **ampulla**, **-ae**, *f*, jar, bottle)
2. Tantae cūrae amīcitiae nostrae impendent!
3. Quis ad tolerandum labōrem erat melior?
4. Quid optandum gēns illa fert?
5. "Prior" inquit lībertīnus "Ego adsum. Cūr timeam dēfendere locum meum?"
6. In agrīs agricolae dīvitis vidēbis plūrima animālia. In hōc agrō vidēbis plūs quam in illō. Hīc quam plūrima vidēbis.
7. Ūber est vitiōrum cōpia. Quandō ūberior erat vitiōrum cōpia quam nunc? Quam plūrima est cōpia.
8. In prīmā parte domūs erant tabulae. In ūnā tabulā bonī diēs inscriptī sunt. Nec pessimī nec peiōrēs diēs notātī ibi sunt. (**tabula**, **-ae**, *f*, tablet)
9. Illud satis est, sī nōbīs ūnīs datur is diēs quem illa lapide candidiōre notat. (**lapis**, **lapidis**, *m*, stone; **candidus**, **-a**, **-um**, white)
10. Ad sinistram [manum] intrantibus canis ingēns (ingentissimus) in parietē erat pictus. (**pariēs**, **-etis**, *f*, wall)
11. Numquam vīdī melius cōnsilium darī. Numquam oculīs meīs vīdī peius cōnsilium darī.

12. Nōn istō modō vīvimus quō tū putās; domus hāc nec honestior ūlla est nec magis aliēna hīs malīs.
13. Quī haec dīcant magnopere ā vēritāte errāvisse videantur.
14. In istō homine est satis ēloquentiae, parum sapientiae.
15. Agitābātur magis magisque animus iste saevus.
16. Fēlix quī potuit cīvium potentiōrum līmina vītāre.
17. Videō mē ad saxa ferrī saeviōribus undīs. Saevius mē ferunt. Saevissimē mē ferunt.
18. Ex omnibus hominibus pauperiōribus, nēmō est pauperior quam ego. Pauperrimus sum omnium pauperōrum.
19. Nihil est māius amīcitiā: nihil ūberius, nihil dulcius. Nūlla amīcitia māior erat quam nostrā.
20. Voluptās nūlla est nautīs māior quam ex altō terram vidēre.
21. Phōcion pauper fuit cum dīvitissimus esse posset. (**Phōcion**, **-ionis**, *m*, an Athenian general)
22.

Phasellus ille quem vidētis, hospitēs,
aït fuisse nāvium celerrimus. . . .
tibi haec fuisse et esse cognitissima
aït phasellus. . . . *(Catullus 4)*

(**phasellus**, -ī, *m*, a light sailing vessel, skiff; **aït** (pronounced 'a-it'), he (she/it) says; **nāvis**, **-is**, *f*, ship)

Legenda

The Roman Experience (3): Freedmen and Social Mobility

Although the poorer citizens of Rome participated in the trades and tilled the land, a very large source of labor was the slave population. The economy of Rome, as of Greece, was based upon the labor of slaves, the "machines of the ancient world."[6] They were used for every kind of non-political human activity, skilled and unskilled. The main use of slave labor, however, was in the domestic sphere, and in mining and agriculture.

Legally, slaves had none of the rights and duties accorded to a "person" in the modern legal sense of that word. Perhaps the greatest incentive for a slave was the hope of freedom (manumission), which was more common in domestic and urban employments than in mining or agriculture. The act of manumission at a single stroke completely transformed a slave from a piece of property to a person with rights.[7] Sometimes Roman

[6] B. Nicholas, *An Introduction to Roman Law* (Oxford, 1969), p. 70.

[7] W. M. Calder and J. M. Cook, *Oxford Classical Dictionary*, 2d ed. (Oxford, 1970), s.v. "Slavery."

The Via Sacra, as it passes through the Roman Forum.

masters provided their slaves with a **pecūlium**, a voluntary grant of money (rather like parents giving their children an allowance), which ambitious slaves could save until they had accumulated enough money to purchase their own freedom. Often the master would free a slave for his own reasons, either during the master's lifetime or in his will. After manumission the slave-owner and his freedmen frequently maintained a close relationship similar to the patron-client relationship existing at Rome between freeborn men of differing financial circumstances.

By the time of the emperor Nero, it was a commonplace that many **equitēs** and even senators were the descendants of slaves. Some freedmen became very wealthy: a favorite example is Trimalchio, the ostentatious nouveau riche of Petronius' delightful novel, the *Satyricon*. The *Satyricon* was written during the first century A.D., at the time of Nero and Seneca, a time when "the primary aim of the ripest civilization in the world was money-making."[8] In the following passage, Encolpius, who has come to dine with Trimalchio, describes the entrance to Trimalchio's house. On the wall inside the entrance Trimalchio has had his entire personal history painted, for the edification of his visitors.

[8] W. H. D. Rouse, *Petronius* (Cambridge, Mass., 1961), p. xiii.

Since this picture was taken (in 1935) about two-thirds of these announcements, painted on the walls at Pompeii, have disintegrated, leaving (on the right):

(SA)TRI   *DEDIC(ATIONE)*
I VALENTINIS FILI   *OPERIS TABULARIUM CN ALLEIUS NIGIDIUS MAIUS*
POMPA VENATIO ATHLETAE

SATRIUM
QUINQ(UENNALEM) O(RO) V(OS) F(ACIATIS)

The two top announcements proclaim gladiatorial games and athletic contests (**pompa, vēnātiō, āthlētae**), *the first arranged for April 8 by D. Lucretius Satrius Valens, and the second arranged by Cnaeus Alleius Nigidius Maius for June 13. The lower announcement is an election appeal: "Vote for Satrius as* **duovir quīnquennālis.**" *The sign-painter Ocella signed his name in the O of* **dēdicātiōne.**

1. Ad sinistram intrantibus canis ingēns, catēnā * vinctus, in pariete * erat pictus superque quadrātīs * litterīs scriptum est "CAVĒ CANEM." Ego tōtum parietem * pervīdī. Erat vēnālīcium * cum titulīs * pictum et ipse Trimalchiō * capillātus * cādūceum * tenēbat Minervāque * dūcente Rōmam intrābat. Hinc quemadmodum ratiōcinārī * didicisset, dēnique dispēnsātor *

1: **catēna**, **-ae** *f* chain
1, 3: **pariēs**, **parietis** *m* wall
2: **quadrātus**, **-a**, **-um** square
3: **vēnālicium**, **-iī** *n* slave market
titulus, **-ī** *m* name, title
cum titulīs "along with names" (identifying the persons being sold as slaves)
3–4: **Trimalchiō**, **-iōnis** *m* a proper name
4: **capillātus**, **-a**, **-um** having hair; "with a fine head of hair"
cādūceum, **-ī** *n* a herald's staff
Minerva, **-ae** *f* Minerva, goddess of wisdom
5: **ratiōcinārī** (pres. active infinitive) to compute, calculate
dispēnsātor, **-ōris** *m* steward, manager

factus esset, omnia dīligenter * pictor cum inscriptiōne reddiderat. In dēficiente porticū * sublātum mentō * in tribūnal * Mercurius * eum rapiēbat. Aderat Fortūna cornū abundantī * cōpiōsa * et trēs Parcae * aurea pēnsa * torquentēs *.

(After Petronius, Satyricon *29)*

2. Nōs iam ad trīclīnium * vēnerāmus, in cuius parte prīmā prōcūrātor * ratiōnēs accipiēbat. Ibi fascēs * erant cum secūribus fīxī * et erat scriptum: "C. POMPEIŌ * TRIMALCHIŌNĪ, SEVIRŌ AUGUSTĀLĪ, CINNĀMUS DISPENSĀTOR *."

In utrōque poste * duae * tabulae * fīxae sunt *, quārum altera *, sī bene meminī, hoc habēbat inscriptum: "III * ET PRIDIĒ KALENDĀS IANUĀRIĀS C. NOSTER FORAS CĒNAT *," altera * lūnae * cursum stellārumque septem * imāginēs pictās; et quī diēs bonī quīque incommodī * essent, bullīs * notābantur.

(After Petronius Satyricon *30)*

3. Trimalchio tries to impress his guests by boasting about the size of his library, and by dropping a few references to literature and mythology, but he gets his stories confused.

6: **dīligenter** (adv.) carefully
6–7: **in dēficiente porticū** "at the point where the wall space of the entrance ended"
porticus, -ūs *f* a walkway covered by a roof
7: **mentum, -ī** *n* the chin
tribūnal, -ālis *n* high official seat
Mercurius, -ī *m* Mercury, the god of traders and thieves, bestower of prosperity
8: **abundō, -āre** overflow
cōpiōsus, -a, -um well-supplied, plentiful, rich
trēs Parcae the three Fates
pēnsum, -ī *n* a quantity of wool to be spun or woven
9: **torqueō, -ēre, torsī, torsus** twist, spin

1: **trīclīnium, -ī** *n* dining room
prōcūrātor, -ōris *m* steward, manager
2: **fascis, -is** *m* bundle of wood; in the plural, **fascēs** are a bundle carried before the highest magistrates as a symbol of office; the bundle consists of rods (**fascēs**) and an ax (**secūris, -is,** *f*) with which criminals were punished.
2, 5: **fīgō, -ere, fīxī, fixus** fix, fasten, post
3–4: **"C. POMPEIŌ . . . CINNĀMUS DISPENSĀTOR"** "(from) Cinnamus the steward to Caius Pompeius Trimalchio, Priest of the College of Augustus"
5: **postis, postis** *m* door-post
duo, duae, duo two
tabula, -ae *f* tablet
5, 7: **altera . . . altera** "the one . . . the other"
6–7: **"III ET PRIDIĒ . . . CĒNAT"**: "Our master Caius is out to supper on December 30th and 31st"
7: **lūna, -ae** *f* moon
8: **septem** (indeclinable) seven
incommodus, -a, -um inconvenient, unlucky
9: **bulla, -ae** *f* knob, marker

Cavē Canem: *Mosaic of a dog on a leash. From Pompeii.*

"Nē mē putēs studium ōdisse, duās* bibliothēcās* habeō, ūnam Graecam, alteram Latīnam. Dīc ergō, sī mē amās, peristasim* dēclāmātiōnis* tuae." Cum dīxisset hospes, "Pauper et dīves inimīcī* erant," inquit Trimalchiō, "Quid est pauper?" "Urbānē*" inquit hospes.

1: **duo, duae, duo** two
bibliothēca, -ae *f* library
2: **peristasim** (acc. *f* s.) surrounding circumstances
2–3: **dēclamātiō, -iōnis** *f* speech
3: **inimīcus, -ī** *m* enemy
4: **urbānē** (adv.) wittily, elegantly [said]

A Roman banquet, as depicted in the movie, "Fellini Satyricon."

"Rogō", inquit Trimalchiō, "mihi cārissime, tenēsne memoriā duodecim* aerumnās* Herculis, aut dē Ulixe* fābulam, quemadmodum illī Cyclops* pollicem* forcipe* extorsit*? Solēbam haec ego puer apud Homērum legere. Nam Sibyllam* quidem Cūmīs* ego ipse oculīs meīs vīdī in ampullā* pendēre et cum illī puerī dīcerent, '*Sibulla, ti theleis*?'* respondēbat illa: '*apothanein thelō*.'*"

(After Petronius, Satyricon *48)*

5–6: **duodecim** (indeclinable) twelve
6: **aerumna**, **-ae** *f* labor, task
Ulixēs, **-is** *m* Odysseus, hero of Homer's *Odyssey*
7: **Cyclops**, **Cyclōpis** *m* the one-eyed giant whom Odysseus blinded
pollex, **-icis** *m* the thumb
forceps, **-cipis** *f* tongs, pincer
extorqueō, **-ēre**, **extorsī**, **extorsus** remove with a twist or jerk
8: **Sibylla**, **-ae** *f* the Sibyl (an aged prophetess) at Cumae (**Cūmīs** is locative). Trimalchio here has mixed together details about the Sibyl and the story of Aurora (the dawn) and Tithonus, Aurora's husband, who was granted immortality but not eternal youth. Consequently he shrivelled into, by some accounts, a grasshopper.
9: **ampulla**, **-ae** *f* a pear-shaped bottle for holding oil, ointment, wine, etc.
***Sibulla, ti theleis*?**: Trimalchio now tries to impress his guest by saying in Greek: "Sibyl, what do you want?" Her answer is "I want to die" (**apothanein thelō**).

4. In the very early days of Rome the relationship called the "patron-client" system developed between the richer and the poorer classes. In this system a member of a ruling family would agree to be a **patrōnus**, a "protector" of another person, that is, to protect that person by making him a **cliēns**, a "follower" or "retainer." The patron would give his client financial or legal assistance, and in return the client would give his patron his political support and, in general, would be available as part of his patron's retinue of well-wishers and admirers. Over the centuries, other forms of the patronage system developed at Rome. Under the emperors the system became distorted, as men of great wealth kept large numbers of parasitic clients for the sake of show. There are numerous accounts of hordes of **clientēs** visiting their patron not even in the hope of being invited to dinner, but in the hope of obtaining the **sportula**, the basket of food (eventually it contained money) which patrons had taken to distributing to their followers.[9]

Writing early in the second century A.D., the satirist Juvenal depicts the social upheaval and excesses caused by the influx of new wealth, and the breakdown of class distinctions, as members of once-proud Roman families contend with former slaves for the basket of favors distributed daily at Rome, and observes, "**difficile est saturam nōn scrībere**" ("It is difficult not to write satire"). This adaptation is not in meter.

Ex quō [tempore] Deucalion *, nimbīs * mare tollentibus,
nāvigiō * montem ascendit sortēsque poposcit
paulātimque animā * caluērunt * mollia saxa,
et Pyrrha * puellās maribus * ostendit,
quidquid agunt hominēs—vōtum, timor, īra, voluptās,
gaudia, discursus *—farrāgo * nostrī libellī * est.
Et quandō ūberior erat vitiōrum cōpia? Alea * quandō
tot animōs habuit? Neque enim * cum sacculīs * īmus
ad cāsum tabulae *, sed dēpositā arcā * lūdimus.

1, 4: **Deucalion**, **-iōnis** *m*; **Pyrrha**, **-ae** *f* in Greek mythology, Deucalion and Pyrrha were the only survivors of the great flood.
1: **nimbus**, **-ī** *m* rain-cloud
2: **nāvigium**, **-ī** *n* ship, boat
3: **anima**, **-ae** *f* the breath of life
caleō, **-ēre**, **caluī**, —— be warm, grow warm
4: **mās**, **māris** *m* male (male of the species)
6: **discursus**, **-ūs** *m* a running to and fro
farrāgo, **-inis** *f* mixed fodder for cattle; here: a medley, a hodge-podge
libellus, **-ī** *m* little book
7: **alea**, **-ae** *f* the game with dice; gambling
8: **neque enim** "nor indeed"
sacculus, **-ī** *m* little sack, bag; purse
9: **tabula**, **-ae** *f* the gaming-table
arca, **-ae** *f* box of money, strongbox, treasure chest

[9] Sportello persists in Italian, as "ticket window."

The Sibyl at Cumae, by the artist Michaelangelo.

Proelia quanta illīc dispēnsātōre * vidēbis
armigerō *! . . . Nunc sportula * prīmō
līmine parva sedet turbae * rapienda togātae *.

10–11: **dispēnsātōre armigerō** (ablative absolute) "with the master's steward as armour-bearer." The "armour" in this case is the master's accounts.

11: **sportula**, **-ae** *f* basket

12: **turbae togātae** (dat. of agent) "by the toga-clad crowd"; the toga was the regular garment of a Roman citizen in time of peace.

ille tamen faciem prius īnspicit et trepidat* nē
suppositus* veniās* ac falsō nōmine poscās*: agnitus*
accipiēs. iubet vocārī ipsōs Trōiugenās*, nam vexant*
līmen et ipsī nōbīscum. "Da* praetōrī, da deinde
tribūnō*." Sed lībertīnus prior est. "Prior," inquit,
"ego adsum. Cūr timeam dubitemve locum dēfendere?
Quid optandum purpura māior* confert?"

(After Satire *I.81–109)*

Probanda XIII–XV

A. Supply the comparative and superlative forms of the following adjectives. Translate each form.

cārus	bellus	dīversus
crudēlis	gravis	mollis
difficilis	levis	sacer
formōsus	tristis	suāvis

B. Supply the missing forms (positive, comparative, and/or superlative) of the following adjectives:

melior
maximus
minor
multus
malus

C. Supply the adverbs of the positive, comparative and superlative degrees of the following:

bonus	potēns
malus	pulcher
magnus	miser
parvus	impudīcus
multus	fortis
cupidus	gravis
tardus	fēlix

D. Translate the following sentences into Latin:

1. They urgently asked that we make our journey as quick as possible.
2. Never more willingly did anyone ask to be made consul.

13–14: **trepidat nē veniās** . . . **ac** . . . **poscās**: "trembles (in fear) that you come **suppositus** (representing someone else)"
ac poscās: "and (in fear that) you make your request. . . ."
14: **agnitus** (from **agnoscō**): "if you are recognized"
15: **ipsōs Trōiŭgĕnās**: the noble families traced their roots back to the Trojans.
Trōiugena, **-ae** (adj., *m* or *f*), of Trojan descent.
vexō, **-āre** shake, agitate; plague, harass
16: **Da praetōrī** . . . **deinde tribūnō** "Pay the praetor first, then the tribune"
19: **purpura māior** the broad purple stripe down the breast of the tunic worn by senators and their sons.

3. The people became more and more afraid, but the consul was even more afraid than the people (were).
4. For a very long time our home has been much farther from Rome than your (sing.) home.
5. For a rather long time he did not explain that he was going to receive a very learned guest.
6. We ask you (sing.) to forgive a very devoted friend.
7. Very often we forgive our enemies much more quickly than we forgive our friends.
8. The general ordered his troops to snatch victory from the enemy.
9. This advice is easy to give but difficult to accomplish.
10. She took the poet's hand to welcome him. (Translate three ways: with **ad** + gerundive; with purpose clause; with genitive of gerundive + **causā**.)
11. The slave touched the ground to turn away evil. (Translate three ways, as in 10.)
12. By touching the ground, they will turn away evil. (Translate two ways: with gerund and with gerundive.)
13. For a very long time, I was without all these things. (Use **dēsum**, **dēesse**.)
14. We must spare our friends and forgive our enemies. (Translate two ways: with passive periphrastic and with **dēbeō**.)
15. The slave served his master for many years, and the master saved the slave from danger.

PROBANDA XII–XV: KEY

A. cārior, cārius (more/rather dear/precious), cārissimus, -a, -um (very/most dear/precious)

crudēlior, crudēlius (more/rather cruel), crudēlissimus, -a, -um (very/most cruel)

difficilior, difficilius (more/rather difficult), difficillimus, -a, -um (very/most difficult)

formōsior, formōsius (more/rather beautiful), formōsissimus, -a, -um (most/very beautiful)

bellior, bellius (more/rather beautiful), bellissimus, -a, -um (most/very beautiful)

gravior, gravius (heavier/weightier/more serious; rather heavy/weighty/serious), gravissimus, -a, -um (very/most heavy/weighty/serious)

levior, levius (more/rather light/trivial), levissimus, -a, -um (very/most light/trivial)

tristior, tristius (more/rather sad), tristissimus, -a, -um (most/very sad)

mollior, mollius (rather/more soft, gentle), mollissimus, -a, -um (very/most soft, gentle)

sacrior, sacrius (more/rather sacred/cursed), sacerrimus, -a, -um (very/most sacred/cursed)

suāvior, suāvius (more/rather sweet), suāvissimus, -a, -um (very/most sweet)

B. bonus, (melior), optimus
magnus, māior, (maximus)
parvus, (minor), minimus
(multus), plūs, plurimus
(malus), pēius, pessimus

C. (bonus): bene, melius, optimē
(malus): male, peius, pessimē
(magnus): magnopere, magis, maximē
(parvus): parum, minus, minimē
(multus): multum, plūs, plurimum
(cupidus): cupidē, cupidius, cupidissimē
(tardus): tardē, tardius, tardissimē
(potēns): potenter, potentius, potentissimē
(pulcher): pulchrē, pulchrius, pulcherrimē
(miser): miserē, miserius, miserrimē
(impudīcus): impudīcē, impudīcius, impudīcissimē
(fortis): fortiter, fortius, fortissimē
(gravis): graviter, gravius, gravissimē
(fēlix): fēlīciter, fēlīcius, fēlīcissimē

D.
1. Poposcērunt ut iter quam celerrimum facerēmus.
2. Numquam quisquam lībentius petīvit/poposcit/quaesīvit ut cōnsul fieret.
3. Populus magis magisque timēbat sed cōnsul (timēbat) magis etiam populō/quam populus.
4. Diūtissimē fuit nostra domus longius Romā quam tua (domus).
5. Diūtius nōn exposuit sē hospitem doctissimum acceptūrum esse.
6. Poscimus tē/Petimus ā tē ut amīcō amantissimō ignoscās.
7. Saepissimē hostibus multō celerius quam amīcīs ignoscimus.
8. Dux cōpiīs suīs imperāvit ut victoriam ex hostibus ēriperent.
9. Hoc cōnsilium est facile datū, confectū/perfectū difficile. (Supine)
10. Manum poētae rapuit ad eum accipiendum/ut eum acciperet/eius accipiendī causā.
11. Servus terram tetigit ad mala āvertenda/malōrum āvertendōrum causā/ut mala āverteret.
12. Terram tangendō/terrā tangendā mala āvertent.
13. Diūtissimē haec omnia mihi dēerant.
14. Nōbīs sunt amīcī parcendī, hostēsque ignoscendī; Amīcīs parcere hostibusque ignoscere dēbēmus.
15. Multōs annōs servus dominō serviēbat, dominusque servum ā perīculō servābat.

XVI

Deponent Verbs; Subjunctive Mood: Optative; *Quīn*, Quōminus; Ablative Case (3): Summary of Uses

Deponent Verbs

A large number of verbs are passive in form but active or reflexive in meaning. These are called deponent verbs, from **dē-pōnere**, "to lay aside."[1] You have already encountered some of these verbs in earlier reading passages:

> Usque **sequar** tē.
> I'll *follow* you all the way.
>
> **Moriēris** stāmine nōndum abruptō.
> You *will die* before the thread is broken (i.e., before your time).
>
> Iam nunc obstās et vōta **morāris**.
> Even now you stand in the way and *delay* his prayers.
>
> Plūrēs hominēs **sequuntur** passiōnēs.
> The majority of men *follow* their passions.
>
> Hinc pictor reddiderat quōmodo Trimalchiō **ratiōcinārī** didicisset.
> Here the painter had rendered how Trimalchio had learned *to compute*.

There are no new forms to be learned for deponent verbs. What is important here is to recognize that they are deponent, so that you will translate them as if they had active endings. Here are partial paradigms of a first and a third conjugation verb. (For complete paradigms, see Appendix B.)

cōnor, cōnārī, cōnātus sum	**loquor, loquī, locūtus sum**
try, attempt	*say, speak, tell*

[1] "To lay aside"—what? Some will answer "their active forms"; others reply, "their passive meanings." Both answers are of course correct, with the final result that deponent verbs have only half as many forms as other, regular verbs.

Indicative

PRESENT

cōnor, I try	loquor, I say
cōnāris, conare, you try	loqueris, loquere, you say
cōnātur, he tries	loquitur, he says
cōnāmur, we try	loquimur, we say
cōnāmini, you try	loquiminī, you say
cōnantur, they try	loquuntur, they say

IMPERFECT

cōnābar, I used to try	loquēbar, I used to say
cōnābāris, -re	loquēbāris, -re
etc.	etc.

FUTURE

cōnābor, I shall try	loquar, I shall say
cōnāberis, -re	loquēris, -re
etc.	etc.

PERFECT

cōnātus sum, I tried	locūtus sum, I said
cōnātus es	locūtus es
etc.	etc.

PLUPERFECT

cōnātus eram, I had tried	locūtus eram, I had said
etc.	etc.

FUTURE PERFECT

cōnātus erō, I shall have tried	locūtus erō, I shall have said
etc.	etc.

Subjunctive

PRESENT

cōner	loquar
cōnēris, cōnēre	loquāris, loquāre
cōnētur	loquātur
cōnēmur	loquāmur
cōnēminī	loquāminī
cōnentur	loquantur

IMPERFECT

cōnārer	loquerer
cōnārēris, cōnārēre	loquerēris, loquerēre
cōnārētur	loquerētur
cōnārēmur	loquerēmur
cōnārēminī	loquerēminī
cōnārentur	loquerentur

PERFECT

cōnātus sim	locūtus sim
etc.	etc.

PLUPERFECT

cōnātus essem	locūtus essem

IMPERATIVE

cōnāre	try!	loquere	speak!
cōnāminī	try!	loquiminī	speak!

INFINITIVES

Present	cōnārī, to try	loquī, to speak
Perfect	cōnātus esse, to have tried	locūtus esse, to have spoken
Future	cōnātūrus esse, to be about to try	locūtūrus esse, to be about to speak

PARTICIPLES

Present Active	cōnāns, trying	loquēns, saying
Perfect Active	cōnātus, having tried	locūtus, having said
Future Active	cōnātūrus, about to try	locūtūrus, about to say
Future Passive	cōnandus, must be tried	loquendus, must be said

Just as the alternate second person singular form of true passives can present difficulties in interpretation, a deponent verb ending in **-re** can also be a source of confusion. This is never the infinitive ending of a deponent verb. It will be either the singular imperative or the alternative second person singular, indicative or subjunctive.

Deponent verbs have the same participial forms other verbs have. Observe, however, that:

1. The present participle is active in form as well as in meaning.

2. Unlike other verbs, deponents have perfect participles which are active in meaning.

3. Deponent verbs have both active and passive future participles: the future passive participle is in fact the only form of a regular deponent verb which is passive in meaning.

Deponents Governing the Ablative Case

There are five deponent verbs which, along with some of their compounds, govern the ablative case. These verbs are reflexive in meaning, and the ablative they govern was originally an ablative of means or instrument. The most frequently encountered of these are **ūtor**, **ūtī**, **ūsus sum**, "use," and its compounds, and **fruor**, **frui**, **fructus sum**, "enjoy."[2] **Utor** with the ablative originally meant "I employ myself by means of," and **fruor** meant something like "I get fruit/enjoyment by means of." These earlier meanings, for the most part, have been lost, and consequently these verbs have come to mean simply "use" and "enjoy," respectively.

[2] The other three deponent verbs governing the ablative case are **fungor**, **fungī**, **functus sum**, "perform, function"; **potior**, **potīrī**, **potītus sum**, "take possession of, possess"; and **vescor**, **vescī**, ——, "feed oneself, eat."

Ūtar **vestrā benignitāte**.
I shall make use of *your kindness*.

Salvā rē pūblicā fruimur.
We enjoy a *secure state*.

Cum Hannibal **victōriā** fruī posset, ūtī māluit.
Although Hannibal was able to enjoy *victory*, he preferred to make use of it.

Scrībenda

cōnor, **-ārī**, **cōnātus sum** try, attempt

fruor, **fruī**, **fructus sum** (+ abl.) enjoy, delight in

gradior, **gradī**, **gressus sum** take steps, walk, go

aggredior, **aggredī**, **aggressus sum** go to, approach, attack

ēgredior, **ēgredī**, **ēgressus sum** go out, come out, come forth

ingredior, **ingredī**, **ingressus sum** go into, enter

hortor, **hortārī**, **hortātus sum** (+ indirect command) encourage, urge

loquor, **loquī**, **locūtus sum** speak, talk (**cum aliquō**)

mīror, **mīrārī**, **mīrātus sum** marvel at, be astonished at, admire

morior, **morī**, **mortuus sum** (future passive participle is **moritūrus**) die

moror, **morārī**, **morātus sum** delay, linger, loiter

nascor, **nascī**, **nātus sum** be born, be begotten

patior, **patī**, **passus sum** bear, endure, suffer

sequor, **sequī**, **secūtus sum** follow, pursue

ūtor, **ūtī**, **ūsus sum** (+ abl.) use, enjoy

A. Identify the conjugation (first, second, third, third **-iō**, fourth) of each of the deponent verbs in the above list.

B. List all the participles (present, perfect, and future active and passive) and their meanings for the following verbs:

ūtor	hortor	moror
fruor	mīror	patior

C. List the present, perfect, and future infinitives and their meanings for the following verbs:

morior	loquor
mīror	ēgredior
moror	fruor
nascor	ūtor
patior	sequor

D. Translate the following deponent verbs, and then change them to the tenses indicated, retaining the original mood, person, and number of the verb given:

Present	*Imperfect*	*Future*	*Perfect*	*Pluperfect*
cōnātur				
cōnāris				
cōner				
ingreditur				
aggrediātur				
ēgrediantur				
gradiuntur				
hortāmur				
hortēmur				
loqueris				
loquāris				
mirēmur				
mirāmur				
moriāmur				
sequiminī				
ūtere (indicative)				
fruuntur				
fruantur				

E. Form the singular and plural imperative of each of the following:

loquor
hortor
aggredior
patior
ūtor
sequor
mīror

F. Translate the following sentences:

1. Quid est, Catulle? Quid morāris morī?
2. Nōn es quae ūtāris excusātiōne muliebris nōminis. (**excusatiō**, **-iōnis** *f*, excuse, alibi; **muliebris**, **-e**, of a woman)
3. Vince loquendō, nōn bellō gerendō.
4. Tacent omnēs, nec rhētor loquitur nec altera mulier. (**rhētor**, **rhētoris** *m*, teacher of rhetoric)
5. Rēs publica fruī dēbet summī virī vītā atque virtūte.
6. Minima corpora mobilitāte fruuntur. (**mobilitās**, **-tātis** *f*, mobility, ability to move)
7. Sī graderēre tantum quantum loquere, iam essēs ad forum. (**forum**, **-ī** *n*, marketplace)
8. Alia animālia gradiendō, alia serpendō ad cibum accēdunt. (**serpō**, **-ere**, crawl, creep)
9. Ēgredere ex urbe, Catilīna. (**Catilīna**, **-ae** *m*, a proper name)
10. Illum ē nāvī ēgredientem duxī ad cēnam. (**nāvis**, **nāvis** *f*, ship)
11. Hortātus sum ut is quid scīret sine timōre mōnstrāret. (Why are **monstrāret** and **scīret** in the subjunctive?)
12. Iuvenēs hortantibus dictīs vocat.

13. Nōlī mīrārī sī tū mihi suādeās.
14. Eandem virtūtem et ōderant et mīrābantur.
15. Haec atque huiusmodī sum multa passa.
16. Sī idem faciant ceterī, invidiā nōs minōre ūtāmur.
17. Dum fīlius bestiās sequitur, invenit mātrem, quae stat rīdēns, quasī vēnātōrem cognoscēns. Ille autem oculōs sē sine fīne sequentēs nescius timēbat. (**vēnātor**, **-tōris** *m*, hunter)

Optative Subjunctive

The subjunctive used in an independent clause to express a wish is called the *optative subjunctive*. Frequently the optative subjunctive is preceded by **utinam** (shortened form **ut** or **utī**), "I wish that" or "would that," particularly in the imperfect and pluperfect tenses. The negative is **nē**.

The present tense in the optative subjunctive indicates that the wish is possible:

Dī tē **ament**.	*May* the gods *love* you.
Stet fortūna domūs.	*May* the fortune of the home *stand* (i.e., continue).

The imperfect tense in the optative subjunctive indicates that the wish was not accomplished in the present:

Utinam hīc **essēs**.	I wish that *you were* here. ("Would that *you were* here.")
Utinam **nē** vērē **scrīberem**.	I wish *I were not writing* the truth.

The pluperfect indicates that the wish was not accomplished in the past:

Nātumque patremque cum tōtō genere **exstinxissem**.
I should have wiped out the son and the father, along with the entire race.

Īdem dolor eademque hōra nōs ambās **tulisset**.
The same grief and the same hour (of death) *should have taken* us both.

Utinam mē ad fāta eadem **vocāvissēs**.
I wish *you had summoned* me to the same fate.

Noun Clauses after Verbs of Fearing or Prevention. Expressions of fear and of prevention are followed by subjunctive clauses. Contrary to what you might expect, clauses following expressions of fear are introduced by **nē** if the subjunctive clause is positive, and by **ut** if it is negative.

Timeō **nē** mē sequāris.	I fear that you *will* follow me.
Verēmur **ut** tibi possīmus parēre.	We fear that we *cannot* obey you.
Magnus est metus **ut** Caesar veniat.	There is great fear that Caesar will *not* come.

This apparently paradoxical construction is the result of the subordination of what was originally an optative subjunctive—an expression of wishing—which has become the object of an expression of fear:

Nē mē sequāris! Timeō.	May you not follow me! I fear (that you will).
Ut tibi possīmus parēre! Verēmur.	May we be able to obey you! We fear (that we will not).
Ut Caesar veniat! Magnus est metus.	May Caesar come! There is great fear (that he won't).

Quīn, Quōminus

Quīn (**quī** + **nē**) is used as an adverb or as a conjunction. As an adverb, it can introduce a question whose verb is indicative or subjunctive, and can be translated "Why not?"

1. When used with the indicative, **quīn** sometimes has the force of a command:

Quīn fugitis dum tūta via est?
Why don't you flee while the path is safe?

2. With the subjunctive, it often introduces a deliberative question:

Quīn ego hōc rogem?
Why shouldn't I ask this?

Quīn redeāmus?
Why shouldn't we return?

These deliberative questions anticipate a negative answer:

Nūlla est causa (quīn ego hoc rogem).
There is no reason why I shouldn't ask this.

Nēmō nōs prohibēbit (quīn redeāmus).
No one will prevent us from returning.

3. Negative verbs or expressions of prevention are frequently followed by a subordinated subjunctive clause introduced by **quīn** or **quōminus** ("but that," "by which the less," "why not"; sometimes a smoother English translation will simply be "from"):

Tenērī nōn potest **quīn** obsit tibi.
He cannot be kept *from* opposing you.

Istum nōn prohibēbis **quōminus** bellum gerat.
You won't keep him *from* waging war.

4. Expressions of doubt are followed by indirect questions. If the expression of doubt contains a negating word (**nōn**, **num**, etc.), the indirect question is introduced by **quīn** ("that, but that"):

Dubitō num pater eius tibi det fīliam.
I doubt whether her father will give you his daughter.

Negative:

Nōn dubium est **quīn** pater eius tibi det fīliam.
There is no doubt (*but*) *that* her father will give you his daughter.

Dubitō an tē sequar.
I am uncertain whether I should follow you.

Negative:

Num dubitās **quin** tē sequar?
Do you doubt (*but*) *that* I will follow you? (negative answer anticipated by **num**)

5. **Quōminus** or **nē** is frequently found instead of **quīn**, when the verbs of hindering or refusing are positive:

Plūra **nē dīcam** tuae mē lacrimae impediunt.
Your tears prevent me *from speaking* further.

Iste impedit **quōminus** id facere possīmus.
That man hinders us *from being able* to do it.

6. **Quīn** (**quī**, **quae**, **quod** + **nōn**) is sometimes used after a negative statement to introduce a clause of result or characteristic:

Result: Nihil tam difficile est **quīn** quaerendō investigārī possit.
Nothing is so difficult *that* it can*not* be tracked down by research.

Characteristic: Hōrum nēmō est **quīn** peritūrus sit.
There is none of these *who* will *not* perish.

Summary: Uses of the Ablative Case

As you learned in Chapter III, the ablative case can be divided into the three basic categories of separation ("from"), location in time or place, and sociative-instrumental uses ("with" or "by"). Included in the following summary you will find some uses which you have not yet encountered marked by an asterisk (*). Although these uses have not previously been discussed, they are fairly obvious and should present little difficulty.

Ablative Proper. Under the category of the ablative proper are included uses of the ablative case to indicate separation, source, agent, or comparison.

1. The ablative of separation usually occurs with **ab**, **dē**, or **ex**. All three prepositions signify separation, and to that extent can be used interchangeably. Additionally, **dē** can indicate a downward motion, and **ex** can indicate motion out of or from within.

Mēns **ā metū** ad fortunam trānsierat.
His thinking had progressed *from dread* to (tne hope of) good fortune.

Cadunt **altīs dē montibus** umbrae.
Shadows are drifting down *from the high mountains*.

Piscātōrēs cibum **ē marī** captāmus.
We fishermen snatch our meal *from the sea*.

The ablative of separation also occurs with verbs meaning "keep away from," "free from," "deprive," or "lack." These verbs sometimes use a preposition, but just as often they omit the preposition:

Līberā nōs **ā malō**.
Free us *from evil*.

Cīvēs erant **metū** vacuī.
The citizens were free *of fear*.

Pecūniā egeō.
I need *money* (I am without *money*).

2. The ablative of source denotes the source from which anything is derived or the material of which it consists. This is sometimes further subdivided into source, origin (as in the second example), and material.

Rhēnus orītur **ex Lepontiīs**. (source)
The Rhine rises *in* (*from*) *the country of the Lepontii*.

Iove nātus haec faciet. (source or origin)
The son *of* (*the person born from*) *Jupiter* will do these things.

Templum **dē marmore** pōnam. (material)
I will build a temple *of* (*out of, consisting of*) *marble*.

3. The ablative of agent occurs with a verb in the passive voice. It is used only of persons or of things that have been personified, and is always introduced by the preposition **ā** or **ab**:

Laudātur **ab hīs**, culpātur **ab illīs**.
He is praised *by these people*, blamed *by those*.

4. The ablative of comparison is used interchangeably with the construction **quam** plus the case of the thing being compared. Thus, the first example below could also be expressed **quam Cicerōnem**, and the second could be **quam aurum**, **quam virtūtēs**:

Putāsne Catōnem esse **Cicerōne** ēloquentiōrem?
Do you think that Cato is more eloquent *than Cicero*?

Vīlius argentum est **aurō**, **virtūtibus** aurum.
Silver is less precious *than gold*, gold *than virtue*.

Location in Place or Time. The ablative case is also used to specify time or place.

1. The ablative of time when or within which denotes the point in time or the range of time within which the action takes place. Time when or within which is expressed without a preposition:

Illō tempore rex eī pepercit. (when)
At that time the king spared him.

Ūnā hōrā incipiet. (within which)
He will begin *within one hour*.

2. Relations of place are expressed by prepositions and the accusative or ablative cases they govern. The prepositions **ab**, **dē**, **ex** and **in**, when governing the ablative case, can indicate the place where or within which. (Note that the names of cities, towns, small islands, **domus**, and **rūs**, which are discussed in length in Chapter VII, are not introduced by these

prepositions.) **Ab**, **dē** or **ex** plus the ablative express place from which; **dē** additionally can express motion downwards, and **ex** can express motion from within. **In** plus the ablative indicates place where or in which.

Ex Asiā vēnit.
He came *from Asia*.
Ab Italiā discēdent.
They will leave *Italy*.
Ista numquam fiant **in Italiā**.
May such things never happen *in Italy*.

Sociative-Instrumental. The sociative-instrumental category includes a wide range of uses, all of which describe the person, thing, or behavior associated with the action.

1. The ablative of accompaniment, introduced by the preposition **cum**, indicates the person(s) in whose company something is done:

Cum coniugibus et līberīs vēnērunt.
They came *with their wives and children*.

2. No preposition introduces the ablative of means or instrument, which indicates by what means or with what instrument an action is performed.

Vī victa vīs, vel potius oppressa **virtūte** audācia est.
Violence was overcome *by violence*, or rather, boldness was put down *by courage*.
Quis humum **flōrentibus herbīs** sparget?
Who will strew the ground *with wild flowers*?
Quō usque tandem **nostrā patientiā** abūtēris?
To what end will you abuse *our patience*? (Ablative with compound of special deponent verb **ūtor**)

3. The ablative of cause occurs with or without a preposition. It frequently overlaps in meaning with other ablatives, particularly the ablative of means or instrument. In such cases the intended sense must be deduced from context. **Causa** and **grātia** in the ablative, when preceded by a genitive noun, pronoun, or gerund or gerundive, meaning "for the sake of," properly belong in this category.

Gubernātōris ars **ūtilitāte**, nōn **arte ipsā**, laudātur.
The Helmsman's skill is praised *because of its usefulness*, not *because of the skill itself*.
Eā causā tē metuō.
I fear you *for that reason* (*because of that reason*).
Rēī pūblicae causā omnia haec facienda sunt.
All these things must be done *for the sake of the republic*.
Exemplī grātiā (abbreviated "e.g."), *for example*.

4. The ablative of manner is introduced by the preposition **cum**. If the noun it governs is modified by an adjective, however, **cum** may or may not be used:

Cum celeritāte vēnit.
He came *swiftly* (*with speed*).
Summā (**cum**) **celeritāte** vēnit.
He came *very swiftly* (*with the greatest speed*).

5. A noun modified by an adjective may be used to describe another noun. The describing noun and its modifier will be in the ablative or the genitive case and is known, accordingly, as the ablative or genitive of quality or description. Either case can be used in expressions of quality, but the ablative case tends to be used more often for the description of physical qualities:

Cācus septem taurōs **eximiā pulchritūdine** ēduxit.
Cacus led away seven bulls *of rare beauty*.
Aristotelēs erat vir **summō ingeniō**.
Aristotle was a man *of very great genius*.

6. The price of a thing is expressed by the ablative of price*, especially when the specific amount of the price or value is indicated. No preposition is used here.

Antōnius regna addīxit **pecūniā**.
Antony sold thrones *for money*.
Agrum vendidit **sestertium sex mīlibus**.
He sold the land *for 6000 sesterces*. (**sestertium** is a partitive genitive)
Servum **vīgintī minīs** ēmī.
I bought the servant *for twenty minae*.

7. The ablative of specification* denotes that in respect to which anything is what it is, or in respect to which it is done:

Virtūte praestant.
They excel *in virtue*.
Ūnus vir, Vergilius **nōmine**, haec scrīpsit.
One man, Vergil *by name*, wrote these things.
Verbīs erat sapiēns, **vītā** nōn ita.
He was wise *in words*, but not *in his* [*mode of*] *life*.

8. The ablative absolute, finally, consists of a subject and a predicate in the ablative case, neither of which has any grammatical connection with the main clause of the sentence. The predicate may be a participle, noun, pronoun or adjective. When the predicate is not a participle, the present participle of the verb **esse** is implied:

Deucalion, **nimbīs mare tollentibus**, montem nāvigiō ascendit.
Deucalion, *when the storm-clouds were raising the sea*, climbed a mountain with a ship.
Trimalchiō, **Minervā dūcente**, Rōmam intrābat.
Trimalchio was entering Rome led by Minerva (*with Minerva leading*).
Tē duce, terra sceleris nostrī vestigiīs solvētur.
With you as leader, the earth will be freed from the traces of our crime.

Scrībenda

dēterreō, **-ēre**, **-uī**, **-itus** frighten from, deter, hinder, prevent
dubitō, **-āre**, **-āvī**, **-ātus** (+ infinitive) hesitate; (+ subjunctive) doubt
prohibeō, **-ēre**, **prohibuī**, **prohibitus** prevent, deter, prohibit
impediō, **-īre**, **-īvī**, **-ītus** hinder, entangle, impede
metuō, **-ere**, **metuī**, **metūtus** fear, be afraid of
vereor, **-ērī**, **veritus sum** revere, feel awe of, fear, be afraid of
utinam (adv.) (+ subjunctive) if only, how I wish that

A. Translate the following sentences:

1. Nē vīvam sī sciō cūr id fēcerit.
2. Nē redīre sit nefās.
3. Nē istud Iuppiter optimus maximus sīverit. (**sinō**, **-ere**)
4. Utinam nē hīc accessissent! (**ad** + **cēdō**)
5. Illud utinam nē vērē scrīberem.
6. Tibur sit meae sēdēs utinam senectae. (**Tibur**, **Tiburis** *n*, ancient town of Latium; **senecta**, **-ae** *f*, old age; **sēdēs**, **-is** *f*, seat; pl., dwelling)
7. Utinam revocēs animum paulātim ab īrā! (**re-vocō**)
8. Utinam aut hic surdus aut haec mūta facta sit! (**surdus**, **-a**, **-um**, deaf; **mūtus**, **-a**, **-um**, mute)
9. Homō hic ēbrius est, ut opīnor. —Utinam ita essem. (**opīnor**, **-ārī**, be of the opinion, suppose)
10. Utinam hic adesset atque audīret haec.
11. Ars utinam mōrēs fingere posset.
12. Eius exemplum utinam imperatōrēs nostrī sequī voluissent!
13. Cupīvērunt fessī discēdere bellō; fēcissentque utinam!
14. Utinam minus vītae cupidī fuissēmus!
15. Utinam ūnus vestrum fuissem!
16. Ille timet nē falsō nōmine veniās.
17. Metuō nē nōn sit surda. (**surda**, see sentence 8)
18. Vereor nē mulier mē absente corrupta sit. (**corrumpō**, **-ere**, **corrūpī**, **corruptus**, corrupt)
19. Perīculum est nē opprimāmur.
20. Dubitāte, sī potestis, ā quō sit ille interfectus.

B. Translate the following sentences into Latin:

1. He attempted to speak to (**loquor cum**) the strange man in Greek.
2. Wherever the poet walked (**gradior**), the other person followed.
3. You are afraid that I will try to follow you.
4. Son of Jupiter, how I wish you had saved me from this annoying person!
5. I fear you will die if you speak to that chatterbox. (**garriō**, **-īre**, **-īvī**, **-ītus**, chatter, talk excessively; use the present active participle of this verb for "chatterbox.")

Verba tenenda

Verbs

accēdō, **-ere**, **-cessī**, **-cessus** go or come to, approach
aggredior, **aggredī**, **aggressus sum** go to, approach, attack
animadvertō, **-ere**, **-vertī**, **-versus** direct one's attention to; consider, regard, notice
audeō, **-ēre**, **ausus sum** have the courage (to do something); dare (to do something)
circumstō, **-stāre**, **-stetī**, —— stand around
cōnor, **-ārī**, **cōnātus sum** undertake, attempt, try
dēstituō, **-ere**, **dēstituī**, **dēstitūtus** leave alone, abandon; set down
dēterreō, **-ēre**, **-uī**, **-itus** frighten from, deter, hinder, prevent
ēgredior, **ēgredī**, **ēgressus sum** go out, come out, come forth
fīgō, **-ere**, **fīxī**, **fīxus** drive in, fix in, pierce; fasten to; fix in position
fruor, **fruī**, **fructus sum** (+ abl.) have the enjoyment of; enjoy
gradior, **gradī**, **gressus sum** take steps, walk, go
hortor, **-ārī**, **hortātus sum** encourage, urge
impediō, **-īre**, **-īvī**, **-ītus** hinder, entangle, impede
ingredior, **ingredī**, **ingressus sum** go into, enter
iūrō, **-āre**, **-āvī**, **-ātus** swear, take an oath
loquor, **loquī**, **locūtus sum** say, speak, tell, converse
metuō, **-ere**, **metuī**, **metūtus** fear, be afraid of
mīror, **-ārī**, **mīrātus sum** marvel at, be astonished at, admire, wonder
morior, **morī**, **mortuus sum** die; **moritūrus**, **-a**, **-um** (future active participle) about to die
moror, **-ārī**, **morātus sum** delay, linger, loiter
nascor, **nascī**, **nātus sum** be born, come into being
orior, **orīrī**, **ortus** rise, get up; (of heavenly bodies) rise, become visible; come forth; rise, spring from; **oritūrus**, **-a**, **-um** (future active participle) about to rise
patior, **patī**, **passus sum** bear, endure, suffer
prōgredior, **prōgredī**, **prōgressus sum** come forth, go forth, proceed
prōhibeo, **-ēre**, **prohibuī**, **prohibitus** prevent, deter, prohibit
sequor, **sequī**, **secūtus sum** follow, pursue
ūtor, **ūtī**, **ūsus sum** (+ abl.) use, make use of
vēlō, **-āre**, **-āvī**, **-ātus** cover, wrap up, veil
vereor, **-ērī**, **veritus sum** revere, feel awe of; fear, be afraid of
vulnerō, **-āre**, **-āvī**, **-ātus** wound, injure

Nouns

adventus, **-ūs** *m* approach, arrival
coniūrātus, **-ī** *m* conspirator
ferrum, **-ī** *n* iron; sword; any weapon or tool made of iron
fidēs, **-eī** *f* good faith, honesty, fidelity
hostis, **-is** *m* foreigner, stranger; enemy

noxa, **-ae** *f* injurious conduct; harm, injury
pectus, **-oris** *n* chest, breast
saeculum, **-ī** *n* a generation, lifetime; an age (of thirty-three years); a century
scelus, **-eris** *n* crime
senātus, **-ūs** *m* the Senate
testis, **-is** *m* witness
vulnus, **-eris** *n* wound

Adjectives

dexter, **dextra**, **dextrum** situated on the right-hand side; favorable;
  dextra, **-ae** *f* the right hand
fidēlis, **-e** faithful, trustworthy
nōbilis, **-e** well-known, famous; of high birth, noble
scelerātus, **-a**, **-um** wicked, vicious, accursed
singulī, **-ae**, **-a** (distributive; plural only) single, separate, one by one
tūtus, **-a**, **-um** safe, secure, carefully guarded

Adverbs

haud not at all, by no means
quīn why not?; indeed
undique in all directions; at random
utinam (+ subjunctive) would that, I wish that

Conjunctions

dōnec while, until
etsī even if; although
quīn but that, that not
quōminus (by which the less), that not

Notanda

audeō, like the verb **soleō**, frequently governs a complementary infinitive. Both verbs become deponent in the perfect tenses: **solitus sum**, "I have been accustomed"; **ausus sum**, "I dared." These verbs are thus known as "semi-deponent" (i.e., half-deponent).

"Circumstance" (from **circumstāre**) suggests all the myriad details surrounding or "standing around" a situation.

gradior and its compounds have numerous derivatives in English: "regress (regressive)," "egress," "progress," "gradient," "grade," "gradual," etc.

ēloquentia is an ability to speak "out" (from **ē-loquor**). **Loquor** is a basic verb with numerous derivatives in Latin and in English. "Loquacious," "eloquence," "colloquium," and "colloquial" are common English derivatives.

Does the English word "moratorium" derive from **morī**, "to die," or **morārī**, "to delay"?

orior signifies rising, frequently with reference to heavenly bodies. **Ortus**, its perfect participle, is also a common fourth declension noun which you have already learned. From the present participle, **oriēns**, **-ntis** come the English words "orient" and "oriental," referring to the rising of the sun (just as "occidental" refers to the setting of the sun).

"Passive" derives from the perfect participle of the deponent verb **patior**, as does "patience."

coniūrātus is the perfect passive participle of the verb, **coniūrāre**, which means "to join in taking an oath" (compare **iūrāre**), whether for good or evil intent.

ferrum is anything made of iron, whether a sword, a tool, an instrument: this same word, therefore, can mean "ploughshare" (a symbol of peace) or "sword" (a symbol of war).

"**Fundamentum iustitiae est fidēs**," writes Cicero in the *Dē officiīs*. Trust is inevitably a basic element in any workable system of laws. The adjective is **fidēlis**.

hostis, "stranger or enemy," has English derivatives reflecting both meanings: compare "hostile" and "hostel," the latter formerly an inn, now a supervised lodging for young itinerants.

noxa derives from **nocēre**, "to harm," and has broad legal application. In Roman Law, "noxal liability" attached to a wrongdoer or the person liable for the behavior of the wrongdoer. **Noxa caput sequitur**: if a slave, for example, committed an injury, and then the slave were sold, the new owner would be liable, and would be required to make restitution for the injury.

The Senate was so called because originally its members were the elders of the state. The abbreviation **SPQR**, which can still be seen stamped on public works in Rome, stands for **Senātus Populusque Rōmānus**.

In English, "vulnerable" (from **vulnus**, compare the verb **vulnerāre**) means "capable of being wounded," either physically or morally.

Instead of saying **manus dextra**, Romans tended to drop the noun and simply use the feminine **dextra** to mean "right hand" and thence a "pledge," since an oath is taken with the right hand.

nōbilis, derived from **noscō**, **nōtus**, means "known" for some reason: accomplishments, high office, or family rank. The adjective in Latin as well as in English often refers to a person's high birth.

The adjective **tūtus**, "safe," is the perfect participle of the deponent verb **tueor**, "to look upon," frequently with the added implication "to look after," i.e., to protect.

Ante legenda

Translate:

1. Aliquid tēcum loquī volō. Nescioquid velle loquī tē mēcum dīxistī. Meminī bene, sed meliōre tempore dīcam.
2. L. Catilīna, nōbilī genere nātus, fuit magnā vī et animī et corporis, sed ingeniō malō prāvōque. Huic ab adulēscentiā bellum cīvile placuit. (**L. Catilīna**, **-ae** *m*, a proper name; **prāvus**, **-a**, **-um**, deformed, perverse; **adulēscentia**, **-ae** *f*, the time of young manhood)
3. Rēs ipsa hortārī vidētur ut rogem quō modo rēs pūblica, ex pulcherrimā atque optimā mutāta, pessima ac flāgitiōsissima facta sit. (**flāgitiōsus**, **-a**, **-um**, shameful, profligate)
4. Ego mē iam cēnsēbam esse in terrā atque in tūtō locō, sed videō me ad saxa ferrī saevīs undīs. Loquere quid sit actum.

5. Lūgēte*, Ō Venerēs Cupīdinēsque,
et quantum est hominum venustiōrum*.
passer* mortuus est meae puellae,
passer*, dēliciae meae puellae,
quem plūs illa oculīs suīs amābat.
(Catullus 3)

(**lūgeō**, **-ēre**, mourn, grieve; **venustus**, **-a**, **-um**, elegant, charming; **passer**, **passeris** *m*, a sparrow [Lesbia's pet])

6. Pater et vir cum singulīs amīcīs vēnērunt.

7. Fac nōs singulōs, quid sumus? praeda animālium et victimae. (**praeda**, **-ae** *f*, plunder, booty, prey; **victima**, **-ae** *f*, victim)

8. Date dextrās [manūs] fidemque haud impūnē scelus illātum esse. (**impūnē**, adv., without punishment)

9. Iūrō per hunc sanguinem, vōsque, dī, testēs faciō mē istum secūtūrum esse nec scelerātōs istīus līberōs regnāre passūrum esse.

10. Dum vulgus tē laudat, saepe tibi dīc, "Meminī post glōriam invidiam sequī."

11. Locus inter Ērigonēn Chēlāsque sequentēs panditur. (**Ērigonēn**, acc., the constellation Virgo; **Chēlae**, **-ārum** *f*, claws of the constellation Scorpio)

12. Iam nunc nātum prohibēs quīn vōta sequātur. Nātus patrem vōta morārī nōn patiētur.

13. Moriēmur inultae, sed moriāmur. (**inultus**, **-a**, **-um**, unavenged)

14. Mālō morī quam hunc patī saevīre leōnem in mē. (**saeviō**, **-īre**, roar savagely; **leō**, **leōnis** *m*, lion)

15. Nunc ad relicta prōgrediar. Ad relicta prōgrediāmur. Prōgressī sunt ad relicta.

16. Nescīs quid malī praeterīeris quī numquam es ingressus mare.

17. Oculōs suōs ad caelum tollere cōnāta est. Saepe illa moritūra, oculōs gravēs tollere cōnāta, dēfēcit.

18. Per suprēmī rēgis regnum iūrō et Iūnōnem, quam ego et vereor et metuō. Quis neget sē Iūnōnem et verērī et metuere? (**regnum**, **-ī** *n*, kingdom)

19. Verēmur quidem vōs et, sī ita vultis, etiam timēmus; sed plūs et verēmur et timēmus deōs.

20. Ego nec tumultum
nec morī per vim metuam tenente
Caesāre terrās.
(Horace, Odes *3.14.14–16)*

(**tumultus**, **-ūs** *m*, disorder, violent commotion)

21. Illud in hīs rēbus vereor, nē forte reāris
impia tē ratiōnis inīre elementa viamque
ingredī sceleris.
(Lucretius 1.80–82)

(**reor**, **reārī**, **rātus sum**, believe, suppose)

Legenda

The Roman Experience (4): The Deaths of Lucretia and Julius Caesar—The Beginning and End of the Republic

The mythological date of the founding of Rome was 753 B.C., when Romulus and Remus chose the site for their new settlement. Between its founding and its fall in the fifth century A.D., Rome experienced three very different forms of government: monarchy, republic, and empire. The earliest rulers were kings. Tarquinius Superbus, the last of the Etruscan Tarquinii to rule, was expelled, the monarchy was abolished, and an aristocratic republic was established in 509 B.C. Two annually elected consuls governed in consultation with the Roman senate. The Republican form of government lasted until the accession of Julius Caesar, who, as dictator, introduced the principle of autocracy into the Roman constitution. The turmoil that followed his assassination was only one in a series of civil disruptions over the preceding century. Octavian, later renamed "Augustus," finally emerged from the conflict as the leader of the Roman world.

Augustus (emperor 27 B.C.–A.D. 14) thus founded the Roman Empire, but for three centuries after its foundation the state was nominally a republic, with the government shared between the Emperor (the predominant partner) and the Senate. The republican disguise fell away completely before the end of the third century A.D. under Constantine. In A.D. 330 a new capital of the Empire was established at Byzantium, which was renamed *Constantinopolis*, or Constantinople. The fall of the Roman Empire in the west to Germanic invaders is usually dated A.D. 476. In the east the Byzantine Empire lasted for another thousand years, until the fall of Constantinople in 1453.

1. Romans expelled the last king in about 509 B.C.; they were moved to do this, according to tradition, after his brutal son, exploiting his inherited position of power, raped Lucretia, the wife of the patrician Collatinus. After revealing the rape to her husband, Lucretia took her own life. Her suicide so outraged Collatinus' companion, Lucius Junius Brutus, that he led an uprising against the monarchy. Subsequently Brutus and Collatinus became the first consuls of the Roman Republic. In the following passage, Lucretia reveals the crime committed against her.

Lucrētia tristis tantō malō nuntium* Rōmam ad patrem virumque mittit* ut cum singulīs fidēlibus amīcīs veniant; rem* atrōcem factam

1: **nuntium**, -ī *n* message;

1–2: **nuntium mittit** here governs indirect command **ut veniant**: "She sends them a message to come . . .";

2–3: **rem atrōcem factam esse** continues the message in indirect statement: "a terrible thing has happened."

The assassination of Julius Caesar.

esse*. Pater et vir cum amīcīs Valeriō* Brūtōque veniunt. Lucrētiam sedentem tristem in cubiculō* inveniunt. Adventū suōrum lacrimās fundit, quaerentīque virō "Satisne salvēs?" "Minimē" inquit; "quid enim salvī est mulierī amissā pudīcitiā*? Vestīgia* virī aliēnī, Collātīne, in lectō* sunt tuō; corpus est violātum* sed animus est insōns*; mors testis erit. Sed date dextrās manūs fidemque haud impūnē* adulterō* futūrum esse. Sextus* est Tarquinius* quī hostis prō hospite priōre nocte vī armātus* mihi sibique, sī vōs virī estis, pestiferum* hinc abstulit gaudium." Dant

3: **Valerius** accompanies the father; **Brutus** accompanies the husband Collatinus.
4: **cubiculum**, -ī *n* bedroom
6: **pudīcitia**, **-ae** *f* chastity, virtue
vestīgium, -ī *n* track, footprint, trace
lectus, -ī *m* bed
7: **violō**, **-āre** injure, dishonor, outrage
insōns, **insontis** guiltless, innocent
8: **impūnē** (adv.) without punishment
adulter, **adulterī** *m* adulterer
9: **sextus Tarquinius** the king's wicked son
armō, **-āre** arm, bear weapons
10: **pestiferus**, **-a**, **-um** pestilential, destructive

omnēs fidem; consōlantur * eam āvertendō noxam ab coactā in auctōrem sceleris; "Vōs", inquit, "Vīderitis * quid illī dēbeātur: ego mē etsī ā culpā solvō, suppliciō * nōn līberō; nec ūlla deinde impudīca Lucrētiae exemplō vīvet." Cultrum *, quem sub veste cēlātum habēbat, in pectore fīgit, prōlāpsaque * in vulnus moritūra cecidit. Clāmant vir paterque.

Brūtus cultrum * ex vulnere Lucrētiae extractum prae sē tenēns, "Per hunc" inquit "castissimum * ante rēgium * sanguinem iūrō, vōsque, dī, testēs faciō mē L. Tarquinium * Superbum cum scelerātā coniuge et omnī līberōrum stirpe * ferrō ignī quācumque dēhinc * vī possim secūtūrum esse, nec illōs nec alium quemquam regnāre Rōmae passūrum esse."

(After Livy 1.57–60)

2. The great weakness of the Roman Republic was the senate's lack of real power, particularly where foreign policy was concerned. During periods when a strong leader was needed, regular constitutional procedures would be suspended legally, by appointment of a dictator. Sometimes popular leaders, such as the Gracchi or Marius, became sufficiently strong to oppose the predominant oligarchy, but it was not until Julius Caesar came to power that the Roman Republic finally came to an end.

Julius Caesar had already been consul once (59 B.C.) when his famous clash with the Roman Senate led to the Senate's order that he lay down his command, and his refusal to comply. On January 10, 49 B.C., Caesar crossed the Rubicon river, which formed the border between Cisalpine Gaul (one of his assigned provinces) and eastern Italy. In order to avoid violating the Roman law of treason, he would have had to disband his army and return unarmed to Rome. His deed was the culmination of a decade of disintegration of the republic under an autocratic triumvirate, and plunged Rome into civil war. Caesar defeated his enemies and, in 46 B.C., was appointed dictator for ten years. In 44 B.C. the appointment was extended to the duration of his life. Shakespeare's *Julius Caesar* is about the reaction of republican loyalists to this appointment, and the civil war that followed their assassination of him. The following account of the assassination is given by the Roman biographer Suetonius (born c. A.D. 69).

Ob quaedam signa diū cunctātus * est an ea quae apud senātum prōposuerat differret. Tandem quintā * ferē hōrā * prōgressus est. Deinde plū-

11: **consōlor, -ārī, -ātus sum** console
12: **vīderitis** perfect subjunctive, jussive
13: **supplicium, -ī** *n* punishment
14, 16: **culter, -trī** *m* knife
14–15: **prōlābor, lābī, prōlāpsus sum** fall forward
17: **castus, -a, -um** chaste, pure
rēgius, -a, -um royal
18: **Lucius Tarquinius Superbus** the king
19: **stirps, stirpis** *m* stock, race, family, lineage
dēhinc (adv.) henceforth, from this time

1: **cunctor, -ārī, cunctātus sum** delay action, hesitate, doubt. The subject is Julius Caesar (**Caesar, Caesāris** *m*)
2: **quintā ferē hōrā** "at about the fifth hour," i.e., about eleven A.M.

ribus hostiīs * caesīs *, cum litāre * nōn posset, intrāvit cūriam *, sprētā * religiōne *, Spurinnamque * rīdēns et ut falsum appellāns, quod sine ūllā suā noxā Īdūs * Martiae adessent; quamquam * is vēnisse quidem eās dīceret, sed nōn praeterīsse *.

Et eum sedentem coniūrātī speciē officiī * circumstetērunt, īlicōque * Cimber Tillius *, quī prīmās partēs suscēperat, quasi aliquid rogātūrus propius accessit renuentīque * et gestū * in aliud tempus differentī * ab utrōque umerō * togam * cēpit; deinde eum clāmantem "Ista quidem vīs est!" alter * ē Cascīs * āversum vulnerat paulum * infrā * iugulum *. Caesar * Cascae * bracchium raptum graphiō * fīxit * cōnātusque prōsilīre * aliō vulnere impedītus est; utque animadvertit undique sē strictīs * pugiōnibus * petī, togā caput vēlāvit, simul sinistrā manū sinum * ad īma * crūra * dēdūxit, ut honestius caderet etiam inferiōre corporis parte vēlātā. Atque ita tribus * et vīgintī plāgīs * confossus * est, ūnō modo ad prīmum ictum * gemitū * sine vōce ēdītō, etsī trādidērunt quīdam Marcō Brūtō *

3: **hostia**, **-ae** *f* victim
caedō, **-ere**, **cecīdī**, **caesum** cut, kill
litō, **-āre** obtain favorable omens
cūria, **-ae** *f* hall, senate-house
spernō, **-ere**, **sprēvī**, **sprētum** scorn
4: **religiō**, **-iōnis** *f* religious ritual
Spurinna, **-ae** *m* the soothsayer who warned Caesar to beware the ides (15th) of March
5: **Īdūs**, **-uum** *f* Ides
5–6: **quamquam** . . . **praeterisse** "and yet he (Spurinna) said (**dīceret**) . . ."
7: **speciē officiī** "with a pretence of duty," i.e., as if to pay their respects.
īlicō (adv.) straightway
8: **Cimber Tillius** a proper name
9: **renuō**, **-ere** refuse
renuentī . . . **differentī** a dative of reference ("of disadvantage") of the present participle in agreement with the implied **Caesārī**; "as Caesar refused and put him off, . . ."
gestus, **-ūs** *m* gesture
10: **umerus**, **-ī** *m* the shoulder
toga, **-ae** *f* the toga was the formal outergarment of free-born Romans; it consisted of a large semicircular piece of woolen cloth wrapped around the body
11: **alter ē Cascīs** "one of the two Cascas" (**Casca**, **-ae** *m*)
paulum (adv.) a little
infrā (+ acc.) below
iugulum, **-ī** *n* throat, neck
11–12: **Caesar** . . . **fīxit** "Caesar pierced the seized arm of Casca," that is, Caesar seized Casca's arm and pierced it.
12: **graphium**, **-ī** *n* stylus
prōsiliō, **-īre** leap forward
13: **stringō**, **-ere**, **strinxī**, **strictus** draw, unsheath
13–14: **pugiō**, **-iōnis** *m* dagger
14: **sinus**, **-ūs** *m* bosom, lap (here, of his toga)
īmus, **-a**, **-um** the lowest (part of)
15: **crus**, **crūris** *n* leg
16: **tribus et vīgintī plāgīs** "with three and twenty blows"
confodiō, **-ere**, **confōdī**, **confossus** stab
17: **ictus**, **-ūs** *m* strike, blow
gemitus, **-ūs** *m* groan
Marcus Brūtus one of the conspirators

irruentī* dīxisse: "*Kai* * *su teknon* *?" Exanimis*, fugientibus cunctīs, diūtissimē iacuit*, dōnec lecticae impositum*, pendente bracchiō, trēs* servī domum retulērunt. Nec in tot vulneribus, ut Antistus* medicus* existimābat*, lētāle* ūllum repertum est, nisi quod secundō* locō in pectore accēperat.

Fuerat animus coniūrātīs corpus occīsī* in Tiberim* trahere, sed metū Marcī Antōniī* cōnsulis et magistrī equitum Lepidī* dēstituērunt.

(After Suetonius, Dē vītā Caesārum, I: Dīvī Iuliī *81.4ff.)*

3. The death of Julius Caesar was followed by a long and bitter civil war, which was finally settled in 31 B.C. at Actium, when Augustus defeated Mark Antony and became the sole ruler of the Roman Empire. Augustus was in fact the first emperor, even though he carefully maintained the appearance of having restored the republican constitution. His long reign is often referred to as the "golden age" of Rome, for it was a period of relative stability, when order was restored to the lives of Roman citizens and the arts and literature flourished. During his reign lived the historian Livy, as well as the greatest Roman poets—Vergil, Horace, Propertius, Tibullus, and Ovid. Most of these writers grew up during the civil war, and consequently their attitude toward the new emperor was colored by their youthful experiences during that traumatic period. Hence, when Vergil writes of the youthful emperor as the great hope of the future, we should bear in mind that he writes as one who has known little peace or stability in his own lifetime. In the following passage, a reference to the sun as a source of weather signs triggers a digression on the trauma of the civil wars. This passage is taken from the *Georgics*, Vergil's poem on farming. The *Georgics* are written in dactylic hexameter. This adaptation is not in meter.

Sōlem quis dīcere falsum audeat*? ille etiam
caecōs* instāre tumultūs* saepe monet . . .

18: **irruō**, **-ere** rush up
"*Kai su teknon*?": Caesar's words are Greek, "you, too, my child?"
exanimis, **-e** lifeless
19: **iaceō**, **-ēre**, **iacuī** lie, lie still
lecticae impositum "placed on a litter"
trēs (nom. *m* pl.) three
20: **Antistus**, **-ī** *m* the doctor (**medicus**, **-ī** *m*)
21: **existimō**, **-āre** think, judge, assess
lētālis, **-e** deadly, fatal
secundus, **-a**, **-um** second
23: **occīsī** "of the murdered man"
Tiberim (acc.) the river Tiber
24: **Marcus Antōnius** and **Lepidus,** along with Octavian, became Caesar's avengers.

1: **audeat** is deliberative subjunctive, "who would dare to say." Romans were very superstitious, and read meanings into many signs from nature. Here Vergil refers to atmospheric disturbances following the death of Caesar, possibly caused by volanic eruptions, which caused the sun to have a reddish cast. It is as if all of nature is distraught by the assassination.
2: **caecus**, **-a**, **-um** unseen
tumultus, **-ūs** *m* uproar, violent commotion, tumult
3: **exstinguō**, **-ere**, **exstinxī**, **exstinctus** extinguish, destroy

ille etiam exstinctō* miserātus* Caesāre Rōmam,
cum caput obscūrā nitidum* ferrūgine* vēlāvit,
impiaque aeternam timuērunt saecula noctem.
tempore quamquam* illō multa signa dabantur.
quotiēns* Cyclōpum* effervere* in agrōs vīdimus
undantem* ruptīs* fornācibus* Aetnam*!
armōrum sonum tōtō Germānia* caelō audīvit;
īnsolitīs* tremuērunt mōtibus Alpēs*.
Et simulācra* modīs pallentia* mīrīs*
vīsa sub obscūrum noctis; pecudēsque* locūtae,
infandum*!

(After Georgics *I.463ff.)*

miseror, -ārī, miserātus sum lament; (+ acc.) feel pity for
4: **nitidus, -a, -um** shining
ferrūgo, -inis *f* iron-rust; the color of iron-rust
6: **quamquam** (conj.) although
7: **quotiēns** (adv.) how often, how many times
7–8: **Cyclōps, -ōpis** *m* the belief was that the Cyclopes, the huge one-eyed giants of Greek myth, were housed beneath Mt. Aetna (**Aetna, -ae**), where they worked their forges, producing arms and lightning bolts for the gods. When Mt. Aetna, which is a volcano, rumbled threats of an eruption, the Cyclopes were believed to be working at their **fornācēs**. **Undantem** refers to the flowing lava following the actual eruption (**ruptīs fornācibus**).
7: **effervō, -ere** boil up, boil over
8: **undō, -āre** rise in waves, undulate; overflow
rumpō, -ere, rūpī, ruptus burst, break open
fornāx, fornācis *f* furnace, forge
9: **Germānia, -ae** *f* Germany
10: **īnsolitus, -a, -um** unusual
Alpēs, -um the Alps
11: **simulācrum, -ī** *n* statue
palleō, -ēre turn pale
mīrus, -a, -um wondrous, surprising
12: **pecus, -udis** *f* herding animal; pl., cattle
13: **infandum**! "an unspeakable thing!"

Numbers; Impersonal Verbs; Noun Clauses; Definitive and Descriptive Conjunctions

Roman Numbers

Latin cardinal numbers are usually indeclinable.[1] Most of these numbers are best learned as vocabulary items. **Ūnus**, **-a**, **-um**, "one," which you have already learned, is an exception to the general rule that numbers are indeclinable, as are **duo**, **duae**, **duo**, "two" and **trēs**, **tria**, "three," the hundreds above one hundred, and **mille** when used as a noun. The hundreds are declined like **magnus**, **-a**, **-um**. **Mille**, a thousand, is indeclinable in the singular; in the plural it is declined like other third declension neuter **i**-stem nouns (**mīlia**, **mīlium**, **mīlibus**, **mīlia**, **mīlibus**). You already know the declension of **ūnus**. Learn now the declension of **duo** and **trēs**:

Nom.	duo	duae	duo	trēs	tria
Gen.	duōrum	duārum	duōrum	trium	trium
Dat.	duōbus	duābus	duōbus	tribus	tribus
Acc.	duōs	duās	duo	trēs	tria
Abl.	duōbus	duābus	duōbus	tribus	tribus

The Latin system of numerals consists of three kinds of numerical adjectives: the cardinal numbers (one, two, three, etc.), most of which are indeclinable; the ordinal numbers, which signify sequence or order (first, second, third, etc.); and the distributive numbers, signifying how many at a time (**singulī**, **-ae**, **-a**, "one at a time"; **bīnī**, **-ae**, **-a**, "two at a time"; **ternī**, **-ae**, **-a**, "three at a time," etc.). There are also numerical adverbs, indicating how many times: **semel**, "once"; **bis**, "twice"; **ter**, "three times," etc.

[1] You are probably already familiar with roman numerals, which consist of seven basic signs: **I** = one, **V** = five, **X** = 10, **L** = 50, **C** = 100, **D** = 500, **M** = 1000. **I** represents a single stroke, **V** represents the spread of a hand, and **X** the spread of two hands. The remaining signs are believed to be Greek in origin. For more information about Roman numerals, see J. M. Reynolds, "Numbers, Roman" in the *Oxford Classical Dictionary* (Oxford, 1970), pp. 741–2, and references there.

Familiarize yourself with the following numbers, only some of which will be included as regular vocabulary items. For other numbers, refer to Appendix C:

Roman	Cardinal	Ordinal
I.	ūnus, -a, -um	prīmus, -a, -um
II.	duo, duae, duo	secundus (alter)
III.	trēs, tria	tertius
IV.	quattuor	quartus
V.	quinque	quintus
VI.	sex	sextus
VII.	septem	septimus
VIII.	octo	octāvus
IX.	novem	nōnus
X.	decem	decimus
XI.	ūndecim	ūndecimus
XII.	duodecim	duodecimus
XIII.	tredecim	tertius decimus
XIV.	quattuordecim	quartus decimus
XV.	quindecim	quintus decimus
XVI.	sēdecim	sextus decimus
XVII.	septendecim	septimus decimus
XVIII.	duodēvīgintī	duodēvīcēsimus
XIX.	ūndēvīgintī	ūndēvīcēsimus
XX.	vīgintī	vīcēsimus
XXI.	vīgintī ūnus	vīcēsimus prīmus, etc.
L.	quinquāgintā	quinquāgēsimus
C.	centum	centēsimus
CI.	centum et ūnus	centēsimus prīmus

Impersonal Verbs

Some verbs, because of their meaning, have no personal subject. Consequently they appear only in the third person singular, the infinitive, and the gerund, in all tenses, and are called "impersonal verbs." In addition, many verbs that are not ordinarily impersonal, especially intransitive verbs in the passive voice, are often used in the same way. In English translation, "it" is often given as the subject of these verbs, although grammatically the real or apparent subject is an infinitive or a noun clause.

Nōn **licet** arma capere.
It is not permitted to take arms. (The subject of **licet** is **capere**.)

Neque vīvere **libet** neque morī **licet**.
He does not wish (lit., *it is not pleasing*) to live and he cannot (lit., *it is not permitted to*) die.
(**vīvere** and **morī** are the subjects of **libet** and **licet**, respectively.)

Impersonal verbs that take the infinitive as an apparent subject may express an agent in the accusative or the dative case, depending on the expression. When the agent is in the accusative case, it is the apparent subject of the infinitive; the accusative subject and the infinitive verb, in turn, together form the actual "subject" of the impersonal verb, as in the second example above.

With **libet**, "it is pleasing," **placet**, which also means "it is pleasing" (sometimes with the added sense that something is agreed upon or resolved), and **vīsum est**, "it seemed good, it seemed right," a personal subject is expressed with the dative case:

Mihi nunc esse hoc vērum **libet**.
It is pleasing to me that this is now true.

Obsecrō ut mea ad mē reddantur. —**Placet**.
I request that my things be returned to me. —*Granted.*

Vīsum est mihi ut eius sententiam temptārem.
I thought it was a good idea (*it seemed best to me*) to test his opinion.

With **oportet**, "it is proper, obligatory," **pudet**, "it causes shame," and **piget**, "it causes displeasure, revulsion," a personal subject is expressed by the accusative case.

Quid **mē oportet** facere?
What *should I* do?

Pudet mē prōdīre ad tē, pater.
I am ashamed to come before you, father.

Nōn **mē** meminisse **pigēbit**.
Remembering will not *displease me.*

The personal subject can be expressed by the accusative or the dative case with **licet**, "it is permitted," **necesse est**, "it is necessary," and **decet**, "it is right, fitting, becoming."

Nōn **licet hominem** esse saepe ut volt.
A person is not often *permitted* to be as he wishes.

Nōn **sōlīs Mycēnīs licet** arma capere.
The Myceneans are not the *only ones* who *are permitted* to take arms.

Necesse est mē Rōmā abīre.
I must leave Rome today.

Mihi necesse est Rōmā abīre.
I must leave Rome.

Haec facite, ut **fortēs mīlitēs decet**.
Do these things, as *is fitting* (for) *brave soldiers.*

Haec ōrātiō **amantī** plūs **decuit**.
This speech *was* more *appropriate for a lover.*

Many of the intransitive verbs you have learned, such as **īre**, **currere**, **parēre**, and **venīre**, are used impersonally in the passive voice. **Curritur** means "there is running," or more generally, "people run"; **itur**, "there is a going" or "people go." **Parētur mihi**, accordingly, means "I am obeyed," and **ventum est** means "there has been a coming," or "people (in a general, non-specific sense) have come":

Ventum erat ad templum Vestae.
People had come to the temple of Vesta.

Itur ad cāsum tabulae.
People approach the peril of the gaming table.

Impersonal verbs are frequently used to express events in nature, such as **pluit**, it rains, **ningit**, it snows, **tonat**, it thunders. In addition, verbs of feeling such as **miseret** (cf. **miser**), "it arouses pity," **paenitet**, "it causes repentance," **piget**, "it displeases, causes revulsion," **pudet** (cf. **pudīcus**), "it shames," and **taedet**, "it wearies," are often used impersonally. Here the person who experiences the feeling becomes the object of the verb, and whatever gives rise to the feeling is expressed by the objective genitive:

Fratris mē **pudet**.
I am ashamed of my brother.

Miseret mē huius hominis.
I pity this person.

Instead of the objective genitive, many of these verbs will indicate the cause of the emotion aroused with an infinitive or noun equivalent as their apparent subject: **miseret mē meminisse**, "remembering grieves me" (**mē meminisse** is the apparent subject).

Noun Clauses with Impersonal Verbs

A subjunctive clause introduced by **ut** can function as a noun equivalent—serving as the subject, predicate, or object of a verb, or standing in apposition to a noun, adjective, or pronoun. Subjunctive noun clauses are particularly common with impersonal verbs, serving as the apparent subject or predicate of the impersonal verb:

Accidit **ut esset lūna plēna**.
It happened *that the moon was full.*
(**ut** . . . **plēna** is subject of **accidit**.)

Quid fit **ut nēmō contentus vīvat**?
Why does it happen *that no one is content with his own life*?
(**ut** . . . **vīvat** is subject of **fit**.)

Est mōs hominum **ut eundem plūribus rēbus excellere nōlint**.
People usually *do not* (it is the custom of human beings *not to*) *want the same person to be outstanding in many things.*
(**ut** . . . **nōlint** is predicate to **est mōs**.)

Effice **ut quidquid corpore contīgerō vertātur in aurum**.
Bring it about *that whatever I touch with my body is changed into gold.*
(**ut** . . . **vertātur** is the object of **effice**.)

Illud nātūra nōn patitur, **ut aliōrum spoliīs nostrās copiās augeāmus**.
Nature does not permit one thing (**illud**), *that we increase our own wealth from the spoils of others.*
(**ut** . . . **augeāmus** is in apposition to **illud**.)

The negative is ordinarily **ut nōn**, since these clauses are commonly clauses of result. Sometimes, however, the negative clause will be introduced by **nē**, indicating that purpose rather than result is in the speaker's mind. Noun clauses of purpose rather than result are most often found with verbs of effecting (especially **faciō**, **efficiō**, **perficiō**), which will tend to take the noun clause as their object:

> Sī potest virtūs efficere **nē miser quis sit**, . . .
> If virtue can bring it about *that someone is not miserable*, . . .
> (**nē** . . . **sit** is negative purpose which, it is implied, **virtūs** intends.)

Compare:

> Potestis efficere **nē male moriar**, sed **ut nōn moriar** efficere nōn potestis.
> You can bring it about *that I do not die a painful death*, but you cannot keep *me from dying*.
> (**nē** . . . **moriar** shows purpose, **ut nōn** . . . **moriar** shows result.)

Scrībenda

accidit, **-ere**, **accidit** it happens, it chances
constat, **-stāre**, **-stitit**, —— it agrees with, it is consistent
convenit, **-īre**, **convēnit**, —— it is agreed
efficiō, **-ere**, **effēcī**, **effectus** bring to pass, accomplish, effect
ēvenit, **-īre**, **ēvēnit**, —— it results, it turns out
libet, **-ēre**, **libuit** or **libitum est** it is pleasing
licet, **-ēre**, **licuit** or **licitum est** it is permitted; one may
necesse est it is necessary
paenitet, **-ēre**, **paenituit** it causes regret
piget, **-ēre**, **piguit** it displeases, causes revulsion
pudet, **-ēre**, **puduit** it causes shame
taedet, **-ēre**, **taeduit** or **taesum est** it wearies

A. Translate the following into English. Identify any noun clauses and indicate whether the noun clause is the subject or the object of the main verb:

1. Necesse est ut haec faciās.
2. Perfice ut Crassus haec nōbīs expōnat.
3. Efficiet ut Cicerō fīat cōnsul.
4. Hominēs suōrum errōrum pudeat ac paeniteat.
5. Rērum obscūritās, nōn verbōrum, facit ut nōn intellegātur ōrātiō.
6. Cācus perfēcit ut bovēs nōn vidērentur.
7. Movendō fīlium cum mātre in caelum, Iuppiter fēcit nē rēs nefanda fieret. (**nefandus**, **-a**, **-um**, unspeakable, abominable)
8. Accidit ut ūnā nocte omnia simulācra tollerentur. (**simulācrum**, **-ī** *n*, statue)
9. Opus erat ut Cācus perīret.
10. Sī bene mē nōveris, pigeat fūgisse, et mē retinēre labōrēs. (**retineō**, **-ēre**, detain, hold fast)
11. Cavendum est in prīmīs nē studia ōderint discipulī.

12. Apud scriptōrēs plūrimōs convenit ut in mediō mundī stet terra.
13. Iam vērō ūnum et ūnum duo, duo et duo quattuor ōdiōsum canticum mihi erat, et dulcissimum spectaculum erat equus ligneus armātis plēnus et Trōiae incendium atque umbra Creūsae. (Augustine) (**ōdiōsus**, **-a**, **-um**, hateful, odious; **ligneus**, **-a**, **-um**, of wood; **incendium**, **-ī** *n*, burning; **umbra**, **-ae** *f*, shade, ghost; **Creusa**, **-ae** *f*, Aeneas' first wife, who was killed at the fall of Troy)
14. Tribus et vīgintī plāgīs Caesar confossus est. (**plāga**, **-ae** *f*, blow; **confodiō**, **-ere**, **-fōdī**, **-fossus**, stab)
15. Da mihi bāsia* mille, deinde centum,
dein mille altera, dein secunda centum,
deinde usque* altera mille, deinde centum,
dein, cum mīlia multa fēcerimus,
conturbābimus* illa, nē sciāmus,
aut nē quis malus invidēre possit,
cum tantum sciat esse bāsiōrum.
(Catullus 5.7–13)
(**bāsium**, **-ī** *n*, kiss; **conturbō**, **-āre**, throw into confusion) (**usque**, adv., continuously)

B. Translate into Latin:

1. Do they pity us?
2. We are not permitted to make errors.
3. I grow weary waiting for you.
4. We agreed to be his dinner guests.
5. We ought (use **oportet**) to go (use **aggredior**) to Athens.

Definitive and Descriptive Conjunctions

In Chapter XII you learned that **cum** with the subjunctive can mean "because," "although," or "when." Several other conjunctions in Latin convey this range of meaning. Some govern only the indicative, some govern only the subjunctive, and some govern either the indicative or the subjunctive, with their meaning differing to reflect the mood they govern. When any of this last group of conjunctions is used with the indicative, it generally defines or identifies objectively a cause, fact, or time. When it is used with the subjunctive, it describes the situation from a subjective perspective.

Consider first the temporal conjunctions. Those which define the time when something happens are **cum**, **quandō**, **ubi**, and **postquam**. **Ubi** and **postquam** always govern the indicative mood, but **cum** plus the subjunctive will instead refer to the circumstances rather than the time. **Quandō** usually governs the indicative:

Fīlius fugit **cum** pater domum **redit**. (Indicative)
The son runs away *when* (whenever) the father *comes* home.

Fīlius fūgit **cum** pater domum **redīret**. (Subjunctive)
The son ran away *when* (under the circumstances of) the father *returned* home.

Fīlius fugit **quandō** pater domum **redit**. (Indicative)
The son runs away *whenever* the father *comes* home.

Antequam[2] and **priusquam**, "before," can refer either to simple time, with one event preceding another, or to the anticipation of something happening afterwards. The subjunctive indicates the latter.

Illa discessit **antequam** vir **advēnit**. (Indicative)
(Illa **ante** discessit **quam** vir **advēnit**.)
She left *before* her husband *arrived*.

Illa discessit **antequam** vir **advenīret**. (Subjunctive)
She left *before* her husband (*could*) *arrive*. (anticipation)

Prius respondēs **quam rogō**. (Indicative)
You answer *before* I *ask* the question.

Prius respondistī **quam rogārem**. (Subjunctive)
You (deliberately) answered *before* I *asked* the question. (anticipation)

Dōnec and **dum**, both meaning "while" or "until," are used with the indicative to limit the time in which the action of the main verb can take place. **Dōnec** with the subjunctive shows an intended or anticipated limit for the action of the main verb. **Dum**, used with the present or imperfect subjunctive, means "until," "as long as," or "provided that" some anticipated action will happen. **Dummodo** and **modo ut** only occur with the subjunctive, and mean "provided that"; **sī modo**, on the other hand, governs the indicative, and means "if at least."

Nē surgātis **dōnec erit** signum **datum**. (Indicative)
Don't get up *until* the signal *is* given.

Elephantī nihil trepidābant, **dōnec** continentī velut ponte **agerentur**. (Subjunctive)
The elephants were afraid of nothing *while* (*as long as*—but only as long as) *they were being driven* over a seemingly continuous bridge.

Dum anima **est**, spēs esse dīcitur. (Indicative)
While (*as long as*) *there is* life, there is said to be hope.

Ille multa passus est, **dum conderet** urbem **inferret**que deōs Latiō. (Subjunctive)
He suffered many things *until* (in anticipation of the time when) *he would found* a city and *bring* his gods to Latium.

Omnia forīs resonent, **dum** intus nihil tumultūs **sit**. (Subjunctive)
Let everything outside ring noisily, *provided there is* no disturbance within.

Quidquid vīs lege, **dummodo** nihil **recitēs**. (Subjunctive)
Read whatever you like, *provided only that you* do not *read it aloud*.

Discēs, **modo ut** tacēre **possīs**. (Subjunctive)
You will learn, *provided you can* be silent.

[2] **ante** and **prius** are sometimes separated from the **quam**. In these cases, they still translate with the **quam**: **ante hoc nōvī quam tū nātus es**, "I learned this before you were born."

Cum sint dī—**sī modo sunt**, ut profectō sunt, . . . (Indicative)
Since the gods exist—*if at least they do exist*, as surely they do, . . .

"Since" or "because" is expressed by **quoniam**, **quandō**, **quod** and **quia** with the indicative mood. **Quod** and **quia** can also govern the subjunctive mood, when an alleged reason (as opposed to simple fact) is being asserted. **Cum** occurs with the subjunctive to express cause.

Quoniam (**quandō**/**quod**/**quia**) ipse prō sē dīcere nōn **posset**, verba fēcit frater eius.
Since he could not speak for himself, his brother spoke for him.

Cum pater **redeat**, fīlius discēdit.
The son is leaving *because* the father *is returning*.

Quod (**quia**) pater **redeat**, fīlius discēdit.
Because the father *is returning* (for this alleged reason, not necessarily the actual reason), the son is leaving.

Concession, "although, granting that," is indicated by **cum** or **quamvīs** with the subjunctive. **Quamquam** plus the indicative also means "although," but the concession refers to an admitted fact.

Nē tibi regnandī veniat tam dīra cupīdō, **quamvīs** campōs talēs aliī **mīrentur**.
Let not so dire a longing to reign come to you, *however much* (*although*) others *admire* such fields.

Cum pater domum **nōn redīret**, fīlius tamen fūgit.
Although the father *did not return* home, the son nevertheless ran away.

Sī tantus est vōbīs amor cāsūs cognoscere nostrōs, **quamquam** animus meminisse **horret**, incipiam.
If you have so great a longing to learn our misfortunes, *although* my mind *dreads* remembering, I shall begin.

Scrībenda

Identify the mood governed by the underlined conjunction, and then translate the entire sentence:

1. Cum patriam amīsī, tum mē perīsse putēs.
2. Cum rosam vīderat, tum incipere ver arbitrābātur. (**rosa**, **-ae** *f*, rose; **ver**, **veris** *n*, spring) (**arbitror**, **-ārī**, **arbitrātus sum**, think, judge)
3. Quandō peribimus? Sōlus amāns nōvit quandō peritūrus sit.
4. Tū Rōmam salvus quandō vēnistī, omnia haec vidēbis.
5. Nihil fierī dē nihilō posse fātendum est, quandō omnibus rēbus est opus sēmine. (**fateor**, **-ērī**, **fassus sum**, confess, admit; **sēmen**, **-inis** *n*, seed, primary physical substance)
6. Ubi vidēbitur mulier quae ingeniō est bonō?
7. Quid, ubi reddēbās aurum, dīxistī patrī? (**aurum**, **-ī** *n*, gold)
8. Sīdera nunc autumnī dīcam, ubi iam est brevior diēs. (**autumnus**, **-ī** *m*, autumn)

9. Nōn rediī domum postquam hanc rem invēnī.
10. Postquam [Naevius] Orchī trāditus [est] thēsaurō, oblitī sunt Rōmae loquī lingua Latina. (**Naevius, -ī** *m*, early Roman poet; **Orchi thesaurus**, the underworld; **oblīvīscor, oblīvīscī, oblītus sum**, forget)
11. Antequam viam ingredior, pauca mihi dīcenda sunt.
12. Hominēs ante invēnērunt artem quam docuērunt.
13. Hostis ante adesse potest quam quisquam eum ventūrum esse suspicārī potest. (**suspicor, -ārī, -ātus sum**, suspect)
14. Ante venī quam [veniat] vir; nec quid, sī vēneris ante,
possit agī videō, sed tamen ante venī.
15. Quam bene Sāturnō vīvēbant rēge, priusquam
tellūs in longās est patefacta viās.

(**Sāturnus, -ī** *m*, the legendary ruler during the Golden Age; **tellūs, tellūris** *f*, the earth; **patefaciō, -ere, -fēcī, -factus**, open, make accessible)

16. Nōn omnēs sedēbunt dōnec cantor 'vōs plaudīte' dīcat. (**cantor, -ōris** *m*, singer; stage director; **plaudō, -ere, plausī, plausus**, applaud)
17. Adde manūs in vincula meās dum furor omnis abit, sī quis amīcus ades.
18. Vīxit, dum vīxit, bene.
19. Ōderint, dum metuant.
20. Similitūdine, dum brevis sit, ūtēmur. (**similitūdo, -inis** *f*, comparison, simile)
21. Dummodo rīsum excutiat, nōn sibi nec cuiquam amīcō parcet. (**rīsus, -ūs** *m*, laughter; **excutiō, -ere**, shake out, provoke)
22. Quae futūra sint loquar multō melius quam illī loquī possunt, cum sim Iuppiter.
23. Quoniam ego adsum, faciet nēmō iniūriam.
24. Sīc ut possumus faciēmus, quandō ut volumus facere nōn licet.
25. Istud scriptōrēs nōn vetant quia nōn liceat, sed quia nōn putent esse istud ūtile. (**vetō, -āre**, forbid; **ūtilis, -e**, useful)
26. Brūtus, quia rēgēs ēiēcit, cōnsul prīmus factus est. (**ēiciō, -ere, ēiēcī, ēiectus**, throw out)
27. Nisī abeās, quamquam tū pulchra es, malum tibi magnum iam dabō.

Verba tenenda

Verbs

accidit, -ere, accidit it happens, it chances

arbitror, -ārī, arbitrātus sum make a decision; think, suppose; be of the opinion, believe

condō, **-ere**, **condidī**, **conditus** found, establish; bury
constō, **-stāre**, **-stitī**, —— stand together; stand still; exist; remain unchanged; stand firm; agree with, be consistent with
conveniō, **-īre**, **convēnī**, **conventus** assemble, meet; come together;
convenit (impersonal) it is agreed
decet, **-ēre**, **decuit**, —— it is right, proper, fitting; it is becoming
efficiō, **-ere**, **effēcī**, **effectus** make; cause to occur, bring about, accomplish; deduce from premises:
efficit ut it follows that
ēveniō, **-īre**, **ēvēnī**, **ēventus** come out; fall by lot; happen, come about
exstō, **exstāre**, **exstitī**, —— stand out, be conspicuous
for, **fārī**, **fātus sum** speak, talk; say, tell
incolō, **-ere**, **incoluī**, —— inhabit, dwell in
iūdicō, **-āre**, **-āvī**, **-ātus** judge; decide; estimate
iungō, **-ere**, **iunxī**, **iunctus** join, connect
libet, **-ēre**, **libuit** or **libitum est** it is pleasing
licet, **ēre**, **licuit** or **licitum est** it is permitted; one may
miseret, **-ēre**, **miseruit** or **miseritum est** move someone (acc.) to feel pity for something (gen.)
oportet, **-ēre**, **oportuit** it is proper, right, inevitable
paenitet, **-ēre**, **paenituit**, —— cause someone (acc.) to feel dissatisfaction or regret for something (gen.)
piget, **-ēre**, **piguit** or **pigitum est** affect someone (acc.) with revulsion or disgust for something (gen.)
praebeō, **-ēre**, **praebuī**, **praebitus** put forward, offer, provide; show
prōvideō, **-ēre**, **-vīdī**, **-vīsus** act with foresight; foresee, discern
pudet, **-ēre**, **puduit** or **puditum est** cause someone (acc.) displeasure or revulsion for someone or something (gen.)
taedet, **-ēre**, **taeduit** or **taesum est** it wearies

Nouns

fātum, **-ī** *n* fate
infāns, **infantis** *m* or *f* infant
initium, **-ī** *n* beginning; first part, origin
mille *n* (indeclinable) a thousand; **mīlia**, **mīlium** *n* pl. thousands or (in a vague sense) any large number
mōns, **mōntis** *m* mountain
prōvidentia, **-ae** *f* foresight; the power of seeing in advance; provision (for)
regnum, **-ī** *n* kingdom, realm
status, **-ūs** *m* posture, stature; condition, station, rank; position, place; constitution (e.g., of a state)
victor, **victōris** *m* conqueror, victor

Adjectives

caecus, **-a**, **-um** blind, unseeing; invisible, unseen
centum one hundred
decem ten
dīligēns; **dīligentis** (gen.) careful, diligent, accurate
duo, **duae**, **duo** two

excellēns; **excellentis** (gen.) eminent, distinguished, outstanding
memorābilis, **-e** memorable, worthy of being remembered
mille (indeclinable) a thousand
rēgius, **-a**, **-um** having to do with the king or queen; royal
secundus, **-a**, **-um** the second in a sequence; following, favoring, supportive
trēs, **tria** three
ultimus, **-a**, **-um** farthest, most distant; the last
vīgintī twenty

Adverbs

bis twice
necesse (used only in predicative position) essential, inevitable:
  necesse est it is necessary
semel once
ter three times

Conjunctions

dummodo (+ subjunctive) provided that
dum (+ subjunctive) until (showing expectation); provided that
  (+ indicative) while, as long as, until
modo ut (negative, **modo nē**) provided that, if only
  sī modo if at least
  quī modo provided that he
priusquam before
quamquam although
quamvīs although
quoniam since, because

Notanda

An **arbiter** (like English "arbitrator") is a person who makes a judgment based upon what he has seen or heard. The deponent verb **arbitror** means "make a judgment" or "be of the opinion" (as opposed to having certain knowledge).

The verb **incolō** can be transitive or intransitive, but has no fourth principal part. Observe that the prefix **in-** can mean "in," as it does here, or it can negate a word (e.g., the adjective **incultus**, also formed from **colō**, means "not cultivated").

The Latin adverb **libenter**, "gladly," "with pleasure," is related to the impersonal verb **libet**.

A "license" (from **licet**) is a formal "permit."

The basic meaning of the preposition **prō**, "before," carries over into the prefix **prō-**, as in **prōvideō** and **prōvidentia**. In English, a "prudent" (ultimately from **prōvidēns**) person is one who looks ahead or "foresees" the effects of his or her actions.

taedet is the Latin root of English "tedium," a wearisomeness: a "tedious" activity is something that is long and tiresome.

fātum literally means, "the thing said," implicitly, by the gods: a person's fate is decreed when (s)he is born, and cannot thereafter be "unsaid." An infant is a person who has not reached the age where it can speak (**in-fāns**). **Fāma** is rumor, the talk that sometimes seems to propel itself. A **fābula** is a story that is told; it can also be the plot of a play.

Note how the genders of **regnum** (neuter), **rēx** (masculine), and **rēgīna** (feminine), all related to the verb **regere**, help to distinguish their respective meanings. The adjective is **rēgius**.

Secundus, "second," derives from **sequor**, inasmuch as the second in a series "follows" the first. It also frequently means "favoring," "going along with," like a favoring breeze that fills the sails of a ship.

Ante legenda

Translate:

1. Sī umquam ūllum fuit tempus, māter, cum ego voluptātī tibi fuerim, ōrō ut nunc tē misereat meī.
2. Singula sequī nōn est necesse.
3. Ego beātōs esse eōs putō quibus deōrum mūnere datum est aut facere scrībenda aut scrībere legenda, beātissimōs vērō quibus utrumque datum est.
4. Nīl mē paeniteat sānum patris huius.
5. Mē piget parum pudēre tē!
6. Nunc dē narrātiōne dīcendum esse vidētur. Oportet igitur eam trēs habēre rēs: ut brevis, ut aperta, ut probābilis sit. Brevis erit, sī unde necesse est inde initium sūmētur et nōn ab ultimō repetētur. (**apertus**, **-a**, **-um**, clear; **probābilis**, **-e**, plausible; **re-petō**)
7. Tum vērō infēlix Dīdō mortem ōrat; taedet caelī convexa tuērī. (**in-fēlix**, unhappy; **Dīdō**, **-ōnis** *f*, queen of Carthage; **convexa**, **-ōrum** *n*, vault, arch; **tueor**, **tuērī**, gaze upon)
8. Tot mīlia gentēs arma ferunt Italae. (**Italus**, **-a**, **-um**, Italian)
9. Sed perīsse semel satis est.
10. Nōn ego cuncta meīs amplectī versibus optō, nōn, mihi sī linguae centum sint ōraque centum. (**amplector**, **amplectī**, **amplectus sum**, encompass, treat) (**ōs**, **ōris** *n*, mouth)
11. Cum virgo quaedam fīliōs duo genuisset, rex imperāvit ut puerī in fluentem aquam mitterentur.
12. Cum aqua infantēs in alveō dēstituisset, lupa eōs clamantēs invēnit. (**alveus**, **-ī** *m*, hollow vessel, tub; river bank; **lupa**, **-ae** *f*, she-wolf)
13. Nūllus homō tantō ingeniō umquam nātus est ut rēs nūlla eum fugeret.
14. Urbī locus est eī quī diuturnam rem pūblicam condere conātur dīligentissimē prōvidendus. (**diuturnus**, **-a**, **-um**, long-lasting)

15. Eī quī incolunt urbēs maritimās nōn haerent in suīs sēdibus, sed semper rapiuntur ā domō longius, atque quamquam manent corpore, animō tamen exulant. (**maritimus**, **-a**, **-um**, on the seacoast; **haereō**, **-ere**, cling, adhere; **sēdēs**, **sēdis** *f* pl., home; **exulō**, **-āre**, be banished, live in exile)

Legenda

The Roman Experience (5): Romulus and Remus

1. Romans believed they were descended from the few Trojans who survived the fall of Troy during the thirteenth century B.C. Led by Aeneas, a small band of Trojans came to Italy in search of a new home.

Rome was founded many generations after Aeneas arrived in Italy. Aeneas' son Ascanius left Lavinium and founded a town known as Alba Longa, which his descendants ruled for many generations. One of these descendants, Amulius, overthrew his older brother, the rightful heir, and seized the throne of Alba. He then proceeded to inflict violence upon his brother's children, and appointed his brother's daughter, Rhea Silvia, a Vestal Virgin. The appointment was not the honor it appeared: Amulius' intent was to preclude the chance of her bearing an heir to his throne. The Vestal Virgin was raped, however, and gave birth to twin boys, Romulus and Remus. Consequently the king imprisoned the new mother, and ordered that the boys be drowned in the river, but the river overflowed, and the boys were rescued by a she-wolf:

Dēbēbātur, ut opīnor*, fātīs tantae urbis orīgo* maximīque imperiī prīncipium. Cum Vestālis* geminum* partum* ēdidisset, nec* dī nec hominēs* aut ipsam aut puerōs ā crūdēlitāte* rēgiā servant: puerōs in fluentem aquam mittī iubet. Forte super rīpās* Tiberis* fūsa aqua infantēs spem ferentibus dabat. Vastae* tum in hīs locīs sōlitūdinēs* erant. Tenet fāma, cum fluitantem* alveum*, quō expositī erant puerī, tenuis*

1: **opīnor**, **-ārī**, **-ātus sum** think, believe
2: **orīgō**, **orīginis** *f* the coming into being, rise
Vestālis [**Virgo**] Vestal Virgin; a priestess dedicated to the cult of Vesta, Roman goddess of the domestic hearth
geminus, **-a**, **-um** twin
partus, **-ūs** *m* offspring, progeny
2–3: **nec dī nec hominēs** An allusion to the claim that the god Mars was the father of the twins. Livy elsewhere reports the claim, but is skeptical about its authenticity.
3: **crūdēlitās**, **-tātis** *f* cruelty
4: **rīpa**, **-ae** *f* river-bank
Tiber, **Tiberis** *m* the river Tiber
5: **vastus**, **-a**, **-um** empty, unoccupied; desert
sōlitūdo, **-inis** *f* a lonely place; wilderness
6: **fluitō**, **-āre** float
alveus, **-ī** *n* hollow vessel, tub
tenuis, **-e** thin; shallow

Etruscan statue (c. 500 B.C.) of the wolf that suckled Romulus and Remus. The statues of the infants were added during the Renaissance.

in siccō* locō aqua dēstituisset, lupam* sitientem* ex montibus ad puerilem* vāgītum* cursum vertisse; eam infantibus adeo mītem praebuisse mammās*, ut linguā lambentem* puerōs magister rēgiī pecoris* invēnerit.

(After Livy I.4)

2. When the twins grew to manhood, they returned to Alba Longa, overthrew the wicked king, and restored their grandfather to his rightful throne. They then set out for the site where they had been exposed, and founded a new settlement. A dispute arose between them, however, during which Romulus killed his brother. The new city was named after the surviving

7: **siccus**, **-a**, **-um** dry
lupa, **-ae** *f* she-wolf
sitiēns, **sitientis** thirsty
7–8: **puerilis**, **-e** childish
8: **vāgītus**, **-ūs** *m* cry of distress, wail
9: **mamma, -ae** *f* breast; udder (in animals), dug, teat
lambō, **-ere**, **lambī**,—— lick
pecus, **pecoris** *n* herd

twin. The success of the new city has been attributed to many factors, including its location. In the following passage, the statesman Scipio Africanus the Younger is depicted musing over the wisdom of the selection of the site of Rome:

2a. Catō* dīcere solēbat ob hanc causam statum nostrae cīvitātis praestāre ceterīs cīvitātibus, quod in illīs singulī fuissent ferē* quī constituissent suam rem pūblicam lēgibus atque institūtīs suīs, nostra autem rēs pūblica nōn unīus ingeniō, sed multōrum, nec ūnā* hominis vītā* sed aliquot* saeculis et aetatibus constitūta esse.

Nam neque ūllum ingenium tantum umquam exstitisse dīcēbat, ut quisquam aliquandō* fuisset quem rēs nūlla fugeret, neque cuncta ingenia collāta in ūnum hominem ūnō tempore prōvidēre posse ut omnia comprehenderet sine rērum ūsū ac vetustāte*.

(After Cicero, Dē rē pūblicā, *2.1)*

2b. Urbī autem locum, quod* est eī quī diuturnam* rem pūblicam serere* cōnātur dīligentissimē prōvidendum*, Rōmulus sapienter lēgit. Neque enim ad mare mōvit, quod eī fuit factū facillimum, sed hic vir cum excellentī prōvidentiā sēnsit ac vīdit nōn esse opportūnissimōs* sitūs* maritimōs* urbibus eīs quae ad spem diuturnitātis* conderentur atque imperiī, prīmum quod essent urbēs maritimae* nōn sōlum multīs perīculīs oppositae sed etiam caecīs. Nam terra continēns* adventūs hostium nōn modo exspectātōs*, sed etiam repentīnōs* multīs indiciīs* et quasi fragōre* quōdam et sonitū* ipsō ante nuntiat; neque vērō quisquam potest hostis advolāre* terrā quīn eum nōn modo esse, sed etiam quis et unde sit, scīre possimus. Maritimus* vērō ille et nāvālis* hostis adesse

1: **Catō, Catōnis** *m* eminent Roman statesman
2: **ferē** (adv.) generally
4: **ūnā . . . vītā** ablative of time
5: **aliquot** (indeclinable) several
7: **aliquandō** (adv.) at some time
9: **vetustās, -tātis** *f* the state of having existed a long time; age; antiquity

1–2: **quod est eī . . . prōvidendum** "because he who . . . must have foresight." (**prōvideō** is used impersonally.)
1: **diuturnus, -a, -um** lasting for a long time
1–2: **serō, -ere, sēvī, satus** plant, sow; (here) found
4: **opportūnus, -a, -um** (+ dat.) suitable (for)
situs, -ūs *m* site, location
5, 6, 11: **maritimus, -a, -um** on the seacoast
5: **diuturnitas, -tātis** *f* long duration
7: **terra continēns** "the mainland"
8: **exspectō, -āre** look out for, expect
repentīnus, -a, -um sudden, hasty
indicium, -ī *n* sign, indication
9: **fragor, -ōris** *n* crash, noise, din
sonitus, -ūs *m* sound
10: **advolō, -āre** fly toward
11: **nāvālis, -e** naval, of or belonging to ships

potest antequam quisquam eum ventūrum esse suspicārī* possit, nec vērō cum venit, prae sē fert aut quis sit aut unde veniat aut etiam quid velit, dēnique nē nōta* quidem ūlla, pacātus an hostis sit, cernī ac iūdicārī potest.

(After Cicero, Dē rē pūblicā, *2.2)*

2c. Est autem maritimīs* urbibus etiam quaedam corruptēla* ac mutātiō* mōrum: miscentur enim novīs sermōnibus* ac disciplīnīs* et importantur* nōn mercēs* sōlum adventiciae*, sed etiam mōrēs, ut nihil possit in patriīs* institūtīs manēre integrum. Iam eī quī incolunt eās urbēs nōn haerent* in suīs sēdibus* sed volucrī* semper spē et cōgitātiōne rapiuntur ā domō longius, atque etiam cum manent corpore, animō tamen exultant* et vagantur*. Sed tamen in hīs vitiīs inest illa magna commoditās*, ut ad eam urbem rēs quāscumque velint adnāre*, et rursus* ut id quod agrī efferant suī, portāre* possint ac mittere.

(After Cicero, Dē rē pūblicā, *2.4)*

12: **suspicor**, -**ārī**, **suspicātus sum** suspect
14: **nōta**, -**ae** *f* sign, mark

1: **maritimus**, -**a**, -**um** [see passage 2b.]
corruptēla, -**ae** *f* a corrupting, seduction
1–2: **mutātiō**, -**iōnis** *f* change
2: **sermō**, -**ōnis** *m* conversation, talk
disciplīna, -**ae** *f* instruction, learning
2–3: **importō**, -**āre** bring or carry into
3: **merx**, **mercis** *f* goods, wares, merchandise
adventicius, -**a**, -**um** coming from abroad, foreign
4: **patrius**, -**a**, -**um** of or belonging to one's native country, native
5: **haereō**, -**ēre** hold fast, cling, adhere
sēdēs, **sēdis** *f* seat, residence, home
volucer, **volucris**, **volucre** flying, winged
6–7: **exulō**, -**āre** be banished; live in exile
7: **vagor**, -**ārī**, **vagātus sum** wander about, be unsettled
commoditās, -**tātis** *f* convenience, advantage
8: **adnō**, -**āre** swim to; come to, approach
rursus (adv.) again
9: **portō**, -**āre** carry

Alternate Forms; Accusative: Additional Uses; Genitive Case (2): Summary of Uses

Alternate Forms

You have now learned enough Latin grammar to be able to read most of the Latin authors without too much difficulty. You will find that each author and period has peculiarities of style and diction, but none should be beyond your grasp. It may be helpful to consider here, however, some of the alternate forms and constructions you will encounter.

You have already encountered some alternate forms in earlier chapters. The second person singular passive ending **-ris**, for example, is sometimes replaced by **-re** (e.g., **amāre** = **amāris**). You have also encountered, in third declension **i**-stem nouns, the accusative plural ending **-īs** as an alternate for the regular accusative ending **-ēs** (e.g., **noctīs** = **noctēs**). Two other forms you should be able to recognize are the third person plural ending **-ēre** as an alternate for **-ērunt**, and **fore** as an alternate for **futūrum esse**.

-ēre = ***-ērunt***. An alternate form for **-ērunt**, **-ēre** is sometimes mistaken for a present active infinitive. Usually the perfect stem to which it is affixed precludes any confusion. Consider the following examples:

Perfect Active	Present Infinitive
amāvēre = amāvērunt	amāre
tenuēre = tenuērunt	tenēre
vēnēre = vēnērunt	venīre
cēpēre = cēpērunt	capĕre
fūgēre = fūgērunt	fŭgĕre
bibēre = bibērunt	bibĕre

Notice that the only time confusion may arise between this form and the present active infinitive is in the third conjugation, and then only when the present stem and the perfect stem are identical, as in **bibēre**. At first

fūgēre looks like the present infinitive too, until we recall that the **-u-** in the perfect stem is long. In both cases, however, **bibēre** and **fūgēre** differ from their present infinitives because of their long **-ē-**.

fore = futūrum esse. **Fore** is simply a shortened form of the future active infinitive **futūrum esse**: **dīcit tē fore cōnsulem** and **dīcit tē futūrum esse cōnsulem** both mean "he says you will be consul." You will sometimes see personal endings added to **fore** (**forem**, **forēs**, **foret**, **forēmus**, **forētis**, **forent**). In such cases it is functioning as an alternate form for the imperfect subjunctive of **esse**.

Syncope. Syncope is the omission of one or more short vowels between consonants. **Saeculum**, for example, sometimes loses the first **-u-** by syncopation, leaving **saeclum**. You should especially be aware of the tendency of this phenomenon to occur in the perfect stems of verbs: the entire syllable **-ve-** or **-vi-** sometimes drops from the perfect stem, producing forms such as **nōram** for **nōveram** and **nōsse** for **nōvisse**.

Future Imperative. In addition to the present imperative, Latin sometimes employs the future imperative, which occurs in the third person singular and plural as well as the second person singular and plural. Future imperative endings are:

	Active		Passive	
	SING.	PL.	SING.	PL.
Second	**-tō**	**-tōte**	**-tor**	——
Third	**-tō**	**-ntō**	**-tor**	**-ntor**

The future imperative occurs mainly where there is a clear reference to future time, in general maxims, and in legal documents. Additionally, the verbs **sciō**, **meminī**, and **habeō** tend to use the future imperative more commonly than the present imperative:

Future:	Dīc quibus in terrīs inscriptī nōmina regum nascantur flōrēs, et Phyllida sōlus **habētō**. Tell me in what lands the names of kings are inscribed naturally in flowers, and then you alone *shall have* Phyllis. *(Vergil,* Eclogue *III.107)*
Maxim:	Terram multō ante **mementō** excoquere. *Remember* to dry out the soil well in advance. *(Vergil,* Georgics, *II.259)*
Legal Document:	Hominem mortuum in urbe nē **sepelitō** neve **uritō**. *One shall not bury* nor *burn* a dead man within the city. *(*Lex XII Tabulārum, *X.1)*

The future imperative forms of **meminī** are **mementō** and **mementōte**:

Tū regere imperiō populōs, Rōmāne, **mementō**.
Remember, Roman, to lead nations with a rule of law. *(Vergil,* Aeneid, *VI.854)*

Accusative: Additional Uses

Accusative of Inner Object. You have learned that the most basic uses of the accusative case are as the direct object of the verb, the object of a preposition, and the subject of an infinitive. A direct object can be external, showing the thing or person directly affected by the verb (***mē vidēs***, "you see me"). It can also show something that the verb itself causes or produces; in this case it is known as an internal accusative, or accusative of the inner object.

Frequently this accusative consists of neuter pronouns and adjectives which explain more fully the contents of the verb:

magnum sonāns	making a *loud* noise
dulce sonāns	making a *sweet* sound
Quid morāris?	Why do you delay? (*What* is the *delay* you are making?)
Nihil mē terrēbis.	You will not frighten me. (You will cause *no* fright in me.)
Id nōs ad tē vēnimus.	*That is why* we have come to you.

This is the origin of many of the irregular adverbs which have the same form as the neuter accusative singular adjective (e.g., **multum**, **plūrimum**, **prīmum**, **sōlum**, **vērum**, **facile**, **difficile**, **forte**).

If the object has the same origin as the verb or has a related meaning, it is called a *cognate* accusative. This occurs most often with verbs that tend to be used intransitively, e.g., ***vītam vīvere***, "to live a *life*"; ***curram currere***, "to run a *race*."

Verbs of taste or smell frequently take an accusative of the inner object which is an extension of the cognate accusative:

Piscis sapit **mare**.	The fish has the taste *of the sea*.
Nōn omnēs possunt olēre **unguenta exotica**.	Not all men can smell of *exotic perfumes*.

Double Accusative. As you learned in Chapter XIV, verbs of asking, requesting, concealing, and teaching govern two accusatives, one of the person, the other of the thing.

Tē pecūniam orāmus.	We are asking *you for money*.
Caesārem auxilium poposcērunt.	They asked *Caesar for assistance*.
Puerōs elementa docuit.	He taught *children the alphabet*.

Verbs of naming, making, choosing, showing, and taking may also govern two accusatives, of the person and of the thing:

Urbem Acestam appellābunt.	They will call *the city Acesta*.
Illum virum cōnsulem fēcērunt.	They made *that man consul*.

Accusative of Respect. The accusative of respect,[1] found with passive or intransitive verbs or verbal adjectives, indicates the part of the body affected:

> Scissa **comam** caelum questibus implet.
> Tearing *her hair*, she fills heaven with her cries.
> nūda **genū** nōdōque **sinūs** collecta **fluentīs**
> her *knee* naked and the *flowing folds of her toga* gathered in a knot

Accusative of Exclamation. The accusative is used in exclamations:

Ō **tempora**, Ō **mōrēs**!	Oh *the times*, Oh *the customs*!
Mē miseram!	*Wretched me*!

Summary: Uses of the Genitive Case

In Chapter VII you encountered the possessive, objective, descriptive, and partitive genitives. These are the main uses of the genitive. Others that you will need to know but have not yet encountered are included in the following summary. The common characteristic of them all is that they show a relationship between two nouns.

1. The possessive genitive indicates the possessor (e.g., **Rōmulī frāter**, "the brother of Romulus"). Instead of the possessive genitive of the first person, second person, and reflexive pronouns, possessive adjectives are usually used (**meus**, **tuus**, **suus**, **noster**, **vester**). The possessive genitive and the possessive adjective can be used in the predicate with **esse**: **dōnum est Caesāris**, "the gift is Caesar's"; **dōnum est meum**, "the gift is mine."

One idiomatic use of the possessive genitive in this predicate construction is the genitive of characteristic, frequently translated, "it is the mark of . . ." or "it is characteristic of . . .":

> **Est vestrae magnitūdinis** mē sīc hortārī.
> *It is characteristic of/the mark of your generosity* to encourage me in this way.

2. The subjective and objective genitives are the names given to two related but distinct uses of the genitive. As you have learned, the objective genitive is governed by the verbal ideal in its governing noun. Thus, in the phrase **amor patriae**, **patriae** is the direct object of the verbal idea in **amor**. To indicate the subject of this verbal idea, Latin can use the possessive adjectives **meus**, **tuus**, **suus**, **noster**, and **vester**. Accordingly, **meus amor patriae** signifies "the love that I feel for my country." If we

[1] Also known as the "Greek accusative"; the accusative functions as a direct object of the Greek middle voice.

choose to name the person, however, Latin uses the subjective genitive: **Caesāris amor patriae**, or **puerī amor patriae**. Here Caesar in one case, and the boy in the other, are the persons who feel love for their country. The genitive pronouns **meī**, **tuī**, **suī**, **nostrī**, **vestrī** are used in the objective sense; hence, "my love for Caesar" would be **meus amor Caesāris**, while "Caesar's love for me" would be **Caesāris amor meī**.

3. The partitive genitive or genitive of the whole indicates the entirety of something, and the word governing it indicates that it is a part of this entirety, e.g., ***plūs sapientiae***, "more (out of the whole of) wisdom." Neuter pronouns frequently govern this genitive. The partitive genitives **nostrum** and **vestrum** refer to groups of persons (**ūnus nostrum**, **multī vestrum**, "one of us, many of you"). **nostrī** and **vestrī** are ordinarily used as objective genitives, but sometimes occur in the partitive sense, referring to individuals: **melior pars nostrī hoc facere recūsat**, "the better part of us refuses to do this."

4. A noun modified by an adjective may be used to describe another noun. The descriptive noun and its modifier may be in the genitive or ablative case (see also Chapter XVI, Ablative of Description):

vir **summae sapientiae**	a man *of the highest wisdom*	(genitive)
vir **summō ingeniō**,	a man *of the greatest genius*	(ablative)

The ablative of description is more commonly used to express physical qualities than is the genitive:

Nullum **istā faciē** vēnisse hūc scīmus.	We know that no one *of that appearance* has come here.
Sunt **capite candidō**.	They are *white-headed*.

The genitive of description tends to be confined to expressions of measure, number, and to nouns modified by **magnus**, **maximus**, **summus**, or **tantus**. In particular, it is found with the adjectival phrases **eius modī** or **eius generis**, both meaning "of this or that kind," and **cuius modī** or **cuius generis**, "of what kind." The genitive of description is also used with numerals to define measure:

fossa **trium pedum**,	a trench *of three feet*
mūrus **sēdecim pedum**,	a wall *of sixteen feet*

5. Whereas the ablative is used to denote a price or value of a specific amount, the genitive of indefinite value is used with neuter adjectives expressing quantity to indicate a value which is not specific. **Magnī**, **parvī**, **tantī**, **quantī**, **plūris**, **minōris** are regularly used to express indefinite value:

Ista vīta est **parvī** mihi.	That life is *of little value* to me.
Potestne haec lūx esse **tantī** tibi?	Can this life be *of such worth* to you?

The idioms **nihilī**, "of no worth," **assis**, "of a penny's worth," and **floccī**, "(worth) a lock of wool" (more idiomatic English would say, "worth a hair" or "a bit"), are also used regularly in the genitive to express indefinite value:

Nōn **floccī** faciō.	I don't care *a bit*.
rūmōrēs senum **nihilī** aestimēmus.	Let us consider the rumors of old men *worth nothing*.

6. The genitive followed by the ablative **causā** or **gratiā**, "for the sake of," is used to express purpose:

exemplī gratiā	for the sake of an example
honōris causā	for the sake of honor

Adjectives and Verbs Governing the Genitive. In addition to these clear categories, a number of adjectives and verbs regularly govern the genitive case. It is best to learn these occurrences as you learn the words, since these cases are not easily categorized. There are, however, some indications to watch out for:

1. Adjectives containing the ideas of desire, knowledge, memory, power, sharing, guilt, and their opposites will govern the genitive:

memorem vestrī, oblītum **suī**	mindful *of you*, forgetful *of himself*
insōns **culpae**	innocent of *guilt*

2. Some adjectives of likeness, nearness, or belonging, which ordinarily govern the dative case, will govern a possessive genitive when these adjectives are used as nouns. Most notable here is **similis**, **simile**:

Dominī similis est.	He is *like* his *master*. (He is his master's likeness.)

Other adjectives in this category are **amīcus**, **inimīcus**, **commūnis**, **pār**, **proprius** (regularly governs the possessive genitive), **sacer** and **vīcīnus**.

3. Verbs of remembering and forgetting may govern either the accusative or the genitive:

Multa ab aliīs audīta meminērunt.	They remember *many things* which they heard from others.
Nec mē meminisse pigēbit **Elissae**.	Nor shall I feel displeasure remembering *Elissa*.

4. Verbs of reminding take the accusative of the person and the genitive of the thing:

Catilīna admonēbat **alium egestātis**, **alium cupiditātis suae**.
Catiline reminded *the one of his need*, *the other of his greed*.

If the thing of which one is being reminded, however, is expressed by a neuter pronoun, the thing will also be in the accusative (see Accusative of Inner Object, above):

Eōs **hōc** moneō.	I warn them *of this*. (I give them this warning.)

5. Verbs of accusing, condemning, and acquitting take the genitive of the charge or penalty:

Illī damnātī sunt **caedis**.	They were condemned *for homicide*.	(charge)
Pecūniae damnātī sunt.	They were condemned *to pay money*.	(penalty)
Arguit tē **furtī**.	He accuses you *of theft*.	(charge)

6. Verbs of feeling take the genitive of the object which arouses the feeling:

> Miserēre **animī** nōn digna ferentis.
> Pity *the soul* that suffers unworthy things.

The impersonal verbs, **miseret**, **paenitet**, **piget**, **pudet**, and **taedet**, take the genitive of the thing causing the feeling, and the accusative of the person feeling the emotion:

> Miseret deōs **animī** nōn digna **ferentis**.
> The gods pity *the soul that suffers* unworthy things.
>
> **Fratris** me pudet pigetque.
> *My brother* makes me ashamed and displeased.

Scrībenda

A. Identify the kind of genitive underlined, and then translate the sentence.

1. Vīve memor lētī.
2. Valē nostrī memor.
3. Possumne ego nātūrae nōn meminisse tuae?
4. Ita oblītus sum meī ut nesciam unde eam neque ubi eam. (**oblīvīscor**, **oblīvīscī**, **oblītus sum**, forget, be forgetful)
5. Ō crūdēlis Alexī, nōnne nostrī miserēre? (**Alexī**, vocative of Alexis)
6. Ō rem miseram, fīliō meō est amīca!
7. Miserārum est nōn amōrī dare lūdum.
8. Nōn omnis moriar, multaque pars meī vītābit Libitīnam. (**Libitīna**, **-ae** *f*, goddess of funerals)
9. Fēlīx est ille quī potuit rērum cognoscere causās.
10. Nōn enim probandī causā sed movendī gratiā dīcam.
11. Admittenda est hominum cuiusque modī multitūdo.
12. Num quid erit eiusmodī quod sine sumptū corrigī possit? (**sumptus**, **-ūs** *m*, expense; **corrigō**, **-ere**, correct)
13. Dominus putat meam operam esse parvī pretiī. (**pretium**, **-ī** *n*, price, value)
14. Dum nē ob male facta peream, id esse parvī putō.
15. Nōn similis virgo illa est virginum nostrārum, quās matrēs student dīmissīs umerīs esse, vinctō pectore, ut gracilēs sint. (**dīmissus**, **-a**, **-um**, drooping; **vinctō pectore**, with bound breast)
16. Neque aqua aquae neque lac est lactis similius quam hic tuī est. (**lac**, **lactis** *n*, milk)
17. Iam tibi formae, iamque est tibi cūra placendī.
18. Ego contemptūs essem patientior huius, sī fugerēs omnēs. (**contemptus**, **-ūs** *m*, scorn, disdain)
19. Māter stetit, fīliō vīsō, et alicuius cognoscentis similis fuit.

20. Alfene, iam tē nōn miseret, dūre, tuī dulcis amīcī? Nec facta impia fallācum hominum caelicolīs placent. Sī tū oblītus es, at dī meminērunt, meminit Fidēs, quae tē ut paeniteat postmodo factī faciet tuī. (**Alfenus**, **-ī** *m*, a proper name; **fallax**, **-ācis**, deceptive; **caelicola**, **-ae** *m* or *f*, inhabitant of heaven; a god. **postmodo**, adv., afterwards; **oblīvīscor**, **oblīvīscī**, **oblītus sum**, forget)
21. Sīsyphus est damnātus longī labōris. Linquenda est terra et domus et placēns uxor, neque hārum quās colis arborum tē praeter invīsās cupressōs ūlla brevem dominum sequētur. (**Sīsyphus**, **-ī** *m*; **invīsus**, **-a**, **-um**, hateful; **cupressus**, **-ī** *f*, cypress tree, used at funerals; **damnō**, **-āre** + gen., condemn (to); **linquō**, **-ere** = **relinquō**, **-ere**)

B. Translate into Latin:

1. Are you ashamed to be one of my friends?
2. The teacher made the students study literature full of bad examples.
3. What kind of father would cause the destruction of his own child?
4. I don't care at all what sort of life she leads.
5. For the father's sake, the sons were permitted to return home.

Verba tenenda

Verbs

cubō, **-āre**, **-uī**, **-itus** recline, lie down
emō, **-ere**, **ēmī**, **emptus** buy, purchase
fodiō, **-ere**, **fōdī**, **fossus** pierce; dig; dig away
habitō, **-āre**, **-āvī**, **-ātus** live in; inhabit; dwell
ignōrō, **-āre**, **-āvī**, **-ātus** have no knowledge of; fail to recognize
oblīvīscor, **oblīvīscī**, **oblītus sum** (+ gen.) forget, be forgetful
opīnor, **-ārī**, **-ātus sum** hold as an opinion; think, believe
vendō, **-ere**, **-didī**, **-ditus** sell
volitō, **-āre**, **-āvī**, **-ātus** fly about; fly to and fro, flutter about

Nouns

argentum, **-ī** *n* silver; money
aurum, **-ī** *n* gold; money
campus, **-ī** *m* field, plain; an even, flat place
carmen, **-inis** *n* song; poem
somnus, **-ī** *m* sleep; **in somnīs**: in sleep (with reference to dreams)
somnium, **-ī** *n* dream

Adjectives

improbus, **-a**, **-um** improper; shameless; unreasonable
stultus, **-a**, **-um** foolish, stupid
vīlis, **-e** cheap, inexpensive; worthless

Adverbs

repentē suddenly
vix scarcely

Legenda

The Roman Experience (6): Life in the City

The center of Roman civic life was the Forum, a public square in the heart of the city. Here Romans conducted official business, emperors dedicated monuments, and public and private personages from all ranks came for their various purposes. Surrounding the Forum were tall, closely constructed living quarters, so close, Martial tells us, you could reach out the window and touch your next door neighbor. In this chapter we see a collection of characters, including some encountered in earlier chapters, that one might meet in the great city.

1. The poet Martial, who lived in Rome during the first century A.D., gently teases his neighbor Novius, who lives very close by, but whom Martial never gets to see.

Vīcīnus meus est manūque tangī
dē nostrīs Novius * potest fenestrīs *.
quis nōn invideat mihi putetque
hōrīs omnibus esse mē beātum,
iunctō cui liceat fruī sodāle * ?
Tam longē est mihi quam Terentiānus *,
quī nunc Nīliacam * regit Syēnen *.
Nōn convīvere *, nec vidēre,
nōn audīre licet, nec urbe tōtā
quisquam est tam prope tam proculque nōbīs.
Migrandum * est mihi longius vel illī.
Vīcīnus Noviō * vel inquilīnus *
sit, sī quis Novium * vidēre nōn vult.

(Martial 1.86)

2. At Trimalchio's lavish dinner party, the guests begin exchanging drunken insults and boasts.

"Quid rīdēs", inquit, "vervēx * ? An tibi nōn placent lautitiae * dominī meī? Tū enim beātior es et vīvere melius solēs. Nōn mehercule̅s soleō

2, 12, 13: **Novius**, **-ī** *m* a proper name
2: **fenestra**, **-ae** *f* window
5: **sodālis**, **-is** *m* or *f* a mate, comrade, friend
6: **Terentiānus**, **-i** *m* governor of **Syēnē**, in Egypt, (modern Aswan) (**Syēnen**, acc.)
7: **Nīliacus**, **-a**, **-um** on the River Nile
8: **convīvō**, **-ere** dine together
11: **migrō**, **-āre** move (from a house), emigrate
12: **inquilīnus**, **-ī** *m* a tenant, lodger

1: **vervēx**, **vervēcis** *m* a castrated male sheep: a term of abuse for a stupid person: "mutton-head," "jerk"
lautitia, **-ae** *f* elegance, luxury

cito fervēre *, sed in mollī carne * vermēs * nascuntur. Rīdet. Quid habet quod rīdeat? Num pater tuus fētum * ēmit lāmnā * ? Eques * Rōmānus es: et ego rēgis fīlius. 'Quārē ergō servīvistī?' Quia ipse mē dedī in servitūtem * et māluī cīvis Rōmānus esse quam tribūtārius *. Et nunc spērō mē sīc vīvere, ut nēminī iocus * sim. Homō inter hominēs sum, capite apertō * ambulō; assem * aerārium * nēminī dēbeō; nēmō mihi in forō dīxit 'redde quod dēbēs.' Vīgintī ventrēs * pascō * et canem; contubernālem * meam redēmī*, nē quis in sinū * illīus manūs tergēret * ; mīlle dēnāriōs * prō eius capite solvī. Spērō, sīc moriar, ut mortuus nōn ērubēscam *.

(After Petronius, Satyricon *57)*

3. The slave Tranio tries to keep Philolaches' father, Theopropides, from entering his house until the party within can be disbanded. Theopropides begins to believe that he has made a bad investment in real estate.

TRANIO: Tetigistīne forēs * ? Occīdistī * hercle omnēs tuōs.
Metuō tē atque istōs expiāre * ut possīs. . . .
Aedēs nē tangās. Tange quoque terram. . . .
THEOPROPIDES: Loquere, quid ita? nōn intellegō.
TRAN: Scelus, inquam, factum est iam diū, antīquum et vetus.
THEO: Quid istud est scelus? aut quis id fēcit?
TRAN: Hospēs necāvit hospitem captum manū;—
Iste, ut opīnor, quī hās tibi aedēs vendidit.
Postquam tuus nātus rediit ā cēnā domum,
abīmus omnēs cubitum. . . .
Atque ille clāmat repentē maximē.

3: **ferveō, -ēre** be intensely hot; be angry
carō, carnis *f* flesh (of animals)
vermis, -is *m* worm, maggot
4: **fētus, -ūs** *m* offspring
lām[i]na, -ae *f* a thin sheet of metal; money, cash
eques, equitis *m* one who rides on horseback; a member of the equestrian order: i.e., a person having the property to qualify for membership in this class
5–6: **servitūs, -tūtis** *f* servitude, slavery
6: **tribūtārius, -a, -um** one who pays taxes (as a provincial)
7: **iocus, -ī** *m* joke
apertus, -a, -um uncovered; not concealed
8: **as, assis** *m* a copper coin
aerārius, -a, -um made of copper
9: **venter, ventris** *m* stomach, belly
pascō, -ere feed, pasture
contubernālis, -is *m* or *f* a slave's "mate" (having the relationship but not the legal status of husband or wife)
10: **redimō, -ere, -ēmī, -emptus** purchase, buy the release (of someone) from slavery.
sinus, -ūs *m* the part of the garment that covers the breast
tergeō, -ēre wipe, rub clean, polish
dēnārius, dēnāriī *m* a silver coin equal to ten **assēs**
11: **ērubēscō, -ere** blush for shame

1: **foris, -is** *f* door
occīdō, -ere, occīdī, occīsus cause the death of, kill
2: **expiō, -āre** make atonement for

THEO: Quis erat homō? An nātus meus?
TRAN: st! tacē, audī modo.
Inquit vēnisse illum in somnīs ad sē mortuum.
. . . Inquit illum hōc modō sibi dīxisse
mortuum esse:
'Ego trānsmarīnus * hospēs sum Diapontius *.
Hīc habitō, haec mihi data est habitātiō *.
Nam mē Accheruntem * recipere Orcus * nōluit,
quia praematurē * vītā egeō. Per fidem
dēceptus * sum: hospēs mē hic necāvit isque mē
condidit insepultum * clam * in hīs aedibus,
scelestus *, aurī causā. Nunc tū hinc ēmigrā *.
scelestae * hae sunt aedēs, impia est habitātiō *.'
Quae hīc mōnstra fiunt annō vix possum loquī.

(After Plautus, Mostellaria *463–504)*

4. When all mortal creatures sleep, do they retain their peculiar quirks and ambitions? Petronius, author of the *Satyricon*, offers a commonly held view about the persistence of the individual personality. The poem is in dactylic hexameter.

Somnia quae mentēs lūdunt volitantibus umbrīs,
nōn dēlūbra * de[ōr]um nec ab aethere * nūmina * mittunt,
sed sibi quisque facit. Nam cum prōstrāta * sopōre
urget * membra quiēs * et mēns sine pondere * lūdit,
quidquid lūce fuit tenebrīs * agit. Oppida * bellō
quī quatit * et flammīs miserandās * ēruit * urbēs,

17: **trānsmarīnus, -a, -um** belonging to a country overseas; "from across the sea"
Diapontius, -ī *m* a proper name (the Greek equivalent of **transmarīnus**)
18, 24: **habitātiō, -iōnis** *f* residence, lodging
19: **Accherūns, -ntis** *m* the Underworld
Orcus, -ī *m* ruler of the Underworld
20: **praematurē** (adv.) too soon
21: **dēcipiō, -ere, -cēpī, -ceptus** deceive
22: **insepultus, -a, -um** not buried with proper funeral rites
clam (adv.) secretly
23, 24: **scelestus, -a, -um = scelerātus**
23: **ēmigrō, -āre** move out

2: **dēlūbrum, -ī** *n* temple, shrine
aether, -eris *n* the air
nūmen, -inis *n* the divine powers
3: **prōsternō, -ere, -strāvī, -strātus** throw on the ground, prostrate
4: **urgeō, -ēre, ursī** push, force, impel
quiēs, quiētis *f* rest, repose, quiet
pondus, ponderis *n* weight
5: **tenebrae, -ārum** *f* darkness (of the night) (here, ablative of time)
oppidum, -ī *n* town
6, 12: **quatiō, -ere, ——, quassus** shake, cause to tremble
miserandus, -a, -um pitiable
ēruō, -ere, ēruī, ērūtus overthrow, destroy

tēla * videt versāsque aciēs * et fūnera * rēgum
atque exundantēs * prōfūsō sanguine campōs.
quī causās ōrāre solent, lēgēsque forumque
et pavidī * cernunt inclūsum chorte * tribūnal *.
Condit avārus * opēs * dēfossumque * invenit aurum.
Vēnātor * saltūs * canibus quatit *. Ēripit * undīs
aut premit ēversam * peritūrus nāvita * puppem *.
Scrībit amātōrī meretrix *, dat adultera * mūnus:
et canis in somnīs leporis * vestīgia lustrat *.
In noctis spatium miserōrum vulnera dūrant *.

(Petronius, 121 P.L.M.)

5. The poet bids farewell to his book of poems, which is about to be published. The poem is in elegiac meter.

Argīlētanās * māvīs habitāre tabernās *,
    cum tibi, parve liber, scrīnia * nostra vacent.
nescīs, heu, nescīs dominae fastīdia * Rōmae:
    crēde mihī, nimium Martia * turba * sapit *.

7: **tēlum**, **-ī** *n* weapon
aciēs, **aciēī** *f* the front of an army: the army drawn up in battle array
fūnus, **-eris** *n* funeral, burial
8: **exundō**, **-āre** overflow
10: **pavidus**, **-a**, **-um** trembling, fearful
c[o]hors, **c[o]hortis** *f* crowd, throng of attendants
tribūnal, **-ālis** *n* the raised platform on which the seats of magistrates were placed
11: **avārus**, **-a**, **-um** greedy; avaricious
opes, **opum** *f* pl. wealth, treasure
dē-fodiō, **-ere**, **dēfōdī**, **dēfossus** dig up
12: **vēnātor**, **-tōris** *m* hunter
saltus, **-ūs** *m* forest-pasture; woodland
ēripiō, **-ere**, **-ripuī**, **-reptus** snatch out, pull out
13: **ēvertō**, **-ere**, **ēvertī**, **ēversus** turn upside down
nāvita = **nauta**
puppis, **-is** *f* the stern (back) of a ship
14: **meretrīx**, **-trīcis** *f* prostitute; courtesan
adultera, **-ae** *f* paramour
15: **lepus**, **leporis** *m* a hare
lustrō, **-āre** go around, encircle, traverse
16: **dūrō**, **-āre** become hard; endure, continue to exist

---

1: **Argīlētanus**, **-a**, **-um** of the Argileturn, the name of a district of Rome which contained many booksellers' shops.
taberna, **-ae** *f* an inn or a shop
2: **scrīnium**, **-ī** *n* a case for papyrus-rolls in a bookshop or library
3: **fastīdium**, **-ī** *n* aversion; disdain; haughtiness
4: **Martius**, **-a**, **-um** Roman (The Romans believed they were descended from Mars, by way of Romulus)
turba, **-ae** *f* crowd, throng
sapiō, **-ere**, **sapiī**, —— be wise, intelligent; know

māiōrēs nusquam * rhonchī * : iuvenēsque senēsque
    et puerī nāsum * rhīnocerōtis * habent.
audieris cum grande * 'sophōs!' *, dum bāsia * iactās,
    ībis ab excussō * missus in astra sagō *,
sed tū nē totiēns * dominī patiāre litūrās *
    nēve notet lūsūs * tristis harundo * tuōs,
aetheriās *, lascīve *, cupīs volitāre per aurās * :
    ī, fuge; sed poterās tūtior esse domī.

(Martial 1.3)

Probanda XVI–XVIII

A. Deponent Verbs: The following verbs are all in the present tense, indicative mood. Translate each verb, and then write a complete synopsis of each verb, retaining the number and person of the verb given:

1. nascitur
2. sequitur
3. mīrātur
4. moreris
5. morāris
6. utiminī
7. hortāminī
8. prōgredimur
9. loquuntur
10. sequuntur

B. Translate the following sentences:

1. Multa patiētur.
2. Multa passī sunt.
3. Multī ibi mortuī sunt.
4. Illa vulnerāta moritūraque cum hoste loquī cōnāta est.

5: **nusquam** (adv.) nowhere
rhoncus, **-ī** *m* noisy discharge through the nostrils; a snort (of disdain)
6: **nāsus**, **-ī** *m* nose
rhīnocerōs, **-ōtis** *m* rhinocerus
7: **grandis**, **-e** great in degree; loud
'sophōs!' the Greek word meaning "wise"; an exclamation of applause: "bravo!"
bāsium, **-ī** *n* kiss
8: **excutiō**, **-ere**, **-cussī**, **-cussus** shake out, throw
sagum, **-ī** *n* a coarse woolen cloak, worn by soldiers, foreigners, etc.
9: **totiēns** (adv.) so many times
litūra, **-ae** *f* the smearing of wax on a writing-tablet (in order to make a deletion); an erasure
10: **lūsus**, **-ūs** *m* play, game, amusement
harundo, **-inis** *f* a reed pen
11: **aetherius**, **-a**, **-um** of or in the air above
lascīvus, **-a**, **-um** playful, frisky, frolicsome
aura, **-ae** *f* air, breeze

5. Quis nostrum id patiātur? Num quis id patiētur?
6. Senātus pōpulusque Rōmānus prōhibuit nē quis cum istō virō loquerētur.
7. Nōn dubitō quīn hostis tibi nocēre velit.
8. Hostis tibi nocēre nōn dubitābit.
9. Sequitur ut plurimī hominēs sīderibus regantur, quia crēdunt sē eīs regī posse. Sīderibus parent quia sīdera omnia regant. Sīdera autem nōn omnia regunt.
10. Utinam omnibus meliōribus ūtāris. Nē cāsūs pēiōrēs patiāre.
11. Metuimus ut tūtus Rōmam ingrediāris. Vereor nē hostis hanc urbem ingressūrus sit. Hostibus ingressīs, urbs cadet.
12. Nihil mē tam dēterrēbit quīn hostēs igne ferrōque sequar.
13. Vōbis fidēlibus, numquam timēbō nē hostis mihi noceat.
14. Nihil me impediēt quōminus noxam facerēm.
15. Cum amīcīs singulīs locūta est.
16. Da mihi dextram iūrāque tē iste scelus numquam passūrum esse.
17. Sōle ortō, ipsa ē thalamō ēgredī incēpit.
18. Sōle nōndum occisō, hostibus sequentibus nocēre cōnābitur.
19. It fāma per urbem. Fēminam morī cupientem piget caelum vidēre.
20. Pater, mihi ignosce mēque miserēre huius mortis!

C. Vocabulary. Match the verbal forms on the right with their first principal part in the left-hand column:

absum	abit, abes, absēns, abeuntēs, abiēns,
auferō	ablātus, attulī, allātūrus,
abeō	aderit, abierit, aditūrus, abeundus,
adsum	āfutūrus, affutūrus
afferō	
adeō	

Probanda XVI–XVIII: Key

A. Deponent Verbs.

1. nascitur: he is being born; nascēbātur, nascētur, nātus est, nātus erat, nātus erit; subjunctive: nascātur, nascerētur, nātus sit, nātus esset.
2. sequitur: he follows; sequēbātur, sequētur, secūtus est, secūtus erat, secūtus erit; subjunctive: sequātur, sequerētur, secūtus sit, secūtus esset.
3. mīrātur: he admires; mīrābātur, mīrābitur, mīrātus est, mīrātus erat, mīrātus erit; subjunctive: mīrētur, mīrārētur, mīrātus sit, mīrātus esset.
4. moreris: you are dying; moriēbāris, moriēris, mortuus es, mortuus erās, mortuus eris; subjunctive: moriāris, morerēris, mortuus sīs, mortuus essēs.
5. morāris: you delay; morābāris, morāberis, morātus es, morātus erās, morātus eris; subjunctive: morēris, morārēris, morātus sīs, morātus essēs.
6. ūtiminī: you (pl.) use: ūtēbāminī, ūtēminī, ūsī estis, ūsī erātis, ūsī eritis; subjunctive: ūtāminī, ūterēminī, ūsī sītis, ūsī essētis.
7. hortāminī: you (pl.) urge/encourage: hortābāminī, hortābiminī; hortātī estis, hortātī erātis, hortātī eritis; subjunctive: hortēminī, hortārēminī, hortātī sītis, hortātī essētis.
8. prōgredimur: we go forth; prōgrediēbāmur, prōgrediēmur, prōgressī sumus, prōgressī erāmus, prōgressī erimus; subjunctive: prōgrediāmur, prōgrederēmur, prōgressī sīmus, prōgressī essēmus.

9. loquuntur: they speak; loquēbantur, loquentur, locūtī sunt, locūtī erant, locūtī erint; subjunctive: loquantur, loquerentur, locūtī sint, locūtī essent.
10. sequuntur: they follow; sequēbantur, sequentur, secūtī sunt, secūtī erant, secūtī erint; subjunctive: sequantur, sequerentur, secūtī sint, secūtī essent.

B. Translations:

1. He will endure/suffer many things.
2. They endured/suffered many things.
3. Many men died there.
4. She, wounded and about to die, tried to speak with the stranger/her enemy.
5. Which one of us (partitive genitive) would endure that? Surely no one (**quis** = **aliquis**) will endure that?
6. The Senate and the Roman People prevented anyone from speaking with that man.
7. I do not doubt that the enemy wishes to harm you.
8. The enemy will not hesitate to harm you.
9. It follows that most men are ruled by the stars because (in fact) they believe they can be ruled by them. They obey the stars because (allegedly) the stars rule everything. But (in fact) the stars do not rule everything.
10. May you enjoy all the better things. May you not suffer worse misfortunes.
11. We fear you may not enter Rome safe(ly). I fear the enemy is going to enter this city. Once (when) the enemy has entered (ablative absolute), the city will fall.
12. Nothing will so hinder me that I will not pursue the enemy with fire and sword/Nothing will prevent me from pursuing . . .
13. If you (pl.) are faithful, I will never fear that the enemy will harm me.
14. Nothing will prevent me from doing harm.
15. She spoke with her friends one by one (**singulīs**).
16. Give me your right hand and swear that you will never endure (tolerate) that crime.
17. When the sun had arisen, she herself began to leave her bedchamber.
18. When the sun has not yet set, he will try to injure the pursuing enemy.
19. Rumor goes through the city. Seeing the sky disgusts the woman who is longing to die.
20. Father, forgive me and pity me this death (of mine)!

C.

absum:	abes, absēns, āfutūrus
aufer:	ablātus
abeō:	abit, abeuntes, abiēns, abierit, abeundus
adsum:	aderit, affutūrus
affer:	attulī, allātūrus
adeō:	aditūrus

Appendix A: Parts of Speech

The parts of speech in English are the *noun*, *adjective*, *pronoun*, *verb*, *adverb*, *preposition*, *conjunction*, and *interjection*.

1. A *noun* names a person, place, thing, or abstract quality, action, or idea. A proper noun is the name of a particular person or thing. A common noun is a name shared by an entire class of persons or things. An abstract noun names a quality, idea, state, or action, as opposed to some material person or thing. A collective noun names a group of persons or things as a single unit. A substantive is a noun or any word or group of words used as a noun. A *gerund* is a verbal noun, active in meaning, and ending with -ing: "doing, singing, working."

2. A *pronoun* is a word that substitutes for the name of a person or thing. The antecedent is the noun for which the pronoun is a substitute. The personal pronouns in English are "I," "you," "he," "she," "it," "we," and "they," and their inflected forms. The relative pronouns are "who," "which," and "that," and their inflected forms. The interrogative pronouns are "who?" "what?" and "which?" The reflexive pronouns include "myself," "yourself," etc., pronouns referring back to the subject of the clause in which they appear. The demonstrative pronouns are "this," "that," "these," and "those," and the indefinite pronouns are those without a clear antecedent, such as "someone," "something," etc.

3. An *adjective* describes, limits, qualifies, or modifies the meaning of a noun or its substitute. A participle is a verbal adjective: a "*piercing* cry," "a *crumbled* wall."

4. A *verb* denotes an action, process, or state of being. It makes a statement, asks a question, or makes a command. A verb has a subject, which is expressed in the first person singular ("I") or plural ("we"), the second person singular ("you") or plural ("you"), or the third person singular ("he, she, it") or plural ("they"). The *number* of a verb, referring to its subject, is either singular or plural.

The *tense* of a verb indicates the time of the action (present, past, or future).

The *voice* of a verb is active or passive. In an active verb, the subject of the verb is the agent of the action. In a passive verb the subject of the verb is the recipient of the action.

The *mood* of a verb refers to the manner by which the action of the verb is indicated. The *indicative mood* signals an objective statement of fact. The *imperative mood* commands that the action be done. The *subjunctive mood* conveys a number of nuances, including purpose, result, wish, possibility, and command.

Transitive verbs are verbs that can take a direct object ("sing a *song*"). An *intransitive* verb is one that cannot take a direct object, either because of meaning (e.g., "go," "come") or because it is merely functioning as a connective between two words ("be," "seem," "become"). This latter verb is known as a *copula*.

A *participle* is an adjective formed from a verb. Like a verb, it has voice (active or passive) and tense (present, future, or past).

5. An *adverb* limits, qualifies, or modifies the meaning of a verb: "He sings *well*." "The poet sang *loudly*." In English, adverbs frequently end with "-ly," but not always.

6. A *conjunction* is a connecting word. Examples of conjunctions are "and," "but," "although," and "neither . . . nor." The conjunction can carry relatively little meaning beyond its connective purpose, or it can show a wide range of reactions to what has preceded or will follow: "He tried to sing, *but* his voice failed" shows the adversative or opposing force of "but." In "he began to sing *and* dance," on the other hand, "and" is a simple connective between the two verbs.

7. A *preposition* is a word governing a noun or pronoun, known as the "object" of the preposition. It shows the relationship between the object of the preposition and some other part of the sentence. The preposition is usually placed before its object, and thus its name (from **prae** + **positus**, "placed before").

8. An *interjection* expresses an emotional response or gives emphasis. It generally has no grammatical connection with the other words of the sentence.

Appendix B: Summary of Verb Forms

PRINCIPAL PARTS

First conjugation:	**amō, amāre, amāvī, amātus** love
Second conjugation:	**teneō, tenēre, tenuī, tentus** hold
Third conjugation:	**dūcō, dūcere, dūxī, ductus** lead
*Third -**iō**:*	**capiō, capere, cēpī, captus** seize
Fourth conjugation:	**audiō, audīre, audīvī, audītus** hear, listen

INDICATIVE ACTIVE

PRESENT

amō	teneō	dūcō	capiō	audiō
amās	tenēs	dūcis	capis	audīs
amat	tenet	dūcit	capit	audit
amāmus	tenēmus	dūcimus	capimus	audīmus
amātis	tenētis	dūcitis	capitis	audītis
amant	tenent	dūcunt	capiunt	audiunt

IMPERFECT

amābam	tenēbam	dūcēbam	capiēbam	audiēbam
amābās	tenēbās	dūcēbās	capiēbās	audiēbās
amābat	tenēbat	dūcēbat	capiēbat	audiēbat
amābāmus	tenēbāmus	dūcēbāmus	capiēbāmus	audiēbāmus
amābātis	tenēbātis	dūcēbātis	capiēbātis	audiēbātis
amābant	tenēbant	dūcēbant	capiēbant	audiēbant

FUTURE

amābō	tenēbō	dūcam	capiam	audiam
amābis	tenēbis	dūcēs	capiēs	audiēs
amābit	tenēbit	dūcet	capiet	audiet
amābimus	tenēbimus	dūcēmus	capiēmus	audiēmus
amābitis	tenēbitis	dūcētis	capiētis	audiētis
amābunt	tenēbunt	dūcent	capient	audient

PERFECT

amāvī	tenuī	dūxī	cēpī	audīvī
amāvistī	tenuistī	dūxistī	cēpistī	audīvistī
amāvit	tenuit	dūxit	cēpit	audīvit
amāvimus	tenuimus	dūximus	cēpimus	audīvimus
amāvistis	tenuistis	dūxistis	cēpistis	audīvistis
amāvērunt	tenuērunt	dūxērunt	cēpērunt	audīvērunt

PLUPERFECT

amāveram	tenueram	dūxeram	cēperam	audīveram
amāverās	tenuerās	dūxerās	cēperās	audīverās
amāverat	tenuerat	dūxerat	cēperat	audīverat
amāverāmus	tenuerāmus	dūxerāmus	cēperāmus	audīverāmus
amāverātis	tenuerātis	dūxerātis	cēperātis	audīverātis
amāverant	tenuerant	dūxerant	cēperant	audīverant

FUTURE PERFECT

amāverō	tenuerō	dūxerō	cēperō	audīverō
amāveris	tenueris	dūxeris	cēperis	audīveris
amāverit	tenuerit	dūxerit	cēperit	audīverit
amāverimus	tenuerimus	dūxerimus	cēperimus	audīverimus
amāveritis	tenueritis	dūxeritis	cēperitis	audīveritis
amāverint	tenuerint	dūxerint	cēperint	audīverint

Subjunctive Active

PRESENT

amem	teneam	dūcam	capiam	audiam
amēs	teneās	dūcās	capiās	audiās
amet	teneat	dūcat	capiat	audiat
amēmus	teneāmus	dūcāmus	capiāmus	audiāmus
amētis	teneātis	dūcātis	capiātis	audiātis
ament	teneant	dūcant	capiant	audiant

IMPERFECT

amārem	tenērem	dūcerem	caperem	audīrem
amārēs	tenērēs	dūcerēs	caperēs	audīrēs
amāret	tenēret	dūceret	caperet	audīret
amārēmus	tenērēmus	dūcerēmus	caperēmus	audīrēmus
amārētis	tenērētis	dūcerētis	caperētis	audīrētis
amārent	tenērent	dūcerent	caperent	audīrent

PERFECT

amāverim	tenuerim	dūxerim	cēperim	audīverim
amāveris	tenueris	dūxeris	cēperis	audīveris
amāverit	tenuerit	dūxerit	cēperit	audīverit
amāverimus	tenuerimus	dūxerimus	cēperimus	audīverimus
amāveritis	tenueritis	dūxeritis	cēperitis	audīveritis
amāverint	tenuerint	dūxerint	cēperint	audīverint

PLUPERFECT

amāvissem	tenuissem	dūxissem	cēpissem	audīvissem
amāvissēs	tenuissēs	dūxissēs	cēpissēs	audīvissēs
amāvisset	tenuisset	dūxisset	cēpisset	audīvisset
amāvissēmus	tenuissēmus	dūxissēmus	cēpissēmus	audīvissēmus
amāvissētis	tenuissētis	dūxissētis	cēpissētis	audīvissētis
amāvissent	tenuissent	dūxissent	cēpissent	audīvissent

Imperative Active

		PRESENT			
Second sing.	amā	tenē	dūc[1]	cape	audī
Second pl.	amāte	tenēte	dūcite	capite	audīte
		FUTURE			
Second sing.	amātō	tenētō	dūcitō	capitō	audītō
Third sing.	amātō	tenētō	dūcitō	capitō	audītō
Second pl.	amātōte	tenētōte	dūcitōte	capitōte	audītōte
Third pl.	amantō	tenentō	dūcuntō	capiuntō	audiuntō

Indicative Passive

		PRESENT		
amor	teneor	dūcor	capior	audior
amāris (-re)	tenēris (-re)	dūceris (-re)	caperis (-re)	audīris (-re)
amātur	tenētur	dūcitur	capitur	audītur
amāmur	tenēmur	dūcimur	capimur	audīmur
amāminī	tenēminī	dūciminī	capiminī	audīminī
amantur	tenentur	dūcuntur	capiuntur	audiuntur
		IMPERFECT		
amābar	tenēbar	dūcēbar	capiēbar	audiēbar
amābāris (-re)	tenēbāris (-re)	dūcēbāris (-re)	capiēbāris (-re)	audiēbāris (-re)
amābātur	tenēbātur	dūcēbātur	capiēbātur	audiēbātur
amābāmur	tenēbāmur	dūcēbāmur	capiēbāmur	audiēbāmur
amābāminī	tenēbāminī	dūcēbāminī	capiēbāminī	audiēbāminī
amābantur	tenēbantur	dūcēbantur	capiēbantur	audiēbantur
		FUTURE		
amābor	tenēbor	dūcar	capiar	audiar
amāberis (-re)	tenēberis (-re)	dūcēris (-re)	capiēris (-re)	audiēris (-re)
amābitur	tenēbitur	dūcētur	capiētur	audiētur
amābimur	tenēbimur	dūcēmur	capiēmur	audiēmur
amābiminī	tenēbiminī	dūcēminī	capiēminī	audiēminī
amābuntur	tenēbuntur	dūcentur	capientur	audientur
		PERFECT		
amātus[2] sum	tentus sum	ductus sum	captus sum	audītus sum
amātus es	tentus es	ductus es	captus es	audītus es
amātus est	tentus est	ductus est	captus est	audītus est
amātī sumus	tentī sumus	ductī sumus	captī sumus	audītī sumus
amātī estis	tentī estis	ductī estis	captī estis	audītī estis
amātī sunt	tentī sunt	ductī sunt	captī sunt	audītī sunt

[1] **dūc** is irregular; the regular third conjugation second singular imperative ending is **-e** (e.g., **mitte**).

[2] The participial portion of all verbs in the perfect system agrees in number, gender, and case with the subject of the verb (e.g., **amātus**, **-a**, **-um sum**; **amātī**, **-ae**, **-a sumus**; **mīrātus**, **-a**, **-um sum**; **mīrātī**, **-ae**, **-a sumus**).

PLUPERFECT

amātus eram	tentus eram	ductus eram	captus eram	audītus eram
amātus erās	tentus erās	ductus erās	captus erās	audītus erās
amātus erat	tentus erat	ductus erat	captus erat	audītus erat
amātī erāmus	tentī erāmus	ductī erāmus	captī erāmus	audītī erāmus
amātī erātis	tentī erātis	ductī erātis	captī erātis	audītī erātis
amātī erant	tentī erant	ductī erant	captī erant	audītī erant

FUTURE PERFECT

amātus erō	tentus erō	ductus erō	captus erō	audītus erō
amātus eris	tentus eris	ductus eris	captus eris	audītus eris
amātus erit	tentus erit	ductus erit	captus erit	audītus erit
amātī erimus	tentī erimus	ductī erimus	captī erimus	audītī erimus
amātī eritis	tentī eritis	ductī eritis	captī eritis	audītī eritis
amātī erunt	tentī erunt	ductī erunt	captī erunt	audītī erunt

Subjunctive Passive

PRESENT

amer	tenear	dūcar	capiar	audiar
amēris (-re)	teneāris (-re)	dūcāris (-re)	capiāris (-re)	audiāris (-re)
amētur	teneātur	dūcātur	capiātur	audiātur
amēmur	teneāmur	dūcāmur	capiāmur	audiāmur
amēminī	teneāminī	dūcāminī	capiāminī	audiāminī
amentur	teneantur	dūcantur	capiantur	audiantur

IMPERFECT

amārer	tenērer	dūcerer	caperer	audīrer
amārēris (-re)	tenērēris (-re)	dūcerēris (-re)	caperēris (-re)	audīrēris (-re)
amārētur	tenērētur	dūcerētur	caperētur	audīrētur
amārēmur	tenērēmur	dūcerēmur	caperēmur	audīrēmur
amārēminī	tenērēminī	dūcerēminī	caperēminī	audīrēminī
amārentur	tenērentur	dūcerentur	caperentur	audīrentur

PERFECT

amātus[2] sim	tentus sim	ductus sim	captus sim	audītus sim
amātus sīs	tentus sīs	ductus sīs	captus sīs	audītus sīs
amātus sit	tentus sit	ductus sit	captus sit	audītus sit
amātī sīmus	tentī sīmus	ductī sīmus	captī sīmus	audītī sīmus
amātī sītis	tentī sītis	ductī sītis	captī sītis	audītī sītis
amātī sint	tentī sint	ductī sint	captī sint	audītī sint

PLUPERFECT

amātus essem	tentus essem	ductus essem	captus essem	audītus essem
amātus essēs	tentus essēs	ductus essēs	captus essēs	audītus essēs
amātus esset	tentus esset	ductus esset	captus esset	audītus esset
amātī essēmus	tentī essēmus	ductī essēmus	captī essēmus	audītī essēmus
amātī essētis	tentī essētis	ductī essētis	captī essētis	audītī essētis
amātī essent	tentī essent	ductī essent	captī essent	audītī essent

Imperative Passive

	PRESENT				
Second sing.	amāre	tenēre	dūcere	capere	audīre
Second pl.	amāminī	tenēminī	dūciminī	capiminī	audīminī
	FUTURE				
Second sing.	amātor	tenētor	dūcitor	capitor	audītor
Third sing.	amātor	tenētor	dūcitor	capitor	audītor
Second pl.	——	——	——	——	——
Third pl.	amantor	tenentor	dūcuntor	capiuntor	audiuntor

Infinitives

	ACTIVE	PASSIVE
Present	amāre	amārī
Perfect	amāvisse	amātus, -a, -um esse
Future	amātūrus, -a, -um esse	amātum īrī[3]
Present	tenēre	tenērī
Perfect	tenuisse	tentus, -a, -um esse
Future	tentūrus, -a, -um esse	tentum īrī
Present	dūcere	dūci
Perfect	dūxisse	ductus, -a, -um esse
Future	ductūrus, -a, -um esse	ductum īrī
Present	capere	capī
Perfect	cēpisse	captus, -a, -um esse
Future	captūrus, -a, -um esse	captum īrī
Present	audīre	audīrī
Perfect	audīvisse	audītus, -a, -um esse
Future	audītūrus, -a, -um esse	audītum īrī

Participles

	ACTIVE	PASSIVE
Present	amāns, amantis	——
Perfect	——	amātus, -a, -um
Future	amātūrus, -a, -um	amandus, -a, -um
Present	tenēns, tenentis	——
Perfect	——	tentus, -a, -um
Future	tentūrus, -a, -um	tenendus, -a, -um
Present	dūcēns, dūcentis	——
Perfect	——	ductus, -a, -um
Future	ductūrus, -a, -um	dūcendus, -a, -um
Present	capiēns, capientis	——
Perfect	——	captus, -a, -um
Future	captūrus, -a, -um	capiendus, -a, -um

[3] The future passive infinitive consists of the accusative supine plus the passive infinitive of **eō**, **īre**, "to go," and translates as "to be going to be loved," etc.

	ACTIVE	PASSIVE
Present	audiēns, audientis	——
Perfect	——	audītus, -a, um
Future	audītūrus, -a, um	audiendus, -a, um

Deponent Verbs

PRINCIPAL PARTS

First conjugation:	**mīror, mīrārī, mīrātus sum** admire
Second conjugation:	**mereor, merērī, meritus sum** deserve
Third conjugation:	**loquor, loquī, locūtus sum** speak
*Third -**iō**:*	**gradior, gradī, gressus sum** step, walk
Fourth conjugation:	**ordior, ordīrī, orsus sum** begin

Indicative

PRESENT

mīror	mereor	loquor	gradior	ordior
mīrāris (-re)	merēris (-re)	loqueris (-re)	graderis (-re)	ordīris (-re)
mīrātur	merētur	loquitur	graditur	ordītur
mīrāmur	merēmur	loquimur	gradimur	ordīmur
mīrāminī	merēminī	loquiminī	gradiminī	ordīminī
mīrantur	merentur	loquuntur	gradiuntur	ordiuntur

IMPERFECT

mirābar	merēbar	loquēbar	gradiēbar	ordiēbar
mirābāris (-re)	merēbāris (-re)	loquēbāris (-re)	gradiēbāris (-re)	ordiēbāris (-re)
mirābātur	merēbātur	loquēbātur	gradiēbātur	ordiēbātur
mirābāmur	merēbāmur	loquēbāmur	gradiēbāmur	ordiēbāmur
mirābāminī	merēbāminī	loquēbāminī	gradiēbāminī	ordiēbāminī
mirābantur	merēbantur	loquēbantur	gradiēbantur	ordiēbantur

FUTURE

mīrābor	merēbor	loquar	gradiar	ordiar
mīrāberis (-re)	merēberis (-re)	loquēris (-re)	gradiēris (-re)	ordiēris (-re)
mīrābitur	merēbitur	loquētur	gradiētur	ordiētur
mīrābimur	merēbimur	loquēmur	gradiēmur	ordiēmur
mīrābiminī	merēbiminī	loquēminī	gradiēminī	ordiēminī
mīrābuntur	merēbuntur	loquentur	gradientur	ordientur

PERFECT

mīrātus† sum	meritus sum	locūtus sum	gressus sum	orsus sum
mīrātus es	meritus es	locūtus es	gressus es	orsus es
mīrātus est	meritus est	locūtus es	gressus est	orsus est
mīrātī sumus	meritī sumus	locūtī sumus	gressī sumus	orsī sumus
mīrātī estis	meritī estis	locūtī estis	gressī estis	orsī estis
mīrātī sunt	meritī sunt	locūtī sunt	gressī sunt	orsī sunt

†See note[2], page 353.

PLUPERFECT

mīrātus eram	meritus eram	locūtus eram	gressus eram	orsus eram
mīrātus erās	meritus erās	locūtus erās	gressus erās	orsus erās
mīrātus erat	meritus erat	locūtus erat	gressus erat	orsus erat
mīrātī erāmus	meritī erāmus	locūtī erāmus	gressī erāmus	orsī erāmus
mīrātī erātis	meritī erātis	locūtī erātis	gressī erātis	orsī erātis
mīrātī erant	meritī erant	locūtī erant	gressī erant	orsī erant

FUTURE PERFECT

mīrātus erō	meritus erō	locūtus erō	gressus erō	orsus erō
mīrātus eris	meritus eris	locūtus eris	gressus eris	orsus eris
mīrātus erit	meritus erit	locūtus erit	gressus erit	orsus erit
mīrātī erimus	meritī erimus	locūtī erimus	gressī erimus	orsī erimus
mīrātī eritis	meritī eritis	locūtī eritis	gressī eritis	orsī eritis
mīrātī erunt	meritī erunt	locūtī erunt	gressī erunt	orsī erunt

SUBJUNCTIVE

PRESENT

mīrer	merear	loquar	gradiar	ordiar
mīrēris (-re)	mereāris (-re)	loquāris (-re)	gradiāris (-re)	ordiāris (-re)
mīrētur	mereātur	loquātur	gradiātur	ordiātur
mīrēmur	mereāmur	loquāmur	gradiāmur	ordiāmur
mīrēminī	mereāminī	loquāminī	gradiāminī	ordiāminī
mīrentur	mereantur	loquantur	gradiantur	ordiantur

IMPERFECT

mīrārer	merērer	loquerer	graderer	ordīrer
mīrārēris (-re)	merērēris (-re)	loquerēris (-re)	graderēris (-re)	ordīrēris (-re)
mīrārētur	merērētur	loquerētur	graderētur	ordīrētur
mīrārēmur	merērēmur	loquerēmur	graderēmur	ordīrēmur
mīrārēminī	merērēminī	loquerēminī	graderēminī	ordīrēminī
mīrārentur	merērentur	loquerentur	graderentur	ordīrentur

PERFECT

mīrātus[2] sim	meritus sim	locūtus sim	gressus sim	orsus sim
mīrātus sīs	meritus sīs	locūtus sīs	gressus sīs	orsus sīs
mīrātus sit	meritus sit	locūtus sit	gressus sit	orsus sit
mīrātī sīmus	meritī sīmus	locūtī sīmus	gressī sīmus	orsī sīmus
mīrātī sītis	meritī sītis	locūtī sītis	gressī sītis	orsī sītis
mīrātī sint	meritī sint	locūtī sint	gressī sint	orsī sint

PLUPERFECT

mīrātus essem	meritus essem	locūtus essem	gressus essem	orsus essem
mīrātus essēs	meritus essēs	locūtus essēs	gressus essēs	orsus essēs
mīrātus esset	meritus esset	locūtus esset	gressus esset	orsus esset
mīrātī essēmus	meritī essēmus	locūtī essēmus	gressī essēmus	orsī essēmus
mīrātī essētis	meritī essētis	locūtī essētis	gressī essētis	orsī essētis
mīrātī essent	meritī essent	locūtī essent	gressī essent	orsī essent

IMPERATIVE

			PRESENT		
Second sing.	mīrāre	merēre	loquere	gradere	ordīre
Second pl.	mīrāminī	merēminī	loquiminī	gradiminī	ordiminī
			FUTURE		
Second sing.	mīrātor	merētor	loquitor	graditor	ordītor
Third sing.	mīrātor	merētor	loquitor	graditor	ordītor
Second pl.	——	——	——	——	——
Third pl.	mīrantor	merentor	loquuntor	gradiuntor	ordiuntor

	PARTICIPLES		INFINITIVES
	ACTIVE	PASSIVE	
Present	mīrāns, mīrantis	——	mīrārī
Perfect	mīrātus, -a, -um	——	mīrātus, -a, -um esse
Future	mīrātūrus, -a, -um	mīrandus, -a, -um	mīrātūrus, -a, -um esse
Present	merēns, mērentis	——	merērī
Perfect	meritus, -a, -um	——	meritus, -a, -um esse
Future	meritūrus, -a, -um	merendus, -a, -um	meritūrus, -a, -um esse
Present	loquēns, loquentis	——	loquī
Perfect	locūtus, -a, -um	——	locūtus, -a, -um esse
Future	locūtūrus, -a, -um	loquendus, -a, -um	locūtūrus, -a, -um esse
Present	gradiēns, gradientis	——	gradī
Perfect	gressus, -a, -um	——	gressus, -a, -um esse
Future	gressūrus, -a, -um	gradiendus, -a, -um	gressūrus, -a, -um esse
Present	ordiēns, ordientis	——	ordīrī
Perfect	orsus, -a, -um	——	orsus, -a, -um esse
Future	orsūrus, -a, -um	ordiendus, -a, -um	orsūrus, -a, -um esse

IRREGULAR VERBS (1): **VOLŌ, NŌLŌ, MĀLŌ**

volō, **velle**, **voluī** wish, be willing
nōlō, **nōlle**, **nōluī** be unwilling
mālō, **mālle**, **māluī** prefer

INDICATIVE			SUBJUNCTIVE		
			PRESENT		
volō	nōlo	mālō	velim	nōlim	mālim
vīs	nōn vīs	māvīs	velīs	nōlīs	mālīs
vult	nōn vult	māvult	velit	nōlit	mālit
volumus	nōlumus	mālumus	velīmus	nōlīmus	mālīmus
vultis	nōn vultis	māvultis	velītis	nōlītis	mālītis
volunt	nōlunt	mālunt	velint	nōlint	mālint

IMPERFECT

volēbam	nōlēbam	mālēbam	vellem	nōllem	māllem
volēbās	nōlēbās	mālēbās	vellēs	nōllēs	māllēs
volēbat	nōlēbat	mālēbat	vellet	nōllet	māllet
volēbāmus	nōlēbāmus	mālēbāmus	vellēmus	nōllēmus	māllēmus
volēbātis	nōlēbātis	mālēbātis	vellētis	nōllētis	māllētis
volēbant	nōlēbant	mālēbant	vellent	nōllent	māllent

FUTURE

volam	nōlam	mālam	——
volēs	nōlēs	mālēs	
volet	nōlet	mālet	
volēmus	nōlēmus	mālēmus	
volētis	nōlētis	mālētis	
volent	nōlent	mālent	

PERFECT

voluī	nōluī	māluī	voluerim	nōluerim	māluerim
voluistī	nōluistī	māluistī	volueris	nōlueris	mālueris
voluit	nōluit	māluit	voluerit	nōluerit	māluerit
voluimus	nōluimus	māluimus	voluerimus	nōluerimus	māluerimus
voluistis	nōluistis	māluistis	volueritis	nōlueritis	mālueritis
voluērunt	nōluērunt	māluērunt	voluerint	nōluerint	māluerint

PLUPERFECT

volueram	nōlueram	mālueram	voluissem	nōluissem	māluissem
voluerās	nōluerās	māluerās	voluissēs	nōluissēs	māluissēs
voluerat	nōluerat	māluerat	voluisset	nōluisset	māluisset
voluerāmus	nōluerāmus	māluerāmus	voluissēmus	nōluissēmus	māluissēmus
voluerātis	nōluerātis	māluerātis	voluissētis	nōluissētis	māluissētis
voluerant	nōluerant	māluerant	voluissent	nōluissent	māluissent

FUTURE PERFECT

voluerō	nōluerō	māluerō	——
volueris	nōlueris	mālueris	
voluerit	nōluerit	māluerint	
voluerimus	nōluerimus	māluerimus	
volueritis	nōlueritis	mālueritis	
voluerint	nōluerint	māluerint	

IMPERATIVE

PRESENT

Second sing.	——	nōlī	——
Second pl.	——	nōlīte	——

FUTURE

Second sing.	——	nōlītō	——
Third sing.	——	nōlītō	——
Second pl.	——	nōlītōte	——
Third pl.	——	nōluntō	——

	Participles			Infinitives		
Present	volēns	nōlēns	——	velle	nōlle	mālle
Perfect	——	——	——	voluisse	nōluisse	māluisse

Irregular Verbs (2): **Sum, Possum, Fīō, Eō, Ferō**

sum, esse, fuī, futūrus be
possum, posse, potuī, —— be able
fīō, fierī, factus sum become
eō, īre, iī or **īvī, itus** go
ferō, ferre, tulī, lātus bring, carry, bear

Indicative

				Active	Passive
		PRESENT			
sum	possum	fīō	eō	ferō	feror
es	potes	fīs	īs	fers	fereris (-re)
est	potest	fit	it	fert	fertur
sumus	possumus	fīmus	īmus	ferimus	ferimur
estis	potestis	fītis	ītis	fertis	feriminī
sunt	possunt	fīunt	eunt	ferunt	feruntur
		IMPERFECT			
eram	poteram	fīēbam	ībam	ferēbam	ferebar
erās	poterās	fīēbās	ībās	ferēbās	ferēbāris (-re)
erat	poterat	fīēbat	ībat	ferēbat	ferēbātur
erāmus	poterāmus	fīēbāmus	ībāmus	ferēbāmus	ferēbāmur
erātis	poterātis	fīēbātis	ībātis	ferēbātis	ferēbāminī
erant	poterant	fīēbant	ībant	ferēbant	ferēbantur
		FUTURE			
erō	poterō	fīam	ībō	feram	ferar
eris	poteris	fīēs	ībis	ferēs	ferēris (-re)
erit	poterit	fīet	ībit	feret	ferētur
erimus	poterimus	fīēmus	ībimus	ferēmus	ferēmur
eritis	poteritis	fīētis	ībitis	ferētis	ferēminī
erunt	poterunt	fīent	ībunt	ferent	ferentur
		PERFECT			
fuī	potuī	factus† sum	iī, īvī[4]	tulī	lātus sum
fuistī	potuistī	factus es	īstī	tulistī	lātus es
fuit	potuit	factus est	iit	tulit	lātus est
fuimus	potuimus	factī sumus	iimus	tulimus	lātī sumus
fuistis	potuistis	factī estis	īstis	tulistis	lātī estis
fuērunt	potuērunt	factī sunt	iērunt	tulērunt	lātī sunt

[4] The perfect stem of **eō** is either **ī**- or, less often, **īv**-. Before -**s**, the **ī**- of the shorter perfect stem contracts with -**i**, becoming **ī**-, so that * **iisse** becomes **īsse**, * **iistī** becomes **īstī**, etc.
†See note[2], page 353.

PLUPERFECT

fueram	potueram	factus eram	ieram	tuleram	lātus eram
fuerās	potuerās	factus erās	ierās	tulerās	lātus erās
fuerat	potuerat	factus erat	ierat	tulerat	lātus erat
fuerāmus	potuerāmus	factī erāmus	ierāmus	tulerāmus	lātī erāmus
fuerātis	potuerātis	factī erātis	ierātis	tulerātis	lātī erātis
fuerant	potuerant	factī erant	ierant	tulerant	lātī erant

FUTURE PERFECT

fuerō	potuerō	factus erō	ierō	tulerō	lātus erō
fueris	potueris	factus eris	ieris	tuleris	lātus eris
fuerit	potuerit	factus erit	ierit	tulerit	lātus erit
fuerimus	potuerimus	factī erimus	ierimus	tulerimus	lātī erimus
fueritis	potueritis	factī eritis	ieritis	tuleritis	lātī eritis
fuerint	potuerint	factī erunt	ierint	tulerint	lātī erunt

Subjunctive

PRESENT				ACTIVE	PASSIVE
sim	possim	fīam	eam	feram	ferar
sīs	possīs	fīās	eās	ferās	ferāris (-re)
sit	possit	fīat	eat	ferat	ferātur
sīmus	possīmus	fīāmus	eāmus	ferāmus	ferāmur
sītis	possītis	fīātis	eātis	ferātis	ferāminī
sint	possint	fīant	eant	ferant	ferantur

IMPERFECT

essem	possem	fierem	īrem	ferrem	ferrer
essēs	possēs	fierēs	īrēs	ferrēs	ferrēris (-re)
esset	posset	fieret	īret	ferret	ferrētur
essēmus	possēmus	fierēmus	īrēmus	ferrēmus	ferrēmur
essētis	possētis	fierētis	īrētis	ferrētis	ferrēminī
essent	possent	fierent	īrent	ferrent	ferrentur

PERFECT

fuerim	potuerim	factus† sim	ierim	tulerim	lātus sim
fueris	potueris	factus sīs	ieris	tuleris	lātus sīs
fuerit	potuerit	factus sit	ierit	tulerit	lātus sit
fuerimus	potuerimus	factī sīmus	ierimus	tulerimus	lātī sīmus
fueritis	potueritis	factī sītis	ieritis	tuleritis	lātī sītis
fuerint	potuerint	factī sint	ierint	tulerint	lātī sint

PLUPERFECT

fuissem	potuissem	factus essem	īssem	tulissem	lātus essem
fuissēs	potuissēs	factus essēs	īssēs	tulissēs	lātus essēs
fuisset	potuisset	factus esset	īsset	tulisset	lātus esset
fuissēmus	potuissēmus	factī essēmus	īssēmus	tulissēmus	lātī essēmus
fuissētis	potuissētis	factī essētis	īssētis	tulissētis	lātī essētis
fuissent	potuissent	factī essent	īssent	tulissent	lātī essent

†See note[2], page 353.

			IMPERATIVE			
			PRESENT			
Second sing.	es	——	fī	ī	fer	ferre
Second pl.	este	——	fīte	īte	ferte	ferimini
			FUTURE			
Second sing.	estō	——	fītō	ītō	fertō	fertor
Third sing.	estō	——	——	ītō	fertō	fertor
Second pl.	estōte	——	——	ītōte	fertōte	——
Third pl.	suntō	——	——	euntō	feruntō	feruntor

	PARTICIPLES		INFINITIVES	
sum				
Present	——		esse	
Perfect	——		fuisse	
Future	futūrus, -a, -um		futūrus, -a, -um esse	
possum				
Present	potēns		posse	
Perfect	——		potuisse	
Future	——		——	
fīō				
Present	——		fierī	
Perfect	factus, -a, -um		factus, -a, -um esse	
Future	faciendus, -a, -um		factum īrī	
	ACTIVE	PASSIVE	ACTIVE	PASSIVE
ferō				
Present	ferēns	——	ferre	ferri
Perfect	——	lātus, -a, -um	tulisse	lātus, -a, -um esse
Future	lātūrus, -a, -um	ferendus, -a, -um	lātūrus, -a, -um esse	lātum īrī
eō				
Present	iēns, euntis	——	īre	īrī
Perfect	——	itus, -a, -um	īsse (īvisse)	——
Future	itūrus, -a, -um	eundus, -a, -um	itūrus, -a, -um esse	——

Appendix C: Nouns, Adjectives, Pronouns

Nouns

FIRST DECLENSION

	bestia, **bestiae** *f* *animal*		**nauta**, **nautae** *m* *sailor*	
	SING.	PL.	SING.	PL.
Nom.	bestia	bestiae	nauta	nautae
Gen.	bestiae	bestiārum	nautae	nautārum
Dat.	bestiae	bestiīs	nautae	nautīs
Acc.	bestiam	bestiās	nautam	nautās
Abl.	bestiā	bestiīs	nautā	nautīs
Voc.	bestia	bestiae	nauta	nautae

SECOND DECLENSION

	amīcus, **amīcī** *m* *friend*	**liber**, **librī** *m* *book*	**puer**, **puerī** *m* *boy*	**dōnum**, **dōnī** *n* *gift*
		SINGULAR		
Nom.	amīcus	liber	puer	dōnum
Gen.	amīcī	librī	puerī	dōnī
Dat.	amīcō	librō	puerō	dōnō
Acc.	amīcum	librum	puerum	dōnum
Abl.	amīcō	librō	puerō	dōnō
Voc.	amīce	liber	puer	dōnum
		PLURAL		
Nom.	amīcī	librī	puerī	dōna
Gen.	amīcōrum	librōrum	puerōrum	dōnōrum
Dat.	amīcīs	librīs	puerīs	dōnīs
Acc.	amīcōs	libros	puerōs	dōna
Abl.	amīcīs	librīs	puerīs	dōnīs
Voc.	amīcī	librī	puerī	dōna

THIRD DECLENSION

dux, **ducis** *m* *leader*	**lībertās**, **lībertātis** *f* *freedom*	**homō**, **hominis** *m* or *f* *human being*	**tempus**, **temporis** *n* *time*

	SINGULAR			
Nom.	dux	lībertās	homō	tempus
Gen.	ducis	lībertātis	hominis	temporis
Dat.	ducī	lībertātī	hominī	temporī
Acc.	ducem	lībertātem	hominem	tempus
Abl.	duce	lībertāte	homine	tempore

	PLURAL			
Nom.	ducēs	lībertātēs	hominēs	tempora
Gen.	ducum	lībertātum	hominum	temporum
Dat.	ducibus	lībertātibus	hominibus	temporibus
Acc.	ducēs	lībertātēs	hominēs	tempora
Abl.	ducibus	lībertātibus	hominibus	temporibus

PARISYLLABICS

	cīvis, **cīvis** *m* *citizen*		**aedēs**, **aedis** *f* *temple*	
	SING.	PL.	SING.	PL.
Nom.	cīvis	cīvēs	aedēs	aedēs
Gen.	cīvis	cīvium	aedis	aedium
Dat.	cīvī	cīvibus	aedī	aedibus
Acc.	cīvem	cīvēs (-īs)	aedem	aedēs (-īs)
Abl.	cīve	cīvibus	aede	aedibus

TWO CONSONANTS

	pars, **partis** *f* *part*		**dēns**, **dentis** *m* *tooth*	
	SING.	PL.	SING.	PL.
Nom.	pars	partēs	dēns	dentēs
Gen.	partis	partium	dentis	dentium
Dat.	partī	partibus	dentī	dentibus
Acc.	partem	partēs (-īs)	dentem	dentēs (-īs)
Abl.	parte	partibus	dente	dentibus

	NEUTER IN **-E**, **-AL**, **-AR**		IRREGULAR
	animal, **animālis** *n* *animal*	**mare**, **maris** *n* *sea*	**vīs**, **vīs** *f* *force*
	SINGULAR		
Nom.	animal	mare	vīs
Gen.	animālis	maris	(vīs) *
Dat.	animālī	marī	(vīs) *
Acc.	animal	mare	vim
Abl.	animālī	marī	vī

		PLURAL	
Nom.	animālia	maria	vīrēs
Gen.	animālium	marium	vīrium
Dat.	animālibus	maribus	vīribus
Acc.	animālia	maria	vīrēs (-īs)
Abl.	animālibus	maribus	vīribus

FOURTH DECLENSION

	versus, versūs *m* *row, line; verse*	**manus, manūs** *f* *hand, fist;* pl., *band of men*	**cornū, cornūs** *n* *horn*
		SINGULAR	
Nom.	versus	manus	cornū
Gen.	versūs	manūs	cornūs
Dat.	versuī	manuī	cornū
Acc.	versum	manum	cornū
Abl.	versū	manū	cornū
		PLURAL	
Nom.	versūs	manūs	cornua
Gen.	versuum	manuum	cornuum
Dat.	versibus	manibus	cornibus
Acc.	versūs	manūs	cornua
Abl.	versibus	manibus	cornibus

FIFTH DECLENSION

	rēs, reī *f* *thing*	**diēs, diēī** *m* *day*	**faciēs, faciēī** *f.* *appearance*
		SINGULAR	
Nom.	rēs	diēs	faciēs
Gen.	reī	diēī	faciēī
Dat.	reī	diēī	faciēī
Acc.	rem	diem	faciem
Abl.	rē	diē	faciē
		PLURAL	
Nom.	rēs	diēs	faciēs
Gen.	rērum	diērum	faciērum
Dat.	rēbus	diēbus	faciēbus
Acc.	rēs	diēs	faciēs
Abl.	rēbus	diēbus	faciēbus

Adjectives

FIRST AND SECOND DECLENSION

bonus, bona, bonus *good*

	SINGULAR			PLURAL		
	M.	F.	N.	M.	F.	N.
Nom.	bonus	bona	bonum	bonī	bonae	bona
Gen.	bonī	bonae	bonī	bonōrum	bonārum	bonōrum
Dat.	bonō	bonae	bonō	bonīs	bonīs	bonīs
Acc.	bonum	bonam	bonum	bonōs	bonās	bona
Abl.	bonō	bonā	bonō	bonīs	bonīs	bonīs
Voc.	bone	bona	bonum	bonī	bonae	bona

Third Declension

ADJECTIVES OF THREE ENDINGS:

celer, celeris, celere *swift*

	SINGULAR			PLURAL		
	M.	F.	N.	M.	F.	N.
Nom.	celer	celeris	celere	celerēs	celerēs	celeria
Gen.	celeris	celeris	celeris	celerium	celerium	celerium
Dat.	celerī	celerī	celerī	celeribus	celeribus	celeribus
Acc.	celerem	celerem	celere	celerēs (-īs)	celerēs (-īs)	celeria
Abl.	celerī	celerī	celerī	celeribus	celeribus	celeribus

ADJECTIVES OF TWO ENDINGS:

dulcis, dulce *sweet*

	SINGULAR		PLURAL	
	M. AND F.	N.	M. AND F.	N.
Nom.	dulcis	dulce	dulcēs	dulcia
Gen.	dulcis	dulcis	dulcium	dulcium
Dat.	dulcī	dulcī	dulcibus	dulcibus
Acc.	dulcem	dulce	dulcēs (-īs)	dulcia
Abl.	dulcī	dulcī	dulcibus	dulcibus

ADJECTIVES OF ONE ENDING:

sapiēns; sapientis *wise, knowing*

	SINGULAR		PLURAL	
	M. AND F.	N.	M. AND F.	N.
Nom.	sapiēns	sapiēns	sapientēs	sapientia
Gen.	sapientis	sapientis	sapientium	sapientium
Dat.	sapientī	sapientī	sapientibus	sapientibus
Acc.	sapientem	sapiēns	sapientēs (-īs)	sapientia
Abl.	sapientī	sapientī	sapientibus	sapientibus

Comparative

	SINGULAR		PLURAL	
	M. AND F.	N.	M. AND F.	N.
Nom.	dulcior	dulcius	dulciōrēs	dulciōra
Gen.	dulciōris	dulciōris	dulciōrum	dulciōrum
Dat.	dulciōrī	dulciōrī	dulciōribus	dulciōribus
Acc.	dulciōrem	dulcius	dulciōrēs	dulciōra
Abl.	dulciōre	dulciōre	dulciōribus	dulciōribus

IRREGULAR COMPARATIVE

	SINGULAR (NEUTER NOUN)	PLURAL M. AND F.	PLURAL N.
Nom.	plūs	plūrēs	plūra
Gen.	plūris	plūrium	plūrium
Dat.	——	plūribus	plūribus
Acc.	plūs	plūrēs	plūra
Abl.	plūre	plūribus	plūribus

Pronouns

PERSONAL PRONOUNS

	FIRST	SECOND	THIRD			REFLEXIVE
Nom.	egŏ̄	tū	is	ea	id	——
Gen.	meī	tuī	eius	eius	eius	suī
Dat.	mihĭ̄	tibĭ̄	eī	eī	eī	sibĭ̄
Acc.	mē	tē	eum	eam	id	sē
Abl.	mē	tē	eō	eā	eō	sē
Nom.	nōs	vōs	eī, iī	eae	ea	——
Gen.	nostrī nostrum	vestrī vestrum	eōrum	eārum	eōrum	suī
Dat.	nōbīs	vōbīs	eīs	eīs	eīs	sibĭ̄
Acc.	nōs	vōs	eōs	eās	eōs	sē
Abl.	nōbīs	vōbīs	eīs	eīs	eīs	sē

RELATIVE PRONOUNS

	SINGULAR			PLURAL		
	M.	F.	N.	M.	F.	N.
Nom.	quī	quae	quod	quī	quae	quae
Gen.	cuius	cuius	cuius	quōrum	quārum	quōrum
Dat.	cuī	cuī	cuī	quibus	quibus	quibus
Acc.	quem	quam	quod	quōs	quās	quae
Abl.	quō	quā	quō	quibus	quibus	quibus

INTERROGATIVE PRONOUNS

	SINGULAR		PLURAL		
	M. AND F.	N.	M.	F.	N.
Nom.	quis	quid	qui	quae	quae
Gen.	cuius	cuius	quōrum	quārum	quōrum
Dat.	cuī	cuī	quibus	quibus	quibus
Acc.	quem	quid	quōs	quās	quae
Abl.	quō	quō	quibus	quibus	quibus

Demonstrative Pronouns

hic *this* / **ille** *that*

SINGULAR

	M.	F.	N.	M.	F.	N.
Nom.	hic	haec	hoc	ille	illa	illud
Gen.	huius	huius	huius	illius	illius	illius
Dat.	huic	huic	huic	illī	illī	illī
Acc.	hunc	hanc	hoc	illum	illam	illud
Abl.	hōc	hāc	hōc	illō	illā	illō

PLURAL

	M.	F.	N.	M.	F.	N.
Nom.	hī	hae	haec	illī	illae	illa
Gen.	hōrum	hārum	hōrum	illōrum	illārum	illōrum
Dat.	hīs	hīs	hīs	illīs	illīs	illīs
Acc.	hōs	hās	haec	illōs	illās	illa
Abl.	hīs	hīs	hīs	illīs	illīs	illīs

iste *this, that, that . . . of yours*

	SINGULAR			PLURAL		
	M.	F.	N.	M.	F.	N.
Nom.	iste	ista	istud	istī	istae	ista
Gen.	istius	istius	istius	istōrum	istārum	istōrum
Dat.	istī	istī	istī	istīs	istīs	istīs
Acc.	istum	istam	istud	istōs	istās	ista
Abl.	istō	istā	istō	istīs	istīs	istīs

īdem *the same*

	SINGULAR			PLURAL		
	M.	F.	N.	M.	F.	N.
Nom.	īdem	eadem	idem	eīdem	eaedem	eadem
Gen.	eiusdem	eiusdem	eiusdem	eōrundem	eārundem	eōrundem
Dat.	eīdem	eīdem	eīdem	eīsdem	eīsdem	eīsdem
Acc.	eundem	eandem	idem	eōsdem	eāsdem	eadem
Abl.	eōdem	eādem	eōdem	eīsdem	eīsdem	eīsdem

Indefinite Adjectives/Pronouns

aliquis, **aliquid** someone, something; anyone, anything
nescioquis, **nescioquid** someone, something
quīcumque, **quaecumque**, **quodcumque** whoever, whatever
quīdam, **quaedam**, **quiddam** (*n* adj., **quoddam**) someone, something; a certain person, a certain thing
quisquam, **quidquam** (or **quicquam**) anyone, anything
quisque, **quaeque**, **quidquid** (*n* adj., **quodque**) each person, each thing
quisquis, **quidquid** whoever, whatever
quīvīs, **quaevīs**, **quidvīs** (*n* adj., **quodvīs**) anyone, anything
uterque, **utraque**, **utrumque** each person, each thing (of two)

Appendix D: Numerals

ROMAN	CARDINAL (USUALLY INDECLINABLE)	ORDINAL (DECLINED)	DISTRIBUTIVES (DECLINED)
I	ūnus, -a, -um	prīmus, -a, -um	singulī, -ae, -a
II	duo, duae, duo	secundus, -a, -um	bīnī, -ae, a
III	trēs, tria	tertius, -a, -um	ternī, -ae, -a
IV	quattuor	quārtus, -a, -um	quaternī, -ae, -a
V	quinque	quīntus, -a, -um	quīnī, -ae, -a
VI	sex	sextus, -a, -um	sēnī, -ae, -a
VII	septem	septimus, -a, -um	septēnī, -ae, -a
VIII	octo	octāvus, -a, -um	octōnī, -ae, -a
IX	novem	nōnus, -a, -um	novēnī, -ae, -a
X	decem	decimus, -a, -um	dēnī, -ae, -a
XI	undecim	undecimus, -a, -um	ūndēnī, -ae, -a
XII	duodecim	duodecimus, -a, -um	duodēnī, -ae, -a
XIII	tredecim (decem [et] trēs)	tertius decimus (decimus [et] tertius)	ternī denī
XIV	quattuordecim	quārtus decimus	quaternī dēnī
XV	quīndecim	quīntus decimus	quīnī dēnī
XVI	sēdecim	sextus decimus	sēnī dēnī
XVII	septendecim	septimus decimus	septēnī dēnī
XVIII	duodēvīgintī (octōdecim)	duodēvīcēsimus (octāvus decimus)[1]	octōnī dēnī (duodēvīcēnī)
XIX	ūndēvīgintī (novendecim)	ūndēvīcēsimus (nōnus decimus)	novēnī dēnī (ūndēvīcēnī)
XX	vīgintī	vīcēsimus (vīgēnsimus)	vīcēnī
XXI	vīgintī ūnus (ūnus et vīgintī) (etc.)	vīcēsimus prīmus (ūnus et vīcēsimus) (etc.)	vīcēnī singulī (etc.)
XXX	trīgintā	trīcēsimus	trīcēnī
XL	quadrāgintā	quadrāgēsimus	quadrāgēnī

[1]The forms in **-ēsimus** are often written **-ēnsimus**.

L	quīnquāgintā	quīnquāgēsimus	quīnquāgēnī
LX	sexāgintā	sexāgēsimus	sexāgēnī
LXX	septuāgintā	septuāgēsimus	septuāgēnī
LXXX	octōgintā	octōgēsimus	octōgēnī
XC	nōnāgintā	nōnāgēsimus	nōnāgēnī
C	centum	centēsimus	centēnī
CI	centum (et) ūnus (etc.)	centēsimus prīmus	centēnī singulī
CC	ducentī, -ae, a	ducentēsimus	ducēnī
CCC	trecentī, -ae, -a	trecentēsimus	trecēnī
CCCC	quadringentī, -ae, -a	quadringentēsimus	quadringēnī
D	quīngentī, -ae, -a	quīngentēsimus	quīngēnī
DC	sescentī, -ae, -a	sescentēsimus	sescēnī
DCC	septingentī, -ae, -a	septingentēsimus	septingēnī
DCCC	octingentī, -ae, -a	octingentēsimus	octingēnī
DCCCC	nōngentī, -ae, -a	nōngentēsimus	nōngēnī
M	mīlle	mīllēsimus	mīllēnī

Appendix E: Chronological Table

This table lists persons and events referred to in Legenda. Brackets indicate other major events and historical figures during this period. For more detail, see M. Cary and H. H. Scullard, *A History of Rome* (New York, 1975).

DATE	EVENT
753 B.C.	Approximate date of founding of Rome
c. 600	[Sappho on Lesbos]
509	Traditional date of expulsion of the last of the Tarquins; beginning of Roman Republic
404	[End of Peloponnesian War; fall of Athenian Empire]
341–270	Epicurus
323	[Death of Alexander the Great]
315–240	Aratus
311–298	Euhemerus
	THIRD AND SECOND CENTURIES B.C.
218–201	Second Punic War (Hannibal invades Italy)
c. 214–184	Comedies of Plautus
c. 190–159	Comedies of Terence
133	Tribunate and assassination of Tiberius Gracchus
123–2	Tribunates and assassination of Gaius Gracchus (Traditional beginning of decline of Roman Republic)
	FIRST CENTURY B.C.
	Early first-century poets: Catullus, Lucretius First-century historians: Julius Caesar, Sallust
81	Dictatorship of Sulla
70	Consulship of Pompey and Crassus
63	Consulship of Cicero
59	First consulship of Julius Caesar
58–51	Caesar's Gallic War
53	Crassus defeated and killed by Parthians
	Late first-century poets: Vergil, Horace, Propertius, Tibullus, Sulpicia, Ovid; Livy begins his history
49–45	Civil war; Caesar defeats Pompey
44	Caesar becomes perpetual dictator, is assassinated
42	Death of Brutus and Cassius after defeat at Philippi
31	Battle of Actium: Octavian and Agrippa defeat Antony and Cleopatra
27	Octavian becomes Augustus, rules empire 27 B.C.–A.D. 14

A.D.	FIRST CENTURY A.D.
c. 6	[Birth of Jesus]
	Early first-century poets: Manilius, Ovid; Livy writing history
14–37	Tiberius is emperor
c. 30–33	[Jesus is crucified]
37–41	Caligula is emperor
41–54	Claudius is emperor
	Late first-century authors: Seneca, Petronius, Juvenal, Quintilian, Pliny the Younger, Tacitus
54–68	Nero is emperor
68–69	Civil war; Galba, then Otho, then Vitellius is emperor
69–79	Vespasian is emperor
79–81	Titus is emperor
79	Pompeii and Herculaneum destroyed by eruption of Mt. Vesuvius
81–96	Domitian is emperor
96–98	Nerva is emperor
	SECOND CENTURY A.D.
98–117	Trajan is emperor
	Early second-century writers: Pliny, Suetonius, Tacitus, Juvenal [in Alexandria, the Greek astronomer Ptolemy]
117–138	[Hadrian is emperor]
	FOURTH CENTURY A.D.
	Fourth-century writers and grammarians: Jerome, Ausonius, Augustine, Donatus, Servius
324–330	[Byzantium becomes Constantinople]
	FIFTH CENTURY A.D.
	Fifth-century writers: Macrobius, Orosius, Boethius
404	[Ravenna becomes capital of the western empire]
410	[Capture of Rome by Alaric the Visigoth]
475–476	[Romulus Augustulus, last western emperor (at Ravenna)]
	SIXTH CENTURY A.D.
	Sixth-century writers: Priscian
527–565	[Justinian is emperor]
590–604	[Pope Gregory I the Great]
	SEVENTH CENTURY A.D.
	Seventh-century writers: Isidore of Seville, Bede
800	[Charlemagne becomes emperor]
	TENTH CENTURY A.D.
	Tenth-century writers: Hrotsvitha, Anselm
1204–1261	[Crusaders occupy Constantinople]
1225–1274	Thomas Aquinas
1400–1600	Renaissance in Italy and Western Europe
1453	[Fall of Constantinople to Ottoman Turks]
1473–1543	Copernicus
1564–1642	[Galileo]
1571–1630	[Kepler]

Appendix F: Proper Names

For more detailed information see the *Oxford Classical Dictionary* listings for each of the following.

Agrippa, Marcus Vipsanius, 63–12 B.C.; Roman statesman, general, engineer.

Alexandrian poetry Greek poetry composed between 300 B.C. and 30 B.C.; the term reflects the dominance of Alexandria during this period as the literary capital of the Greek world.

Antonius, Marcus (Mark Antony), 83–30 B.C.; Roman general and friend of Julius Caesar.

Aquinas, Thomas, c. A.D. 1225–1274; Italian philosopher and Christian theologian.

Aratea Latin translation into verse of Aratus' *Phaenomena*.

Aratus c. 315–240/239 B.C.; Greek poet, who wrote *Phaenomena*, an astronomical poem describing the constellations.

Augustinus, Aurelius (St. Augustine), 354–430; leader of the early Christian Church; bishop of Hippo in North Africa; author of *City of God* and *Confessions*.

Augustus (Gaius Octavius), born 63 B.C.; emperor 27 B.C.–A.D. 14; first of the Julio–Claudian emperors; before 27 B.C. referred to as Octavian.

Ausonius, Decimus Magnus, c. 300–395; teacher, poet, and politician in Roman Gaul.

Boccaccio, Giovanni, 1313–1375; Italian writer and poet.

Boethius 475–525; Roman philosopher and statesman.

Brutus, Lucius Junius, consul in 509 B.C.; assassin of the last Etruscan king of Rome.

Brutus, Marcus Junius, 85–42 B.C.; Roman provincial administrator and one of the assassins of Julius Caesar.

Caesar, Gaius Julius, 100–44 B.C.; Roman general, statesman, and historian, whose assassination marked the end of the Roman Republic. The title "Caesar" was also bestowed on Roman emperors, from Augustus to Hadrian.

Caligula (Gaius Caesar Germanicus), A.D. 12–41; eldest son of Germanicus and Agrippina; emperor A.D. 37–41.

Carolingian period mid–eighth through tenth centuries; named after the Frankish dynasty which reigned in France from 751 to 987, and in Germany until 911; the most famous member of this dynasty was

Charlemagne, "Charles the Great," king of the Franks 768–814, and, as Charles I, emperor of the Holy Roman Empire, 800–814.

Cato, Marcus Porcius ("the Elder" or "the Censor"), 234–149 B.C.; Roman statesman, soldier, and writer; vociferous supporter of Roman tradition in the face of foreign influence.

Chaldaei a people of Assyria, distinguished for their knowledge of astronomy and astrology.

Cicero, Marcus Tullius, 106–43 B.C.; Roman statesman, orator, and writer.

Cinna, Lucius, consul 87–84 B.C.; opponent of Sulla.

Claudius (Tiberius Claudius) 10 B.C.–A.D. 54; emperor A.D. 41–54.

Copernicus, Nicolaus, 1473–1543; great Polish astronomer; founder of modern astronomy.

Crassus, Marcus Licinius, consul 70 B.C.; in 53 B.C. he was killed during a military expedition in Parthia (now part of Iran).

Donatus, Aelius, famous fourth-century grammarian.

Epicurus 341–270 B.C.; moral and natural Greek philosopher, whose philosophy was the subject of *Dē rērum nātūrā*, Lucretius' didactic poem.

Euhemerus 311–298 B.C.; Greek philosopher who maintained that the gods were once outstanding mortals, who were subsequently worshipped by people grateful to them.

Galileo, Galilei, 1564–1642; Italian physicist and astronomer.

Germanicus, Julius Caesar, 15 B.C.–A.D. 19; nephew of Tiberius and father of Caligula; wrote an *Aratea*.

Gracchi Tiberius Sempronius Gracchus and his younger brother, Gaius Sempronius Gracchus, assassinated in 133 and 122 B.C., respectively, after introducing bills intended to alleviate poverty (which were legal but which undermined traditional bases of power at Rome). Their assassinations traditionally mark the beginning of the disintegration of the republican form of government at Rome.

Hannibal Carthaginian general in Second Punic War (218–201).

Hellenistic the term refers to the Greek language or culture after the time of Alexander the Great, when foreign elements were introduced into their society.

Helvia mother of the philosopher Seneca.

Horace 65 B.C.–8 B.C.; Roman poet.

Hrotsvitha tenth-century German nun and playwright.

Humanists scholars of the Renaissance who sought to elevate man and his values and turned to the cultures of ancient Greece and Rome for models.

Isidore of Seville c. 560–635; Spanish archbishop and Latin encyclopedist.

Jerome, St. 348–420; monk and scholar of the Church; translator of the Latin (Vulgate) Bible.

Justinian (The Great) 483–565; Byzantine emperor 527–565; under him leading jurists codified Roman law. (This codification is known as the "Justinian Code.")

Juvenal c. A.D. 50/64–127; Roman satiric poet.

Kepler, Johann, 1571–1630; German astronomer.

Lepidus, Marcus, consul 46 B.C.; joined forces with Antony and Octavian to avenge assassination of Julius Caesar.

Livy 59/64 B.C.–A.D. 17/12; Roman historian.

Lucretius c. 99–55 B.C.; Latin poet; wrote didactic poem *Dē rērum nātūrā* to explain the philosophy of Epicurus.

Macrobius, Ambrosius Theodosius, fifth-century writer; his *Saturnalia* (c. 430) is important for the history of early Vergilian scholarship.

Manilius, Marcus, first-century A.D. poet; author of didactic poem on astrology, *Astronomica*, written under Augustus and Tiberius.

Marius, Gaius, 157–86 B.C.; Roman general and consul six times; opponent of Sulla; created the client army; important popular leader.

Martial, c. A.D. 40–c. 104; Roman poet, best known for his books of *Epigrams*.

Nero (Nero Claudius Caesar) A.D. 37–68; emperor 54–68; son of Agrippina and stepson of the emperor Claudius; notorious for his cruelty and corruption; last of the Julio–Claudian emperors.

Ovid (Publius Ovidius Naso) 43 B.C.–A.D. 17; Roman poet; was exiled to Tomis on the Black Sea by the emperor Augustus because of an unknown crime and died in exile.

Petronius Arbiter first-century A.D. poet/novelist; author of *Satyricon*.

Plautus, Titus Maccius, c. 254–184 B.C.; Roman comic dramatist.

Piny the Younger (Gaius Plinius Caecilius Secundus) c. A.D. 61–112; Roman writer, statesman, and orator; known primarily from his published letters.

Pompey (Gnaeus Pompeius Magnus) 106–48 B.C.; Roman general and statesman.

Priscian (Priscianus) early sixth-century grammarian.

Propertius, Sextus, c. 54/47–2 B.C.; Roman elegiac poet.

Ptolemy (Claudius Ptolemaeus) (flourished A.D. 127–48); Greek astronomer, mathematician, and geographer.

Quintilian (Marcus Fabius Quintilianus) A.D. 40–c. 100; Roman teacher, writer, and practitioner of rhetoric.

Sallust (Gaius Sallustius) c. 86–35 B.C.; Roman historian.

Salutati, Coluccio, d. 1406; Italian Humanist.

Sappho c. 600 B.C.; Greek lyric poetess who lived on the island of Lesbos.

Sejanus (Lucius Aelius Seianus) d. A.D. 31; as Prefect of the Praetorian Guard (the bodyguard of Republican Roman generals, then of the Emperor), he wielded enormous power at Rome during Tiberius' retirement to the island of Capreae in A.D. 27.

Seneca, Lucius Annaeus, c. A.D. 1–65; philosopher, poet, and advisor to the emperor Nero.

Suetonius Tranquillus, Gaius, born c. A.D. 69; Roman biographer.

Sulla, Lucius Cornelius, c. 138–78 B.C.; Roman general and dictator (82–79 B.C.).

Sulpicia first-century A.D. Roman elegiac poetess.

Tacitus, Cornelius, c. 56–115 A.D.; Roman historian.

Tarquinii Etruscan kings who ruled Rome until 509 B.C.

Terence (Publius Terentius Afer) c. 190–159 B.C.; Roman comic dramatist.

Tiberius (Tiberius Julius Caesar Augustus) 42 B.C.–A.D. 37; emperor A.D. 14–37.

Tibullus, Albius, c. 55/48–c. 19 B.C.; Roman elegiac poet.

Vergil (Vergilius, Publius Maro) 70–19 B.C.; Roman poet.

Latin-English Vocabulary

A number following the English definition indicates that these words are included in Verba Tenenda, and the chapter in which the word was assigned. For nouns, the nominative and genitive cases and gender are given. Third declension adjectives with one ending are followed by a semicolon (;) and by the genitive singular, for example: **ingēns**; **ingentis**.

A

ā, **ab** (*prep.* + *abl.*) from, away from, by *III*
abeō, **abīre**, **abiī** (**abīvī**), **abitum** go away (from), depart *VIII*
absēns; **absentis** (*present participle of* **absum**) absent
abrumpō, **-ere**, **abrūpī**, **abruptus** break, break off, sever
absum, **abesse**, **āfuī**, **āfutūrus** be away from, be absent *IX*
absurdus, **-a**, **-um** preposterous, ridiculous
ac (*conj.*) and, also *IV*
accēdō, **-ere**, **-cessī**, **-cessus** go or come to, approach *XVI*
accendō, **-ere**, **accendī**, **accensum** set on fire; inflame
accidit, **-ere**, **accidit** (*impersonal*) it happens; it chances *XVII*
accipiō, **-ere**, **-cēpī**, **-ceptus** take, accept, receive *III*
accommodō, **-āre**, **-āvī**, **-ātus** fit or adapt one thing to another; accommodate
accumbō, **-ere**, **accumbuī**, **accumbitus** recline, lie down
acer, **acris**, **acre** sharp, pointed, piercing; keen *XI*
acerbus, **-a**, **-um** bitter, sour; hostile
actiō, **-iōnis** *f* a doing, acting, action
actus, **-ūs** *m* motion; performance, act; the deed *XII*
ad (*prep.* + *acc.*) to, toward, near *IV*
addō, **-ere**, **-didī**, **-ditus** bring to, add to, augment *IX*
adeō, **adīre**, **adiī** (**adīvī**), **aditum** go to, approach *VIII*
adeō (*adv.*) so, so far, to such a degree *IX*
adhūc (*adv.*) to this place, thus far; until now; yet *XIII*
adiciō, **-ere**, **adiēcī**, **adiectus** throw to; apply to; add
adsum, **adesse**, **adfuī**, **adfutūrus** be present, be at hand; (+ *dat.*) aid, assist *IV*
adulescēns, **-ntis** *m* young man
adultus, **-a**, **-um** grown, adult *VII*
adveniō, **-īre**, **-vēnī**, **-ventus** come to, arrive at *III*
adventus, **-ūs** *m* approach, arrival *XVI*
adversus, **-a**, **-um** turned face to face; opposite, contrary *XI*
advigilō, **-āre**, **-āvī**, **-ātus** keep guard over, be watchful

advocātus, **-ī** *m* advocate, lawyer; witness
aedēs, **-is** *f* building for habitation; temple;
pl. dwelling for men *XI*
Aegyptius, **-a**, **-um** Egyptian
aemula, **-ae** *f* rival
aequāliter (*adv.*) equally
aequus, **-a**, **-um** equal, even, fair;
aequum est it is right, fair, just *V*
āēr, **āeris** *m* air *X*
aetās, **-tātis** *f* time of life, age; lifetime of a human being; a generation, an age *X*
aeternus, **-a**, **-um** eternal, without beginning or end *X*
aevum, **-ī** *n* time; an age; a generation
affectus, **-ūs** *m* affection, mood, disposition (*a state of body and of mind produced by some outside influence*) *XII*
afficiō, **-ere**, **-fēcī**, **-fectus** exert an influence on, influence, affect *XIII*
afferō, **afferre**, **attulī**, **allātus** bring near, bring to, report *XII*
aggredior, **aggredī**, **aggressus sum** go to, approach, attack *XVI*
ager, **agrī** *m* field *II*
agitō, **-āre**, **-āvī**, **-ātus** set in motion, disturb, rouse *VI*
agitō mēcum I deliberate, I consider *VI*
agnoscō, **-ere**, **-nōvī**, **-nitus** recognize; acknowledge as one's own; acknowledge *XIII*
agō, **agere**, **ēgī**, **actus** lead, drive; do, make; act, spend *III*
vītam agere live, spend one's life
grātiās agere (+ *dat.*) give thanks (to); thank *III*
age; **agedum** come, now! *III*
agricola, **-ae** *m* farmer *II*
ait, **aiunt** (*defective verb, present tense only*) he (she/it) says; they say
aliēnus, **-a**, **-um** belonging to someone else, foreign;
aliēnus ā + *abl.* different from *X*
aliquandō (*adv.*) at whatsoever time
aliquis, **aliquid** (*indefinite pronoun*) someone, something; anyone, anything *XII*
alius, **alia**, **aliud** other, another *III*
alligō, **-āre**, **-āvī**, **-ātus** bind to; bind, oblige
alō, **-ere**, **aluī**, **alitus** *and* **altus** feed, nourish, support
alter, **altera**, **alterum** the other (of two); the second *III*
altus, **-a**, **-um** high, lofty, noble; deep, profound *IX*
amāns, **amantis**, *m* or *f* a lover
amātus, **-a**, **-um** loved, beloved *II*
amēns; **amentis** mad, senseless
ambiō, **ambīre**, **ambiī** (**ambīvī**), **-itum** go about; solicit *VIII*
ambulō, **-āre**, **-āvī**, **-ātus** walk, take a walk *IV*
amīca, **-ae** *f* girl-friend, sweetheart *II*
amīcitia, **-ae** *f* friendship; bond of friendship *XV*
amīcus, **-ī** *m* friend *II*
āmittō, **-ere**, **āmīsī**, **āmissus** send away, dismiss, lose *VI*

amō, **-āre**, **-āvī**, **-ātus** love *I*
amor, **amōris** *m* love *IX*
amplius (*adv.*) more, besides
amplius, **-a**, **-um** large, spacious; distinguished
an (*introducing a direct question*) can it be that?
(*introducing a second question*) or can it be that?
(*introducing an alternative*) or, or perhaps *VI*
anima, **-ae** *f* breath of life, soul *X*
animadvertō, **-ere**, **-vertī**, **-versus** direct one's attention to; consider, regard, notice *XVI*
animal, **animālis** *n* animal *XI*
animus, **-ī** *m* soul, mind;
pl. courage, high spirits *IV*
annus, **-ī** *m* year *VIII*
ante (*prep.* + *acc.*) before, in front of
(*adv.*) before, previously *IV*
(*or* **ante** . . . **quam**)
antequam (*conj. and adv.*) before *VI*
antīquus, **-a**, **-um** old, ancient, former *X*
antrum, **-ī** *n* cave
aperiō, **-īre**, **aperuī**, **apertus** uncover, lay bare, disclose *XIII*
appareō, **-ēre**, **apparuī**, **apparitus** become visible, appear, come into sight *XII*
appellō, **-āre**, **-āvī**, **-ātus** address, speak to; call, name *III*
apertus, **-a**, **-um** clear, uncovered
appetītus, **-ūs** *m* attack; longing for, desire for; faculty of desire
aptus, **-a**, **-um** (+ *dat.*) fit (for), suitable, proper *XIII*
apud (*prep.* + *accus.*) at; near; among; in the presence of; at the house of *X*
aqua, **-ae** *f* water *IV*
ara, **-ae** *f* altar *XI*
arbitror, **-ārī**, **arbitrātus sum** make a decision; think, suppose; be of the opinion, believe *XVI*
arbor, **arboris** *f* tree *VIII*
ardeō, **-ēre**, **arsī**, **arsus** be on fire, burn, blaze *IX*
argentum, **-ī** *n* silver, money *XVIII*
arma, **-ōrum** *n* arms, weapons *X*
ars, **artis** *f* skill, trade, art *XI*
ascendō, **-ere**, **ascendī**, **ascēnsus** climb, ascend
astrum, **-ī** *n* star, constellation *XII*
at (*conj.*) but, but indeed *XII*
Athēnae, **-ārum** *f* Athens *VIII*
atque (*conj.*) and, and also, and even *IV*
auctor, **-ōris** *m* author
auctōritās, **-tātis** *f* leadership, influence, authority
audācia, **-ae** *f* boldness, daring; courage *V*
audeō, **-ēre**, **ausus sum** have the courage (*to do something*), dare (*to do something*); be bold *XVI*

audiō, **-īre**, **audīvī**, **audītus** hear, listen (to) *III*
auditor, **-tōris** *m* listener; pupil, scholar, disciple *VIII*
auferō, **auferre**, **abstulī**, **ablātus** take away, carry off, remove *XII*
augeō, **-ere**, **auxī**, **auctus** increase; cause to grow or increase; augment, strengthen *XI*
Augustus, **-ī** *m* the emperor Augustus
augustus, **-a**, **-um** majestic, august, worthy of honor *XI*
aura, **-ae** *f* air, breeze
aureus, **-a**, **-um** golden, of gold *XVI*
aurum, **-ī** *n* gold; money XVIII
aut (*conj.*) or
  aut . . . aut either . . . or *IV*
autem (*postpositive conj.*) however, on the other hand; but, yet *VII*
auxilium, **-iī** *n* help, aid, assistance *II*
avertō, **-ere**, **-vertī**, **-versus** turn (*something*) away from; avert, hinder; put to flight *VII*

B

barbarus, **-a**, **-um** foreign; uncivilized
basium, **basiī** *n* kiss
beātus, **-a**, **-um** blessed, fortunate *XV*
bellum, **-ī** *n* war *XI*
bellus, **-a**, **-um** pretty, handsome, charming *XIII*
bene (*adv.*) well *IV*
beneficium, **-iī** *n* kindness, favor, benefit *X*
benevolentia, **-ae** *f* good-will, benevolence; favor, kindness *VII*
bestia, **-ae** *f* wild animal, beast *II*
bibō, **-ere**, **bibī**, —— drink, imbibe *III*
bis (*adv.*) twice
bonus, **-a**, **-um** *good II*
bōs, **bovis** *m* or *f* (*gen. pl.* **boum**, *dat./abl. pl.*, **būbus** or **bōbus**) ox, bull, cow *IX*
bracchium, **-iī** *n* arm *XII*
brevis, **-e** short, brief, concise; close together *XI*
brevitās, **-tātis** *f* brevity, shortness, conciseness *VIII*
breviter (*adv.*) short, briefly
bucca, **-ae** *f* cheek, mouth

C

Cācus, **-ī** *m* Cacus
cadō, **-ere**, **cecidī**, **cāsus** fall, fall down *III*
caecus, **-a**, **-um** blind, unseeing; invisible, unseen *XVII*
caelestis, **-e** having to do with the heavens: found in heaven, heavenly, celestial *XII*
caelum, **-ī** *n* sky; weather *II*
campus, **-ī** *m* field, plain; an even, flat place *XVIII*
candidus, **-a**, **-um** bright, white, fair (*implying beauty*)

canis, **canis** *m* or *f* (*gen. pl.* **canum**) dog *XIV*
canō, **-ere**, **cecinī**, **cantus** sing, sing of, celebrate; prophesy *XI*
canticum, **-ī** *n* song; monody *VI*
cantō, **-āre**, **-āvī**, **-ātus** sing *I*
capiō, **-ere**, **cēpī**, **captus** take, seize *III*
captō, **-āre**, **-āvī**, **-ātus** try to seize, catch, capture *I*
caput, **capitis** *n* head *XI*
carmen, **carminis** *n* song; poem *XVIII*
Carthāgo, **-inis** *f* Carthage
cārus, **-a**, **-um** dear, precious, expensive *XIII*
castra, **-ōrum** *n* military encampment; camp
cāsus, **-ūs** *m* (*from* **cadō**) a falling, a falling down; accident, misfortune; mistake *XII*
Catullus, **-ī** *m* the poet Catullus
cauda, **-ae** *f* tail of an animal *IX*
causa, **-ae** *f* cause, reason; lawsuit, case *IV*
caveō, **-ēre**, **cāvī**, **cautus** (+ *acc.*) be on guard, take heed, beware (of) *XV*
cēdō, **-ere**, **cessī**, **cessus** go, move, yield; withdraw, depart; (+ *dat.*) submit to, yield to, grant, concede *IV*
celer, **celeris**, **celere** swift, fleet, quick *XI*
celeriter (*adv.*) quickly
cēlō, **-āre**, **-āvī**, **-ātus** conceal, keep secret, hide *V*
cēna, **-ae** *f* meal, dinner
cēnō, **-āre**, **-āvī**, **-ātus** take a meal, dine, eat
cēnseō, **-ēre**, **cēnsuī**, **cēnsus** tax, assess, estimate; think *V*
centum (*indeclinable*) one hundred *XVII*
Cerēs, **Cereris** *f* Ceres, goddess of grain; bread
cernō, **-ere**, **crēvī**, **crētus** separate; distinguish (*visually*), perceive, discern *XIV*
certē (*adv.*) certainly *IV*
certus, **-a**, **-um** certain, sure *VIII*
cessō, **-āre**, **-āvī**, **-ātus** delay, cease from, be inactive; give over, yield
ceterī, **-ae**, **-a** the others, the rest (of) *IV*
Chēlae, **-ārum** *f. pl.* the claws of the constellation Scorpio; also identified as the constellation Libra, the "Scales."
cibus, **-ī** *m* food *IV*
circiter (*adv.*) nearly, about, almost
circum (*prep.* + *acc.* or *adv.*) around, about *XI*
circumdō, **-are**, **-dedī**, **-datus** put or place around; surround
circumstō, **-stāre**, **-stetī**, —— stand around *XVI*
cito (*adv.*) quickly *XI*
cīvīlis, **-e** pertaining to citizens; civil, civic *XI*
cīvis, **cīvis** *m* or *f* citizen *XI*
cīvitās, **-tātis** *f* the state, the citizens united into the body politic; the state *X*
clam (*adv.*) secretly, under cover
clāmō, **-āre**, **-āvī**, **-ātus** cry out, shout *XIV*

clārus, **-a**, **-um** clear, bright; famous *II*
claudō, **-ere**, **clausī**, **clausus** close, shut *VII*
claustrum, **-ī** *n* lock, bar, bolt; an enclosure, a place that is shut up; a cloister or monastery
cliēns, **clientis** *m* or *f* dependent; client
coepī, **coepisse**, **coeptus** (*defective verb*; *no present stem*) begin
cōgitātiō, **-iōnis** *f* a thinking, thought, meditation *X*
cōgitō, **-āre**, **-āvī**, **-ātus** think, plan, deliberate *I*
cognoscō, **-ere**, **cognōvī**, **cognitus** learn, become acquainted with; (*in perfect tense*) know *IV*
cōgō, **-ere**, **coēgī**, **coactus** compel, force; collect, bring together, assemble *V*
colligō, **-ere**, **collēgī**, **collectus** gather, collect
collis, **-is** *m* hill
colō, **-ere**, **coluī**, **cultus** cultivate, till, tend; inhabit; cherish, care for; worship *X*
comedō, **-ere**, **-ēdī**, **-ēsus** eat up, eat, consume; waste *X*
commemorō, **-āre**, **-āvī**, **-ātus** recall; recall in speech, mention
commendō, **-āre**, **-āvī**, **-ātus** entrust, commit to one's care; recommend *V*
commereō, **-ēre**, **-meruī**, **-meritus** fully deserve
committō, **-ere**, **-mīsī**, **-missus** bring together; join; entrust
commodus, **-a**, **-um** convenient, suitable; opportune; desirable
commūnis, **-e** common, public, general *XI*
complūrēs, **-es**, **-a** (*pl.*) quite a number of, many, several
compōno, **-ere**, **-posuī**, **-positus** put together; compose, arrange; compare
concēdō, **-ere**, **-cessī**, **-cessus** grant, yield; go, depart *XIV*
concilium, **-iī** *n* a popular assembly; public meeting; council
conclūdō, **-ere**, **-clūsī**, **-clūsus** shut up closely, enclose; confine *VII*
condō, **-ere**, **condidī**, **conditus** found, establish; bury *XVII*
conferō, **-ferre**, **-tulī**, **collātus** bring together, compare
sē conferre go, betake oneself *XII*
conficiō, **-ere**, **-fēcī**, **-fectus** complete, accomplish, produce
confīdō, **-ere**, **confīsus sum** put one's trust in, be confident
confirmō, **-āre**, **-āvī**, **-ātus** strengthen; make firm; assure
coniciō, **-ere**, **coniēcī**, **coniectus** throw together, unite
coniūrātus, **-ī** *m* conspirator *XVI*
coniunctiō, **-iōnis** *f* a joining together, union; conjugal connection, relation;
(*as grammatical term*) conjunction
coniugium, **-iī** *n* marriage, connection by marriage *X*
coniunx, **coniugis** *m* husband; *f* wife *XVIII*
conloquium, **-iī** *n* talk, conversation
cōnor, **-ārī**, **cōnātus sum** undertake, attempt, try *XVI*
cōnsequor, **-ī**, **cōnsecūtus sum** go or come after, follow; succeed in time; follow as a consequence
cōnsilium, **-iī** *n* advice; plan, purpose; judgment *IV*

cōnsistō, **-ere**, **-stitī**, —— stop moving, come to a halt
cōnstō, **-stāre**, **-stitī**, —— stand together; stand still; exist; remain unchanged; stand firm; agree with; be consistent with;
cōnstat (*impersonal*) it is agreed *XVII*
cōnstituō, **-ere**, **-uī**, **-tūtus** place, establish, appoint, set up; decide, determine, resolve *VIII*
cōnsuescō, **-ere**, **cōnsuēvī**, **cōnsuētus** become accustomed to, form a habit
cōnsuētūdō, **-tūdinis** *f* custom, habit, usage
cōnsul, **cōnsulis** *m* consul (*one of two Roman magistrates elected annually*) *VIII*
cōnsulō, **-ere**, **cōnsuluī**, **cōnsultus** consider, reflect, deliberate
cōnsulātus, **-ūs** *m* office of the consul, consulship
cōnsūmō, **-ere**, **-sumpsī**, **-sumptus** take up completely; consume, devour, squander
contemnō, **-ere**, **-tempsī**, **-temptus** value little, despise, disdain, scorn; defy *VII*
contendō, **-ere**, **contendī**, **contentus** hasten, go quickly; engage in contest; exert, strain
continentia, **-ae** *f* adjoining places; mainland
contineō, **-ēre**, **-tinuī**, **-tentus** hold together, enclose, contain, limit, retain *X*
continuus, **-a**, **-um** uninterrupted, continued
contrā (*adv.*) in opposition, in turn, in return;
(*prep.* + *acc.*) against, contrary to *VII*
contrōversia, **-ae** *f* controversy, quarrel, debate
conveniō, **-īre**, **-vēnī**, **-ventus** assemble, meet, come together;
convenit (*impersonal*) it is agreed; it is arranged; it is suitable *XVII*
convertō, **-ere**, **-vertī**, **-versus** turn around, reverse *IX*
convīva, **-ae** *m* or *f* guest, dinner or drinking companion *III*
convīvō, **-ere**, **convīxī**, —— live with, banquet together
cōpia, **-ae** *f* abundance; wealth, power; supply;
pl. troops *XIV*
cor, **cordis** *n* heart *XI*
cornū, **cornūs** *n* horn (*of an animal*); wing of an army *XII*
corporālis, **-e** having to do with the body; physical, corporeal *XII*
corporeus, **-a**, **-um** corporeal
corpus, **corporis** *n* body, flesh; substance *VIII*
cōtīdiē (*adv.*) every day; day by day
crēber, **crēbra**, **crēbrum** closely set, at frequent intervals, crowded
crēdō, **-ere**, **crēdidī**, **crēditus** (+ *dat.*) believe, trust *V*
crescō, **-ere**, **crēvī**, **crētus** grow, increase in size *VII*
crīmen, **crīminis** *n* charge, accusation
crūdēlis, **-e** hard, unmerciful, cruel *XIII*
cruciō, **-āre**, **-āvī**, **-ātus** inflict torture on; torture
cubō, **-āre**, **-uī**, **-itus** recline, lie down *XVIII*
cuiusmodī (*gen.*) of what sort

culcitra, **-ae** *f* pillow
culpa, **-ae** *f* crime, fault, blame
cum (*prep. + abl.*) with *III*
cum (*conjunction + indicative*) when (*temporal*); whenever *XII*
(*+ subjunctive*) when (*circumstantial*), since, because, although *XII*
cunctus, **-a**, **-um** all, all together, entire *X*
cupīdō, **-inis** *f* or *m* desire, longing;
(*personified*) Cupid, god of Love *XIII*
cupiō, **-ere**, **cupīvī**, **cupītus** long for, desire, wish *XII*
cupidus, **-a**, **-um** (+ *gen.*) desirous (of), longing, eager (for) *XII*
cūr (*adv.*) why *VI*
cūra, **-ae** *f* care, concern, worry *III*
cūrō, **-āre**, **-āvī**, **-ātus** care for, take care of *V*
currō, **-ere**, **cucurrī**, **cursus** run, hasten *XII*
cursus, **-ūs** *m* a running, a course, a passage *XII*
custōs, **custōdis** *m* or *f* guard, guardian, protector
cyathissō, **-āre**, **-āvī**, **-ātus** pour wine
Cyclōps, **Cyclōpis** *m* enormous one-eyed giant

D

datus, **-a**, **-um** (from **dō**, **dare**) given *II*
dē (*prep. + abl.*) from, down from; about, concerning *IV*
dēbeō, **-ēre**, **dēbuī**, **dēbitus** owe;
(*complementary infinitive*) be bound or obliged (*to do something*) *III*
decem (*indeclinable*) ten XVII
decet, **-ēre**, **decuit**, —— it is fitting, right, proper *VII*, *XVII*
dēclāmātiō, **-iōnis** *f* speech
dēclāmō, **-āre**, **-āvī**, **-ātus** speak as an orator, make a speech, declaim *VI*
decōrum, **-ī** *n* propriety; fitness *VII*
decōrus, **-a**, **-um** becoming, fitting, proper *VII*
dēdūcō, **-ere**, **-dūxī**, **-ductus** lead away, bring down *IX*
dēfendō, **-ere**, **dēfendī**, **dēfensus** ward off, defend, protect *XV*
dēfensiō, **-iōnis** *f* a defending; defence *VIII*
dēferō, **-ferre**, **-tulī**, **-lātus** bring down, bring, deliver *XII*
dēficiō, **-ere**, **-fēcī**, **-fectus** desert, fail, forsake; grow faint, disappear *XIII*
dēfluō, **-ere**, **-fluxī**, **-fluxus** flow down, flow
Dēianīra, **-ae** *f* Deianira, wife of Hercules *IX*
deinde (*adv.*) then, next, afterwards *VI*
dēlīberō, **-āre**, **-āvī**, **-ātus** consider, deliberate, take counsel *V*
dēliciae, **-ārum** *f pl.* delight, pleasure *VI*
dēmittō, **-ere**, **dēmīsī**, **dēmissus** send down, let down; drop, lower *XIV*
dēmōnstrō, **-āre**, **-āvī**, **-ātus** show, point out, indicate *IV*
dēnique (*adv.*) finally, at last; and then *XV*
dēns, **dentis** *m* tooth *XI*
dēponō, **-ere**, **-posuī**, **-positus** set down, put down; lay aside, deposit *XIII*
dērīdeō, **-ēre**, **-rīsī**, **-rīsus** laugh at

dēsīderium, **-iī** *n* a longing, a wish for something once possessed: grief, regret; need, necessity
dēsinō, **-ere**, **dēsīvī** (**dēsiī**), —— (+ *infinitive*) cease, desist, stop; end, terminate *X*
dēstituō, **-ere**, **-uī**, **-ūtus** leave alone, abandon; set down *XVI*
dēsum, **dēesse**, **dēfuī**, **dēfutūrus** be absent, be lacking; fail *IV*
dēterreō, **-ēre**, **-uī**, **-itus** frighten from, deter, hinder, prevent *XVI*
dexter, **dextra**, **dextrum** situated on the right-hand side; favorable; right
dextra, **-ae** *f* right hand *XVI*
deus, **-ī** *m* (*nom. pl.* **dī**) god, deity *VI*
dīcō, **-ere**, **dīxī**, **dictus** say, speak *III*
diēs, **diēī** *m* day *XIV*
differō, **-ferre**, **distulī**, **dīlātus** carry in different directions; scatter, disperse; postpone; differ *XII*
difficile (*adv.*) with difficulty *XIII*
difficilis, **-e** difficult *XIII*
difficultās, **-tātis** *f* difficulty, trouble
dignitās, **-tātis** *f* worthiness, merit; grandeur, dignity, rank, authority
dignus, **-a**, **-um** (+ *abl.*) worthy, deserving *VI*
dīligēns; **-ntis** (*adj.*) careful, diligent, accurate; fond of, devoted *XVII*
dīligentia, **-ae** *f* carefulness
dīmittō, **-ere**, **-mīsī**, **-missus** send out, let go, dismiss
dīrus, **-a**, **-um** dire, dread
discēdō, **-ere**, **-cessī**, **-cessus** depart, leave; divide, separate *XII*
disciplīna, **-ae** *f* teaching, training; a brand of study, a discipline
discipula, **-ae** *f* (*female*) student *VI*
discipulus, **-ī** *m* (*male*) student *VI*
discō, **-ere**, **didicī**, —— learn *VI*
dispōnō, **-ere**, **-posuī**, **-positus** distribute; arrange; place here and there *XIII*
disputō, **-āre**, **-āvī**, **-ātus** dispute, argue *VI*
dissimilis, **-e** (+ *dat.*) unlike, dissimilar *XIII*
distrahō, **-ere**, **-traxī**, **-tractus** tear into pieces, separate forcibly; divide, separate; perplex *V*
diū (*adv.*) for a long time *XI*
diūtius (*adv.*) for a rather long time *XV*
diutissimē (*adv.*) for a very long time *XV*
dīversus, **-a**, **-um** turned different ways, opposite, contrary *XIII*
dīvēs; **dīvitis** rich, wealthy, sumptuous, costly *XV*
dīvīnus, **-a**, **-um** of or belonging to a diety, divine *IX*
dīvitiae, **-arum** *f pl.* riches, wealth *VI*
dīvus, **-a**, **-um** divine, of a deity *XI*
dō, **dare**, **dedī**, **datus** give *I*
doceō, **-ere**, **docuī**, **doctus** teach, instruct, inform *VI*
doleō, **-ēre**, **doluī**, **doliturus** suffer pain, grieve
dolor, **dolōris** *m* pain, grief *IX*

dominus, **-ī** *m* master, ruler *II*
domus, **-ūs** *f* (also **domus**, **-ī** *f*) home *XII*
  domī (*adv.*) at home *VIII*
  domō (*adv.*) (from) home *VIII*
  domum (*adv.*) (to) home *VIII*
dōnō, **-āre**, **-āvī**, **-ātus** (+ *dat.*) give as a present, present
dōnec (*conj.*) while; until *XVI*
dōnum, **-ī** *n* gift, present *II*
dormiō, **-īre**, **-īvī**, **-ītus** sleep
dubitātiō, **-iōnis** *f* hesitation
dubitō, **-āre**, **-āvī**, **-ātus** doubt, be uncertain; (+ *infinitive*) hesitate *XIV*
dubius, **-a**, **-um** doubtful, uncertain *XIV*
dūcō, **-ere**, **dūxī**, **ductus** lead, conduct, guide, reckon *III*
dulcis, **-e** sweet, pleasant, charming *XI*
dum (+ *indicative*) while, as long as *II*, *XVII*
  (+ *subjunctive*) provided that *XVII*
  (+ *subjunctive*) (*showing anticipation*) until *XVII*
dummodo (*conj.* + *subj.*) provided that *XVII*
duo, **duae**, **duo** two *XVII*
duodecim (*indeclinable*) twelve
dūrus, **-a**, **-um** hard, harsh, rough; stern *IX*
dux, **ducis** *m* leader, general *VIII*

E

ē, **ex** (*prep.* + *abl.*) from, out of *V*
ēbrius, **-a**, **-um** drunk, inebriated *III*
ecce behold
eccum behold him
ecquis anyone?
edepol by pollux!
ēdō, **-ere**, **ēdidī**, **ēditus** give out, put forth, bring forth *XIII*
efferō, **-ferre**, **extulī**, **ēlātus** bring out, carry out; set forth, publish, proclaim *XII*
efficiō, **-ere**, **-fēcī**, **-fectus** make; cause to occur, bring about, accomplish; deduce from premises
  efficit ut (*impersonal*) it follows that *XVII*
egeō, **-ēre**, **eguī**, —— (+ *abl.*) be in want, be in need; need, lack, be without *X*
egŏ (*pronoun*) I *III*
ēgredior, **ēgredī**, **ēgressus** go out; come out; go forth *XVI*
ēgregius, **-a**, **-um** outstanding, excellent, splendid
ēlegāns; **ēlegantis** luxurious, fastidious; fine, neat, elegant *XI*
elementum, **-ī** *n* first principle, element; *pl.* the alphabet *VI*
ēloquentia, **-ae** *f* eloquence *VI*

em ahem!
emō, **-ere**, **ēmī**, **emptus** buy, purchase *XVIII*
enim (*postpositive conj.*) for, indeed, truly, for indeed *V*
enimvērō (*conj.*) yes indeed, certainly
eō (*adv.*) there
eō, **īre**, **iī** (**īvī**), **itum** go *VIII*
eōdem (*adv.*) to the same place
epistula, **-ae** *f* letter, epistle
eques, **-itis** *m* horseman, rider; a member of the equestrian order, a "knight"; one able to provide his own horse
equus, **-ī** *m* horse *V*
era, **-ae** *f* mistress
ergō (*adv.*) consequently, therefore *V*
ēripiō, **-ere**, **ēripuī**, **ēreptus** snatch out, tear out, take away *XIII*
errō, **-āre**, **-āvī**, **-ātus** err, make a mistake, wander *I*
error, **errōris** *m* error, mistake
erus, **-ī** *m* master
et (*conj.*) and, even *II*
  et . . . et both . . . and *II*
etiam even, also *V*
etsī (*conj.*) even if; although *XVI*
ēveniō, **-īre**, **ēvēnī**, **ēventus** come out;
  ēvenit ut (*impersonal*) it happens, it turns out that *XVII*
ex, **ē** (*prep.* + *abl.*) from, out of *V*
exanimō, **-āre**, **-āvī**, **-ātus** deprive of life, kill
excēdō, **-ere**, **-cessī**, **-cessus** go from, depart *X*
excellēns; **excellentis** eminent, distinguished, excellent *XVII*
excipiō, **-ere**, **-cēpī**, **-ceptus** take out; except, make an exception of; catch, capture *XIII*
exclūdō, **-ere**, **exclūsī**, **exclūsus** shut out, remove, put out *VII*
exemplar, **-āris** *n* example, pattern *XI*
exemplum, **-ī** *n* example, pattern, paradigm *VI*
exerceō, **-ēre**, **-uī**, **-itus** exercise, train *VI*
exercitus, **-ūs** *m* army, troops *XII*
existimō, **-āre**, **-āvī**, **-ātus** value, esteem; think, suppose
exitus, **-ūs** *m* departure, exit *XII*
exorior, **-īrī**, **exortus sum** come into view, present oneself; appear on horizon; arise; come into existence
expellō, **-ere**, **expulī**, **expulsus** throw out, expel *X*
ex(s)pectō, **-āre**, **-āvī**, **-ātus** wait for, expect
experior, **-īrī**, **expertus sum** make a trial of, test
expleō, **-ēre**, **explēvī**, **explētus** fill up, complete, satisfy
expōnō, **-ere**, **exposuī**, **expositus** put out; expose; explain *XIII*
ex(s)tō, **ex(s)tāre**, **ex(s)titī**, —— stand out, project; be conspicuous *XVII*
extrahō, **-ere**, **extraxī**, **extractus** drag out; extract; release *V*
extrēmus, **-a**, **-um** situated at the end; occurring last; extreme in degree

F

fābula, **-ae** *f* a narration, account, story; the subject of common talk; fictitious story; a drama *VI*
faciēs, **-ēī** *f* face, appearance *XIV*
facile (*adv.*) easily *XIII*
facilis, **-e** easy *XIII*
facinus, **-oris** *n* deed, wicked deed, crime
faciō, **-ere**, **fēcī**, **factus** do, make *III*
factum, **-ī** *n* deed, fact *VIII*
facultās, **facultātis** *f* ability, capacity; easiness
fallō, **-ere**, **fefellī**, **falsus** deceive, trick
falsus, **-a**, **-um** deceptive, feigned, false *IX*
fāma, **-ae** *f* rumor, reputation *VI*
famēs, **-is** *f* hunger; starvation
familia, **-ae** (or **-ās** *gen.*) all persons in a household subject to one man's control; household
familiāriter (*adv.*) intimately
fās (*indeclinable*) that which is right or permissible by divine law; that which is right; right; an obligation *XIV*
fātum, **-ī** *n* a prophetic utterance; destiny, fate *XVII*
faveō, **-ēre**, **fāvī**, **fautus** (+ *dat.*) be favorable toward, favor, protect *XV*
fēlix; **fēlīcis** fruitful; lucky, happy, fortunate *XI*
fēmina, **-ae** *f* woman *IV*
ferē (*adv.*) approximately; almost; in most cases, as a rule
ferō, **ferre**, **tulī**, **lātus** bring, carry, bear, report *XII*
ferus, **-a**, **-um** not tame, wild; unrestrained
ferrum, **-ī** *n* iron; *any tool or weapon made of iron*: sword, plough, *etc.* *XVI*
fessus, **-a**, **-um** exhausted, tired *IX*
fētus, **-ūs** *m* offspring, progeny
fictus, **-a**, **-um** false, fictitious *VI*
fidēlis, **-e** faithful, loyal, trustworthy *XVI*
fidēs, **fideī** *f* good faith, honesty, fidelity, trust *XVI*
fidūcia, **-ae** *f* trust, reliance, confidence
fīlius, **-ī** *m* son *II*
fīlia, **-ae** *f* daughter *II*
fīgō, **-ere**, **fīxī**, **fīxus** drive in, fix in, pierce; fasten to, fix in position *XVI*
figūra, **-ae** *f* form, image; symbol *X*
fingō, **-ere**, **finxī**, **fictus** form, fashion, make; imagine *X*
fīniō, **-īre**, **-īvī**, **-ītus** limit, enclose within boundaries; finish, end, terminate; set a limit *XIII*
fīnis, **-is** *m* boundary, limit, border; end; *pl.* territory *XI*
fīō, **fierī**, **factus sum** become, be made, happen *XIV*
flamma, **-ae** *f* flame, blaze, fire *IX*
fleō, **-ēre**, **flēvī**, **flētus** weep, shed tears; weep over *IX*
flōreō, **-ēre**, **flōruī**, —— bloom, flower; flourish, be prosperous, be distinguished *VI*

flūmen, **-inis** *n* river, stream
fluō, **-ere**, **fluxī**, **fluxus** flow *IX*
fluvius, **-iī** *m* stream, river *IX*
fodiō, **-ere**, **fōdī**, **fossus** pierce; dig; dig away *XVIII*
folium, **-iī** *n* leaf
for, **fārī**, **fātus sum** speak, talk; say, tell *XVII*
foris, **foris** *f* door of a building
forīs (*adv.*) on the outside of a building; outside
forma, **-ae** *f* form, shape; appearance; beauty *X*
formō, **-āre**, **-āvī**, **-ātus** shape, give form to *VI*
formōsus, **-a**, **-um** beautiful, lovely, handsome *XIII*
fors, **fortis** *f* chance, luck
fortasse (*adv.*) perhaps
forte (*adv.*) by chance, by accident *XIII*
fortis, **-e** brave, strong *XI*
fortūna, **-ae** *f* fortune, luck *V*
forum, **-ī** *n* public market place *XI*
frāter, **frātris** *m* brother *XIII*
fraus, **fraudis** *f* cheating, deceit, deception, fraud
frōns, **frontis** *f* forehead, brow *IX*
fruor, **fruī**, **fructus sum** (+ *abl.*) have the enjoyment of; enjoy *XVI*
frustrā (*adv.*) in vain; to no purpose; needlessly
fugiō, **-ere**, **fūgī**, **fugitus** flee, run away (from), avoid, escape *III*
fulgeō, **-ēre**, **fulsī**, —— flash, shine, gleam
fulvus, **-a**, **-um** yellow, tawny, yellow gold
fundō, **-ere**, **fūdī**, **fūsus** pour, pour out, shed *IX*
fungor, **fungī**, **functus sum** perform one's function

G

gaudeō, **-ēre**, **gāvīsus sum** rejoice, (+ *abl.*) take pleasure in, delight in *XIV*
gaudium, **-iī** *n* joy, delight *XIII*
gēns, **gentis** *f* a race, a clan; kind, a class *XI*
genū, **genūs** *n* the knee *XII*
genus, **generis** *n* race, stock, sort, species; kind, gender *VIII*
gerō, **-ere**, **gessī**, **gestus** do, accomplish; carry, bring; wear *VI*
  sē gerere behave, conduct oneself *VIII*
  mōrem gerere (+ *dat.*) comply with someone's wishes *VIII*
gignō, **-ere**, **genuī**, **genitus** beget, bring forth, produce; (*passive*) be born, arise *X*
gladius, **-iī** *m* sword
glōria, **-ae** *f* glory, fame, renown *VII*
gracilis, **-e** slender, thin *XIII*
gradior, **gradī**, **gressus sum** take steps, walk, go *XIV*
Graecia, **-ae** *f* Greece
Graecus, **-a**, **-um** Greek, of Greece
grammaticus, **-ī** *m* teacher of grammar and literature *VII*

grātia, **-ae** *f* favor, regard, friendship; esteem, charm, grace *III*
grātiās agere (+ *dat.*) to give thanks
grātus, **-a**, **-um** grateful; pleasant, appealing
gravis, **-e** heavy, weighty, serious, important *XIII*
grex, **gregis** *m* flock, herd *IX*

H

habeō, **-ēre**, **habuī**, **habitus** have, hold; consider, regard *IV*
habitō, **-āre**, **-āvī**, **-ātus** live in; inhabit; dwell *XVIII*
haud (*adv.*) not, not at all, by no means, scarcely *XVI*
hem well! (*expression of surprise*)
hercle by Hercules!
Herculēs, **-is** *m* Hercules *IX*
herculeus, **-a**, **-um** of Hercules *IX*
heri (*adv.*) yesterday
heu alas!
hīberna, **-ōrum** *n* winter encampment
hiems, **hiemis** *f* winter; winter weather
hīc (*adv.*) here *III*
hic, **haec**, **hoc** this man, this woman, this thing; the latter *IX*
hinc (*adv.*) from here, from this place *XV*
hōdiē (*adv.*) today *IV*
Horātius, **-ī** *m* the poet Horace
Homērus, **-i** *m* the poet Homer
homō, **hominis** *m* or *f* human being *VIII*
honestus, **-a**, **-um** honorable *VI*
honor, **-ōris** *m* honor, esteem; public office *X*
hōra, **-ae** *f* hour *VIII*
hortor, **-ārī**, **-ātus sum** encourage, urge *XVI*
hortus, **-ī** *m* garden
hospes, **hospitis** *m* guest, visitor *XV*
hostis, **-is** *m* foreigner, stranger; enemy *XVI*
hūc (*adv.*) to this place, here; to this end or purpose
hūmānus, **-a**, **-um** having to do with human beings; of human beings, human *IX*
humilis, **-e** humble, lowly, poor *XIII*
hūmor, **hūmōris** *m* liquid, moisture, fluid
humus, **-ī** *f* soil, ground

I

iaceō, **-ēre**, **iacuī**, **iacitus** lie, lie ill, be sick; be inactive
iaciō, **-ere**, **iēcī**, **iactus** throw, hurl *V*
iactō, **-āre**, **-āvī**, **-ātus** toss, throw, hurl, scatter; mention, discuss; **sē iactāre** boast *XI*
iam (*adv.*) now, already, soon *III*
iānua, **-ae** *f* door *III*
ibi (*adv.*) there *III*

ibidem (*adv.*) in the same place
id *see* **is, ea, id**
idcircō (*adv.*) on that account, for that reason, therefore *X*
īdem, eadem, idem the same *IX*
idōneus, -a, -um suitable
igitur (*conj.*) therefore *X*
ignārus, -a, -um not knowing, unaware *IX*
ignis, -is *m* fire *IX*
ignōrō, -āre, -āvī, -ātus have no knowledge of; fail to recognize *XVIII*
ignoscō, -ere, -nōvī, -nōtus (+ *dat.*) forgive *XV*
ignōtus, -a, -um unknown *IV*
ille, illa, illud (*demonstrative pron. and adj.*) that man, that woman, that thing; the former
illīc (*adv.*) from there, from that place *XV*
illūc (*adv.*) to that place
imāgō, -inis *f* an image, likeness, copy; statue; ghost *XI*
imbuō, -ere, imbuī, imbūtus moisten; dye; stain; give initial instruction, introduce (to) *VI*
imitātiō, -iōnis *f* imitation
immortālis, -e immortal *XI*
immortālitās, -tātis *f* immortality
immūtō, -āre, -āvī, -ātus change, alter
imparātus, -a, -um unprepared
impediō, -īre, -īvī, -ītus hinder, entangle, impede *XVI*
impendeō, -ēre, —— hang over, impend, be imminent; threat *V*
imperium, -iī *n* an order, command; power of command; authority; dominion, empire *XI*
imperō, -āre, -āvī, -ātus (+ *dat.*) order, command, give orders to *XIII*
impetus, -ūs *m* attack
impius, -a, -um irreverent, impious *X*
impleō, -ēre, -plēvī, -plētus fill *VI*
impōnō, -ere, -posuī, -positus (+ *dat.*) place upon, set upon, impose *XIII*
impressiō, -iōnis *f* impression; impression on the mind, influence
imprimō, -ere, impressī, impressus press into, stamp, imprint; impress; influence *XII*
improbus, -a, -um improper; shameless; unreasonable *XVIII*
impudīcus, -a, -um unchaste, immodest *VI*
in (+ *abl.*) in, on;
(*prep.* + *acc.*) into *II*
incendō, -ere, -cendī, -cēnsus set fire to, kindle; burn; rouse, excite *IX*
incertus, -a, -um uncertain, doubtful *V*
incitō, -āre, -āvī, -ātus set in rapid motion; stimulate
incipiō, -ere, -cēpī, -ceptus begin *III*
inclūdō, -ere, -clūdī, -clūsus shut in, confine
incolō, -ere, incoluī, —— inhabit, dwell in *XVII*
incolumis, -e safe, intact
inde (*adv.*) from that place, from that time, then *XI*

indecōrus, **-a**, **-um** unbecoming, disgraceful, shameful *VII*
indulgentia, **-ae** *f* indulgence, gentleness, kindness
induō, **-ere**, **induī**, **indūtus** put on (*an article of clothing*)
inēlegāns; **inēlegantis** tasteless, inelegant *XI*
ineō, **inīre**, **iniī** (**-īvī**), **initum** go into, enter *VIII*
infāns, **infantis** *m* and *f* infant, little child *XVII*
infantia, **-ae** *f* infancy *VI*
infēlix; **infēlīcis** unhappy; unfruitful
inferior; **inferiōris** lower
inferō, **-ferre**, **-intulī**, **-illātus** carry in, bring in; (+ *dat.*) inflict upon, attack *XII*
infīnītus, **-a**, **-um** unlimited, boundless, infinite *XIII*
ingenium, **ingeniī** *n* natural ability, talent, genius *VII*
ingēns; **ingentis** huge, enormous, large *XII*
ingredior, **ingredī**, **ingressus sum** go into, enter *XVI*
inhonestus, **-a**, **-um** dishonorable, disgraceful, shameful *VI*
inimīcitia, **-ae** *f* hostility
inimīcus, **-a**, **-um** hostile
  inimīcus, **-ī** *m* enemy
inīquus, **-a**, **-um** uneven; not equal; not level
initium, **-iī** *n* a beginning, first part, origin *XVII*
iniūria, **-ae** *f* harm; injury, wrong *anything contrary to what is right and just VIII*
inquam, **inquis**, **inquit** (*defective third conjugation* **-iō** *verb*) I say, you say, he (she/it) says *XIII*
insānus, **-a**, **-um** not of sound mind; raving, insane, foolish *IV*
inscrībō, **-ere**, **inscripsī**, **inscriptus** write in, upon; inscribe *XV*
inscriptiō, **-iōnis** *f* inscription; title *XV*
insidiae, **-ārum** *f pl.* treachery; ambush
insignis, **-e** clearly visible; remarkable in appearance; noteworthy
inspiciō, **-ere**, **-spexī**, **-spectus** inspect, examine *XV*
instituō, **-ere**, **-uī**, **-ūtus** establish; teach, instruct *VI*
instō, **-āre**, **institī**, —— (*fut. act. part.*: **instatūrus**) stand upon, in; approach, threaten; urge, press upon
insula, **-ae** *f* island
insum, **inesse**, **infuī**, —— be in; be contained in; belong in *VIII*
integer, **-gra**, **-grum** untouched, unimpaired, whole, fresh
  in (**ad**) **integrum** to a former or original state *V*
intellectus, **-ūs** *m* intellect; perception *XII*
intellegentia, **-ae** *f* understanding, knowledge, perception *XI*
intellegō, **-ere**, **-lexī**, **-lectus** perceive, understand, comprehend *XI*
inter (*prep.* + *acc.*) amid, among, between *IX*
intereā (*adv.*) meanwhile
interficiō, **-ere**, **-fēcī**, **-fectus** kill, destroy *X*
intrō, **-āre**, **-āvī**, **-ātus** go into, walk into *XV*
inveniō, **-īre**, **invēnī**, **inventus** come upon, find, discover *III*
invideō, **-ēre**, **invīdī**, **invīsus** (+ *dat.*) envy, be jealous of; look askance at; begrudge *something* (*acc.*) *to someone* (*dat.*) *XIV*

invidia, **-ae** *f* envy, jealousy; ill-will, spite *II*
invītus, **-a**, **-um** unwilling, reluctant *V*
ipse, **ipsa**, **ipsum** (*intensive pron.*) himself, herself, itself; the very *IX*
īra, **-ae** *f* anger, wrath *XI*
īrātus, **-a**, **-um** (+ *dat.*) angry with
is, **ea**, **id** he, she, it; this or that person, this or that thing *VII*
iste, **ista**, **istud** that (*man*, *woman*, *thing*) (of yours) *IX*
ita (*adv.*) in this manner, in this way, so, thus *IX*
Ĭtalia, **-ae** *f* Italy *VIII*
item (*adv.*) likewise *VIII*
iter, **itineris** *n* a going, a journey; walk, way, path, road *XIV*
iubeō, **-ēre**, **iussī**, **iussus** order, command *IV*
iūcundus, **-a**, **-um** pleasant
iūdiciālis, **-e** judicial *XI*
iūdicō, **-āre**, **-āvī**, **-ātus** judge, decide, estimate *XVII*
iungō, **-ere**, **iunxī**, **iunctus** join, connect *XVII*
Iūno, **-ōnis** *f* Juno (*queen of the gods*), wife of Jupiter *IX*
Iuppiter, **Iovis** *m* Jupiter (*ruler of the gods*) *IX*
iūs, **iūris** *n* (natural) right, law, justice *VIII*
  iūs iūrandum, **iūris iūrandī** oath
iūrō, **-āre**, **-āvī**, **-ātus** swear, take an oath *XVI*
iustus, **-a**, **-um** just, equitable, lawful *VII*
iuvenis, **is** *m* (*gen. pl.* **iuvenum**) young man *XII*

L

labrum, **-ī** *n* lip *VI*
labor, **labōris** *m* labor, toil *IX*
labōrō, **-āre**, **-āvī**, **-ātus** labor, take pains, exert oneself; work, toil *VI*
lacrima, **-ae** *f* tear *XIII*
lapis, **lapidis** *m* stone, pebble
Latīnus, **-a**, **-um** Latin *III*
latus, **-eris** *n* side (*of the body*); lungs
lātus, **-a**, **-um** broad, wide
laus, **laudis** *f* praise *XI*
laudō, **-āre**, **-āvī**, **-ātus** praise *V*
legō, **-ere**, **lēgī**, **lectus** choose, gather, select; read *III*
lēnis, **-e** gentle, mild
levis, **-e** light (*in weight*); slight, trivial *XIII*
lētum, **-ī** *n* death *VII*
lex, **lēgis** *f* a bill which has become law; law *VIII*
libenter (*adv.*) willingly *X*
liber, **librī** *m* book *II*
līber, **līberī** *m* (*usually in the plural*) child
līber, **-era**, **-erum** free *II*
Līber, **Līberī** *m* Liber, *Italian god associated with Bacchus*
līberō, **-āre**, **-āvī**, **-ātus** (*with or without* **ab** + *abl.*) free (from), liberate *IX*
lībertās, **-tātis** *f* freedom *VIII*
lībertīnus, **-ī** *m* freedman *XV*

libet, **-ēre**, **libuit** or **libitum est** (*impersonal*) it is pleasing *XVII*
lībra, **-ae** *f* balance, pair of scales
licet, **-ēre**, **licuit** or **licitum est** (*impersonal*) it is permitted; one may *XVII*
līmen, **-inis** *n* threshold, edge *XV*
lingua, **-ae** *f* tongue, language *III*
linquō, **-ere**, **līquī**, —— go away from, leave, abandon
littera, **-ae** *f* letter (of alphabet);
pl. letter *VI*
lītus, **lītoris** *n* shore, coastline
locō, **-āre**, **-āvī**, **-ātus** place, set, arrange *X*
locus, **-ī** *m X* place
loca, **-ōrum** *n pl.* places, locations
locī, **-ōrum** *m pl.* passages (*in literature*)
longus, **-a**, **-um** long, lengthy, far *VIII*
loquor, **loquī**, **locūtus sum** say, speak, tell, converse *XVI*
luctus, **-ūs** *m* sorrow, grief
lūdō, **-ere**, **lūsī**, **lūsus** play, play at a game; make sport of, mock *VI*
lūdus, **-ī** *m* game, play, sport; school *VI*
lūgeō, **-ēre**, **luxī**, **luctus** mourn, lament
lūmen, **lūminis** *n* light;
pl. (*metaphorically*) eyes *XII*
lūna, **-ae** *f* the moon
lux, **lūcis** *f* light (*of the sun and other heavenly bodies*); daylight, light *X*

M

magis (*adv.*) more *XV*
magister, **-trī** *m* teacher, master *II*
magistrātus, **-ūs** *m* office of a magistrate
magnitūdō, **-tūdinis** *f* greatness, size, bulk
magnopere (*adv.*) greatly *XV*
magnus, **-a**, **-um** large, big, great *II*
māior, **māius** larger, greater; *XV*
nostrī māiōrēs *pl.* ancestors
māior nātū elder; older (*in age*)
male (*adv.*) badly *VI*
malitia, **-ae** *f* wickedness
mālō, **mālle**, **māluī**, —— prefer *VI*
malus, **-a**, **-um** bad *II*
mandō, **-āre**, **-āvī**, **-ātus** order, command, give a command; entrust *XIII*
māne (*adv.*) in the morning
maneō, **-ēre**, **mānsī**, **mānsūrus** remain, stay; await *V*
manus, **-ūs** *f* hand; band of men *XII*
mare, **-is** *n* the sea *XI*
marītus, **-ī** *m* husband; married man
marmor, **marmoris** *n* marble; surface of the sea
marsuppium, **-iī** *n* purse, pocket-book
māter, **mātris** *f* mother *XIII*

māteria, **-ae** *f* substance, material
mātrimōnium, **-iī** *n* marriage
maximus, **-a**, **-um** greatest, largest *XV*
mē (*acc. abl. sing.*) me *II*
medicus, **-ī** *m* doctor
medius, **-a**, **-um** middle, the middle (of) *VIII*
mehercle by Hercules!
melior, **-ius** better *XV*
membrum, **-ī** *n* limb *IX*
memor; **memoris** mindful (of), remembering *XI*
memorābilis, **-e** memorable, worthy of being remembered *XVII*
memoria, **-ae** *f* memory *VI*
memorō, **-āre**, **-āvī**, **-ātus** recall to mind, remind of; recount, narrate, mention *XI*
meminī, **meminisse** (*defective verb*) remember *VI*
mēns, **mentis** *f* the mind *XI*
mēnsis, **mēnsis** *m* month *XI*
mereō, **-ēre**, **meruī**, **meritus** deserve, earn; be worthy of *XI*
mereor, **-ērī**, **meritus sum** deserve, earn
metuō, **metuere**, **metuī**, **metūtus** fear, be afraid of *XVI*
metus, **-ūs** *m* fear, dread *XIII*
meus, **-a**, **-um** my, mine *II*
mihĭ̄ (*dat. sing.*) to/for me
mīles, **mīlitis** *m* soldier *X*
mille (*indeclinable neuter noun*) one thousand *XVII*
  mīlia, **mīlium** *n pl.* thousands
minimus, **-a**, **-um** smallest, least *XV*
minor, **minus** smaller *XV*
minus (*adv.*) less
mīror, **-ārī**, **mīrātus sum** marvel at, be astonished at, admire; wonder *XVI*
mīrus, **-a**, **-um** wondrous, surprising, remarkable
misceō, **-ēre**, **miscuī**, **mixtus** mingle, intermingle; unite, mix *XIII*
miser, **-era**, **-erum** unhappy, wretched, miserable *II*
miseret, **-ēre**, **miseruit**, —— (*impersonal*) move *someone* (*acc.*) to feel pity for *something* (*gen.*); it causes pity *XVII*
mītis, **-e** mild, gentle, kind; sweet-tasting
mittō, **-ere**, **mīsī**, **missus** send *III*
modo (*adv.*) only, but
  nōn modo . . . **sed etiam** not only . . . but also
  modo ut (+ *subjunctive*) provided that *XVII*
  sī modo (+ *indicative*) if at least *XVII*
  quī modo (+ *indicative*) provided that he *XVII*
modus, **-ī** *m* manner, method, way; measure, limit; rhythm *V*
moenia, **-ium** *n* defensive walls of a town
molestus, **-a**, **-um** annoying, irksome *IV*
mollis, **-e** soft, flexible, tender, gentle *XIV*
moneō, **-ēre**, **monuī**, **monitus** warn, advise, remind *I*

mōns, **montis** *m* mountain *XVII*
mōnstrō, **-āre**, **-āvī**, **-ātus** show, point out, indicate *IX*
mōnstrum, **-ī** *n* omen, wonder, monster *IX*
mordeō, **-ēre**, **momordī**, **morsus** bite, sting *I*
morior, **morī**, **mortuus sum** (*fut. act. part.* **moritūrus**) die *XVI*
mora, **-ae** *f* delay
moror, **-ārī**, **morātus sum** delay, linger, loiter *XVI*
mors, **mortis** *f* death *XI*
mortālis, **-e** mortal, subject to death *XI*
mōs, **mōris** *m* custom, habit;
pl. character; customs, habits
mōrem gerere (+ *dat.*) comply with the wishes (*of someone*) *VIII*
mōtus, **-ūs** *m* motion, movement; emotion *XII*
moveō, **-ēre**, **mōvī**, **mōtus** move
mox (*adv.*) soon *VI*
muliĕbris, **-e** of a woman, having to do with a woman
mulier, **mulieris** *f* woman, wife, female *XIII*
multitūdo, **-tūdinis** *f* multitude *VIII*
multum (*adv.*) much *XV*
multus, **-a**, **-um** much, many *IV*
mundus, **-ī** *m* universe, world *VI*
muniō, **-īre**, **-īvī**, **-ītus** fortify
mūnus, **mūneris** *n* function, duty; gift, offering *XIII*
mūrus, **-ī** *m* wall; city wall
Mūsa, **-ae** *f* Muse, a goddess presiding over the arts
mūtō, **-āre**, **-āvī**, **-ātus** alter, change *VI*
myrtus, **-ī** *f* myrtle tree

N

nam (*conj.*) for (*confirms or explains a preceding statement*) *IV*
narrātiō, **-iōnis** *f* a relating, a narrative; the (*formal*) narrative section of a speech *VIII*
nascor, **nascī**, **nātus sum** be born, come into being *XVI*
nāsus, **-ī** *m* (or **nāsum**, **-ī** *n*) nose
nātālis, **-e** having to do with one's birth *XII*
nātiō, **-iōnis** *f* a people; a nation; the birth of a child *XI*
nātūra, **-ae** *f* nature *VI*
nātūrālis, **-e** natural, in keeping with nature *XII*
nātūrāliter (*adv.*) naturally *XII*
nātus, **-ī** *m* son *X*
nauta, **-ae** *f* sailor *II*
nāvis, **-is** *f* ship
nē (+ *subj.*) that . . . not; in order not to *IV*
nē . . . **quidem** not even *X*
-ne (*enclitic, introduces a question*) *I*
-ne . . . **an** (*introduces a double question*: "? or . . . ?") *VI*
nec (*conj.*) and not, also not *IV*
nec . . . **nec** neither . . . nor

necesse est (*impersonal*) it is necessary *XVII*
necessitās, **-tātis** *f* force, compulsion
necō, **-āre**, **-āvī**, **-ātus** kill, put to death, destroy
nefandus, **-a**, **-um** unspeakable, abominable
nefās (*indeclinable neuter noun*) contrary to divine law, sinful, unlawful; sin, crime *XIV*
neglegentia, **-ae** *f* carelessness, negligence
neglegō, **-ere**, **-lexi**, **-lectus** neglect, disregard
negō, **-āre**, **-āvī**, **-ātus** deny; say no, refuse
(*with acc. + infin.*) say that . . . not *XIII*
negōtium, **-ī** *n* business, employment; labor *VII*
nēmō, **nēminis** *m* or *f* no one, nobody *IX*
Neptūnus, **-ī** *m* Neptune, *god of the sea*
neque (*conj.*) and not, also not
neque . . . **neque** neither . . . nor *IV*
nesciō, **-īre**, **nescīvī**, **-ītus** not know, be unknowing *III*
nescioquis, **nescioquid** (*indefinite pronoun*) someone, something *XI*
nescius, **-a**, **-um** not knowing, unaware *IX*
neuter, **-tra**, **-trum** neither of two *III*
nihil or **nīl** (*indeclinable*) nothing *V*
nimis (*adv.*) excessively
nimium (*adv.*) excessively
nisi unless, if not *IV*
nitidus, **-a**, **-um** bright, shining, gleaming
nōbilis, **-e** well-known, famous; of high birth; noble *XVI*
noceō, **-ēre**, **nocuī**, **nocitus** (+ *dat.*) do harm to, harm *X*
nōlī, **nōlīte** (+ *infinitive*) don't *I*
nōlō, **nōlle**, **nōluī**, —— be unwilling *VI*
nōmen, **nōminis** *n* name; appellation; noun *VIII*
nōn (*adv.*) not *I*
nōndum (*adv.*) not yet
nōnne: *introduces a question which expects an answer in the affirmative* *V*
nōs (*nom.* or *acc. pl.*) we, us *III*
noscō, **-ere**, **nōvī**, **nōtus** learn, become acquainted with;
(*in perfect tense*) know *IV*
noster, **-tra**, **-trum** our *II*
notō, **-āre**, **-āvī**, **-ātus** mark, indicate, denote, signify; pay attention to *XV*
novem (*indeclinable*) nine
novus, **-a**, **-um** new; recent; unusual, strange *VIII*
nox, **noctis** *f* night *XI*
noxa, **-ae** *f* injurious conduct; harm, injury *XVI*
nūbēs, **-is** *f* cloud *XI*
nūllus, **-a**, **-um** no, none *III*
num (*introducing direct question*) *anticipates negative answer*
(*introducing indirect question*) whether, if *V, VI*
nūmen, **-inis** *n* divine will, power of the gods; a deity
numerus, **-ī** *m* number, meter *II*
numquam (*adv.*) never *IV*

nunc now *IV*
nuntiō, **-āre**, **-āvī**, **-ātus** announce *XI*
nuntius, **-ī** *m* messenger
nuptiae, **-ārum** *f pl.* marriage, wedding *V*
nuptiālis, **-e** nuptial, of or belonging to a marriage
nusquam (*adv.*) nowhere

O

ob (*prep.* + *acc.*) on account of, because of, for the purpose of *XI*
oblītus: from **oblīvīscor**
oblīvīscor, **oblīvīscī**, **oblītus sum** (+ *gen.*) forget, be forgetful *XVIII*
oboleō, **-ēre**, **oboluī**, —— emit a scent, smell of something
obscūrus, **-a**, **-um** dark, shady, obscure, hidden *XI*
obsequium, **-iī** *n* (+ *gen.*) obedience (to); compliance *XIII*
obsum, **obesse**, **offuī**, **offutūrus** (+ *dat.*) hinder, injure
obtineō, **-ēre**, **-uī**, **-tentum** obtain
occāsus, **-ūs** *m* a fall, a setting (of the sun) *XII*
occidō, **-ere**, **occidī**, **occāsus** fall down, fall; perish *III*
octo (*indeclinable*) eight
oculus, **-ī** *m* eye *VII*
ōdī, **ōdisse** (*defective verb*) hate, despise; dislike *XIII*
offerō, **-ferre**, **obtulī**, **oblātus** present, show, bring forward, offer *XII*
officium, **-iī** *n* duty, responsibility; office *VII*
ōlim (*adv.*) formerly, once, once upon a time *IX*
omnis, **-e** every, all *XI*
omnīnō (*adv.*) entirely, altogether
onus, **oneris** *n* burden
opera, **-ae** *f* service, exertion, work, labor
opīniō, **-iōnis** *f* opinion, conjecture, belief *VIII*
opīnor, **-ārī**, **opīnātus sum** hold as an opinion; think, believe *XVIII*
oportet, **-ēre**, **oportuit** it is proper, right, inevitable, bound to happen *XVII*
oppōnō, **-ere**, **-posuī**, **-positus** set against; oppose *XII*
opportūnus, **-a**, **-um** (*with* **ad** + *acc.*) fit, suitable (for); convenient *VIII*
opprimō, **-ere**, **oppressī**, **oppressus** overwhelm, oppress *IX*
opprobrium, **-ī** *n* reproach, scandal, disgrace *V*
oppugnō, **-āre**, **-āvī**, **-ātus** attack
ops, **opis** *f* power; means;
pl. wealth, resources
opus, **operis** *n* work, labor; the result of work; need
opus est (+ *gen. or abl.*) there is need (*of*)
opus est (+ *infinitive*) there is a need, it is necessary (*to do*) *X*
optimus, **-a**, **-um** best *XV*
optō, **-āre**, **-āvī**, **-ātus** desire, wish for, want *I*
ōrātiō, **-iōnis** *f* speech *VIII*
ōrātor, **ōrātōris** *m* speaker; orator, *the person making a speech* *VIII*
orbis, **is** *m* round surface, sphere, circle, ring
orbis terrārum the world *XI*

ordior, **ordīrī**, **orsus sum** begin
ordō, **ordinis** *m* order, rank; arrangement in a line
orior, **orīrī**, **ortus sum** (*future act. participle*: **oritūrus**) rise, get up; (*of heavenly bodies*) rise, become visible; come forth; rise, spring from *XVI*
ōrō, **-āre**, **-āvī**, **-ātus** ask, beg, pray, plead *XIII*
ortus, **-ūs** *m* a rising; rise, beginning, origin *XII*
ōs, **ōris** *n* the mouth; an opening; the face
osculum, **-ī** *n* kiss *XIII*
ostendō, **-ere**, **-tendī**, **-tentus** show, reveal *VI*
ōtium, **-iī** *n* leisure, peace *VII*

P

pacō, **-āre**, **-āvī**, **-ātus** make peaceful, pacify *XI*
paedagōgus, **-ī** *m* child attendant; paedagogue *VI*
paene (*adv.*) almost *XV*
paenitet, **-ēre**, **paenituit**, —— (*impersonal*) cause *someone* (*acc.*) to feel dissatisfaction or regret for *something* (*gen.*); it causes repentence *XVII*
palātum, **-ī** *n* the palate
pandō, **-ere**, **pandī**, **passus** spread, spread out, unfold, expand, extend *XII*
pār; **pāris** (+ *dat.* or *gen.*) equal (to) *XIII*
parcō, **-ere**, **pepercī**, **parsūrus** (+ *dat.*) be sparing to, spare *XV*
pareō, **-ēre**, **paruī**, **paritus** (+ *dat.*) be obedient to, obey, comply with *XV*
parēns, **-ntis** *m* or *f* parent
parō, **-āre**, **-āvī**, **-ātus** prepare, provide *I*
pars, **partis** *f* part; direction *IX*
parum (*indeclinable neuter noun* or *adverb*) (+ *partitive genitive*) a little; too little; not enough VII
parvus, **-a**, **-um** small, little *II*
pater, **patris** *m* father *VIII*
patior, **patī**, **passus sum** bear, endure, suffer *XVI*
patria, **-ae** *f* fatherland, native land *VII*
patrius, **-a**, **-um** of one's father or native land, ancestral
patrimōnium, **-iī** *n* an estate inherited from a father; inheritance *X*
pastor, **pastōris** *m* shepherd; herdsman
paucī, **paucae**, **pauca** (*pl.*) few, a few *XII*
paulātim (*adv.*) little by little *XV*
paulisper (*adv.*) for a little while
paulum (*adv.*) only to a small extent; only for a short time
pauper; **pauperis** poor, not wealthy; of small means *XV*
pax, **pācis** *f* peace *X*
pectus, **-oris** *n* chest, breast *XVI*
pecus, **pecoris** *n* herd, flock;
pl. farm animals, especially cattle or sheep
pecūnia, **-ae** *f* money *IV*
pēior, **pēius** worse *XV*

pellō, **-ere**, **pepulī**, **pulsus** push, hurl, drive out *X*
pendeō, **-ēre**, **pependī**, —— be suspended, hang; be weighed *XV*
per (*prep.* + *acc.*) through; through the agency of *X*
pereō, **perīre**, **periī** (**perīvī**), **peritum** perish, pass away, be destroyed *VIII*
perficiō, **-ere**, **-fēcī**, **-fectus** accomplish, complete, do thorougly, perfect *X*
perfidia, **-ae** *f* treachery, faithlessness, falsehood
perīculum, **-ī** *n* danger, peril *X*
permittō, **-ere**, **-mīsī**, **-missus** surrender; commit; allow, grant, permit *XIV*
perpetuus, **-a**, **-um** constantly occurring; continuous
persōna, **-ae** *f* personage, character; a mask *VII*
perspiciō, **-ere**, **-spexī**, **-spectus** look through, look at
persuādeō, **-ēre**, **-suāsī**, **-suāsus** (+ *dat.*) win over by talking, persuade *XV*
perveniō, **-īre**, **-vēnī**, **-ventus** arrive
pervertō, **-ere**, **-vertī**, **-versus** overturn, overthrow, subvert *IX*
perversus, **-a**, **-um** not right; turned the wrong way, distorted, askew *VII*
pervideō, **-ēre**, **-vīdī**, **-vīsus** look over, survey, examine
pēs, **pedis** *m* foot (*of a person or animal*) *XI*
pessimus, **-a**, **-um** worst *XV*
petō, **-ere**, **-īvī**, **-ītus** seek, ask *III*
philosophia, **-ae**, *f* philosophy
philosophor, **-ārī**, **-ātus sum** philosophize
philosophus, **-ī** *m* philosopher *VII*
pictor, **-tōris** *m* painter *XV*
pietās, **-tātis** *f* reverence, piety, devotion *XIII*
piget, **-ēre**, **piguit**, —— (*impersonal*) affect *someone* (*acc.*) with revulsion or disgust for *something* (*gen.*); it disgusts *XVII*
pingō, **-ere**, **pinxī**, **pictus** paint, embroider, adorn; represent pictorially *XV*
pīnus, **-ī** *f* pine tree
placeō, **-ēre**, **placuī**, **placitus** (+ *dat.*) be pleasing to, please *XV*
planta, **-ae** *f* plant, shoot, slip of a plant *VII*
plantō, **-āre**, **-āvī**, **-ātus** to plant *VII*
plebs, **plēbis** *f* the general body of citizens at Rome
plēnus, **-a**, **-um** (*adj.* + *abl.* or *gen.*) filled (with), full (of) *VII*
plūrimum (*adv.*) most, very much *XV*
plūrimus, **-a**, **-um** most *XV*
plūs, **plūris** *n* (*sing.*: *neuter noun*) more;
(*adv.*) more
plūrēs, **plūra** (*pl.*: *irregular comparative adj.*) more *XV*
poena, **-ae** *f* punishment, penalty
Poenus, **-ī** *m* Carthaginian
poēta, **-ae** *m* poet *II*
poēticus, **-a**, **-um** poetic; after the manner of poets *VII*

polliceor, -**ērī**, **pollicitus sum** promise
pōnō, -**ere**, **posuī**, **positus** put, place *IV*
populus, -**ī** *m* (*collective noun*) the people, nation *VII*
porticus, -**ūs** *f* colonnade, covered walkway, porch *XIV*
poscō, -**ere**, **poposcī**, —— ask urgently for; beg, request; demand *XIV*
possum, **posse**, **potuī**, —— (+ *complementary infin.*) be able *III*
post (*prep.* + *acc.*) after *XI*
posteā (*adv.*) afterwards
posterī, -**ōrum** *m pl.* descendants, posterity
posterus, -**a**, -**um** later
postquam (*conj.*) after *IX*
potēns; **potentis** powerful, able *XI*
potentia, -**ae** *f* might, force, power *X*
potestās, -**tātis** *f* ability, power *XIII*
potior, -**īrī**, **potītus sum** (+ *abl.*) get possession of
prae (*adv.*) before
(*prep.* + *abl.*) before, in front of *IX*
praebeō, -**ēre**, **praebuī**, **praebitus** put forward, offer, provide; show *XVII*
praecēdō, -**ere**, -**cessī**, -**cessus** go before, precede *IX*
praedīco, -**ere**, -**dīxī**, -**dictus** foretell, predict
praesēns; **praesentis** present; in person
praestō, -**stāre**, -**stitī**, -**stitus** (+ *dat.*)
(*intrans.*) stand in front of; stand out, be superior;
(*trans.*) show, exhibit; make good, perform, fulfill *XV*
praesum, -**esse**, -**fuī**, —— (+ *dat.*) be before; preside over, have charge of *XI*
praeter (*prep.* + *accus.*) beyond, in addition to
praetereō, -**īre**, -**iī** (**īvī**), -**itum** pass by, pass over, omit *VIII*
premō, -**ere**, **pressī**, **pressus** hold fast, bear down, press *IX*
pretium, -**iī** *n* price, value
prīmō (*adv.*) at first, in the first place *XV*
prīmum (*adv.*) at first, in the first place *XV*
prīmus, -**a**, -**um** first *XIII*
prīnceps, -**cipis** *m* the chief; head person; the first member of the Senate; the ruler, emperor *XI*
prīncipium, -**iī** *n* beginning, commencement *XI*
prior, **prius** former *XV*
priusquam (*or* **prius** . . . **quam**) (*conj.*) before *XVII*
prō (*prep.* + *abl.*) for, in behalf of; before, in front of; in proportion *VII*
probābilitās, -**tātis** *f* probability *VIII*
probō, -**āre**, -**āvī**, -**ātus** approve (of), find acceptable *VII*
prōcēdō, -**ere**, -**cessī**, -**cessus** go forward, go forth, proceed; advance *XII*
prōcreō, -**āre**, -**āvī**, -**ātus** bring forth, beget, generate
procul (*adv.*) at a distance *XI*
prōdeō, -**īre**, -**iī** (-**īvī**), -**itum** go or come forth *VIII*
prōdest: *see* **prōsum**
proelium, -**iī** *n* battle, combat *XV*

prōficiō, **-ere**, **-fēcī**, **-fectus** advance, make progress, accomplish; be useful, contribute *VII*
profugus, **-a**, **-um** fugitive, exiled
prōfundō, **-ere**, **-fūdī**, **-fūsus** pour out, pour forth; cause to flow *VII*
prōgredior, **-gredī**, **-gressus sum** come or go forth, proceed *XVI*
prohibeō, **-ēre**, **-uī**, **-itus** prevent, deter, prohibit *XVI*
prope (*adv.*) near, nearly;
(*prep.* + *acc.*) near *IX*
prōpōnō, **-ere**, **-posuī**, **-positus** propose, offer; state a proposition; set before the mind *VI*
proprius, **-a**, **-um** special, particular, one's own; not common with others *XII*
propter (*adv.*) near, close by;
(*prep.* + *acc.*) on account of; through
prosperus, **-a**, **-um** favorable, fortunate, prosperous *XI*
prōsum, **prōdesse**, **prōfuī**, **prōfutūrus** (+ *dat.*) be useful (to), do a good thing (to), benefit *X*
prōtinus (*adv.*) straightway, immediately *XIII*
prōveniō, **-īre**, **-vēnī**, **-ventus** come forth, appear *VII*
prōvidentia, **-ae** *f* foresight, the power of seeing in advance; provision (for) *XVII*
prōvideō, **-ēre**, **-vīdī**, **-vīsus** act with foresight; foresee, discern *XVII*
prōvincia, **-ae** *f* a province; territory governed by Rome *XI*
pūblicus, **-a**, **-um** public (*as opposed to private*); of or belonging to the community *VII*
pudet, **-ēre**, **puduit**, —— (*impersonal*) cause *someone* (*acc.*) displeasure or revulsion *for someone or something* (*gen.*); it causes displeasure *XVII*
pudīcus, **-a**, **-um** bashful, shamefaced; chaste, pure, undefiled; modest *VI*
puella, **-ae** *f* girl; daughter; sweetheart, mistress *II*
puer, **puerī** *m* boy; child; slave *II*
pugnō, **-āre**, **āvī**, **-ātus** fight *X*
pulcher, **-chra**, **-chrum** beautiful, handsome *II*
pulchritūdō, **-tūdinis** *f* beauty *IX*
pulsō, **-āre**, **-āvī**, **-ātus** strike, beat, knock *III*
Pūnicus, **-a**, **-um** Carthaginian
purpura, **-ae** *f* purple
pūrus, **-a**, **-um** pure, clean, honest, unstained *VI*
putō, **-āre**, **-āvī**, **-ātus** think *VII*
pyra, **-ae** *f* funeral pyre *IX*

Q

quā (**viā**) where, by what way
quaerō, **-ere**, **quaesīvī**, **quaesītus** seek, look for, ask, inquire *IV*
quālis, **-e** of what sort, of what kind *XI*

quam (*interrog. adv.*) how? to what degree; *VI*
(*exclamatory adv.*) how! *XIII*
(*with comparisons*) than; *XIII*
(*with superlatives*) as . . . as possible *XIII*
quam ob rem why; why?; wherefore *VI*
quamquam (*conjunction*) although *XVII*
quamvīs (*conjunction*) although *XVII*
quandō (*adv.* and *conjunction*) when? when; because, since *VI*
quantus, **-a**, **-um** how great, how large, how much *V*
quartus, **-a**, **-um** fourth
quattuor (*indeclinable*) four
quārē wherefore, why; why? *VI*
quasi as if, like
-que (*enclitic conjunction*) and *V*
quemadmodum (*adv.*) how, in what way *XV*
quī, **quae**, **quod** (*relative pronoun*) who, which *VI*
quia (*conjunction*) because *X*
quīcumque, **quaecumque**, **quodcumque** (*indefinite pronoun*) who(so)ever, what(so)ever *XII*
quid (*interrogative adv. or pronoun*) what? why? *III*, *VI*
quid ita how so?
quīdam, **quaedam**, **quiddam** (*adj.* **quoddam**) (*indefinite pronoun*) someone, something; a certain person, a certain thing *XII*
quidem indeed (*gives emphasis, usually by contrasting one thing with another*)
nē . . . (*x*) . . . **quidem** not even *x* *X*
quī modo (*conj.*) provided that he
quīn (*conj.*) but that, that not;
(*adv.*) why not?, indeed *XVI*
quis, **quid** (*interrogative pronoun*) who? what? *III*, *VI*
quis, **quid** (*after* **sī**, **nisī**, **num**, **nē**) = **aliquis**, **aliquid**
quisquam, **quidquam** (**quicquam**) (*indefinite pron. used mainly after negative expression, whether implied or expressed*) anyone, anything *XII*
quisque, **quaeque**, **quidque** (*adj.*: **quodque**) (*indef./distrib. pron.*) each person, each thing (of more than two persons or things) *XII*
quisquis, **quisquid** whoever, whatever *XII*
quīvīs, **quaevīs**, **quidvīs** (*adj.*: **quodvīs**) anyone, anything *XII*
quod because *III*
quōminus that not;
(*after verbs of preventing, hindering*) from *XVI*
quō (*adv.*) where, to what place *XIV*
quō modo how, in what way *VI*
quondam (*adv.*) once, formerly, at one time
quoniam (*conj.*) since, because *XVII*
quoque also, too *X*
quot how many *V*

R

rapiō, **-ere**, **rapuī**, **raptus** seize and carry off, carry off by force; seize, snatch, take *X*
ratiō, **-iōnis** *f* account, reckoning, calculation; reason, reasoning; system
ratiōnem reddere give an account *X*
recēns; **recentis** recent
recipiō, **-ere**, **-cēpī**, **-ceptus** take back, recover, accept *XI*
rectus, **-a**, **-um** straight; right, correct *X*
reddō, **reddere**, **reddidī**, **redditus** give back, restore, return *IX*
redeō, **redīre**, **rediī** (**redīvī**), **reditum** return, go or come back *VIII*
redigō, **-ere**, **redēgī**, **redactus** drive or send back, restore
redimō, **-ere**, **-ēmī**, **-emptus** buy back, purchase
reditus, **-ūs** *m* a returning, return *XII*
referō, **-ferre**, **-tulī**, **-lātus** carry back, bring back; report *XII*
sē referre return, withdraw
rēgīna, **-ae** *f* queen
rēgius, **-a**, **-um** royal; of the king *XVII*
regnō, **-āre**, **-āvī**, **-ātus** rule, reign
regnum, **-ī** *n* kingdom, realm *XVII*
regō, **-ere**, **rexī**, **rectus** guide, direct, rule, manage *X*
religiō, **-iōnis** *f* religious awe, reverence
relinquō, **-ere**, **relīquī**, **relictus** leave, abandon, leave behind *X*
reliquus, **-a**, **-um** the rest, the remaining
remaneō, **-ēre**, **-mānsī**, **-mānsūrus** remain, stay behind *V*
remedium, **-iī** *n* remedy, cure, solution *V*
remittō, **-ere**, **-mīsī**, **-missus** let go, send back
removeō, **-ēre**, **-mōvī**, **-mōtus** remove, move back, set aside *VIII*
repente (*adv.*) suddenly *XVIII*
reperiō, **-ere**, **repperī**, **repertus** find, meet with
reprimō, **-ere**, **-pressī**, **-pressus** press back, check, curb, restrain *IX*
rēs, **rēī** *f* thing, matter, event; property; situation
rēs pūblica commonwealth, republic *XIV*
respiciō, **-ere**, **-spexī**, **-spectus** look back, turn one's attention
respondeō, **-ēre**, **respondī**, **respōnsus** reply, answer; give a legal opinion *III*
reus, **-ī** *m* defendant
rex, **rēgis** *m* king, ruler *XI*
rīdeō, **-ēre**, **rīsī**, **rīsus** laugh, laugh at *XIII*
rīdiculus, **-a**, **-um** foolish
rīpa, **-ae** *f* bank of a river
rogō, **-āre**, **-āvī**, **-ātus** ask *VI*
Rōma, **-ae** *f* Rome *VIII*
Rōmānus, **-a**, **-um** Roman, of Rome *VIII*
Rōmulus, **-ī** *m* Romulus (*founder of Rome*)
rūmor, **-ōris** *m* common talk, gossip, report
rumpō, **-ere**, **rūpī**, **ruptus** split open, cause to burst
rursum (*adv.*) again

rūs, **rūris** *n* countryside *VIII*
rūre from the countryside *VIII*
rūrī in the countryside *VIII*
rūs to the countryside *VIII*

S

sacer, **sacra**, **sacrum** sacred, holy; cursed XIV
saeculum, **-i** *n* generation, lifetime; an age (of thirty-three years); a century *XVI*
saepe (*adv.*) often *I*
saevus, **-a**, **-um** raging, cruel, savage *V*
saltem (*adv.*) at least
salūtō, **-āre**, **-āvī**, **-ātus** keep safe, preserve; greet, wish health
salveō, **-ēre**, ——, —— be well, be in good health
salvē! (*sing.*), **salvēte!** (*pl.*) hello! good morning! how are you?; goodbye! fare well! be well! *IV*
salvus, **-a**, **-um** safe, unharmed, well *III*
sanguis, **sanguinis** *m* blood, gore; bloodshed; blood-relation *IX*
sānus, **-a**, **-um** sound, whole, healthy *IV*
sapiēns; **sapientis** wise, knowing *XI*
sapiēns, **sapientis** *m* a wise person; a philosopher
sapientia, **-ae** *f* wisdom; philosophy *VI*
satis (*adv.*; *indeclinable n. noun or adjective*) enough *IV*
saucius, **-a**, **-um** wounded, sick
saxum, **-ī** *n* large stone, rock *XV*
scelus, **-eris** *n* crime, wicked deed *XVI*
scelerātus, **-a**, **-um** wicked, vicious, accursed *XVI*
scelestus, **-a**, **-um** see **scelerātus**
schola, **-ae** *f* learned conversation; a place for learned conversation; school *VI*
scīlicet (*adv.*) it is evident, of course *XI*
scindō, **-ere**, **scidī**, **scissus** cut, tear, split *IX*
sciō, **-īre**, **scīvī**, **scītus** know, understand, perceive *III*
Scorpius, **-iī** *m* the constellation Scorpio
scrībō, **-ere**, **scrīpsi**, **scrīptus** write *VI*
scriptor, **-tōris** *m* writer, author *XI*
sē (*acc.* or *abl.*, *sing.* or *pl. reflexive pronoun*) himself, herself, themselves *VII*
secundus, **-a**, **-um** the second in a sequence; following; favoring, supportive *XVII*
sēcūrus, **-a**, **-um** free from care *VII*
sed (*conj.*) but *II*
sedeō, **-ēre**, **sēdī**, **sessus** sit, continue sitting; sit down *VI*
sedulus, **-a**, **-um** diligent, careful
semel (*adv.*) once; once and for all; simultaneously *XVII*
semper (*adv.*) always *XIII*
senātus, **-ūs** *m* the Senate *XVI*

senectus, **-tūtis** *f* old age *XIII*
senex, **senis** *m* old man
sēnsus, **-ūs** *m* sense, feeling *XII*
sententia, **-ae** *f* opinion, judgment; way of thinking *V*
sentiō, **-īre**, **sēnsī**, **sēnsus** perceive, discern by the senses; feel *III*
septem (*indeclinable*) seven
sequor, **sequī**, **secūtus sum** follow, pursue *XVI*
serō, **-ere**, **sēvī**, **satus** sow, plant
serviō, **-īre**, **servīvī** (**serviī**), **servītus** (+ *dat.*) serve, to be a servant to *XV*
servitūs, **-tūtis** *f* slavery, servitude
servō, **-āre**, **-āvī**, **-ātus** save; retain; preserve, protect, keep safe *VI*
servus, **-ī** *m* slave, servant *II*
seu (*conj.*) (= **sīve**) or if
 seu . . . **seu** whether . . . or *VI*
sevērus, **-a**, **-um** strict, stern, serious, grave *VII*
sex (*indeclinable*) six
sī (*conj.*) if *III*
sīc (*adv.*) so, thus, in this or that way, to such a degree; as follows *IV*, *IX*
sīcut (*adv.*) as, as if, just as *X*
sīdus, **sīderis** *n* constellation, star *XII*
signum, **-ī** *n* mark, token, sign; signal; statue; constellation *XII*
silentium, **-iī** *n* stillness, freedom from disturbance; silence, stillness *XI*
silva, **-ae** *f* a wood, forest, woodland *XIV*
similis, **-e** (+ *dat.* or *gen.*) like, similar *XIII*
sī modo (*conj.*) if at least
simul (*adv.*) at the same time, together *V*
sine (*prep.* + *abl.*) without *III*
singulī, **-ae**, **-a** (*distributive adjective*, *pl. only*) single, separate, one by one *XVI*
sinister, **-tra**, **-trum** left, on the left side; of bad omen *XV*
sinō, **-ere**, **sīvī**, **situs** let, allow, suffer
sinus, **-ūs** *m* curve, fold (*of toga*); lap; bosom; gulf, bay
sīve (*conj.*) or if
 sīve . . . **sīve** whether . . . or
socia, **-ae** *f* female partner
socius, **-ī** *m* companion, partner, ally
sōl, **sōlis** *m* the sun *X*
soleō, **-ēre**, **solitus sum** (+ *complementary infinitive*) to be accustomed, to be used (to) *VII*
solum, **-ī** *n* foundation; soil; sole of a shoe
sōlum (*adv.*) only *IV*
 nōn sōlum . . . **sed etiam** not only . . . but also *V*
sōlus, **-a**, **-um** alone, only *III*
solvō, **-ere**, **solvī**, **solūtus** loosen, relax; set free; weaken; dissolve *VI*
somnium, **-iī** *n* dream *XVIII*

somnus, -ī *m* sleep; *XVIII*
in somnīs in sleep
sonō, **-āre**, **-uī**, **-itus** make a noise, make a sound *VI*
sonus, -ī *m* a noise, a sound *VI*
sopor, **sopōris** *m* sleep, drowsiness *IX*
soror, **sorōris** *f* sister *XIII*
sors, **sortis** *f* lot, share, chance, fortune *XIV*
spatium, -iī *n* space
spectāculum, -ī *n* show, sight, spectacle
spectātus, **-a**, **-um** examined, tried, tested
spectō, **-āre**, **-āvī**, **-ātus** look at, behold, observe *XIII*
spēlunca, **-ae** *f* cave, cavern, den *IX*
spērō, **-āre**, **-āvī**, **-ātus** hope (for) *I*
spēs, **spēī** *f* hope
spīrō, **-āre**, **-āvī**, **-ātus** breathe *I*
stāmen, **stāminis** *n* thread
status, **-ūs** *m* posture, stature, condition, station, rank; position, place; constitution (*of a state*) *XVII*
stella, **-ae** *f* star *II*
stilus, -ī *m* a long, sharp, pointed piece of metal, especially one used for writing: a pen
stō, **stāre**, **stetī**, **status** stand upright, stand firm, remain *IX*
struō, **-ere**, **struxī**, **structus** pile up, construct
studeō, **-ēre**, **studuī**, —— (+ *dat.*) be zealous for, be eager for; study *VIII*
studium, **studiī** *n* enthusiasm; interest; study *VI*
stultitia, **-ae** *f* stupidity
stultus, **-a**, **-um** foolish, stupid, slow-witted *XVIII*
suādeō, **-ēre**, **suāsī**, **suāsus** (+ *dat.*) urge, advise, persuade *XIII*
suāvis, **-e** sweet, pleasant, agreeable *XIV*
sub (*prep.* + *acc.*) under, below, beneath (*motion toward*)
(+ *abl.*) underneath, below, beneath (*place where*) *XI*
subdō, **-ere**, **-didī**, **-ditus** put under, place under, subject, subdue *IX*
subeō, **-īre**, **-iī** (**īvī**), **-itus** (= **sub** + **eō**) come or go under, approach, undergo, submit to *XIII*
subiciō, **-ere**, **-iēcī**, **-iectus** subject, bring or place under, set below *XI*
subigō, **-ere**, **-ēgī**, **-actus** bring under, subjugate, compel
subitō (*adv.*) suddenly
sublātus, **-a**, **-um** *see* **sufferō**, **tollō**
subveniō, **-īre**, **-vēnī**, **-ventus** come to someone's assistance, aid, assist
sufferō, **sufferre**, **sustulī**, **sublātus** carry under; bear, support, sustain; undergo, suffer *XII*
sum, **esse**, **fuī**, **futūrus** to be *III*
summus, **-a**, **-um** highest *XV*
summa, **-ae** *f* summit, top; main thing, chief point; substance; the whole
sūmō, **-ere**, **sumpsī**, **sumptus** take, take up, lay hold of, assume *XI*

super (*adv.*) up above *XV*
(*prep.* + *acc.* or *abl.*) above
superbus, **-a**, **-um** haughty, proud, insolent *X*
superior, **superius** higher
superō, **-āre**, **-āvī**, **-ātus** overcome, conquer *IX*
supersum, **-esse**, **-fuī**, **-futūrus** remain; exist still, survive; be in abundance *IV*
superus, **-a**, **-um** situated above, upper; heavenly
superī, **-ōrum** *m pl.* the gods (above) *XI*
suprā (*adv.*) above, on top
suprēmus, **-a**, **-um** last, highest *XV*
surdus, **-a**, **-um** deaf
surgō, **-ere**, **surrexī**, **surrectus** raise, lift; rise, arise, get up *XII*
suscipiō, **-ere**, **-cēpī**, **-ceptus** support, hold up; take up; take, receive; undertake, begin
sustulī *see* **sufferō**; **tollō**
suus, **-a**, **-um** (*third person reflexive possessive adj.*) of or belonging to himself, herself, itself, themselves *VII*

T

taceō, **-ēre**, **tacuī**, **tacitus** be silent, be still *XIV*
taedet, **-ēre**, **taeduit** or **taesum est** (*impersonal*) it makes (*one*) weary, it makes (*one*) sick (*of something*) *XVII*
tālis, **-e** of such a sort, of such a kind *XIII*
tālis . . . **quālis** of such a sort . . . as *XIII*
tam (*adv.*, *modifies an adjective or adverb*) so *IX*
tam . . . **quam** as much . . . as, as well . . . as
nōn tam . . . **quam** not so much . . . as *XII*
tamen (*adv.*) nevertheless
tandem (*adv.*) finally, at last *XIII*
tangō, **-ere**, **tetigī**, **tactus** touch, handle; strike; border on or be contiguous to *XIV*
tantus, **-a**, **-um** of such a size or measure; so great *V*
tantus . . . **quantus** as great (large) . . . as *V*
tardus, **-a**, **-um** slow, sluggish; late *XII*
tē (*acc.*, *abl. sing.*) you *II*
tē amābō "please"
tegmen, **tegminis** *n* a covering, cover
tegō, **-ere**, **texī**, **tectus** cover
tempestās, **-tātis** *f* season, period of time, weather, storm
tempus, **temporis** *n* time *VIII*
tenebrae, **-ārum** *f pl.* darkness
teneō, **-ēre**, **tenuī**, **tentus** hold, grasp *I*
ter (*adv.*) three times *XVII*
tergum, **-ī** *n* the back, rear
terra, **-ae** *f* earth, land, soil *III*
terreō, **-ēre**, **-uī**, **-itus** terrify, frighten

testis, **-is** *m* witness *XVI*
thalamus, **-ī** *m* an inner room; bedchamber; marriage-bed *XIII*
tibĭ (*dat. sing.*) to/for you
timeō, **-ēre**, **timuī**, —— fear, be afraid of *I*
timidus, **-a**, **-um** fearful, afraid, timid *V*
timor, **-ōris** *m* fear, dread, anxiety
titulus, **-ī** *m* inscription; title; notice
tolerō, **-āre**, **-āvī**, **-ātus** tolerate, endure, bear, sustain *VII*
tollō, **-ere**, **sustulī**, **sublātus** lift, raise, elevate; take away, destroy, kill, abolish *X*
tot (*indeclinable numerical adjective*) so many
  tot . . . **quot** so many . . . as *V*
totidem (*indeclinable*) the same number of; as many
totiēns (*adv.*) so often, so many times
tōtus, **-a**, **-um** whole, entire, total *III*
trādō, **-ere**, **-didī**, **-ditus** hand over, transmit, deliver; report; betray *IX*
trahō, **-ere**, **traxī**, **tractus** draw, drag, pull *V*
trāns (*prep.* + *acc.*) across, over, beyond, through *IX*
trānseō, **-īre**, **-iī** (**-īvī**), **-itus** go over or across, cross over, pass over, pass through
trēs, **tria** three *XVII*
tristis, **-e** sad, gloomy, unhappy *XIII*
tū (*nom. sing. pron.*) you *III*
tueor, **tuērī**, **tūtus sum** gaze at, look upon; protect
tulī *see* **ferō**
tum (*adv.*) then, at that time *III*
turba, **-ae** *f* crowd, throng
turbō, **-āre**, **-āvī**, **-ātus** disturb, upset, discompose *XI*
turpis, **-e** loathsome; ugly; foul
tūtēla, **-ae** *f* protection, care, guardianship; tutelage of minors
tūtus, **-a**, **-um** safe, secure, protected *XVI*
tuus, **-a**, **-um** your (*sing.*), of you *II*

U

ūber; **ūberis** full, fruitful, fertile, plentiful *XV*
ubi (*adv.*) where, when *III*
ubi (*interrog. adv.*) where? *III*
ūllus, **-a**, **-um** any *III*
ulmus, **-ī** *f* elm tree
ultimus, **-a**, **-um** farthest, most distant; the last *XVII*
ultrō (*adv.*) of one's own accord, voluntarily; in addition to everything else
umbra, **-ae** *f* shade, shadow *XIV*
umquam (*adv.*) ever *IV*
ūna (*adv.*) at the same time
unda, **-ae** *f* wave;
  pl. the sea; waves, water *XV*
unde (*adv.*) from where, from what place *VI*

undique (*adv.*) in all directions, at random *XVI*
ūnus, **-a**, **-um** one *III*
urbs, **urbis** *f* city *XI*
ūrō, **-ere**, **ussī**, **ustus** burn *XIII*
ūsus, **-ūs** *m* use, exercise, practice; need, necessity *XIV*
usque (*adv.*) all the way (to)
ut (+ *indic.*) (*adv.*) as, like; when; how *IV*
(+ *subj.*) (*conj.*) (*with purpose clauses*) in order to, in order that, so that *IV*
(*with result clauses*) that, with the result that *IX*
uter, **utra**, **utrum** which (*of two*) *III*
uterque, **utraque**, **utrumque** each (*of two*) person, each (*of two*) thing; one as well as the other *XII*
utī = **ut**
ūtilis, **-e** useful
utinam (+ *subj.*) Would that, I wish that, If only *XVI*
ūtor, **ūtī**, **ūsus sum** (+ *abl.*) use, make use of *XVI*
utrum . . . **an** (*adv.*) whether . . . or *VI*
uxor, **uxōris** *f* wife, spouse *XIII*

V

vae! alas!
vah! ugh! (*expression of disgust*)
vacō, **-āre**, **-āvī**, **-ātus** (+ *abl.*) be empty, be without
vacuus, **-a**, **-um** empty
vagor, **-ārī**, **vagātus sum** wander, roam
valeō, **-ēre**, **valuī**, **valitūrus** be strong, well, healthy
valē! valēte! farewell! goodbye! *V*
varius, **-a**, **-um** varied, diverse, different *IX*
-ve (*enclitic conj.*) or
vehō, **-ere**, **vexī**, **vectus** convey, carry
vel (*conj.*) or; perhaps, at least;
vel . . . **vel** either . . . or *X*
vēlō, **-āre**, **-āvī**, **-ātus** cover, wrap up, veil *XVI*
vēnātor, **-tōris** *m* hunter
vendō, **-ere**, **vendidī**, **venditus** sell *XVIII*
veniō, **-īre**, **vēnī**, **ventus** come *III*
ventus, **-ī** *m* wind
Venus, **-eris** *f* Venus (*goddess of Love*); love
verbum, **-ī** *n* word *II*
Vergilius, **-iī** *m* the poet Vergil
vēritās, **-tātis** *f* truth *VIII*
vereor, **-ērī**, **veritus sum** revere, feel awe of; fear, be afraid of *XVI*
vērō (*adv.*) in truth, in fact, certainly
(*as corroborating adversative*) but in truth, but in fact; however *XII*
versus, **-ūs** *m* a furrow; a line; a line of writing; a verse *XII*

vertō, **-ere**, **vertī**, **versus** turn, turn round *VII*
  sē vertere to turn (one's self)
verū, **verūs** *n* spit, broach (for roasting upon)
vērum (*adv.*) yes, certainly
  (*conj.*) but, but in truth, but still
vērus, **-a**, **-um** true, real, actual *IX*
vescor, **vescī**, —— (+ *abl.*) eat, fill oneself with food *XVI*
vester, **-tra**, **-trum** your (*pl.*), of you *II*
vestīgium, **-iī** *n* footprint; *pl.* traces, tracks *IX*
vestis, **vestis** *f* clothing, cloak, attire *IX*
vetō, **-āre**, **-uī**, **-itus** forbid
vetus; **veteris** aged, ancient, long-existing
via, **-ae** *f* way, road, path; journey *II*
vīcīnus, **-a**, **-um** (*adj.* + *dat.* or *gen.*) near (to), neighboring *XIII*
  vīcīna, **-ae** *f* or **vīcīnus**, **-ī** *m* neighbor *VI*
victor, **-tōris** *m* conqueror, victor *XVII*
victōria, **-ae** *f* victory *XI*
videō, **-ēre**, **vīdī**, **vīsus** see, understand *I*
vigilō, **-āre**, **-āvī**, **-ātus** be awake, keep awake; be watchful
vīgintī (*indeclinable*) twenty *XVII*
vīlis, **-e** of small price or value; cheap, inexpensive; worthless *XVIII*
villa, **-ae** *f* farmhouse
vincō, **-ere**, **vīcī**, **victus** conquer, subdue, defeat *X*
vīnum, **-ī** *n* wine *IX*
violentia, **-ae** *f* violence, ferocity
vinculum, **-ī** *n* chain, bond, rope *II*
vir, **virī** *m* man, husband *II*
virgō, **virginis** *f* maiden, unmarried girl
  Virgō constellation Virgo in the zodiac *XII*
virtūs, **-tūtis** *f* virtue, manliness, excellence; strength, courage *VIII*
vīs, **vis** *f* force, energy, violence
  vīrēs, **vīrium** *pl.* physical strength *XI*
vīsus, **-a**, **-um** seen *II*
vīsus, **-ūs** *m* a seeing, looking; sight; the thing seen: appearance *XII*
vīta, **-ae** *f* life *III*
vītō, **-āre**, **-āvī**, **-ātus** avoid *VIII*
vitium, **-iī** *n* fault, defect, imperfection; moral fault, vice *VI*
vīvō, **-ere**, **vīxī**, **vīctus** live *III*
vīvus, **-a**, **-um** alive, living *X*
vix (*adv.*) scarcely *XVIII*
vocō, **-āre**, **-āvī**, **-ātus** call, summon *IV*
volitō, **-āre**, **-āvī**, **-ātus** fly about; fly to and fro, flutter about *XVIII*
volō, **velle**, **voluī**, —— wish, want, intend *VI*
volō, **-āre**, **-āvī**, **-ātus** fly
voluntās, **-tātis** *f* free will, choice *XII*
voluptās, **-tātis** *f* satisfaction, enjoyment, pleasure *XV*

volvō, **-ere**, **volvī**, **volūtus** (*active*) roll, turn over; (*passive*) revolve *XII*
vōtum, **-ī** *n* solemn promise, vow; prayer *XV*
vox, **vōcis** *f* voice, sound, cry; tone *IX*
Vulcānus, **-ī** *m* Vulcan (*god of fire and of craftsmanship*)
vulgus, **-ī** *n* the great mass, the multitude; the public, the (common) people *VIII*
vulnerō, **-āre**, **-āvī**, **-ātus** wound, injure *XVI*
vulnus, **-eris** *n* wound *XVI*

English-Latin Vocabulary

A

abandon relinquō, -ere, relīquī, relictus
able (*verb*) *see* **can**
able (*adjective*) potēns; potentis
accomplish perficiō, -ere, -fēcī, -fectus; conficiō, -ere, -fēcī, -fectus
across trāns + *acc.*
advise moneō, -ere, monuī, monitus; hortor, -ārī, -ātus
afraid: **be afraid (of)** timeō, -ēre, -uī, ——
aid auxilium, -iī *n*
almost paene
alone sōlus, -a, -um
animal bestia, -ae *f*; animal, animālis *n*
ancestors māiōrēs, māiōrum *m pl.*
anger īra, -ae *f*
  in anger, **angry** īrātus, -a, -um
annoying molestus, -a, -um
any ūllus, -a, -um
anyone, **anything** quisquam, quidquam; aliquis, aliquid
art ars, artis *f*
ashamed (**be ashamed**) (*impersonal verb*) pudet
ask for petō, -ere, -īvī, -ītus; quaerō, -ere, quaesīvī, quaesītus
ask urgently poscō, -ere, poposcī, ——
assistance auxilium, -iī *n*
at all: *see genitive of indefinite value, ch. XVIII*
attempt conor, -ārī, -ātus
Athens Athēnae, -ārum *f*
avoid vītō, -āre, -āvī, -ātus; fugiō, -ere, fūgī, fugitus

B

bad malus, -a, -um
beautiful pulcher, -chra, -chrum
become fīō, fierī, factus sum
begin incipiō, -ere, incēpī, inceptus
believe crēdō, -ere, crēdidī, crēditus
book liber, librī *m*
boy puer, puerī *m*
brief brevis, -e
bring ferō, ferre, tulī, lātus; afferō, afferre, attulī, allātus

C

call appellō, -āre, -āvī, -ātus, vocō, -āre, -āvī, -ātus
can, could possum, posse, potuī, ——
care (*noun*) cūra, -ae *f*
(*verb*) floccī faciō
carefully cum cūrā
carry gerō, -ere, gessī, gestus
cattle bōs, bovis, *m* or *f*
certain certus, -a, -um
"a certain . . ." quīdam, quaedam, quiddam/quoddam
chain vinculum, -ī *n*
change mūtō, -āre, -āvī, -ātus
child puer, -ī *m*; puella, -ae *f*
children līberī, līberorum *m*
citizen cīvis, cīvis *m* or *f*
city urbs, urbis *f*
clear clārus, -a, -um
clearly clārē
come veniō, -īre, vēnī, ventus
complete conficiō, -ere, -fēcī, -fectus; perficiō, -ere, -fēcī, -fectus
conceal cēlō, -āre, -āvī, -ātus
country patria, -ae *f*
countryside rūs, rūris *n*
cry fleō, -ēre, flēvī, flētus

D

day diēs, diēī *m*
daughter fīlia, -ae *f*
death mors, mortis *f*
Dēianīra Dēianīra, -ae *f*
decide cōnstituō, -ere, cōnstituī, cōnstitūtus
depart cēdō, -ere, cessī, cessus
destruction *use noun clause* (ut + pereō)
devoted amāns; amantis
difficult difficilis, -e
die morior, morī, mortuus
dinner guest convīva, -ae *m* or *f*
do agō, -ere, ēgī, actus; faciō, -ere, fēcī, factus
don't nōlī *or* nōlīte + *infinitive*

E

each quisque, quidque
earth terra, -ae *f*
easy facilis, -e
endure ferō, ferre, tulī, lātus
enemy hostis, -is *m*
envy invidia, -ae *f*

escape fugiō, -ere, fūgī, fugitus; vītō, -āre, -āvī, -ātus
estimate cēnseō, -ēre, cēnsuī, cēnsus
evil malus, -a, -um
example exemplum, -ī *n*
expect spērō, -āre, -āvī, -ātus
explain expōnō, -ere, exposuī, expositus

F

fall cado, -ere, cecidī, casus
far longus, -a, -um
farmer agricola, -ae *m*
father pater, patris *m*
fear timeō, -ēre, timuī, ——
feel sentiō, -īre, sēnsī, sēnsus
find inveniō, -īre, invēnī, inventus
follow sequor, sequī, secūtus
forgive ignoscō, -ere, ignōvī, ignōtus
former ille, illa, illud
freedman lībertīnus, -ī *m*
friend amīcus, -ī *m*; amīca, -ae *f*
full plēnus, -a, -um
(**full of** plenus, -a, -um + *gen.*)

G

game lūdus, -ī *m*
general dux, ducis *m*
gift dōnum, -ī *n*
give dō, dare, dedī, datus
glory glōria, -ae *f*
go eō, īre; cēdō, -ere, cessī, cessus; gradior, gradī, gressus sum
good bonus, -a, -um
goodbye valē!; valēte!
great magnus, -a, -um
so great tantus, -a, -um
Greek graecus, -a, -um
ground terra, -ae *f*

H

habit mōs, mōris *m*
hand manus, -ūs *f*
hard dūrus, -a, -um
head caput, capitis *n*
hear audiō, -īre, -īvī, -ītus
hello salvē!; salvēte!
help auxilium, -iī *n*
give help auxilium dare
Hercules Herculēs, -is *m*

highest *use* summus, -a, -um
his, her *use genitive of* is, ea, id *or* (*if reflexive*) suus, -a, -um
hold teneō, -ēre, tenuī, tentus
home domus, -ūs *f*
horn cornu, cornūs *n*
horse equus, -ī *m*
hour hōra, -ae *f*
how (*in what way*) quō modo
how (*exclamatory*) quam
however autem (*postpositive*)
husband marītus, -ī *m*

I

I egŏ (meī, mihi, mē, mē)

J

judge cēnseō, -ēre, cēnsuī, cēnsus
Jupiter Iuppiter, Iovis *m*

K

kill interficiō, -ere, interfēcī, interfectus
kind modus, -ī *m*; genus, generis *n*
know sciō, scīre, scīvī, scītus *or perfect tense of* noscō

L

language lingua, -ae *f*
large magnus, -a, -um
last ultimus, -a, -um; extrēmus, -a, -um
latter hic, haec, hoc
laugh rīdeō, -ēre, rīdī, rīsus
lawyer advocātus, -ī *m*
lay aside dēpōnō, -ere, dēposuī, dēpositus
lead dūcō, -ere, dūxī, ductus; agō, -ere, ēgī, actus
learn discō, -ere, didicī, ——
leave (**abandon, leave behind**) relinquō, -ere, relīquī, relictus;
  depart from abeō, abīre, abīvī, abitus; discēdō, -ere, discessī, discessus
listen (**to**), **hear** audiō, -īre, -īvī, -ītus
literature litterae, -ārum *f*
live vīvō, -ere, vīxī, vīctus; *or* vītam agere
long longus, -a, -um
  for a long time (*adv.*) diū
love amō, -āre, -āvī, -ātus

M

man vir, virī *m or* homō, hominis *m*
marriage nuptiae, -ārum *f pl.*

master dominus, -ī *m*
me *see* "I"
miserable miser, misera, miserum
misery miseria, -ae *f*
money pecūnia, -ae *f*
mother māter, mātris *f*
mourn lūgeō, -ēre, lūxī, luctus
move moveō, -ēre, mōvī, mōtus
my meus, -a, -um

N

never numquam
no nūllus, -a, -um
no one nēmō, nēminis *m* or *f*
not nōn;
  not only nōn sōlum *or* nōn modo
nothing nihil

O

observe videō, -ēre, vīdī, vīsus
offer ostendō, -ere, ostendī, ostentus; offerō, offerre, obtulī, oblātus
one ūnus, -a, -um
other alius, -a, -um
  the other (*of two*) alter, altera, alterum
ought dēbeō, -ēre, dēbuī, dēbitus; (*impersonal verb*) oportet, -ēre, oportuit
overcome superō, -āre, -āvī, -ātus; vincō, -ere, vīcī, victus

P

paedagogue paedagōgus, -ī *m*
pain dolor, dolōris *m*
part pars, partis *f*
pass over praetereō, -īre, -īvī (-iī), -itus
people populus, -ī *m*; hominēs (*pl.*); gēns, gentis *f*
permit (*impersonal verb*) licet, -ēre, licuit
perceive sentiō, -īre, sēnsī, sēnsus
pity (*impersonal verb*) miseret, -ēre, miseruit
place (*noun*) locus, -ī *m*
  (*verb*) pōnō, -ere, posuī, positus; locō, -āre, -āvī, -ātus
"**please**" tē amābō
  be pleasing placeō, -ēre, -uī
poem carmen, carminis *n*
poet poēta, -ae *m*
point out, show ostendō, -ere, ostendī, ostentus
power vīs, vis *f*
praise laudō, -āre, -āvī, -ātus
prefer mālō, mālle, māluī, ——

Q

quick celer, celeris, celere
quickly celeriter

R

read legō, -ere, lēgī, lectus
receive accipiō, -ere, accēpī, acceptus
return redeō, redīre, redīvī (rediī), reditus
reveal ostendō, -ere, ostendī, ostentus; aperiō, -īre, aperuī, apertus
river fluvius, -ī *m*
Roman Rōmānus, -a, -um
Rome Rōma, -ae *f*
run currō, -ere, cucurrī, cursus
run away fugiō, -ere, fūgī, fugitus

S

sailor nauta, -ae *m*
sake (**for the sake of**) *genitive* + causā; *genitive* + gratiā
save servō, -āre, -āvī, -ātus
say dīcō, -ere, dīxī, dictus
sea mare, maris *n*
see videō, -ēre, vīdī, vīsus
send mittō, -ere, mīsī, missus
sense sentiō, -īre, sēnsī, sēnsus
serious gravis, -e
servant servus, -ī *m*
serve serviō, -īre, -īvī, -ītus + *dative*
short brevis, -e
sing canō, -ere, cecinī, cantus
slave servus, -ī *m*
snatch rapiō, -ere, rapuī, raptus
some (**people**) . . . **others** aliī . . . aliī
someone quisquam; aliquis
son fīlius, -ī *m*
sort; **of that sort** eius generis; eius modī
spare parcō, -ere, pepercī, parsūrus (+ *dative*)
speak dīcō, -ere, dīxī, dictus
speaker ōrātor, -ōris *m*
speech ōrātiō, -iōnis *f*
state rēs pūblica, reī pūblicae *f*; cīvitās, cīvitātis *f*
strange novus, -a, -um
strength vīrēs, vīrium *f*
student discipulus, -ī *m*
such great, **so great** tantus, -a, -um
suffer patior, patī, passus sum
summon vocō, -āre, -āvī, -ātus

survive supersum, superesse, superfuī, superfutūrus
sweet dulcis, -e

T

tail cauda, -ae *f*
take rapiō, -ere, rapuī, raptus; capiō, -ere, cēpī, captus; sūmō, -ere, sumpsī, sumptus
teach doceō, -ēre, docuī, doctus
teacher magister, -trī *m*
tell dīcō, -ere, dīxī, dictus
think putō, -āre, -āvī, -ātus; cēnseō, -ere, cēnsuī, cēnsus
thank (I) gratiās agō + *dative*
that *demonstrative pronoun, or* ut + *subjunctive, or indirect statement*
time tempus, temporis *n*
  for a long time diū (*adv.*)
troops cōpiae, -ārum *f*
truth vēritās, -tātis *f*
try cōnor, -ārī, -ātus sum

U

understand intellegō, -ere, intellēxī, intellēctus; videō, -ēre, vīdī, vīsus
unhappy miser, misera, miserum
urge hortor, -ārī, hortātus

V

victory victōria, -ae *f*
visit vīsō, -ere, vīsī, ——

W

wait for exspectō, -āre, -āvī, -ātus
want optō, -āre, -āvī, -ātus; volō, velle, voluī, ——
we nōs, nostrum/nostrī, nōbīs, nōs, nōbīs
weary, **grow weary** (*impersonal verb*) taedet, -ēre, taeduit *or* taesum est
welcome accipiō, -ere, accēpī, acceptus
whenever cum + *indic.* or *subj.*; quandōcumque
willing libēns; libentis;
  be willing volō, velle, voluī, ——
  willingly (*adv.*) libenter
with cum + *ablative* or *ablative without a preposition*
who *relative pronoun* quī, quae, quod or
  interrogative pronoun quis, quid
word verbum, -ī *n*
work (*verb*) labōrō, -āre, -āvī, -ātus
work (*noun*) opus, operis *n*
worthy dignus, -a, -um

wounded saucius, -a, -um
write scrībō, -ere, scrīpsī, scrīptus

Y

yes certē; certē sciō; sīc
you tu (*sing.*); vōs (*pl.*)
your tuus, -a, -um (*sing.*); vester, -tra, -trum (*pl.*)

Illustration Credits

The Bettmann Archive, pages 33, 53, 111, 112, 228, 230, 269, 289.

Museo Nazionale, Naples, page 55.

New York Public Library Picture Collection, pages 74, 161, 209, 257, 313, 331.

Julian Brown/Brandeis University, page 91.

Art Resource, pages 139, 183, 253, 286, 287, 292.

Committee of the Egypt Exploration Society, page 134.

The Granger Collection, New York, page 203.

The Metropolitan Museum of Art, Harris Brisbane Dick Fund, 1951, page 204.

Springer/Bettmann Film Archive, page 290.

Index

Numbers refer to pages unless otherwise stated. For summaries of verb forms see Appendix B, pp. 351 ff. For summaries of noun, adjective and pronoun forms, see Appendix C, pp. 363 ff.

Table of Contents

The Imperial Oil Company Limited
is honoured to be associated
with a cultural manifestation
so prestigious as the
publication of this volume.

Preface

This is the first volume in a series we have titled *A Survey of Creators*. Thanks to the generous participation of the Imperial Oil Company, *Vie des Arts* is in a position to produce a project that has been dear to our hearts for a long time: to cast, with the help of a publication more permanent than a periodical, new light on artists of our time, by showing their ways of living and working. What the artists are coincides with their creation. But their work also harmonizes with their manner of creating, with their immediate environment, with all that weaves the web of everyday life, with constant immersion in the interior world.

Our goal in calling upon the double testimony of the photographer and the writer was simple: to foster comprehension through the eye and to give free rein to the interpretive premises that have the works as object.

We asked our photographers to capture the artist in his studio, in his home, in his moments of relaxation, in some of his habits, convinced in advance that our hunters of images would bring revealing snapshots, each in his own way. Each photographer has his own approach, his style. As things developed, it became evident that each has, besides, his own ways of persuasion, the artist being easily rebellious at any intrusion into his personal life.

We also invited sixteen art critics and historians to present the painters dealt with in the present volume, leaving them free to treat their subject as they saw fit. Some remained faithful to their own method of analysis: others were more interested in the human side of the experiment. From this variety of interpretation, from these ideas and these images, from this meeting of writer and photographer, there results a living document that speaks to us of artists who all have in common the circumstance of having been born in Quebec, even if they live in Toronto or Paris. These creators draw inspiration from the same source, their roots are in the same soil, they live in their work. It is not necessary here to seek an historical perspective or a classification in order of importance; other volumes will come, as eloquent in their choice. It is the unique feature of each artistic experiment that interests us.

To see the world with the eyes of the artist is a way of loving without possessing, it is to share a vision that goes always further, that tries constantly to force back the barriers of ignorance. The artist teaches us the world because he does not rest until he has exhausted all resources, that is to say almost never.

It is easy to feel in the pages that follow how much familiar surrounding things are a source of wonder for him. Affectionate relationships are established with the most humble objects, with landscapes, with close persons. But it is still in action, at his easel, that the artist best reveals himself. There the process of creation finds its outcome and, as the creator does not know this kind of respite, he remains to the end prisoner of his interrogations, his anguish, his hopes.

Let the pleasure of the eye open new horizons for us and, especially, let it bring us close to a world where art is born. Where living forces dwell, and vitality. Art is a matter of the senses, of the mind, and the eye leads us toward unexplored regions.

Andrée PARADIS